Success in PreHealth and Beyond with Critical Thinking

Custom Publication for
Georgian College

MCGRAW-HILL RYERSON LIMITED

Selected Materials From:

Power Learning and Your Life: Essentials of Student Success, First Edition, by Robert Feldman and Danica Lavoie.
ISBN 0-07-092351-5

THiNK, Third Edition, by Judith Boss.
ISBN 0-07-803843-X

Cover photo: Doug Crawford

Product Development Manager - Custom: Jason Giles
Product Developer - Custom: Corinne Mohr
Regional Learning Solutions Manager: Julie Robertson

Cover Design: Corinne Mohr

Printed and bound in Canada

Table of Contents

Power Learning and Your Life: Essentials of Student Success, **First Edition,** by Andrea Hendricks

THiNK, **Third Edition,** by Judith Boss

Success in PreHealth and Beyond

1

P.O.W.E.R. Learning: Becoming an Expert Student

Learning Outcomes

By the time you finish this chapter, you will be able to

» LO **1.1** Discuss the benefits of a post-secondary education.

» LO **1.2** List the skills, attitudes, and behaviours valued by Canadian employers.

» LO **1.3** Identify the basic principles of P.O.W.E.R. Learning and the ways in which expert students use P.O.W.E.R. Learning to set goals and achieve academic success.

» LO **1.4** Compare and contrast learning styles, striving styles, and multiple intelligences. Identify your own styles, and reflect on how they relate to your academic success.

The day has started off with a bang. Literally. As Nandini Singh reaches sleepily to turn off her clock radio's continual buzzing at 6:35 A.M., she knocks the clock off the table next to her bed. The loud bang it makes as it hits the floor wakes her fully, and it rouses her daughters sleeping in the next room, who grumble resentfully.

Struggling out of bed, Nandini reflects on the day ahead. It's one of her most intense days—two shifts at two different part-time jobs on different sides of town. She also must get her children ready for school and then take them to swimming lessons in the afternoon.

And on top of all that, she has an exam that morning at the college she attends.

After a quick shower, Nandini manages to get her daughters off to school, and then joins her fellow paralegal students on campus. She glances at her paralegal textbook and feels a wave of anxiety flood over her: Will I do well enough on my exam? How will I manage to hold down two jobs, take care of my family, and have enough time to study? Will I find a job as a paralegal after graduation? Will I make my children proud? . . . And underlying them all is a single challenge: Will I be successful in college and in my career?

Looking Ahead

Whether academic pursuits are a struggle or come easily to you . . . whether you are returning to post-secondary education or attending for the first time . . . whether you are gaining new skills for your current job or have been at home caring for your children and are now starting on a whole new career path . . . whether you are attending college or university in your own hometown or have travelled from another country to be here—whatever your situation, pursuing post-secondary education is a challenge. Every one of us has concerns about our own capabilities and motivation; and new situations—like starting college or university—make us wonder how well we'll succeed.

That's where this book comes in. It is designed to help you learn the most effective ways to approach the challenges you encounter, not just in college or university, but in your career, too. It will teach you practical strategies, and it will provide hints and tips that can lead you to success, all centred on an approach to achieving classroom and career success. That approach is called P.O.W.E.R. Learning.

This book is designed to be useful in a way that is different from other texts. It presents information in a hands-on format. It's meant to be used, not just read. Write on it, underline words and sentences, use a highlighter, circle key points, and complete the questionnaires right in the book. The more exercises you do, the more benefit you'll get from the book. The ideas in this book will help you throughout your post-secondary education and throughout your career, so it's a good idea to invest your time here and now. If the learning techniques you master here become second nature, the payoff will be enormous.

In the first part of this chapter, you'll read about the benefits of post-secondary education and examine the skills, attitudes, and behaviours valued by Canadian employers. After that, you'll be introduced to the basics of the P.O.W.E.R. Learning process, a process that is used throughout the book and is a fundamental building block in achieving academic and career success. Finally, in the last half of the chapter, you'll discover a number of interactive tools that will help you uncover the ways in which you learn best, what you truly value, and how you can use your learning style, striving style, and multiple intelligences to become an expert student.

figure 1.1
Canada is one of the most multicultural countries in the world. (Wordle created at **www.wordle.net.**)

≫ LO 1.1 The Benefits of a Post-secondary Education

Congratulations. You are enrolled in an institution of higher learning. Clearly, you agree with Canadians who, when surveyed by the Canadian Council on Learning in 2008, overwhelmingly agreed that adult learning is critical to success

Try It!

Why Are You Going to College or University?

Place a 1, a 2, and a 3 by the three most important reasons that you have for attending college/university:

_____ I want to get a good job when I graduate.

_____ I want to make my family proud.

_____ I couldn't find a job.

_____ I want to try something new.

_____ I want to get ahead at my current job.

_____ I want to pursue my dream job.

_____ I want to improve my reading and critical thinking skills.

_____ I want to become a more cultured person.

_____ I want to make more money.

_____ I want to learn more about things that interest me.

_____ A mentor or role model encouraged me to go.

_____ I want to prove to others that I can succeed.

Now consider the following:

1. What do your answers tell you about yourself?
2. What reasons besides these did you think about when you were applying to college or university?
3. How do you think your reasons compare with those of your fellow students?

To Try It online, go to Connect for *P.O.W.E.R. Learning and Your Life.*

in life and to satisfaction with one's life. The reasons that people go to college or university vary from the practical ("I need new skills for my job"), to the noble ("I want to build a better life for my family"), to the vague ("Why not? I don't have anything better to do"). Consider your own reasons for enrolling, as you complete **Try It! 1,** "Why Are You Going to College or University?"

It's likely that one of your primary motivations for pursuing post-secondary education is to further your career. In fact, a survey of first-year college students found that almost three-quarters of them want to learn about things that interest them, get training for a specific career, land a better job, and make more money (see **Figure 1.2** on page 4). Statistics clearly demonstrate that a post-secondary education helps people find better jobs. On average, college and university graduates earn about 75 percent more than high school graduates over their working lifetime.[1] That difference adds up: Over the course of their working lifetimes, college graduates earn close to a million dollars more than those with only a high school diploma. Furthermore, as jobs become increasingly complex and technologically sophisticated, a post-secondary education is becoming an entry-level requirement for many jobs.

There are many reasons for pursuing a college or university education:

▸ **You'll learn to think critically.** Here's what one student said about his college experience after he graduated: "It's not about what you major in or which classes you take. . . . It's really about learning to think. Wherever you end up, you'll need to be able to analyze and solve problems—to figure out what needs to be done and do it."[2] Education improves your ability to understand the world—to understand it as it now is, and to prepare to understand it as it will be.

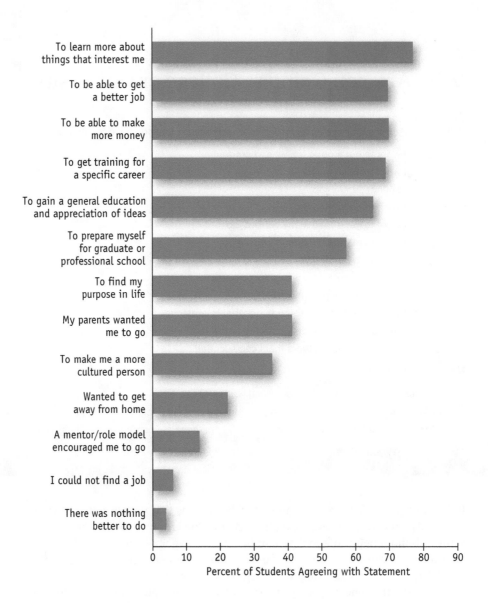

figure 1.2
Choosing College
These are the most frequently cited reasons that first-year college students gave when asked in a U.S. survey why they had enrolled in college.[2]

> **You'll learn how to communicate better.** Post-secondary institutions provide you with the opportunity to communicate your thoughts and ideas orally and in writing; teachers provide important feedback on how to do this well. As you learn in the next section of this chapter, communication is a skill that is highly valued by Canadian employers.

> **You'll be able to better deal with advances in knowledge and technology that are changing the world.** Genetic engineering . . . drugs to reduce forgetfulness . . . foods that make us smarter—no one knows what the future will hold. But you can prepare for it through a post-secondary education. Education can provide you with intellectual tools that you can apply regardless of the specific situation in which you find yourself.

> **You'll learn to adapt to new situations.** College and university are different worlds from high school or the workplace. They present new experiences and new challenges. Your adjustment to the culture of your college or university will prepare you for future encounters with new situations.

> **You'll be better prepared to live in a world of diversity.** The ethnic composition of Canada is changing rapidly. Whatever your ethnicity, chances are

you'll be working and living with people whose backgrounds, lifestyles, and ways of thinking may be entirely different from your own.

You won't be prepared for the future unless you understand others and their cultural backgrounds, as well as how your own cultural background affects you.

> **You'll make learning a lifelong habit.** Higher education isn't the end of your education. Education will build upon your natural curiosity about the world, and it will make you aware that learning is a rewarding and never-ending journey.

> And finally, the obvious: **You will boost your career prospects.** You will acquire skills, attitudes, and behaviours that Canadian employers value; and you will earn more money over the course of your lifetime than someone who has not obtained a diploma or degree.

» LO 1.2 What Canadian Employers Value

Forging a successful career depends, as much as anything else, on the "fit" between what employers are looking for and what you have to offer. In this section, we focus on uncovering the main skills, attitudes, and behaviours sought by Canadian employers. Later, we will provide you with an opportunity to examine how you can best harness your talents to offer employers what they are seeking.

Canadian employers are a diverse lot. They span the public and private sectors, large and small businesses, and every industry imaginable. Is it really possible that they can come to an agreement on the qualities they look for in an employee? They can, and they have. The result is the Employability Skills 2000+, a publication of the Conference Board of Canada, which can be found in **Figure 1.3** on page 6. It divides the skills desired by employers into three main categories: fundamental skills, personal management skills, and teamwork skills.

To accompany the Employability Skills 2000+, the Conference Board has developed a Skills Assessment and Portfolio Building Tool (SCT) for students, employees, and job-seekers. The SCT allows you to assess your own essential skills and employability attitudes and behaviours and to create a printout that you can share with your professor. To access the Skills Assessment and Portfolio Building Tool, go to **http://conferenceboard.checkboxonline.com/Survey.aspx?s=b5cfd4c7ef204b5cb3e6a6c1f7e07628**.

To help you develop the skills, attitudes, and behaviours valued by Canadian employers, it's time to introduce you to a fundamental process that will help you achieve success, both in school and in life beyond: P.O.W.E.R. Learning.

» LO 1.3 P.O.W.E.R. Learning: Five Key Steps to Achieving Success

P.O.W.E.R. Learning
A system designed to help people achieve their goals, based on five steps: **P**repare, **O**rganize, **W**ork, **E**valuate, and **R**ethink

The term **P.O.W.E.R. Learning** is an acronym—a word formed from the first letters of a series of steps—for an approach to learning that will help you take in, process, and make use of the information you'll acquire in college or university. It will help you to achieve your goals, both while you are in school and after you graduate.

Employability Skills 2000+

The skills you need to enter, stay in, and progress in the world of work—whether you work on your own or as a part of a team.

These skills can also be applied and used beyond the workplace in a range of daily activities

Fundamental Skills	Personal Management Skills	Teamwork Skills
The skills needed as a base for further development	The personal skills, attitudes and behaviours that drive one's potential for growth	The skills and attributes needed to contribute productively

You will be better prepared to progress in the world of work when you can:

Communicate

- read and understand information presented in a variety of forms (e.g., words, graphs, charts, diagrams)
- write and speak so others pay attention and understand
- listen and ask questions to understand and appreciate the points of view of others
- share information using a range of information and communications technologies (eg., voice, e-mail, computers)
- use relevant scientific, technological and mathematical knowledge and skills to explain or clarify ideas.

Manage Information

- locate, gather and organize information using appropriate technology and information systems
- access, analyze and apply knowledge and skills from various disciplines(e.g.,arts, languages, science, technology, mathematics, social sciences and the humanities)

Use Numbers

- decide what needs to be measured or calculated
- observe and record data using appropriate methods, tools and technology
- make estimates and verify calculations

Think & Solve Problems

- assess situations and identify problems
- seek different points of view and evaluate them based on facts
- recognize the human, interpersonal, technical, scientific and mathematical dimensions of a problem
- identify the roof cause of a problem
- be creative and innovative in exploring possible solutions
- readily use science, technology and mathematics as ways to think, gain and share knowledge, solve problems and make decisions
- evaluate solutions to make recommendations or decisions
- implement solution
- check to see if a solution works, and act an opportunities for improvement

You will be able to offer yourself greater possibilities for achievement when you can:

Demonstrate Positive Attitudes & Behaviours

- feel good about yourself and be confident
- deal with people, problems and situations with honesty, integrity and personal ethics
- recognize your own and other people's good efforts
- take care of your personal health
- show interest, initiative and effort

Be Responsible

- set goals and priorities balancing work and personal life
- plan and manage time, money and other resources to achieve goals
- assess, weigh and manage risk
- be accountable your actions and the actions of your group
- be socially responsible and contribute to your community

Be Adaptable

- work independently or as a part of a team
- carry out multiple tasks or projects
- be innovative and resourceful: identify and suggest alternative ways to achieve goals and get the job done
- be open and respond constructively to charge
- learn from your mistakes and accept feedback
- cope with uncertainty

Learn Continuously

- be willing to continuously learn and grow
- assess personal strengths and areas for development
- set your own learning goals
- identify and access learning sources and opportunities
- plan for and achieve your learning goals

Work Safely

- be aware of personal and group health and safety practices and procedures, and act in accordance with these

You will be better prepared to add value to the outcomes of a task, project or team when you can:

Work with Others

- understand and work within the dynamics of a group
- ensure that a team's purpose and objectives are clear
- be flexible: respect, be open to and supportive of the thoughts, opinions and contributions of other in a group
- recognize and respect people's diversity, individual differences and perspectives
- accept and provide feedback in a constructive and considerate manner
- contribute to a team by sharing information and expertise
- lead or support when appropriate, motivating a group for high performance
- Understand the role of conflict in a group to reach solutions.
- manage and resolve conflict when appropriate

Participate in Projects & Tasks

- plan, design or carry out a project or task from start to finish with well-defined objectives and outcomes
- develop-a plan, seek feedback, test, revise and implement
- work to agreed quality standards and specifications
- select and use appropriate tools and techonology for a task or project
- adapt to changing requirements and information
- continuously monitor the success of a project or task and identify ways to improve

The Conference Board of Canada

255 Smyth Road, Ottawa
ON K1H 8M7 Canada
Tel. (613) 526-3280
Fax (613) 526-4857

Internet: www.conferenceboard.ca/education

figure 1.3

Conference Board of Canada's Employability Skills 2000+

The Conference Board's Employability Skills 2000+ tells you what most Canadian employers are looking for, and it is also a great resource when you are writing your resumé!

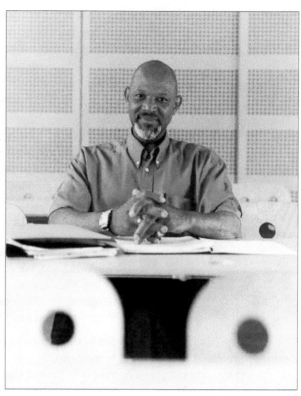

Students go to school for their own individual reasons. Gwen recently visited a friend in the hospital and was struck by how much she wanted to be a part of the health-care community. John has survived several rounds of layoffs at his job and wants to make himself more marketable.

Prepare, Organize, Work, Evaluate, and Rethink. That's it. It's a simple framework, but an effective one. Using the systematic framework that P.O.W.E.R. Learning provides (illustrated in the P.O.W.E.R. Plan diagram in the margin) will increase your chances of success at any task, from writing a paper to buying the weekly groceries to filling out a purchase order.

Keep this in mind: P.O.W.E.R. Learning isn't a product that you can simply pull down off the shelf and use without thinking. P.O.W.E.R. Learning is a process, and you are the only one who can make it succeed. Without your personal investment in the process, P.O.W.E.R. Learning consists of just words on paper.

Relax, though. You already know each of the elements of P.O.W.E.R. Learning; and you may discover that you are already putting this process, or parts of it, to work for you. You've applied and been accepted at an institution of higher learning. You may have also held down a job, started a family, and paid your monthly bills. Each of these accomplishments required that you use P.O.W.E.R. Learning. What you'll be doing throughout this book is becoming more aware of these methods and how they can be used to help you in situations you will encounter in school and your career.

P Prepare

Chinese philosopher Lao Tzu said that travellers taking a long journey must begin with a single step. But even before they take that first step, travellers need to know several things: what their destination is, how they're going to get there, how they'll know when they reach the destination, and what they'll do if they have trouble

P.O.W.E.R. Plan

along the way. In the same way, you need to know where you're headed as you embark on the academic journeys involved in pursuing a post-secondary education. Whether you are performing a major, long-term task, such as landing a new and better job, or a more limited activity, such as getting ready to complete a paper due in the near future, you'll need to prepare for the journey.

Setting Goals

From the perspective of . . .

A STUDENT What goals did you set when you decided to go school? What can you do to ensure that you meet these goals?

Before we seek to accomplish any task, all of us do some form of planning. The trouble is that most of the time such planning is done without conscious thinking, as if we are on autopilot. However, the key to success is to make sure that planning is systematic.

The best way to plan systematically is to use goal-setting strategies. In many cases, goals are clear and direct. It's obvious that our goal in washing dishes is to have the dishes end up clean. We know that our goal at the gas station is to fill the car's tank with gas. We go to the post office to buy stamps and mail letters.

Other goals are not so clear-cut. In fact, often the more important the task—such as going to college or university—the more complicated our goals may be.

What's the best way to set appropriate goals? Here are some guidelines:

Long-term goals
Aims relating to major accomplishments that take some time to achieve

Short-term goals
Relatively limited steps toward the accomplishment of long-term goals

> **Set both long-term and short-term goals. Long-term goals** are aims relating to major accomplishments that take some time to achieve. **Short-term goals** are relatively limited steps you would take on the road to accomplishing your long-term goals. For example, one of the primary reasons you're enrolled in a post-secondary institution is to achieve the long-term goal of helping your career. But in order to reach that goal, you have to accomplish a series of short-term goals, such as completing a set of required courses and earning your diploma or degree. Even these short-term goals can be broken down into shorter-term goals. In order to complete a required course, for instance, you have to accomplish a series of short-term goals, such as completing a paper, taking several tests, and so on. For practice in setting long- and short-term goals, complete **Try It! 2**, "What Are Your Goals?", on page 9, "What Are Your Goals?"

The **SMART approach to goal setting** has been around for a long time. The acronym SMART reminds us that goals must be Specific, Measurable, Achievable, Realistic, and Time-Bound. Let's look at each of these in turn.

SMART approach to goal setting
A framework for goal setting that emphasizes that goals should be specific, measurable, achievable, realistic, time-bound

> **Set goals that are Specific.** Saying that "some day I'll learn a new language" is not specific enough. When you are setting a goal, make it as specific as possible. Which language? Where will you learn it? How will you learn it? Online? In a classroom setting? When will you learn it? The more specific and vivid the goal, the easier it is to achieve it.

> **Set goals that are Measurable.** Goals should represent some measurable change from a current set of circumstances. Your behaviour ought to change in some way that can be expressed in terms of numbers—to show an increase ("raise my grade point average 10 percent"), a decrease ("reduce wasted time by two hours each week"), or a level to be maintained ("keep in touch with my out-of-town friends by writing four email messages each month"), developed ("participate in one workshop on critical thinking"), or restricted ("reduce my phone expenses 10 percent by speaking and texting less").

> "If I had one hour to chop down a tree, I'd spend the first thirty minutes sharpening the saw."
> Abraham Lincoln

Try It!

What Are Your Goals?

Before you begin any journey, you need to know where you are going. To plan your academic journey—and your later career—you first need to set goals. *Short-term goals* are relatively limited objectives that bring you closer to your ultimate goal. *Long-term goals* are aims relating to major accomplishments that take more time to achieve.

In this **Try It!**, think about your short- and long-term academic and career goals for a few minutes, and then list them, using the SMART approach to goal setting. Because short-term goals are based on what you want to accomplish in the long term, first identify your long-term goals. Then list the short-term goals that will help you reach your long-term goals. An example is provided of both a long-term and a short-term goal:

Long-Term Goal #1 *Get a nursing diploma or degree* _____
  Related Short-Term Goals:
  • *Complete four courses with a grade of B or above each term*
  • _____
  • _____
  • _____

Long-Term Goal #2: _____
  Related Short-Term Goals:
  • _____
  • _____
  • _____
  • _____

Long-Term Goal #3: _____
  Related Short-Term Goals:
  • _____
  • _____
  • _____
  • _____

Long-Term Goal #4: _____
  Related Short-Term Goals:
  • _____
  • _____
  • _____
  • _____

Long-Term Goal #5: _____
  Related Short-Term Goals:
  • _____
  • _____
  • _____
  • _____

After you complete the lists, consider how easy or difficult it was to identify your long-term goals.

1. How many of your long-term goals relate to your education, and how many to your future career?
2. Do any of your short-term goals relate to more than one long-term goal?
3. In what ways will using the SMART approach to goal setting help you achieve your goals?

To Try It online, go to Connect for *P.O.W.E.R. Learning and Your Life.*

> **Set goals that are <u>A</u>chievable.** Someone once said, "A goal without a plan is but a dream." Everyone would like to win gold medals at the Olympics or star in videos or write best-selling novels. Unfortunately, you are unlikely to achieve such goals. It isn't enough to have a goal. Depending on the goal, you may also need the physical, emotional, or intellectual capacity, *and* the motivation and determination required to achieve it.

> **Set goals that are <u>R</u>ealistic.** We all want world peace and an end to poverty. Few of us have the resources or capabilities to bring either about. On the other hand, it is realistic to want to work in small ways to help others, such as by becoming a Big Brother or Big Sister or by volunteering at a local food bank. Be honest with yourself. There is nothing wrong with having big dreams. But it is important to be realistically aware of all that it takes to achieve them. If your long-term goals are unrealistic and you don't achieve them, the big danger is that you may incorrectly conclude that you are inept and lack ability, and you may then use this as an excuse for giving up. If goals are realistic, you can develop a plan to attain them, spurring you on to attain more.

> **Set goals that are <u>T</u>ime-bound.** As mentioned earlier, the more specific the goal, the better. This also applies to timing. When setting a goal, you should have a specific time frame in mind for achieving it. Procrastination is all too easy; before you know it, that goal you set five years ago is pushed far down your priority list, overtaken by more pressing matters and new responsibilities.

Finally, recognize that your goals should not be independent of one another. Instead, they should fit together into a larger dream of who you want to be. Every once in a while, step back and consider how what you're doing today relates to the kind of career and life that you would ultimately want to have.

By determining where you want to go and expressing your goals in terms that can be measured, you have already made a lot of progress.

The next step in P.O.W.E.R. Learning is to organize the tools you'll need to accomplish your goals. Building upon the goal-setting work you've undertaken in the preparation stage, it's time to determine the best way to accomplish the goals you've identified.

How do you do this? Suppose you've decided to build a set of bookshelves for one room in your house. Let's say that you've already determined the kind of bookshelves you like and you've figured out the basic characteristics of the ones you will build (the preparation step in P.O.W.E.R. Learning). The next stage involves gathering the necessary tools, buying the wood and other building materials, sorting the construction supplies, and preparing the room for your building project—all aspects of organizing for the task.

Similarly, your academic success will hinge to a large degree on the thoroughness of your organization for each academic task that you face. In fact, one of the biggest mistakes that students make is plunging into an academic project—studying for a test, writing a paper, completing an in-class assignment—without being organized.

Looking at the Big Picture

It's natural to view college or university as a series of small tasks—classes to attend, a certain number of pages to read each week, a few papers due during the term, quizzes and final exams to study for, and so on.

But such a perspective may lead you to miss what college and university, as a whole, are all about. Using the P.O.W.E.R. Learning framework can help you to take the long view of your education, considering how it helps you achieve your long- and short-term goals for your professional and personal life (the *Prepare* step) and what you'll need to do to maximize your success (the *Organize* step). By preparing and organizing even before you set foot in the classroom for the first time, you'll be able to consider what it is that you want to get out of your post-secondary experience and how it fits into your life as a whole.

Course
Connections

Two Kinds of Organization: Physical and Mental

Physical organization involves the mechanical aspects of task completion. For instance, you need to ask yourself if you have the appropriate tools, such as pens, paper, and a calculator. If you're using a computer, do you have access to a printer? Do you have a way to back up your files? Do you have the books and other materials you'll need to complete the assignment? Will the campus bookstore be open if you need anything else? Will the library be open when you need it? Do you have a comfortable place to work?

Mental organization is even more critical. Mental organization is accomplished by considering and reviewing the academic skills that you'll need to complete the task at hand successfully. You are an academic general in command of considerable forces—the basic skills, knowledge, and resources that you have at your command. You will need to make sure your forces are at their peak of readiness. For example, if you're working on a math assignment, you'll want to consider the basic math skills that you'll need and brush up on them. Thinking about these skills actively will help you organize mentally. Similarly, you'll want to mentally review your knowledge of engine parts before beginning car repair work (either for a class project class or at the side of the road!).

Why does producing mental organization matter? The answer is that it provides a context for when you actually begin to work. Organizing paves the way for better subsequent performance.

Too often, students or workers on the job are in a hurry to meet a deadline and figure they had better just dive in and get it done. Organizing can actually save you time, because you're less likely to be anxious and end up losing your way as you work to complete your task.

Much of this book is devoted to strategies for determining—*before* you begin work on a task—how to develop the mental tools for completing an assignment. However, as you'll see, all of these strategies share a common theme: that success comes not from a trial-and-error approach, but from following a systematic plan for achievement. Of course, this does not mean that there will be no surprises along the way, nor that simple luck is never a factor in great accomplishments. But it does mean that we often can make our own luck through careful preparation and organization.

W	Work

You're ready. The preliminaries are out of the way. You've prepared and you've organized. Now it's time to start actually doing the work.

In some ways, work is the easy part, because—if you have conscientiously carried out the preparation and organization stage—you should know exactly where you're headed and what you need to do to get there.

It's not quite so easy, of course. How effectively you'll get down to the business at hand depends on many factors. Some may be out of your control. There may be a power outage that closes down the library or a massive traffic jam that delays you getting to the office. But most factors should be under your control. Instead of getting down to work, however, you may find yourself thinking up "useful" things to do—like finally cleaning underneath the couch—or simply sitting captive in front of the TV. This kind of obstacle to work relates to motivation.

Finding the Motivation to Work

"If only I could get more motivated, I'd do so much better with my _____" (*school-work, job, diet, exercising*—you fill in the blank).

All of us have said something like this at one time or another. We use the concept of **motivation**—or its lack—to explain why we just don't work hard at a task. But when we do that, we're fooling ourselves. We all have some motivation, that inner power and psychological energy that directs and fuels our behaviour. Without any motivation, we'd never get out of bed in the morning.

We've also seen evidence of how strong our motivation can be. Perhaps you're an avid runner and you love to jog in the morning and compete in weekend races. Or maybe your love of music helped you learn to play the guitar, making practising for hours a pleasure rather than a chore. Or perhaps you're a single parent, juggling work, school, and family; and you get up early every morning to make breakfast for your kids before they go off to school.

All of us are motivated. The key to success in the classroom and on the job is to tap into, harness, and direct that motivation.

If we assume that we already have all the motivation we need, P.O.W.E.R. Learning becomes a matter of turning the skills we already possess into a habit. It becomes a matter of redirecting our psychological energies toward the work we wish to accomplish.

In a sense, everything you'll encounter in this book will help you to improve your use of the motivation that you already have. But there's a key concept that underlies the control of motivation: you have to view success as a consequence of effort. In Canadian writer Malcolm Gladwell's book *Outliers,* for example, Gladwell notes that to become a true master in a field—the Sidney Crosby of hockey or the Measha Brueggergosman of opera, for example—requires about 10 000 hours of concentrated effort.

Effort produces success.

Suppose, for example, you've gotten a good performance review from your new supervisor. The boss beams at you as she discusses your results. How do you feel?

You will be pleased, of course. But at the same time you might think to yourself, "Better not get a swollen head about it. It was just luck." Or perhaps you explain your success by thinking, "The new boss just doesn't know me very well."

If you often think this way, you're cheating yourself. Using this kind of reasoning when you succeed, instead of patting yourself on the back and thinking with satisfaction, "All my hard work really paid off," is sure to undermine your future success.

Motivation
The inner power and psychological energy that directs and fuels behaviour

A great deal of psychological research has shown that thinking you have no control over what happens to you sends a powerful and damaging message to your self-esteem—that you are powerless to change things. Just think of how different it feels to say to yourself, "Wow, I worked at it and I did it," as compared with "I lucked out" or "It was so easy that anybody could have done it."

In the same way, we can delude ourselves when we try to explain our failures. People who see themselves as the victims of circumstance may tell themselves, "I'm just not smart enough," when they don't do well on an academic task. Or they might give an excuse: "My co-workers don't have children to take care of."

The way in which we view the causes of success and failure is, in fact, directly related to our success. Students who generally see effort and hard work as the reason behind their performance usually do better in college and university. Workers who see their job performance in this way usually do better in their careers. It's not hard to see why: When such individuals are working on a task, they feel that the greater the effort they put forth, the greater their chances of success. So they work harder. They believe that they have control over their success; and if they fail, they believe they can do better in the future.

The great golfer Gary Player said it best: "The harder I work, the luckier I get." Here are some tips for keeping your motivation alive, so you can work with your full energy behind you:

> **Take responsibility for your failures—and successes.** When you do poorly on a test, don't blame the teacher, the textbook, or a job that kept you from studying. When you miss a work deadline, don't blame your boss or your incompetent co-workers. Analyze the situation, and see how you could have changed what you did to be more successful in the future. At the same time, when you're successful, think of the things you did to bring about that success.

> **Think positively.** Assume that the strengths that you have will allow you to succeed and that, if you have difficulty, you can figure out what to do.

> **Accept that you can't control everything.** Seek to understand which things can be changed and which cannot. You might be able to get an extension on a paper due date, but you are probably not going to be excused from an institution-wide requirement.

To further explore the causes of academic success, consider the questions in **Try It! 3**, "Examining the Causes of Success and Failure," discussing them with your classmates.

E Evaluate

"Great! I'm done with the work. Now I can move on."

It's natural to feel relief when you've finished the work necessary to fulfill the basic requirements of a task. After all, if you've written the five double-spaced pages required for an assignment or balanced a complicated office budget, why shouldn't you heave a sigh of relief and just hand in your work?

The answer is that if you stop at this point, you'll almost be guaranteed a mediocre result. Did Shakespeare dash off the first draft of *Hamlet* and, without another glance, send it off to the Globe Theatre for production? Do professional athletes just put in the bare minimum of practice to get ready for a big game? Think of one of your favourite songs. Do you think the composer wrote it in one sitting and then performed it in a concert?

> "Words are mighty things, when you live them. If you just read them, you may as well just stay in bed."
>
> Canadian singer—songwriter Jann Arden

It's all too easy to make excuses for our own failures. Can you think of a time when you shifted blame away from yourself for a failure? Was it a reasonable course of action? Why or why not?

Try It!

WORKING IN A GROUP

3 Examining the Causes of Success and Failure

Complete this Try It! while working in a group. First, consider the following situations:

1. Although he researched his report thoroughly, Farrukh is told by his professor that he has not referenced it properly. Farrukh is disgusted with himself and says, "I'll never be good at writing research reports. I might as well give up trying."

2. Yuqi's English professor suggested that she apply for a scholarship offered to first-year students. She wins the scholarship but later finds out that only five people applied for it. She decides she only succeeded because she had no real competition.

3. Usually an A student, Alicia's grades this semester are lower than she expected. Her financial circumstances have forced her to take a part-time job, and while she no longer worries about money, she is disappointed with her performance at school. Distressed, she considers quitting school entirely, because she thinks that she'll never be able to achieve the high marks she is accustomed to.

Now consider the following questions about each of the situations:

1. What did each person conclude was the main cause of his or her performance?

2. What effect does this conclusion seem to have on the person?

3. Taking an outsider's point of view, what would *you* think was probably the main cause of each person's performance?

4. What advice would you give to each?

Now consider these broader questions:

1. What are the most important reasons why some people are more successful than others?

2. How much does ability determine success? How much does luck determine success? How much do circumstances determine success?

3. If someone performs poorly at a job, what are the possible reasons for his or her performance? If someone performs well, what are the possible reasons for his or her performance? Is it harder to find reasons for good performance or for poor performance? Why?

To Try It online, go to Connect for *P.O.W.E.R. Learning and Your Life*.

Evaluation

An assessment of the match between a product or activity and the goals it was intended to meet

In every case, the answer is no. Even the greatest creation does not emerge in perfect form, immediately meeting all the goals of its producer. Consequently, the fourth step in the P.O.W.E.R. process is **evaluation**, which consists of determining how well the product or activity we have created matches our goals for it. Let's consider some steps to follow in evaluating what you've accomplished:

> **Take a moment to congratulate yourself and feel some satisfaction.** Whether studying for a test, writing a paper, completing a report, or drafting a memo, you've done something important. You've moved from ground zero to a spot that's closer to your goal.

> **Compare what you've accomplished with the goals you're seeking to achieve.** Think back to the goals, both short-term and long-term, that you're seeking to achieve. How closely does what you've done match what you're aiming to do? For instance, if your short-term goal is to complete a math problem set with no errors, you'll need to check over the work carefully to make sure you've made no mistakes.

> ▸ **Evaluate your accomplishments as if you were a respected mentor from your past.** If you've written a paper, reread it from the perspective of a favourite teacher. If you've prepared a report, imagine you're presenting it to a boss who taught you a lot. Think about the comments you'd give if you were this person.

> ▸ **Evaluate what you've done as if you were your current instructor or supervisor.** This time, consider what you're doing from the perspective of the person who gave you the assignment. How would he or she react to what you've done? Have you followed the assignment to the letter? Is there anything you've missed?

> ▸ **Based on your evaluation, revise your work.** If you're honest with yourself, it's unlikely that your first work will satisfy you. So go back to the Work stage and revise what you've done. But don't think of it as a step back: Revisions you make as a consequence of your evaluation bring you closer to your final goal. This is a case where going back moves you forward.

R Rethink

They thought they had it perfect. But they were wrong.

In fact, it was a $1.5 billion mistake—a blunder on a grand scale. The finely ground mirror of the Hubble space telescope, designed to provide an unprecedented glimpse into the vast reaches of the universe, was not so finely ground after all.

Despite an elaborate system of evaluation designed to catch any flaws, there was a tiny blemish in the mirror that was not detected until the telescope had been launched into space and started to send back blurry photographs. By then, it seemed too late to fix the mirror.

Or was it? NASA engineers pondered the problem for months, devising and discarding one potential fix after another. Finally, after bringing a fresh eye to the situation, they formulated a daring solution that involved sending a team of astronauts into space. Once there, a space-walking Mr. Goodwrench would install several new mirrors in the telescope, which could refocus the light and compensate for the original flawed mirror.

Although the engineers could not be certain that the $629 million plan would work, it seemed like a good solution, at least on paper. It was not until the first photos were beamed back to Earth, though, that NASA knew their solution was A-OK. These photos were spectacular.

It took months of reconsideration before NASA scientists could figure out what had gone wrong and devise a solution to the problem they faced. Their approach exemplifies—on a grand scale—the final step in P.O.W.E.R. Learning: rethinking.

Rethinking what you've accomplished earlier means bringing a fresh—and clear—eye to what you've done. It involves using **critical thinking**, thinking that involves reanalyzing, questioning, and challenging our underlying assumptions. While evaluation means considering how well what we have done matches our initial goals, rethinking means reconsidering not only the outcome of our efforts, but also our goals and the ideas and process we've used to reach them. Critically rethinking what you've done involves analyzing and synthesizing ideas, and seeing the connections between different concepts.

Rethinking involves considering whether our initial goals are practical and realistic or if they require modification. It also requires asking yourself what you would do differently if you could do it over again.

Critical thinking
A process involving reanalysis, questioning, and challenge of underlying assumptions

P.O.W.E.R. Learning and the World of Work

As we've discussed, the P.O.W.E.R. Learning process has applications both in the classroom and on the job. In **Career Connections** boxes, we'll highlight ways in which the principles we're discussing can help you excel in the workplace. Take a look at these "help wanted" advertisements and online postings. They illustrate the importance of the components of P.O.W.E.R. Learning in a wide variety of fields.

We'll be considering critical thinking throughout this book, examining specific strategies in every chapter; but the following steps provide a general framework for using critical thinking to rethink what you've accomplished:

> **Reanalyze, reviewing how you've accomplished the task.** Consider the approach and strategies you've used. What seemed to work best? Do they suggest any alternatives that might work better the next time?

> **Question the outcome.** Take a "big picture" look at what you have accomplished. Are you pleased and satisfied? Is there something you've somehow missed?

> **Identify your underlying assumptions; then challenge them.** Consider the assumptions you made in initially approaching the task. Are these underlying assumptions reasonable? If you had used different assumptions, would the result have been similar or different?

> **Consider alternatives rejected earlier.** You've likely discarded possible strategies and approaches prior to completing your task. Now's the time to think about those approaches once more and determine if they might have been more appropriate than the road you've followed.

> **What would you do differently if you had the opportunity to try things again?** It's not too late to change course.

> **Finally, reconsider your initial goals.** Are they achievable and realistic? Do your goals, and the strategies you used to attain them, need to be modified? Critically rethinking the objectives and goals that underlie your efforts is often the most effective route to success.

Completing the Process

The rethinking step of P.O.W.E.R. Learning is meant to help you understand your process of work and to improve the final product if necessary. But mostly it is meant to help you grow, to become better at whatever it is you've been doing. Like a painter looking at his or her finished work, you may see a spot here or there to touch up; but don't destroy the canvas. Perfectionism can be as paralyzing as laziness. Keep in mind these key points:

> **Know that there's always another day.** Your future success does not depend on any single assignment, paper, or test. Don't fall victim to self-defeating thoughts such as "If I don't do well on this particular assignment, I'll never graduate" or "Everything is riding on this one project." Nonsense. In school, on the job, and in life, there is almost always an opportunity to recover from a failure.

> **Realize that deciding when to stop work is often as hard as getting started.** Knowing when you have put in enough time studying for a test, revising a paper, or reviewing your figures on an estimate is as much a key to success as preparation. If you've carefully evaluated what you've done and if you've seen that there's a close fit between your goals and your work, it's time to stop work and move on.

> **Use the strategies that already work for you.** Although the P.O.W.E.R. Learning framework provides a proven approach to attaining success, employing it does not mean that you should abandon strategies that have brought you success in the past. Using multiple approaches, and personalizing them, is the surest road to success.

»LO 1.4 Learning More about Yourself

Consider what it would be like to be a member of the Trukese people, a small group of islanders in the South Pacific. Trukese sailors often sail hundreds of miles on the open sea. They manage this feat with none of the navigational equipment used by Western sailors. No compass. No chronometer. No sextant. They don't even sail in a straight line. Instead, they zigzag back and forth, at the mercy of the winds and tides. Yet they make few mistakes. Almost always they are able to reach their destination with precision. How do they do it?

They can't really explain it. They say it has to do with following the rising and setting of the stars at night. During the day, they take in the appearance, sound, and feel of the waves against the side of the boat. But they don't really have any idea of where they are at any given moment, nor do they care. They just know that ultimately they'll reach their final destination.

It would be foolhardy to suggest that the Trukese don't have what it takes to be successful sailors. The fact that they don't use traditional Western navigational equipment when they're sailing does not mean that they are any less able than Western navigators.

What about academic or career success? Isn't it reasonable to assume that there are different ways to reach academic goals and professional goals? Wouldn't it be surprising if everyone learned in exactly the same way?

Doing well in college or university and, ultimately, on the job, depends on an awareness of yourself. How do you learn? What are your strengths? What are your weaknesses? What do you value? What do you do better than most people, and what are your areas for improvement? If you can answer such questions, you'll be able to harness the best of your talents and anticipate challenges you might face. The interactive tools provided in this section of the chapter will go a long way towards helping you better understand what makes you unique and how to make the most of your potential.

Each of us has preferred ways of learning, approaches that work best for us either in the classroom or on the job. And our success is not just dependent on how well we learn, but on *how* we learn.

A **learning style** reflects a person's preferred manner of acquiring, using, and thinking about knowledge. We don't have just one learning style, but a variety of styles. Some involve our preferences regarding the way information is presented to us, some relate to how we think and learn most readily, and some relate to how our personality traits affect our performance. An awareness of your learning styles will help you in college by allowing you to study and learn course material more effectively. On the job, knowing your learning styles will help you master new skills and techniques, ensuring you can keep up with changing office practices or an evolving industry.

We'll start by considering the preferences we have for how we initially perceive information.

What Is Your Preferred Learning Style?

One of the most basic aspects of learning styles concerns the way in which we initially receive information from our sense organs. People have different strengths in terms of how they process information and which of their senses they prefer to use in learning. Specifically, there are four different types of learning styles:

Read/write learning style. If you have a **read/write learning style,** you prefer information that is presented visually in a written format. You feel most comfortable reading, and you may recall the spelling of a word by thinking of how the word looks. You probably learn best when you have the opportunity to read about a concept rather than listening to a teacher explain it.

> **Visual/graphic learning style.** Those with a **visual/graphic learning style** learn most effectively when material is presented visually in a diagram or picture. You might recall the structure of an engine or a part of the human body by reviewing a picture in your mind, and you might benefit from instructors who make frequent use of visual aids in class such as videos, maps, and models. Students with visual learning styles find it easier to see things in their mind's eye—to visualize a task or concept—than to be lectured about them.

> **Auditory/verbal learning style.** Have you ever asked a friend to help you put something together by having her read the directions to you while you worked? If you did, you may have an **auditory/verbal learning style.** People with auditory/verbal learning

Learning style
One's preferred manner of acquiring, using, and thinking about knowledge

Read/write learning style
A style that involves a preference for written material, favouring reading over hearing and touching

Visual/graphic learning style
A style that favours material presented visually in a diagram or picture

Auditory/verbal learning style
A style that favours listening as the best approach to learning

Steven Spielberg, an award-winning filmmaker, is a self-admitted visual learner. How can you use your own learning style to influence your career decisions?

styles prefer listening to explanations rather than reading them. They love class lectures and discussions, because they can easily take in the information that is being talked about.

> **Tactile/kinesthetic learning style.** Those with a **tactile/kinesthetic learning style** prefer to learn by doing—touching, manipulating objects, and doing things. For instance, some people enjoy the act of writing because of the feel of a pencil or a computer keyboard—the tactile equivalent of thinking out loud. Or they may find that it helps them to make a three-dimensional model to understand a new idea.

Learning styles have implications for effective studying or for learning new skills on the job:

> If you have a **read/write style,** consider writing out summaries of information, highlighting and underlining written material, and using flash cards. Transform diagrams and math formulas into words.

> If you have a **visual/graphic style,** devise diagrams and charts. Translate words into symbols and figures.

> If you have an **auditory/verbal style,** recite material out loud when trying to learn it. Work with others in a group, talking through the material, and consider recording lectures, with your professor's approval, of course.

> If you have a **tactile/kinesthetic style,** incorporate movement into your study. Trace diagrams, build models, arrange flash cards and move them around. Keep yourself active when learning, taking notes, drawing charts, and jotting down key concepts.

Table 1.1 presents a summary of the features of these learning styles, and **Try It! 4,** "What's Your Learning Style?" will help you figure out which of the four is your preferred learning style.

Tactile/kinesthetic learning style
A style that involves learning by touching, manipulating objects, and doing things

From the perspective of . . .

A NURSING ASSISTANT
You shouldn't see your learning style as a limitation. Repeating instructions aloud is one way for nursing assistants who are auditory learners to ensure they are comprehending instructions. How can you adapt your learning style in multiple career settings?

table 1.1 The Four Learning Styles

Category	Type	Description	Using the Style
Learning Styles	Read/write	A style that involves a preference for material in a written format, favouring reading over hearing and touching.	Read and rewrite material, take notes and rewrite them; organize material into tables; transform diagrams and math formulas into words.
	Visual/graphic	A style that favours material presented visually in a diagram or picture.	Use figures and drawings; replay classes and discussions in your mind's eye; visualize material; translate words into symbols and figures.
	Auditory/verbal	A style in which the learner favours listening as the best approach.	Recite material out loud; consider how words sound; study different languages; record lectures or training sessions; work with others, talking through the material.
	Tactile/kinesthetic	A style that involves learning by touching, manipulating objects, and doing things.	Incorporate movement into studying; trace figures and drawings with your finger; create models; make flash cards and move them around; keep active during class and meetings, taking notes, drawing charts, jotting down key concepts.

 Try It!

 PERSONAL STYLES

What's Your Learning Style?

Read each of the following statements and rank them in terms of their usefulness to you as learning approaches. Base your ratings on your personal experiences and preferences, using the following scale:

1 = Not at all useful

2 = Not very useful

3 = Neutral

4 = Somewhat useful

5 = Very useful

	1	2	3	4	5
1. Studying alone					
2. Studying pictures and diagrams to understand complex ideas					
3. Listening to class lectures					
4. Performing a process myself rather than reading or hearing about it					
5. Learning a complex procedure by reading written directions					
6. Watching and listening to film, computer, or video presentations					
7. Listening to a book or lecture on tape					
8. Doing lab work					
9. Studying teachers' handouts and lecture notes					
10. Studying in a quiet room					
11. Taking part in group discussions					
12. Taking part in hands-on demonstrations					
13. Taking notes and studying them later					
14. Creating flash cards and using them as a study and review tool					
15. Memorizing how words are spelled by spelling them "out loud" in my head					
16. Writing down key facts and important points as a tool for remembering them					
17. Recalling how to spell a word by seeing it in my head					
18. Underlining or highlighting important facts or passages in my reading					
19. Saying things out loud when I'm studying					
20. Recalling how to spell a word by "writing" it invisibly in the air or on a surface					
21. Learning new information by reading about it in a book					
22. Using a map to find an unknown place					
23. Working in a study group					
24. Finding a place I've been to once by just going there without directions					

(continued)

4

Scoring: The statements cycle through the four learning styles in this order: (1) read/write; (2) visual/graphic; (3) auditory/verbal; and (4) tactile/kinesthetic.

To find your primary learning style, disregard your 1, 2, and 3 ratings. Add up your 4 and 5 ratings for each learning style (i.e., a "4" equals 4 points and a "5" equals 5 points). Use the following chart to link the statements to the learning styles and to write down your summed ratings:

Learning Style	Statements	Total (Sum) of Rating Points
Read/write	1, 5, 9, 13, 17, and 21	23
Visual/graphic	2, 6, 10, 14, 18, and 22	24
Auditory/verbal	3, 7, 11, 15, 19, and 23	14
Tactile/kinesthetic	4, 8, 12, 16, 20, and 24	24

The total of your rating points for any given style will range from a low of 0 to a high of 30. The highest total indicates your main learning style. Don't be surprised if you have a mixed style, in which two or more styles receive similar ratings.

To Try It online, go to Connect for *P.O.W.E.R. Learning and Your Life*.

What Is Your Striving Style™?

Figuring out how best to leverage your college or university education begins with understanding who you are meant to be. Investing several years of your life in study only to find out that the work you have studied for does not align with your needs and values is a depressing thought. No matter which diploma or degree you want to pursue, what you strive to be influences how you learn and achieve. The Striving Styles™ Personality Assessment, developed by Canadian psychotherapist Dr. Anne Dranitsaris, helps you understand how to best approach learning by identifying what Dranitsaris calls your striving style and the predominant need that must be met for you to feel confident and secure. In **Try It! 5**, "What Is Your Striving Style?" you can determine your striving style. For a more in-depth report on your striving style, visit the Connect site for *P.O.W.E.R. Learning and Your Life* or **www.striving-styles.com**. **Table 1.2** on page 25 contains a summary of each striving style along with a description of how people of each style learn best.

Striving Style
A mode of thought and behaviour driven by a predominant need that directs the way in which we seek satisfaction from our lives.

Try It!

PERSONAL STYLES

What Is Your Striving Style?

STRIVING STYLES™ SELF-ASSESSMENT–Student Version*

Rate how *often* the description in each of the following sentences applies to you	
Section A Never = 0; Rarely = 1; Infrequently = 2; Frequently = 4; Always = 5	
1. I prefer to have the choice and responsibility for making my own decisions.	5
2. Others turn to me to know what to do in most situations.	4
3. I look for chances to be in charge of people and activities.	4
4. I usually know what is best for my friends and expect them to listen to my advice.	5
5. I find it hard to see the point of people getting emotional or creating drama.	5
6. I like to have goals for myself for school and my future.	5
7. For me, doing my school work and projects is more important than my social life.	4
8. I am uncomfortable when I have to let others be in charge.	3
Section A Total	37
Section B Never = 0; Rarely = 1; Infrequently = 2; Frequently = 4; Always = 5	
1. I like being with people and easily make friends with others.	5
2. I have many friends and I enjoy introducing people to each other.	2
3. When I am involved in group activities, I tend to talk a lot and get others involved.	5
4. I have a hard time saying no to invitations from friends. My social calendar is usually pretty full.	5
5. I like to see the positive in people and have a hard time understanding when they hurt my feelings.	5
6. I can sometimes get so involved with my friends and their problems that I forget about my own chores or homework.	4
7. I like giving compliments to people and letting my friends know how special they are to me.	5
8. I see everyone I meet as a potential friend.	4
Section B Total	37
Section C Never = 0; Rarely = 1; Infrequently = 2; Frequently = 4; Always = 5	
1. I enjoy being the center of attention and look for chances to be there.	4
2. I have many talents and do lots of things well.	4
3. I am very conscious of how I look and work hard to make sure I look good.	5
4. I often try to act like other people tell me I should act.	5
5. I believe I am meant to do something important.	5
6. I like to let people know what I can do and special things I have done.	1
7. When I'm having fun, I will lose track of time and force myself to stay awake even if I'm tired so I don't miss anything.	2
8. I often end up doing things that make others notice me.	4
Section C Total	23
Section D Never = 0; Rarely = 1; Infrequently = 2; Frequently = 4; Always = 5	
1. I like to be involved in a lot of activities most of the time.	4
2. I have a strong need for adventure, excitement, and new and different experiences.	4
3. I don't like having to do the same thing the same way twice.	3

5

4. I tend to be outgoing, friendly, and sociable with many friends and acquaintances.	5
5. I like to be where the action is.	2
6. I am good when a problem needs to be solved or when there is trouble happening.	4
7. I don't really think about how what I do might make other people feel.	0
8. I need a lot of freedom and don't like it when people try to make me follow rules.	5
Section D Total	27

Section E	Never = 0; Rarely = 1; Infrequently = 2; Frequently = 4; Always = 5	
1. I seek beauty, originality, and creativity in all I do.		5
2. Others describe me as being moody and emotional.		4
3. I tend to have only a few friends, but I am very close with them.		5
4. I don't feel it is important to conform to what others or society thinks I should do.		45
5. I tend to be a perfectionist and am self-critical.		4
6. I feel that most people do not understand me.		5
7. I look calm on the outside even though there is a lot going on inside of me.		5
8. I enjoy spending time alone in nature.		4
Section E Total		37

Section F	Never = 0; Rarely = 1; Infrequently = 2; Frequently = 4; Always = 5	
1. I get absorbed in things that interest me, spending hours alone with them.		5
2. I like to know as much as I can about how things work. I also like to do things well		5
3. When I am tired or feel pressure, I tend to withdraw from others and spend a lot of time alone.		5
4. I believe I'm different than others and I don't like it when others try to make me conform.		5
5. I will challenge people in authority (such as teachers or parents) by disagreeing or questioning them.		5
6. I don't like to talk about myself and others find me difficult to know.		5
7. I am not naturally curious about what I feel or how others feel.		0
8. I say what's on my mind and sometimes people think I'm being critical, even when I'm not.		4
Section F Total		34

Section G	Never = 0; Rarely = 1; Infrequently = 2; Frequently = 4; Always = 5	
1. My friends often come to me for my opinions on things.		4
2. I enjoy schoolwork where I can independently research, investigate, or create new ideas about how things might be in the future.		4
3. I try to understand the deeper meaning of things.		5
4. I prefer to figure out how something works than to ask for help.		5
5. I sometimes know things are going to happen before they do.		5
6. I am talented at solving problems and dealing with things that are complicated.		5
7. I sometimes focus too much on little, unimportant things and avoid what I really need to do.		5
8. When I am tired or stressed I tend to overindulge in food, alcohol, or other things that aren't really good for me.		5
Section G Total		35

(continued)

5 *(concluded)*

Section H Never = 0; Rarely = 1; Infrequently = 2; Frequently = 4; Always = 5	
1. Others would describe me as loyal, hardworking, and predictable.	2
2. I don't like change because it's more comfortable when things stay the same.	4
3. I try to do what is expected of me and am respectful of authority.	1
4. I tend to say no when asked to try new things, preferring to stay with what I am familiar with.	1
5. I have a hard time saying no when people ask me to do important things for them.	0
6. I prefer to be with the friends I know well rather than meeting new people.	4
7. I sometimes worry and can imagine terrible things when I think about the future.	2
8. I tend to focus more on doing things with people and less on getting to know who those people are (what they like, what they think about things, etc.)	2
Section H Total	16

Overall Totals

Once you have answered the questions in each of the sections, place your scores in the <u>first column below.</u> Your striving style is the style in which you have scored highest. If you have two similar scores, read the descriptions of each of the striving styles and determine which most accurately describes how you see yourself.

Total Scores	Striving Style	Predominant Need	Key Characteristics
Section A Total 31	Leader	To be in Control	Analytical, driven, goal oriented, implements, organizes others
Section B Total 31	Socializer	To be Connected	Sociable, outgoing, sentimental, seeks personal and social success
Section C Total 23	Performer	To be Recognized	Extro verted, innovative, seeks novelty, goal and achievement driven
Section D Total 27	Adventurer	To be Spontaneous	Adventurous, hands-on, impulsive, pleasure-seeking, straightforward
Section E Total 37	Artist	To be Creative	Inaccessible, holistic, enigmatic, self-contained, seeks inner intensity
Section F Total 34	Intellectual	To be Knowledgeable	Solitary, introspective, seeks knowledge, expert, aloof
Section G Total 38	Visionary	To be Perceptive	Idealistic, creative thinker, futuristic revolutionary, discovering
Section H Total 16	Stabilizer	To be Secure	Intense, obsessive, detached, authoritarian, dutiful

*Based on the Striving Styles™ Personality System © Sage, Kahuna Enterprises 2010

To Try It online, go to Connect for *P.O.W.E.R. Learning and Your Life.*

table 1.2 The Eight Striving Styles

Category	Type	Description	How this Style Learns
Striving Styles	Leader	Self-directed, can experience difficulty accepting opinions of others.	Enjoy logical discussions in study groups, but dislike tangents. Have high expectations of self and others, including the teacher.
	Socializer	Skilful communicators, tend to take criticism personally.	Learn best in structured settings where you can discuss with your peers.
	Performer	Success-oriented, enthusiastic learners, like recognition.	Engage in learning through discussions with teacher and other students.
	Adventurer	Spontaneous, enjoy constant activity, enjoy group work.	Learn by doing, like to challenge teachers.
	Artist	Diligent, motivated to learn mainly about subjects that interest them.	Struggle to assess quality of your own work; learn best when you get to know and can consult with the teacher.
	Intellectual	Enjoy the learning process.	Need to have respect for the teacher, prefer to learn at your own pace.
	Visionary	Strong work ethic, dislike memorization.	Learn though interaction with others, whether in person or through reading.
	Stabilizer	Tenacious and persistent with their studies, need to master fundamentals before moving on.	Learn best in well-structured environment with clear, precise assignments.

Multiple Intelligences: Showing Strength in Different Domains

Do you feel much more comfortable walking through the woods than navigating city streets? Are you an especially talented musician? Is reading and using a complicated map second nature to you?

If so, in each case you may be demonstrating a special and specific kind of intelligence. According to psychologist Howard Gardner, rather than asking "How smart are you?", we should be asking "How are you smart?" To answer the latter question, Gardner has developed a theory of multiple intelligences that offers a unique approach to understanding learning styles and preferences.

The multiple intelligences view says that we have eight different forms of intelligence, each relatively independent of the others and linked to a specific kind of information processing in our brains:

> **Logical-mathematical intelligence** involves skills in problem solving and scientific thinking.

> **Linguistic intelligence** is linked to the production and use of language.

> **Spatial intelligence** relates to skills involving spatial configurations, such as those used by artists and architects.

> **Interpersonal intelligence** is found in learners with particularly strong skills involving interacting with others, such as sensitivity to the moods, temperaments, motivations, and intentions of others.

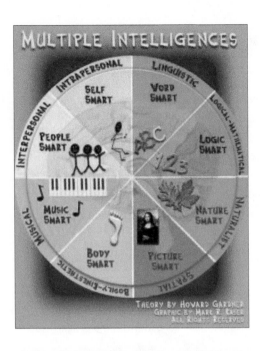

> **Intrapersonal intelligence** relates to a particularly strong understanding of the internal aspects of oneself and having access to one's own feelings and emotions.
> **Musical intelligence** involves skills relating to music.
> **Bodily kinesthetic intelligence** relates to skills in using the whole body or portions of it in the solution of problems or in the construction of products or displays, exemplified by dancers, athletes, actors, and surgeons.
> **Naturalist intelligence** involves exceptional abilities in identifying and classifying patterns in nature.

All of us have the same eight kinds of intelligence, although to varying degrees; and they form the core of our learning styles and preferences. While relatively independent of one other, these separate intelligences do not operate in isolation. Instead, any activity involves several kinds of intelligence working together. **Table 1.3** describes each of the types of intelligence and shows how each is used. Later on in this book, we'll also introduce you to the notion of "emotional intelligence" which, while not part of Howard Gardner's model, is a valuable addition to the work done in this area.

table 1.3 Multiple Intelligences

Category	Type	Description	Using the Intelligence
Multiple Intelligences	Logical-mathematical	Strengths in problem solving and scientific thinking.	Express information mathematically or in formulas.
	Linguistic	Strengths in the production and use of language.	Write out notes and summarize information in words; construct stories about material.
	Spatial	Strengths involving spatial configurations, such as those used by artists and architects.	Build charts, graphs, and flowcharts.
	Interpersonal	Found in learners with particularly strong skills involving interacting with others, such as sensitivity to the moods, temperaments, motivations, and intentions of others.	Work with others in groups.
	Intrapersonal	Strengths in understanding the internal aspects of oneself and having access to one's own feelings and emotions.	Build on your prior experiences and feelings about the world; use your originality.
	Musical	Strengths relating to music.	Write a song or lyrics to help remember material.
	Bodily kinesthetic	Strengths in using the body or parts of it in the solution of problems or in the construction of products or displays, exemplified by dancers, athletes, actors, and surgeons.	Use movement in studying; build models.
	Naturalist	Exceptional strengths in identifying and classifying patterns in nature.	Use analogies based on nature.

Put It All Together

Here are some key facts to remember about learning styles, striving styles, and multiple intelligences:

> **You have a variety of styles.** As you can see in the summaries in **Tables 1.1** (page 19), **1.2** (page 25), and **1.3** (page 26), there are several types of learning styles, striving styles, and intelligences. For any given task or challenge, some types may be more relevant than others. Furthermore, success is possible even when there is a mismatch between what you need to accomplish and your own pattern of preferred styles. It may take more work, but learning to deal with situations that require you to use less-preferred styles is important for college or university and for your career.

> **Your style reflects your preferences regarding which abilities you *like* to use—not the abilities themselves.** Styles are related to our preferences and the mental approaches we like to use. You may prefer to learn in a tactile way, but that in itself doesn't guarantee that the products that you create in that way will be good. You still have to put in work! Conversely, you can produce very good results using approaches that are difficult and uncomfortable for you.

> **Your style may change over the course of your life.** You can learn new styles and expand the range of learning experiences in which you feel perfectly comfortable. In fact, you can conceive of this book as one long lesson in learning styles because it provides you with strategies for learning more effectively in a variety of ways.

> **You should work on improving your less-preferred styles.** Although it may be tempting, don't always make choices that increase your exposure to preferred styles and decrease your practice with less-preferred styles. The more you use approaches for which you have less of a preference, the better you'll be at developing the skills associated with those styles.

> **Work cooperatively with others who have different styles.** If your instructor or supervisor asks you to work cooperatively, seek out classmates or co-workers who have styles that are different from yours. Working with people with differing styles will help you to achieve collective success, and you can also learn from observing others' approaches to tackling tasks.

Deal with Learning Disabilities

If you, like millions of people in North America, have a learning disability of any kind, the process of becoming an expert student will present additional challenges. **Learning disabilities** are defined as difficulties in processing information when listening, speaking, reading, or writing; in most cases, learning disabilities are diagnosed when there is a discrepancy between learning potential and actual academic achievement.

One of the most common kinds of learning disabilities is *dyslexia,* a reading disability that produces the misperception of letters during reading and writing, unusual difficulty in sounding out letters, spelling difficulties, and confusion between right and left. Although its causes are not yet completely understood, one likely explanation is a problem in the part of the brain responsible for breaking words into the sound elements that make up language.

Another common disability is *attention deficit hyperactivity disorder* (or *ADHD*), which is marked by inattention, an inability to concentrate, and a low

Learning disabilities
Difficulties in processing information when listening, speaking, reading, or writing, characterized by a discrepancy between learning potential and actual academic achievement

tolerance for frustration. For the 1 to 3 percent of adults who have ADHD, planning, staying on task, and maintaining interest present unusual challenges. Not only are these challenges present in college or university, but they also affect job performance.

People with learning disabilities are sometimes viewed as unintelligent. Nothing could be further from the truth: There is no relationship between learning disabilities and IQ. For instance, dozens of well-known and highly accomplished individuals suffered from dyslexia, including physicist Albert Einstein, Virgin Group founder Richard Branson, Apple founder Steve Jobs, and actors Will Smith, Orlando Bloom, and Keanu Reeves.

By the time they reach a post-secondary institution, most people with learning disabilities have already been diagnosed. If you have a diagnosed learning disability and you need special services, it is important to disclose your situation to your instructors and counsellors and to take advantage of the support they can offer.

In some cases, students with learning disabilities have not been appropriately evaluated prior to college or university. If you have difficulties such as mixing up and reversing letters frequently and suspect that you have a learning disability, there will likely be an office on campus that can provide you with guidance. One place to start is your campus counselling or health centre.

Many sorts of treatments, ranging from learning specific study strategies and the use of specially designed computer software to the use of medication, can be effective in dealing with learning disabilities. However, just because you are having trouble with reading assignments doesn't automatically mean that you have a learning disability. The kind of reading you do in college or university is more difficult than in other contexts, and there's also more of it; so you can expect to find academic reading challenging. It's only when reading represents a persistent, long-term problem—one that won't go away no matter how much work you do—that a learning disability becomes a possible explanation. An excellent Canadian website for post-secondary students with learning disabilities can be found at **www.youth2youth.ca**.

A learning disability in no way dictates what you are able to accomplish.

Time to Reflect: What Did I Learn?

1. Look back at the Employability Skills 2000+ list (Figure 1.3 on page 6), which describes the skills valued by Canadian employers. Which of these skills do you already possess? Which need more work?

2. Before reading this chapter, had you ever considered the fact that there are many different kinds of intelligence? How can knowing this have an impact on how you see other people?

3. Canadian writer Malcolm Gladwell has put forth the notion that to be a true master in any field requires about 10 000 hours of concentrated effort, which translates into about 3 hours a day, every day, for 10 years. What do you enjoy doing that would make you want to put in that kind of effort? Could you see yourself committing to that amount of time and effort? Why or why not?

Looking
Back

What are the benefits of a post-secondary education?

- The reason first-year college students most often cite for attending college is to get a better job, and college graduates do earn more on average than non-graduates.
- A post-secondary education provides many benefits in addition to improved career prospects. These include becoming well educated, learning to think critically and communicate effectively, understanding the interconnections among different areas of knowledge and our place in history and the world, and understanding diversity.

What do Canadian Employers value in a potential employee?

- Canadian employers are seeking a set of skills, attitudes, and behaviours relating to three main categories: fundamental skills, personal management skills, and teamwork skills.

What are the basic principles of P.O.W.E.R. Learning?

- P.O.W.E.R. Learning is a systematic approach people can easily learn, using abilities they already possess, to acquire successful habits for learning and achieving personal goals.
- P.O.W.E.R. Learning involves **p**reparation, **o**rganization, **w**ork, **e**valuation, and **r**ethinking.

How do expert students use P.O.W.E.R. Learning?

- To *prepare,* learners set both long-term and short-term goals, making sure that their goals are realistic, measurable, and under their control—and will lead them toward their final destination.
- They *organize* the tools they will need to accomplish those goals.
- They get down to *work* on the task at hand. Using their goals as motivation, expert learners also understand that success depends on effort.
- They *evaluate* the work they've done, considering what they have accomplished in comparison with the goals they set for themselves during the preparation stage.
- Finally, they *rethink,* reflecting on the process they've used, taking a fresh look at what they have done, and critically reassessing their goals.

How can I use knowledge about my learning and striving styles and multiple intelligences to be more successful?

- People have patterns of diverse learning styles—characteristic ways of acquiring and using knowledge.
- Learning styles include read/write, visual/graphic, auditory/verbal, and tactile/kinesthetic styles.
- Striving styles include leader, socializer, performer, adventurer, artist, intellectual, visionary, and stabilizer.
- The multiple intelligences view suggests that we have eight different forms of intelligence, each relatively independent of the others.
- Knowing more about how you learn, how you are smart, and how you like to interact with the world around you can help you identify the specific techniques that will allow you to master material in class and on the job more effectively.

[KEY TERMS AND CONCEPTS]

Auditory/verbal learning style (p. 18)

Bodily-kinesthetic intelligence (p. 26)

Critical thinking (p. 15)

Evaluation (p. 14)

Interpersonal intelligence (p. 25)

Intrapersonal intelligence (p. 26)

Learning disabilities (p. 27)

Learning style (p. 18)

Linguistic intelligence (p. 25)

Logical-mathematical intelligence (p. 25)

Long-term goals (p. 18)

Motivation (p. 12)

Musical intelligence (p. 26)

Naturalist intelligence (p. 26)

P.O.W.E.R. Learning (p. 5)

Read/write learning style (p. 18)

Short-term goals (p. 8)

SMART approach to goal setting (p. 8)

Spatial intelligence (p. 25)

Striving style™ (p. 21)

Tactile/kinesthetic learning style (p. 19)

Visual/graphic learning style (p. 18)

[RESOURCES]

ON CAMPUS

Every college and university provides a significant number of resources to help its students succeed and thrive, ranging from the activities coordination office to a multicultural centre to writing labs to career centres. You can check them out on your institution's website, or in the calendar or phone directory.

Here's a list of some typical campus resources, many of which we'll be discussing in future chapters:

- Activities/clubs office
- Adult and re-entry centre
- Advising centre
- Alumni office
- Art gallery
- Bookstore
- Career centre
- Chaplain/religious services
- Child care centre
- Cinema/theatre
- Computing centre/ computer labs
- Continuing education
- Disability centre (learning or physical disabilities)

- Financial aid office
- Fitness centre/ gymnasium
- Health centre
- Honours program
- Housing centre
- Information centre
- Intramural sports
- Language lab
- Lost and found
- Math lab
- Multicultural centre
- Museum
- Online education (distance learning) office
- Off-campus housing and services
- Ombudsperson/ conflict resolution

- Photography lab
- Police/campus security
- Post office
- Printing centre
- Registration office
- Residential life office
- School newspaper
- Student government office
- Student affairs office
- Study abroad/ exchange programs
- Testing centre
- Volunteer services
- Work-study centre
- Writing lab

If you are commuting to school, your first "official" encounters on campus are likely to be with representatives of the college or university's Student Affairs Office or its equivalent. The Student Affairs Office has the goal of maintaining the quality of student life, helping to ensure that students receive the support they need. Student Affairs personnel are often in charge of student orientation programs that help new students familiarize themselves with their new institution.

Whatever representatives you deal with during your first days on campus, remember that their job is to help you. Don't be shy about asking questions about what you may expect, how to find things, and what you should be doing.

Above all, if you are experiencing any difficulties, be certain to make use of your institution's resources. Success in post-secondary education does not come easily for anyone, particularly when it demands juggling responsibilities of work and family. You should make use of whatever support your college or university offers.

IN PRINT

To learn more about Canadian writer Malcolm Gladwell's 10 000 hour theory, take a look at his fascinating book *Outliers: The Story of Success* (Little, Brown and Company, 2008).

For a practical guide on surviving your first year, check out *Off to College: Now What? A Practical Guide to Surviving and Succeeding Your First Year of College,* a paperback book authored by Jessica Linnell (Atlantic Publishing Company, 2009).

Are you an international student who is new to the Canadian education system? You'll want to examine *Succeeding as an International Student in the United States and Canada* by author Charles Lipson (University of Chicago Press, 2008).

Gail Wood's book *How to Study: Use Your Personal Learning Style to Help You Succeed When It Counts* (Learning Express Press, 2000) provides an introduction to learning styles, offering tips and suggestions for making use of the way that you learn.

ON THE WEB

The following websites provide the opportunity to extend your learning about the material in this chapter.

▸ Macleans.ca's on-campus website (**http://oncampus.macleans.ca/education/**) offers students up-to-the-minute news, advice, blogs, information on student finance, scholarships, and co-op. It serves as the companion site to *Maclean's* magazine's annual University Ranking issue.

▸ *Campus Life* magazine's online site (**www.campuslifemagazine.ca**) is 100% student driven, from the writing to the cover models. The site offers a broad selection of articles of interest to post-secondary students.

▸ GlobeCampus (**www.globecampus.ca/**) is *The Globe and Mail*'s site dedicated to undergraduate education in Canada, and is a companion site to *The Globe and Mail*'s annual Canadian University Report, a survey of over 40 000 students across Canada.

▸ To examine each of the Striving Styles in more depth, visit **www.annedranitsaris.com**.

▸ If you haven't yet done so, be sure to visit the Conference Board of Canada's free "Skills Credentialing Tool for Individuals" at **www.conferenceboard.ca/topics/education/default.aspx**.

TAKING IT TO THE NET

1 Find out what percentage of the Canadian population of has received a college diploma or undergraduate degree, by visiting the Education, Training and Learning section of Statistics Canada's website at **www.statcan.gc.ca**. The site provides information about the Canadian population based on the Canadian census, which is conducted every five years in Canada (the latest one was conducted in 2011). How many men have received a post-secondary diploma or certificate? How many women?

2 Do you control your destiny, or are you controlled by it? This *Psychology Today* "Locus of Control" test assesses how you view the relative impact of hard work versus luck on achieving success. (**http://psychologytoday.tests.psychtests.com/take_test.php?idRegTest=1317**)

The Case of . . .
Vexed in Vancouver

It was during the second week of classes that the questioning started. Until then, Jian had been fairly confident in his decision to enrol at a college in the Vancouver suburbs to gain training to be a medical technician. He had been excited to try something new and to start a new career, but more and more he was wondering if he'd made the right choice.

To get to campus, Jian had to take a 45-minute bus ride, because his wife needed the car to get to her office in downtown Vancouver. Jian was also keeping his part-time job as an executive assistant at a doctor's office, a job that meant another long commute. And on top of that, Jian needed to find time among work, classes, and studying to help care for his five-year-old son.

Maybe, Jian was beginning to think, college hadn't been such a good idea. True, he could earn more money as a medical technician and begin a more promising career. But was it really worth all this added time and stress? Plus, Jian had never done very well academically. Why would college be any different? If he wanted to make more money, he could just add more shifts at his current job.

Why bother with college? Jian thought to himself. What an expense, and what a hassle. For what?

1. What arguments could you provide Jian as to the value of a college education?

2. Do you think that Jian's doubts are common?

3. What might you suggest that Jian do to help deal with his doubts about the value of college?

4. Why might a student's doubts about the value of college be especially strong during the beginning weeks of college?

5. Do you share any of Jian's concerns about the value of a college education? Do you have additional ones?

2 Making the Most of Your Time

Learning Outcomes

By the time you finish this chapter, you will be able to

» LO 2.1 Explain why it is important to manage time more effectively and discuss techniques that can help you better manage your time.

» LO 2.2 Analyze how to handle competing priorities.

» LO 2.3 Identify strategies for dealing with surprises and distractions.

As Jen Wong waits in line for her morning cup of coffee, she mentally goes over the things she needs to get done during the day: *Get to the gym at 8:00 A.M. for her morning yoga class . . . study for her anatomy quiz over lunch at 12:30 . . . from 1:30 to 4:30, go to classes at the college where she's studying for her massage therapist diploma . . . meet her boyfriend at 5:00 to watch his son's soccer game . . . go home, make dinner, finish an assignment, and spend some time catching up with her friends on Facebook.* She has the nagging feeling that there's something else she needs to do, but she can't put her finger on it.

Jen finally gets to the head of the line to pay for her double-double, which she starts drinking even before she pays for it. Glancing at a clock as she leaves the Tim Hortons, she gives up the thought of getting in some last-minute studying for her anatomy quiz before her yoga class. It will be a minor miracle if she even makes it to the gym on time.

Jen has been up less than an hour, and already she is running behind schedule.

Looking Ahead

Are your days like Jen's? Are you constantly trying to cram more activities into less time? Do you feel as if you never have enough time?

You're not alone: Most of us wish we had more time to accomplish the things we need to do. However, some people are a lot better at juggling their time than others. What's their secret?

There is no secret. No one has more than 24 hours a day and 168 hours a week. The key to success lies in figuring out our priorities and better using the time we do have.

Time management is like juggling a bunch of tennis balls: For most of us, juggling doesn't come naturally; but it is a skill that can be learned. Not all of us will end up perfect jugglers (whether we are juggling tennis balls or time); but, with practice, we can become a lot better at it.

The P.O.W.E.R Plan in this chapter starts where every P.O.W.E.R. Plan starts—with Preparation—where you learn to account for the ways you currently use—and misuse—time. Then, it helps you Organize, by providing you with tools that help you track your time and strategies that help you manage your priorities and competing goals. After that comes Work—where you implement the tools and give the strategies a try. Then it's time to Evaluate—how are the tools and strategies working for you? How are you dealing with the inevitable interruptions and counterproductive personal habits that can sabotage your best intentions? And finally, it's time to Rethink—to reflect on how your personal style of time management affects you and others in your life, and to examine some of the special challenges involved in juggling the priorities of school and work with other aspects of life, such as child rearing or hobbies. The P.O.W.E.R. Plan in this chapter will provide you with skills that are important not only for success in post-secondary education and on the job, but in your personal life as well.

≫LO2.1 Managing Your Time Effectively

Without looking up from the page, answer this question: What time is it?

Most people are pretty accurate in their answer. And if you don't know for sure, it's very likely that you can find out. Your cellphone may display the time; there may be a clock on the wall, desk, or computer screen; or maybe you're riding in a car that shows the time in the instrument panel. Time is something from which we can't escape. Even if we ignore it, it's still going by, ticking away, second by second, minute by minute, hour by hour. So the main issue in using your time well is this: Who's in charge? We can allow time to slip by and let it be our enemy. Or we can take control of it and make it our ally.

By taking control of how you spend your time, you'll increase your chances of becoming more successful in your post-secondary education and in your career. Here's another way to look at it: The better you are at managing the time you devote to your studies and your job, the more time you will have to spend on your outside interests. How you approach time and time management will undoubtedly be a reflection of the learning style, striving style, and multiple intelligences you uncovered in Chapter 1. You can get a sense of your own personal "time style" by completing **Try It! 1**, "Find Your Time Style," on the next page.

The goal of time management is not to schedule every moment so we become pawns of a timetable that governs every waking moment of the day. Instead, the goal is to permit us to make informed choices as to how we use our time. Rather than letting the day slip by, largely without our awareness, the time management procedures we'll discuss can make us better able to harness time for our own ends. In short, time management doesn't confine us. On the contrary, it frees us to do the things we want and need to do.

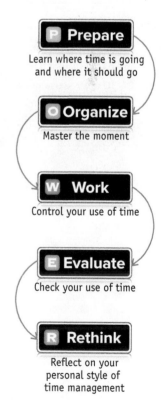

P Prepare
Learn where time is going and where it should go

O Organize
Master the moment

W Work
Control your use of time

E Evaluate
Check your use of time

R Rethink
Reflect on your personal style of time management

P.O.W.E.R. Plan

Try It! PERSONAL STYLES

Find Your Time Style

Rate how well each of the statements below describes you.   Use this rating scale:

1 = Doesn't describe me at all

2 = Describes me only slightly

3 = Describes me fairly well

4 = Describes me very well

	1	2	3	4
1. I often wake up later than I should.				
2. I am usually late for classes and appointments.				
3. I am always in a rush getting places.				
4. I put off big tasks and assignments until the last minute.				
5. My friends often comment on my lateness.				
6. I am easily interrupted, putting aside what I'm doing for something new.				
7. When I look at a clock, I'm often surprised at how late it is.				
8. I often forget appointments and have to reschedule them.				
9. When faced with a big task, I feel overwhelmed and turn my mind away from it until later.				
10. At the end of the day, I have no idea where the time went.				

Rate yourself by adding up the points you assigned. Use this scale to assess your time style:

10–15 = Very efficient time user

16–20 = Efficient time user

21–30 = Time use needs work

31–40 = Victim of time

To Try It online, go to Connect for *P.O.W.E.R. Learning and Your Life.*

 **Prepare**   ## Learn Where Your Time Is Going

Before you get somewhere, you need to know where you're starting from and where you want to go. So the first step in improving your time management skills is figuring out how you're managing your time *now.*

"Where did the day go?" If you've ever said this to yourself, one way of figuring out where you've spent your time is

> "You may delay, but time will not."
>
> Benjamin Franklin

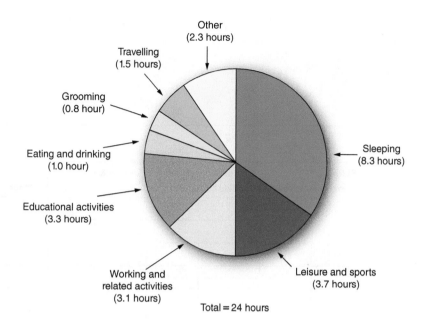

figure 2.1
Time Use of Full-Time University and College Students on an Average Weekday
Source: Courtesy of U.S. Bureau of Labor Statistics

to create a time log. A time log is the most essential tool for improving your use of time.

A **time log** is simply a record of how you actually have spent your time—including interruptions. It doesn't have to be a second-by-second record of every waking moment. But it should account for blocks of time in increments as short as 15 minutes. By looking at how much time you spend doing various activities, you now know where your time goes. How does it match with your perceptions of how you spend your time? Be prepared to be surprised, because most people find that they're spending time on a lot of activities that just don't matter very much.

Let's take a look at the results of a study of time use for full-time university and college students. As you can see from **Figure 2.1**, surprisingly little time—about 3.3 hours of every day—is actually spent on activities related to education. Perhaps it's not so surprising when you consider that, according to a study done in 2009 by Nielsen Online, the total number of minutes spent worldwide on Facebook alone increased by 566% over a one-year period; and involvement with social networking sites is only expected to increase. How does the pie chart in Figure 2.1 compare to how *you* spend your time?

Look at the blank time log in **Try It! 2**, Create a Time Log." As you fill out the log, be specific, indicating not only what you were doing at a given time (for example, "studying for economics quiz") but also the interruptions that occurred (such as "answered cellphone twice" or "switched to Internet for 10 minutes").

Time log

A record of how one spends one's time

From the perspective of . . .

A STUDENT Time logs can be helpful tools when determining how you spend your time; they can also help you find more time for the activities you enjoy doing. In what areas of your life do you wish you had more time to spend?

»LO 2.2 Handling Competing Priorities

By this point you should have a good idea of what's taking up your time. But you may not know what you should be doing instead.

To figure out the best use of your time, you need to determine your priorities. **Priorities** are the tasks and activities you need and want to do, rank-ordered from most important to least important. Your priorities should be rooted in your

Priorities

The tasks and activities that one needs and wants to do, rank-ordered from most important to least important

Try It!

Create a Time Log

Time Log

Day: _____   Date: _____

	Grooming	Eating & Drinking	Travelling	Educational Activities	Work & Related	Leisure & Sports	Sleep	Other
6–7 a.m.								
7–8 a.m.								
8–9 a.m.								
9–10 a.m.								
10–11 a.m.								
11 a.m.–Noon								
Noon–1 p.m.								
1–2 p.m.								
2–3 p.m.								
3–4 p.m.								
4–5 p.m.								
5–6 p.m.								
6–7 p.m.								
7–8 p.m.								
8–9 p.m.								
9–10 p.m.								
10–11 p.m.								
11 p.m.–Midnight								
Midnight–6 a.m.								
Total hours spent per category								

Keep track of the way you spend your time across seven days on time logs. Insert the amount of time you spend on each activity during each one-hour period for a single day. Do the same thing for every day of the week on separate time logs. Be sure to make copies of this log before you fill it in for the first day, or you can print out copies at the *P.O.W.E.R. Learning* website.

   Analyze your log: After you complete your log for a week, the next step is to analyze how you spend your time according to the major categories on the log, a task that will appeal particularly to those of you with strong logical-mathematical intelligence. Add up the number of hours you spend on each category, and divide the number of hours for each category by 168, which is the number of hours you have in a week. This will give you a percentage for the week for each category. Those of you who are visual/graphic learners will probably want to go one step further and transform these percentages into a pie chart like the one shown in **Figure 2.1.**

Now consider the following:

1. What do you spend most of your time on?

2. Are you satisfied with the way that you are using your time? Are there any areas that seem to use up excessive amounts of time?

3. Do you see some simple fixes that will allow you to use time more effectively?

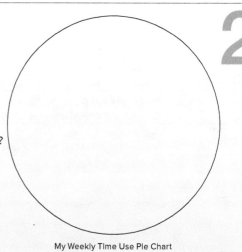

My Weekly Time Use Pie Chart

 WORKING IN A GROUP

Compare your use of time during an average week with those of your classmates and the students who were surveyed in Figure 2.1. What are the major similarities and differences in the use of time?

To Try It online, go to Connect for *P.O.W.E.R. Learning and Your Life.*

values and your goals. There are no right or wrong priorities; you have to decide for yourself what you wish to accomplish. Maybe spending time on your studies is most important to you, or working to earn more money, or maybe your top priority is spending time with your family. Only you can decide. Furthermore, what's important to you at this moment may be less of a priority to you next month, next year, or five years from now. Revisiting your priorities, and assessing whether they still fit with your values and goals, is something that should be done on a regular basis.

For the purpose of effective time management in college or university, the best procedure is to start off by identifying priorities for an entire term. What do you need to accomplish? Don't just choose obvious, general goals, such as "passing all my classes." Instead, think about your priorities in terms of the SMART approach to goal setting introduced in Chapter 1: specific, measurable activities, such as "studying ten hours before each exam"—not "studying harder," a goal which is too vague. (Look at the example of a priority list in **Figure 2.2** and also the **Course Connections** feature on page 40.)

Write your priorities on the chart in **Try It! 3**, "Set Priorities," on page 41. After you've filled out the chart, organize it by giving each priority a ranking from 1 to 3. A "1" represents a priority that absolutely must be done; without it, you'll suffer a major setback. For instance, showing up for work should receive a "1" for a priority

Priority	Ranking
Study for each class at least 30 minutes/day	1
Start each major paper 1 week in advance of due date	2
Hand in each paper on time	1
Review for test starting a week before test date	2
Be on time for job	1
Check in with Mom once a week	3
Work out 3x/week	3

figure 2.2
Sample List of Priorities

ranking; carving out time to take those guitar lessons you always wanted to take might be ranked a "3" in terms of priority. The important point is to rank-order your priorities to reveal what is and is not important to accomplish during the term.

Setting priorities will help you to determine how to make the best use of your time. No one has enough time to complete everything; prioritizing will help you make informed decisions about what you can do to maximize your success.

Recognize What Is Important and What Is Urgent

Every priority is not as important as every other, and all priorities are not equally urgent. For example, suppose an economics assignment worth 2% of your final mark is due Wednesday morning and you also have a marketing test scheduled

Course Connections

Study Time: How Much Is Enough?

What would you guess is the average number of hours instructors think you should be studying each week? In the view of instructors queried in a national survey, students should spend, on average, six hours per week preparing for each class in which they're enrolled. And if they're taking courses in the sciences and engineering, instructors expect their students to put in even more hours.[1]

Keep in mind that study time does *not* include actual class time. If you add that in, someone taking four classes would need 24 hours of outside class preparation and would be in class for 16 hours—for a total of 40 hours, or the equivalent of full-time employment. If you are enrolled in a fast-track program or career college, where the training is even more intense and fast-paced, you may find yourself working the equivalent of two full-time jobs!

If you've underestimated the amount of time instructors believe is necessary to devote to class preparation, you may need to rethink the amount of time you'll need to allocate to studying. You might also speak to your individual instructors to see what they believe is an appropriate amount of preparation. Although they may not be able to give exact figures, their estimates will help you to prioritize what you need to do to be a successful student.

Try It!

Set Priorities

3

Set your priorities for the term. They may include getting to class on time, finishing papers and assignments by their due dates, maintaining a good reputation with your boss, or spending time with your family. To get started, list your priorities in any order. Be sure to consider priorities relating to your classes, work, family, social obligations, and health. After you list them, assign a number to each one indicating its level—giving a "1" to the highest priority items, a "2" to medium priority items, and a "3" to the items with the lowest priority.

List of Priorities	
Priority	**Priority Ranking**

Now redo your list, putting your number 1s first, followed by as many of your number 2s and 3s as you feel you can reasonably commit to.

Final List of Priorities
Priority
1.
2.
3.
4.
5.
6.
7.
8.
9.
10.

1. What does this list tell you about your greatest priorities? Are they centred around school, career, friends and family, or some other aspect of your life?

2. Do you have so many "1" priorities that they will be difficult or impossible to accomplish successfully? How could you go back to your list and trim it down even more?

3. What does this listing of priorities suggest about how successful you'll be during the upcoming term?

To Try It online, go to Connect for *P.O.W.E.R. Learning and Your Life.*

Try It!

4

Urgent? Important?

Fill in the quadrants in **Figure 2.3** to help you figure out what is truly urgent and what is really important. Revisit the priorities you identified in **Try It! 3**, but this time distinguish the important priorities from the less important and the urgent from the not-so-urgent, taking into account *what* and *who* will be impacted if a priority is not addressed in time.

figure 2.3
Priority Setting:
The Importance of
Distinguishing What is
Important and What Is
Urgent
(adapted from Covey,
Stephen [2004]. *The Seven*
Habits of Highly Successful
People [Fireside])

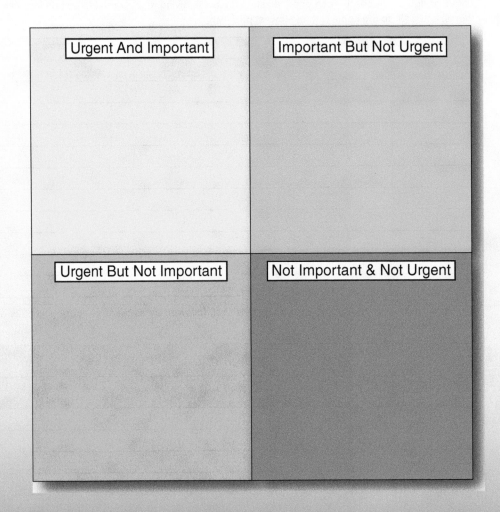

To Try It online, go to Connect for *P.O.W.E.R. Learning and Your Life.*

Wednesday afternoon, worth 25% of your final mark. While both may be urgent, they should not receive the same amount of attention. How much time you spend on each should reflect its relative impact on your grades.

Similarly, if you are working on a group project and everyone is supposed to submit a draft of his or her part by a specific date, not meeting this deadline will have an impact not only on you, but also on everyone else in your group. With even one section missing, the entire project could be delayed. Tasks of this nature, where a missed deadline has a detrimental impact on a lot of other people, should take on greater importance and urgency than those that affect only you.

With these ideas in mind, work through **Try It! 4**, "Urgent? Important?"

▣ Organize Master the Moment

Having completed the first step of your time management P.O.W.E.R. Plan, preparation, you now know where you've lost time in the past; and your new list of priorities is telling you where you need to head in the future.

It's time to move to step 2: Organize. This is a major step.

Being organized is key to taking control of your time; to do it well requires a few tools.

> ▸ A **master calendar** that shows all the weeks of the term in one place. Those of you who have a tactile/kinesthetic learning style should probably purchase a large, inexpensive erasable/wipe-off calendar from your local office supply store and place it above your workspace. Another alternative is to create an electronic master calendar using templates you can find readily on the Internet or by using programs like Microsoft Outlook or Google Calendar. Whether you choose an erasable or electronic calendar, you can use different colours to indicate different types of activities; i.e., red for school due dates, blue for social activities, and so on. Storing your calendar electronically is a particularly efficient approach to time management, because you can access it from anywhere and download it to your iPod, Blackberry, or other electronic organizer.
>
> The important point about your master calendar is that it should include every week of the term and seven days per week. In other words, it should capture your entire life for the next few months, at a glance. You should put assignment due dates and quiz and test dates into this calendar; and you should also include statutory holidays, medical and dental appointments, important birthdays and anniversaries, upcoming trips, and social activities. In this way, you can readily identify the bottlenecks, those times when you have too much going on at once and will need to consider getting something done ahead of schedule. (See the example of a master calendar in **Figure 2.4** on page 44.)
>
> ▸ A **weekly timetable** is a master grid with the days of the week across the top and the hours along the side. It will permit you to write in all your regularly scheduled activities, as well as one-time appointments when they arise. (A blank weekly timetable is provided in **Figure 2.5** on page 45. You can also find it online at Connect for *P.O.W.E.R. Learning and Your Life,* or use the one that comes with your calendar software.)
>
> ▸ A **daily to-do list** can be integrated into your online calendar program; it can be written on a small, portable calendar that includes a separate page for each day of the week; or it can simply be a small notebook, with a separate sheet of paper for every day of the week. Whatever form your daily to-do list takes, make sure it's portable, because you'll need to keep it with you all the time.

Master calendar
A schedule showing the weeks of a longer time period, such as a term or semester, with all assignments and important activities noted on it

Weekly timetable
A schedule showing all regular, prescheduled activities due to occur in the week, together with one-time events and commitments

Daily to-do list
A schedule showing the tasks, activities, and appointments due to occur during the day

September 2012

Sun	Mon	Tue	Wed	Thu	Fri	Sat
						1 Camping
2	3 Labour Day	4 Classes start	5	6	7	8
9	10	11 English Quiz 5%	12 Psych Quiz 10%	13	14	15
16	17	18	19	20 Acctg Quiz 5%	21	22 8 p.m. Tiff's birthday party
23	24 Math test 20%	25 English quiz 5%	26 Mktg Report due, 15%	27	28 9 a.m. Dentist	29 Study Group Mtg
30						

October 2012

Sun	Mon	Tue	Wed	Thu	Fri	Sat
	1	2	3	4 English quiz 5%	5	6
7	8 Thanksgiving	9 English midterm 20%	10 Mktg midterm 25%	11 Acctg midterm 20%	12 Psych midterm 20%	13
14 Brunch with Maria	15	16	17	18 Acctg quiz 5%	19	20 Study Group Mtg
21	22	23 English quiz 5%	24 Mkting Report Due 15%	25	26	27 Halloween party at pierre's
28	29	30	31			

November 2012

Sun	Mon	Tue	Wed	Thu	Fri	Sat
				1 Acctg Quiz 5%	2	3 Weekend in montreal
4 Montreal	5	6 English quiz 5%	7 Mktg Test 25%	8	9	10 Study Group Mtg
11	12	13	14	15 Acctg quiz 5%	16 Psych quiz 10%	17
18	19	20	21	22	23	24
25	26	27	28 Mktg Report due, 15%	29 Acctg Quiz 5%	30 Psych quiz 10%	

December 2012

Sun	Mon	Tue	Wed	Thu	Fri	Sat
						1 Study Group Mtg
2	3 Martin's Birthday	4	5 Group Report Due, 30%	6	7	8
9	10 Final Exam Week	11	12	13	14	15 Xmas Shopping
16	17	18	19	20	21	22
23	24	25 Christmas	26 Boxing Day	27	28	29
30	31					

figure 2.4
A Sample Master Calendar

The basic organizational task you face is filling in these three schedules. You'll need at least an hour to do this, so set the time aside. In addition, there will be some repetition across the three schedules, and the task may seem a bit tedious. But every minute you invest now in organizing your time will pay off in hours that you will save in the future.

Follow these steps in completing your schedule. The steps are similar, whether you track your appointments on paper or electronically:

> **Start with the master calendar, which shows all the weeks of the term on one page.** Write on the master calendar every class assignment, quiz, or test you have for the entire term, noting it on the date that it is due. Use your course outline or syllabus as your guide. Where due dates are not provided, ask your professor for guidance. Also include major events at work, such as days when you might need to work overtime. In addition, include important activities from your personal life and student activities, drawn from your list of priorities. For instance, if your spouse or child has a performance or your college or university has a sporting event you want to attend, be sure to mark it down.

Finally, schedule some free time—time when you promise yourself you will do something that is just plain fun. Consider these days to be written in stone, and promise yourself that you won't use them for anything else except for something enjoyable. Just knowing that you have some down time planned will help you to throw yourself into more demanding tasks. In addition, getting into the habit of allowing yourself time to relax and reflect on your life is as important as any other time management skill you may learn.

You now have a good idea of what the next few weeks have in store for you. You can identify just by looking at your master calendar the periods when you are going to be especially busy. You can also note the periods when you will have less to do.

Use the off-peak periods to get a head start on future assignments! In this way, your master schedule can help you head off disaster before it occurs.

> **Now move to the blank weekly timetable provided in Figure 2.5** on page 46. Fill in the times of all your fixed, prescheduled activities—the times when your classes are scheduled, when your study groups meet, when you have to be at work, or when you have to pick up your child at daycare, as well as any other regularly recurring appointments. In electronic calendars like Microsoft Outlook, it is very easy to schedule any type of recurring appointment—whether it occurs weekly, biweekly, monthly, or even annually—the latter being particularly useful for remembering birthdays, anniversaries, or your annual medical checkup.

Short- and long-term priorities may not always match. What would you do if a test scheduled in a class you needed to graduate conflicted with your daughter's weekly soccer game?

Once you've filled in the weekly timetable, as in the sample version provided in **Figure 2.6**, you get a bare-bones picture of the average week. You will still need to take into account the specific activities that are required to complete the assignments on the master calendar.

To move from your "average" week to specific weeks, make photocopies of the weekly timetable that now contains your fixed appointments. Make enough copies for every week of the term. On each copy, write the week number of the term and the specific dates it covers.

Using your master calendar, add assignment due dates, tests, and any other activities on the appropriate days of the week. Then pencil in blocks of time necessary to prepare for those events.

How much time should you allocate for schoolwork? One very rough rule of thumb holds that every one hour that you spend in class requires, on average, two hours of study outside of class to earn a B and three hours of study outside of class to earn an A. Do the arithmetic: If you are taking five 3-hour courses weekly or 15 credits (with each credit equivalent to an hour of class per week), you'll need to plan for 30 hours of studying each week to earn a B average—an intimidating amount of time. Of course, the amount of time you must allocate to a specific class will vary from week to week, depending on what is happening in the class.

If you estimate that you'll need five hours of study for a midterm exam in a certain class, pencil in those hours. Don't set up a single block of five hours. People remember best when their studying is spread out over shorter periods

Week #

	14 Sunday	15 Monday	16 Tuesday	17 Wednesday	18 Thursday	19 Friday	20 Saturday
7 am							
8 00							
9 00							
10 00							
11 00							
12 pm							
1 00							
2 00							
3 00							
4 00							
5 00							
6 00							
7 00							
8 00							
9 00							
10 00							
11 00							

figure 2.5
A Weekly Timetable Template

Week

	14 Sunday	15 Monday	16 Tuesday	17 Wednesday	18 Thursday	19 Friday	20 Saturday
7 am							
8 00							
9 00		Economics Room D3-02		Economics Room D3-02	Study Group Meeting MKTG Library	Work Tim Hortons	
10 00							
11 00			Statistics Room B1-02	Study Group Meeting ECON Library	Statistics Room B1-02		
12 pm							
1 00		Lunch	Lunch with Drew	Lunch	Lunch		Yoga Class Hot Yoga Centre
2 00		Human Resources D3-06	Marketing C3-26	Human Resources D3-06	Marketing C3-26		
3 00							
4 00							
5 00			Soccer Practice Recreating				
		Supper		Supper			
6 00							
7 00		Work Tim Hortons	Supper	Work Tim Hortons	Supper	Supper out with friends Restaurant	
8 00			Volunteer Work Community Centre		Finance-Night course A2-15		
9 00							
10 00							
11 00							

figure 2.6
A Sample Weekly Timetable

Sometimes it is okay (and even necessary) just to relax. Make sure that you make time to unwind!

rather than attempted in one long block of time. Besides, it will probably be hard to find a block of five straight hours on your weekly calendar.

Has your professor assigned a major project that isn't due until the end of the term? Unfortunately, many students assume that they can pull off a major project by turning their attention to it a few days before it is due. This is *not* the best way to approach a major project. Like anything else that takes a lot of effort, time for a major project should be planned out and inserted into your weekly timetable.

Whether it's a group or individual project, you should begin by breaking up any major project into its component parts and identifying a reasonable amount of time required for completion of each task. A major group research project might involve, for example, 4 group meetings of 1 hour each, 10 hours of research, 5 hours of writing, 3 hours of editing, 1 hour of proofreading, and 1 hour to put together an integrated bibliography. Once you've identified the tasks and the time they require, put the tasks into the logical order in which they must be accomplished, noting which tasks involve time overlap. If it's a group project, allocate the tasks by putting a group member's name beside each one.

Now, starting with the LAST task, and taking into account how long each task takes, work your way *backwards* from the project due date. Do this with the next-to-last task, and so on, until you've worked your way back to the very first task. You will now know the very latest date on which work on the project must begin. You have just created a "**workback**" from the project's due date, and can transfer these tasks into your weekly timetable.

Keep in mind that estimates are just that: estimates. Don't think of them as set in stone, but don't deliberately under- or over-estimate the amount of work required either. And remember: It's crucial not to over-schedule yourself. You'll still need time to eat, to talk with your friends, to spend time with your family, and to enjoy yourself in general. If you find that your life is completely filled with things that you feel you must do in order to survive and that there is no room for fun, then take a step back and cut out something to make some time for yourself in your daily schedule. Finding time for yourself is as important as carving out time for what others want you to do. Besides, if you are overworked, you're likely to "find" the time by guiltily goofing off without really setting aside the time and enjoying it.

Workback

Planning when to start a project by working your way back from its due date.

To-Do List for
_____

Mon 17/10/2011

☐	!	📎	Task Subject	Status	Due Date	Priority	% Complete	Done
☑			Call Navendra about quiz	Not Started	Mon 17/10/2011	▇ 2	0 %	
☑			Finish Marketing Assignment	In Progress	Mon 17/10/2011	1	60 %	
☑			Call dentist for appt	Not Started	Mon 17/10/2011	▇ 3	0 %	
☑			Meet with Prof. Lavoie	Done	Mon 17/10/2011	1	100 %	✔
☑			Pick up Megan at school	Done	Mon 17/10/2011	1	100 %	✔
☑			Bring book to library	Done	Mon 17/10/2011	▇ 2	100 %	✔
☑			Do laundry	Not Started	Mon 17/10/2011	▇ 3	0 %	
☑			Work on outline Economics	In Progress	Mon 17/10/2011	▇ 2	30 %	

figure 2.7
Sample Daily To-Do List

> **If you've taken each of the previous steps, you're now in a position to work on the final step of organization for successful time management: completing your daily to-do list.** Unlike the master calendar and weekly timetable—both of which you develop weeks or even months in advance—complete your daily to-do list just one day ahead of time, preferably at the end of the day.

List all the things that you intend to do the next day, and their level of priority. Start with the things you know you *must* do and which have fixed times, such as classes, work schedules, and appointments. These are your first priority items. Then add in the other things that you *should* accomplish, such as an hour of study for an upcoming test or a trip to the garage to have the oil changed in your car. Finally, list things that are lower priority but still desirable—setting aside time for a run or a walk, for example. If you use an electronic to-do list, like the one in Microsoft Outlook, turn on the auditory reminder function to remind you when a task is scheduled to begin.

Don't schedule every single minute of the day. That would be counterproductive, and you'd end up feeling as if you'd failed if you deviated from your schedule. Instead, think of your daily to-do list as a path through a forest. If you were hiking, you would allow yourself to deviate from the path, occasionally venturing onto side tracks when they looked interesting. But you'd also be keeping tabs on your direction so you would end up where you needed to be at the end of the hike, rather than miles away from your car or home.

Like the sample daily to-do list in **Figure 2.7** above, include a column to check or cross off after you've completed an activity. There's something very satisfying in acknowledging what you have accomplished.

From the perspective of . . .

A WORKING PARENT
The balancing act between work and family can be a challenge. How can a weekly timetable help you ensure all areas of your life are getting the attention they deserve?

≫ LO2.3 **W Work** Dealing with Surprises and Distractions

We've now reached Step 3 of the P.O.W.E.R. Plan for managing your time: Work. The good news is that you've already done a lot of the work, because much of work in time management is in the preparation and organization. The work involved in time management is to follow the schedules and to-do lists that you've prepared and organized. But it won't be easy. Our lives are filled with surprises. Things take longer than we've planned. A friend we haven't spoken to in a while calls to chat, and it seems rude to say that we don't have time to talk. Crises occur; buses are late; computers break down; kids get sick.

The difference between effective and ineffective time management lies in 1) how well you take control of your environment, 2) how efficiently you work, 3) how well you deal with procrastination, and 4) how well you balance competing responsibilities.

Take Control of Your Environment

It is up to you to take active control of your environment and not let it take control of you. Here are a few suggestions to help you do just that:

> **Just say no.** You don't have to agree to every request and every favour that others ask of you. You're not a bad person if you refuse to do something that will eat up your time and prevent you from accomplishing your goals. And if you do decide to do someone else a time-consuming favour, try to come up with the most efficient way of accomplishing it. Don't let all your time get taken up by the priorities of others. This advice is especially important for those of you with strong interpersonal intelligence, who tend to put the needs of others ahead of your own.

> **Get away from it all.** Go to the library. Lock yourself into your bedroom. Find a quiet, out-of-the-way coffee shop. Any of these places can serve to isolate you from everyday distractions and thereby permit you to work on the tasks that you wish to complete. Try to adopt a particular spot as your own, such as a corner desk in a secluded nook in the library. If you use it enough, your body and mind will automatically get into study mode as soon as you seat yourself there.

> **Enjoy the sounds of silence.** Although many people insist they accomplish most while a television, radio, or CD is playing, scientific studies suggest otherwise: We are able to concentrate best when our environment is silent. So even if you're sure you work best with a soundtrack playing, experiment and work in silence for a few days. Even those of you with strong musical intelligence may be surprised to find out that you get more done in less time than you would in a more distracting environment.

> **Take a break from e-distractions.** Text messages, phone calls, Facebook status updates, instant messages, email. Who doesn't love to hear from others? We may not control when communications arrive, but we can make the message wait until we are ready to receive it. Take a break and shut down your communication distractions for a period of time. When it comes to emails and social networking sites like Facebook, set aside a specific time each day to deal with them, rather than turning your attention to the computer every time an email is received or a friend's status is updated. Consider turning off audible or visual notifications entirely, so you won't be distracted by them.

> **Expect the unexpected.** Interruptions and crises, minor and major, can't be eliminated. However, they can be prepared for.

> How is it possible to plan for surprises? Though it may still be too early in the term to get a clear picture of what sorts of unanticipated events you'll encounter, you should keep an eye out for patterns. Perhaps one instructor routinely gives surprise assignments. Maybe you're asked to work extra hours on the weekends because a certain co-worker doesn't show up for his or her shift.

> You'll never be able to escape the interruptions and surprises that will require your attention. But by trying to anticipate them, and by thinking about how you'll react to them, you'll be positioning yourself to react more

effectively when they do occur. Another way to prepare for the unexpected is to stick to your to-do list as best you can; that way, the time that you need to deal with the unexpected will be available to you.

Work Smarter, Not Harder

Thanks to smart phones, computers, and the Internet, you are never more than a click away from a massive encyclopedia of the world's knowledge. Learning to leverage this knowledge is one of the most important investments you can make. Here are some additional strategies for working smarter rather than harder:

> **Accomplish the task in the most efficient way possible.** We tend to do things the way we've always done them, without considering whether there might be a more efficient way to accomplish what we've set out to do. For example, you may consider heading out to your local bookstore to see whether they have a particular book. Why not check online first or phone ahead? You'll save time and gas, and you'll also avoid the possibility of wasting even more time browsing once you reach the bookstore!

> **Match the amount of effort you expend to the importance of the task.** You probably wouldn't spend just ten minutes deciding which car to buy, but you might spend ten minutes selecting a pair of shoes. The same goes for school work. The amount of time you put into a report worth 25% of your mark should differ significantly from the time you spend studying for a weekly 1% quiz.

> **Develop a consistent approach to tasks you do regularly.** Whether it's folding towels or developing a business presentation, there are efficiencies to be gained by approaching tasks that you do regularly in the same way each time. When it comes to your school work, reuse presentation or report templates that have worked well for you in the past. Examine some of the templates available in Microsoft Word or PowerPoint to get ideas. Why reinvent the wheel if someone has already put time and effort into developing something that you can use as a foundation?

> **Use electronic devices to help you manage your time—and your life—more effectively.** Use your smart phone or computer calendar's "reminder" functions whenever it makes sense to do so. Input due dates for upcoming assignments, then ask to be reminded about the task a few days and/or hours in advance. Invest an hour of your life putting important birthdays and anniversaries into your electronic calendar; use the "recurring annually" function with no end date, and you will never forget these dates again. Add in a reminder a week in advance of the date to prepare an e-card and purchase a gift online, a timesaver if ever there was one. And if you are an auditory/verbal learner, go one step further by making that reminder an auditory one.

Deal with Procrastination

Procrastination, the habit of putting off tasks that need to be accomplished, is like a microscopic parasite. It is invisible to the naked eye, but it eats up your time nonetheless.

Procrastination
The habit of putting off tasks that need to be accomplished

You can't control interruptions and crises that are imposed upon you by others. But even when no one else is throwing interruptions at us, we make up our own. Ever wonder how much time the average Canadian spends on social networking sites? A study by Ipsos Reid revealed that the average Facebook user, for instance, spends 5.9 hours per week on the site. How do you compare? Check out **Figure 2.8** to find out.

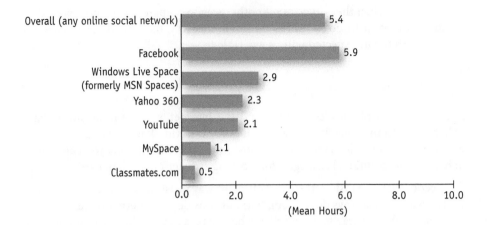

figure 2.8
Ipsos Reid Poll on
Time Spent on Social
Networking Sites[2]

The problem with procrastinating is that you are merely delaying the inevitable. Eventually, the task *must* get done, and you *know* it must get done. The longer you delay, the more stressed you get, and the more you open yourself up to any number of potential problems: not finding the information you are looking for, running out of printer ink, not having time to ask the professor for clarification, and so forth. Procrastinating when working on a group project is even more stressful—perhaps not for you, but certainly for the people you are working with. Professors usually expect group projects to have a unified look and to read as though they were written by one person. To accomplish this requires careful editing and proofreading—tasks which take time, and which cannot wait for procrastinators to get their act together!

To identify whether you are a procrastinator, find your "Procrastination Quotient" in **Try It! 5**, "Find Your Procrastination Quotient," on page 53.

If you find yourself procrastinating, several strategies can help you:

> **Break large tasks into small ones.** People often procrastinate because a task they're seeking to accomplish appears overwhelming. If writing a 15-page paper seems nearly impossible, think about writing a series of five 3-page papers. If reading a 750-page book seems impossible, think of it as reading several 250-page books.

> **Start with the simplest part of a task, and then do the harder parts.** Succeeding initially on the easy parts can make the harder parts of a task less daunting, and make you less apt to procrastinate in completing the task.

> **Just begin!** Sometimes the hardest part of an activity is simply getting started. So take the leap and begin the task, and the rest may follow easily.

> **Work with others.** Just being in the same physical location with others can motivate you sufficiently to accomplish tasks that you consider unpleasant and on which you might be tempted to procrastinate. For instance, filling out tedious order forms can be made easier if you collaborate with co-workers. Beware, though: If you spend too much time socializing, you lower the likelihood of success.

> **Keep the costs of procrastination in mind.** Procrastination doesn't just result in delay; it may also make the task harder than it would have been if you hadn't procrastinated. Not only will you ultimately have less time to complete the task, but you also may have to do it so quickly that its quality may be diminished. In the worst case scenario, you won't be able to finish it at all. And if others are involved in the task, you will be making their lives difficult as well, something they will remember the next time you are looking to work in their group.

Try It!

5

Find Your Procrastination Quotient

Do you procrastinate? To find out, circle the number that best applies for each question:

1. I invent reasons and look for excuses for not acting on a problem.

Strongly agree 4 3 2 1 **Strongly disagree**

2. It takes pressure to get me to work on difficult assignments.

Strongly agree 4 3 2 1 **Strongly disagree**

3. I take half measures that will avoid or delay unpleasant or difficult tasks.

Strongly agree 4 3 2 1 **Strongly disagree**

4. I face too many interruptions and crises that interfere with accomplishing my major goals.

Strongly agree 4 3 2 1 **Strongly disagree**

5. I sometimes neglect to carry out important tasks.

Strongly agree 4 3 2 1 **Strongly disagree**

6. I schedule big assignments too late to get them done as well as I know I could.

Strongly agree 4 3 2 1 **Strongly disagree**

7. I'm sometimes too tired to do the work I need to do.

Strongly agree 4 3 2 1 **Strongly disagree**

8. I start new tasks before I finish old ones.

Strongly agree 4 3 2 1 **Strongly disagree**

9. When I work in groups, I try to get other people to finish what I don't.

Strongly agree 4 3 2 1 **Strongly disagree**

10. I put off tasks that I really don't want to do but know that I must do.

Strongly agree 4 3 2 1 **Strongly disagree**

Scoring: Total the numbers you have circled. If the score is below 15, you are not a chronic procrastinator and you probably have only an occasional problem. If your score is 16–25, you have a minor problem with procrastination. If your score is above 25, you procrastinate quite often and should work on breaking the habit.

Now, consider the following:

- If you do procrastinate often, why do you think you do it?
- Are there particular kinds of assignments that you are more likely to procrastinate on?
- Is there something that you are putting off doing right now? How might you get started on it?

 WORKING IN A GROUP

Think about the last time you procrastinated. Describe it as completely as you can. What was the task? What did you do rather than doing what needed to be done? What could you have done to avoid procrastinating in this situation? Ask others what strategy they might suggest for avoiding procrastinating.

To Try It online, go to Connect for *P.O.W.E.R. Learning and Your Life.*

Balance Competing Responsibilities

Balance school and work demands

Juggling school and a job can be a real challenge. Not only must you manage your time to complete your schoolwork, but in many cases you'll also face time management demands while you are on the job. Here are some tips to help you keep everything in balance:

> "I had a friend who was taking classes to become a paralegal. He always complained about how he didn't have enough time between taking classes and holding down his job. But he was always inviting me and his other friends out to movies, insisting we stay at the bar for one more round. It wasn't a surprise when he eventually dropped out of school. It wasn't that he didn't have enough time. It was that he spent it on all the wrong things."
>
> **Bell Hansom, restaurant manager**

- **If you have slack time on the job, get some studying done.** Try to keep at least some of your textbooks, class notes, or notecards always with you so you can refer to them. Of course, you should never do school work without your employer's prior agreement. If you don't get permission, you may jeopardize your job.

- **Use your lunch hour effectively.** Although it's important to eat a nutritious lunch and not to wolf your food down, you may be able to use some of the time allotted to you for lunch to fit in some studying.

- **Ask your employer about flextime.** If your job allows it, you may be able to set your own hours, within reason, as long as the work gets done. If this is an option for you, use it. Although it may create more time management challenges for you than would a job with set hours, it also provides you with some flexibility.

- **Accept new responsibilities carefully.** If you've barely been keeping up with the demands of work and school, don't automatically accept new job responsibilities without carefully evaluating how they fit with your long-term priorities. If your job is temporary and you're not planning to stay, you might want to respectfully decline substantial new duties or an increase in the number of hours you work. On the other hand, if you plan to continue in the job once you're done with school, accepting new responsibilities may be more reasonable.

Balance School and Work Obligations with Family Demands

If you have a job and are a student and you also have caregiver responsibilities for children or other family members, time management is especially challenging. Your family demands—and deserves—substantial quantities of your time, and juggling school and work along with family obligations can prove to be exhausting. However, there are some specific strategies that can help.

- **Dealing with child-care demands:**

  Provide activities for your children. Kids enjoy doing things on their own for part of the day. Plan activities that will keep them happily occupied while you're doing school work.

  Make spending time with your children a priority. Carve out "free play" time for your kids. Even 20 minutes of good time devoted to your children will give all of you—you *and* them—a lift. No matter how busy you are, you owe it to your children, and to yourself, to spend time as a family.

  Enlist your child's help. Children love to play adult and, if they're old enough, you can ask them to help you study. Maybe they can help you clear a space to study. Perhaps you can give them "assignments" that they can work on while you're working on your assignments.

  Encourage your child to invite friends over to play. Some children can remain occupied for hours if they have a playmate.

On-the-Job Time Management

Career Connections

In the business world, schedules are unpredictable. Crises occur, perhaps due to manufacturing problems or client demands, which require sudden flurries of work. Perhaps you have a demanding boss who may, without warning, give you an urgent assignment due the next morning. Time is always at a premium. You may be forced to drop everything you normally work on and pitch in on a sudden new task. As a result, your plans to complete your everyday work may be disrupted completely.

Simply put, time management is an essential survival skill when developing your career. Learning the basic principles of time management now will help you well beyond your years in college or university, throughout your later career. You'll also want to learn new time-management strategies specific to the working world. For instance, if you supervise other employees, it may be possible to delegate some work to them, allowing them to help you complete assignments on time. Or sometimes it may be possible to deflect assignments brought to you by a boss to some other unit or department. Always keep in mind what you can do alone and what you cannot complete without the aid of co-workers. Don't be afraid to ask for help. In the working world, the end result is what counts above all.

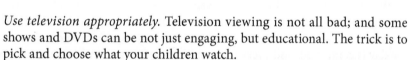

Use television appropriately. Television viewing is not all bad; and some shows and DVDs can be not just engaging, but educational. The trick is to pick and choose what your children watch.

Find the best child care or babysitters that you can. The better the care your children are getting, the better you'll be able to concentrate on your classes or your job. You may still feel guilty that you're not with your children as much as you'd like, but accept that guilt. Remember, your attendance in class and good performance at work builds a better future for your children.

Use your children's "downtime" effectively. If your children are young, use their nap time as a chance to catch up on work or chores. Or consider getting up early, before your children wake up, for a period in which you will have fewer interruptions than later in the day.

▸ **Dealing with the elder-care demands:**

Encourage as much independence as possible on the part of older adults for whom you are responsible. Not only will it take some of the pressure off you, but it will be helpful to the older adult.

Ask for support from your siblings and other family members. Caring for an ill or aging parent should be a family affair, not a burden that falls on any one individual.

Determine what community resources are available. Local centres for the aged may provide assistance not only to the elderly but also to their caregivers.

Respect your own needs. Remember that your own priorities are important. Elders for whom you are responsible will understand that you will sometimes need to put yourself first.

 ## Check Your Use of Time

Your time management P.O.W.E.R. Plan is on track. Now it's time to Evaluate your progress. Evaluating how you use your time is pretty straightforward: You either accomplished what you intended to do in a given period, or you didn't. Did you check off all the items on your daily to-do list? If you go over your list at the end of every day, you will know how successful your time management efforts have been, and you will be able to incorporate any activities you missed into the next day's to-do list.

Checking off the completed items on your to-do list is important because it provides an objective record of what you have accomplished on a given day. Just as important, it provides you with concrete reinforcement for completing the task. There are few things more satisfying than gazing at a to-do list with a significant number of check marks.

Of course, you won't always accomplish every item on your to-do list. That's not surprising, nor even particularly bad, especially if you've included some second- and third-level priorities that you don't absolutely have to accomplish anyway.

Give yourself a pat on the back for completing the things that you've accomplished. Successful time management is not easy, and if you've improved at all, you deserve to feel some personal satisfaction.

 ## Reflect on Your Personal Style of Time Management

At the end of the day, after you've evaluated how well you've followed your time management plan and how much you've accomplished, it's time to Rethink where you are. Maybe you've accomplished everything you set out to do. Every task for the day is completed, and every item on your to-do list has a check mark next to it.

Or maybe you have the opposite result. Your day has been a mess, and you feel as if nothing has been accomplished. Because of a constant series of interruptions and chance events, you've been unable to make headway on your list.

Or—most likely—you find yourself somewhere in between these two extremes. Some tasks got done, while others are still hanging over you. Now is the time to rethink in a broad sense how you manage your time by doing the following:

> **Reassess your priorities.** Are your long- and short-term goals appropriate? Are you expecting too much of yourself, given the constraints in your life? Reassess your priorities in order to be sure you're attempting to do what is most important to you.

> **Reconsider your personal style of time management.** We've outlined one method of time management. Although it works well for most people, it isn't for everyone. Some people just can't bring themselves to be so structured and scheduled. They feel hemmed in by to-do lists.

  If you're one of those people, fine. You don't need to follow the suggestions presented in this chapter exactly. In fact, if you go to your campus bookstore or any office supply store, you'll find lots of other aids to manage your time. Publishing companies produce elaborate planners, such as Daytimers. In addition, software companies produce computerized time management software, such as Microsoft's Outlook or Novell's GroupWise, that reside on computers and on wireless handheld devices such as the BlackBerry or iPhone. Many cellphones contain a calendar system and alarm, and they can be set to provide periodic reminders.

However you choose to manage your time, the important thing is to do so consistently. And remember that whatever approach to time management you take, it will work best if it is compatible with your own personal values and strengths. Keep experimenting until you find an approach that works for you.

> **Consider doing less.** If you keep falling behind, do less. There are only 24 hours in the day, and we need to sleep for about a third of the time. In the remaining hours, it is impossible to carry a full load of classes and work full-time and care for a child and still have some time left to have a normal life.

Consequently, if you consistently fall behind in your work, it may be that you are just trying to do too much. Reassess your goals and your priorities, and make choices. Determine what is most important to you. It's better to accomplish less, if it is accomplished well, than to accomplish more, but poorly.

> **Use your free time well.** Although it is a problem that many of us would envy, some people have too much time on their hands. Their classes may not be too demanding, or work demands may suddenly slacken off. If this happens to you, take advantage of it. For example, you might use the extra time to simply relax and enjoy your more unhurried existence. There is a lot to be said for having time to let your thoughts wander. We need to take time out to enjoy our friends, admire the flowers in the park, exercise, and consider the spiritual side of our lives.

> "Our costliest expenditure is time."
>
> Theophrastus, quoted in Diogenes Laertius's *Lives and Opinions of Eminent Philosophers*, tr. R. D. Hicks

On the other hand, if you consistently have more time than you know what to do with, reflect on what you want to accomplish and add some activities that help you reach your goals. For example, consider becoming involved in an organization on campus. Volunteer your time to the community. Think about taking an extra course during the next term.

But whatever you decide to do, make a real decision. Don't let the time slip away. Once it's gone, it's gone forever.

Time to Reflect: What Did I Learn?

1. Generally speaking, how would you characterize your time management skills?

2. What would be the benefit to you personally if you could manage time more effectively; i.e., what goals might you accomplish if you had more time at your disposal?

3. Based on what you learned about time management in this chapter, what do you plan to do differently in the future? Be specific.

Looking Back

How can I manage my time most effectively?

▸ Decide to take control of your time.

▸ Become aware of the way you use your time now.

▸ Set clear priorities.

▸ Distinguish the important priorities from the not-so-important and the urgent from the not-so-urgent.

▸ Use time management tools such as a master calendar, a weekly timetable, and a daily to-do list.

How can I control my environment?

▸ Control your environment by saying no, getting away from it all, working in silence, taking control of communications, and leaving some slack in your schedule to accommodate the unexpected.

How can I work smarter, instead of harder?

▸ Accomplish tasks in the most efficient way possible, match the amount of effort you expend to the importance of the task, develop a consistent approach to tasks you do regularly, and use electronic devices to help you manage your time.

How can I avoid procrastination?

▸ Avoid procrastination by breaking large tasks into smaller ones, starting with the easiest parts of a task first; working with other people; and calculating the true costs of procrastination.

How can I balance competing priorities?

▸ Consider how your competing priorities relate to one another.

▸ Manage work time carefully, use slack time on the job to perform school assignments, use flextime, accept new responsibilities thoughtfully, and assign the proper priority to work.

[KEY TERMS AND CONCEPTS]

Daily to-do list (p. 43)
Master calendar (p. 43)
Priorities (p. 37)

Procrastination (p. 51)
Time log (p. 37)

Weekly timetable (p. 43)
Workback (p. 48)

[RESOURCES]

ON CAMPUS

The person who determines when classes meet is usually known as the registrar. If you are having difficulty in scheduling your classes, the registrar's office may be helpful. In addition, your academic adviser can help you work out problems in enrolling in the classes you want.

For help with such issues as planning a study schedule for the upcoming term, dealing with multiple assignments and obligations on the same date, or tips on dealing with competing academic and work demands, consult with your campus learning centre. The staff can help you sort out the various options you may have.

IN PRINT

Stephen Covey's *The Seven Habits of Highly Successful People* (Fireside, 2004) and Alan Axelrod and Brian Tracy's *Eat That Frog! 21 Great Ways to Stop Procrastinating and Get More Done in Less Time* (Berrett-Kohler, 2007) offer practical, hands-on guides to time management.

How to Do Everything with Microsoft Outlook (Osborne-McGraw-Hill, 2007), by Bill Mann, provides a quick, hands-on introduction to Microsoft's Outlook software, a popular time management program that is part of the Microsoft Office Suite.

Finally, Veronique Vienne and Erica Lennard's *The Art of the Moment: Simple Ways to Get the Most Out of Life* (Clarkson Potter, 2002) is an antidote to the impulse to schedule every minute of our days. The book celebrates taking time out and devoting it to oneself, providing a practical guide to rest and relaxation.

ON THE WEB

Connect for P.O.W.E.R. Learning and Your Life provides online versions of all the time management forms present in this chapter. You can complete the forms online or download them and print out as many copies as you need. The following websites provide the opportunity to extend your learning about the material in this chapter.

> The University of Victoria's Office of Counselling Services provides two useful sites:

- Effective hints on how to plan study time, ideas about when to study, as well as tips on how to study (**www.coun.uvic.ca/learning/time-management/**).

- A handy self-management checklist that allows visitors to the site to better achieve their goals with the time that they have (**www.coun.uvic.ca/learning/motivation/self-management.html**). It also provides effective techniques for avoiding procrastination and distractions, two major obstacles to effective time management.

> From Penn State University, try this nifty online interactive time management exercise (**http://pennstatelearning.psu.edu/resources/study-tips/time-mgt/exercise**). This site also includes comprehensive links to a number of comments on how to manage your time while in college or university.

TAKING IT TO THE NET

1 Complete a weekly organizer online. Find a site on the Web that offers shareware or freeware featuring a weekly planner (for example, **www.printablecalendar.ca/** or **www.studygs.net/schedule/weekly.htm**). Create a weekly schedule sheet for yourself based on this design. Be sure to write in all of your classes, job obligations, and any other regular responsibilities that you have. Be sure to set specific times in your daily schedule to study. (If you already use Outlook or another kind of communications software, use its calendar function to do the same thing.)

2 Make a master calendar for the term, using the same software you used for the exercise above. If your calendar does not provide this information automatically, you can go to Yahoo! (**dir.yahoo.com**), click on "Reference," then again on "Calendars." Here you'll find many links to different calendar-related information such as when holidays occur. Be sure to indicate dates when important assignments are due and when exams occur.

The Case of . . .

Time Crunched

Paul Misir couldn't believe it. He was working overtime at his delivery job because one of his co-workers was on vacation. During a break from his shift, he got a text message from a classmate asking if he wanted to study the next day for the exam they had to take the following Monday. Paul had forgotten all about the exam.

Even worse, Paul couldn't study with his classmate the next day because he'd promised his girlfriend he would join her to visit her grandmother, who lived an hour's drive from the city. Although he wasn't looking forward to the two-hour round trip, he knew his girlfriend would be furious if he broke his promise. And on top of all that, he also had to find time in the next few days to work on a term paper due in one of his other classes.

As he was driving home thinking about all this, his car started to sputter and then stalled. He was unable to get it started. That was it. He sat there on the side of the road, feeling as if his life had completely fallen apart and wondering how he'd ever get it back together again.

1. What might you tell Paul that could help solve his predicament?

2. What specific time management techniques might Paul have employed in the past to avoid these problems?

3. Is there anything else Paul could have done to prevent the situation he now faces from occurring in the first place?

4. What strategies might Paul use now to take control over his limited time during the coming days?

5. What advice could you give Paul to try to prevent problems in time management for his next term?

3 Reading and Remembering

Learning Outcomes

By the time you finish this chapter, you will be able to

» LO 3.1   Identify the essential elements of successful reading, and explain how to improve concentration when reading.

» LO 3.2   Demonstrate the use of techniques for memorizing large amounts of information.

» LO 3.3   Analyze how best to retain what you have read.

"Read the next chapter in the textbook by Tuesday." "Read the first two articles in the course pack by next class." "The test will cover the first hundred pages in your book, so be sure you've read them."

One day, three different reading assignments, Jessica Knowles thought as the instructor of her last class of the day delivered this last instruction. It would be hard enough for Jesssica to complete all this reading during an ordinary week. But this week she had to finish painting her bedroom and she had volunteered to help her brother move. On top of that, there was her part-time job as a cashier—and, Jessica suddenly remembered, she'd agreed to work overtime on Friday.

Still, Jessica figured that even with all her work, family, and household obligations, she could still find time to do all her reading—except Jessica believed she was an unusually slow reader. When she pushed herself to read more quickly and absorb more, she actually read and retained less. For Jessica, the problem wasn't just completing the reading—it was remembering it when test time rolled around.

For people like Jessica, reading assignments are the biggest challenge in college or university. The amount of required reading is often enormous. Even skilled readers may find themselves wishing they could read more quickly and effectively. On the job, too, many people struggle with all the memos, emails, manuals, and other documents that they need to read.

Fortunately, there are ways to improve your reading skills. In this chapter, we'll go over a number of strategies to make your reading more effective.

We'll also discuss ways to improve memory skills, not just as they relate to reading, but in general. Most of us have experienced the challenge of memorizing a seemingly impossible amount of information, and we tend to focus on our failures far more than on our successes. But the truth is that our memory capabilities are truly astounding. For instance, if you are like the average college or university student, your vocabulary contains some 50 000 words, you know hundreds of mathematical facts, and you can recall detailed images from events you witnessed years ago. In this chapter, you'll learn how to harness the power of your memory.

» LO 3.1 Sharpening Your Reading Skills

One of the reasons many people struggle with reading, especially in college or university, is they feel they *shouldn't* have to struggle with it. Reading, after all, is something almost all of us master as children, right?

In fact, it is not so simple. Reading, as we will see in this chapter, involves more than just recognizing words. The task of reading large amounts of information and remembering the essential points takes time to master.

To begin, consider the way you read now. In other words, what kind of reader are you? Ask yourself first of all about your reading preferences: What do you *like* to read, and why? What makes you pick up a book and start reading—and what makes you put one down?

Before going any further, reflect on your striving style and how it might affect how you read and remember material. Then, examine the suggestions and recommendations provided in the sidebar.

Read for Retention, Not Speed

You may have come across advertisements on the Web promoting reading "systems" that promise to teach you to read so quickly that you'll be reading entire books in an hour and whizzing through assigned readings in a few minutes.

Unfortunately that's not going to happen. Research has shown that claims of speed-reading are simply groundless. But even if it were physically possible to read a book in an hour, ultimately it probably doesn't matter very much. If we read too quickly, comprehension and ultimately retention plunge. Reading is not a race, and the fastest readers are not necessarily the best readers.

The act of reading is designed to increase our knowledge and open up new ways of thinking. It can help us achieve new levels of understanding and get us to think more broadly about the world and its inhabitants. Speed matters far less than what we take away from what we've read. That's not to say we shouldn't try to become more efficient readers who comprehend and recall more effectively. Ultimately, though, the key to good reading is comprehension, not speed.

Reading and Remembering and Striving Styles

Leaders

Try not to get impatient with reading. Set up reading and memorizing challenges to stay engaged. Reading out loud helps focus.

Socializers

Passive learning, such as reading, is de-energizing. Use of visual tools and acronyms are helpful. Helping others helps reinforce learning.

Performers

Read, then review, and talk with others about the subject. Use a visual organizer. Start well in advance and take plenty of breaks.

Adventurers

Try reading while walking or on a treadmill to increase focus. Reading and discussing can help as can having fun with acronyms and word games.

Artists

Take lots of time and space to read and reflect. Use memory cards and repetition to help with rote learning. Connect reading to something personal.

Intellectuals

Checking for inconsistencies when reading is a time-consuming distraction. Use a timer to keep track of time. Make lots of notes.

Visionaries

Read where there are no distractions. Difficulty with rote memory can cause anxiety about remembering. Make plenty of notes and use visual aids.

Stabilizers

Have others help with theory and complex subjects. Take plenty of time to absorb. Check to ensure understanding of exactly what is expected.

P.O.W.E.R. Plan

P **Prepare**
Approach the written
word thoughtfully

O **Organize**
Gather the tools
of the trade

W **Work**
Get the most out
of your reading

E **Evaluate**
Put it into context of
what you already know

R **Rethink**
Get it the second time

SQ3R approach
Model for reading and
comprehension based on these
five steps: Survey, Question,
Read, Recite, and Review

Advance organizers
Broad, general ideas related to
material that is to about to be
read or heard, which pave the
way for subsequent learning

In describing how you can use the principles of P.O.W.E.R. Learning to become a better reader with a more complete memory of what you read, we'll focus on the type of reading that is typically called for in academic pursuits—textbook chapters, articles, handouts, and the like. However, the same principles will help you get more benefit and enjoyment out of your recreational reading as well. In addition, the reading skills you learn and employ in the classroom will help you read more efficiently and effectively on the job.

P **Prepare**   Plan Your Approach

Preparation for reading isn't difficult, and it won't take very long; but it's a crucial first step in applying P.O.W.E.R. Learning (summarized in the P.O.W.E.R. Plan here). In fact, preparation is the first step in the **SQ3R approach to reading,** a model developed during World War II by Professor Francis Robinson, a psychology professor at Ohio State University. His SQ3R model—an acronym for **S**urvey, **Q**uestion, and the three Rs, which in this case stand for **R**ead, **R**ecite, and **R**eview—was developed in response to an urgent need to train soldiers to read and understand thousands of pages of complicated technical manuals in preparation for war. The summary table shown below outlines the main points of the model, which we discuss in more detail throughout the chapter.

SQ3R

S	Survey	Familiarize yourself with the materials that surround the core text
Q	Question	Question the point of view of the material you are reading *and* the credibility of the person writing it
R	Read	Read the material
R	Recite	Recite the material aloud as you read it
R	Review	Go back and review what you've read, along with any notes you've taken

The "S" in SQ3R is for **S**urveying, or familiarizing yourself with the materials that surround the core text. These **advance organizers**—which include prefaces, chapter previews, outlines and overviews, learning outcomes, and other clues to the meaning and organization of new material—are built into most textbooks; for example, every chapter in this book includes a Learning Outcomes list and a Looking Ahead section. You can also create your own advance organizers by skimming material to be read and sketching out the general outline of the material you'll be reading. Another tip is to examine end-of-chapter review material before reading the chapter, as it will point you towards what is most important in the chapter.

Advance organizers pave the way for subsequent learning. They help you tie information that you already know to new material you're about to encounter. This connection between old and new material is crucial in helping build memories of what you read. If you approach each new reading task as something entirely new and unrelated to your previous knowledge, you'll have enormous difficulty recalling it. On the other hand, if you connect it to what you already know, you'll be able to recall it far more easily.

Try It! P.O.W.E.R.

Discover How Advance Organizers Help

Read this passage. What do you think it means?

> The procedure is actually quite simple. First you arrange items into different groups. Of course, one pile may be sufficient, depending on how much there is to do. If you have to go somewhere else due to lack of facilities, that is the next step; otherwise, you are pretty well set. It is important not to overdo things. That is, it is better to do too few things at once than too many. In the short run, this may not seem important; but complications can easily arise. A mistake can be expensive as well. At first, the whole procedure will seem complicated. Soon, however, it will become just another facet of life. It is difficult to foresee any end to the necessity for this task in the immediate future, but then one can never tell. After the procedure is completed, one arranges the materials into different groups again. Then they can be put into their appropriate places. Eventually, they will be used once more and the whole cycle will then have to be repeated. However, this is a part of life.[1]

If you're like most people, you don't have a clue about what this all means and you won't be able to remember anything about it in five minutes. Now, suppose you have been given some context in advance, and you know before reading it that the description has to do with doing laundry. Now does it all fall into place? Do you think it will be easier to remember? Read the passage once more, and see how having an advance organizer (in this case, *doing laundry*) helps out.

To Try It online, go to Connect for *P.O.W.E.R. Learning and Your Life.*

In short, the more we're able to make use of advance organizers and our own prior knowledge and experiences, the better we can understand and retain new material. (To prove the value of advance organizers to yourself, complete **Try It! 1**, "Discover How Advance Organizers Help.")

Identify the Purpose of the Reading Assignment

The "Q" in SQ3R involves questioning the purpose of the material you are about to read, and your goal in reading it. Will you be reading a textbook on which you'll be thoroughly tested? Is your reading supposed to provide background information that will serve as a context for future learning but that won't itself be tested? Is the material going to be useful to you personally? Realistically, how much time can you devote to the reading assignment?

Your goal for reading will help you determine which reading strategy to adopt. You aren't expected to read everything with the same degree of intensity. Some material you may feel comfortable skimming; for other material you'll want to put in the maximum effort.

Understand the Author's Point of View

The "Q" in SQ3R also extends to questioning the point of view of the material you are reading and the credibility of the person writing it. What are you reading? Is it a textbook, an essay, an article, a blog? If it is an essay, article, or blog, why was it written? To prove a point? To provide information? To express the author's personal feelings? Knowing the author's purpose (even if his or her specific point and message aren't yet clear) can help you put the material in context. Knowing something about the author can help you determine if the material is based purely on the author's own experience, and, therefore, might suffer from an inherent bias, or whether it is drawn from a broad body of professional research.

Start with the Frontmatter

The preface, introduction, and table of contents of a book

If you'll be using a text or other book extensively throughout the term, start by surveying the preface and/or introduction and scanning the table of contents—what publishers call the **frontmatter.** Instructors often don't formally assign the frontmatter; but reading it can be a big help because it is there that the author has a chance to step forward and explain, often more personally than elsewhere in an academic book, what he or she considers important. Knowing this will give you a sense of what to expect as you read.

Create Advance Organizers

To provide a context for your reading, you can create your own advance organizers by skimming through the table of contents, which provides the main headings of what you will be reading. Textbooks often have chapter outlines, listing the key topics to be covered, and these also provide a way of previewing the chapter content. As you read over the outline, you can begin to consider how the new material in the book may relate both to what you know and to what you expect to learn—from the reading assignment itself and from the course.

Textbooks also often have end-of-chapter summaries, and many articles include a final section in which the author states his or her conclusions. Take a look at these ending sections as well. Even though you haven't read the material yet and the summary probably won't make complete sense to you, by reading the summary, you'll get an idea of what the author covers and what is important.

Your instructor may also provide an advance organizer for readings. Sometimes instructors will mention things to pay particular attention to or to look for, such as "When you read Thomas Paine's *Common Sense,* notice how he lays out his argument and what his key points are." Sometimes they will tell you why they assigned a particular reading. Such information provides clues that can help you develop a mental list of the reading's key ideas.

However you construct advance organizers, be sure they provide a framework and context for what you'll be reading; this framework and context can spell the difference between fully comprehending what you read and misunderstanding it.

Now it's time to put all these ideas to good use. Create an advance organizer for a textbook chapter by working through **Try It! 2**, "Create an Advance Organizer," on page 67.

Identify What You Need to Remember

No matter how important a reading assignment is to a course, you will not be expected to remember every word of it—nor should you try! The average textbook chapter has something like 20 000 words. Recalling every word of the chapter would be nearly impossible. Furthermore, no matter how much of a perfectionist you may be, memorizing every word would be a waste of your valuable time. Being able to spew out paragraphs of material is quite different from the more important ability to recall and deeply understand material in meaningful ways.

Within those 20 000 words, there may be only 20 different concepts that you need to learn. And perhaps there are only 10 keywords. *Those* are the pieces of information that should be the focus of your efforts to memorize.

How do you know what's so important that you need to recall it? One way is to use the guides built into most textbooks. Key concepts and terms are often highlighted or in boldface type. Chapters often have summaries that recap the most important information. Use such guideposts to understand what's most critical in

Try It! 2

Create an Advance Organizer

Use any information you have available to create an advance organizer for a chapter in a text that you are using this term. Skim the section headings in the chapter, read the chapter summary, consult the book's frontmatter, and recall anything your instructor may have said about the chapter.

Complete the following statements to prepare your organizer:

1. The general topics that are covered in the chapter are . . .

2. The most critical topics and concepts in the chapter are . . .

3. The most difficult material in the chapter includes . . .

4. Words, phrases, and ideas that are unfamiliar to me include . . .

5. Ways that the material in this chapter relates to other material that I've previously read in the text include . . .

Use this Try It! as a starting point for advance organizers for future chapters in the book.

To Try It online, go to Connect for *P.O.W.E.R. Learning and Your Life.*

a chapter. Another approach is to use the journalist's trick of asking the Ws—who, what, when, where, and why.

Write down what you determine is important. Putting critical information in writing helps you manage what you need to remember, and the very act of writing it down makes it easier to memorize the information later.

In short, the first step in building a better memory of what you read is to determine just what it is that you wish to recall. By extracting what is important from what is less crucial, you'll be able to limit the amount and extent of the material that you need to recall. You'll be able to focus on what you need to remember.

 **Organize**   **Gather the Tools of the Trade**

It's obvious that the primary item you'll need to complete a reading assignment is the material that you're reading. But there are other essential tools you should gather, potentially including the following:

> Pencils or pens to write notes in the margin.

> Highlighters to indicate key passages in the text.

> A copy of the assignment, so you'll be sure to read the right material.

> A pad of paper and/or index cards for note-taking if the material is particularly complex. If you routinely use a computer to take notes, get it ready.

> A dictionary. You never know what new words you'll encounter while you're reading. If a dictionary is not handy, you'll be tempted to skip over unfamiliar words—a decision that may come back to haunt you. Note that some word-processing software includes a dictionary; there are also many good dictionaries available online (e.g., Merriam-Webster's at **www.m-w.com,** where you will also find an online thesaurus). The point is to use what's available—but use something!

Give Yourself Time

There's one more thing you need in order to prepare successfully for a reading assignment: enough time to complete it. The length of reading assignments is almost never ambiguous. You will typically be given a specific page range, so you will know just how much material you will need to cover.

Now get a watch and time yourself as you read the first three pages of your assignment, being sure to pay attention to the material, not the time! Timing how long it takes to read a representative chunk of material provides you with a rough measure of your reading speed for the material—although it will vary even within a single reading assignment, depending on the complexity of the material.

You'll also need to consider an aspect of your personal learning style: your reading attention span. **Attention span** is the length of time that a person usually is able to sustain attention. People with a long attention span can read for relatively lengthy periods without getting jumpy, while those with a shorter attention span can only maintain attention for a short while. Get a general sense of your own attention span by completing **Try It! 3,** "Discover Your Attention Span," on page 69.

You can use the three pieces of information you now have—the length of the assignment, your per-page reading speed at full attention, and your typical attention span—to estimate roughly how long it will take you to complete the reading assignment. For example, if you are asked to read 12 pages, you have found that you need approximately 4 minutes to read a page, and your reading attention span is, on average, 25 minutes long, you can expect your reading to take at least 60 minutes, assuming you'll take a short break when your attention begins to fade after 25 minutes.

In addition, you may need to interrupt your reading to look up words in the dictionary, get a drink, stretch, or answer the phone. You may also decide to break your reading into several short sessions, in which case your total reading time may be greater since you will have to get reacquainted with the reading assignment each time you approach it.

You can use this strategy for estimating the amount of time you will need for reading tasks outside the classroom, too. If your employer asks you to read a set of customer feedback forms, for example, you can figure out how much time in your day you'll need to block off to complete the work by factoring in the total length of all the forms, your per-page reading speed, and your attention span. Remember, though, that reading on the job is different from reading in a college or university library or at your desk at home. You can expect many more distractions as you try to read—co-workers asking questions, emails coming in, the phone ringing. Take into account these inevitable workplace distractions when making your reading time estimate.

Attention span
The length of time that attention is typically sustained

Discover Your Attention Span

You should be aware of your attention span, the length of time you usually are able to sustain attention to a task, as you prepare for reading assignments. To get an idea of the length of your current attention span for reading, perform this exercise over the next few days.

1. Choose one of the textbooks that you've been assigned to read this semester.
2. Start reading a chapter, without any preparation, noting in the chart below the time that you start reading.
3. As soon as your mind begins to wander and think about other subjects, stop reading and note the time on the chart below.
4. Using the same textbook, but not the same passage, repeat this process four more times over the course of a few days, entering the data on the chart below.
5. To find your reading attention span, calculate the average number of minutes across the five trials.

Trial #1   Starting time: _____   Ending time: _____

Number of minutes between start and end times: _____

Trial #2   Starting time: _____   Ending time: _____

Number of minutes between start and end times: _____

Trial #3   Starting time: _____   Ending time: _____

Number of minutes between start and end times: _____

Trial #4   Starting time: _____   Ending time: _____

Number of minutes between start and end times: _____

Trial #5   Starting time: _____   Ending time: _____

Number of minutes between start and end times: _____

Reading attention span (the average of the number of minutes in the last column, found by adding up the five numbers and dividing by 5) = _____ minutes

---

Ask yourself these questions about your reading attention span:

1. Are you surprised by the length of your reading attention span? In what way?
2. Does any number in the set of trials stand out from the other numbers? For instance, is any number much higher or much lower than the average? If so, can you account for this? For example, what time of day was it?
3. Do the numbers in your trials show any trend? For instance, did your attention span tend to increase, decrease, or stay the same over the course of the trials? Can you explain any trend you may have noted?
4. Do you think your attention span times would be very different if you had chosen a different textbook? Why or why not?
5. What things might you do to improve your attention span?

To Try It online, go to Connect for *P.O.W.E.R. Learning and Your Life.*

 **Work**

Get the Most out of Your Reading

Once you've familiarized yourself with the material as a whole and gathered the necessary tools, it's time to get down to work and start reading. Here are several things that will help you get the most out of the reading process.

Stay Focused

The TV show you watched last night . . . your husband forgetting to meet you at the bus stop . . . the new toothbrush you need to buy for your daughter . . . your grumbling stomach. There are a million and one distractions that can invade your thoughts as you read. Your job is to keep distracting thoughts at bay and focus on the material you are supposed to be reading. It's not easy, but the following are things you can do to help yourself stay focused:

> **Read in small bites.** If you think it is going to take you four hours to read an entire chapter, break up the four hours into more manageable time periods. Promise yourself that you'll read for one hour in the afternoon, another hour in the evening, and the final two hours spaced out during the following day. One hour of reading is far more manageable than a four-hour block.

> **Take a break.** Plan to take several short breaks to reward yourself while you're reading. During your breaks, do something enjoyable—eat a snack, watch a bit of a ball game on television, send a text message to a friend. Just try not to get drawn into your break activity to the point that it takes over your reading time.

> **Deal with mental distractions.** Sometimes problems have a way of popping into our minds and repeatedly distracting us. If a particular problem keeps interrupting your concentration—such as a difficulty you're having on the job—try to think of an action-oriented strategy to deal with it. You might even write your proposed solution down on a piece of paper. Putting it down on paper can get the problem off your mind, making it less intrusive.

> **Manage interruptions.** You can't prevent your children from getting into a fight and needing immediate attention. But there are some things you can do to reduce interruptions and their consequences. For instance, you can schedule reading to coincide with periods when you know you'll be alone. You can also plan to read less critical parts of assignments (such as the summaries or book frontmatter) when distractions are more likely, saving the heavier reading for later. Or, if you are a parent with small children, you can get your children involved in an activity that they can perform independently so you'll be free to concentrate.

Write and Recite While You Read

For those of you who are avid readers or who have a read/write learning style, simply reading the material, which is the first "R" in SQ3R, might be enough to help you remember it. But if you lean more towards a visual/graphic or tactile/kinesthetic learning style, the physical act of writing as you read will actually be an important part of your approach to remembering what you read. If you haven't underlined, jotted notes to yourself, placed check marks on the page, drawn arrows,

If you are reading a long assignment, taking a break can be a reward and reinvigorate you.

Textbook Tips: Starting Off on the Right Page

You've just come back from the bookstore, weighted down with a knapsack filled with textbooks and other materials for the upcoming term. Now is the time to take some preliminary steps to make the most of your investment.

- Make sure you've bought the correct textbooks. Look at each syllabus or course outline from your classes to ensure you've bought the appropriate text. Sometimes there are multiple sections of a course, and each section uses a different text or a particular edition. Be sure the book you've bought matches the description in the syllabus.

- Make the book your own. Write your name, email address, and/or telephone number in the front of the book. If you misplace your book during the term, you want the person who finds it to be able to return it to you easily.

- Orient yourself to each of your textbooks. Take a quick look at each of the books, examining the table of contents, introduction, and/or preface (as we discussed earlier). Get a sense of the content and the general reading level of the book.

- Get yourself online. Many textbooks contain a card or insert with a password that gives you access to online material. Follow the directions and enter the book's website, making sure the password allows you to register. If you have trouble making the site work, call the tech support number that should be included with the password.

Course Connections

constructed diagrams, and otherwise defaced and disfigured your book while you're reading, you're not doing your job as a P.O.W.E.R. reader.

The idea of writing on a book page may go against everything you've been taught in the past. (And, of course, you should never write on a library book or one that you've borrowed.) However, once you've bought your book, you own it and you should make it your own. Don't keep your textbooks spotless so they will fetch a higher price if you sell them later. Instead, think of textbooks as documents recording your active learning and engagement in a field of study. In addition, you should look at your textbooks as the foundation of your personal library, which will grow throughout your lifetime. In short, writing extensively in your book while you're reading is an important tactic for achieving success. (For more on using textbooks, see the **Course Connections** feature above.)

If you have an auditory/verbal learning style, an effective technique is to recite the material aloud as you read it—and recite, coincidentally, is the second "R" in SQ3R. As you learned in Chapter 1, auditory learners prefer to listen to material aloud or hear explanations rather than read them. For this type of learner, it is

worth the extra effort to locate an audiobook version of the novel you are reading in English class, or search for a podcast on a particular topic you are discussing in class to reinforce your learning.

The ability to add your own personal notes, underline, and make other annotations to a clean text while you're reading is one of the reasons it usually pays to buy new, rather than used, textbooks. Why would you want a stranger's comments on something you own? Can you really trust that person's judgment over your own regarding what's important enough to underline? You can mark up new books in your own personal style, without the distraction of competing voices.

What should you be writing while you are reading? There are several things you should write down:

> **Rephrase key points.** Make notes to yourself, in your own words, about what the author is trying to get across. Don't just copy what's been said. Think about the material, and rewrite it in words that are your own.
>
> Writing notes to yourself in your own words has several consequences, all good. First, you make the material yours; it becomes something you now understand and part of your own knowledge base. This is an aid to memorization. When you try to recollect your reading, you won't be trying to summon the thoughts of someone else; rather, you'll be trying to remember *your own* thinking.
>
> Second, trying to summarize a key point in your own words will clarify for you whether you truly understand it. It's easy to be fooled into thinking we understand something as we're reading along. But the true test is whether we can explain it to ourselves (or someone else) on our own, without referring to the book or article.
>
> Third, the very act of writing engages an additional type of perception, involving the physical sense of moving a pen or pressing a keyboard. This will help you learn the material in a more active way.
>
> Finally, writing notes and phrases will help you study the material later. The key points will be highlighted, and your notes will also quickly bring you up to speed regarding your initial thoughts and impressions.
>
> **Highlight or underline key points.** Very often the first or last sentence in a paragraph, or the first or last paragraph in a section, will present a key point. Before you highlight anything, though, read the whole paragraph through. Then you'll be sure that what you highlight is, in fact, the key information. Topic sentences do not always fall at the beginning of a paragraph.
>
> Be selective in your highlighting and underlining. A page covered in yellow highlighter may be artistically appealing, but it won't help you understand the material any better. Highlight only the key information. You might find yourself highlighting only one or two sentences or phrases per page. That's fine. In highlighting and underlining, less is more. One guideline: No more than ten percent of the material should be highlighted or underlined.
>
> Keep in mind as you highlight and underline that the key material you are marking is the material you will likely need to remember for exams or assignments. To aid in your recall of such material, read it over a time or two after you've marked it, and consider reading it aloud as well. This will reinforce the memories you are building of the essential points in the assignment.
>
> **Use arrows, diagrams, outlines, tables, timelines, charts, and other visuals to help you understand and later recall what you are reading.** If there are three examples given for a particular point, number them. If a paragraph discusses a situation in which an earlier point does not hold, link the original point to the exception by an arrow. If a sequence of steps is presented, number each step.

From the perspective of . . .

A STUDENT To truly retain what you are reading, you must give your reading your undivided attention. Make a list of your biggest distractions and consider strategies for avoiding those distractions when you read.

"What is reading but silent conversation?"

Walter Savage Landor,
"Aristoteles and Callisthenes,"
Imaginary Conversations **(1824–53)**

Highlight or underline key points.

① Topic sentence

Read whole paragraph before highlighting

Highlight or underline key points. Very often the first or last sentence in a paragraph, or the first or last paragraph in a section, will present a key point. Before you highlight anything, though, read the whole paragraph through. Then you'll be sure that what you highlight is, in fact, the key information. Topic sentences do not always fall at the beginning of a paragraph.

Be selective in your highlighting and underlining. A page covered in yellow highlighter may be artistically appealing, but it won't help you understand the material any better. Highlight only the key information. You might find yourself highlighting only one or two sentences or phrases per page. That's fine. In highlighting and underlining, less is more. One guideline: No more than ten percent of the material should be highlighted or underlined.

Reread key points to help memory

Keep in mind as you highlight and underline that the key material you are marking is the material you will likely need to remember for exams or class discussions. To aid in your recall of such material, read it over a time or two after you've marked it, and consider also reading it aloud. This will reinforce the memories you are building of the essential points in the assignment.

② Use visuals →

Use arrows, diagrams, outlines, tables, timelines, charts, and other visuals to help you understand and later recall what you are reading. If three examples given for a particular point, number them. If a paragraph discusses a situation in which an earlier point does not hold, link the original point to the exception by an arrow. If a sequence of steps is presented, number each step.

For example, after you have annotated this page of *P.O.W.E.R. Learning*, the annotations might look something like the handwritten notes shown in **Figure 3.1**.

Particularly if your learning style is a visual one, representing the material graphically will get you thinking about it—and the connections and points in it—in new and different ways. Rather than considering the material solely in verbal terms, you can now add visual images. The act of creating visual annotations will both help you to understand the material better and help you to recall it later. Practise this technique on the sample textbook page in If there are **Try It!** 4 on page XX.

Look up words in dictionary →

Look up unfamiliar words in a dictionary Even though you may be able to figure out the meaning of an unfamiliar word from its context, use a dictionary anyway. This way you can be sure that what you think it means is correct A dictionary will also tell you what the word sounds like, which may be important if your instructor uses the word in class.

figure 3.1
Sample of Annotated Page

For example, if **Figure 3.1** were a single page of *P.O.W.E.R. Learning*, the annotations might look something like the handwritten notes in the left margin.

Particularly if your learning style is a visual one, representing the material graphically will get you thinking about it—and the connections and points in it—in new and different ways. Rather than considering the material solely in verbal terms, you now add visual images. The act of creating visual annotations will both help you to understand the material better and help you to recall it later. Practise this technique on the sample textbook page in **Try It! 4,** "Mark Up a Book Page," on pages 74 and 75.

▸ **Look up unfamiliar words in a dictionary.** Even though you may be able to figure out the meaning of an unfamiliar word from its context, use a dictionary anyway. This way you can be sure that what you think it means is correct. A dictionary will also tell you what the word sounds like, which may be important if your instructor uses the word in class.

Mark Up a Book Page

First, working alone, read the excerpt in **Figure 3.2** on the opposite page. Then use the techniques we've discussed for marking up a page to highlight its key points.

Next, working in a group, compare and contrast your annotations with those of some classmates, and answer the following questions:

1. How do others' annotations differ from yours?

2. Why did they use the annotations they did?

3. Which annotation techniques worked best for you? Which did others prefer? Why?

4. How might these annotations help you to remember what is important?

5. If there were different sorts of material presented on the page, such as mathematical formulas, would you use different kinds of annotations?

To Try It online, go to Connect for *P.O.W.E.R. Learning and Your Life.*

4

world, not ... put our foot in our mouths every chance we get." Although a TV ad and commentary from a few politicians do not define the Canadian identity, the flavour of these does reflect distinctions within regional cultures in Canada.

The Self and Culture

So, imagine we replaced the word "Canadian" in the scale we did with some other word from our earlier list (maybe Catholic, or Muslim, or Aboriginal, or any other word that describes a group you belong to). Most of us have multiple identities (e.g., male, Muslim, Canadian and gay; Female, Baptist, Black, and straight), However, can these different identities cause conflict? Do you see conflict in the multiple identities that define who you are? Many immigrants, or children of recent immigrants, report high levels of inter-role conflict. Often, their life satisfaction and well-being is related to their ability to balance the values of their traditional culture with their new language and cultural reality (Lee & Chen, 2000; Liebkind & Jasinskaja-Lhati, 2000; Sam, 2000).

Culture The enduring behaviours, attitudes, and traditions shared by a large group of people and transmitted from one generation to the next.

Culture can be defined as the enduring behaviours, attitudes, and traditions shared by a large group of people and transmitted from one generation to the next For some people, especially those in industrialized Western cultures, individualism prevails as the self-concept. The psychology of Western culture assumes that your life will be enriched by defining your possible selves (that is, the person you could be) and believing in your power of personal control. By the end of the 20th century, individualism had become the dominant voice in Western culture.

Individualism The concept of giving priority to one's own goals over group goals and defining one's identity in terms of personal attributes rather than group identifications.

Cultures native to Asia, Africa, and Central and South America place a greater value on collectivism. They nurture what Shinobu Kitayama and Hazel Markus (1995) call the *interdependent self*. People are more self-critical and have less need for positive self-regard (Heine et al., 1999). Identity is defined more in relation to others. Malaysians, Indians, Japanese, and traditional Kenyans such as the Maasai, for example, are much more likely than Australians, Americans, and the British to complete an "I am..." statement with their group identities (Bochner, 1994; Dhawan et al., 1995; Ma & Schoeneman, 1997; Markus & Kitayama, 1991).

Collectivism Giving priority to the goals of one's groups (often one's extended family or work group) and defining one's identity accordingly.

However, making general statements about a culture's individualistic or collectivist orientations is oversimplified. Even within Canada, there are regional and ethnic differences as well. For example, people in Québec and Ontario tend to be more liberal, whereas people in Western Canada (particularly Alberta) tend to be more individualistic. Conservatives tend to be economic individualists ("don't tax or regulate me") and moral collectivists ("do legislate against immorality"). Liberals tend to be economic collectivists and moral individualists.

With an *inter*dependent self, one has a greater sense of belonging. Uprooted and cut off from family, colleagues, and loyal friends, interdependent people would lose the social connections that define who they are. They have not one self but many selves: self-with-parents, self-at-work, self-with-friends (Cross et al., 1992). As Figure 3-1 suggests, the interdependent self is embedded in social memberships. Conversation is less direct and more polite (Holtgraves, 1997). The goal of social life is not so much to enhance one's individual self as to harmonize with and support one's communities.

www.mcgrawhill.ca/ole/myers

figure 3.2
Sample Page to Annotate

Reading Goes Digital

When computers were first introduced in the 1980s, many people sounded the death knell of books and magazines, and the idea of the "paperless office" was born. The reality, however, has been quite different. Fast forward 30 years and the paperless office is nowhere to be seen; and even with the introduction of cheaper e-texts, many students in the first decade of the twenty-first century continued to opt for tangible textbooks.

As we enter the second decade of this century, however, the reading landscape is undergoing a dramatic change. Tools like the Apple iPad, the Sony Reader, Amazon's Kindle, and the Kobo sold through Chapters/Indigo, have made the ability to read anything, anywhere, anytime, a reality for many. In fact, in the first 28 days that the Apple iPad was introduced to the United States market in the spring of 2010, one million were sold, or about one per 300 households. That means more and more of us are going to be doing our reading on electronic devices—and many of these devices incorporate features that will make remembering material even easier. The iPad, for instance, incorporates features that allow you to change font size, highlight and search text, and bookmark specific sections that you can return to later. For auditory learners, there is a built-in screen reader that will read you the page aloud. As more and more applications are built for these devices, you can expect that the task of remembering what you read will only become easier.

When reading material on a traditional computer, there are already a number of tools and techniques available that can make the task easier. The simplest approach is to cut and paste material from the screen into an application like Microsoft Word, and use the "Insert," "Review," and "References" menus to reference the source, research additional material, add comments and insert your own notes, embed images, and so forth. Microsoft also has software called OneNote which is an add-on to its Microsoft Office suite, which provides you with a seamless, organized approach to keeping all of your course materials, including notes, images, and videos, in one place. OneNote has the added advantage of being both shareable with other users (great for group projects!), and searchable by keyword. To download a trial version of OneNote, visit the main Microsoft website.

Web pages are becoming increasingly cluttered with photos, frames, sponsored advertisements, and the like, making it difficult to pinpoint what you actually want to read. A tool that can make reading online easier is Arc90's Readability, a "bookmarklet" that allows you to remove the clutter from any Web page, leaving you with only the text you want to read. To learn more about Readability, view the short video at **www.readability.com**. A similar tool called Readable is also available.

LO3.2 Memorizing Key Material

Many of the reading strategies discussed earlier will help fix key material in your mind. Rephrasing key points, highlighting or underlining essential material and then rereading it, and creating visuals will all help you recall the information you've read.

Sometimes, though, these strategies are not enough. You may need to memorize a great deal of information, more than you'll be able to recall just through the process of reading, underlining, and so forth. Many people find extensive memorization daunting. But one of the good things about the work of memorization is that you have your choice of literally dozens of techniques. Depending on the kind of material you need to recall and how much you already know about the subject, you can turn to any number of methods.

As we sort through the various options, keep in mind that no one strategy works by itself. (And some strategies don't seem to work; for example, forget about supplements like gingko biloba—there's no clear scientific evidence that they are effective.[2]) Instead, try the following proven strategies and find those that work best for you. Feel free to devise your own strategies or add those that have worked for you in the past.

Rehearsal

Say it aloud: rehearsal. Think of it in terms of the three syllables that make up the word: re—hear—sal. OK, one more time—say the word "rehearsal."

If you're scratching your head over the last paragraph, it's to illustrate the point of **rehearsal:** to transfer material that you encounter into memory. If you don't rehearse information in some way, it will end up like most of the information to which we're exposed—on the garbage heap of lost memory.

Rehearsing is the equivalent of **R**eciting in SQ3R. To test if you've succeeded in transferring the word "rehearsal" into your memory, put down this book and go off for a few minutes. Do something entirely unrelated to reading this book. Have a snack, catch up on the latest sports scores on TSN, or read the front page of the newspaper.

Are you back? If the word "rehearsal" popped into your head when you picked up this book again, you've passed your first memory test. You can be assured that the word "rehearsal" has been transferred into your memory.

Many of us can sing along to popular songs on the radio and know the lyrics by heart. That is because we hear and/or sing the songs over and over again. Rehearsal is the key strategy in remembering information. If you don't rehearse material, it will never make it into memory. Repeating the information, summarizing it, associating it with other memories, and above all thinking about it when you first come across it will ensure that rehearsal will be effective in pushing the material into memory. If you scored high on musical intelligence, try developing a rap or rhyme to help you remember course material.

Rehearsal
The process of practising and learning material to transfer it into memory

Mnemonics

This odd word (pronounced in an equally odd fashion, with the "m" silent—"neh MON ix") describes formal techniques used to make material more readily remembered. **Mnemonics** are the tricks of the trade that professional memory experts use, and will probably appeal most to people with an auditory/verbal learning style and a high score on linguistic intelligence.

Among the most common mnemonics are **acronyms.** You're already well acquainted with acronyms—words or phrases formed by the first letters of a series of terms. For instance, although you may not have known it, the word "laser" is actually an acronym for "light amplification by stimulated emissions of radiation," and "radar" is an acronym for "radio detection and ranging." If you took music lessons, you may know that FACE spells out the names of the notes that appear in the spaces on the treble clef of the music staff ("F," "A," "C," and "E," starting at the bottom of the staff).

The benefit of acronyms is that they help us to recall a complete list of items. P.O.W.E.R. stands for—well, by this point in the book, you probably remember.

Mnemonics
Formal techniques used to make material more readily remembered

Acronym
A word or phrase formed by the first letters of a series of terms

POWER Try It! 5

Do-it-yourself Acronyms and Acrostics

In the first part of this Try It!, work individually to create an acronym and an acrostic.

1. Figure out an acronym to remind you of the names of the five Great Lakes, using the first letters of their names (Erie, Huron, Michigan, Ontario, Superior).

2. The eight multiple intelligences you learned about in Chapter 1 are the following: naturalist, interpersonal, intrapersonal, musical, bodily-kinesthetic, logical-mathematical, spatial, and linguistic. Here is an acrostic to help you remember them: **N**umerous **I**dealistic **I**nventors **M**ake **B**itter **L**e**M**ons **S**weet and **L**uscious. Now, devise your own acrostic to help you remember the learning styles: read/write, visual/graphic, auditory/verbal, and tactile/kinesthetic. Then create another to help you remember the eight striving styles: leader, socializer, performer, adventurer, artist, intellectual, visionary, and stabilizer.

After you've tried to create the acronym and the acrostic, meet in a group and discuss these questions:

1. How successful were you in devising effective acronyms and acrostics?

2. Do some of the group members' creations seem more effective than others? Why?

3. Is the act of creating them an important component of helping to remember what they represent, or would having them created by someone else be as helpful in recalling them?

For your information, a common acronym for the Great Lakes is HOMES (**H**uron, **O**ntario, **M**ichigan, **E**rie, **S**uperior).

To Try It online, go to Connect for _P.O.W.E.R. Learning and Your Life._

After learning to use the acronym "FACE" to remember the notes on the spaces of the music staff, many beginning musicians learn that the names of the lines on the staff form the acrostic, "Every Good Boy Deserves Fudge." Another type of mnemonic is an **acrostic**—a sentence in which the first letters correspond to something that needs to be recalled. The benefits—as well as the drawbacks—of acrostics are similar to those of acronyms. (You can explore acronyms and acrostics in **Try It! 5**, "Do-it-yourself Acronyms and Acrostics.")

Although mnemonics are helpful, keep in mind that they have a number of significant shortcomings. First, they don't focus on the meaning of the items being remembered. Because information that is learned in terms of its surface characteristics, such as first letters that form a word, is less likely to be retained than information that is learned in terms of its meaning, mnemonic devices are an imperfect route to memorization.

Acrostic

A sentence in which the first letters of the words correspond to material that is to be remembered

There's another problem with mnemonics: Sometimes it takes as much effort to create a mnemonic device as it would to memorize the material in the first place. And because the mnemonic itself has no meaning, it can be forgotten.

Despite their drawbacks, mnemonics can be useful. They are particularly helpful when the material being memorized includes a list of items or a series of steps.

Involve Multiple Senses

No matter what your learning style, the more senses you can involve when you're trying to learn new material, the better you'll be able to remember. Here's why: Every time we encounter new information, all of our senses are potentially at work. For instance, if we witness a car crash, we receive sensory input from the sight of the two cars hitting each other, the sound of the impact, and perhaps the smell of burning rubber. Each piece of sensory information is stored in a separate location in the brain, and yet all the pieces are linked together in extraordinarily intricate ways.

What this means is that when we seek to remember the details of the crash, recalling a memory of one of the sensory experiences—such as what we heard—can trigger recall of the other types of memories. For example, thinking about the *sound* the two cars made when they hit can bring back memories of the way the scene looked.

When you learn something, use your body. Don't sit passively at your desk. Instead, move around. Stand up; sit down. Touch the page. Trace figures with your fingers. Talk to yourself. Think out loud. It may seem strange, but doing this increases the number of ways in which the information is stored.

Visualize

Visualization is a technique by which images are formed to ensure that material is recalled. For instance, memory requires three basic steps: the initial recording of information, the storage of that information, and, ultimately, the retrieval of the stored information. As you read the three steps, you probably see them as logical and straightforward processes. But how do you remember them?

You might visualize a computer, with its keyboard, disks, and monitor (see **Figure 3.3**). The keyboard represents the initial recording of information. The disk represents the storage of information, and the monitor represents the display of information that has been retrieved from memory. If you can put these images in your mind, it will help you to remember the three basic memory steps later.

Overlearn

Think back to when you were learning your basic multiplication facts ($1 \times 1 = 1$; $2 \times 2 = 4$; and so forth). Let's suppose you had put each multiplication problem on a flash card, and you decided to go through your entire set of cards, trying to get every problem right.

The first time you went through the set of cards and answered all the problems correctly, would you

Visualization
A memory technique by which images are formed to help recall material

figure 3.3
Visualizing Memory

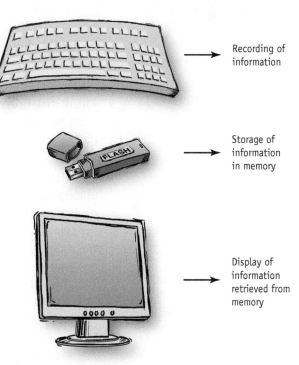

Recording of information

Storage of information in memory

Display of information retrieved from memory

feel as if you'd memorized them perfectly and believe that you'd never again make an error? You shouldn't. You would need several instances of perfect performance to be sure you had learned the multiplication facts completely.

Lasting learning doesn't come until you have overlearned the material. **Overlearning** consists of studying and rehearsing material past the point of initial mastery. Through overlearning, recall becomes automatic. Rather than searching for a fact, going through mental contortions until perhaps the information surfaces, overlearning permits us to recall the information without even thinking about it.

To put the principle of overlearning to work, don't stop studying at the point when you can say to yourself, "Well, I'll probably pass this test." You may be right, but that's all you'll do—pass. Instead, spend extra time learning the material until it becomes as familiar as an old pair of jeans.

Overlearning
Studying and rehearsing material past the point of initial mastery to the point at which recall becomes automatic

»LO 3.3 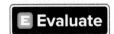 Evaluating What You Have Read

Evaluation is a crucial step in reading. You need to be able to answer the seemingly simple question, "What does all this mean?"

But there's another aspect to evaluation. You need to evaluate, truthfully and honestly, your own level of understanding. This process of evaluation will help you to retain what you have read. What do you know as a result of your reading? Evaluation, then, consists of the following steps:

> **Identify the main ideas and themes and their value to you personally.** Try to determine the take-home message of the material you've read. For example, the take-home message of a chapter on accounting ethics might be, "In the long run, honest accounting practices benefit the long-term health of any business."
>
> Sometimes the main ideas and themes are spelled out, and at other times you will have to deduce them for yourself. Evaluating the main ideas and themes in terms of how they relate to you personally will help you understand and remember them more easily.

> **Prioritize the ideas.** Of all the information that is presented, which is the most crucial to the main message and which is the least crucial? Make a list of the main topics covered and try to rank them in order of importance.

> **Think critically about the arguments presented in the reading.** Do they seem to make sense? Are the author's assertions reasonable? Are there any flaws in the arguments? Would authors with a different point of view dispute what is being said? How would they build their own arguments?

> **Explain the material to someone else.** There is no better way to know if you understand the material than by trying to explain it to someone else. Try explaining the material to a fellow classmate who missed the assignment. In the absence of another person, you can pretend you are explaining the material, talking—out loud!—about what you read. This is one time when talking out loud when no one else is around is not only acceptable, but beneficial.
>
> Talking out loud does two things. First, it helps you identify weak spots in your understanding and recall; talking to yourself will help you nail down concepts that are still not clear in your own mind. Second, and equally important, because you are transforming the written word into the spoken word, you are thinking about the information in another way, which will help you remember it better.

From the perspective of . . .

AN EDITORIAL ASSISTANT The ability to discern what is important within what you read is a key job function for editors. How might you apply your reading evaluation skills to an author's first draft?

The Job of Reading

Memos. Annual reports. Instructions. Continuing education assignments. Professional journals.

Each of these items illustrates the importance of developing critical reading skills for on-the-job success. Virtually every job requires reading expertise; and for some professions, reading is a central component. Polishing your reading skills now will pay big dividends when you enter the world of work. The better you are at absorbing and remembering written information, the better you'll be at carrying out your job.

For instance, in many corporations, vital information is transmitted through the written word, via emails, hard-copy memos, technical reports, or Web-based material. The job of repairing broken appliances or automobiles requires the reading of numerous service manuals to master the complex computer diagnostic systems that are now standard equipment. Nurses and others in the health-care field must read journals and reports to keep up with the newest medical technologies.

Furthermore, because not all supervisors are effective writers, you'll sometimes need to read between the lines and draw inferences and conclusions about what you need to do. You should also keep in mind that there are significant cultural differences in the way in which people write and the type of language they use. Being sensitive to the cultural background of colleagues will permit you to interpret and understand what you are reading more accurately.

In short, reading is a skill that's required in virtually every profession. Developing the habit of reading critically while you are in college or university will pave the road for future career success.

> **Use in-text and online review questions and tests.** Many textbook chapters end with a quiz or a set of review questions about the material or make these available on a companion website. Don't ignore them! Such questions indicate what the writer of the book thought was important for you to learn, and they can also provide an excellent opportunity for evaluating your memory.

> **Team up with a friend or use a study group.** When it comes to evaluating your understanding of a reading, two heads (or more!) are often better than one, particularly if you scored high on interpersonal intelligence back in Chapter 1. Working with a classmate or study group—especially others who may have a different preferred learning style from your own—can help you test the limits of your understanding and memory of material and assess areas in which you need work.

> **Be honest with yourself.** Most of us are able to read with our minds on cruise control. But the net result is not much different from not reading the passage at all. If you have drifted off while you've been reading, go back and reread the passage.

R Rethink   Getting It the Second Time

You're human, so—like the rest of us—when you finish a reading assignment you'd probably like nothing more than to heave a sigh of relief and put the book away.

As an experienced P.O.W.E.R. learner, by now you know that there's a key last step you should take that will assist you in cementing what you've learned into memory: rethinking what you've read. If you do it within 24 hours of first reading the assignment, it can save you hours of work later. This review process also happens to be the third "R" in SQ3R: Going back to something you've read and reviewing it, along with any notes you've taken, is one of the most effective ways of remembering what you have read.

> "Reading furnishes the mind only with materials of knowledge; it is thinking that makes what we read ours."
>
> John Locke, *Of the Conduct of the Understanding,* 1706

Yeah, right, you're probably thinking. *Like I have time for that.* The goal, though, is not a literal rereading. It isn't necessary to reread word for word. You already know what's important and what's not important, so you can skim some of the less important material. But it is wise to review the more difficult and important material carefully, making sure that you fully understand what is being discussed and ensuring that you'll remember the key details.

What's most critical, though, is that you think deeply about the material, considering the take-home message of what you've read. You need to be sure that your understanding is complete and that you're able to answer any questions that you had earlier about the material. Rethinking should be the central activity as you reread the passage and your notes.

The benefits of rethinking the material can't be overstated. Rethinking transfers material from your short-term memory to your long-term memory. It solidifies information so that it will be remembered far better over the long haul.

Time to Reflect: What Did I Learn?

1. Think about times when you read for pleasure compared with times when you read material for a class. How do the ways you read the two types of material differ?

2. Do you prefer reading traditional textbooks or e-books? Why?

3. Based on what you learned about reading and remembering in this chapter, what do you plan to do differently to help you remember what you read in the future? Be specific.

Looking **Back**

What are the essential elements of successful reading?

▸ The most important aspect of reading is comprehension, not speed. Finishing a reading assignment quickly is far less important than understanding it fully.

▸ One problem people have with reading is a limited attention span. However, attention span can be increased with self-awareness and practice.

How can I improve my concentration and read more effectively?

▸ Reading should be approached with a clear sense of purpose and goals, which will vary from assignment to assignment. Examining the frontmatter of a book and creating advance organizers are useful strategies.

▸ As your read, identify and focus on the key material you will need to remember later. Don't try to memorize everything you read.

▸ Maintain focus by breaking down the reading into small chunks, taking breaks as needed, dealing with distractions, and writing while reading.

What are some techniques I can use for memorizing large amounts of information?

▸ Many memory techniques are available to improve memorization. Rehearsal is a primary one, as is the use of mnemonics such as acronyms and acrostics.

▸ Other memory techniques are visualization and the use of multiple senses while learning new material.

▸ Overlearning is a basic principle of memorization.

How can I best retain what I have read?

▸ Understanding of reading assignments can be cemented in memory by identifying the main ideas, prioritizing them, thinking critically about the arguments, using in-text questions and tests, and explaining the writer's ideas to someone else.

▸ Quickly rereading assignments and the notes you took as you read can greatly help in solidifying your memory of the material.

[KEY TERMS AND CONCEPTS]

Acronym (p. 77)

Acrostic (p. 78)

Advance organizers (p. 64)

Attention span (p. 68)

Frontmatter (p. 66)

Mnemonics (p. 77)

Overlearning (p. 80)

Rehearsal (p. 77)

SQ3R (p. 64)

Visualization (p. 79)

[RESOURCES]

ON CAMPUS

If you are experiencing unusual difficulties in reading or remembering material, you may have a learning disability, as discussed in Chapter 1. If you suspect this is the case, take action. Many colleges and universities have an office that deals specifically with learning disabilities. You can also talk to someone at your college or university counselling centre; he or she will arrange for you to be tested, and this process can determine whether you have a problem.

IN PRINT

The fourth edition of Joe Cortina and Janet Elder's book, *Opening Doors: Understanding College Reading* (McGraw-Hill, 2008), provides a complete set of guidelines for reading textbooks and other kinds of writing that you will encounter during college or university. Another useful volume is the seventh edition of *Breaking Through: College Reading* (Longman, 2009) by Brenda Smith.

In *Improving Your Memory* (Johns Hopkins, 2005), Janet Fogler and Lynn Stern provide an overview of practical tips on maximizing your memory. Barry Gordon and Lisa Berger provide insight into the functioning of memory and how to improve it in *Intelligent Memory* (Penguin, 2004).

Finally, *The Memory Doctor* by Douglas Mason and Spencer Smith (New Harbinger Publications, 2005) offers simple techniques for improving memory.

ON THE WEB

The following websites provide the opportunity to extend your learning about the material in this chapter.

➤ Check out this excellent 3-minute video on how to help remember what you read. It is an interview with Dr. Cynthia R. Green, psychologist and author of *Total Memory Workout: Eight Easy Steps to Maximum Memory Fitness* (**www.howdini.com/howdini-video-6635124.html**)

➤ *Increasing Textbook Reading Comprehension by Using SQ3R* is the title of this site offered by Virginia Tech University (**www.ucc.vt.edu/lynch/TextbookReading.htm**). Offered here is a clear and detailed outline on how to use the SQ3R reading method, as well as links to other reading comprehension aids such as critical reading, proofreading, and selective reading.

➤ Need a mnemonic? Have one you'd like to share? Then just go to **www.mnemonic-device.com/**, a site devoted entirely to mnemonics. This fun and educational site covers a variety of subjects from astronomy to weather.

➤ *Mind Tools* is a website worth visiting. It offers a number of free online articles on a wide range of topics including reading strategies (**http://www.mindtools.com/rdstratg.html**), techniques for improving memory (**www.mindtools.com/memory.html**) and the SQ3R approach to reading (**http://www.mindtools.com/pages/article/newISS_02.htm**).

TAKING IT TO THE NET

1 Go to a newspaper's website, such as that of *The Globe and Mail* (**www.theglobeandmail.com**) or the *Calgary Herald* (**www.calgaryherald.com/**), and read one of the current editorials, which you can find in the Opinions section. Highlight key points of the editorial. Look up unfamiliar words in the dictionary. Make notes on what you've read. Review your notes. Then, with a classmate, recount the main points made in the editorial.

2 Practise the rehearsal technique for storing information in memory. Go to **http://canadaonline.about.com/od/premiers/Provincial_Premiers_in_Canada.htm** to find the names of five Canadian premiers. Repeat the names several times. Now explore another, unrelated site on the Web. After a few minutes, write down the names of the five premiers from memory. How did you do?

The Case of . . .

The Five-Pound Reading Packet

The instructor dropped the thick packet of course readings on Anjana Garud's desk. It landed with a loud *thunk*.

"We'll be reading this packet over the next four weeks," the instructor announced.

But staring at the packet, all Anjana could think was, *I don't think I could even lift that, let alone read it in just a month!*

Sure, Anjana was interested in the topics of the readings. They all dealt with the history of computer programming, and Anjana was in university to get her degree in that field. She told herself a lot of the information in the readings would probably be very useful, both in university and throughout her programming career.

But all Anjana could focus on as she stared at the packet were nagging questions: How could she possibly read all of it in four weeks? How would she remember all that material for tests or on the job? And perhaps most urgently of all, how would she even get the massive packet home?

1. How would you advise Anjana to prepare for her course reading?

2. How would you suggest Anjana organize her time so she could finish the readings in the allotted four weeks?

3. How might Anjana stay focused on her reading? How might she most effectively use writing as a way to accomplish her task?

4. What techniques might Anjana use to memorize long lists or other key material from her reading?

5. In what ways can Anjana use rethinking techniques to improve her understanding of the readings in the packet?

4 Taking Notes

Learning Outcomes

By the time you finish this chapter, you will be able to

» **LO 4.1**   Identify the characteristics of effective notes.

» **LO 4.2**   Demonstrate the various methods of note-taking: outlining, the Cornell method, concept mapping, and using a PowerPoint handout.

» **LO 4.3**   Demonstrate how to take study notes, which are created for the purpose of reviewing material.

A s he took a seat in the front row of his marketing class in his second term of college, Matt Ortiz realized that something fundamental had changed.

For the whole first term, Matt had sat in the back of the room during classes, just as he'd done in high school. He figured that just showing up to class was all that mattered. What difference did it make where he sat? And what difference would it make if he occasionally sent text messages on his cellphone?

But then he had received mostly Cs in his first-term courses.

In a note-taking workshop Matt enrolled in afterward, he learned the importance of active listening and taking good notes in class. He also learned that one way to become more engaged in class is to sit close to the instructor.

Trying out the strategies he was taught in the workshop, Matt found—a bit to his surprise—that they helped. By the end of the term, he'd pulled his grades way up.

Looking Ahead

Matt Ortiz's move from the back to the front of the classroom is both a source and a symbol of his academic success. Matt's ability to take good notes is also likely to pay future dividends, because note-taking skills not only help produce academic success in college but also contribute to career success.

In this chapter, we discuss effective strategies for taking notes during class lectures, during other kinds of oral presentations, and from written sources such as textbooks. There's a lot more to good note-taking than you probably think—and a lot less if you view note-taking as "getting everything down on paper." As we explore the ins and outs of note-taking, we'll pause along the way to discuss the tools of the note-taking trade, how to be an active learner, and how to think your way to good notes.

Prepare
Consider your goals

Organize
Get the tools of note-taking together

Work
Process—don't just copy—information

Evaluate
Think critically about your notes

Rethink
Review your notes shortly after class to activate your memory

P.O.W.E.R. Plan

» LO 4.1 Taking Notes in Class

You know the type: the student who desperately tries to write down everything the instructor says. No spoken word goes unwritten. And you think to yourself, "If only I took such thorough notes—I'd do much better in my classes."

Contrary to what many students think, good note-taking does not mean writing down every word that an instructor utters. With note-taking, less is often more. We'll see why as we consider the basic steps in P.O.W.E.R. note-taking.

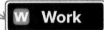 **Prepare** Consider Your Goals

As with other academic activities, preparation is a critical component of note-taking. The following steps will prepare you for action:

> **Identify the instructor's goals for the course.** On the first day of class, most instructors talk about their objectives, what they hope you'll get out of the class, and what you'll know when it's over. Most instructors restate the information on the class syllabus or course outline, the written document that explains the learning outcomes for the course, the learning objectives for each class, and the reading and assignments for the term. For example, they may say that they want you to "develop an appreciation for the ways that statistics are used in everyday life." The information you get during that first session and through the syllabus is critical. If the instructor's goals aren't stated explicitly, you should consider going up after class and discussing them with the instructor.

> **Identify your own goals for the course.** In addition to those "external" goals, you should have your own goals. What is it you want to learn from the course? What kind of grade do you want, and what are you prepared to do to obtain it? How will the information from the course help you to enhance your knowledge, improve your career prospects, and achieve your dreams?

> **Complete assignments before coming to class.** Always go to class prepared. Complete all of your reading and other assignments beforehand. Instructors assume that their students have done what they've assigned, and their lectures are based upon that assumption. It's virtually impossible to catch on to the gist of a lecture if you haven't completed the assignments. Good note-taking requires being prepared to listen to the material.

> **Be willing to make suggestions to the instructor that can help enhance your note-taking.** For example, if you have a visual/graphic learning style, you may

want to suggest that the instructor put an agenda or outline of the main topics on the board at the beginning of class, to help you follow how the information being presented that day is connected. Students with an auditory/verbal learning style may want to ask for permission to record the lecture, or they may want to find out if a podcast is available.

> **Accept the instructor, whatever his or her teaching style.** Not every instructor teaches in the same way. Accept the fact that, just as students have different learning styles, instructors may approach teaching in different ways. Ultimately, it's your responsibility to adapt to an instructor's teaching style. Where an instructor's teaching style does not fit well with your learning style, you must not use this as an excuse to do poorly or to give up. You cannot afford to let this get in the way of your education or let it interfere with your goals. If you need extra help or clarification, don't be afraid to approach the instructor and ask for it. If need be, investigate whether your college or university offers tutoring, which is often provided at no cost to you.

> **Perform a pre-class warm-up.** No, this doesn't mean doing stretches just before each class. As you head to class or settle into your seat, skim your notes from the previous lecture, looking over what the instructor said and where that lecture left off. You should also briefly review the main headings or summary section of the readings you've been assigned.

> The warm-up doesn't have to be long. The goal is simply to refresh yourself, to get yourself into the right frame of mind for the class.

> **Choose a seat that will promote good note-taking.** You should certainly choose a seat that permits you to see and hear clearly, but there's more to your choice than that. Picking the right seat in a classroom can make a big difference.

> Where is the best place to sit? Usually it's front and centre. Instructors make more eye contact with the people near them, and they often believe that the best, most-engaged students sit closest.

> "The highest result of education is tolerance."
> Helen Keller

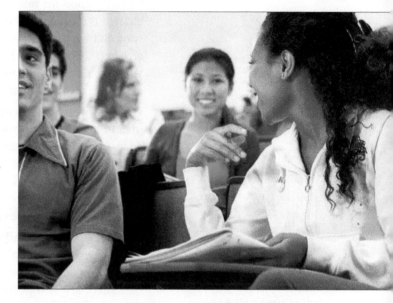

Sometimes distracting seats have less to do with location and more to do with the person sitting next to you. Don't be afraid to put some physical distance between yourself and a distracting neighbour.

Furthermore, sitting in the back of the class may make you feel disengaged and out of touch with what is happening at the front of the room. In turn, this lack of engagement may make it easier for your mind to wander.

 **Organize**

Get the Tools of Note-Taking Together

Do you have a favourite pen? A preferred type of notebook?

Most of us have distinct tastes in the type of tools we use for various tasks: a favourite screwdriver, a preferred style of mouse, a brand of running shoes we find most comfortable. You should determine your preferred classroom "tools," too. Taking your favourite kind of notebook and pen to class can give you the confidence and focus you need to take effective notes.

There are several things to consider as you prepare for class:

> **Choose the appropriate writing utensil.** Generally, using a pen is better than using a pencil. Ink is less likely to smudge, and what you produce with ink is usually brighter and clearer—and therefore easier to use when studying. On the other hand, for math and accounting classes, where you may be copying down or even working through formulas in class, a pencil might be better, because it's easier to erase if you make a mistake when copying detailed, complex information.
>
> Sometimes you may want to use a combination of pen and pencil. And in some cases you might use several different pen colours, or highlighting markers. One colour might signify important information that the instructor mentions will be on the test. Another colour might be reserved for definitions or material that is copied from the board. And a third might be used for general notes on the lecture.

> **Choose a notebook that assists in note-taking.** Loose-leaf notebooks are particularly good for taking notes because they permit you to go back later and change the order of the pages or add additional material in the appropriate spot. But whatever kind of notebook you use, use only one side of the page for writing: keep one side free of notes. There may be times when you're studying when you'll want to spread your notes in front of you, and it's much easier if no material is written on the back of pages.

> **Consider the benefits of taking your textbook to class.** It's generally a good idea to take your textbook to class, unless your instructor advises you otherwise. Sometimes instructors will refer to information contained in it, and they may assign in-class exercises that are in the text. Sometimes it's useful to have the textbook handy to clarify information that is being discussed. You can also use it to look up key terms that may momentarily escape you. But don't, under any circumstances, use class time as an opportunity to read the textbook!

> **Consider the pros and cons of using a laptop computer to take notes in class.** There are several advantages: Legibility problems are avoided, and it's easy to go back and revise or add material after you've taken the notes.
>
> There are also potential pitfalls. You may end up keyboarding more and thinking less. Or you may succumb to the temptation to check your email or surf the Web, rather than listening to your instructor.
>
> Because of their drawbacks, some instructors have strong feelings against the use of laptops in class. Consequently, be sure to ask for permission before using your laptop to take notes.

From the perspective of . . .

A STUDENT Using a laptop is advantageous for students who type faster than they write. What are some of the advantages of taking handwritten notes? Of using a laptop to take notes?

 **Work**

Process—Don't Just Copy—Information

With pen poised, you're ready to begin the work of note-taking. The instructor speaks, and you start to write as quickly as you can, taking down as many of the instructor's words as possible.

Stop! You've made your first mistake. The central act in taking notes is not writing; listening and thinking are far more important. The key to effective note-taking is to write down the right amount of information—not too much and not too little.

Successful note-taking involves not just *hearing* what is said, but *listening actively*. **Hearing** is the involuntary act of sensing sounds. The annoying drip of

Hearing
The involuntary act of sensing sounds

Determine Your Listening Style

Consider the following pairs of statements. Place a check next to the statement in each pair that more closely describes your classroom listening style.

- [ ] 1a. When I'm listening in class, I lean back and get as comfortable as possible.
- [ ] 1b. When I'm listening in class, I sit upright and even lean forward a little.
- [ ] 2a. I let the instructor's words wash over me, generally going with the flow of the lecture.
- [ ] 2b. I try to guess in advance what the instructor is going to say and what direction the lecture is taking.
- [ ] 3a. I regard each lecture as a separate event, not necessarily related to what the instructor has said before or will say the next time.
- [ ] 3b. As I listen, I regularly ask myself how this lecture relates to what was said in previous classes.
- [ ] 4a. When I take notes, I try to reproduce the instructor's words as closely as possible.
- [ ] 4b. When I take notes, I try to interpret and summarize the ideas behind the instructor's words.
- [ ] 5a. I don't usually question the importance of what the instructor is saying or why it's the topic of a lecture or discussion.
- [ ] 5b. I often ask why the content of the lecture is important enough for the instructor to be speaking about it.
- [ ] 6a. I rarely question the accuracy or logic of a presentation, assuming that the instructor knows the topic better than I do.
- [ ] 6b. I often ask myself how the instructor knows something and find myself wondering how it could be proved.
- [ ] 7a. I rarely make eye contact with the instructor.
- [ ] 7b. I often make eye contact with the instructor.

If you tended to prefer the "a" statements in most pairs, you have a more passive listening style. If you preferred the "b" statements, you have a more active listening style. Wherever you selected "a" statements, go back and examine the corresponding "b" response to consider ways that you can become a more active listener.

To Try It online, go to Connect for *P.O.W.E.R. Learning and Your Life*.

a faucet, or the grating sound of a co-worker's voice speaking on the phone in the next cubicle are two examples of how hearing is both involuntary and often meaningless. In contrast, **active listening** is the intentional act of focusing on what is being said, making sense of it, and thinking about it in a way that permits it to be recalled accurately. Listening involves concentration. It also requires shutting out competing thoughts, such as what we need to pick up at the grocery store or why our date last night was so terrific. (To get a sense of your own listening skills, complete **Try It! 1,** "Determine Your Listening Style.")

Keeping the importance of active listening in mind, consider the following recommendations for taking notes in class:

> **Listen for the key ideas.** Not every sentence in a lecture is equally important, and one of the most useful skills you can develop is separating the key ideas from supporting information. Good instructors strive to make just a few main points. The rest of what they say consists of explanation, examples, and other supportive material that expands upon the key ideas.

> Your job, then, is to distinguish the key ideas from their support. To do this, you need to be alert and always searching for your instructor's **meta-message**—that is, the underlying main ideas that a speaker is seeking to convey, or the meaning behind the overt message you hear.

Active listening
The intentional act of focusing on what is being said, making sense of it, and thinking about it in a way that permits it to be recalled accurately

Meta-message
The underlying main ideas that a communicator is seeking to convey; the meaning behind the overt message

How can you discern the meta-message? One way is to listen for key phrases. Instructors know what's important in their lecture; your job is to figure it out, not just from what they say but from how they say it.

For instance, listen for clues about the importance of material. Pay attention to phrases like "don't forget . . . ," "be sure to remember that . . . ," "you need to know . . . ," "the most important thing that must be considered . . . ," "there are four problems with this approach . . . ," and—a big one—"this will be on the test"! These phrases should cause you to sit up and take notice. Another sign of importance is repetition. If an instructor says the same thing in several ways, it's a clear sign that the material being discussed is important.

> **Be on the lookout for nonverbal signals.** Does an instructor get excited about a particular topic? Does he or she seem unenthusiastic when talking about something? Use nonverbal cues to gauge the importance of a particular part of a message relative to other things being said. Listen also for what is *not* being said. Sometimes silence is not just golden, but informative as well. By noting what topics are not being covered in class, or are presented only minimally, you can gauge the relative importance of ideas in comparison with one another.

This is where preliminary preparation *and* organization come in. The only way to know what's left out of a lecture is to have done the assigned readings in advance. Also, don't be fooled into thinking that if a topic is not covered in class, it's totally unimportant: Most instructors believe students are responsible for all material that is assigned, whether or not it's explicitly covered in class.

> **Use short, abbreviated phrases—not full sentences—when taking notes.** Forget everything you've ever heard about always writing in full sentences. If you try to write notes in complete sentences, you'll soon become bogged down, paying more attention to your notes than to your instructor. In fact, if you use full sentences, you'll be tempted to try transcribing every word the instructor utters, which, as you now know, is not a good idea at all.

Instead, write in phrases, using only keywords or terms. Save full sentences for definitions or quotations that your instructor clearly wants you to know word for word. For example, consider the following excerpt from a lecture:

> *There are two kinds of job analyses used by human resource experts: First, there are job- or task-oriented analyses, and second, there are worker- or employee-oriented analyses. Job analyses just describe the tasks that need to be accomplished by a worker; for example, heart surgeons need to be able to perform heart bypass surgery in order to carry out their jobs. In contrast, employee-oriented job descriptions describe knowledge, skills, and abilities the employee must have to get the job done; for example, surgeons need to understand the different types of blood vessels in the heart in order to be successful. Most job analyses include elements of both job-oriented and employee-oriented types.*

If you were taking notes, you might produce the following:

2 kinds job analyses:
    1. Job-oriented (=task-oriented): tasks needed to get job done. Ex: heart surgeon operates
    2. Worker-oriented (=employee-oriented): knowledge, skills, abilities, etc. necessary to do job. Ex: surgeon knows blood vessels
Most j.a. a combination

Note how the lecturer used almost 120 words, while the notes used only around 35 words—less than a third of the lecture.

> **Use abbreviations.** One way to speed up the note-taking process is through the use of abbreviations. These are among the most common:

and	*& or +*	with	*w/*	without	*w/o*
care of	*c/o*	leads to; resulting in	$\longrightarrow$	as a result of	$\longleftarrow$
percent	*%*	change	Δ	number	*#*
that is	*i.e.*	for example	*e.g.*	and so forth	*etc.*
no good	*n.g.*	question	*?*	compared with	*c/w*
page	*p.*	important!	*!!*	less than	*<*
more than	*>*	equals, same as	*=*	versus	*vs.*

> **Copy key information written on the board or projected from overheads or PowerPoint slides.** If your instructor provides a definition, quotation, or formula, you probably should copy it. In fact, such prominently displayed material has "test item" written all over it. You might want to highlight such material in some way in your notes.

> **Pay particular attention to the points raised by instructors at the end of classes.** Instructors often provide a summary of the discussion, which is worthy of inclusion in your notes.

> **Ask questions.** One of the most important things you can do during a class is to ask questions. Raising questions will help you evaluate, clarify, and ultimately better understand what your instructor is saying. And if you are having trouble understanding something, you can bet there are others just like you who have the same question.

Questions also serve several other purposes. For one thing, raising questions will help you to personalize the material being covered, permitting you to draw it more closely into your own framework and perspective. Furthermore, when you ask a question and it is answered, you become personally engaged in what the instructor is saying. In very large classes, asking questions may be the only way that an instructor can get a sense of you as an individual.

Questioning also increases your involvement in the class as a whole. If you sit back and never raise questions in class, you are much less likely to feel a real part of the class. Becoming an active questioner will rightly make you feel as if you have contributed something to the class. Remember, if you are unclear about some point, it is likely that others share your lack of clarity.

Finally, by asking questions in class, you serve as a role model for other students. Your questions may help break the ice in a class, making it easier for others to raise issues that they have about the material. And ultimately the answers that the instructor provides to others' questions may help you to better understand and/or evaluate your understanding of the material.

» LO 4.2 Note-taking Methods to Use in Class

Over the years, several note-taking methods have been developed and used successfully by students at all levels of learning. Having a consistent way of taking notes for each of your classes will save you time in the long run. It is, therefore,

figure 4.1
Note-taking in
Outline Form

```
  I.  Difficulties faced by college students seeking affordable housing
      A. Students subjected to high rents close to campus
          1. Forced to share apartments
          2. Sometimes must live far from campus
      B. Made to sign harsh leases
 II.  Possible solutions
      A. College offers subsidized housing
          1. Advantage: Housing costs can be lowered
          2. Potential problems
              a. College becomes students' landlord
              b. College uses funds for housing instead of investing
                 in education
      B. Rent control
          1. Advantage: Can provide fixed, reasonably priced rents
          2. Disadvantages
              a. Creates permanent expensive rent-control bureaucracy
              b. Landlords may neglect rent-control property
              c. Little incentive for owners to increase the number of
                 rental units
              d. Strong competition for rent-fixed units
III.  Summary
      A. Advantages and disadvantages to both solutions
      B. May need new, creative solutions
```

worthwhile to explore the various approaches to note-taking to determine which one works best for *you*. The methods we will discuss in this section are the following: outlining, the Cornell method, concept mapping, and using a PowerPoint handout. It is worth trying out each of them before settling on one note-taking method, or perhaps deciding to use a combination.

▷ **Take notes in outline form.** It's often useful to take notes in the form of an outline. The **outline method of note-taking** summarizes ideas in short phrases and indicates the relationship among concepts through the use of indentations.

When outlining, you can be formal about it, using roman numerals, regular numbers, and capital and small letters (see the example in **Figure 4.1** above). Or, if you prefer, you can also simply use outlining indentations without assigning numbers and letters (as in the short handwritten note on page 92).

Outlining serves a number of functions. It forces you to try to determine the structure of the lecture. Organizing the key points and noting the connections among them helps you remember the material better because you have processed it more. The effort involved in outlining also keeps your mind from drifting away from the lecture.

Use **Try It! 2**, "Outline a Lecture," on page 95, to practise your outlining skills.

**outline method
of note-taking**

A method of taking notes that summarizes ideas in short phrases and indicates the relationship among concepts through the use of indentations.

WORKING IN A GROUP Try It! **P.O.W.E.R**

2

Outline a Lecture

Working with others in a group, take turns slowly reading sections of the following lecture to each other.[2] As the paragraph is being read, outline the main arguments in the space below.

In 1985 Joseph Farman, a British earth scientist working in Antarctica, made an alarming discovery. Scanning the Antarctic sky, he found less ozone than should be there—not a slight depletion but a 30% drop from a reading recorded 5 years earlier in the Antarctic!

At first the scientist thought that this "ozone hole" was an as-yet-unexplained weather phenomenon. Evidence soon mounted, however, pointing to synthetic chemicals as the culprit. Detailed analysis of chemicals in the Antarctic atmosphere revealed a surprisingly high concentration of chlorine, a chemical known to destroy ozone. The source of the chlorine was a class of chemicals called chlorofluorocarbons (CFCs). CFCs have been manufactured in large amounts since they were invented in the 1920s, largely for use as coolants in air conditioners, propellants in aerosols, and foaming agents in making Styrofoam™. CFCs were widely regarded as harmless because they were chemically unreactive under normal conditions. But in the thin atmosphere over Antarctica, CFCs condense on to tiny ice crystals; warmed by the sun in the spring, they attack and destroy ozone without being used up.

The thinning of the ozone layer in the upper atmosphere 25 to 40 kilometres above the surface of the earth is a serious matter. The ozone layer protects life from the harmful ultraviolet (UV) rays from the sun that bombard the earth continuously. Like invisible sunglasses, the ozone layer filters out these dangerous rays. When UV rays damage the DNA in skin cells, it can lead to skin cancer. Every 1% drop in the atmospheric ozone concentration is estimated to lead to a 6% increase in skin cancers. The drop of approximately 3% that has already occurred worldwide, therefore, is estimated to have led to as much as a 20% increase in skin cancers.

Write your outline here.

_____
_____
_____
_____
_____
_____
_____
_____
_____
_____
_____
_____
_____
_____
_____
_____
_____
_____

After you have outlined the passage, compare your outline with that of others who took notes on the same passage.

1. Did you all agree on the main ideas of each passage?

2. How do your notes differ from others? How are they similar?

3. How might you improve your notes to better capture the main points?

4. Would a different topic produce greater or fewer difficulties?

Collectively, produce what you believe is the ideal outline, and compare it with the outlines produced by other groups.

To Try It online, go to Connect for *P.O.W.E.R. Learning and Your Life.*

figure 4.2
Cornell Note-taking Method

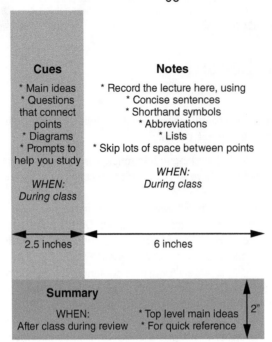

Cues

* Main ideas
* Questions that connect points
* Diagrams
* Prompts to help you study

WHEN: During class

Notes

* Record the lecture here, using
* Concise sentences
* Shorthand symbols
* Abbreviations
* Lists
* Skip lots of space between points

WHEN: During class

2.5 inches   6 inches

Summary

WHEN: After class during review   * Top level main ideas
* For quick reference   2"

Cornell method of note-taking

A method of structuring one's written notes into three categories: main notes, cues and questions, and a summary.

> Use the **Cornell method of note-taking.** If the outline method isn't working for you, you might want to try the Cornell approach to note-taking. This method divides a sheet of paper into three parts, with areas for main notes, cues and questions, and a summary at the bottom, as in **Figure 4.2**, drawn from the Lifehacker website. The site also includes instructions on how to create your own Cornell note-taking templates in Microsoft Word (**http://lifehacker.com/202418/geek-to-live-take-study+worthy-lecture-notes**).

Concept mapping

A method of structuring written material by graphically grouping and connecting key ideas and themes

> A third approach to note-taking, one that will appeal particularly to visual learners, is to create **concept maps.** Concept mapping (sometimes called "mind mapping") is a method of structuring written material by graphically grouping and connecting key ideas and themes. In contrast to an outline, a concept map visually illustrates how related ideas fit together. The pictorial summary gives you another handle for storing the information in memory, and it focuses your thinking on the key ideas from the lecture.

In a concept map, each key idea is placed in a different part of the page, and related ideas are placed near it—above, below, or beside it. What emerges does not have the rigid structure of an outline. Instead, a "finished" concept map looks something like a map of the solar system, with the largest and most central idea in the centre (the "sun" position), and related ideas surrounding it at various distances. It has also been compared to a large tree, with numerous branches and sub-branches radiating out from a central trunk. (**Figure 4.3** presents a sample concept map.)

> The final note-taking method we will discuss is the option of creating PowerPoint handouts, where you can take advantage of PowerPoint slides provided by your instructor. Some instructors will post online their PowerPoint slides

From the perspective of . . .

A MEDICAL ASSISTANT Learning abbreviations is an important aspect of life in a medical office. How can taking notes with abbreviations while in school help you learn important notations for your medical career?

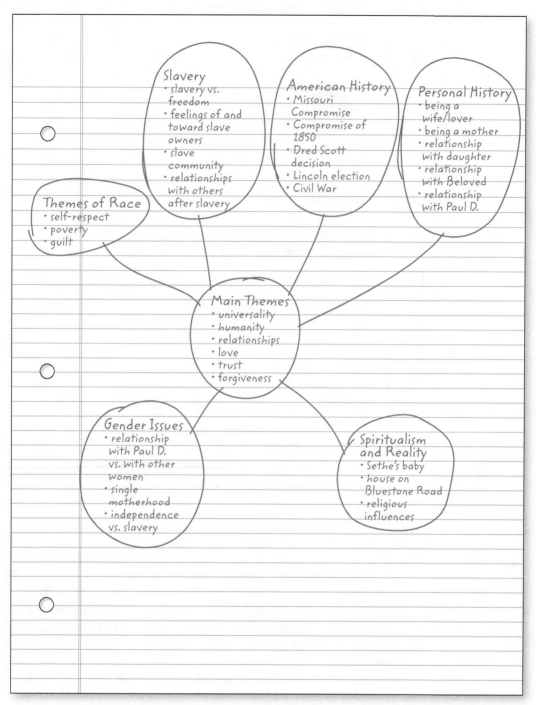

figure 4.3
A Concept Map of Toni Morrison's *Beloved*

before class. (See **Figure 4.4** on page 98 for a sample PowerPoint handout.) To make the most of this opportunity, save the slides to your computer. Then, open them up in PowerPoint and using the print function within PowerPoint, select the option called "handout," and then select "three to a page." This format will produce a sheet containing three slides per page, with a few blank lines next to each slide for your notes.

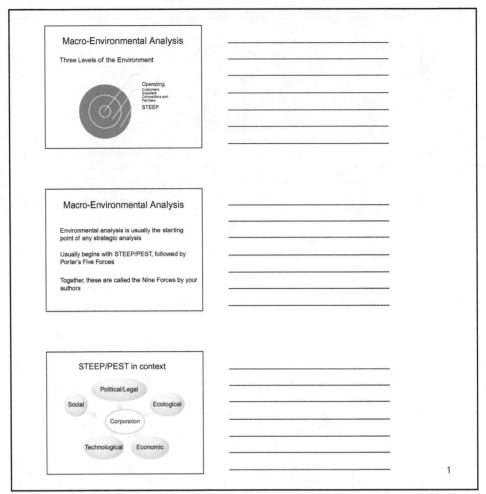

figure 4.4
A PowerPoint Handout, three slides to a page with a place for notes

Create a package of handouts for each chapter, and bring it to class. Then, instead of writing furiously to capture what is on the slide as the teacher speaks, you can listen actively to the value-added explanation and examples provided by your instructor and summarize these next to each slide. The combination of your notes and the PowerPoint slides will be invaluable when reviewing and studying the material later on.

Even if your instructor doesn't post the slides until after class, it's still a good idea to print them out and keep them with the notes you create in class. If your instructor doesn't post slides *at all,* you may want to approach him or her about doing so, explaining the value it provides for all students to be able to create handouts. Students for whom English is a second language find the PowerPoint handout approach to note-taking invaluable, and should approach the instructor on that basis.

Cope with Different Instructional Styles

He talks too fast . . . her accent is difficult to understand . . . he puts people down when they ask a question . . . she rambles . . . he goes off on boring tangents . . . she explains things in a way that doesn't make much sense . . . he won't give me a straight answer.

Not every instructor comes to class with a clear, compelling lecture and then presents it beautifully. All of us have sat through lectures that are deficient in one or more ways. What should you do when you find yourself in such a situation?

> **Remember that "this too shall pass."** First, keep in mind that this is a temporary condition; your experience usually won't last more than one term. Most instructors are conscientious and well prepared; and unless you have enormously bad luck, the unpleasant experience you're having now will not be routine.

> **Ask questions about the material.** Even if you have no idea what is going on in class—or especially if you have no idea—ask questions. You are not the only one struggling with the instructor's shortcomings. You will be doing everyone in the class a favour if you admit you're not following what an instructor is saying and ask for clarification.

> **Ask—privately and politely—for the instructor to alter the way material is presented.** If an instructor has a habit of speaking too quickly, approach him or her privately after class to discuss it. Instructors sometimes get carried away with enthusiasm about their subject and begin speaking faster and faster without being aware of it. Very often a reality check from a student will be welcome. But don't couch your comment in a way that makes the instructor feel inept ("Could you slow down; you're going too fast and losing me"). Instead, keep the comment neutral, without placing blame. For instance, you might simply say, "I'm having trouble keeping up with you; would it be possible for you to speak a little more slowly?"

> **Pool your resources.** Get together with other students in the class and work out a strategy for dealing with the situation. If an instructor speaks too fast and you just can't keep up with the flow of information, meet with your fellow students and compare what you've gleaned from the class. They may have understood or noted material that you missed, and vice versa. (**Figure 4.5** on page 100 shows how two students might take notes on the same material.) Together, you may be able to put the pieces of the puzzle together and get a fuller understanding of the material.

If you've ever been totally lost following a lecture, you may have discovered that speaking with your instructor immediately after class was helpful. Most instructors are very happy to go over and clarify key points that they've covered during class. They also appreciate your initiative and interest.

> **Talk with the instructor after class.** If you feel totally lost after a lecture, or even if you've missed only a few points, speak with the instructor after class. Ask for clarification and get him or her to explain again any points that you missed. Such a dialogue will help you to understand the material better.

Find a Balance between Too Many Notes and Too Few Notes

The key to effective note-taking is to keep a balance between too many and too few notes.

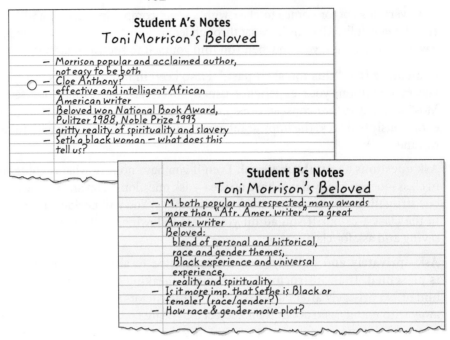

figure 4.5
Sharing lecture notes with classmates can help ensure that your notes are complete.

Student A's Notes
Toni Morrison's Beloved

- Morrison popular and acclaimed author, not easy to be both
○ - Cloe Anthony?
- effective and intelligent African American writer
- Beloved won National Book Award, Pulitzer 1988, Noble Prize 1993
- gritty reality of spirituality and slavery
- Seth a black woman — what does this tell us?

Student B's Notes
Toni Morrison's Beloved

- M. both popular and respected; many awards
- more than "Afr. Amer. writer" — a great
- Amer. writer
  Beloved:
    blend of personal and historical,
    race and gender themes,
    Black experience and universal experience,
    reality and spirituality
- Is it more imp. that Sethe is Black or female? (race/gender?)
- How race & gender move plot?

The best way to achieve this balance is by paying close attention in class. By being alert, engaged, and involved in class, you'll be able to make the most of the techniques we've discussed. The result: notes that capture the most important points raised in class and that will optimize your recall and mastery of the course subject matter.

E Evaluate

Think Critically about Your Notes

Toward the end of class, take a moment to look over your notes. Now's the time—before the class has ended—to evaluate what you've written.

After being sure you can answer yes to the most basic question—can I read what I've written?—ask yourself these questions:

> Do my notes do a good job of representing what was covered in class?

> Do they reflect the emphases of the instructor?

> Are there any key points that are not entirely clear?

> Do I need help clarifying any of the points my instructor made?

Evaluating your notes is a critical part of the note-taking process. You can get a sense of how effective your note-taking has been while you still have a chance to ask your instructor to clarify anything that is not clear.

Perhaps, for example, you've left out a key word in a definition. Maybe you don't understand a concept fully, even though you've written about it in your notes. Possibly you've left out the third step in a list of six steps necessary to accomplish something.

If you look over your notes while you're still in class, you have time to ask your instructor for clarification. Or you can wait until the end of class and raise

Try It!

Evaluate Your Class Notes

3

Take a set of notes you made recently during one of your classes and evaluate it using the following criteria.

Statement	Not Even Slightly	Slightly	Moderately	Pretty Well	Very Well
1. I can read my notes (i.e., they are legible).					
2. Someone else can read my notes.					
3. My notes are complete; I missed nothing important.					
4. My notes represent the key points that were covered in class.					
5. My notes reflect the instructor's emphases.					
6. The instructor's key points are clear and easy to understand.					
7. The notes contain only important points, with no extraneous material.					
8. I understand not only the notes but also the class content they reflect.					
9. Using only the notes, I will be able to reconstruct the essential content of the class in 3 months.					

 WORKING IN A GROUP

1. What do your answers tell you about the effectiveness of your note-taking skills?

2. What might you do differently the next time you take notes?

3. Evaluate and compare the notes you took during the previous 20 minutes of the class you are in now. How do your notes compare with those of the other members of your group?

To Try It online, go to Connect for *P.O.W.E.R. Learning and Your Life.*

your question privately. Most instructors will be happy to answer questions from students who have obviously been actively listening. Just make sure that you add what they tell you to your notes so you'll be able to refer to them later. (To practise evaluating your notes, complete **Try It! 3,** "Evaluate Your Class Notes.")

Note-taking: A Collaborative Approach

Different people take notes differently. Some students understand some topics better than others. And let's face it, not everyone is "awake" for every minute of every class. The bottom line is that for every class, students in the same class are unlikely to have the same notes, and most will have notes that are not complete. So why not share? Consider collaborating with other like-minded students and form a note-taking and study group. You can each take notes for a different subject, or for the same class, or for a different part of the same class. Start by trying it out for a week and get together to compare notes, to ensure you are all getting what you expect from each other; if your classmates are not living up to your expectations, set out some guidelines. Note-taking is one student task where sharing can be a good thing!

R Rethink   ## Activate Your Memory

The lecture has ended, and class is over. You put the top on your pen, close your notebook, stash everything in your bag, and head out for a cup of coffee before your next class.

Wait! Before you close up your notebook, finish the P.O.W.E.R. process. Rethink what you've heard. Spending five or ten minutes reconsidering what you've written right now can save you *hours* of work later. The reason: Rethinking promotes the transfer of information into long-term memory (something we already discussed in Chapter 3). As you integrate the new information you've taken down with what you already know, you plug this information into your memory in a much more meaningful way, which means you can remember it better and more easily.

> "I'd think to myself, 'I don't need to write that down; I'll remember it.' A few days later, it was like, 'What did he say . . .?'"
>
> **Student, Duke University[3]**

If you looked over your notes to clarify and evaluate the information in them in class, you've already begun the process. But once class is over, you need to review the material more formally. Here's how to do it:

> **Rethink as soon as possible.** Time is of the essence! The rethinking phase of note-taking doesn't have to take long; five to ten minutes are usually sufficient. The more critical issue is *when* you do it. The longer you wait before reviewing your notes, the less effective the process will be.
>
> There's no doubt that the best approach is to review the material just after the class has ended. As everyone else is leaving, you can just stay seated and go over your notes. This works fine for classes late in the day, when no other class is scheduled in the room. But what if you must vacate the room immediately after class? The next best thing is to find a quiet space somewhere nearby and do your rethinking there.
>
> In any case, don't let the day end without examining your notes. In fact, reconsidering material just before you go to sleep can be particularly effective.

> **Make rethinking an active process.** Some people feel the notes they take in class are akin to historical documents in a museum, with Do Not Touch! signs hanging on them. On the contrary, think of your notes as a construction project and yourself as the project manager.
>
> When you review your notes, do so with an eye to improving them. If any information is not entirely clear, change the wording in your notes, adding to

Try It! P•O•W•E•R

Practise Your Note-taking Skills

4

Practise your note taking skills, using any techniques you find helpful, in one of the classes in which you are enrolled this term. Analyze your notes to answer these questions:

1. Which specific techniques did I use in taking notes?

2. Which of the note-taking techniques detailed in this chapter was I unable to use, and why?

3. Could I take the notes I made in class and redo them, using one of the techniques in this chapter, such as creating a concept map?

After you have taken notes, use the techniques discussed in this chapter to evaluate and rethink them. Creating a concept map on a separate sheet of paper may be particularly helpful.

To Try It online, go to Connect for *P.O.W.E.R. Learning and Your Life.*

or amending what's there. If certain words are hard to read, fix them. It won't be any easier to read them the night before a test; chances are you'll have even more trouble.

If, on rethinking the material, you don't understand something, ask your instructor or a friend to clarify it. And when you receive an explanation, add it to your notes so you won't forget it. (You might want to use a different-coloured pen for additions to your notes, so you'll know they came later.)

‣ **Think critically about the material in your notes.** As you review the information, think about the material from a critical point of view. Go beyond the facts and pieces of information, integrating and evaluating the material.

In addition, as you rethink your notes, don't think of them only in terms of a single lecture or a single class. Take a longer view. Ask yourself how they fit into the broader themes of the class and the goals that you and the instructor have for the term. How will the information be useful to you? Why did the instructor emphasize a particular point?

To practise the techniques we've been discussing, see **Try It! 4**, "Practise Your Note-Taking Skills."

≫ LO 4.3 Creating Study Notes

Weighing as much as five pounds, bulky and awkward, and filled with more information than you think anyone could ever need to know, it's the meat and potatoes of post-secondary work: your course textbook. You might feel intimidated by its size; you might be annoyed at its cost; you might think you'll never be able to read it, let alone understand, learn, and recall the material in it. How will you manage?

The answer involves taking **study notes,** notes taken for the purpose of reviewing material. They are the kind of notes that you take now to study from later.

Several strategies are useful for taking study notes from written material such as books, magazines, journals, and websites. Which approach works best depends on whether you're able to write directly on the material on which you wish to take notes.

Study notes
Notes taken for the purpose of reviewing material

Take Notes on Material You Can Write On

Here are some suggestions for creating study notes for material you own, material you are free to mark up:

> **Integrate your text notes into your study notes.** Start by annotating the pages, using the techniques that work best for you: highlighting, underlining, circling, and/or making marginal notes. Keep in mind that writing on the text, by itself, is not sufficient to promote learning; it's what you do *next* that counts.
>
> Specifically, after you've finished reading and annotating the material, create study notes. The study notes should provide a summary of the key points, in outline form or in the form of concept maps. Either form of summary should supplement the annotations you've made on the printed page.
>
> Furthermore, any notes you take should stand on their own; that is, they should include enough information to be useful whether or not you have the book or article on hand.

> **Use flash cards.** If you feel confident that the annotations you've written in the book are sufficiently comprehensive, you might consider taking notes on flash cards. **Flash cards** are simply index cards that contain key pieces of information that you need to remember.
>
> Flash cards are particularly useful in subjects that present many small bits of information to remember, such as technical vocabulary words or scientific formulas. When you need to learn a new term, for instance, you can write the term on one side of a card and its definition on the other side.
>
> One of the greatest virtues of flash cards is their portability. Because they are small, they can fit into your pocket or handbag, and you can look at them at odd times when you have a spare moment.

> **Create a separate glossary or definitions page.** Having all the definitions in one place can make studying easier.

> **Keep your notes organized by the chapter they refer to.** Put the date of the lecture on them. Add a reference in your notes to the textbook page they refer to, and vice versa, making it easier for you when it comes time to study and review for a quiz or test.

Flash cards
Index cards that contain key pieces of information to be remembered

Take Notes on Material You Cannot Write On

Taking notes on material that can't be written on is a different story. Library books, magazines, journal articles, and materials on library reserve that are shared with others require a different approach.

> **Approach the written material as you would a class lecture.** The techniques we discussed earlier for taking notes in class can all be adapted for taking notes from written material. In fact, the task is often easier than class note-taking, because the material is in black and white in front of you, and you can refer to it directly.

Taking Notes on the Job: Meetings of the Minds

The principles of good note-taking discussed in this chapter are useful in the classroom, and they can also help you as you make your way in your career. For instance, you may need to take notes on lengthy memos or reports that detail company procedures you will need to master your job.

Further, one of the most important settings in which you'll want to take effective notes is in meetings. Meetings take up a good part of many people's professional workdays and being able to take effective notes can provide a significant career advantage.

Meetings are similar to class discussions. During a meeting, you will want to look for key topics and make note of the ideas that receive the most emphasis or enthusiastic response. Note these areas and keep them in mind as likely priorities.

During meetings, tasks are often assigned. You will want to note clearly what you are supposed to do and when you are supposed to do it; and keeping track of what others are doing will also be helpful, because you may need to get information from them or otherwise coordinate efforts. For instance, if you are assigned the task of managing the development of your company's website, you'll want to clarify in your notes which person has agreed to do what portion of the task.

Taking notes when others are speaking also shows that you are paying attention to what the speaker is saying. It's a kind of compliment that suggests you find what the speaker is saying to be so important that you will want to refer to it later.

Finally, note-taking plays another role: It can make seemingly interminable meetings appear to proceed faster by providing something for you to do that's more active than simply listening. In short, not only can note-taking provide you with a clear record of what occurred in a meeting, but it can also keep you engaged in what is going on.

> ▸ **Laptops can be especially helpful in creating study notes.** If you're a good keyboarder, it's often easier and quicker to take notes using your laptop. On the other hand, don't be lured into typing too much. You need to be just as selective in what you input into your computer as you would be in taking notes during a class lecture.

> ▸ **Use the tricks of the trade we discussed earlier for taking notes from a class lecture.** Look for key ideas, definitions, quotations, and formulas, and include them in your notes. Use the headings that are included in the text, such as chapter and section titles. Bold or italic type is also a clue that an important point is being made. Graphs and charts often provide critical information.

> ▸ **Use the same form of note-taking that you use in class lectures.** If you are a read/write learner and write your notes in outline form, create an outline based on the written material. If you are a visual/graphic learner and prefer to create graphics such as concept maps, create them now. The point is to produce notes that are consistent with those you take during class lectures.

Time to Reflect: What Did I Learn?

1. Overall, how effective are your current note-taking techniques?

2. Describe the way(s) in which you think your note-taking style is a reflection of your learning style.

3. Based on what you learned about note-taking in this chapter, what do you plan to do differently in the future? Be specific.

Looking
Back

What is effective note-taking?

> The central feature of good note-taking is listening and distilling important information, rather than writing down everything that is said.

How can I take good notes in class?

> Prepare for taking notes by identifying the instructor's and your own goals for the course, completing all assignments before arriving in class, and "warming up" for class by reviewing the notes and assignments from the previous class.

> Before writing notes, listen to the instructor and carefully process the information that the instructor is attempting to deliver.

> One note-taking method is to take down notes as brief phrases rather than full sentences and, if possible, in outline form to reveal the structure of the lecture. Other methods include the Cornell method, concept mapping, and PowerPoint handouts. Material written on the board should usually be copied word for word.

> Before leaving class, evaluate your notes, verifying that they are complete and easy to understand, while there is still time to correct them. As soon as possible after class, actively rethink your notes.

What techniques apply to taking notes from written materials?

> Taking good study notes from written materials involves many of the principles that apply to taking good notes from oral presentations, although the source material can be consulted repeatedly, making it easier to get the information down accurately.

> Concept maps and flash cards can be helpful tools for taking notes from textbooks.

[KEY TERMS AND CONCEPTS]

Active listening (p. 91)
Concept mapping (p. 96)
Cornell method of note-taking (p. 96)

Flash cards (p. 104)
Hearing (p. 90)
Meta-message (p. 91)

Outline method of note-taking (p. 94)
Study notes (p. 104)

[RESOURCES]

ON CAMPUS

If you are having difficulty taking class notes effectively, talk with your course instructor. Bring your notes with you soon after a class has ended, and let the instructor assess what you are doing correctly and what could stand improvement.

If your problems persist, and you have great difficulty translating the spoken word into notes, then there's a small possibility that you suffer from an auditory learning disability. Be tested by your campus learning disabilities office or counselling office to rule this out.

IN PRINT

Judy Kesselman-Turkel and Franklynn Peterson's *Note-Taking Made Easy* (University of Wisconsin Press, 2003) provides a broad overview of how to take good notes in class, as does Bobbi DePorter and Mike Hernacki's *Quantum Notes* (Learning Forum, 2000).

ON THE WEB

The following websites provide the opportunity to extend your learning about the material in this chapter.

›   Mount Royal University in Calgary provides some excellent note-taking tips on their website. (**www.mtroyal.ca/AcademicSupport/ResourcesServices/StudentLearning Services/StudyingWritingEffectively/notetaking.htm**)

›   California Polytechnic State University offers a good overview of several note-taking systems: Cornell, outline, mapping, charting, and sentence methods. (**http://www. sas.calpoly.edu/asc/ssl/notetakingsystems.html**)

›   For online note-taking, you may want to consider a tool like Evernote, which automatically processes, indexes, and allows you to organize and search text-based notes, photos of notes (i.e., notes on a whiteboard), webpages, and screenshots. (**http://www.evernote.com/about/home.php**)

TAKING IT TO THE NET

1   The best way to improve note-taking skills is to practise. One possible strategy is to go to the home page for Canoe.ca, a well-known Canadian website (**http:// en.canoe.ca/home.html**). Click on one of the categories (e.g., News, Sports, Showbiz, Money, Life, etc.), and look for a story that sounds interesting. Locate a story of interest on the Internet and take notes while reading it.

2   Taking notes during lectures is an important part of classroom learning, but keeping up with a speaker for an entire hour can be difficult. You can improve your note-taking skills for lectures by taking notes while listening to recorded speeches on the Internet. For example, go to the TED site (**http://www.ted.com/ talks/steve_jobs_how_to_live_before_you_die.html**) and listen to Apple and Pixar co-founder Steve Jobs's inspiring commencement speech to a Stanford graduating class. Take notes while listening to the speech. Afterward, go back and indicate the key points and terms. You can check your comprehension by comparing the speech to news articles reporting on it. (You can also check the articles for bias!)

The Case of . . .
Not Missing a Thing

Some people write down a few things in class. Others write down most things. Jennifer Beck wrote down *everything*.

The woman was virtually a human dictation machine. She spent her time in class in a whirlwind of note-taking, writing down in a clear, meticulous script seemingly every word her instructor uttered. By the end of a term, her notebooks were so lengthy that they approached the size of telephone books from a small city.

Yet despite her thorough notes, Jennifer was only a mediocre student. She was a hard worker and studied her many notes thoroughly before tests. But she never managed to get grades higher than a C+. It seemed unbelievable to her. She worked incredibly hard in class taking good notes. Why wasn't it paying off?

1. How do you think Jennifer defines "good note-taking"?

2. Why does Jennifer's method of note-taking produce such poor results? What is she missing?

3. If you asked Jennifer to summarize the instructor's main ideas after a class lecture, how successful do you think she would be? Why?

4. Do you think it would be easy or hard to study for a final exam using Jennifer's notes? Why?

5. Do you think Jennifer evaluates her notes during or after class? Do you think she ever rethinks them? What questions would you ask to help her perform these steps?

6. In general, what advice would you give Jennifer on note-taking?

5 Taking Tests

Learning Outcomes

By the time you finish this chapter, you will be able to

>> LO **5.1**   Employ various strategies to prepare for tests.

>> LO **5.2**   Discuss effective strategies for writing tests.

>> LO **5.3**   Analyze the strengths and weaknesses of your performance on a test.

Months of study and classes and reading and commuting to and from his college . . . and now it all came down to a test.

That was the thought that ran through Darvinder's head as he sat down to take the final exam in his computer programming course. Darvinder knew the test would count for 65 percent of his final grade. If he passed, he would have enough credits to get the graphic design diploma he'd been working toward for years. If he failed—well, Darvinder tried not to think about that.

He'd taken tests before, but the stakes had never been so high for a single exam. Although he was fairly confident—he had studied hard—he couldn't altogether relax. He told himself that he had always done well on tests in the past; he wasn't going to fail now. But still, Darvinder couldn't help but feel as if his entire school career, maybe his entire future, was on the line.

Looking
Ahead

Although most tests are not as critical as Darvinder's computer programming final, tests do play a significant role in everyone's academic life. Students typically experience more anxiety over tests than over anything else in their college or university careers. If you're returning to post-secondary education after a long break, or perhaps struggled with tests earlier in your academic career, you may find the prospect of taking a test especially intimidating.

But tests don't have to produce so much anxiety. There are strategies and techniques you can learn to reduce your fear of test-taking. In fact, learning how to take tests is, in some ways, as important as learning the content that they cover. Taking tests effectively involves mastering information, but it also requires mastering specific test-taking skills.

One of the most important goals of this chapter is to take the mystery out of the whole process of taking tests. To do that, you'll learn about the different types of tests and about strategies you can start using even before you take a test. You'll gain insight into how different kinds of tests work and how best to approach them. As well, you'll learn about the various types of test questions and strategies for responding most effectively to each type.

This chapter also explores two aspects of test-taking that may affect your performance: test anxiety and cramming. You will learn ways to deal with your anxiety and strategies to keep cramming to a minimum—but you will also learn how to make the most of cramming, if you do have to resort to it.

The chapter ends with suggestions for evaluating your performance toward the end of a test as well as after it's been graded, to learn how to improve your performance the next time around.

What Tests Measure

Tests may be the most unpopular part of college and university life. Students hate them because they produce fear, anxiety, apprehension about being evaluated, and a focus on grades instead of learning for learning's sake. Instructors often don't like them very much either, because they produce fear, anxiety, apprehension about being evaluated, and a focus on grades instead of learning for learning's sake. That's right: Students and instructors dislike tests for the very same reasons.

But tests are also valuable. A well-constructed test identifies what you know and what you still need to learn. Tests help you see how your performance compares with that of others. And knowing that you'll be tested on a body of material is likely to motivate you to learn the material more thoroughly.

However, there's another reason you might dislike tests: You may assume that tests have the power to define your worth as a person. If you do badly on a test, you may be tempted to believe that you've received some fundamental information about yourself from the instructor and the educational institution, information that says you're a failure in some significant way.

This is a dangerous—and wrong-headed—assumption. If you do badly on a test, it doesn't mean you're a bad person. Or stupid. Or that you don't belong in college or university. If you don't do well on a test, you're the same person you were before you took the test—no better, no worse. You just did badly on a test. Period.

In short, tests are not a measure of your value as an individual. They are only a measure of how well (and how much) you studied, and your test-taking skills.

Tests are tools; they are indirect and imperfect measures of what we know. Someone with a great deal of knowledge can do poorly on a test; tension or going at too slow a pace can lead to unwelcome results in some cases. Another person may know considerably less and still do well on the test simply because he or she has learned some test-taking skills along the way.

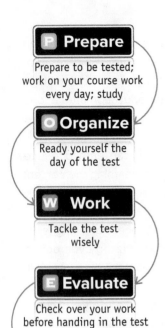

P Prepare

Prepare to be tested;
work on your course work
every day; study

O Organize

Ready yourself the
day of the test

W Work

Tackle the test
wisely

E Evaluate

Check over your work
before handing in the test

R Rethink

Reflect on what you've learned
when you get the test back

P.O.W.E.R. Plan

How we do on a test depends on a number of considerations: the kind of test it is, the subject matter involved, our understanding of test-taking strategies, and, above all, how well we prepare for it. Let's turn, then, to the first step in test-taking: preparation. (The five steps are summarized in the P.O.W.E.R. Plan on the left.)

LO 5.1 **P Prepare**

Preparing to Be Tested

Preparation for tests requires a number of strategies. Many of the most important are listed below.

Course Work as Test Preparation

Many of the things you do during a course will help to prepare you for a test. There is no surer way to get good grades on tests than to take these steps:

> **Read** assigned chapters before every class

> **Attend** class faithfully and pay attention while you are there

> **Review** your notes following each class

> **Create** a set of study notes, as described in Chapter 4

> **Complete** all assignments and review the instructor's feedback when you receive the assignment back

Preparing for tests is a long-term proposition. It's not a matter of "giving your all" the night before the test. Instead, it's a matter of "giving your all" to *every* aspect of the course, throughout the semester.

Know What to Prepare For

Determine as much as you can about the test before you begin to study for it. The more you know about a test beforehand, the more efficient your studying will be.

To find out about an upcoming test, ask these questions of your instructor:

> Is the test called a "test," "exam," "quiz," or something else? As you can see in **Table 5.1,** the names imply different things. For simplicity's sake, we'll use the term "test" throughout this chapter; but you need to know that these distinctions exist, and they should affect the way you prepare.

> What material will the test cover?

> How many questions will be on it?

> How much time is it expected to take? A full class period? Only part of a period?

> What kinds of questions will be on the test?

> How will it be graded?

> Will sample questions be provided?

> Are tests from previous terms available?

> How much does the test contribute to your final course grade?

While an instructor is highly unlikely to tell you what will be on a test, if you can "think like an instructor," you may be able to figure it out yourself. Look for clues in the course outline, in the content of assignments, and in the way the instructor introduces or summarizes certain topics. If the instructor says things like "this is very important" or "you need to pay special attention to the concept I am about to introduce," he or she will probably test on this material. Put an asterisk beside it so it will stand out when you are ready to study for the test.

table 5.1	Quizzes, Tests, Exams, Assignments, Term Projects . . . What's in a Name?

Although they may vary from one instructor to another, the following definitions are most commonly used.

Quiz: A *quiz* is a brief assessment, usually covering a relatively small amount of material. Some quizzes cover as little as one class's worth of reading. Although a single quiz usually doesn't count very much, instructors often add quiz scores together, and collectively they can become a significant part of your final course grade.

Test: A *test* is a more extensive, more heavily weighted assessment than a quiz, covering more material. A test may come every few weeks of the term, often after each third or quarter of the term has passed; but this varies with the instructor and the course.

Exam: An *exam* is the most substantial kind of assessment. In many courses, just one exam is given—a final exam at the end of the term. Sometimes there are two exams, one at the midpoint of the term (called, of course, a midterm) and the second at the end. Exams are usually weighted quite heavily because they are meant to assess your knowledge of all the course material covered up to that point.

Assignment: An *assignment* is usually something that is done individually outside of class, has a relatively narrow focus, and is not usually worth more than 10–15% of your final grade. It may involve researching a specific topic or reading a particular article and providing your own perspective on it. Where possible, you should ask the instructor if a "marking rubric" is available for the assignment, so you can see how marks will be allocated and as a result, how to allocate your time and effort.

Term project: A *term project* is completed outside of class, may be done individually or in a group, and spans the full semester or term. It is usually broad in focus, and it can be worth a significant portion of your final grade, depending on the course. Undertaking an analysis of the state of an entire industry and the major competitors within it would be an example of a term project. Again, you should ask your instructor if a marking rubric is available, so you can see how marks will be allocated and where you should put most of your effort.

Test-Preparation Strategies

Match Study Methods to Question Types

Test questions come in different types (see **Table 5.2**), and each requires a somewhat different style of preparation.

> **Essay questions.** Essay tests focus on the big picture—ways in which the various pieces of information being tested fit together. You'll need to know not just a series of facts, but also the connections among these facts; and you will have to be able to discuss these ideas in an organized and logical way. A good study tactic is to play instructor: After carefully reviewing your notes and other course materials, think of likely exam questions. Then, without looking at your notes or your readings, answer each potential essay question, either aloud or by writing out the major points an answer should include. After you've answered the questions, check yourself by looking at your notes and the course readings once again.

> **Short-answer and fill-in questions.** Short-answer and fill-in questions are similar to essays in that they require you to recall key pieces of information rather than finding the information on the page in front of you. However, short-answer and fill-in questions—unlike essay questions—typically don't demand that you integrate or compare different types of information. Consequently, the focus of your study should be on the recall of specific, detailed information.

> **Multiple-choice, true–false, and matching questions.** While the focus of review for essay questions should be on major issues and controversies, studying for multiple-choice, true–false, and matching questions requires more attention to the details.

> Almost anything is fair game for multiple-choice, true–false, and matching questions, so you can't afford to overlook anything when studying. True, these kinds of questions put the material right there on the page for you to react to—e.g., Did Jacques Cartier arrive on New Brunswick's Bay of Chaleur in 1534, or

table 5.2	Types of Test Questions
Essay	Requires a fairly extended, on-the-spot composition about some topic. Examples include questions that call on you to describe a person, process, or event, or those that ask you to compare or contrast two separate sets of material.
Multiple-choice	Contains a question or statement, followed by a number of possible answers (usually 4 or 5 of them). You must choose the best response from the choices offered.
True–false	Presents statements about a topic that are either accurate or inaccurate. You are to indicate whether each statement is accurate (true) or inaccurate (false).
Matching	Presents two lists of related information, arranged in column form. Typically, you are asked to pair up the items that go together (e.g., a scientific term and its definition).
Definition	Requires you to provide the meaning of a word.
Short-answer	Requires brief responses (usually a few sentences at most) in a kind of mini-essay.
Fill-in	Requires you to add one or more missing words to a sentence or series of sentences.

not?—rather than asking you to provide the names and dates yourself (as in the case of the essay or short-answer question). Nevertheless, to do well on these tests you must put your memory into high gear and master a great many facts.

It's a particularly good idea to write down important facts on index cards. Remember the advantages of these cards: They're portable and available all the time, and the act of creating them helps drive the material into your memory. Furthermore, you can shuffle them and test yourself repeatedly until you've mastered the material.

Another helpful strategy is to write the name of a particular concept or theory on one side of a note card, and then to write an example of it on the other side. Studying the cards will ensure that you fully understand the concepts and theories and can generalize them to different situations.

Test Yourself

Once you feel you've mastered the material, test yourself on it. There are several ways to do this. Often textbooks are accompanied by websites that offer automatically scored practice tests and quizzes. (*P.O.W.E.R. Learning* does: Visit Connect for *P.O.W.E.R. Learning and Your Life*,)

You can also create a test for yourself, in writing, making its form as close as possible to what you expect the actual test to be. For instance, if your instructor has told you the classroom test will be primarily made up of short-answer questions, your test should reflect that.

You might also construct a test and administer it to a classmate or a member of your study group. In turn, you could take a test that someone else has constructed. Constructing and taking practice tests are excellent ways of studying the material and cementing it into memory. (To be sure you're fully prepared for your next test, complete **Try It! 1**, "Complete a Test Preparation Checklist," on page 116.)

Form a Study Group

Study groups are small, informal groups of students who work together to learn course material and study for a test. Forming such a group can be an excellent way to prepare for any kind of test. Some study groups are formed for particular tests, whereas others meet consistently throughout the term.

Study groups can be extremely powerful tools because they help accomplish several things:

> They help members organize and structure the material to approach their studying in a systematic and logical way.

> They allow students to share different perspectives on the material.

> They make it more likely that students will not overlook any potentially important information.

> They force members to rethink the course material, explaining it in words that other group members will understand.

From the perspective of . . .

A STUDENT You will take many types of courses during your academic career. Can you think of how test-taking strategies will work in an English course versus a science course?

Study group
Small, informal group of students whose purpose is to help members work together and study for a test

Study groups, made up of a few students who study together for a test, can help organize material, provide new perspectives, and motivate members to do their best. Do you think you would function well in a study group? Why or why not?

P O W E R Try It! 1

Complete a Test Preparation Checklist

It takes more than simply learning the material to prepare for a test. You also need a strategy that will help you understand what it is you are studying for. To do that, you need to learn as much as you can about the test. The more you know about the kind of test it is and what it will cover, the better you'll be able to target your studying, and the less anxious you will feel when you first see the test.

To focus your studying, complete the following test preparation checklist before your next test. When it comes to items like the test format or what will be covered, don't be afraid to ask your instructor for input.

TEST PREPARATION CHECKLIST

- ☐ I know whether it's a quiz, test, or exam.
- ☐ I know what kinds of questions will be on the test.
- ☐ I understand what material will be covered.
- ☐ I know how many questions will be on the test.
- ☐ I know how long I will have to complete the test.
- ☐ I know how the test will be graded, and how the grade contributes to my final course grade.
- ☐ I obtained sample questions and/or previous tests, if available.
- ☐ I formed or participated in a study group.
- ☐ I used different and appropriate preparation strategies for different types of questions.
- ☐ I read and studied my class notes.
- ☐ I composed some questions of the kind that will be on the exam.
- ☐ I answered essay questions aloud.
- ☐ I actively memorized facts and details.
- ☐ I made and used index cards.
- ☐ I created and used a test like the real test.

After completing the checklist, ask yourself these questions:

1. How can I use this checklist to study more effectively for tests?
2. How might completing the checklist change the way I study for tests?
3. What new strategies might I follow in order to prepare for tests more effectively in the future?

To Try It online, go to Connect for *P.O.W.E.R. Learning and Your Life*.

There are some potential drawbacks to keep in mind. Study groups don't always work well for students with learning styles that favour working independently. In addition, "problem" members—those who don't pull their weight—may cause difficulties for the group. In general, though, the advantages of study groups far outweigh their disadvantages. To set up your own study group, see **Try It! 2**, "Form a Study Group."

Use On-campus Resources

Many colleges and universities have a learning centre, tutorial centre, or other office that can help you cope with test anxiety and show you how to approach studying for a test. Don't wait until after you do badly on a test to visit your campus learning

WORKING IN A GROUP

Try It!

P O W E R

2

Form a Study Group

The next time you have to prepare for a test, form a study group with three to five classmates. They may have a variety of study habits and skills, but all must be willing to take the group seriously.

The first time you meet, compare notes about what is likely to be on the test and brainstorm to come up with possible test questions. If the instructor hasn't given you detailed information about the test (i.e., number and types of questions, weighting, etc.), one of you should be delegated to ask for it. Plan to meet once more closer to the test date to discuss answers to the questions you've come up with, share any new insights, and quiz each other on the material.

After you've taken the test and gotten your results, meet again. Find out if members felt the group was effective.

1. Did the members feel more confident about the test?

2. Do you all think you did better than you would have without the group?

3. What worked? What didn't?

4. What could you do differently next time?

To Try It online, go to Connect for *P.O.W.E.R. Learning and Your Life.*

or tutorial centres. A visit prior to your first test is a good use of your time, even if you feel it's not essential. Just knowing what resources are available can boost your confidence.

Deal with Test Anxiety

What does the anticipation of a test do to you? Do you feel shaky? Frantic, like there's not enough time to get it all done? Is there a knot in your stomach? Do you grit your teeth?

Test anxiety is a temporary condition characterized by fears and concerns about test-taking. Almost everyone experiences it to some degree, although for some people it's more of a problem than it is for others. The real danger with test anxiety is that it can become so overwhelming that it can hurt test performance.

You'll never eliminate test anxiety completely, nor do you want to. A little bit of nervousness can energize you, making you more attentive and vigilant. Like other competitive events, testing can motivate you to do your best. You might think of moderate test anxiety as a desire to perform at your peak—a useful quality at test time.

On the other hand, for some, anxiety can spiral into the kind of paralyzing fear that makes their minds go blank. There are several ways to keep this from happening to you:

> **Prepare thoroughly.** The more you prepare, the less test anxiety you'll feel. Good preparation can give you a sense of control and mastery, and it will prevent test anxiety from overwhelming you.

> **Take a realistic view of the test.** Remember that your future success does not hinge on your performance on any single test or exam. Think of the big picture: Put the particular test in context, and remind yourself of all the hurdles you've passed so far.

> **Eat right and get enough sleep.** Good mental preparation can't occur without your body being well prepared.

Test anxiety

A temporary condition characterized by fears and concerns about test-taking

3

Measure Your Test-taking Style

Do you feel anxious at the very thought of a test, or are you cool and calm in the face of testing situations? Get a sense of your test-taking style by checking off every statement below that applies to you.

- [ ] 1. The closer a test date approaches, the more nervous I get.
- [ ] 2. I am sometimes unable to sleep on the night before a test.
- [ ] 3. I have "frozen up" during a test, finding myself unable to think or respond.
- [ ] 4. I can feel my hands shaking as I pick up my pencil to begin a test.
- [ ] 5. The minute I read a tough test question, all the facts I ever knew about the subject abandon me and I can't get them back no matter how hard I try.
- [ ] 6. I have become physically ill before or during a test.
- [ ] 7. Nervousness prevents me from studying immediately before a test.
- [ ] 8. I often dream about an upcoming test.
- [ ] 9. Even if I successfully answer a number of questions, my anxiety stays with me throughout the test.
- [ ] 10. I'm reluctant to turn in my test paper for fear that I can do better if I continue to work on it.

If you checked off more than four statements, you have experienced fairly serious test anxiety. If you checked off more than six statements, your anxiety is probably interfering with your test performance. In particular, statements 3, 5, 6, 7, and 10 may indicate serious test anxiety.

If, based on your responses to this questionnaire and your previous experience, your level of test anxiety is high, what are some of the steps described in this chapter that might be helpful to you?

To Try It online, go to Connect for *P.O.W.E.R. Learning and Your Life.*

> **Learn relaxation techniques.** You can learn to reduce or even eliminate the jittery physical symptoms of test anxiety by using relaxation techniques. The basic process is straightforward: Breathe evenly, gently inhaling and exhaling. Focus your mind on a pleasant, relaxing scene such as a beautiful forest or a peaceful farm, or on a restful sound such as the sound of ocean waves breaking on the beach.

> **Visualize success.** Think of an image of your instructor handing back your test marked with a big fat "A." Or imagine your instructor congratulating you on your fine performance the day after the test. Positive visualizations that highlight your potential success can help replace images of failure that may fuel test anxiety.

To assess your own test-taking style and the degree of anxiety around tests that you experience, see **Try It! 3**, "Measure Your Test-taking Style."

What if these strategies don't work? If your test anxiety is so great that it's getting in the way of your success, make use of your campus resources. Most provide a learning resource centre or a counselling centre that can provide you with personalized help. (For more on dealing with test anxiety, particularly where math is concerned, see the **Course Connections** feature on page 119.)

When Anxiety Leads to Cramming

Cramming
Hurried, last-minute studying

You know, of course, that **cramming**—hurried, last-minute studying—is not the way to go. You know that you're likely to forget the material the moment the test is over because long-term retention is nearly impossible without thoughtful study. But . . .

Special Techniques for Dealing with Math Anxiety

For many students, the greatest test anxiety comes when they're taking a test involving math. Math seems to bring out the worst fears in some people, perhaps because it's seen as a discipline in which answers are either totally right or totally wrong, or perhaps because they've felt they've "hit the wall" and they'll never be able to understand a new concept, no matter how hard they try.

Such feelings about math can be devastating, because they can prevent you from doing well even if you know the material. If you suffer from math anxiety, keep these things in mind:

- Math is like any other subject: The greatest component of success is the effort you put in, not whether you have a "math gene" that makes you naturally good at math. It's not true that you are either born "good at math" or not, or that there's some "secret" about math that some people know and others don't.

- It's also not true that there's only one way to solve a math problem. Sometimes there are a variety of routes to coming up with a solution. And keep in mind that the solution to math problems often calls for creativity, not just sheer logic.

- It's a false stereotype that women are not as good at math as men, but it's a stereotype that many women accept. Research has shown that when men do badly on a math test, they're most likely to think that they haven't put in enough effort; but when women don't do well on a math test, they're three times more likely than men to feel that they don't have enough ability to be successful.[1] That's an erroneous view of the world. Don't become a prisoner of stereotypes.

Use these special strategies to deal with math problems on exams:

BEFORE TESTS:

1. Math is cumulative, building on prior concepts and knowledge. Make sure you review math fundamentals before moving on to more advanced topics.
2. Ask questions in class. Don't be afraid that you'll ask the wrong question in the wrong way. Instructors want you to understand their subject.
3. Make use of review sessions and other study resources.
4. Practise, practise, practise. The more experience you have completing math problems under pressure, the better you'll do. Practise math problems using a timer in order to simulate an actual test.

DURING TESTS:

1. Analyze math problems carefully. What are the known quantities or constants, and what pieces of information are missing? What formula(s) or theorem(s) apply?
2. Consider drawing a diagram, graph, or probability tree.
3. Break down calculations into their component parts.
4. Check your math carefully.
5. Be neat and logical in your presentation, and show every step as you solve problems. Your instructor may give you partial credit if you lay out every step you're going through. In addition, some instructors may require you to show your work.

. . . it's been one of those weeks where everything went wrong

. . . the instructor sprang a quiz on you at the last minute

. . . you forgot about the test until the night before it was scheduled.

Whatever the reason, there may be times when you can't study properly. What do you do if you have to cram for an exam?

Don't spend a lot of time on what you're unable to do. Beating yourself up about your failings as a student will only hinder your efforts. Instead, admit you're human and imperfect like everyone else. Then spend a few minutes developing a plan about what you can accomplish in the limited time you've got.

The first thing to do is choose what you *really* need to study. You won't be able to learn everything, so you have to make choices. Figure out the main focus of the course—a detailed course outline can help you with this—and concentrate on it.

Once you have a strategy, prepare a one-page summary sheet with hard-to-remember information. Just writing the material down will help you remember it, and you can refer to the summary sheet frequently over the limited time you do have to study.

Next, read through your class notes, concentrating on the material you've underlined and the key concepts and ideas that you've already noted. Forget about reading all the material in the books and articles you're being tested on. Instead, only read the passages that you've underlined and the notes you've taken on the readings. Finally, maximize your study time. Using your notes, index cards, and concept maps, go over the information. Read it. Say it aloud. Think about it and the way it relates to other information. In short, use all the techniques we've talked about for learning and recalling information.

When the exam is over, material that you have crammed into your head is destined to leave your mind as quickly as it entered. If you've crammed for a midterm, don't assume that the information will still be there when you study for the final. In the end, cramming often ends up taking more time for worse results than does studying with appropriate techniques.

Before going any further, reflect on your Striving Style™ and how it might affect your approach to test-taking. Then, examine the suggestions and recommendations provided in the sidebar on page 121.

 **Reducing Anxiety on the Day of the Test**

You've studied a lot, and you're happy with your level of mastery. Or perhaps you have the nagging feeling that there's something you haven't quite gotten to. Or maybe you know you haven't had enough time to study as much as you'd like, and you're expecting a disaster.

Whatever your frame of mind, it will help to organize your plan of attack on the day of the test. What's included on the test is out of your hands, but you can control what you bring to it. Here's how:

> **Bring the right tools to the test.** Have at least two pens with you. It's usually best to write in pen because, in general, writing tends to be easier to read in pen than in pencil. But you also might want to have pencils and a good eraser on hand. Sometimes instructors will use machine-scored tests that require the use of a pencil. Or there may be test questions that involve computations, and solving them may entail frequent reworking of calculations.

Cramming can be exhausting, but it is on occasion necessary. With the family and personal responsibilities many students face, sometimes it can't be avoided. There are, however, strategies you can use to help you make the best use of limited time.

- ➤ **Bring a watch** to the test, even if there will be a clock on the wall of the class-room. You will want to be able to pace yourself properly during the test. Also, if you usually use a cellphone to determine the time, remember that many instructors will ask you to put it away during the test. If they do so, ask if the instructor can write the time on the board at half-hour intervals.

- ➤ **Bring your study notes, if allowed.** Sometimes instructors permit you to use notes and books during the test. If you haven't brought them with you, they're not going to be much help; so make sure you bring them if they're permitted. (Even for closed-book tests, having such material available when you arrive in the classroom allows you a few minutes of review before the test actually starts.) And don't be lulled into thinking an open-book test is going to be easy. Instructors who allow you to use your notes and books during a test may not give you much time to look things up, so you still need to study.

- ➤ **Resist the temptation to compare notes with your friends** about how much you've studied. Yes, you might end up feeling good because many of your classmates studied less than you did. But chances are you'll find others who seem to have spent significantly more time studying than you, and this will do little to encourage you.

- ➤ **Plan on panicking.** Although it sounds like the worst possible approach, permitting yourself the option of spending a minute feeling panicky will help you to recover from your initial fears.

- ➤ **Listen carefully to what an instructor says before the test is handed out.** The instructor may tell you about a question that is optional or worth bonus marks or inform you of a typographical error on the test. Whatever the instructor says just before the test, you can be sure it's information that you don't want to ignore.

➤➤ LO **5.2**  ## Test-taking Strategies

Take a deep breath—literally.

There's no better way to start work on a test than by taking a deep breath, followed by several others. The deep breaths will help you to overcome any initial panic and anxiety you may be experiencing. It's OK to give yourself over for a moment to panic and anxiety; but, to work at your best, use the relaxation techniques that we spoke about earlier to displace those initial feelings. Tell yourself, "It's OK. I am going to do my best."

Read test instructions carefully. Even if instructors talk about what a test will be like beforehand, at the last minute they may make changes. Consequently, it's critical to read the instructions for the test carefully. In fact, you should skim through the entire exam before you begin. Look at the kinds of questions and pay attention to the way they will be scored. If the weighting of the marks for the various parts of the exam is not clear, ask your instructor to clarify it.

Knowing the weighting of the marks is critical, because it will help you to allocate your time. You don't want to spend 90 percent of your time on an essay that's worth only 10 percent of the marks, and you want to be sure to leave time at the end of the test to check your answers.

An initial read-through will also help you verify that you have every page of the exam and that each one is readable. It may also provide you with

Taking Tests and Striving Styles™

Leaders
Enjoy being tested to demonstrate achievement. Tend to plan and prepare. Prone to over-studying. Organize and lead study groups.

Socializers
Try to do well to please teachers. Study groups lead to more socializing than study. Often unprepared, tend to cram and pull all-nighters.

Performers
Enjoy recognition for achieving top marks but have difficulty disciplining themselves to study. Study sporadically; have difficulty focusing. Will ask for makeup exams.

Adventurers
Dislike studying and exams. Organize study groups which turn into play. Cut corners to get good marks. Would rather show what they know than write about it.

Artists
Diligent around studying because they are afraid of failing. Anxious even when they know their stuff. Perfectionism causes them to underachieve due to pressure they create.

Intellectuals
Enjoy studying subjects they like and will "wing it" on subjects they don't. Can over-focus on one subject and have to cram for others. Don't enjoy study groups.

Visionaries
Do best on theoretical or interpretive tests. Have difficulty memorizing. Have to review excessively to retain facts. Don't trust they know enough.

Stabilizers
Structure and prepare in advance. Excel with factual subjects, have difficulty with theoretical or interpretive. Rarely guess. Feel it is their duty to perform well.

"intratest-knowledge"—sometimes terms defined or mentioned in one part of a test trigger memories that can help answer questions in another part of the test.

If there are any lists, formulas, or other key facts that you're concerned you may forget, jot them down now on the back of a test page or on a piece of scrap paper. You may want to refer to this material later during the test.

Once this background work is out of the way, you'll be ready to proceed to actually answering the questions. These principles will help you to do your best on the test:

> **Answer the easiest questions first.** By initially getting the questions out of the way that are easiest for you, you accomplish several important things. First, you'll be leaving yourself more time to think about the tougher questions. In addition, moving through a series of questions without a struggle will build your confidence. Finally, working through a number of questions will build up a base of marks that may be enough to earn you at least a minimally acceptable grade.

> **Write legibly and only on one side of the paper.** If an instructor can't read what you've written, you're not going to get credit for it, no matter how brilliant your answer. So be sure to keep your handwriting legible.

> It's a good idea to write your answers to essay questions on only one side of a page. This will allow you to go back later and add or revise information.

> **Master machine-scored tests.** Tests will sometimes be scored, in part, by computer. In such cases, you'll usually have to indicate your answers by filling in—with a pencil—circles or squares on a computer answer sheet.

> Be careful! A stray mark or smudge can cause the computer scanner to misread your answer sheet, producing errors in grading. Be sure to bring a good eraser in addition to a pencil; the biggest source of mistakes in machine grading is incomplete erasing. If you find yourself having to erase more than once, you should probably ask for a fresh answer sheet.

> It's best to write your answers not only on the answer sheet, but also on the test itself (if the test is not intended for future reuse). That way you can go back and check your answers easily—a step you should take frequently. It's also a good idea to match up your answers on the test with the numbers on the answer sheet every five or so items. This will help you make sure you haven't skipped a space or gotten off track in some other way. If you catch such problems early, they're easy to fix.

> A variant of machine-scored testing is online testing. In such cases, you'll be taking an exam on a computer outside of class. You shouldn't wait until the final deadline to start this type of test, as technical difficulties may not allow you to log in or may not give you enough time to finish. In addition, be sure to have paper and pencil available. Even though you use the computer to record your answers, you'll want to be able to jot down ideas and notes, and to do calculations the traditional way, by hand.

> "Computerized test-scoring isn't perfect. Smudges can kill you. If your grade seems incorrect, ask to see the answer sheet."
> **Graduate, Physiology, Michigan State University[2]**

Answer Specific Types of Test Questions Appropriately

Every type of question requires a particular approach. Use these strategies:

> **Essay questions.** Essay questions, with their emphasis on description and analysis, often present challenges because they are relatively unstructured.

Unless you're careful, it's easy to wander off and begin to answer questions that were never asked. To prevent that problem, the first thing to do is read the question carefully. If your essay answer will be lengthy, you might want to write a short outline, or a note using the Cornell note-taking method discussed in Chapter 4 (see page 96).

Pay attention to key words that indicate what, specifically, the instructor is looking for in an answer. Certain action words are commonly used in essays, and you should understand them fully. For instance, knowing the distinction between "compare" and "contrast" can spell the difference between success and failure. **Table 5.3** defines common action words.

table 5.3 Action Words for Essays
These words are commonly used in essay questions. Learning the distinctions among them will help you answer essay questions effectively.
Analyze: Examine and break into component parts.
Clarify: Explain with significant detail.
Compare: Describe and explain similarities.
Compare and contrast: Describe and explain similarities and differences.
Contrast: Describe and explain differences.
Critique: Judge and analyze, explaining what is wrong—and right—about a concept.
Define: Provide the meaning.
Discuss: Explain, review, and consider.
Enumerate: Provide a listing of ideas, concepts, reasons, items, etc.
Evaluate: Provide pros and cons of something; provide an opinion and justify it.
Explain: Give reasons why or how; clarify, justify, and illustrate.
Illustrate: Provide examples; show instances.
Interpret: Explain the meaning of something.
Justify: Explain why a concept can be supported, typically by using examples and other types of support.
Outline: Provide an overarching framework or explanation—usually in narrative form—of a concept, idea, event, or phenomenon.
Prove: Using evidence and arguments, convince the reader of a particular point.
Relate: Show how things fit together; provide analogies.
Review: Describe or summarize, often with an evaluation.
State: Assert or explain.
Summarize: Provide a condensed, precise list or narrative.
Trace: Track or sketch out how events or circumstances have evolved; provide a history or timeline.

Use appropriate language in essays. Be brief and to the point in your essay. Avoid flowery introductory language. Compare the two sentences that follow:

"Management techniques have evolved to a point never before seen in the history of our country, or perhaps even our world."

"Many new management techniques have been developed in recent years."

The second sentence says the same thing much more effectively and economically.

Your response should follow a logical sequence, moving from major points to minor ones, or following a time sequence. Essays are improved when they include examples and point out differences. Above all, your answer should address every aspect of the question posed on the test. Because essays often contain several different, embedded questions, you have to be certain that you have answered every part to receive full credit. (After reviewing Table 5.3, complete **Try It! 4**, "Understand Action Verbs in Essay Questions," on page 125.)

➤ **Short-answer and fill-in questions.** Short-answer and fill-in questions require you to generate and supply specific information. Unlike essays, which are more free-form and may have several possible answers, short-answer and fill-in questions are usually quite specific, requiring only one answer.

Use both the instructions for the questions and the questions themselves to determine the level of specificity that is needed in an answer. Try not to provide too much or too little information. Usually, brevity is best. Be guided by the mark allocation when deciding how much information to include.

➤ **Multiple-choice questions.** If you've ever looked at a multiple-choice question and said to yourself, "But every choice seems right," you understand what can be tricky about this type of question. However, there are some simple strategies that can help you deal with multiple-choice questions.

First, read the question carefully. Note any specific instructions. In most cases, only one answer will be correct; but some questions will you ask you to select multiple items.

Then, before you look at the possible answers, try to answer the question in your head. This can help you avoid confusion over inappropriate choices.

Next, carefully read through every possible answer. Even if you come to one that you think is right, read them all—there may be a subsequent answer that is better.

Look for absolutes like "every," "always," "only," "none," and "never." Choices that contain such absolute words are rarely correct. For example, an answer choice that says, "There has never been a woman prime minister in Canada" is incorrect due to the presence of the word "never." On the other hand, less-absolute words, such as "generally," "usually," "often," "rarely," "seldom," and "typically" may indicate a correct response.

Be especially on guard for the word "not," which negates the sentence ("The one key concept that is not embodied in the Canadian Privacy Principles . . ."). It's easy to gloss over "not"; and if you have the misfortune of doing so, it will be nearly impossible to answer the item correctly.

If you're having trouble understanding a question, underline key words or phrases, or try to break the question into different short sections. Sometimes it is helpful to work backwards, *Jeopardy*-style, and look at the possible answers first to see if you can find one that is clearly accurate or clearly inaccurate.

Use an **educated guessing** strategy—which is very different from wild or random guessing. Unless you are penalized for wrong answers (a scoring rule by which wrong answers are deducted from the points you have earned on other questions, rather than merely not counting at all toward your score), it always pays to guess.

Educated guessing
The practice of eliminating obviously false multiple-choice answers and selecting the most likely answer from the remaining choices

Understand Action Verbs in Essay Questions

Part A: Federal Industry Minister Tony Clement claims that new voluntary long-form census "strikes a fair and reasonable balance between ensuring the federal government has the basic information every government requires, and protecting the privacy of Canadian citizens." **(http://www.charityvillage.com/cv/archive/acov/acov10/acov1024.asp)**

Research this topic, then answer the following three questions about the Canadian government's plan to replace the mandatory "long form" of the census with a voluntary form. As you respond to each question, pay special attention to the different action verbs that introduce each question.

1. **Summarize** the government's position on the long census form.

2. **Analyze** the government's position on the long census form.

3. **Discuss** the government's position on the long census form.

Part B:

1. How do your answers differ for the each of the questions?
2. Which of the questions provoked the lengthiest response?
3. Which of the questions could you answer best?

To Try It online, go to Connect for *P.O.W.E.R. Learning and Your Life.*

The first step in educated guessing is to eliminate any obviously false answers. The next step is to examine the remaining choices closely. Does one response choice include an absolute or qualifying adjective that makes it unlikely; for example, "the probability of a leadership review *always* increases when a Canadian prime minister is facing political difficulties"? Does one choice include a subtle factual error? For example, the answer to a multiple-choice question asking why Columbus took his journey to the new world that says "The French monarchy was interested in expanding its colonial holdings" is wrong because it was not the French monarchy, but the Spanish monarchy, that funded Columbus's journey.

▶ **True–false questions.** Although most of the principles we've already discussed apply equally well to true–false questions, a few additional tricks of the trade may help you with this type of question.

Begin a set of true–false questions by answering the ones you're sure you know. But don't rush; it's important to read every part of a true–false question, because key words such as "never," "always," and "sometimes" often determine the appropriate response.

If you don't have a clue about whether a statement is true or false, here's a last-resort principle: Choose "true." In general, more statements on a true–false test are likely to be true than false.

> **Matching questions.** Matching questions typically present you with two columns of related information, which you must link, item by item. For example, a list of terms or concepts may be presented in one column, along with a list of corresponding definitions or explanations in the second column. The best strategy is to reduce the size of both columns by matching the items you're most confident about first; this will leave a short list in each column, and the final matching may become apparent.

About Academic Honesty

Academic honesty
Completing and turning in only one's own work under one's own name

Plagiarism
Taking credit for someone else's words, thoughts, or ideas

It's tempting: A glance at a classmate's test may provide the one piece of information that you just can't remember. But you owe it to yourself not to do it. Copying from a classmate's paper is no different from reaching over and stealing that classmate's cellphone. It is a violation of **academic honesty,** one of the foundations of civility in the classroom, as well as in society. Unless the work you turn in under your own name is your work, you are guilty of academic dishonesty.

A violation of academic honesty can take many forms. It may involve **plagiarism**—taking credit for someone else's words, thoughts, or ideas. Academic dishonesty may also include using a calculator when it's not allowed, discussing the answer to a question, copying an unauthorized computer file, taking an exam for another person, or stealing an exam. It can take the form of ripping a page out of a book in the library, or lying to an instructor about the reason for a late paper. It includes using your textbook or conferring with a friend when taking a closed-book exam in an online, distance-learning course.

You may feel that "everyone does it," so cheating is not so bad. Wrong! Everyone doesn't do it, just as most people don't embezzle from their companies or steal from others. Although you may know of a few cases of exceptionally dishonest classmates, most of your classmates try to be honest—you just don't notice their honesty.

Whatever form it takes, academic dishonesty is just plain wrong. It makes the grading system unfair, it reduces the meaning of your grade, and it lowers the level of civility in the classroom. It certainly hinders academic and personal growth. It can't help but rob the cheater of self-respect. Don't do it!

Finally, academic dishonesty violates the regulations of every college and university (rules that you should familiarize yourself with), and instructors know it is their obligation to uphold standards of academic honesty. Violations of honesty policies will lead to any number of potentially devastating scenarios: failing the exam on which the cheating has taken place, failing the entire course, being brought before a disciplinary board, having a description of the incident permanently placed on your grade transcript, being placed on academic probation, or even being thrown out of school. A single instance of cheating can permanently prevent you from embarking on the career of your choice. Cheating is simply not worth it.

E Evaluate Check Your Work

The last few minutes of a test may feel like the final moments of a marathon. You need to focus your energy and push yourself even harder. It can be make-or-break time.

Tests for a Lifetime

If you think the last tests you'll ever have to take are the final exams just before you graduate, you're probably wrong.

Increasing numbers of professions require initial licensing exams, and some even require periodic exams to remain in good standing within the profession. For example, in Canada, people who wish to become dental hygienists must pass a licensing exam in the province in which they wish to practise. And even experienced hygienists are expected to remain current with the latest tools and techniques by participating in professional development activities throughout their careers.

In short, good test-taking skills won't just bring you success in college or university. They're something that may benefit you for a lifetime as you pursue your career.

Career Connections

Save some time at the end of a test so you can check your work. You should have been keeping track of your time all along, so plan on stopping a few minutes before the end of the test period to review what you've done. It's an important step, and it can make the difference between a terrific grade and a mediocre one. It's a rare person who can work for an uninterrupted period of time on a test and commit absolutely no errors—even if he or she knows the material backwards and forwards. Consequently, checking what you've done is crucial.

Start evaluating your test by looking for obvious mistakes. Make sure that you've answered every question. If there is a separate answer sheet, check to see that all your answers have been recorded on the answer sheet and are in the right spot.

If the test included essay and short-answer questions, proofread your responses. Check for obvious errors—misspellings, missing words, and repetitions. Make sure that you've responded to every part of each question and that each essay, as a whole, makes sense.

Check over your responses to multiple-choice, true–false, and matching questions. If there are some items that you haven't yet answered because you couldn't remember the necessary information, now is the time to take a stab at them. As we discussed earlier, it usually pays to guess, even randomly if you must. On most tests, no answer and a wrong answer are worth the same amount—nothing!

What about items that you initially guessed at? Unless you have a good reason to change your original answer—such as a new insight or a sudden recollection of some key information—your first guess is likely your best guess.

Know When to Stop

After evaluating and checking your answers, there may still be some time left. What to do? If you're satisfied with your responses, it's simply time to tell yourself, "Let it go."

Permit yourself the luxury of knowing that you've done your best, and hand the test in to your instructor. You don't have to review your work over and over just because there is time remaining and some of your classmates are still working on their tests. In fact, such behaviour is often counterproductive, because you might start over-interpreting and reading things into questions that really aren't there.

On the other hand, what if you've run out of time? It's a nightmarish feeling: The clock is ticking relentlessly, and it's clear that you don't have enough time to finish the test. What should you do?

Stop working! Although this advice may sound foolish, in fact the best thing you can do is take a minute to calm yourself. Take some deep breaths to replace the feelings of panic that are likely welling up inside you. Collect your thoughts, and plan a strategy for the last moments of the test.

If there are essays that remain undone, consider how you'd answer them if you had more time. Then write an outline of each answer. If you don't have time even for that, write a few key words. Writing anything is better than handing in a blank page, and you may get at least some credit for your response. The key principle here: Something is better than nothing, and even one mark is worth more than zero marks.

The same principle holds for other types of questions. Even wild guesses are almost always better than not responding at all to an item. So rather than telling yourself you've certainly failed and giving up, do as much as you can in the remaining moments of the exam.

From the perspective of . . .

A LEGAL ASSISTANT
Even though tests are uncommon in professional careers, deadlines are frequent occurrences. How might test-taking strategies help you when you are faced with a tight schedule?

LO 5.3 R Rethink Post-test Analysis

Your instructor is about to hand the graded exams back. All sorts of thoughts run through your head: How did I do? Did I do as well as my classmates? Will I be happy with my results? Will the results show how much I studied? Will I be embarrassed by my grade?

The first thing you should do when you get your test back is to ensure the instructor has added up your mark correctly; instructors are human, and mistakes are sometimes made. It is always worth checking to be sure you have received all the marks you are due. You may also want to ask your instructor about the class average on the test, so you can determine how well you did relative to the rest of the class.

Most of us focus on the evaluative aspects of tests. We look at the grade we've received on a test as an end in itself. It's a natural reaction.

But there's another way to look at test results: They can help guide us toward future success. By looking at what we've learned (and haven't learned) about a given subject, we'll be in a better position to know what to focus on when we take future exams. Furthermore, by examining the kinds of mistakes we make, we can improve our test-taking skills.

When you get your test back, you have the opportunity to reflect on what you've learned and to consider your performance. Begin by actively listening to what your instructor says as he or she hands back the test. You may learn about things that were generally misunderstood by the class. You also may pick up some important clues about what questions will be on future tests.

Then examine your own mistakes. Chances are they'll jump out at you since they will be marked incorrect. Did you misunderstand or misapply some principle? Was there a certain aspect of the material that you missed? Were there particular kinds of information that you didn't realize you needed to know? Or did you lose some points because of your test-taking skills? Did you make careless errors, such as forgetting to fill in a question or misreading the directions? Was your handwriting so sloppy that your instructor had trouble reading it?

Once you have a good idea of what material you didn't fully understand or remember, get the correct answers to the items you missed—from your instructor, your classmates, or your book. If it's a math test, rework problems you've missed. Finally, summarize—in writing—the material you had trouble with. This will help you study for future exams that cover the same material.

Finally, if you're dissatisfied with your performance, talk to your instructor—not to complain, but to seek help. Instructors should be able to point out problems in your test that you can address readily so you can do better in the future. Demonstrate to your instructor that you want to do better and are willing to put in the work to get there. The worst thing to do is crumple up the test and quickly leave the class in embarrassment. Remember, you're not the first person to get a bad grade, and the power to improve your test-taking performance lies within you. (Now, take a deep breath and complete **Try It! 5**, "Take a Test on Taking Tests," on pages 130–31.)

Take a Test on Taking Tests

Part A: Take the following test on test-taking skills, which illustrates every question type discussed in this chapter.

Before taking the test, think of the test-taking strategies we've discussed in the chapter and try to employ as many of them as possible.

MULTIPLE-CHOICE SECTION

Choose one of the possible responses following each question.

1. Tests are useful tools for which of the following purposes?
   a. Determining people's likely level of future career success.
   b. Indicating strengths and gaps in people's knowledge.
   c. Defining people's fundamental abilities and potentials.
   d. Evaluating people's individual worth and contributions.

2. One of the main advantages of study groups is that
   a. Every individual must contribute equally to the group.
   b. Group members can help each other during the test.
   c. Each member has to memorize only a fraction of the material.
   d. They allow each member to share different perspectives on the material.

3. Which of the following is a good way to deal with test anxiety?
   a. Visualizing success on the test.
   b. Drinking coffee or other stimulants.
   c. Telling yourself to stop worrying.
   d. Focusing on the importance of the test.

MATCHING SECTION

_____1.	Essay question	A.	A question in which the student supplies brief missing information to complete a statement.
_____2.	Multiple-choice question	B.	Hurried, last-minute studying.
_____3.	Matching question	C.	A question in which the student must link information in two columns.
_____4.	Fill-in question	D.	A question requiring a lengthy response in the student's own words.
_____5.	Guessing penalty	E.	Deduction of points for incorrect responses.
_____6.	Cramming	F.	Representing someone else's work as one's own.
_____7.	Plagiarism	G.	A question that requires selection from several response options.

FILL-IN SECTION

1. Fear of testing that can interfere with test performance is called _____.
2. The primary source of error on machine-scored tests is incomplete _____.

5

TRUE–FALSE SECTION

1. The best way to prepare for an essay test is to review detailed factual information about the topic. T _____ F _____

2. True–false questions require students to determine whether given statements are accurate or inaccurate. T _____ F _____

3. You should never permit yourself to feel panicky during a test. T _____ F _____

4. A good evaluation strategy toward the end of a test is to redo as many questions as time permits. T _____ F _____

5. In a multiple-choice question, the words "always" and "never" usually signal the correct response. T _____ F _____

6. If you run out of time at the end of a test, it is best to write brief notes and ideas down in response to essay questions rather than to leave them completely blank. T _____ F _____

SHORT-ANSWER SECTION

1. What are five things you should find out about a test before you take it?

2. What is academic honesty?

ESSAY SECTION

1. Discuss the advantages of using a study group to prepare for an examination.

2. Why is academic honesty important?

(Answers can be found on page 135.)

Part B:
After you have completed the test, consider these questions:

1. Did you learn anything from taking the test that you might not have learned if you hadn't been tested?
2. How effective were the test-taking strategies you employed?
3. Were any types of strategies easier for you to employ than others?
4. Were any types of questions easier for you to answer than others?

 WORKING IN A GROUP

Exchange your essay responses with a classmate, and critique the essays. How do the responses of your partner compare with your own?

To Try It online, go to Connect for *P.O.W.E.R. Learning and Your Life.*

Time to Reflect: What Did I Learn?

1. Generally speaking, how does being tested make you feel?

2. What factors seem to contribute to your success or failure on a particular test or exam? Which of these factors are under your control?

3. What strategies do you plan to use in the future to improve your performance on tests?

Looking Back

What kinds of tests will I encounter in college and university?

> There are several types of tests, including brief, informal quizzes; tests, which are more substantial; and exams, which are even more significant and tend to be administered at the midpoint and end of a course.

> Although tests are an unpopular fact of college and university life, they can provide useful information about your level of knowledge and understanding about a subject.

What are the best ways to prepare for various kinds of tests?

> Good test preparation begins with doing the course assignments, attending class regularly, and paying attention in class. It also helps to find out as much as possible about a test beforehand and to form a study group to review material.

> If cramming becomes necessary, focus on summarizing factual information broadly, identifying key concepts and ideas, and rehearsing information orally.

What can I do during the test to maximize my test results?

> When you first receive the test, you should skim it to see what kinds of questions are asked, figure out how the different questions and sections will be weighted, and jot down complex factual information you might need for the test.

> Answer the easiest questions first, write legibly, use only one side of each sheet of paper, mark answer sheets carefully, and record answers in the test book as well as on the answer sheet.

What are the best strategies for answering specific kinds of test questions?

> For essay questions, you should work to understand each question and each of its parts, interpret action words correctly, write concisely, organize the essay logically, and include examples.

> The best strategy for short-answer and fill-in questions is to be very sure what is being asked. Keep answers complete but brief.

> For multiple-choice items, read the question very carefully and then read all response choices. Educated guessing based on eliminating incorrect response choices is usually a reasonable strategy.

> For true–false and matching questions, answer all the items that you are sure of quickly and then go back to the remaining items.

What can I learn from taking the test?

> Analyzing the graded test will help you to see weaknesses in your understanding of the material tested. You can study these weak areas further before you take your next test or exam on that material.

> You may see places in the test where you have misread questions or misallocated your time. Recognizing these tendencies in yourself can help you to be more "test-wise" in the future.

[KEY TERMS AND CONCEPTS]

[RESOURCES]

ON CAMPUS

Colleges and universities provide a variety of resources for students having difficulties with test-taking. Some offer general workshops reviewing test-taking strategies. As well, if you are planning to take a specific standardized test, you may be able to sign up for a course offered through your college or university (or through such commercial organizations as Princeton Review or Kaplan).

If you are experiencing difficulties in a specific course, you may be able to find a tutor to help you. Some institutions have tutoring centres or campus learning centres that can provide one-to-one assistance. It's also important to speak to your instructor, who has likely encountered many students with similar problems and may have some useful test-taking strategies.

If you find that you are experiencing significant test anxiety when taking a test or in the days leading up to it, talk to one of the professionals at your campus counselling centre or health centre. They can help you learn relaxation techniques and can provide counselling to help make your anxiety manageable.

IN PRINT

If you have difficulty with test anxiety, you'll want to check out *Insider's Guide to Beating Test Anxiety* (Bedford, 2010).

In *How to Ace Any Test* (Wiley, 2004), Beverley Chin provides a variety of techniques designed to improve your performance on any kind of test.

Eileen Tracy's *The Student's Guide to Exam Success* (Open University Press, 2006) gives an overview of strategies for test-taking success.

ON THE WEB

The following websites provide the opportunity to extend your learning about the material in this chapter.

> "The Multiple Choice Exam," an online handout from the University of Victoria's Learning Skills Program (**www.coun.uvic.ca/learning/exams/multiple-choice.html**) offers some valuable suggestions on how to approach multiple-choice exams. Several types of multiple-choice questions are described and strategies for answering them are explained. There are also helpful hints about what to look for in the wording of both the questions and the answer choices.

> "Simplified Plans of Action for Common Types of Question Words," another online handout from the University of Victoria's Learning Skills Program (**www.coun.uvic.ca/learning/essays/simple-answers.html**), gives examples of question words that are often found in essay assignments or in essay questions on exams. Possible "plans of action" for each of the question types are outlined. These outlines can be useful as a starting point for understanding how to approach essay questions.

> "Tactics for Managing Stress and Anxiety" (**www.coun.uvic.ca/personal/stress-anxiety.html**) offers several suggestions that you might find helpful in managing and reducing your level of stress and anxiety. The techniques may help you deal with test-related anxiety as well as academic anxiety in general. Not all of the techniques work for everyone. Try them and adopt the ones that work best for you.

TAKING IT TO THE NET

1 Seeing exams from other classes can help you get an idea of the kinds of questions that are often asked on exams. Use an Internet search engine to locate examples of exams from other colleges and universities. One strategy would be to use the Google search engine at **www.google.ca**, and type "examples of exams" (including the quotation marks) at the search prompt. Look at several exams. How many of the questions on these exams were true–false? How many were multiple-choice? How many were essays?

2 Practise answering essay questions by comparing and contrasting the information different Web pages offer about the same topic. For example, go to Yahoo! (**http://ca.yahoo.com**) and enter the phrase "essay exams" (using quotation marks). Read the strategies for essay exams offered in two different websites. Then write a paragraph describing the information both sites had in common, and another paragraph describing the information that was unique to each site.

ANSWERS TO ITEMS IN TRY IT! 5

Multiple-choice: 1b, 2d, 3a

Matching: 1D, 2G, 3C, 4A, 5E, 6B, 7F

Fill-in: test anxiety, erasing

True–False: 1F, 2T, 3F, 4F, 5F, 6T

Short answer:

1. Possible answers include what the test is called, what it will cover, how many questions will be on it, how much time it will take, what kinds of questions will be on it, how it will be graded, whether sample questions will be provided, and whether tests from prior terms are available.
2. Academic honesty is completing and turning in only one's own work under one's own name.

Essay:

1. Strong essays would include a brief definition of a study group, followed by a discussion of the advantages of using study groups (including such things as helping to organize and structure material, providing different perspectives, and rethinking material). A mention of the disadvantages of study groups would also be reasonable.
2. After starting with a brief definition of academic honesty, the bulk of the answer should concentrate on the reasons why academic honesty is important and the consequences of academic dishonesty.

The Case of . . .
That Sinking Feeling

This is going to be easy, Janelle Ross said to herself as she sat down to take her test, a midterm exam covering the basics of restaurant management. She had spent a few hours the previous night and an hour right before class studying key terms and concepts. She felt she knew the material. She felt ready.

Janelle was surprised to see, though, that the exam had two parts: a multiple-choice section and an essay section. Janelle hadn't really thought about what she might say in an essay. But she figured working on the multiple-choice questions might help give her some ideas.

The first two multiple-choice questions Janelle answered easily, but she got stuck on the third one. She went back and forth over two possible answers and finally decided just to leave that question blank. The pattern was the same for the rest of the multiple-choice questions: A few questions Janelle would answer easily, then she'd get stuck on a hard one.

Finally, Janelle finished the multiple-choice questions and came to the essay. Only then did she notice the instructions that indicated the essay was worth 50 marks, and the multiple-choice questions 25 marks. Then Janelle got another shock: She had only ten minutes left to write her essay! Her mind froze—and Janelle had the horrible feeling that she didn't have enough time to complete the test. Even though she had studied, Janelle now felt certain she would fail.

1. What mistakes did Janelle make in her test preparation that probably harmed her performance?

2. What mistakes did Janelle make during the test that hurt her?

3. What was right about Janelle's initial approach to the test?

4. What should Janelle have done differently in calculating the amount of time to devote to each portion of the test? Why?

5. What specific strategies would have helped Janelle with the multiple-choice questions? What strategies could she have used on the essay?

6. If you were in Janelle's shoes, what would you do with only ten minutes left in the test?

11 Planning Your Career

Learning Outcomes

By the time you finish this chapter, you will be able to

» LO **11.1**   Identify your ideal career.

» LO **11.2**   Prepare a Career Portfolio, including an up-to-date resumé and cover letter.

» LO **11.3**   Explain some effective job search strategies.

» LO **11.4**   Demonstrate your interviewing skills.

» LO **11.5**   Evaluate the impact of your striving style on career choice and career development.

Michelle Isaacs felt ready for her first job interview. In fact, she felt more than ready.

Her interview for a position as a broker in a local real estate firm had been scheduled the week before; and ever since then, Michelle had been mentally preparing answer after answer about her background and about the position. She'd researched the real estate company online, reviewed her own job experience, and even scanned some real estate ads in the local newspaper to try to get a sense of the area real estate market.

But when the interviewer, seemingly out of the blue, asked her, "How many piano tuners are there in your home province?" she was clueless. How should she know? And, more to the point, what did that question have to do with being a real estate broker?

Looking Ahead

Luckily for Michelle, what she later called the "piano crisis" was a turning point. Once she got beyond her initial shock, she realized that the aim of the question was to test not her knowledge of piano tuners but her problem-solving skills. After first considering the population of her home state, and then guessing at how many of those people might own pianos, she was able to come up with a rough estimate of how many piano tuners there might be. The interviewer, clearly satisfied, moved on to other, more predictable questions.

Job interviews can be anxiety-producing events. But they are just one of a series of challenging activities that are part of the process of finding a job. In several chapters of *P.O.W.E.R. Learning,* we've been looking at skills that are usually applied in a classroom setting: note-taking, test-taking, and so forth. In this final, online chapter, we explore strategies that will help you in the world of work. We address ways to identify your career goals and the best methods to achieve them. To put it simply, we consider the things you need to know to get the job you want.

≫ LO 11.1 Career Planning

At this point, you're in college or university to learn the skills to start down a specific career path. That means you've made up your mind about your career . . . right?

In fact, the answer is probably no. Even while enrolled in a particular program at college or university, many students remain unsure about what they want to do career-wise. And that's normal. It's even OK. With most people changing careers many times throughout their lives, there is no way you can plan that much in advance. What you *can* do, on your way to acquiring training to work in a particular field, is think and plan carefully with regard to your professional ambitions.

Imagine you are on your way to earning a degree in accounting, for example. Clearly, you've made an important decision about your career. But consider these questions: Do you want to work independently or as an employee of a business? If you want to work for a business, would you rather it be a small company or a large corporation? Do you want a job that will pay less initially but at which you can advance, or would you rather trade the possibility of moving up the ladder for a better starting salary? Further, do you want to work locally, or would you be willing to relocate for the right job? What kind of hours are you willing to work? What kind of hours *can* you work, given the demands of family and other obligations?

These are just some of the questions people need to answer as they plan their careers. Keep in mind that you don't need to have all the answers right now. Few people know *exactly* how they'd like their professional lives to unfold. What's important to realize is that even if you've chosen a field, you still have lots of decisions to make and options to choose from as you pursue your career. Career planning is not a decision you make once; rather, it is an ongoing process.

P Prepare
Identify your career goals

O Organize
Find and research career opportunities

W Work
Create a career portfolio

E Evaluate
Get feedback on your resumé and cover letter

R Rethink
Rethink your initial career choice

P.O.W.E.R. Plan

 **P Prepare** Identify Your Career Goals

Some people take a job for the money. Some people take a job for the benefits package. Some people show up at work because they love to crunch numbers or treat patients or make a hollandaise sauce. Others go to the office because they believe that hard work is the key to happiness.

Try It!

Identifying Your Long-term Career Goals

Consider each of these areas as you determine your long-term goals:

- Achievement
- Advancement opportunities
- Challenge
- Contribution to society
- Control, power
- Creativity

- Financial rewards
- Friendships with co-workers
- Helping others
- Independence
- Leadership
- Learning new things

- Loyalty
- Prestige
- Recognition from others
- Security
- Variety
- Working with others

Using this list, create a set of your three most important occupational goals. For example, three primary goals might be to (1) be challenged to reach your potential, (2) work with others in a friendly environment, and (3) make a lasting contribution to society. However, don't be influenced by these examples—choose goals that are your own.

My Primary Career Goals Are to:

1.

2.

3.

Stating your career goals up front, even before you consider the range of jobs that you have to choose from, is important. Identifying your goals helps you know what it is that you want out of work. Research will help you determine if the career you have in mind will help you achieve those goals. For example, no matter how glamorous being a chef might sound, most people pursuing this type of career find it involves very long hours including evenings, weekends, and holidays; another consideration is that only the top chefs make a lot of money. Modelling may seem like another glamorous career; but for most models, their career is over by the time they are in their early twenties. Being a flight attendant may also sound appealing because of the travelling; but when you get right down to it, you never see much more than the inside of an airport and a hotel room. It is absolutely critical, therefore, that you assess the pros and cons of your intended career—not just in the short term, when you may be single and carefree, but also in the long term, when you may have a family and the additional responsibilities that come along with it.

Future employers are more interested in what you bring to your job, than in how well a job fulfills your important goals. It's crucial that you consider what has significance to you before making career decisions. If a career opportunity doesn't fulfill your major goals, it will not be a good choice for you.

To Try It online, go to Connect for *P.O.W.E.R. Learning and Your Life*.

These are all valid reasons for doing a job. As you think about the kind of job you want to find, it's essential to consider your own goals. Apart from what you might do during the day, do you want a job that helps others? A job that pays very well? A job with flexible hours? Is having an impact on future generations important to you? Use **Try It! 1**, "Identifying Your Long-term Career Goals," to guide your thinking.

⊙ Organize | Find Career Opportunities

Research, research, research. That's the name of the game when it comes to charting your career. Even if you know the general direction you want your career to take, you'll want to get a feel for the specific opportunities within your chosen field, as well as how your field is developing and changing.

Be sure to keep notes about what you find. Your notes don't have to be elaborately written or suitable for handing in to an instructor. Just keep them simple, legible, and organized; and make sure that they include the source of the information you're recording.

Websites

A good first step in obtaining career information is to examine the Government of Canada's integrated job website at **www.workingincanada.gc.ca**. On the website, you'll find a wealth of information on the demand level for specific jobs, skill requirements, and educational programs for more than 500 different jobs. You can even print out a detailed report for the job you are interested in, tailored to where you would like to work. The site provides information on Canada's National Occupation Codes (NOC), access to labour market projections through the Canadian Occupational Projection Systems (COPS), and an online Career Handbook. Also available on the site are a set of Essential Skill Profiles that identify the degree to which jobs require nine essential skills: The nine skills are these:

- Reading Text
- Document Use
- Numeracy
- Writing
- Oral Communication
- Working with Others
- Continuous Learning
- Thinking Skills
- Computer Use

Do these skills sound familiar? Many of these same skills were mentioned in Chapter 1, in the Conference Board's Employability Skills 2000+.

You are likely to find many career planning tools and resources at your college or university, either in the career centre or in the library. In addition, almost every public library has a reference section on careers, and Service Canada employment centres often have extensive materials to help identify careers.

In addition to books, you may find CD-ROMs, pamphlets, and other helpful material, often including on-site computers with software that can help you gather job-related information. For example, *Choices* is a widely used computer program that has proven helpful to those engaged in career searches.

You'll also want to visit the Canadian version of Yahoo's HotJobs (**http://ca.hotjobs.yahoo.com**), which was co-developed with Monster, a popular job search website.

Personal Interviews

To get an up-close-and-personal look at a profession, another strategy is to talk with people who are already in it. People love to talk about their jobs, whether they love them or hate them; so don't be afraid to ask for an interview. You don't need a

From the perspective of . . .

A STUDENT
Part of your growth as a student involves an honest assessment of career possibilities. What careers appeal to you most?

  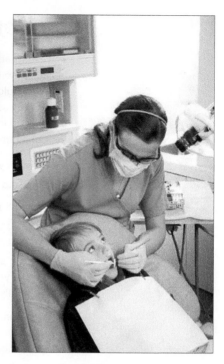

Personal service workers, forensic science technicians, and dental hygienists are all career areas on the rise. Have you considered any of the careers on this list?

lot of their time—just enough to get an inside view of what it's like to work in their profession. Here are some questions you might want to ask:

> What's your typical day like?

> How did you find your job?

> What are the best and worst aspects of being in your profession?

> What do you look for in someone who wants to enter your field?

Keep in mind, of course, that the answers you get will be the opinions of one individual, reflecting his or her unique, personal experience. That's why it is a good idea to talk to several practitioners of a particular occupation, and to consider what they say in the context of other research that you have conducted.

Be sure to write a thank-you note following an interview. Not only is it common courtesy, but it also serves the additional purpose of reinforcing who you are and your interest in their profession. You never know: One day, they might have a job opening, and you might want to ask them for a job!

LO 11.2 Creating a Career Portfolio

The research you've done on career options forms the foundation for creating a Career Development Portfolio. A **Career Portfolio** is a dynamic record that documents your skills, capabilities, achievements, and goals; it also provides a place to keep notes, ideas, and research findings related to careers. Such a portfolio will provide an easy-to-access history of your job-related activities, and it will include material that will be helpful for you and, later, for potential employers. You'll want to maintain and update your Career Portfolio as long as you are pursuing a career.

Career Portfolio
A dynamic record that documents your skills, capabilities, achievements, and goals, and provides a place to keep notes, ideas, and research findings related to careers

Career Guides

You can learn a great deal about career opportunities and the process of getting a job by talking to someone who is pursuing or has pursued a career that interests you. These "career guides" could be your course instructor, someone who guest lectured in your class, the owner of a local business, a friend of your parents, the parents of a friend—in fact, anyone who has experience in your area of interest. You'll want to set up a time to talk with this person, and at the appointment, ask questions such as these:

- What is your educational and professional background?
- How did you get your current job?
- What employees have you had who have been particularly successful in this career? What qualities did they have that set them apart from other employees?
- What general advice do you have for someone looking for a job?
- If your career guide knows you quite well, you can ask them this question: What skills would you encourage me to work on and develop in order to increase my chances of successfully getting a job?

You can gain valuable insights into navigating a career from career guides. After speaking with them, reflect on what they've told you about what it takes to be successful in that field, and compare those attributes to your own strengths and weaknesses. What do you need to work on?

One last thought: Talking with career guides can help you get to know them better, and it may eventually pave the way for them to provide you with letters of recommendation and/or job leads. Not a bad return on an investment of an hour or so of your time!

Your Career Portfolio will consist of two main parts. The first part, background information, will help you keep track of your accomplishments and notes on your research; the second part, which includes your resumé and cover letter, will be material that you share with potential employers.

Your Career Portfolio can either be in a traditional, hard-copy form, or you can create an e-Portfolio online. Some colleges and universities provide online templates or "wizards" that guide you through the process of creating a Career Portfolio. E-Portfolios have the advantage of being easily modified, and—since they reside on the Web—they are accessible anywhere you have access to the Internet.

Career Portfolio, Part I: Background Information

The information in this section of your Portfolio is meant to help you make career-related decisions and record your thinking about your career. This part is for your eyes only. Although you will draw on the material for the "public" part of your Portfolio that potential employers will see, think of it as your own, private repository of information.

- **Basic personal data.** Keep a record of data and identification numbers that you think you'll never forget—even with the best intentions, you can forget them at the least opportune moment. For example, include your social insurance number, addresses (home and school), ID number, and telephone numbers. If you're a renter, keep a record of your landlord's name and address; you might need a credit reference one day.
- **Career research notes.** Whether your notes have been collected from books, Web-based research, or interviews with people in a particular occupation, they belong in your Career Portfolio. They will provide a record of your career-related activities.

- **Syllabus/course outline from courses you have taken.** Include a copy of the syllabus and course outline of every course you take, along with the grade you received in the course. The information contained in a course syllabus and outline will serve to jog your memory about the material the course covered. Without these materials, you're at the mercy of your memory when you're trying to recall the content of a course you may have taken several years earlier but that has direct relevance to your career. Also, you will need copies of course outlines should you ever want to apply for a transfer credit, so they really are something you should keep.

  For further documentation relating to your courses, you could include a copy of the course description from the college or university calendar and, if it contained a list of learning outcomes that students were to attain, you'd want to get a copy of this as well.

- **Transcripts.** Include the most recent version of your transcript, listing the courses you took, credits you earned, and grades you received in your classes.

- **Your personal history.** If someone were to write your biography, what are the key events that you'd want him or her to know about?

  The events that would be included in your biography can form the core of a list that you should make of every significant experience you've had. The list should include every employment-related experience you've had, even part-time jobs or summer jobs when you were in high school. But don't limit yourself only to job experiences; include other accomplishments as well, such as the community service you perform. Personal events that have had a major impact on who you are should also earn a place in your personal history, such as any notable athletic achievements or the car accident you had. Use **Try It! 2**, "Cataloguing Your Personal History," on page 276, to help make this list, some of which you'll use later to create a resumé.

- **Long-term career goals.** Your Career Portfolio should have the statement of the long-term career goals that you developed in **Try It! 1.**

- **Writing samples.** Add examples of your best writing. These can be papers that you've handed in for classes or other writing you have done on your own or on the job. The idea is to have a sample of your writing easily available should a potential employer ask for one.

- **Credentials.** Include copies of any credentials you have earned. For example, place in the Portfolio a copy of diplomas you have earned, certificates from workshops, seminars, or training sessions that you have received, proof of non-credit continuing education courses you have taken, and the like. You never know when an employer might want to see documentation of your accomplishments.

Career Portfolio, Part II: Resumé and Cover Letter

This section of your Career Portfolio encompasses information that you will share with potential employers. Whereas the material in the first part of your Portfolio provides the background for your career planning, this is the public face of your Portfolio.

Think of the components of the first part as the equivalent of the backstage of a play, with a director and crew working behind the scenes to pull things together. In contrast, this second part of the Portfolio is the play the audience sees, the part that should proceed flawlessly. You want the critics to offer nothing less than raves for your production.

Cataloguing Your Personal History

	Describe activity or event, when and where it occurred, your responsibilities and actions, skills and talents used or learned, achievements, and insights gained
Did you work during or before high school?	
Were you a member of any clubs or other organizations in high school?	
How many paid jobs have you held since high school?	
Have you performed any community service?	
Have you provided any services to a religious institution?	
Are you working, while at college or university?	
Are you in any clubs at college or university?	
Have you had any personally significant life experiences?	
Have you ever been called upon to exercise skills or talents you didn't know you had?	
Have you ever solved a tough problem and felt great satisfaction?	
Have you ever worked in a group to solve a problem?	
Have you ever organized a complex task on your own?	
Have you ever led a group in the performance of a large task?	
What is the best thing you have ever done?	

 WORKING IN A GROUP

Compare your responses to those of other students in your class.

1. What unique capabilities do you have which set you apart from others in the group?

2. How could you take advantage of those unique capabilities when you are seeking a job?

To Try It online, go to Connect for *P.O.W.E.R. Learning and Your Life.*

The two primary elements that belong in the second part of your Career Portfolio are your resumé and your cover letter.

Resumé

A resumé (pronounced res-oo-may) is a brief summary of your qualifications for a job. It is the first thing that potential employers see and should serve to arouse their interest in you. Actually, a human may not even initially see it: An increasing number of employers use computers to screen resumés. The computers look for key skills and terminology, so include the verbs used in the National Occupational Classification (NOC) listing (see **www.workingincanada.gc.ca/report-eng.do?action=display-allnoc**). If the appropriate skills are not listed, the computers send an automatic rejection.

Consequently, the resumé must be crafted with great precision and care. If you've created a personal history statement earlier for Part I of your Career Portfolio, use it to get started.

The key elements of a resumé include the following and are illustrated in a sample resumé in **Figure 11.1** on page 278.

> **Contact information.** Include your name, address (current and permanent if they're different), phone number(s), and email address. *Don't* include your sex, age, race, or marital status. These factors are irrelevant to your job performance, and employers are not legally permitted to take them into consideration.

> **Job objective.** If you are targeting a specific job, include a specific objective (such as, "to obtain a position as a buyer for a major retail department store"). However, if you're willing to be flexible, provide a more general job objective (for example, "to obtain an entry-level position in retail sales").

> **Education.** Include the colleges and/or universities you've attended or are currently attending, with the actual or anticipated year of graduation and credential earned.

> **Awards and honours.** If you've won any awards or honours (such as membership in an honours program or inclusion on the Dean's List), mention them. If you have none that you want to include, leave this category off your resumé.

> **Campus and community activities.** Include activities in which you've participated, and indicate any in which you've had a leadership role. You want to demonstrate that you are an involved, contributing member of your community.

> **Professional memberships.** Do you belong to any professional organizations that are relevant to the job you'll be seeking? If so, include them.

> **Work experience.** List your experience, starting with your most recent job and working backward. Include the job title, dates, and your major on-the-job responsibilities.
>
> Don't feel you need to include every job you're ever held (for example, leave out the occasional pet sitting). Instead, focus on the key positions that illustrate your ability to hold a job and to carry out responsibilities. Furthermore, as you present your work experience, always remember that the focus should be on how your past work can get you a job in the profession you want in the future.

- **Particular skills.** Do you know how to program in Linux? Can you speak Tagalog fluently? Are you a certified lifeguard? Can you develop a complex Excel spreadsheet or excellent PowerPoint slides?

  Include a brief list of the special skills you have. Once again, make sure that the skills you list are related to the job you're seeking. For example, if you're seeking a job in information technology, Linux programming is relevant, but it may not be if you're looking for a job in medical services.

ALEJANDRO D. WEBB
1334 Kingston Road, Toronto, Ontario M1A 2B3
416 - 555 - 6677 e: ajdw@gmail.com

JOB OBJECTIVE To obtain a position as an office manager

WORK EXPERIENCE
Law offices of Brandon and Shields, Toronto, Ontario
Office Manager
June 2010 - Present

- Oversaw logistics of law office of twelve people; was responsible for scheduling, filing, copying, and managing administrative staff.
- Devised new office-wide filing system for records of completed cases.
- Researched and implemented new office-wide benefits package.
- Responsible for balancing monthly facilities budget.
- Occasionally accompanied attorneys to court to provide organizational support.

Amelia D. Rafael Law Office, Pickering, Ontario
Administrative Assistant
October 2009 - April 2010

- Managed schedule, correspondence, and files for high-profile Pickering attorney.
- Aided in creating documents and organizing evidence for $13 million class action suit.

EDUCATION
Centennial College, Office Administration, June 2010

HONOURS AND AWARDS
School of Business Dean's List
Board of Governors' Award for Student Achievement

CAMPUS AND COMMUNITY ACTIVITIES
Latino Students Organization
Volunteer, Daily Bread Food Bank

PROFESSIONAL MEMBERSHIP
Association of Administrative Assistants

PARTICULAR SKILLS
Proficient in all Microsoft office programs
Fluent in Spanish

REFERENCES
Available upon request

---

figure 11.1
Sample Resumé

> **References.** A "reference" category is optional; but if you include it, simply say "References available upon request." Don't list specific names, but have them available should an interviewer ask for them. (We'll discuss whom to ask and how to obtain references later in the chapter.)

As you create a resumé, keep in mind some general rules. First, keep your resumé short. In a resumé, less is more. Generally, resumés should be no longer than one page.

Second, make it look good. Your resumé should appear professional. Use plenty of white space, with one-inch margins on every side. Use strong action words, such as those in **Table 11.1**. Avoid articles (such as "the," "a," and "an") and pronouns (such as "I" or "we"); don't write in full sentences.

table 11.1   Action Words

Using strong action words and making sentences short will help you prepare a professional and eye-catching resumé. Here is a list of action words to get you started. Use words that best describe what you do and who you are.

Achieved	Directed	Investigated
Administered	Discovered	Launched
Advised	Drafted	Led
Aided	Edited	Managed
Approved	Educated	Moderated
Arranged	Enabled	Monitored
Archived	Established	Negotiated
Assigned	Evaluated	Operated
Assisted	Examined	Organized
Authored	Expanded	Oversaw
Budgeted	Expedited	Performed
Built	Extracted	Recommended
Calculated	Facilitated	Recruited
Catalogued	Fashioned	Regulated
Chaired	Granted	Remodelled
Classified	Forecasted	Reported
Coached	Formulated	Restored
Collected	Founded	Reversed
Compiled	Generated	Reviewed
Computed	Guided	Saved
Conducted	Identified	Scheduled
Contracted	Illustrated	Solved
Controlled	Improved	Strengthened
Coordinated	Increased	Summarized
Counselled	Influenced	Supervised
Created	Informed	Trained
Critiqued	Initiated	Translated
Delegated	Inspected	Trimmed
Demonstrated	Installed	Tutored
Designated	Instituted	Upgraded
Designed	Instructed	Validated
Developed	Integrated	Worked
Devised	Interviewed	Wrote
Diagnosed	Invented	

Finally, proofread, proofread, proofread. You want to be sure that no typographical errors or misspellings find their way into your resumé.

The same rules hold for the second element of Part II of your Career Portfolio, your cover letter, which we discuss next. Before moving on, though, get a start on creating a resumé by completing **Try It 3**, "Creating a Resumé," on page 280.

3

Creating a Resumé

It's time to use some of the pieces you have been thinking about and working on to create a resumé. You have explored your ideas about your occupational goals (**Try It! 1**), and you have gathered important elements of your personal history (**Try It! 2**). Now put the pieces together by filling in the worksheet below. Then use the worksheet to create a clean, one-page resumé that you can have reviewed and proofread.

Contact Information:

Your name, address, phone number(s), and email address.

Job Objective:

Use your ideas about your occupational goals. Write one statement, beginning with the word "To," that sums up your goals. Be specific ONLY if you are applying for a job you understand and want to focus on; otherwise, state your goals broadly and generally.

Education:

List any colleges and/or universities attended, including your current post-secondary institution, starting with the most recent. If you have taken college or university courses without being formally enrolled, list those too.

Awards and Honours (Optional):

List any honours you have received. Academic honours are of primary importance, but honours and awards from social, religious, and community groups (e.g., 4-H, Red Cross, Rotary Club) may be worth including if they testify to personal characteristics that may help you gain employment, such as leadership, perseverance, or a sense of civic duty.

Campus and Community Activities (Optional):

List any clubs, teams, or activities in which you have participated since high school. Include high school activities only if they were significant and are related to your career goals. Also list community activities in which you have participated, especially those in which you had a leadership role.

3

Professional Memberships (Optional):

List any professional organizations related to your career goals of which you are or have been a member. Professional organizations are groups such as the Canadian Marketing Association, the Canadian Professional Sales Association, the Purchasing Management Association, the Certified General Accountants Association of Canada, and the like.

Work Experience (if You've Had Any):

List all jobs you have had, including paid jobs (on campus and off), apprenticeships, internships, and similar "real" jobs. List your most recent work experience first and work backward through time. Include the title of the job, organization for which you worked, dates of work, and major responsibilities. Understand that you may be asked about any of the jobs you list, including your reasons for moving to the next job.

Particular Skills (Optional):

List anything you are particularly good at that might transfer to a work setting; for example, the ability to speak a foreign language, to fix computer hardware problems, to write and debug software programs, to repair engines, to create websites, and so forth. You can draw this list from your academic, work, and even personal/recreational life.

References:

Available on request.

To Try It online, go to Connect for *P.O.W.E.R. Learning and Your Life.*

Cover letter

Although your resumé is the centrepiece of your presentation to potential employers, your cover letter is no less important. It shows that you can string words together into well-crafted sentences, and it gives you the opportunity to bring life to the list of qualifications on your resumé. It also gives you the opportunity to say how enthusiastic you are about the job for which you're applying and to illustrate how well your qualifications match the job requirements.

In writing a cover letter, keep in mind the perspective of the person who is reading it. Potential employers have a problem that they need to solve: identifying someone to do work that they need done so much that they're willing to pay someone to do it. The better you can provide them with a solution to this problem, the more attractive you will be.

What this means is that your cover letter should be oriented toward helping employers solve *their* problem, not toward how the job will solve *your* problems. Consequently, don't talk about how you think the job will fulfil you as a person or how much you need it to pay your bills. Instead, orient your letter toward describing how well your own unique qualifications match the specific job requirements.

Every cover letter should be tailored to a specific position (see the two sample letters in **Figures 11.2** and **11.3**), but they typically contain the following elements:

> **Introduction: Catching the interest of the reader.** Describe why you are writing, how you learned about the job, and why you are interested in it. Emphasize the connection between the position requirements and your qualifications.

> **Letter body: Drawing in the reader.** Here's where you describe, in very brief terms, who you are and what makes you unique. Highlight major accomplishments and qualifications from your personal history, making the argument that your skills are a close match to the job. Show enthusiasm!

> You can also include information that does not appear on your resumé; for instance, if you paid for your education entirely on your own, you might want to mention that fact. In addition, you can write about what you hope to accomplish on the job.

> Finally, show that you know something about the organization to which you are applying. Do some homework to learn about the employer, and state specifically what you find attractive about them.

> **Conclusion: A call for action.** End the letter by restating your interest in the position and suggesting that you would like to discuss the position further. State that you are available to meet for an interview. Thank the employer for considering your application.

Like your resumé, the cover letter should read well and look good. Before you send it, be sure to proofread it carefully.

Include a sample cover letter in your Career Portfolio. Doing so will ensure that you are ready at a moment's notice to revise the sample and send it off. Job opportunities sometimes appear unexpectedly, and it will be much easier for you to respond quickly, and respond well, if you already have a sample letter on file.

Unless you are certain of the job you'll be seeking in the future, you might want to prepare several cover letters, targeted at the different job possibilities you are considering. In addition, the act of writing cover letters for a variety of professions may actually help you come to a decision regarding the path you ultimately choose to follow.

One final note about your Career Portfolio: Keep in mind that it is a work in progress, a living document that is meant to be revised as your interests and aspirations change. That's why it may be a good idea to keep your Career Portfolio in virtual form, rather than as a hard copy. By creating an e-Portfolio, you will be able to make revisions easily. An e-Portfolio also simplifies the process of producing your resumé and cover letter for an actual job opening.

July 29, 2012

Mr. Reginald Pelly
Assistant Vice President
BooksRUs Publishers
100 Front Street
Winnipeg, MN R9S 8T7

Dear Mr. Pelly:

Jennifer Windsor, Director of Editorial Development at BooksRUs
Publishers, advised me of an opening in your company for an entry-level
trade book editor. From my enclosed resumé, you will find that both my
experience and my education fully meet the requirements you have
outlined for the position.

My current position as a copy editor at a medium-sized daily newspaper
has given me experience in dealing with deadlines and working closely
with others. Having served as a reporter for six years, I can relate to the
needs of writers as well. My colleagues consider me both outgoing and
diplomatic, traits that have served me well in my work as an editor.

I will contact you next week to learn when we can meet for an interview.

Sincerely,

Martina L. Veschova

Enclosure: Resumé

figure 11.2
Sample Cover Letter

 Career Portfolio, Part III:
Get Feedback on Your Resumé
and Cover Letter

After you have created the key elements of your Career Portfolio—your resumé
and cover letter—it's time to evaluate their effectiveness. Start by asking a trusted
person, such as one of your course instructors or someone on the staff of your
college or university's career centre, to review what you've created. Ask them to

Martin L. Chen

555 Comox St,   email: marlchen@mrnr.com   Phone: 604 555-5555
Vancouver, BC
V6E 1K1

July 25, 2012

Ms. Arlene Washington
Director, Human Services
St Peter's Hospital
8088 King Street,
Vancouver, BC
V6Z 6Z6

Dear Ms. Washington:

I am writing in response to the position advertised July 22, 2012, in the Vancouver *Province* seeking a
Lead Cost Analyst Accountant. My professional experience and education match well with the position
requirements listed. Enclosed is my resumé.

In addition to being self-motivated, I work well under pressure and welcome new challenges and
opportunities. Among some of my accomplishments are the following:

- Analyzed, defined, and produced appropriate budgets for wages and salary
  costs, materials, expenses, and workload.
- Provided extensive, timely, and appropriate reporting for all aspects of the
  various budgets.
- Investigated variances from budget.
- Performed cost benefit analyses and assisted with capital expenditure proposals.

My experience in supervising a team of four co-workers has taught me patience and has strengthened
my organizational skills. My greatest satisfaction in a job comes from selecting, training, and
motivating personnel. I believe I have the qualities that can help a department become more efficient
and productive.

I am familiar with St Peter's Hospital from news stories on breakthrough cancer research conducted
there, and I have further researched your hospital and its contributions to medicine. I feel there is a
good fit between my career goals and your needs. I welcome the opportunity to discuss the position
further, and look forward to hearing from you soon. Thank you for your consideration.

Yours truly,
Martin L. Chen

Enclosure

figure 11.3
Sample Cover Letter

provide honest and concrete suggestions, because the more feedback you receive,
the better the finished product will be.

Once you've received an initial review, one of the best strategies is to ask individuals working in the field in which you're interested to review your resumé and
cover letter. Requesting feedback from one or two people who are already working in your desired profession, particularly if they have hired people in the past,
serves several purposes. First, these reviewers will be in the best position to know
what employers are looking for, and they can tell you how to present yourself most

effectively. Not only can they help you say the right things, but they can also help you to avoid saying the wrong thing.

But there's a bonus from seeking advice from someone currently working in the field: You become a known quantity to them; and at some point in the future, they may have a job opening and you may spring to mind. Or if you contact them in the future, they may be able to steer you to a job opening.

 ## Rethink Your Initial Career Choice

Going through the process of identifying your goals, researching careers, and building a Career Portfolio may lead you to solidify your ideas about which occupation you'd like to pursue. That's great—that's the point of career exploration.

But even if you are sure about what you intend to do professionally, it's important to take some time to reconsider your initial choice. The most important thing is to avoid what psychologists call "foreclosure." Foreclosure is making a premature decision and sticking with it so persistently that you ignore other possibilities, even ones that hold considerable promise. For example, let's say you are a fan of the television program *CSI,* and are intent on pursuing a degree in forensic science. You'll want to consider learning opportunities that allow for experiential learning through fieldwork, cooperative education, internships, and volunteering that will bring you into the working environment of a forensic scientist. These types of opportunities allow you to "try on a career for size" and will help you determine if you've indeed made a good career decision or if, in fact, this is not exactly *CSI* and is far from what you had in mind. You need to keep an open mind when it comes to careers: There are so many things you can do for a living that you may never have even thought of.

What if you haven't been able to narrow things down? What if you're still completely up in the air about what path you'd like to pursue? First, realize that it's natural to be undecided. It's almost inevitable that you'll have some uncertainty with regard to decisions as important as where you work.

Also, keep in mind that even if you are certain about the general shape you want your career to take, there will inevitably be moments of backtracking and reconsideration. Very few people take one job at one organization and work there until they retire. The point is that you will have many opportunities to rethink your decisions. Don't feel that any one decision will forever shape the rest of your career, or your life.

If you're close to the point where you need to start work, and you still don't have a clue about what you want to do, then maybe you need to rethink your approach. Assuming you've considered various possibilities, you may want to reconsider the career-planning strategies you've been using. Ask yourself these questions:

> Have you been too restrictive or too selective in considering possibilities?
> Have you done sufficient research?
> Have you rejected job opportunities that seem somewhat interesting without carefully considering what they have to offer?
> Have you underestimated (or overestimated) your skills?
> Have you taken full advantage of all the resources your college or university offers in terms of career planning?

From the perspective of . . .

PURSUING A SECOND CAREER
It is possible to work for years in one field before deciding on a new career path. What are some things to consider if you are contemplating a second career?

"Your true pilot cares nothing about anything on earth but the river, and his pride in his occupation surpasses the pride of kings."
Mark Twain, *Life on the Mississippi,* 1883

LO 11.3 Other Job Search Strategies

Choose Your References Wisely

Getting the job you want sometimes can hinge less on what you say about yourself and more on what others say about you. A good reference can make the difference between getting a job and getting passed over. A bad reference can destroy your chances of being offered a position.

Finding just the right people to supply potential employers with a reference can be the key to obtaining the job you want. That's why it's critical to identify people who are willing to speak on your behalf well before you face a deadline.

Identifying People to Provide References

Several categories of individuals can provide your references, including these:

- Former job supervisors
- Colleagues in previous positions
- Class instructors
- Community service supervisors
- Coaches, club advisers, or heads of professional groups to which you belong
- People who can provide character references (e.g., clergy)

The most effective references come from people who know you well and who can speak to your skills, abilities, accomplishments, motivation, and character. In addition, people who can speak to the specific requirements of the job you're seeking (especially those who have worked with you in environments similar to that of the potential job) are highly effective.

The least effective references are those from family members or friends or, even worse, friends of friends. For instance, a reference from someone famous who happens to play tennis occasionally with your uncle will rarely be helpful, unless that person knows you well. Remember a key rule of references: The ability of a reference provider to describe in detail *your* strengths and *your* accomplishments is considerably more important than the identity, strengths, and accomplishments of the reference provider.

Asking for a Reference

When choosing someone to be a reference, always ask permission. Never give out the names of people who you think will provide references without asking them beforehand. Not only is seeking permission common courtesy, but asking first avoids violating another rule of references: No reference is better than a bad reference. You need to check that the reference someone provides will be an explicitly positive one.

Although you can't directly ask someone if they can provide a positive reference (it's very hard for someone to tell you straight out that they can't), you can approach the issue indirectly. When asking someone to serve as a reference, ask them if they have any reservations. If they do, no matter how minor, turn to someone else to provide the recommendation.

You should also offer some guidelines for those providing recommendations. Let them know why you're asking them in particular, and remind them of the context in which they've known you. If there is something you'd like them to address specifically in providing you with a reference—such as, for example, the unusual creativity you showed in a previous position or the fact that you wrote exceptionally good papers in a class—let them know. The more explicit information you can provide them, the better.

If you've been out of touch with one of your references for quite some time—for example, you've graduated and are now on your second job, but have a professor from several years ago who has served as a reference—be sure to update him or her on what you've been doing lately, and on why you are now undertaking a new job search.

Network, Network, Network

The need for references underscores the importance of knowing how to build and maintain a supportive network. Even while you're in college or university, it's critical to build up a network of people who can vouch for you. To network effectively, be sure to keep in touch with people who know and like you. And try to expand your network of contacts. Attend activities, seminars, or conferences sponsored by your local professional association, which may have student rates. And whenever you're at a social event, on a commuter train, or even flying home for summer break, don't be afraid to talk to people you don't know. You just never know who you might be sitting next to: It could be someone who knows of a job opportunity that is perfect for you, or it could even be the president of a company you've always wanted to work for.

To maintain a list of people who can vouch for you, consider joining a networking website like Linked In (**www.linkedin.com**), which can best be described as a Facebook-type site for the working world.

Use the Web in Your Job Hunt

The Web has changed some of the rules for conducting a job search. It permits you to post your resumé and have the potential for thousands of possible employers to screen it. It also permits employers to post their job needs and have the potential for thousands of possible employees to see them. You can apply for jobs online. Internet services can help you to conduct automated searches, exposing you to job listings in your chosen field and receiving emails containing job postings that fit your skills.

The advantages of electronic job searches—such as the potentially wide exposure of your resumé—come at some potential costs. First, your resumé will quite likely be "read" by a computer. That means you must be extremely precise and follow some specific stylistic rules to avoid its being misread or ignored. Second, there are security issues, since you never know who may be reading your resumé.

In using the Web for a job search, you need to cast your net widely. Although general interest job sites such as **www.canadajobs.com, www.jobbank.gc.ca, monster. ca,** and **careerbuilder.ca** post millions of jobs each year, there are more focused sites that can help you identify possible jobs in specific industries (see **Table 11.2**). In addition, most large companies post job openings on their own websites.

There are several general guidelines to follow when posting your resumé on an online employment site:

> ▸ Be very precise in the words you employ. For example, use action verbs and other words that are standard within an industry. Remember to check the NOC description for your desired job at the Working in Canada website.

Career Connections

Starting Over: Once You Have a Job You Want

What's the best time to start looking for a job? When you already have one and don't need to find a new one.

Even if you feel happy and secure in your job, it makes sense to be prepared for the unexpected. Perhaps you'll get a new boss you can't work well with, or your current job's activities and requirements change for the worse. Or maybe the company will downsize or be merged with another corporation, causing widespread layoffs.

For a variety of reasons, then, you'll want to keep your resumé and Career Portfolio updated, even if you've just started a new job. You will want to stay in contact with the people who have provided you with references in the past. Why not select the same time each year to make the updates and touch base with your references? This will ensure that you are always prepared for the next job search, no matter what happens.

Above all, take every opportunity to learn new skills. As the economy and technology change, you'll want to have cutting-edge skills that will allow you to compete effectively.

In short: Be prepared!

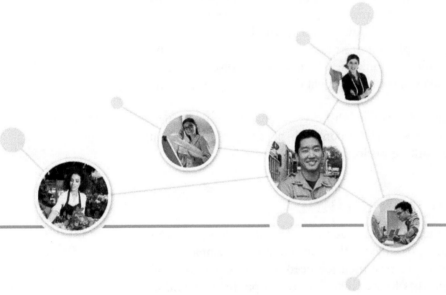

> Use simple font styles, such as Arial or Times New Roman.
> Avoid elaborate formatting, such as tabs or italics.
> Use a standard 80 characters per line.
> As always, proofread, proofread, proofread. A typographical error is more than embarrassing: Computers screening your resumé may reject your application before a human ever sees it because they do not recognize a misspelled word.

» LO 11.4 Job Interviews

For a potential employer who has never met you, a job interview puts a face to what has previously been an impression based on mere words written on a page. The interview is your chance to show who you are, to demonstrate your enthusiasm for a potential position, and to exhibit what you can bring to a position.

table 11.2　Finding the Right Site on the Web

Specific Sites

www.jobs.gc.ca	Jobs in the Canadian government
www.educationcanada.com	Teaching
www.cten.ca	Engineering technology & applied science
www.healthcarejob.ca	Health Care
http://www.pharmahorizons.com/	Pharmaceuticals
www.hrpa.ca/Pages/HireAuthority Canada.aspx	Human resources
www.techjobscanada.com/	Information technology
www.jobsinlaw.ca	Legal
www.aic.ca	Agriculture

The fact that interviews are so important may make them seem intimidating and overwhelming. However, remember that the fact that you've been invited to an interview means you've overcome some of the highest hurdles already. Furthermore, you can follow a variety of concrete strategies to ensure that you maximize the opportunity an interview presents.

Before the Interview

▸ **Learn about the potential employer.** It's important to learn as much as you can about the position and the company that is offering it. Go to the potential employer's website and find out as much as you can about the organization's management style and company culture. Then try to find magazine and newspaper articles to gain a sense of the success and effectiveness of the organization. The bottom line: If an interviewer asks, "What do you know about our organization?" be prepared to answer, "Quite a bit, because I've researched it thoroughly."

▸ **Prepare questions.** Come to the interview prepared with questions. Think up a set of questions and write them down so you can remember them—it's perfectly fine to refer to them during the interview. Having targeted questions shows that you've spent time thinking about the position. For a set of excellent questions to ask a potential employer, see the Web resources at the end of this chapter. By the way, don't ask about salary during the interview; salary issues are usually addressed if you get an actual job offer.

▸ **Prepare answers.** Finally, come prepared with answers to likely questions. For instance, it shouldn't be a surprise if an interviewer asks you to "tell me about yourself." So have an answer ready, a two- or three-minute response that touches on your career goals, your skills, your experiences, and your personality. Obviously, this is a lot to cover in just a few minutes, so practise it until you can do it comfortably within that short time frame. Going longer than three minutes runs the risk of boring your interviewer. Furthermore, don't just practise it by yourself. Have someone else listen to it and give you feedback.

Other favourite interview questions include these:

- ▸ "What are your major strengths and weaknesses?"
- ▸ "Why do you want to leave your current position?"
- ▸ "What are your major qualifications?"
- ▸ "What are your short-term and long-range goals?"
- ▸ "Why should I hire you?"

Although you can't prepare for every possible question in advance, thinking through some of the most likely possibilities will help you feel more confident and ready to deliver polished responses.

During the Interview

- ▸ **Be punctual.** Allow yourself enough time to arrive well ahead of the scheduled interview. That will help you find a parking space, locate the building and room, and compose yourself before the interview.

- ▸ **Dress appropriately.** Wear the right clothes for the interview. Stop by beforehand to see how people dress. If you're unsure of how formal to be, keep in mind that it's almost always better to be overdressed than to be underdressed. This is not the time to make a fashion statement. You want to look professional.

- ▸ **Use your social skills effectively.** Shake hands firmly, and look the interviewer in the eye. Show that you're interested in the interviewer as a fellow human being, not just as someone who might give you a job. Listen attentively to what he or she has to say, and be responsive. Above all, try to think confidently. Thinking positive, confident thoughts will help you appear positive and confident.

- ▸ **Be ready for their questions.** Sam Geist, a consultant based in Markham, Ontario, has developed a set of "Ten Key Questions" that are often posed by potential employers.[1] Before you head off to an interview, take time to reflect on your answers to these important questions:

1. What was your most challenging job? Why? What did you learn from this job?

2. What was your least challenging job? Why? What did you learn from this job?

3. In what situation did you find that you had to overcome major obstacles to meet your objectives? What did you do? Why? What did you learn from the experience?

4. Who do you admire most? Who do you admire least? Why?

5. In what situation did you attempt to do something, but failed? Why did you fail? What did you learn from this situation?

6. Describe a bad experience that happened to you. What did you learn from it?

7. Describe a situation where you tried to help someone change. What strategy did you use? How did the situation end?

8. Describe a mistake you made in dealing with people. What did you learn from it?

9. What was your best learning experience? What was your worst learning experience? What did you learn from each of them?

10. Describe the last major change you made. Why did you do it? How did it work out? What did you learn?

> **Ask questions.** If you have prepared for the interview, you've got some questions to ask about the organization from which you are seeking employment. Be sure to ask them. Interviewers almost always ask if you have any questions; but if they don't, try to work them in when you sense that the interview is almost over. It's also a good idea to ask about the hiring process the employer is using. Ask how long it will be before they will be making a decision and when you can expect to hear from them again.

> **Above all, be yourself and be honest.** You do yourself no favour by pretending to be someone other than who you are. Getting a job under false pretenses virtually guarantees that neither you nor your employer ultimately will be satisfied with your job performance. You may end up doing things you don't like to do and may not be very good at, and neither you nor your employer will find that acceptable for very long. (To get experience dealing with interview questions, complete **Try It! 4**, "Interviewing," on page 292.)

After the Interview

> **Evaluate your interview performance.** Are you pleased with how you presented yourself in the interview? What did you do particularly well? What things could you have done better?

Jot down your impressions of the interview while they're still fresh in your mind and place them in your Career Portfolio. These notes will be valuable when you prepare for future interviews.

> **Consider if you still want the position.** Suppose, for a moment, you were actually offered the job. Do you really want it?

It's important to ask yourself whether, given what you learned about the position, you would accept it if it were offered to you. You probably found out things about the position that interested you, and others that may be worrisome. Evaluate the job; and if there are too many serious negatives, rethink whether you should accept it.

Unless there are so many negatives that you're certain that under no circumstances would you take the job, don't withdraw your application. It may be that if you are offered the job, you could negotiate with your potential employer to eliminate the factors that you find undesirable.

> **Write a thank-you note.** It's common courtesy to send a note to the person who interviewed you, thanking that person for his or her time.

It's also strategically important. It shows that you are polite and can be counted on to do the right thing. It demonstrates your interest in the job. And it gives you one more opportunity to show you have the "right stuff."

Although you shouldn't turn your thank-you note into a sales pitch, do indicate your continued interest in the position. Write about the aspects of the job that were of particular interest to you and explain how you can see yourself fitting in well with the company. Should you send the note by email? Probably not. It's not likely to stand out, whereas a mailed note likely will.

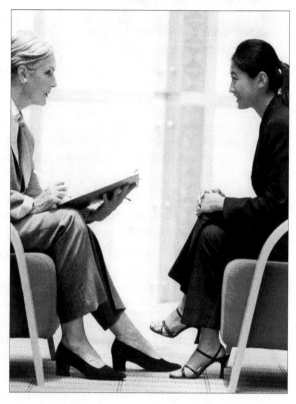

Interviews can be a nerve-wracking experience, but preparation and a cool-headed approach can make all the difference. Don't forget that you are interviewing a potential employer, as well as being interviewed as a potential employee!

"It is not our abilities that show what we truly are; it is our choices."

Professor Dumbledore, in the 2002 film *Harry Potter and the Chamber of Secrets*

Interviewing

Nothing will prepare you better for an upcoming interview than a number of prior interviews. To get practice interviewing, ask an instructor, a person who has had experience in hiring, or even a fellow student, to role-play an interview with you in which they will interview you, the potential job applicant. Prepare for your role carefully and treat the practice interview seriously.

Follow these steps:

- Choose a company or organization that you would like to work for, and provide the person who will interview you with some details about it, such as information from the company website.

- You should also research your chosen company as a potential interviewee would, to gain enough knowledge to answer potential interview questions well.

- Hold the interview. You should be serious and try to play your role well. If you like, you can "dress the part" to help you set the right tone. You may also want to tape-record the session.

- After you've concluded the interview, ask your interviewer for a critique of your performance. Ask the interviewer to make as candid a judgment as he or she can as to which category you would fit into based solely on the interview: (a) Make a job offer; (b) Don't make a job offer; or (c) Call back for another interview to follow up with additional questions.

After you've completed the steps outlined above, answer the following questions:

1. What did you learn from the interview?

2. Critically assess your performance as an interviewee. What was your greatest strength as an interviewee? Your greatest weakness?

3. What would you do differently during an actual interview?

4. How can you better prepare for an actual interview in the future?

To Try It online, go to Connect for *P.O.W.E.R. Learning and Your Life.*

- **Keep records.** Maintain a folder for each potential employer. In this folder, put the results of your research on the employer, business cards of people who've interviewed you, notes you've made following an interview, and any communication either sent or received.

- **Follow up.** If you haven't heard from the employer in a few weeks, and it's past the point where you were told you'd be contacted, it's perfectly reasonable to email or call. The purpose is not to badger the employer into hiring you—that's not going to work—but simply to check up on where the process stands. Of course, it also serves another purpose: to remind a potential employer of your continued interest in the position. You can also use the opportunity to provide additional information or to tell the employer of another job offer.

LO 11.5 Moving Your Career Forward and Striving Styles

Too often students try to figure out what they want to do with their education and career without seeking to understand themselves. While it is true that for some people this knowing comes easy, for most it does not. Seeking to understand what you are meant to do after college or university starts by understanding who you are meant to be. The idea of investing several years of your life in study only to find that the work you have studied for has no intrinsic value or reward for you is a depressing thought. That's why so many young people struggle to make this decision. As already discussed in Chapter 1, the Striving Styles Personality System (SSPS) offers you a way to make this decision knowing that what you are choosing is aligned with your intrinsic needs.

No matter what you want to study or which diploma or degree you want to pursue, how your personality is organized influences how you go about doing this. The Striving Styles Personality Assessment helps you understand how to best approach learning by identifying your Striving Style and the predominant need that must be met in order for you to feel confident and secure. Students often find it difficult to adapt their learning style to fit the standardized way they are expected to learn. The SSPS helps them understand why and the adjustments they have to make to keep them on track.

Understanding and accepting your Striving Style is the first step on the path to self-actualization. The resources available on the Striving Styles website at **http://strivingstyles.com** allow you to deepen your understanding of your striving energy and how you can best use it to self-actualize. It also provides you with specific tips to help you emerge from "survival mode," as well as strategies to pursue for maintaining self-awareness and sustaining forward movement in your development. It will show you how to continue growing and prospering by fulfilling the intrinsic needs of your predominant Striving Style.

As you move forward, we encourage you to further explore your Striving Style in different aspects of your life as well as to learn more about the Striving Styles of others (partners, children, co-workers, family members, etc.)[2]

1. **Take the online Striving Styles Personality Assessment–Level I**

   A more in-depth tool than the quiz you completed in Chapter 1, this provides greater validity around your results and provides you with the ability to order customized or comparison reports. The assessment takes approximately 15 minutes and costs $25 including a 2-page summary report on your style. More detailed reports are also available.

2. **General Report**

   This 32-page report provides a comprehensive overview of your Striving Style as well as valuable descriptions of each of the eight styles. In addition to general information about your Style, the report includes information on how people of your Style behave when self-actualizing as opposed to self-protecting; how you can get your predominant needs met in leisure, in relationships, and at work; situations that push your Style into self-protective behaviour; and a roadmap for personal development based on your Style.

3. **Book an Interpretation Session**

   Learn more about your Striving Style and how to self-actualize in your own life through an individual interpretation session with a SSPS Coach. Conducted over the phone, the interpretation sessions provide you with the opportunity to ask questions about your style and how it relates to your experiences and challenges whether they're related to career, school, relationships, or parenting.

4. **Book an Interpretation Session—Deciding on Your Major**

   Learn more about your Striving Style and how to choose your college or university major to ensure you are selecting something that will meet your predominant need. Conducted over the phone, this session provides you with the opportunity to discuss the need of your style and different educational paths that can help you become the person you are meant to be.

5. **Striving Styles Career Report**

   Find the career you were meant to have. This 15-page report includes specific information on the predominant needs that must be met at work in order for you and other people of your Style to feel satisfied and achieve your potential. The report includes general information on your work style, your strengths and challenges, the best careers and work environments for your style, tips for managing your career, and much more.

6. **Book an Interpretation Session—Career Planning Session**

   Learn more about your Striving Style and how to choose the career that will provide opportunities to meet your predominant need. Conducted over the phone, this session provides you with the opportunity to discuss the need of your Style and different career paths that can help you become the person you are meant to be.

7. **Comparison Report**

   Want to know how your Style compares to someone else's? Want to understand the differences and similarities between your styles in order to improve communication, reduce conflict, and strengthen your relationships?

8. **Striving Styles Coaching Sessions**

   It often takes more than one session to build self-awareness and make important decisions around education and careers. Using the Striving Styles Framework, the coach focuses on removing barriers to decision-making, increasing emotional self-awareness, and shifting to self-actualizing behaviours. These sessions can be conducted in person or over the phone.

9. **Become a Striving Styles Member**

   Gain access to complimentary resources, webinars, and discounts on products, workshops, and assessments. Participate in discussions about your Style. Receive tips and tools to support you to put your knowledge about your predominant need and the needs of others to work for you.

   Visit **http://strivingstyles.com** for many more resources available to help you on your path to self-actualization and to realizing your potential.

Time to Reflect: What Did I Learn?

1. Generally speaking, do you see work as something you must do in order to earn a living, or as something that is a central and important aspect of life, in and of itself? Why is that?

2. Thinking for a moment about your future career, how important is variety in what you do? How important is stability in what you do? What impact do your answers to these questions have on the type of jobs you choose?

3. Based on what you learned about careers in this chapter, what steps can you to take now to ensure that you find work that fulfils you?

Looking Back

How do I identify my ideal job?

- Careful and systematic research is the key to identifying possible career options.
- Know yourself, and match your job searches with your personality and your career goals.
- Books, websites, and informational interviews provide useful information about careers.

What is a Career Portfolio, and why is it important?

- A Career Portfolio can document your skills, capabilities, achievements, and goals, as well as provide a place to keep notes and research findings relating to jobs. It also includes your resumé and cover letter.
- A Career Portfolio helps you to prepare systematically for a job search, and it also ensures that you have all the necessary materials available should you become aware of a job opportunity.

What are the best strategies for finding and getting a job?

- It is important to find appropriate references.
- The Internet provides substantial information about potential jobs and companies, and it can also play an important role in getting a job.
- Network, network, network.

How can I maximize my job interviewing skills?

- Job interviews require a significant amount of preparation.
- Useful interview strategies include being punctual, dressing appropriately, using social skills effectively, asking questions, being yourself, and being honest.
- After an interview, send a thank-you note to the interviewer.

How does my striving style affect my career choices?

- It is important to know yourself well in order to find a career that will satisfy you throughout your life. Understanding yourself and your predominant need will lead you toward the career or careers in which you will feel confident and secure.

[KEY TERM AND CONCEPT]

Career Portfolio   (p. 273)

[RESOURCES]

ON CAMPUS

Your campus almost certainly has an office devoted to career planning. In addition, your college or university library, as well as any public library, will have books that can help you research careers and find a job.

IN PRINT

There are thousands of books that can help you with career planning. One classic is Richard Bolles's *What Color Is Your Parachute?* (Ten Speed Press, 2011), which comes out in a new edition almost every year.

Another useful guide is Frank Satterthwaite and Gary D'Orsi's *The Career Portfolio Workbook* (McGraw-Hill, 2003), which guides you through the process of building a career portfolio.

Acing the Interview: How to Ask and Answer Questions that Will Get You the Job (AMACOM, 2008) offers a variety of pointers to help you prepare for interviews more effectively. And on the same topic, you'll want to read H. Anthony Medley's classic book on interviewing. It's appropriately called *Sweaty Palms: The Neglected Art of Being Interviewed* (Warner Business Books, 2005) and was the first book of its kind to look at interviewing from the perspective of the person being interviewed.

For something altogether different, check out *The Adventures of Johnny Bunko: The Last Career Guide You'll Ever Need* by author Daniel Pink and illustrator Rob Ten Pas. It is a career guide in manga format.

ON THE WEB

The following websites provide the opportunity to extend your learning about the material in this chapter.

> At **www.jobbank.gc.ca**, you'll find a number of tools and resources to help you plan your career, including a Career Navigator, quizzes, and a Blueprint for Life/Work Design.

> Welcome to Resumania (**www.resumania.com/**)—a fun but practical look at those things you shouldn't put into a resumé. The term "Resumania" was coined by Robert Half, founder of the specialized staffing firm Robert Half International Inc. (RHI), to describe errors made by job seekers on resumés, applications, and cover letters.

> The Career Resources section of the Workopolis website at **www.workopolis.com** provides dozens of tips on various topics, including resumé writing, interviewing, networking, and negotiating.

> For questions that *you* might want to ask an interviewer, take a look at **www. workforce.com/section/recruiting-staffing/article/200-questions-job-candidates-may-ask-your-company.html**.

> Because every profession or job requires a different type of resumé, for samples from your field of interest, we suggest you go to Google and type in "best resumé samples" along with your field; e.g. dental hygiene, psychology, etc. Look for best practices in the resumés that you uncover.

TAKING IT TO THE NET

1 Use the Internet to identify two companies that you would be interested in working for (e.g., using **www.monster.ca** or the HotJobs section of **www.yahoo.ca**). Find out what you can about the companies, trying to go beyond the public relations statements that you will find on their websites. Write down your impressions about such features as their location, current financial situation, history, work setting and atmosphere, dress code, and benefits, as well as your need for prior experience in the field, your chances for advancement, and anything else of interest to you. Note similarities and differences between the two companies. Can you tell enough about the two companies to prefer one over the other? Would your preparation for an interview with each company be different? (Remember to put your research findings in your Career Portfolio.)

2 Explore at least two websites that offer advice about interviewing. See if you can find sample questions that are often asked at interviews (including both traditional questions and brainteasers), tips on what to do and what not to do at an interview, hints for making a good impression and improving your chances of success, and other advice. Write down the names of the websites you found helpful and take notes on the advice they offer. (Remember to put your research findings in your Career Portfolio.)

The Case of . . .

Interviewophobia

Jayden had found his dream job.

A few weeks before finishing college to get his degree in Physical Education, he found an online job posting for an entry-level training job with the professional basketball team that played in his area. Jayden had long been a fan of the team. The salary and benefits were excellent. The facility where the team trained was only ten minutes from Jayden's house. In short, the job was perfect; and Jayden was thrilled when, a week after submitting his resumé, he received a call about scheduling an interview.

But then Jayden started to get nervous. He had failed miserably at the only job interview he had ever had, for a sales position at a retail company after he finished high school. He'd actually gotten into an argument with his interviewer. What if the interview for the fitness trainer position went just as poorly?

Other worries started creeping into Jayden's mind. What if the interviewer asked questions about Jayden's limited training experience? What if Jayden forgot to mention the key experiences on his resumé? What if he wore the wrong clothes?

As the interview approached, Jayden went from excited to terrified. He was certain he would blow the interview. So much for my dream job, he thought.

1. What advice would you give Jayden? How is this interview different from the one he experienced just after finishing high school?

2. What steps could Jayden take to prepare himself for the interview? How could he build his confidence?

3. What could Jayden do to prepare for questions about his work experience?

4. What tactics could Jayden employ to make sure the interview remains cordial?

8 Making Decisions and Solving Problems

Learning Outcomes

By the time you finish this chapter, you will be able to

>> LO **8.1**   Outline a framework for decision-making.

>> LO **8.2**   Discuss how critical thinking can be applied to the problem-solving process.

>> LO **8.3**   Apply critical thinking to everyday problems.

Bayani Soriano had a tough decision coming up. In three weeks, he would earn his Construction Engineering Technician diploma. It had taken a great deal of effort and the sacrifice of a lot of free time, but he was almost there. It was what to do next, though, that was giving Bayani problems.

All through college, he had worked for a local contractor, picking up construction jobs when the contractor needed an extra pair of hands. Now that Bayani was graduating as a construction engineering technician, the contractor had offered to make him a permanent member of his construction crew. In short, he was being offered more work at a better salary.

Bayani knew it was a great offer—but it was not his only option. A friend he had met in college wanted to start his own house inspection business, and he wanted Bayani to be his partner. Working together, Bayani's friend said, they could build the business quickly; and they would earn more and have more flexibility than if they worked for someone else.

As graduation approached, Bayani knew he had to make up his mind. But he kept going around in circles. Was security more important than flexibility? How much was running his own business worth to him?

Bayani knew he had to make up his mind. But how?

Looking Ahead

Like Bayani, all of us face important life decisions at one time or another. How can we make the right decisions? The best way is to employ some basic techniques that can help improve the quality of our decision-making.

This chapter gives you a sense of what decision-making is and is not, and it discusses a structured process that can help make your decisions the right ones. But what happens when you make the wrong decision? That's where problem-solving skills come into play. Most students confront a variety of problems as they proceed through college or university and throughout their career. In this chapter, we'll look at a number of proven techniques that will help you find solutions to the problems you might face. We'll also examine some common problems that can affect our thinking and discuss several biases that can make us jump to the wrong conclusions.

≫ LO 8.1 Making Better Decisions: A Framework

Neither making decisions nor solving problems is easy. Sometimes the best decision or solution to a problem is one that we don't see at first; we all have mental blind spots. The best problem-solvers and decision-makers have learned how to use critical thinking to see around these blind spots. To use Robert Ennis's classic definition, "critical thinking is reasonable, reflective thinking that is focused on deciding what to believe or do."[1] In other words, it is the ability to reflect on your views and opinions about the world around you and on what gave rise to these views; i.e., *why* you think the way you do.

Decision-making is the process of deciding among various alternatives. Whether you are trying to decide between a Ford and a Honda, between an apartment that is close to your job and one that is close to family, or simply between a hamburger and a pizza, every choice requires a decision. Some decisions are easily made and have few consequences; but others, such as whether to take one job or another, can involve the deepest examination of our beliefs and values.

Whatever you're deciding, you need to think critically in order to make a reasoned decision. You need to actively apply your past knowledge, synthesize and evaluate alternatives, and reason and reflect on a course of action. The greater your depth of thinking about the components of the decision, the more likely it is that you'll come up with the best choice.

To make a good decision, map out a strategy for making the choice that is best for you. Every decision can benefit from your thinking systematically through the options involved, based on the P.O.W.E.R. Plan illustrated here.

Decision-making

The process of deciding among various alternatives

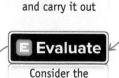

P.O.W.E.R. Plan

Prepare — Examine Your Goals

Every decision starts with the end you have in mind: the goals you wish to accomplish by making the decision.

For example, suppose you are trying to decide on something as simple as where to sit in a classroom. Your long-term goal is to make the Dean's List. You know that sitting near the front of the room means you'll probably pay attention more, the teacher will get to know who you are, and it will be easier to ask or answer questions. On the other hand, sitting at the back means you can sit with your friends; and if the class gets boring, you can text without the teacher noticing. Also, if you are at the back, it's unlikely that the teacher will call on you to answer questions. Your seat selection must be seen in light of your long-term goal: doing well enough to make the Dean's List. Where you sit in each classroom will very likely have an impact on your grade in each course; the closer you sit to the front, the more likely you will be able to reach your goal.

In short, every decision should start with a consideration of what our short- and long-term goals are. Identifying the goals that underlie decisions ensures that we make decisions in the context of our entire lives and not just to provide short-term answers to immediate problems.

Consider and Assess Your Alternatives

Identifying Alternatives

Making a decision requires weighing various alternatives. Determining what those alternatives are, and their possible consequences, is often the most difficult part of decision-making. It's important not only to think thoroughly about the obvious alternatives, but also to consider alternatives that are less obvious. For many decisions, there are choices beyond the "this or that" alternatives that can dominate our thinking. How can you be sure that you've considered all the possible alternatives? Do your research. What have others done in a similar situation? Investigate, either through reading about the life journeys of others in your situation, or by interviewing them personally.

There are also more creative approaches to identifying alternatives that you may wish to consider. If you have a visual/graphic learning style, you might want to use the mind mapping technique introduced in Chapter 7. If your learning style leans more towards read/write, using a technique called freewriting may be the best way to go.

In **freewriting,** you write continuously for a fixed period of time, perhaps five or ten minutes. During this period, the idea is to write as many different ideas as possible, without stopping. It makes no difference whether the alternatives are good or bad or even whether they make sense. All that matters is that you let yourself brainstorm about the topic for a while and get the ideas down on paper.

With freewriting, evaluating the worth of the ideas you've generated comes later. After you have produced as many possibilities as you can, then you go back and sift out the reasonable ones from those that are unlikely or just plain wacky. It's OK if you have to delete quite a few alternatives from your list; the process is likely to have liberated some reasonable alternatives that you might not otherwise have come up with. (Try this technique in **Try It! 1**, "Use Freewriting," on page 194.)

Freewriting
A technique involving continuous writing, without self-criticism, for a fixed period of time

Assessing Alternatives

Once you have generated as extensive a list of alternatives as possible, assess them. You need to follow three key steps when assessing each alternative:

> "Nothing is more difficult, and therefore more precious, than to be able to decide."
>
> **Napoleon I, *Maxims*, 1804–15**

1. **Determine the possible outcomes for each alternative.** Some outcomes are positive, some negative. Consider as many as you can think of. For example, if you are considering ways of solving transportation problems, one alternative might be to purchase a car. That alternative produces several potential outcomes. For example, you know that it will be easier to get wherever you want to go, and you might even have a

Try It!

Use Freewriting

Part A: Use freewriting to think of as many answers as you can to each of the following questions. The ground rules are that you should spend three minutes on each question, generating as many ideas as possible—regardless of whether they are feasible. To give yourself maximum freedom, write each answer on a separate sheet of paper.

1. How can you make room in your schedule to take one more course next term than you're taking this term?

2. Thinking about past relationships, what will you look for in future partners?

3. How can you make some extra money while going to school full-time?

4. What activities can you participate in while in school that will make your resumé more attractive to potential employers?

Part B: After generating ideas, go back and evaluate them.

1. How many were actually feasible?

2. Do you think freewriting led to the production of more or fewer ideas than you would have come up with if you hadn't used the technique?

3. Did the quality of ideas change?

 WORKING IN A GROUP

After you have answered the questions above, form a group and compare your answers with those of others in your group. As a group, try to identify the best answers to each question.

To Try It online, go to Connect for *P.O.W.E.R. Learning and Your Life.*

---

better social life—clearly positive outcomes. But it is also true that buying and owning a car will be expensive, and that it may be difficult to find convenient parking—both significant negative outcomes.

2. **Determine the probability that those outcomes will take place.** Some outcomes are far more likely than others. To take this into account, make a rough estimate of the likelihood that an outcome will come to pass, ranging from 100 percent (you are certain that it will occur) to 0 percent (you are certain that it will never occur). Obviously, the probabilities are just guesses, but going through the exercise of estimating them will make the outcomes more real and will permit you to compare the various alternatives against one another more easily.

3. **Compare the alternatives, taking into account the potential outcomes of each.** Systematically compare each of the alternatives. A simple pro/con list like the one shown in **Figure 8.1**, which examines the decision to get a tattoo, can help you make this comparison. Then ask yourself the key question: Which alternative, on balance, provides the most positive (and most likely) outcomes?

The Pros & Cons of Getting a Tattoo

figure 8.1
Creating a list of pros and cons can help you make a better decision.

Pros

1. It expresses my individuality

2. It would represent something special to me

3. My friends all have one

4. It's the style these days to have a tattoo

5. I think tattoos can be really pretty

6. My style icon, Lady Gaga, has several

Cons

1. My parents would be angry

2. It's expensive to remove

3. I don't like needles or pain

4. There's a risk of infection

5. Will it still look good when I'm 60?

6. It might not look good if I'm in a wedding dress or business attire

Obviously, not every decision requires such an elaborate process. In fact, most won't. But when it comes to major decisions, those that could have a large impact upon you and your life, it's worthwhile to follow a systematic process.

Take a look at **Career Connections** on page 197 for another process that you can follow to help you make a career decision.

Make Your Decision and Carry It Out

Working through the previous steps will lead you to the point of decision: choosing one of the alternatives you've identified. Having carried out the steps will make the actual decision easier, but not necessarily easy.

Choosing among Alternatives

The reason that important decisions are difficult is that the alternatives you have to choose from carry both benefits and costs. Choosing one alternative means that you have to accept the costs of that choice and give up the benefits of the other alternatives. A decision can also mean a "fork in the road": One decision can lead to a number of other decisions; and as you become more and more committed, you find it almost impossible to go backwards. A graphic representation of that process is captured by what is called a "decision tree." Examine the decision tree in **Figure 8.2,** which shows a person who has already taken a fork in the road by deciding to get a tattoo. Now they must decide what the subject of that tattoo should be. They are torn between a text-based tattoo (either a song lyric or a line from a poem) or an illustration of a fish (goldfish or dolphin) or a flower (tulip or rose). As they move through the decision process, they compare one alternative against the other, narrowing their preference down each time and finally coming to the

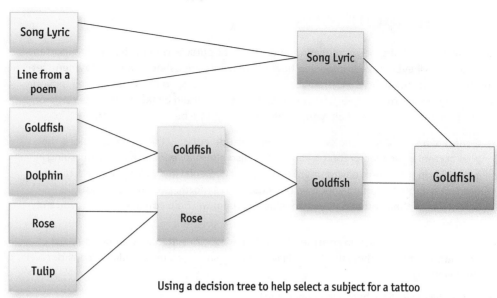

figure 8.2
Developing a decision tree can help you select among a set of alternatives.

Using a decision tree to help select a subject for a tattoo

conclusion that they will get a tattoo of a goldfish. While this decision tree is rather simple, consider what a similar tree might look like as you try to choose between five or six majors at college or university.

What if, after going through the steps of the process laid out here, you still can't make up your mind? Try these strategies:

> **Give the decision some time.** Sometimes waiting helps. Time can give you a chance to think of additional alternatives. Sometimes the situation will change, or you'll have a change in viewpoint.

> **Make a mental movie, acting out the various alternatives.** Many of us have difficulty seeing ourselves in the future and envisioning how various options would play out. One way to get around this difficulty is to cast yourself into a series of "mental movies" that have different endings depending on the decision you make. Working through the different scripts in your head makes potential outcomes far more real and less abstract than they would be if you simply left them as items on a list of various options.

> **Toss a coin.** This isn't as crazy as it sounds. If each alternative seems equally positive or negative to you, pull out a coin—make option A "heads" and B "tails." Then flip it.

> The real power of the coin-toss strategy is that it might help you discover your true feelings. It may happen while the coin is in the air, or it may be that when you see the result of the coin toss, you won't like the outcome and will say to yourself, "No way." In such a case, you've just found out how you really feel.

> **Ask for advice.** Although Western society teaches the virtues of rugged individualism, asking others for their advice is often an excellent strategy. Friends, instructors, parents, or a counsellor can provide helpful recommendations— sometimes because they've had to make similar decisions themselves. You don't have to take their advice, but it can help to listen to what they have to say.

> **Go with your gut feeling.** Call it what you like—gut feeling, intuition, hunch, superstition—but sometimes we need to go with our hearts and not our minds. If you've thought rationally about a decision and have been unable to

From the perspective of . . .

A STUDENT Balancing education and other aspects of life can be fraught with many alternatives and choices. How do you prioritize options when making a decision?

Weighing Options

After choosing what type of education and career to pursue, one of the most important decisions you'll ever make is choosing how to apply this education in an employment setting that will stimulate you and that you will enjoy. Your long-term goals, as well as your personality, your striving style, and your learning style, should all factor into this decision. Here's one method that can help you decide what might be best suited to you:

- Generate a selection of choices to consider. Include not only the obvious options that your current education prepares you for, but also alternative ideas such as pursuing a position in a different environment (e.g., dental hygienist in a public health setting), earning a degree, starting your own business, and so forth. Even if you doubt you'll select one of these other options, considering them will help you assess what you truly want to do.

- Determine life-satisfaction considerations that are important to you. Generate a list of criteria to use in weighing the possibilities. For instance, you might want to consider the following:

  Benefits (vacation, health insurance, etc.)
  Salary
  Spouse's opinion
  Friends' opinions
  Interest in the activity
  Prestige
  Job security
  Flexible hours
  Benefit to society
  Practicality/attainability
  Everyday working conditions
  Clients you will be working with
  Opportunities to learn
  Opportunities to travel

- Determine how well a particular option fulfills each of the life-satisfaction factors you consider important. By systematically considering how a potential path fulfills each of the criteria you use, you'll be able to compare different options. One easy way to do this is to create a chart like the one in **Table 8.1,** which shows an example of how job options for a massage therapist might fulfill the various criteria, using a scale of 1-10, where 1 means worst and 10 means best.

- Compare different choices. Using the chart, evaluate your possibilities. Keep in mind that this is just a rough guide and that it's only as accurate as (a) the effort you put into completing it and (b) your understanding of a given choice. Use the results in conjunction with other things you find out about the jobs—and yourself.

table 8.1	Making Career Decisions		
Life-satisfaction considerations on a scale of 1-10	**Massage therapist at a local spa**	**Sports massage therapist at a university**	**Massage therapist on a cruise ship**
Benefits	4	8	5
Income	8	7	5
Spouse's opinion	8	6	1
Friends' opinions	4	7	7
Interest in the activity	5	6	8
Prestige	5	9	7
Job security	4	7	5
Flexible hours	8	5	6
Benefit to society	6	8	6
Practicality/attainability	9	4	2
Everyday working conditions	7	8	6
Clients you will be working with	5	7	8
Opportunity to learn	3	8	5
Opportunity to travel	1	5	10
Other			
Total	**77**	**95**	**81**

If all else fails, toss a coin to decide what alternative to follow. Tossing a coin at least brings you to a decision. Then, if you find you're unhappy with the result, you'll have gained important information about how you really feel regarding a particular choice.

determine the best course of action but have a gut feeling that one choice is better than another, follow your feelings.

Following a gut feeling does not mean that you don't need to consider the pros and cons of a decision rationally and carefully. In fact, generally our "intuition" is best when informed by the thoughtfulness of a more rational process.

Carrying Out the Decision

Ultimately, decisions must move from thought to action—they have to be carried out. Consequently, the final stage in making a decision is to act upon it. You need to turn your decision into behaviour.

 **Evaluate** Consider the Outcome

Did you make the right decision?

Even if you've spent time and mental effort in thinking through a decision, you still need to consider the results. Even well-considered decisions can end up being wrong, either because you neglected to consider an alternative or because something has changed: either you or the situation.

Remember, it's never too late to change your mind. In fact, even major life decisions are often reversible. That's why it's so important to evaluate your choices. If you chose the wrong alternative, reverse course and reconsider your options.

It's not a bad thing to change your mind. In fact, admitting that a decision was a mistake is often the wisest and most courageous course of action. You don't want to be so rigidly committed to a decision that you're unable to evaluate the consequences objectively. Give yourself permission to be wrong.

> "In any moment of decision, the best thing you can do is the right thing, the next best thing is the wrong thing, and the worst thing you can do is nothing."
> **President Theodore Roosevelt**

 **Rethink**

Reconsider Your Goals and Options

We can get to most places by multiple routes. There's the fastest and most direct route, which will get us to our destination in the smallest amount of time. Then there's the longer, more scenic route, where the trip itself provides pleasure. You can "take the long way home," as the song goes. Is one route better than the other? Often not. Both take us to our destination. How-ever, the experience of reaching our goal will have been very different.

Decisions about how to achieve a goal are similar to travelling down different routes. There's often no single decision that is best, just as there's often no single road to a particular place. Consequently, it's important now and then to reconsider the major decisions that we've made about our lives.

Ask yourself these questions:

> Are my decisions still producing the desired consequences?

> Are my decisions still appropriate, given my circumstances and changes in my life?

> Are my decisions consistent with what I want to get out of life?

Periodically taking stock like this is the best way to make sure that your decisions are taking you where you want to go. Taking stock also helps you to be more effective in making future decisions.

»LO 8.2 Problem-Solving: Applying Critical Thinking to Find Solutions

Two trains are approaching one another, each moving at 60 miles an hour. If the trains continue moving at the same speed, how long will it be before . . .

Problem-solving
The mental activity involved in generating a set of alternative courses of action to enhance decision-making

If this is what comes to mind when you think of problem-solving, think again. **Problem-solving** encompasses more than the abstract, often unrealistic situations portrayed in math texts. It involves everyday, commonplace situations: How do we divide the restaurant bill so that each person pays a fair share? How do I keep my 1-year-old from tumbling down the stairs when there seems to be no way to fasten a gate at the top? How can I stop a faucet from dripping? How do I manage to study for a test and do the laundry the same evening?

While decision-making is most focused on choosing among various alternatives, the central issue in problem-solving is generating alternatives. Since many problems require that decisions be made regarding alternatives, decision-making and problem-solving are related.

What's the Problem?

The first step in solving any problem is to be as clear as you can about what the problem is. This may sound easy, but often it isn't. In fact, it may take some time to figure out just what is at stake. Some problems, such as mathematical equations or the solution to a jigsaw puzzle, are quite precise. Determining how to stop terrorism or finding peace in the Middle East, on the other hand, are big, ill-defined problems. Simply determining what information is required to solve such problems can be a major undertaking.

To determine what the problem is and set yourself on a course for finding a solution, ask yourself these questions:

> What is the initial set of facts?

> What is it that I need to solve? Which parts of the problem am I actually able to solve?

> Which parts of the problem appear to be most critical to finding a solution?

> Is there some information that can be ignored?

> "Problems are only opportunities in work clothes."

Henry J. Kaiser (1882–1967), entrepreneur, *Maxim*

The more systematically you approach a problem, the better. For instance, you can apply the five P.O.W.E.R. steps to problems, similar to the way you can apply them to making decisions. When you consider a problem systematically and think through your options, your choices will become clearer to you.

As you clarify what the problem is, you may find that you have encountered similar problems before. Your experience may suggest the means to the solution of the current problem. For example, consider the problem of the trains rushing toward each other. If you have worked on this kind of problem before, you might know a fairly simple equation you can write to determine how long it will take before they meet. If someone asks you about the problem she has in keeping her toddler from tumbling down the stairs, you might offer your experience in keeping your own children from visiting an off-limits area of your house.

On the other hand, to solve many of the problems we face in our daily lives, we have to do more than reach into our memories of prior situations. Instead, we need to devise novel approaches. How do you do this? There are several strategies you might use.

Strategies for Solving Life's Messier Problems

> **Break the problem down into smaller, more manageable pieces, a process called "chunking."** Divide a problem into a series of sub-goals. As you reach

each sub-goal, you get closer to your overall goal of solving the problem. For example, if your goal is to find a job in Montreal, a sub-goal should be to learn French. By reaching this sub-goal, you move closer to reaching your ultimate goal—a job in a city that interests you.

> **Work backward.** Sometimes you know the answer to the problem, but not how to get there. Then it's best to work backward. A workback strategy starts at the desired solution or goal and works backward, moving away from the goal. For example, if you have a project due in eight weeks, and you aren't sure how to start it, you might imagine the end result—the finished project—and then work backward to consider how to prepare it.

> **Use a graph, chart, or drawing to redefine the problem.** Transforming words into pictures often can help you to devise solutions that otherwise would elude us. For ideas on how drawing pictures can help you solve problems, you'll want to take a look at the international best-seller *The Back of the Napkin: Solving Problems and Selling Ideas with Pictures*, as well as author Dan Roam's website **www.thebackofthenapkin.com.**

> **Consider the opposite.** You can sometimes solve problems by considering the opposite of the problem you're seeking to solve. For example, to define "good mental health," you might try to define "bad mental health."

> **Use analogies.** Some problems can be solved through the use of an **analogy,** which is a comparison between concepts or objects that are alike in some respects, but dissimilar in most others. For instance, if you liken a disastrous family vacation to a voyage on the *Titanic,* you're using an analogy.
>
> Analogies may help us gain additional insight into the problem at hand, and they may provide an alternative framework for interpreting the information that is provided. For instance, the manufacturers of Pringles potato chips found that they could cut packaging costs if they slightly moistened the chips before packaging them—an idea that came when researchers noticed that dry tree leaves, which normally crumble easily, could be packed together tightly when they were wet.

> **Take another's perspective.** By viewing a problem from another person's point of view, it is often possible to obtain a new perspective on the problem that will make it easier to solve.

> **Forget about it.** Sometimes it's best simply to walk away from a problem for a while. Just a few hours or days away from a problem may give us enough of a break to jar some hidden solutions from the recesses of our minds. The idea of "sleeping on it" also sometimes works; we may wake up refreshed and filled with new ideas.

> **Approach it in the spirit of "trial and error."** Whether you are solving a problem or making a decision, recognize that what you choose to do is often reversible. You can "dip your toe in," by volunteering part-time in a field that interests you. If it doesn't turn out the way you expected, you can always change gears later. If you research the requirements in advance, you can even try out a "major" in English, and later switch to Psychology, without losing credits towards your degree.

> **Recognize that NOT making a decision IS making a decision.** Keeping things as they are is as much a decision as choosing to change them, and the status quo can sometimes be a viable alternative. But don't let inaction be the result of procrastination, of letting time slip away without making a decision. Let it be a *true* choice.

Analogy

A comparison between concepts or objects that are alike in some respects but dissimilar in most others

2

Exercise Your Problem-solving Skills

Part A: Working in a group, try to solve these problems.[2] To help you devise solutions, a hint regarding the best strategy to use is included after each problem.

1. A college student has a flat tire on a dark, deserted stretch of country road. He pulls onto the shoulder to change it. After removing the four lug nuts and placing them into the hubcap, he removes the flat tire and takes his spare out of the trunk. As he is moving the spare tire into position, his hand slips and he upsets the hubcap with the lug nuts, which tumble off into the night where he can't find them. What should he do? (*Hint:* Instead of asking how he might find the lug nuts, reframe the problem and ask where else he might find lug nuts.)

2. A construction worker is paving a walk, and needs to add water quickly to the just-poured concrete. She reaches for her pail to get water from a spigot in the front of the house, but suddenly realizes the pail has a large hole in it and cannot be used. As the concrete dries prematurely, she fumbles through her toolbox for tools and materials with which to repair the pail. She finds many tools, but nothing that would serve to patch the pail. The house is locked, and no one is home. What should she do? (*Hint:* When is a pail not a pail?)

3. What day follows the day before yesterday if two days from now will be Sunday? (*Hint:* Break it up, or draw a diagram.)

4. Sadia has four chains, each three links long. She wants to join the four chains into a single, closed chain. Having a link opened costs 2 cents and having a link closed costs 3 cents. How can she have the chains joined for 15 cents? (*Hint:* Can only end links be opened?)

5. What is two-thirds of one-half? (*Hint:* Reverse course.)

6. Toby has three separate large boxes. Inside each large box are two separate medium-sized boxes, and inside each of the medium boxes are four small boxes. How many boxes does Toby have altogether? (*Hint:* Draw it.)

Part B: After working together to solve these problems, consider these questions:

1. Which problems were the easiest to solve, and which were more difficult? Why?

2. Were the hints helpful?

3. Do you think there was more than one solution to any of the problems?

4. Did your initial assumptions about the problem help or hinder your efforts to solve it?

Note: Answers to the problems are found on page 212.

To Try It online, go to Connect for *P.O.W.E.R. Learning and Your Life.*

Test these problem-solving strategies in **Try It! 2**, "Exercise Your Problem-solving Skills," above.

Assess Your Potential Solutions

If a problem clearly has only one answer—a math problem, for example—this step in problem-solving is relatively easy. You should be able to work the problem and figure out whether you've been successful. In contrast, messier problems have several possible solutions, some of which may be more involved and costlier than others. In these cases, it's necessary to compare alternative solutions and choose the best one. For example, suppose you want to surprise your best friend on her birthday. She is studying at a school about 100 kilometres from you, and you need to find a way to get there. You could rent a car, take a bus, or find some other way.

Money is an issue. You will want to figure out how much each alternative costs before choosing one as your solution to the problem. Since every penny you spend getting there is a penny less that you will have to celebrate, you will want to weigh the options carefully.

Finally, spend a bit of time seeing whether there is a way to refine the solution. Is the solution you've devised adequate? Does it address all aspects of the problem? Are there alternative approaches that might be superior? Answering these questions, and refining your solution to address them, can give you confidence that the solution you've come up with is the best. For example, if you're trying to get to your friend's school, you might decide to use the ride board at your school to try to find a ride with someone going there that day. Maybe your friend's family is going to be driving in and could pick you up or could even lend you a car for the trip.

Remember that not every problem has a clear-cut solution. Sometimes we need to be satisfied with a degree of uncertainty and ambiguity. For some of us, such a lack of clarity is difficult, making us uneasy; it may push us to choose a solution—any solution—that seems to solve the problem. Others of us feel more comfortable with ambiguity; but this may lead us to let problems ride without taking steps to resolve the situation.

Either way, it's important to consider what your own problem-solving style is when you seek to identify solutions. And keep in mind that often there is no perfect solution to a problem—only some solutions that are better than others.

Reflect on the Process of Problem-Solving

It's natural to step back and bask in the satisfaction of solving a tough problem. That's fine—but take a moment to consider your success. Each time you solve a problem, you end up a couple steps ahead, but only if you've thought about the process you went through to solve it.

From the perspective of . . .

A PHARMACY TECHNICIAN The ability to ask questions is a trait that will continue to matter in your career. What are some of the potential consequences of not asking questions in a field that presents possible health risks?

Go back and consider what it took to solve the problem. Can the means you used to come up with your solution be applied to more complex kinds of problems? If you arrived at a solution by drawing a chart, would this work on similar problems in the future? Taking a moment to rethink your solution can provide you with an opportunity to become an expert problem solver and, more generally, to improve your critical thinking skills. Don't let the opportunity slip away.

»LO 8.3 Applying Critical Thinking to Everyday Problems

Being able to think clearly and without bias is the basis for critical thinking. As you have probably noticed already, the quality of the thinking you do regarding problems and decisions plays a crucial role in determining how successful you are.

Unfortunately, it is sometimes the alternative you *didn't* think of that can end up being the most satisfactory decision or solution. So how can we learn to think critically and avoid blind spots that hinder us in our decision-making and problem-solving? We can start by considering these common obstacles to critical thinking:

> **Don't assume that giving something a name explains it.** The mere fact that we can give an idea or problem a name doesn't mean we can explain it. Yet we often confuse the two.

For instance, consider the following sequences of questions and answers:

Q. Why do I have so much trouble falling asleep?

A. Because you have insomnia.

Q. Why is he so unsociable?

A. Because he's an introvert.

Q. Why did the defendant shoot those people?

A. Because he's insane.

Q. How do you know he's insane?

A. Because only someone who was insane would shoot people in that way.[3]

It's clear that none of these answers is satisfactory. All use circular reasoning, in which the alleged explanation for the behaviour is simply the use of a label.

> **Don't accept vague generalities dressed up as definitive statements.** Read the following personality analysis and think about how well it applies to you:

You have a need for other people to like and admire you and a tendency to be critical of yourself. You also have a great deal of unused potential that you have not turned to your advantage; but although you have some personality weaknesses, you are generally able to compensate for them. Nonetheless, relating to members of the opposite sex has presented problems to you; and while you appear to be disciplined and self-controlled to others, you tend to be anxious and insecure inside.

If you believe that these statements provide an amazingly accurate description of your unique qualities, you're not alone: Most college and university students believe that the description is tailored specifically to them.[4] But how is that possible? It isn't. The reality is that the statements are so vague that they are virtually meaningless. The acceptance of vague but seemingly useful and significant statements about oneself and others has been called the *Barnum effect,* after showman and circus master P. T. Barnum, who coined the phrase "there's a sucker born every minute."

▸ **Don't confuse opinion with fact.** Opinions are not facts. Although we may be aware of this simple formula, almost all of us can be fooled into thinking that someone's opinion is the same as a fact.

A fact is information that is proven to be true. In contrast, an opinion represents judgments, reasoning, beliefs, inferences, or conclusions. If we accept some bit of information as a fact, we can use it to build our opinions. But if we are presented with an opinion, we need to determine the facts on which the opinion is built to judge its reliability.

The difference between fact and opinion can sometimes be subtle. For instance, compare these two statements:

1. Every student needs to take a writing course during the first term of college or university.

2. Many students need to take a writing course during the first term of college or university.

The first statement is most likely an opinion, because it is so absolute and unqualified. Words such as "every," "all," and "always" are often evidence of opinion. On the other hand, the second statement is more likely a fact, since it contains the qualifier "many." In general, statements that are qualified in some way are more likely to be facts.

Complete **Try It! 3**, "Distinguish Fact from Opinion," on page 206, to see the difficulties sometimes involved in distinguishing between fact and opinion.

▸ **Avoid jumping to conclusions.** Read this riddle and try to answer it:

A father and his son were driving along the Trans Canada Highway when the father lost control of the car, swerved off the road, and crashed into a utility pole. The father died instantly, and his son was critically injured. An ambulance rushed the boy to a nearby hospital. A prominent surgeon was summoned to provide immediate treatment. When the surgeon arrived and entered the operating room to examine the boy, a loud gasp was heard.

"I can't operate on this boy," the surgeon said. "He is my son."

How can this be?

If you find this puzzling, you've based your reasoning on an assumption: that the surgeon is a male. But suppose you had assumed that the surgeon was a female. Suddenly, the riddle becomes a lot easier. It's far easier to guess that the surgeon is the son's mother if we don't leap to embrace a faulty assumption.

Why is it so easy to jump to conclusions? One reason is that we sometimes aren't aware of the assumptions that underlie our thinking. Another is our reliance on "common sense."

▸ **Be skeptical of "common sense."** Much of what we call common sense makes contradictory claims. For example, if you believe in the notion "Absence makes the heart grow fonder," you may assume that your girlfriend, now working at a job in another city, will arrive home at Christmas even more in love with you than before. But what about "Out of sight, out of mind," which

POWER Try It!

3

Distinguish Fact from Opinion

Read the following statements and try to determine which are facts (put "F" on the line that follows the item) and which are opinions (put "O" on the line that follows the item).

1. College and university students should get at least seven hours of sleep every night. _____

2. The average college or university student sleeps less than seven hours a night. _____

3. Nike offers better styling and comfort than any other brand of shoe. _____

4. Two out of five sports figures surveyed preferred Nike over Converse shoes. _____

5. Government figures show spending in Canada is much higher for health than for education. _____

6. Sidney Crosby is the most outstanding, most exciting, and certainly most successful hockey player who ever stepped onto the ice. _____

Items 1, 3, and 6 are opinions; the rest are facts. What are the main differences between opinion and fact?

To Try It online, go to Connect for *P.O.W.E.R. Learning and Your Life*.

Using Critical Thinking in Your Classes

Nowhere is critical thinking more important to use—and demonstrate to your instructors—than when you're in your classes. Here are some strategies to foster your skills as a critical thinker when you are in class:

- **Ask questions.** Most instructors welcome questions. Even if an instructor doesn't have time to provide a full response, the very act of formulating a question will help you think more critically about the course material.

- **Accept that some questions have no right or wrong answers.** Understanding that some questions have no simple answer is a sign of mental sophistication. Sometimes the best an instructor can do is present competing theories. Although you may want to know which theory is right, accept that sometimes no one knows the answer to that question—that's why they're theories, not facts!

- **Keep an open mind.** Your instructor and classmates have their own perspectives and opinions. Even if you disagree with them, try to figure out why they hold their views. It will help you to see the multiple sides of different issues.

- **Don't deny your emotional reactions—manage them.** There may be times when an instructor or classmate says something that is bothersome or even makes you angry. That's OK. But be sure to manage your emotions so that they don't overwhelm your rational self. And use your emotional reactions to gain understanding of what's important to you.

- **Don't be afraid of looking unintelligent.** No one wants to look foolish, especially in front of a roomful of classmates. But don't let self-defeating feelings prevent you from expressing your concerns. Take intellectual risks!

suggests a less positive outcome? Common sense often presents us with contradictory advice, making it a less than useful guide to decision-making and problem-solving.

> **Don't assume that just because two events occur together one causes the other.** Just because two events appear to be associated with one another, we cannot conclude that one event has caused the other to occur. Suppose you read that a study showed that 89 percent of juvenile delinquents use marijuana. Does this mean that smoking marijuana *causes* juvenile delinquency?

No, it doesn't. It is pretty safe to say that 100 percent of juvenile delinquents grew up drinking milk. Would you feel comfortable saying that milk causes delinquency? With the association between marijuana use and delinquent behaviour, it is very likely that there's some third factor—such as the influence of peers—that causes people both to (a) try drugs and (b) engage in delinquent behaviour. The bottom line: We do not know that marijuana use is the cause of the delinquency just because delinquents often smoke marijuana.

In short, we need to be careful in assuming causality. Even if two events or other kinds of variables occur together, it it is not necessarily true that one causes the other. To see this for yourself, take a look at the statements in **Try It! 4**, "What's the Real Explanation?" on page 208.

Try It!

What's the Real Explanation?

Even though two events are related to each other, it doesn't mean that one causes the other. Instead, there is often some other factor that is the actual cause of the relationship.

To see this for yourself, consider each of the following (actual!) findings. What might be a plausible explanation for each one?

1. Ice cream sales and the timing of shark attacks are highly related. Why?

2. The number of cavities children have and the size of their vocabulary are closely related. Why?

3. Skirt hemlines tend to rise as stock prices rise. Why?

4. Women with breast implants have a higher rate of suicide than those without breast implants. Why?

5. People who own washing machines are more likely to die in car accidents than those who don't. Why?

Once you've completed this **Try It!,** look at the possible explanations on page 212. Keep in mind that these are simply theories; we don't know for sure if they're correct.

To Try It online, go to Connect for *P.O.W.E.R. Learning and Your Life.*

Apply Decision-making and Problem-solving Techniques to Everyday Life

In this chapter, you've learned about many tools and techniques that can help you with the problems you encounter and the decisions you have to make while pursuing your post-secondary education. You may be under the impression that it's only worth using these techniques to solve the *big* problems and make the *big* decisions—should you have children, should you change careers, or when should you retire, for example—but they apply equally to the little decisions. And it doesn't stop there. Whether it's a pro/con list, a decision tree, a chart to help you weigh alternatives, or freewriting, you will find that you will return to the techniques introduced in this chapter again and again, in all facets of your life, and through its many stages. For suggestions on the decision-making and problem-solving techniques that best suit your striving style, see the recommendations provided in the sidebar.

Decision-making, Problem-solving, and Striving Styles™

Leaders
Approach problems logically, systematically, and objectively. Weigh options and alternatives. Can be reactive to problems when stressed.

Socializers
Use value judgments to decide (good/bad, right/wrong). Consider impact of decisions on people. Can ignore facts and details.

Performers
Approach problems as a challenge. Great at weighing pros and cons and arguing both sides. Can change their minds many times in process and fail to conclude.

Adventurers
Prefer using instincts to decide. Don't like to delve into weighing options. Need to move to action to attempt to solve the problem.

Artists
Use subjective criteria for decision-making. Value judgments (good/bad, right/wrong) influence approach. Problems that evoke emotion are challenging.

Intellectuals
Gather information to assess alternatives. Can spend too much time weighing options. Can come up with unique solutions and alternatives.

Visionaries
Arrive at a decision intuitively, and then support it with facts and details. Generate lots of options. Try to make facts fit their decision even when they don't.

Stabilizers
Use a prescribed framework for making decisions. Like to decide quickly without too much consideration. Can get overwhelmed by too many alternatives.

Time to Reflect: What Did I Learn?

1. Generally speaking, how would you characterize your decision-making skills?

2. In what way(s) does your approach to decision-making reflect your Striving Style?

3. Based on what you learned about decision-making in this chapter, what do you plan to do differently when making decisions in the future? Be specific.

Looking Back

How can I improve the quality of my decisions?

> A structured process of decision-making can clarify the issues involved, expand your options, and improve the quality of your choices.

> Good decision-making begins with understanding your short- and long-term goals.

> Decision-making is improved if you have a large number of alternatives.

> For difficult decisions, strategies include taking time to make the decision, acting out alternatives, tossing a coin to test your feelings, seeking advice, and acting on gut feelings.

What strategies can I use for problem-solving?

> Problem-solving entails the generation of alternatives to consider.

> You need to first understand and define the problem and to determine the important elements in coming to a solution to a problem.

> Approaches to generating solutions include breaking problems into pieces, working backward, using pictures, considering the opposite, using analogies, taking another's perspective, and "forgetting" the problem.

> Problem-solving ultimately requires the evaluation and refinement of the solutions that have been generated.

What are some problems that affect critical thinking?

> Labelling, using vague generalities, accepting opinion as fact, jumping to conclusions, mistaking common sense for logic, and assuming causation all pose threats to critical thinking.

[KEY TERMS AND CONCEPTS]

Analogy (p. 201)   Decision-making (p. 192)   Problem-solving (p. 200)

Critical thinking (p. 192)   Freewriting (p. 193)

[RESOURCES]

ON CAMPUS

Some colleges and universities offer courses in critical thinking, and they are a good bet to help increase decision-making and problem-solving skills. In addition, courses in logic and philosophy will help improve critical thinking skills.

If you are having a personal problem that is difficult to solve, don't hesitate to turn to staff at the counselling centre at your college or university or to your local mental health centre. Trained counsellors and therapists can help you sort through the different options in an objective manner. They may help you to identify possibilities for solutions that you didn't even know existed. Even if the person with whom you speak initially is not the right one, he or she can direct you to someone who can help.

If you need career counselling, staff at your campus counselling centre or career centre are the people to approach for assistance. They have access to a wide range of resources that can help you narrow down your career choices.

IN PRINT

If you have trouble making good decisions, then check out *Learning to Think Things Through: A Guide to Critical Thinking Across the Curriculum,* by Gerald M. Nosich (Prentice Hall, 2008). It is an excellent, concise guide to improving your decision-making skills.

In addition, *Asking the Right Questions: A Guide to Critical Thinking,* 9th ed. (Prentice Hall, 2009) teaches readers how to effectively consider alternative points of view while making personal choices.

ON THE WEB

The following websites provide the opportunity to extend your learning about the material in this chapter.

> "Guidelines to Problem-Solving and Decision-Making" (**www.managementhelp.org/ prsn_prd/prob_slv.htm**) by Carter McNamara, PhD, provides seven steps to effective problem-solving and decision-making. This site is rich in links to comprehensive approaches to decision-making, critical and creative thinking, time management, and organizing yourself.

> Metropolitan Community College's Critical Thinking Project site (**http://mcckc. edu/main.asp?L=CoreNotesIntro**), coordinated by Michael Connelly of Longview Community College, presents principles of critical thinking with exercises and examples. The site contains a short history of logic and answers the question, "What is the point of studying critical thinking?"

[ANSWERS TO TRY IT! 2 PROBLEMS]

1. Remove one lug nut from each of the other three tires on the car and use these three to attach the spare tire. This will hold until four more lug nuts can be purchased.
2. Dump the tools out of the toolbox and use it as a pail.
3. Thursday.
4. Open all three links on one chain (cost = 6 cents) and use them to fasten the other three chains together (cost = 9 cents; total cost = 15 cents).
5. It is the same as one-half of two-thirds, or one-third.
6. 33 boxes (3 large, 6 medium, 24 small).

[ANSWERS TO TRY IT! 4 PROBLEMS]

1. The actual cause is probably the temperature, which causes both sales of ice cream and ocean swimming to increase.
2. Both the number of cavities children have and the size of their vocabularies are related to their age.
3. Skirt hemlines go up, as does the stock market, when people are feeling less conservative and more optimistic.
4. Having breast implants and committing suicide both may be a result of unhappiness or a poor self-image.
5. People who own washing machines are more likely to own cars, and therefore they stand a higher risk of dying in a car crash.

TAKING IT TO THE NET

1 Making good decisions can depend on distinguishing legitimate appeals (good reasons) from fallacious appeals (bad reasons). Go to San Jose State University's "Mission: Critical," an interactive tutorial in critical thinking (**www.sjsu.edu/depts/ itl/graphics/adhom/appeal.html**). After reading the description of the different kinds of fallacious appeals, do the related exercises.

2 Locate three problem-solving strategies on the Internet. Possible strategy: Go to Yahoo! (**http://ca.yahoo.com**) or AltaVista (**www.altavista.com**), and enter the key phrase "problem-solving." Search the results until you find at least three different problem-solving strategies. Are these strategies similar to the ones described in the book? If not, how are they different?

The Case of . . .
The Missing Roommate

Megha had a problem.

In June, she and her cousin had rented a three-bedroom apartment near the university and had signed a lease for the two semesters from September to April. They had advertised for a third person on the university's website, and had interviewed several applicants, finally settling on a young nursing student called Neha to be their third roommate. That wasn't the problem, though. The problem was that it was now the day after Labour Day and classes were starting, and Neha had still not shown up.

Concerned, Megha called her—and the nursing student brusquely told her she'd found a better place and wouldn't be sharing the apartment with Megha and her cousin after all. Then she hung up. Suddenly Megha was left with an empty room, and without Neha's share of the rent money.

1. Of the problem-solving strategies outlined in this chapter, which would you use to approach this problem?

2. What alternatives does Megha have for dealing with the situation?

3. How should Megha go about evaluating the outcomes for each alternative?

4. Based on your analysis of the problem, what advice would you give Megha for dealing with the situation?

5. Is there anything Megha could have done to avoid this problem in the first place?

Critical Thinking

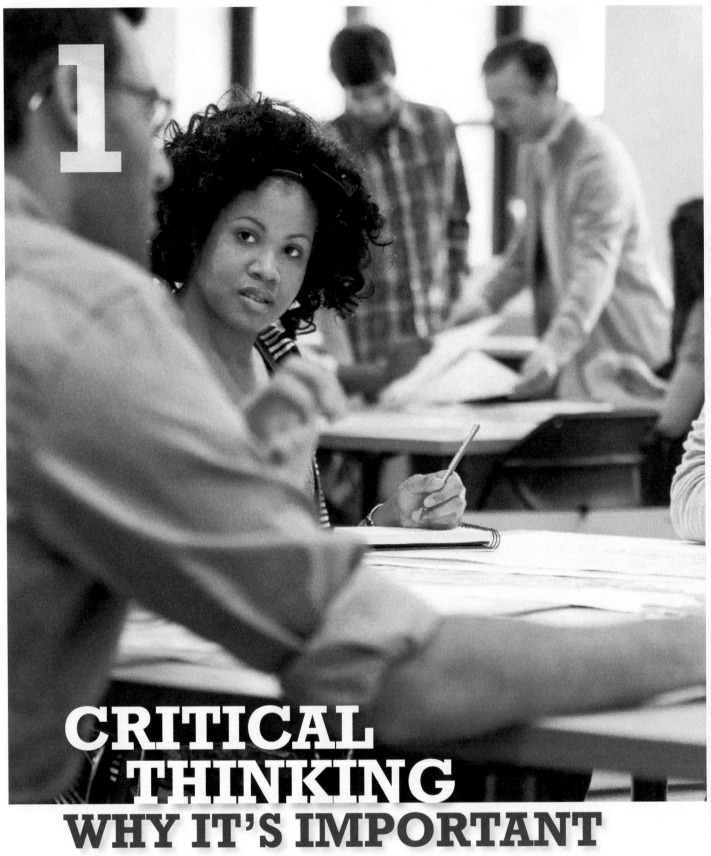

1

CRITICAL THINKING
WHY IT'S IMPORTANT

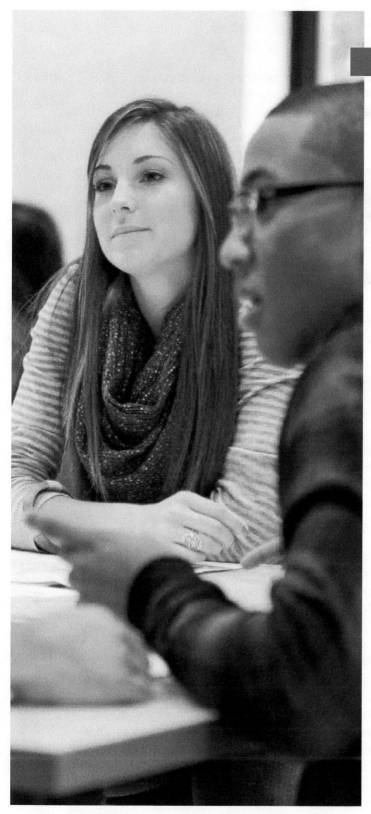

In what ways does sharing ideas with others and listening to their feedback help develop our critical thinking skills?

Nazi war criminal Adolf Eichmann was tried in Israel in 1960 for crimes against humanity. Despite his claim that he was just following the orders of his superiors when he ordered the deaths of millions of Jews, the court found him guilty and sentenced him to death. Was Eichmann an inhuman monster? Or was he, as his defense lawyer claimed, just doing what many of us would do— following orders from our superiors?

To address this question, social psychologist Stanley Milgram of Yale University conducted, between 1960 and 1963, what has become a classic experiment. Milgram placed an advertisement in a newspaper asking for men to take part in a scientific study of memory and learning.[1] Those chosen to participate were told that the purpose of the experiment was to study the effects of punishment on learning—and that their job was to give electric shocks as punishment when the learner gave a wrong answer. The participants were instructed that

3

THiNK FIRST

- What are the characteristics of a skilled critical thinker?
- What are the three levels of thinking?
- What are some of the barriers to critical thinking?

>> the shocks would be given at the direction of the experimenter and would range in intensity from 15 volts to 450 volts. In fact, no shocks were actually being given, but the participants didn't know this.

As the intensity of the shocks "increased," the learner (actually an actor) responded with increased anguish, screaming in pain and pleading with the participant delivering the shocks to stop. Despite the repeated pleas, all the participants gave shocks of up to 300 volts before refusing to go on. In addition, 65 percent continued to deliver shocks of 450 volts simply because an authority figure (a scientist in a white lab coat) told the participants to continue. Most who continued were clearly disturbed by what they were doing. However, unlike the participants who refused to continue, they were unable to provide logical counterarguments to the scientist's insistence that "the experiment requires that you must continue."

How could this happen? Were the results of Milgram's study some sort of aberration? As it turns out, they were not.

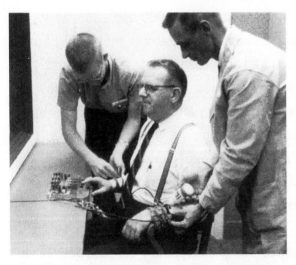

Milgram Experiment **Scene from the Milgram experiment on obedience. The "learner" is being hooked up to the machine that will deliver bogus electric shocks each time he gives a wrong answer.**

Several years later, in 1971, the U.S. Navy funded a study of the reaction of humans to situations in which there are huge differences in authority and power—as in a prison. The study was administered under the direction of psychologist Philip Zimbardo, who selected student volunteers judged to be psychologically stable and healthy.[2] The volunteers were randomly assigned to play the role of either "guard" or "prisoner" in a two-week prison simulation in the basement of the Stanford University building in which the psychology department was located. To make the situation more realistic, guards were given wooden batons and wore khaki, military-style uniforms and mirrored sunglasses that minimized eye contact. The prisoners were given ill-fitting smocks without underwear and rubber thongs for their feet. Each prisoner was also assigned a number to be used instead of a name. The guards were not given any formal instructions; they were simply told that it was their responsibility to run the prison.

The experiment quickly got out of control. Prisoners were subjected to abusive and humiliating treatment, both physical and emotional, by the guards. One-third of the guards became increasingly cruel, especially at night when they thought the cameras had been turned off. Prisoners were forced to clean toilets with their bare hands, to sleep on concrete floors, and to endure solitary confinement and hunger. They were also subjected to forced nudity and sexual abuse—much like what would happen many years later in 2003–2004 at Abu Ghraib prison in Iraq. (see Analyzing Images: Abuse at Abu Ghraib prison, Iraq, page 18). After only six days, the Stanford prison experiment had to be called off.

These experiments suggest that many, if not most, Americans will uncritically follow the commands of those in authority. Like the Milgram study, the Stanford prison experiment demonstrated that ordinary people will commit atrocities in situations where there is social and institutional support for behavior that they would not do on their own and if they could put the blame on others. Milgram wrote:

> Ordinary people, simply doing their jobs and without any particular hostility on their part, can become agents in a terrible destructive process. Moreover, even when the destructive effects of their work become patently clear, and they are asked to carry out actions incompatible with fundamental standards of the majority, relatively few people have the resources needed to resist authority.[3]

What are these resources that people need to resist authority? Good critical-thinking skills are certainly one. Those who refused to continue in the Milgram study were able to give good reasons for why they should stop: for example, "it is wrong to cause harm to another person." In contrast, those who continued, even though they knew what they were doing was wrong, simply deferred to the authority figure even though he was making unreasonable demands of them.[4]

Although most of us may never be in a situation in which our actions have such grim consequences, a lack of critical-thinking skills can still have negative consequences in our everyday decisions. When it comes making to personal, educational, and career choices, we may defer to our parents or cave in to pressure from friends rather than think through the reasons for our decisions. When major life decisions are not carefully thought out, there can be long-lasting consequences, such as dropping out of school or choosing a career in which we are ultimately unhappy. In addition, because critical-thinking skills are transferable across disciplines, improving these skills can have a positive impact on our success in college. In this chapter we'll be looking at some of the components of critical thinking as well as the benefits of developing good critical-thinking skills. We'll conclude by examining some of the barriers to critical thinking. Specifically, we will:

- Define *critical thinking* and *logic*
- Learn about the characteristics of a good critical thinker
- Distinguish between giving an opinion and engaging in critical thinking
- Explain the benefits of good critical thinking
- Relate critical thinking to personal development and our role as citizens in a democracy
- Identify people who exemplify critical thinking in action
- Identify barriers to critical thinking, including types of resistance and narrow-mindedness

At the end of the chapter, we will apply our critical-thinking skills to a specific issue by discussing and analyzing different perspectives on affirmative action in college admissions.

> These experiments suggest that many, if not most, Americans will uncritically follow the commands of those in authority.

5

WHAT IS CRITICAL THINKING?

Critical thinking is a collection of skills we use every day that are necessary for our full intellectual and personal development. The word *critical* is derived from the Greek word *kritikos,* which means "discernment," "the ability to judge," or "decision making." Critical thinking requires learning *how* to think rather than simply *what* to think.

Critical thinking, like logic, requires good analytical skills. **Logic** is part of critical thinking and is defined as "the study of the methods and principles used in distinguishing correct (good) arguments from incorrect (bad) arguments."[5] Critical thinking involves the application of the rules of logic as well as gathering evidence, evaluating it, and coming up with a plan of action. We'll be studying logical arguments in depth, in Chapters 5 through 8.

> **critical thinking** A collection of skills we use every day that are necessary for our full intellectual and personal development.
>
> **logic** The study of the methods and principles used to distinguish correct or good arguments from poor arguments.
>
> **opinion** A belief based solely on personal feelings rather than on reason or facts.

Critical thinking provides us with the tools to identify and resolve issues in our lives. Critical thinking is not simply a matter of asserting our opinions on issues. **Opinions** are based on personal feelings or beliefs, rather than on reason and evidence. We are all certainly entitled to our own opinions. Opinions, however, are not necessarily reasonable. While some may happen to turn out to be correct, opinions, no matter how deeply and sincerely held, may also be mistaken. As a critical thinker you need to be willing to provide logical support for your beliefs.

Uninformed opinions can lead you to make poor decisions in your life and act in ways that you may later come to regret. Sometimes uninformed opinions can negatively impact society. For example, even though antibiotics kill bacteria and have no effect on cold viruses, many people try to persuade their doctors into prescribing them for cold symptoms. Despite doctors telling patients that antibiotics have no effect on viral infections, studies show that about half of doctors give in to patient pressure for antibiotics for viral infections.[6] Such overuse of antibiotics makes bacteria more drug resistant and has led to a decline in the effectiveness of treatment in diseases where they are really needed.[7] This phenomenon

SELF-EVALUATION QUESTIONNAIRE

Rate yourself on the following scale from 1 (strongly disagree) to 5 (strongly agree).

1 2 3 4 5   There are right and wrong answers. Authorities are those who have the right answers.

1 2 3 4 5   There are no right or wrong answers. Everyone has a right to his or her own opinion.

1 2 3 4 5   Even though the world is uncertain, we need to make decisions on what is right or wrong.

1 2 3 4 5   I tend to stick to my position on an issue even when others try to change my mind.

1 2 3 4 5   I have good communication skills.

1 2 3 4 5   I have high self-esteem.

1 2 3 4 5   I would refuse to comply if an authority figure ordered me to do something that might cause me to hurt someone else.

1 2 3 4 5   I don't like it when other people challenge my deeply held beliefs.

1 2 3 4 5   I get along better with people than do most people.

1 2 3 4 5   People don't change.

1 2 3 4 5   I have trouble coping with problems of life such as relationship problems, depression, and rage.

1 2 3 4 5   I tend to sacrifice my needs for those of others.

1 2 3 4 5   Men and women tend to have different communication styles.

1 2 3 4 5   The most credible evidence is that based on direct experience, such as eyewitness reports.

Keep track of your results. As you read this book and gain a better understanding of critical thinking, you'll find out what your responses to each of these statements mean. A brief summary of the meaning of each rating can also be found at the back of the book.

ANALYZING **IMAGES**

"All or Nothing" Thinking

DISCUSSION QUESTIONS

1. *Discuss Calvin's claim that seeing the complexities of knowledge is "paralyzing."*

2. *Think back to a time when you felt, as does Calvin in the cartoon, that life is easier if you can think in dualist terms of black and white rather than "seeing the complexities and shades of gray." Referring back to this and other similar experiences, what are some of the drawbacks of making decisions or taking action on the basis of all-or-nothing thinking? Be specific.*

---

has been linked to the emergence of new, more virulent strains of drug-resistant tuberculosis. In addition, the incidence of some sexually transmitted diseases such as syphilis, which was once treatable by penicillin, is once again on the rise.[8]

The ability to think critically and to make effective life decisions is shaped by many factors, including our stage of cognitive development, the possession of good analytical communication, and research skills and such characteristics as open-mindedness, flexibility, and creativity.

Cognitive Development in College Students

Becoming a critical thinker is a lifelong process. Education researcher William Perry, Jr. (1913–1998) was one of the first to study college students' cognitive development.[9] **Cognitive development** is the process by which each of us "becomes an intelligent person, acquiring intelligence and increasingly advanced thought and problem-solving ability from infancy to adulthood."[10] Perry's work has gained wide acceptance among educators. Although Perry identified nine developmental positions, later researchers have simplified his schemata into three stages: dualism, relativism, and commitment. These three stages are represented by the first three questions

in the Self-Evaluation Questionnaire in the Think Tank feature on page 6.

Stage 1: Dualism. Younger students such as freshmen and many sophomores tend to take in knowledge and life experiences in a simplistic, "dualistic" way, viewing something as either right or wrong. They see knowledge as existing outside themselves and look to authority figures for the answers.

> **cognitive development** The process of acquiring advanced thinking and problem-solving skills from infancy through adulthood.

This dualistic stage is most obvious when these students confront a conflict. Although they may be able to apply critical-thinking skills in a structured classroom environment, they often lack the ability to apply these skills in real-life conflicts. When confronted with a situation such as occurred in the Milgram study of obedience,[11] they are more likely to follow an authority figure even if they feel uncomfortable doing so. In addition, a controversial issue such as affirmative action, where there is little agreement among authorities and no clear-cut right or wrong answers, can leave students at this stage struggling to make sense of it. We'll be studying some perspectives on affirmative action at the end of this chapter.

> **Connections**
>
> **How do you determine if the statistics found in the results of a scientific experiment are credible?**
> *See Chapter 12, p. 382.*

When researching an issue, students at the dualistic stage may engage in **confirmation bias**, seeking out only evidence that supports their views and dismissing as unreliable statistics that contradict them.[12] The fact that their "research" confirms their views serves to reinforce their simplistic, black-and-white view of the world.

confirmation bias At the dualistic stage of research, seeking out only evidence that supports your view and dismissing evidence that contradicts it.

HIGHLIGHTS

COGNITIVE DEVELOPMENT IN COLLEGE STUDENTS

Stage 1: Dualism There are right and wrong answers. Authorities know the right answers.

Transition to Stage 2 There are some uncertainties and different opinions, but these are temporary.

Stage 2: Relativism When the authorities don't have the right answers, everyone has a right to his or her own opinion; there are no right or wrong answers.

Transition to Stage 3 All thinking is contextual and relative but not equally valid.

Stage 3: Commitment I should not just blindly follow or oppose authority. I need to orient myself in an uncertain world and make a decision or commitment.

➤*APPLICATION: Identify an example of thinking at each of three stages in the text.*

Adapted from Ron Sheese and Helen Radovanovic, "W. G. Perry's Model of Intellectual and Ethical Development: Implications of Recent Research for the Education and Counseling of Young Adults," paper presented at the annual meeting of the Canadian Psychological Association (Ottawa, Ontario, June 1984).

In one study, 48 undergraduates, who either supported or opposed capital punishment, were given two fictitious studies to read.[13] One study presented "evidence" contradicting beliefs about the deterrent effect of capital punishment. The other study presented "evidence" confirming the effectiveness of capital punishment as a deterrent. The results showed that students uncritically accepted the evidence that confirmed their preexisting views, while being skeptical about opposing evidence. In other words, despite the fact that both groups read the same studies, rather than modifying their position, the students used the confirming study to support their existing opinion on capital punishment and dismissed the opposing evidence.*

*For more on the debate on capital punishment see pages 261–264.

Students at this stage may also be unable to recognize ambiguity, conflicting values, or motives in real-life situations. In light of this, it is not surprising that young people are most likely to fall victim to con artists, financial fraud, and identity theft, despite the stereotype that the elderly are more vulnerable to scam artists.[14]

Students are most likely to make the transition to a higher stage of cognitive development when their current way of thinking is challenged or proves inadequate. During the transition they come to recognize that there is uncertainty in the world and that authorities can have different positions. Some educators called this period of disorientation and doubting all answers "sophomoritis."[15]

Stage 2: Relativism. Rather than accepting that ambiguity and uncertainty may be unavoidable and that they need to make decisions despite this, students at the relativist stage go to the opposite extreme. They reject a dualistic worldview and instead believe that all truth is relative or just a matter of opinion. People at this stage believe that stating your opinion is the proper mode of expression, and they look down on challenging others' opinions as "judgmental" and even disrespectful. However, despite their purported belief in relativism, most students at this stage still expect their professor to support his or her opinion.

Having their ideas challenged, grappling with controversial issues, encountering role models who are at a higher stage of cognitive development, and learning about their limits and the contradictions in their thinking can all help students move on to the next stage of cognitive development.

Stage 3: Commitment. As students mature, they come to realize that not all thinking is equally valid. Not only can authorities be mistaken but also in some circumstances uncertainty and ambiguity are unavoidable. When students at this stage experience uncertainty, they are now able to make decisions and commit to particular positions on the basis of reason and the best evidence available. At the same time, as independent thinkers, they are open to challenge, able to remain flexible, and willing to change their position should new evidence come to light.

As students mature,
they come to realize that not
all thinking is equally valid.

As we mature and acquire better critical-thinking skills, our way of conceptualizing and understanding the world becomes increasingly complex. This is particularly true of older students who return to college after spending time out in the "real world." Unlike people at the first stage who look to authority for answers, people at the third stage accept responsibility for their interactions with their environment and are more open to challenges and more accepting of ambiguity.

EXERCISE 1-1

STOP AND ASSESS YOURSELF

1. Imagine that you are a participant in Milgram's study of obedience. What would you have done if you protested and the experimenter in charge answered, "The experiment requires that you continue"? Discuss your answer in light of the stages of cognitive development. Discuss also what you might do to make it less likely that you would obey an authority figure in a situation such as the Milgram study.

2. College professor Stephen Satris maintains that the relativism of the second stage of development is not a genuine philosophical position but a means of avoiding having one's ideas challenged. Student relativism, he writes, "is primarily a method of protection, a suit of armor, which can be applied to one's own opinions, whatever they may be—but not necessarily to the opinion of others. . . . It is an expression of the idea that no one step forward and judge (and possibly criticize) one's own opinion."[16] What is your "suit of armor"? Discuss strategies you might take to break out of this "suit of armor." Relate your answer to your own stage of cognitive development.

3. Most college students do not make the transition to the third, or commitment, stage of cognitive development. Why do you think this is so? Discuss ways in which the curriculum and college life in general might be restructured to encourage cognitive growth in students.

4. Today, more people are returning to college after having children and/or having worked for several years. This phenomenon is especially prevalent in community colleges, where the average age is 28.[17] Discuss whether there are differences in how students of different ages in your class think about the world, and how interaction among students at different stages might enrich our thinking.

5. The first three questions of the "Self-Evaluation Questionnaire" in the Think Tank feature represent the three stages of cognitive development. Which stage, or transition between stages, best describes your approach to understanding the world? What are the shortcomings and strengths of your current stage of cognitive development? Develop a plan to improve your skills as a critical thinker. Put the plan into action. Report on the results of your action plan.

CHARACTERISTICS OF A GOOD CRITICAL THINKER

Critical thinking is a collection of skills that enhance and reinforce each other. In this section we'll be discussing some of the more important skills for effective critical thinking.

Analytical Skills

As a critical thinker, you need to be able to analyze and provide logical support for your beliefs rather than simply rely on your opinions. Analytical skills are also important in recognizing and evaluating other people's arguments so that you are not taken in by faulty reasoning. We'll be studying logical argumentation in more depth in Chapter 2 and in Chapters 5 through 9.

Effective Communication

In addition to analytical skills, critical thinking requires communication and reading skills.[18] Communication skills include listening, speaking, and writing skills. Being aware of your own communication style, as well as of cultural variations and differences in the communication styles of men and women, can also go a long way toward improving communication in a relationship. We'll be learning more about communication in Chapter 3, "Language and Communication."

Research and Inquiry Skills

Understanding and resolving issues requires research and inquiry skills such as competence in gathering, evaluating, and pulling together supporting evidence. For example, in researching and gathering information on what would be the best major or career path for you, you need to identify your interests and talents first and then evaluate possible majors and careers in light of these interests and talents. Research skills are also important in understanding and moving toward a resolution of a complex issue such as affirmative action in college admissions.

Inquiry and gaining greater insight requires asking the right questions, as Milgram did in designing his study of obedience. While most people were asking what sort of twisted monsters the Nazis were or why the German people allowed Hitler to have so much power, Milgram asked the more basic question: How far would ordinary citizens go in obeying an authority figure? Despite the fact that experiments such as Milgram's were declared unethical by the American Psychological Association in 1973 because of long-term psychological distress suffered by many of the participants, his scientific experiments still stand as classics in the field.

As critical thinkers we need to avoid confirmation bias and the tendency to selectively see and interpret data to fit into our own world-views, as happened in the study on student's views of capital punishment (see page 8). This is a practice that often leads to stalemates and conflict in personal as well as in political relations. Our research should also be accurate and based on credible evidence. We'll be learning more about researching and evaluating evidence in Chapter 4.

Flexibility and Tolerance for Ambiguity

Too many people defer to others or fail to take a position on a controversial issue simply because they are unable to evaluate conflicting views. As we mature, we become better at making decisions in the face of uncertainty and ambiguity. Effective decision making includes setting clear short-term and long-term goals in our lives and developing a realistic strategy for achieving these goals. Critical thinkers also build flexibility into their life plans so that they can adapt to changes, especially since most of us haven't had sufficient experience to finalize our life plan during our first few years of college. We'll be discussing the process of developing a life plan in more depth later in this chapter.

Connections

How do scientists identify a problem and develop a hypothesis for studying a problem?
See Chapter 12, p. 367.

Open-Minded Skepticism

Critical thinkers are willing to work toward overcoming personal prejudices and biases. They begin with an open mind and an attitude of reflective skepticism. The point is not simply to take a stand on an issue—such as What career is best for me? Is abortion immoral? Does God exist? What should be the role of women in the family?—but rather to critically examine the evidence and assumptions put forth in support of different positions on the issue before coming to a final conclusion. In doing so, effective critical thinkers are able to balance belief and doubt.

First put forward by French philosopher and mathematician René Descartes (1596–1650), the **method of doubt** suspends belief. This method of critical analysis,

René Descartes (1596–1650) proposed the method of doubt, in which we never accept anything as true without evidence and reason to support our conclusion.

which has traditionally been preferred in fields such as science and philosophy, begins from a position of skepticism in which we put aside our preconceived ideas. Descartes wrote regarding the rules for using the method of doubt:

> The first of these [rules] was never to accept anything as true if I did not have evident knowledge of its truth: that is to say, carefully to avoid precipitate conclusions and preconceptions, and to include nothing more in my judgments than what presented itself to my mind so clearly and distinctly that I had no occasion to doubt it.[19]

It is especially important that you be willing to adopt a position of doubt or skepticism when critically examining your own cherished beliefs and the claims of authority figures. Albert Einstein (1879–1955), in developing his theory of relativity, used the method of doubt regarding the generally accepted belief that time is "absolute"—that is, fixed and unchanging.

The **method of belief**, in contrast, suspends doubt. Becoming immersed in a good book, movie, or play often involves what English poet Samuel Taylor Coleridge (1772–1834) called the "willing suspension of disbelief." This approach is also productive when we are discussing issues on which we hold strong views and are not as open as we should be to opposing viewpoints. In dialogues between people who are pro-choice and pro-life, for example, a pro-choice critical thinker, in order to compensate for his or her biases, should be genuinely open to believing what the pro-life person is saying, rather than start from the traditional position of doubt. This task requires empathy, active listening skills, and intellectual curiosity.

Creative Problem Solving

Creative thinkers can view problems from multiple perspectives and come up with original solutions to complex problems. They use their imagination to envision possibilities, including potential future problems, and to develop contingency plans to effectively deal with these scenarios.

When staff members of the U.S. Department of Homeland Security put together a handbook of possible disaster scenarios, they failed to foresee the possibility of civil unrest and social breakdown following a disaster. Because of lack of preparedness for such occurrences as Hurricane Katrina, which struck the Gulf Coast in 2005, hundreds of people died who might have been saved and thousands of others were left homeless and living in chaotic and squalid conditions for weeks and months. Practice in problem-solving for disasters enabled the United States to respond quicker and more effectively when the East Coast was struck by Superstorm Sandy in 2012.

The Tokyo Electric Power Company, operator of the Fukushima Daiichi nuclear power plant, failed to take measures to prevent disasters, like the one that followed an earthquake and tsunami off the coast of Japan in 2011. Rather than taking on the challenge of making the plant secure from such events, they ignored the possibility that there could be such a large tsunami. Consequently, they failed to install adequate backup generators and cooling systems and as a result the power plants experienced a nuclear meltdown spewing toxic radiation into the surrounding area.

Creativity also involves "a willingness to take risks, to cope with the unexpected, to welcome challenge and even failure as a part of the process to arrive at a new and deeper understanding."[20] Instead of giving up when

Connections

Why is having an open mind important in the sciences?
See Chapter 12, p. 368.

method of doubt A method of critical analysis in which we put aside our preconceived ideas and beliefs and begin from a position of skepticism.

method of belief A method of critical analysis in which we suspend our doubts and biases and remain genuinely open to what people with opposing views are saying.

About 20,000 people died as a result of the tsunami that struck Japan in 2011. The tsunami also caused extensive damage to the nuclear power plants on the coast.

times are difficult or resources are lacking, creative critical thinkers are able to make creative use of available resources. In 1976, when he was only 21, Steve Jobs built the first Apple personal computer in his family's garage. His innovative idea of user-friendly software changed the way people perceived computers and heralded the age of personal computing. He later went on to introduce the iPod, which revolutionized portable music players.

Creative thinking is a much sought-after skill in the business world.[21] Because young people are usually less invested in traditional ideas and ways of doing things than are people who have been working in a field for years, they tend to be more open to new ideas. Being able to recognize creative solutions to a problem and to generate and communicate new ideas requires not just creative thinking but also being open-minded, confident, intellectually curious, and an effective communicator.

Attention, Mindfulness, and Curiosity

Critical thinkers are intellectually curious. They are attentive and mindful to what's going on around them and to their own thoughts and feelings. The Buddhist concept of the "beginner's mind" is closely related to the Western concept of the critically open mind, or mindfulness. Zen master Shunryu Suzuki defined the beginner's mind as "wisdom which is seeking for wisdom." He wrote:

> The practice of Zen mind is beginner's mind. The innocence of first inquiry—what am I? . . . The mind of the beginner is empty, free of the habits of the expert, ready to accept, to doubt, and open to all possibilities. . . . If your mind is empty, it is always ready for anything; it is open to everything. In the beginner's mind there are many possibilities. . . .[22]

Like the beginner's mind, good critical thinkers do not reject, without sound reasons, views that conflict with their own. Instead, they are willing to consider multiple perspectives. One of the recent breakthroughs in neuroscience is the discovery that the brains of Buddhist monks who meditate regularly—a practice that involves being mindful, open, and attentive to what is going on in the present moment—are neurally much more active and more resilient in neuroplasticity than are the brains of

people who do not meditate.[23] Many large corporations, including some Fortune 500 companies, are encouraging their executives to take meditation breaks on the job, since it has been found to improve their performance.[24]

Collaborative Learning

Critical thinking occurs in a real-life context. We are not isolated individuals—we are interconnected beings. As critical thinkers we need to move beyond the traditional, detached approach to thinking and develop a more collaborative approach that is grounded in shared dialogue and community.

The failure to take into account context and relationships can lead to faulty decisions that we may later regret. An example of this type of faulty reasoning is the tendency of many individuals to neglect both feedback and complexity. Because of this, they tend not to fully and accurately consider the other side's response. In a relationship we may do something in an attempt to get our partner to pay more attention to us—for example, threatening to leave a partner if he or she doesn't stop spending so much time with friends—only to see this backfire, losing the relationship altogether because we failed to consider how the other person might react.[25]

To use another example, military planners in developing strategies sometimes fail to consider what the enemy might do in return to minimize the effectiveness of these strategies. During the War of 1812, a group of politicians in Washington, D.C., decided the time had come to add Canada to the United States. Their military strategy failed primarily because they did not adequately assess the Canadian response to the U.S. mission to annex Canada. Instead of greeting the American invaders as liberators from British rule, Canadians regarded the war as an unprovoked attack on their homes and lives. Rather than uniting Canada and

Did You Know

The ancient Greek thinker Socrates (469–399 BCE) spent much of his time in the marketplace of Athens surrounded by his young followers. He used this public venue to seek out people in order to challenge their traditional beliefs and practices. He did this by engaging people in a type of critical thinking, now referred to as the Socratic method, in which his probing questions provoked them into realizing their lack of rational understanding and their inconsistencies in thought.

the United States, the War of 1812 gave rise to the first stirring of Canadian nationalism (and even provoked a movement in New England to secede from the United States).[26]

Good critical thinkers adopt a collaborative rather than an adversarial stance, in which they listen to and take others' views into account. Let's go back to the relationship example. Rather than accusing our partner of not spending enough time with us, a good critical thinker would express his or her feelings and thoughts and then listen to the other person's side. Critical thinkers carefully consider all perspectives and are open to revising their views in light of their broader understanding. Using our critical-thinking skills, we might come to realize that

> Good critical thinkers adopt a collaborative rather than an adversarial stance.

our partner's friends are very important to him or her. Perhaps we are being insecure and need to spend more time with our own friends, giving our partner more space. Maybe we can find a solution that meets both our needs. For example, the sports lovers can bring their partners or another friend along once or twice a month to watch the games with them.

HIGHLIGHTS

CHARACTERISTICS OF A SKILLED CRITICAL THINKER

As a skilled critical thinker, you should

- Have good **analytical skills**
- Possess effective **communication skills**
- Be **well informed** and possess good **research skills**
- Be **flexible** and able to **tolerate ambiguity** and **uncertainty**
- Adopt a position of **open-minded skepticism**
- Be a creative **problem solver**
- Be **attentive, mindful, and intellectually curious**
- Engage in **collaborative learning**

➤*APPLICATION: Identify an example of each of the characteristics in the text.*

EXERCISE 1-2

STOP AND ASSESS YOURSELF

1. Watch the Milgram film *Obedience*. Discuss ways in which the participants in the film demonstrated, or failed to demonstrate, good critical-thinking skills.

2. Identifying good role models in your life can help you come up with a picture of the person you would like to be. Think of a person, real or fictional, who exemplifies good critical-thinking skills. Make a list of some of the qualities of this person. Discuss how these qualities help the person in his or her everyday life.

3. Adopt the stance of the Buddhist "beginner's mind." Be attentive only to what is happening in the now. After one minute, write down everything you observed going on around you as well as inside of you (your feelings, body language, and the like). Did you notice more than you might have otherwise? Share your observations with the class. Discuss ways in which this practice of being more attentive to what is going on might enhance your effectiveness as a critical thinker.

4. Working in groups of four to six students, select an issue about which the group is evenly divided into positions for or against it. Each side should adopt a stance of belief and open-mindedness when listening to the other side's position. After the pro side presents its views for two minutes, the anti side takes one minute to repeat back the pro's views without interjecting their own doubts. Repeat the process with the anti side presenting their views. Discuss as a class how this exercise helped you to suspend your biases and to actively listen to views that diverge from your own.

5. Referring to the Self-Evaluation Questionnaire on page 6, share your strengths and weaknesses as well as your plans for improving your critical-thinking skills with others, whether it be friends, family, or in class. Discuss steps you might take or have already taken to work toward or overcome some of your weaknesses.

CRITICAL THINKING AND SELF-DEVELOPMENT

Critical thinking is not just about abstract thought. It is also about self-improvement and your whole development as a person. Working on your self requires that you be honest with yourself and others about your biases, your expectations, your strengths, and your limitations. Are your expectations realistic? Do you have a well thought out plan and goals for your life? People who are inflexible in their thinking may be unable to adapt to changing or new or unusual circumstances and may instead get caught up in rules and inflexible ways of thinking that are inadequate to resolve the situation.

Living the Self-Examined Life

"The unexamined life is not worth living," Socrates said. Often we flounder in college because we have not taken the time to learn about ourselves or develop a plan for our future. The lives of too many people are controlled more by circumstances than by their own choices. Good critical thinkers, in contrast, take charge of their lives and choices rather than opting for the security of fitting into the crowd or simply blindly following an authority figure as happened in the Milgram study at the beginning of this chapter. In addition to being rational thinkers, they are in touch with their emotions and feelings. We'll be looking more at the role of emotion in Chapter 2.

Some psychologists and psychiatrists believe that irrational beliefs and poor critical-thinking skills contribute to many of the "problems of life," such as depression, rage, and low self-esteem.[27, 28] While depression often has a biochemical component that needs to be treated, poor critical-thinking skills can aggravate or even be a major factor in some types of situational depression where a student feels overwhelmed and unable to cope or make a decision in a particular set of circumstances. In a 2011 survey by the American College Health Association, about 30 percent of college students reported that at least once during the past year they felt "so depressed, it was difficult to function." Since people tend to become better at problem-solving as they get older, it is not surprising that depression rates start to drop beginning at age 30. Compared to people over the age of 60, 18–29 year-olds are 70 percent more likely to experience depression.[29]

Although by no means a cure-all, improving critical-thinking skills has been shown to help people deal more effectively with their problems.[30] Rather than view the problems in our lives as being out of our control, we should—as cognitive psychologists in particular counsel us—develop strategies for taking charge of our lives, develop realistic expectations, and commit ourselves to acknowledging and developing the skills to resolve our problems.

Developing a Rational Life Plan

American philosopher John Rawls (1921–2002) wrote that in order to get the most out of life, everyone needs to develop a "rational life plan"—that is, a plan that would be chosen "with full deliberative rationality, that is, with full awareness of the relevant facts and after a careful consideration of the consequences. . . . Someone is happy, when his plans are going well and his more important aspirations are being fulfilled."[31]

In drawing up our life plan, we make a hierarchy, with our most important plans or goals at the top, followed by a list of subplans. Organize your goals according to a schedule when they are to be carried out, although the more distant a goal is, the less specific the plan will be. Of course, we can't predict everything that will happen in life, and there will be times when circumstances hinder us from achieving our goals. Think of a life plan as being like a flight plan. Airplanes are off course about 90 percent of the time because of such factors as weather, wind patterns, and other aircraft. The pilot must constantly correct for these conditions to get the plane back on course. Without a flight plan, the pilots and their planes would be at the mercy of winds and weather, blown hither and thither, and never reaching their destination.

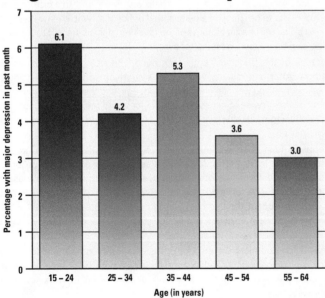

Age Differences in Depression

Percentage with major depression in past month

- 15 – 24: 6.1
- 25 – 34: 4.2
- 35 – 44: 5.3
- 45 – 54: 3.6
- 55 – 64: 3.0

Age (in years)

Source: Santrock (2009) *Life-Span Development,* McGraw-Hill, p. 404.

Begin putting together your life plan by making a list of your values, interests, skills, and talents. Values are what are important to you in life and include things such as financial security, love, family, career, independence, spirituality, health and fitness, education, contributions to society, friends, sense of integrity, and fun. Your goals in life should be rational as well as consistent with your values. According to the 2013 American Freshman Survey, "raising a family," the most important goal for several years, has now taken a back seat to being "able to get a good job," with 87.9 percent of freshman listing this as their top goal, the highest since 1966.[32] Take time to deliberate about your hierarchy of values. It is possible that after careful consideration of the implications of a particular value, such as "being well off financially," you may want to place it lower on your hierarchy of values.

If you are unsure of your skills and talents, go to the career office at your college and take some of the aptitude and personality tests available there, such as the Myers-Briggs Indicator.[33] These tests are useful in helping you to

HIGHLIGHTS
MY LIFE PLAN

In putting together your life plan you need to identify:

1. Your most important values

2. Your strengths (interests, skills, talents, and assets)

3. Your weaknesses (for example, lack of financial resources or skill)

4. Your goals

   a. Short term

   b. Long term

5. A plan of action to achieve short-term goals

6. A plan of action to achieve long-term goals

➤ *APPLICATION: Identify an example of each of the six steps in the text.*

determine which career or careers might be most fulfilling for you. The Web site www.collegeboard.org also provides helpful information on choosing a major and a career.

But don't just list your strengths, assets, and competencies; take note of your weaknesses too. Weaknesses are something we do poorly or something we lack, such as financial resources, information, or technical expertise.

Once you've written down your values, interests, talents, skills, and weaknesses, list your goals. Goals are important in helping you organize your day-to-day life and in giving your life direction. Start out by listing short-term goals, or those that you want to accomplish by the time you graduate from college; for example, choose a major,

maintain a 3.0 average, or get more exercise. These goals should be consistent with your interests, talents, and the type of person you want to be. Also come up with a plan of action to achieve these short-term goals.

Next, list your long-term goals. Ideally your long-term and short-term goals should augment each other. Your plans for achieving the long-term goals should be realistic and compatible with your short-term goals and interests. Think creatively about how certain goals can fit together.

People who are skilled critical thinkers not only have reasonable, well thought out goals and strategies to achieve them but also act from a sense of integrity or personal authenticity and respect for the integrity and aspirations of others in their lives. We are not isolated individuals but social beings whose decisions affect the lives of all those around us.

Connections

How can participation in civic life improve your critical-thinking skills and enhance your personal growth? *See Chapter 13, p. 402.*

What marketing strategies should you be aware of so as to avoid being an uncritical consumer? *See Chapter 10, pp. 311–312.*

Facing Challenges

Sometimes traditional practices and cultural beliefs get in the way of our achieving our life plan. In these cases we may need to develop subgoals that involve challenging the

A life plan is like a flight plan; it helps keep us on course.

Martin Luther King's willingness to go to jail, rather than back down on his goal of equality for all people, made him one of the most effective civil rights leaders in American history.

obstructing beliefs rather than give up our life plan. Openly questioning traditional belief systems and effectively addressing challenges to deeply held beliefs requires courage and self-confidence. The abolitionists and early feminists and civil rights advocates were often ridiculed and even imprisoned because they challenged traditions they believed were unjust. See "Thinking Outside the Box: Elizabeth Cady Stanton, Women's Rights Leader."

When Martin Luther King Jr. was thrown in jail for his role in organizing the 1955 bus boycott in Montgomery, Alabama, he refused to back down despite the beseeching of his fellow clergy. Fortunately, King had the courage to stand by his convictions. In his "Letter from Birmingham Jail," King wrote:

> My Dear Fellow Clergy,
>
> I am in Birmingham because injustice is here. . . .
> We know through painful experience that freedom is never voluntarily given by the oppressor; it must be demanded by the oppressed.
>
> You express a great deal of anxiety over our willingness to break laws. . . . This is a legitimate concern . . . an unjust law is a code that is out of harmony with the moral law. . . . Any law that degrades human personality is unjust. . . . I submit that an individual who breaks a law that conscience tells him is unjust, and willingly accepts the penalty by staying in jail to arouse the conscience of the community over its injustice, is in reality expressing the very highest respect for law.

Critical thinking, as we noted earlier, requires being in touch with our emotions, such as indignation or anger,

elicited by unjust treatment, as in the case of King, or by a shocking image such as the photo showing the abuse at Abu Ghraib prison (see page 18).

In addition to being able to effectively challenge social injustices, as critical thinkers we need to be able to respond thoughtfully to challenges to our own belief systems rather than engaging in resistance. This requires good critical-thinking skills as well as self-confidence.

The Importance of Self-Esteem

Effective critical-thinking skills appear to be positively correlated to healthy self-esteem. Healthy self-esteem emerges from effectiveness in problem solving and success in achieving our life goals. The task of sorting out genuine self-worth from a false sense of self-esteem requires critical thinking. Healthy self-esteem is not the same as arrogant pride or always putting one's own interests first. Nor are people with proper self-esteem habitually self-sacrificing, subverting their interests and judgment to those of others.

People with low self-esteem are more vulnerable to manipulation by others. They experience more "depression, irritability, anxiety, fatigue, nightmares . . . withdrawal from others, nervous laughter, body aches and emotional tension."[34] Some of these traits, such as anxiety and nervous laughter, were seen in the Milgram study participants who complied with the request of the authority figure. Indeed, many of these men later came to regret their compliance and even required psychotherapy.

Good critical-thinking skills are essential in exercising your autonomy. Critical thinkers are proactive. They are aware of the influences on their lives, including family, culture, television, and friends; they can build on the positive influences and overcome the negative ones, rather than be passively carried through life and blaming others if their decisions turn out poorly.

An autonomous person is both rational and self-directing and therefore less likely to be taken in by poor reasoning or contradictions in his own or other's reasoning. Being self-directing entails making decisions on the basis of what is reasonable instead of getting swept up in groupthink or blindly obeying an authority figure. To achieve this end, autonomous critical thinkers seek out different perspectives and actively participate in critical dialogues to gain new insights and expand their own thinking.

Did You Know

Studies show that young people who have positive self-esteem "have more friends, are more apt to resist harmful peer pressure, are less sensitive to criticism or to what people think, have higher IQs, and are better informed."[35]

Thinking Outside the Box

ELIZABETH CADY STANTON, *Women's Rights Leader*

Elizabeth Cady Stanton (1815–1902) was a social activist and leader in the early women's rights movement. In 1840, when she was a young newlywed, Stanton attended the World Anti-Slavery Society convention in London, which her husband was attending as a delegate. It was there that Stanton met Lucretia Mott (1793–1880). At the convention the women delegates from the United States were denied seats after some of the male U.S. delegates vehemently objected. Mott, in response, demanded that she be treated with the same respect accorded any man—white or black. During these heated discussions, Stanton marveled at the way Mott, a woman of 47, held her own in the argument, "skillfully parried all their attacks . . . turning the laugh on them, and then by her earnestness and dignity silencing their ridicule and jeers."*

Following the Civil War, Stanton refused to support passage of the Fifteenth Amendment, which gave voting rights to black men but not to women. She argued that the amendment essentially was based on the fallacy of false dilemma—either black men get the vote (but not women) or only white men can vote. Instead she pointed out that there was a third option: both men and women should have the right to vote. Unfortunately, her line of argument and her challenges to traditional beliefs about the role of women were ridiculed. Although black men received the vote in 1870 with passage of the Fifteenth Amendment, it would be another 50 years before women were finally given the right to vote in the United States. Nevertheless, Stanton's persistence and refusal to back down in her fight for equal opportunity for women paved the way for the final passage of this amendment so that other women could achieve their life plans of equal participation in the political life of the country.

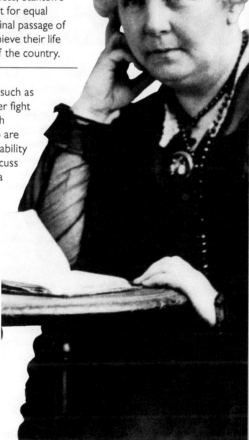

1. Elizabeth Cady Stanton had close friends such as Lucretia Mott and Susan B. Anthony in her fight for women's rights. Discuss ways in which having a support network of people who are skilled critical thinkers can enhance your ability not to use or fall for faulty reasoning. Discuss ways in which you do, or could, serve as a critical-thinking mentor to others.

2. Think of a time when your ability to pursue your goals was compromised by ridicule. Explain, using specific examples. Discuss steps you might take to make yourself less likely to give into faulty reasoning or to give up on an aspect of your life plan under such circumstances.

*Lloyd Hare, *The Greatest American Women: Lucretia Mott* (New York: American Historical Society, 1937), p. 193.

ANALYZING **IMAGES**

Abuse at Abu Ghraib Prison, Iraq Being an autonomous thinker makes it less likely that you will uncritically follow orders or conform to peer pressure. The abuse and humiliation of Iraqi prisoners by U.S. soldiers at Abu Ghraib prison in Iraq in 2003–2004 provides a real-life illustration of what happened in the Milgram and Stanford prison experiments. In 2005, Army reservist and prison guard Charles Graner was convicted and sentenced to 10 years in prison for his role as ringleader in the abuse and humiliation of Iraqi detainees. In his defense he said that he was simply following orders. His defense lawyers also pointed out that the U.S. Army's intelligence units were poorly trained and badly managed, factors that contributed to the reservists' poor judgment. Graner's defense was rejected by the court. Graner was released from prison in 2011 after serving six years of his term.

DISCUSSION QUESTIONS

1. *Was Graner's reason for his treatment of the Iraqi prisoners justified? Should he be held responsible for his actions? Discuss what you might have done had you been a low-ranking guard at Abu Ghraib and had witnessed your fellow soldiers mistreating Iraqi prisoners.*

2. *What was your initial emotional reaction to this image? Discuss how learning to be aware of and critically analyzing your reaction to this or other upsetting images might make you more likely to question authority or rethink some of your world views. Support your response in light of what you know about autonomous thinkers.*

3. *Similar situations have occurred during fraternity and sorority initiation hazings. If you know of, or have been witness to, any situations where this happened, discuss why it most likely happened and what might have been done to prevent it.*

Critical Thinking in a Democracy

Critical-thinking skills are essential in a democracy. **Democracy** literally means rule by the people; it is a form of government in which the highest power in the state is invested in the people and exercised directly by them or, as is generally the case in modern democracies, by their elected officials. As citizens of a democracy, we have an obligation to be well informed about policies and issues so that we can effectively participate in critical discussions and decisions.

Thomas Jefferson wrote, "In a republican nation, whose citizens are to be led by reason and persuasion and not by force, the art of reasoning becomes of the first importance."[36] The purpose of democracy is not to achieve consensus through polling or majority vote but to facilitate open-ended discussion and debates by those with diverse views. Truth, argued British philosopher John Stuart Mill (1806–1873), often is found neither in the opinion of those who favor the status quo nor in the opinion of the noncon-

formist but in a combination of viewpoints. Therefore, freedom of speech and listening to opposing views, no matter how offensive they may be, are essential for critical thinking in a democracy.

Corrupt politicians have been elected or appointed to public office and high-ranking positions in their parties because the

democracy A form of government in which the highest power in the state is invested in the people and exercised directly by them or, as is generally the case in modern democracies, by their elected officials.

ANALYZING **IMAGES**

Student Protestor in Front of Tanks at Tiananmen Square, China

On June 3rd and 4th, 1989, hundreds, possibly thousands, of unarmed demonstrators protesting the legitimacy of China's communist government were shot dead in a brutal military operation to crush a democratic uprising in Beijing's Tiananmen Square. The demonstrators, who were mostly university students, had occupied the square for several weeks, refusing to leave until their demands for democratic reform were met. A photographer captured the above picture of a lone, unnamed demonstrator standing in front of the tanks, bringing to a halt the row of advancing tanks. To this day, no one knows who the demonstrator was or what his fate was.

DISCUSSION QUESTIONS

1. *What do you think the student in the photo is thinking and feeling? What do you think led up to his decision to take this action? Does his action show good critical thinking? Discuss ways in which the student's action demonstrates, or does not demonstrate, good critical-thinking skills. Relate your answer to the actions of reformers such as Stanton and King.*

2. *Imagine yourself in a similar situation. Discuss how you would most likely react and how your reaction is a reflection of your current self-development. What steps could you take in your life to make yourself more likely to engage in civil disobedience, particularly in a case where your life was not at stake?*

What critical-thinking skills do you need to participate in campaigns and elections, influence public policy, and understand the legal system? *See Chapter 13.*

people failed to educate themselves about their activities and ideals. Indeed, in a 1938 poll of Princeton freshmen, Adolf Hitler was ranked first as the "greatest living person"![37] And in New York City in the mid-nineteenth century, politician William Marcy "Boss" Tweed (1823–1878) conned citizens out of millions of dollars. He also managed to get his corrupt associates, known as the Tweed Ring, appointed and elected to high offices.

Unlike totalitarian societies, modern democracies encourage diversity and open discussion of different ideas. Research on the effects of race, ethnicity, class, and diversity on college students reveals "important links between experiences with diversity and increased commitment to civic engagement, democratic outcomes and community participation."[38] Exposure to diversity on campus and in the classroom broadens students' perspectives and improves critical thinking and problem-solving skills.[39]

In his book *The Assault on Reason* (2007), Al Gore argues that there has been a decline in participation by ordinary citizens in the democratic process since television overtook the printed word as the dominant source of information. Television as a one-way source of information appeals mainly to our uncritical emotions rather than requiring critical reflective thought, thus rendering viewers passive consumers of prepackaged information and ideologies. Political engagement tends to rise during a presidential election year and drop off following the election. For example, 39.5 percent of college freshmen in 2008 stated that "keeping up to date with political affairs" was an essential or very important objective for them. However, this figure had dropped to 36 percent one year after the election of Barack Obama.[40]

People who are skilled at critical thinking are less likely to be taken in by faulty arguments and rhetoric. They are also more likely, like the pro-democracy Chinese students in Tiananmen Square, to demand the same clarity and reasonableness of thinking in their leaders that they require in themselves rather than remain passive in the face of government abuses of power. Thus, critical thinking contributes to your own well-being as well as to the well-being of society as a whole, by teaching you how to stand up to authority and irrational thinking.

EXERCISE 1-3

STOP AND ASSESS YOURSELF

1. According to German philosopher Immanuel Kant (1724–1804), one of our primary moral duties is self-respect and the development of proper self-esteem.[41] To truly respect others and their perspectives, we must first respect ourselves. Discuss and relate your answer to how proper self-respect might enhance your critical thinking skills. Use specific examples to support your answer.

2. Choose one of your short-term or long-term goals. Working in small groups, brainstorm about ways each of you might best achieve your goals. Also discuss the role good critical-thinking skills play (or played) in helping you achieve your goals.

3. In small groups, discuss a time when you deferred to the view of someone else and did (or failed to do) something you later came to regret because you were unable to give good reasons at the time for why you should not accept that person's view. Brainstorm with your group about ways in which you might make yourself less prone to this behavior.

4. A June 2004 article in *Altermedia Scotland* states: "America as a nation is now dominated by an alien system of beliefs, attitudes, and values that has become known as 'political correctness.' It seeks to impose a uniformity in thought and behaviour among all Americans and is therefore totalitarian in nature."[42] Do you agree that political correctness imposes "a uniformity of thought and behavior"? Come up with examples of political correctness on college campuses to illustrate your answer. Discuss what role, if any, political correctness might play in increasing respect for diversity and enhancing the democratic process.

5. What is diversity? What are the educational benefits of diversity? Discuss ways in which your college, including your classes, addresses and facilitates diversity.

6. The student pro-democracy movement in Tiananmen Square was unsuccessful in terms of bringing democracy and a more open society to China. Does this failure mean that the movement and the lives that were lost were a waste? Support your answer.

7. Al Gore argues that the "mental muscles of democracy have begun to atrophy."[43] Discuss his claim. Relate your answer to the exercise of your "mental muscles" and those of other college students in political dialogue.

EXERCISE 1-3 CONT.

8. When the *Brown Daily Herald*, the student newspaper at Brown University, ran an ad from conservative activist David Horowitz entitled "Ten Reasons Why Reparation for Slavery Is a Bad Idea—and Racist Too," a coalition of Brown students stole and destroyed nearly 4,000 newspapers at campus distribution points. Defendants of the action argued that the ad was "an attempt to inject blatantly revisionist and, yes, racist arguments into a legitimate debate about black reparations . . . ."[44] Is it ever appropriate to censor views? Did the students have a legitimate right, on the basis of their freedom of speech, to destroy the newspapers? To what extent, if any, do we have an obligation in a democracy to listen attentively to and consider views that we find offensive? What would you have done had your school newspaper decided to publish the ad by Horowitz?

9. What are your strengths and talents? If you are not sure of your talents, go to the career office at your college and ask if you can take some of the personality and aptitude tests available there. These tests are also useful in helping you to determine which career or careers might be most fulfilling for you. Be creative; don't limit or underrate yourself.

BARRIERS TO CRITICAL THINKING

By sharpening your critical-thinking skills, you can become more independent and less susceptible to worldviews that foster narrow-mindedness. In this section we'll be looking at some of the barriers to critical thinking that keep us from analyzing our experiences or worldviews, as well as the experiences and worldviews of others.

The Three-Tier Model of Thinking

The processes used in critical thinking can be broken down into three tiers or levels: experience, interpretation, and analysis. Keep in mind that this division is artificial and merely helps to highlight the critical-thinking process. Although analysis is at the pinnacle of the process, the three-tier model is also recursive and dynamic, with analysis returning to experience for confirmation and interpretation being modified in light of the analysis of the new information. People never have pure experience or engage in pure analysis.

Experience, the first level, includes firsthand experience as well as information or empirical facts that we receive from other sources. Experience is the foundation of critical thinking and argumentation. It provides the material for interpretation and analysis. At this level of thinking we merely describe our experiences rather than try to understand them. For example:

1. I was turned down for the job I interviewed for.
2. Mark held the door open for me when I was leaving class.
3. Human cloning is illegal in the United States.
4. Although blacks represent only 12.8 percent of the U.S. population, they make up 37 percent of the prison inmates.[45]

Interpretation, the second level, involves trying to make sense of our experiences. This level of thinking includes individual interpretations of experiences as well as collective and cultural worldviews. Some of our interpretations may be well informed; others may be based merely on our opinions or personal feelings and prejudices.

Connections

How has the Internet enhanced your ability to participate in political life? *See Chapter 11, pp. 347–348.* In what ways is the news media biased? *See Chapter 11, pp. 344–345.* How can we as citizens participate in the law-making process? *See Chapter 13, p. 408.*

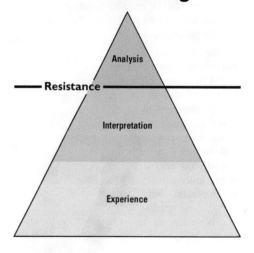

The Three Levels of Thinking

Some possible interpretations of the experiences previously listed are

1. I didn't get the job because I didn't have the right connections.
2. Mark is a chauvinist pig who thinks women are too weak to open their own doors.
3. If human cloning is illegal, it must be immoral.
4. Black men make up such a large percentage of the prison population because black men are innately more violent than white men.

Analysis, the third level, requires that we raise our level of thinking and critically examine our interpretations of an experience, as well as those of others, refusing to accept either narrow interpretations of an experience or interpretations that are too broad. Analysis is most productive when it is done collectively because we each bring different experiences and interpretations, as well as skills in analysis, to the table. Analysis often begins by asking a question. The following are examples of questions we might ask in order to begin our analysis of the interpretations:

1. Was it my lack of connections or my poor interviewing skills or lack of job qualifications that caused me not to get the job?
2. What was Mark's intention in holding the door open for me?
3. Why is human cloning illegal? Are there circumstances in which human cloning might be acceptable?
4. Is there evidence that black men are innately more violent, or is it possible that black men are simply discriminated against more than white men? Or are other factors at work to account for their overrepresentation in the prison population?

The three-tier model of thinking provides a dynamic model of critical thinking in which analysis is always returning to experience for confirmation. As critical thinkers, it is not only our reasoning process that is important but also that our reasoning is connected to reality.

Connections

How can you use the three-tier model of thinking to analyze media messages? *See Chapter 11, p. 352.*

What model of thinking do scientists use? *See Chapter 12, p. 367.*

Resistance

Because most of us hate to be proven wrong, we may create barriers to keep our cherished worldviews from being challenged. Resistance, defined as "the use of immature defense mechanisms that are rigid, impulsive, maladaptive, and nonanalytical," can act as a barrier to critical thinking.

Almost all of us use defense mechanisms when we feel overwhelmed. Resistance, however, becomes a problem when it is used as a habitual way of responding to issues. Such habitual use interferes with our self-development, since it involves avoiding novel experiences and ideas that challenge our world-views. People who hold views that are backed by public opinion or the law may be particularly likely to resist when these views are challenged: They don't want to see the status quo upset.

> People who hold views that are backed by public opinion or the law may be particularly likely to resist when these views are challenged: They don't want to see the status quo upset.

In addition, resistance can create anxiety, since it puts us in a defensive mode and can shield us from the ideas and viewpoints of others, thus preventing us from working collaboratively and coming up with a well thought out plan of action.

Types of Resistance

There are several types of resistance, including avoidance, anger, clichés, denial, ignorance, conformity, struggling, and distractions.

Avoidance. Rather than seeking out different points of view, we may avoid certain people and situations. Some people who hold strong opinions but are insecure in their ability to defend these positions hang out only with people who agree with them or read literature and watch television news shows that support their worldview. I attended a church service during which the minister in her sermon lambasted Mel Gibson's movie *The Passion of the Christ* (2004) as a violent and inaccurate depiction of the betrayal and death of Jesus. I asked her after the service if she had seen the movie, and she said no. When I told her that I liked the movie, she frowned and quickly moved on to talk to someone else. As a form of resistance, avoidance can lead to a serious lack of communication and even hostility among people who hold opposing points of view.

Anger. We cannot always avoid people who disagree with us. Rather than using critical thinking when confronted with an opposing viewpoint, some people respond with anger. People with physical and/or social power are more likely than those without it to use anger to silence those who disagree with them. Anger may be expressed overtly by glares, threats, physical violence, gang activity, or even war.

Not all anger is resistance. We may feel anger or moral indignation when we hear that one of our favorite professors was denied tenure because he is Arab. This anger may motivate us to correct this injustice by writing a letter of protest to the local newspaper. We'll be looking more at the positive role of emotion in critical thinking in Chapter 2.

Clichés. Resorting to clichés—often-repeated statements such as "Don't force your views on me," "It's all relative," "To each his own," "Things always work out for the best," and "I have a right to my own opinion"—can keep us from thinking critically about issues. Advertisers and politicians often use clichés as a means of sidetracking us from considering the quality of the product or the issue at hand.

Resistance to analyzing one's position is seen in the abortion debate where each side has become entrenched in the clichés pro-choice or pro-life, with the pro-choice side focused on having few or no legal restrictions and the pro-life side wanting abortion to be illegal, at least in most cases. To overcome this divisive thinking, the term "reproductive justice" was coined by a group of black feminists to address the concerns of African-American women, whose abortion rate is three and one-half times that of white women. Loretta Ross, cofounder of the group SisterSong Women of Color Reproductive Justice Collective, maintains that we need to think differently about the abortion debate. "Those of us in the reproductive justice movement, would say, 'Let's ask why there is such a high rate of unintended pregnancies in our community: What are the factors driving it?'"[46]

Used sparingly, clichés can be helpful to illustrate a point. However, the habitual use of clichés acts as a barrier to critical thinking.

Denial. According to the U.S. National Center for Injury Prevention and Control, alcohol-related motor vehicle accidents kill someone every 30 minutes and account for 41 percent of all traffic-related deaths.[47] Despite these startling statistics, people who drink and drive often deny that they are drunk. They may refuse to let someone else drive, claiming that they are quite capable of doing so.

Many Americans are also in denial about the possibility that world oil reserves may soon run out. Despite improved exploration technology, discovery of new oil reserves peaked in 1962 and has been dropping ever since. According to some predictions, active oil reserves may run out by anywhere from 2020 to 2030.[48] Yet, faced with declining fossil-fuel sources, many Americans continue to drive large vehicles and to live in large homes that cost more and more to heat.

Ignorance. Confucius taught that "Ignorance is the night of the mind." The modern Hindu yogi Swami Prabhavananda wrote, "Ignorance creates all the other obstacles." People are more likely to think critically about

Connections

How can our critical-thinking skills help us recognize misleading advertisements? *See Chapter 10, p. 321.*

ANALYZING IMAGES

Is Ignorance Bliss?

DISCUSSION QUESTIONS

1. *Has there even been a time when, like the man in the picture above, you've preferred ignorance to being informed? Why? Support your answer with specific examples.*

2. *Some people accuse college students of taking the attitude that "ignorance is bliss" when it comes to participation in public life. Analyze this claim using research findings as well as examples to support your answer.*

issues about which they have knowledge in depth. In certain situations, we are ignorant about an issue simply because the information about it is not available to us. However, sometimes we just don't want to know.

Ignorance is a type of resistance when we intentionally avoid learning about a particular issue, about which information is readily available, in order to get out of having to think or talk about it. Ignorance is often used as an excuse for inaction. For example, Joe told his colleagues that he wanted to make a donation to help the Haitians following the 2010 earthquake but he didn't because "you just can't tell which charities are ripping you off and keeping most of the money for themselves." In fact, there are websites such as www.charitynavigator.org that inform potential donors exactly how much money each major charitable organization uses directly for charity and how much goes to administrative and fundraising costs. Some people believe that being ignorant excuses them from having to think critically about or take action on an issue. As a result, the issue is not resolved or even becomes worse.

How does the news media influence and reinforce narrow-minded worldviews? *See* Chapter 11, pp. 353–354.

Connections

Conformity. Many people fear that they will not be accepted by their peers if they disagree with them. Even though they may actually disagree, they go along with the group rather than risk rejection. We've probably all been in a situation where someone at work or a party makes a racist or sexist joke or an offensive comment about gays or women. Rather than speaking up, many people keep quiet or even laugh, thus tolerating and perpetuating bigotry and negative stereotypes.

Other people conform because they don't have a point of view of their own on an issue. Saying "I can see both sides of the issue" often masks a reluctance to think critically about it. Martin Luther King Jr. once pointed out, "Many people fear nothing more terribly than to take a position which stands out sharply and clearly from prevailing opinion. The tendency of most is to adopt a

view that is so ambiguous that it will include everything, and so popular that it will include everyone."

Struggling. During the Nazi occupation of France in World War II, the people of the village of Le Chambonsur-Lignon provided refuge for Jews who were fleeing the Nazis. When Pierre Sauvage, director of *Weapons of the Spirit*—a documentary about the people and resistance movement of Le Chambon—was asked by PBS television's Bill Moyers years later why they did this when other people were still struggling about what to do, Sauvage replied, "Those who agonize don't act; those who act don't agonize."[49]

It is appropriate to struggle with or agonize over difficult issues before coming to a tentative stand. However, some people get so caught up in the minute details and "what ifs" of an issue—a situation sometimes referred to as "analysis paralysis"—that nothing gets accomplished. Procrastinators are most likely to use this type of resistance. Although struggling with an issue as part of the analytical process of coming up with a resolution and plan for action is an important component of critical thinking, when the struggle becomes an end-in-itself, we are engaging in resistance, not critical thinking.

Distractions. Some people hate silence and being left alone with their own thoughts. Many of us use television, loud music, partying, work, drugs, alcohol, or shopping to prevent our minds from critically thinking about troublesome issues in our lives. People may overeat instead of examining the causes of their cravings or unhappiness. Mental hindrances like distractions, according to Buddhist teaching, keep us from clear understanding. Instead, Buddhist philosophy values stillness and contemplation as means of achieving wisdom and understanding.

Narrow-Mindedness

Like resistance, narrow-mindedness and rigid beliefs, such as absolutism, egocentrism, and ethnocentrism can become barriers to critical thinking.

Absolutism. As we noted earlier, we may find ourselves acting contrary to our deeply held moral beliefs—as happened to most of the subjects in the Milgram study—simply because we do not have the critical-thinking skills necessary for standing up to unreasonable authority. In particular, college students at the first stage of cognitive development, where they regard information as either right or wrong, have an "expectation that authorities provide them with absolutely correct knowledge."[50]

When confronted with a situation like the one faced by those who administered electric shocks in Milgram's study, such students lack the critical-thinking skills to counter the authority's reasoning. For more on the stages of moral development, see Chapter 9.

THINKING Outside the Box

STEPHEN HAWKING, *Physicist*

Stephen Hawking (b. 1942) is perhaps the most famous physicist alive. Shortly after graduating from college, he learned that he had ALS (Lou Gehrig's disease), a devastating and incurable neurological disease. About half of the people with it die within three years. After enduring depression and waiting to die, Hawking pulled himself together and decided to live his life to his fullest rather than give up. He enrolled in graduate school, married, and had three children. He writes: "ALS has not prevented me from having a very attractive family and being successful in my work. I have been lucky that my condition has progressed more slowly than is often the case. But it shows that one need not lose hope."

In 2004, Hawking publicly recanted a position he had held for the past 30 years that the gravity of black holes is so powerful that nothing can escape it, not even light.* In doing so, he conceded, with some regret, that CalTech astrophysicist John Preskill had been right all along about black holes. Preskill theorized that information about objects swallowed by black holes is able to leak from the black holes, a phenomenon known as the "black hole information paradox." Hawking paid Preskill off with an agreed-upon prize—an encyclopedia of baseball.

1. Discuss what characteristics of a good critical thinker, listed in the text, are demonstrated by Hawking's response to adversity and uncertainty.

2. Think of a position that you held (or still hold) against all evidence. Compare and contrast Hawking's action with how you respond when someone challenges your views or position. Discuss what extent resistance and/or narrow-mindedness is responsible for your reluctance to change or modify your position.

*See Mark Peplow, "Hawking Changes His Mind about Black Holes," http://www.nature.com/news/2004/040712/full/news040712-12.html.

Fear of Challenge. We may also fail to stand up to others because we fear that others will challenge our beliefs. Some people believe that is it a sign of weakness to change their position on an issue. Good critical thinkers, however, are willing to openly change their position in light of conflicting evidence. Unlike physicist Stephen Hawking, who is described in "Thinking Outside the Box: Stephen Hawking, Physicist," many people—especially those with low self-esteem or an egocentric personality—resist information and evidence that are at odds with what they believe. They may view the expression of opposing views or evidence as a personal attack.

Egocentrism. Believing that you are the center of all things is called **egocentrism**. Egocentric, or self-centered, people have little regard for others' interests and thoughts. Studies of cognitive development in college students suggest that as students develop cognitively and become better at critical thinking, they are less likely to view themselves egocentrically.[51] Although we all tend to fall for compliments and be skeptical of criticism, this tendency is especially true of egocentric people. Flattery impedes our ability to make sound judgments and increases our chances of being persuaded by the flatterer. Advertisers and con artists are well aware of this human tendency and thus use flattery to try to get us to go along with them or to buy products that we wouldn't otherwise buy.

> **egocentrism** The belief that the self or individual is the center of all things.
>
> **ethnocentrism** The belief in the inherent superiority of one's own group and culture.
>
> **anthropocentrism** The belief that humans are the central or most significant entities of the universe.

Ethnocentrism. An uncritical or unjustified belief in the inherent superiority of one's own group and culture is called **ethnocentrism**. It is characterized by suspicion of and a lack of knowledge of foreign countries and cultures.[52] Ethnocentric people often make decisions about other groups, cultures, and countries on the basis of stereotypes and opinions rather than on factual information. In addition, we tend to remember evidence that supports our worldview or stereotypes and forget or downplay that which doesn't. (See page 119 for more on self-serving biases in our thinking.)

Since the September 11, 2001 terrorist attacks on New York City and the Pentagon, Arab Americans have been subjected to hate crimes as well as to racial profiling by police and federal officials, despite official policies against this practice.

According to the U.S. Department of Justice, anti-Muslim crimes soared in 2010 to the highest level since 2001. This increase was due in part as a response to the "Ground Zero Mosque" (which was in fact a community center, not a mosque) in New York City and because of the incendiary rhetoric of groups such as "Stop Islamization of America." Hundreds of Muslims and Americans of Arab descent have been detained without charges and imprisoned under the USA Patriot Act, which was extended by President Obama in 2011. These types of hasty reactions can lead to misunderstandings and even increased hostility.

Uncritical nationalism—a form of ethnocentrism—can blind us to flaws and deteriorating conditions in our own culture. Americans who engage in this type of narrow-mindedness, for example, may bristle at the mere suggestion that the United States may not be the greatest and freest nation ever. Yet according to the Worldwide Governance Indicators 2011 report, which ranks governments by the amount of freedom citizens have to voice opinions and select their government, the United States, ranks lower than Canada, Australia, and most European nations.[53] This represents a drop from 2005, in part because of increased restrictions on freedom of the press.

Anthropocentrism. A belief that humans are the central or most significant entities of the universe, called **anthropocentrism**, can blind people to the capabilities of other animals. In his theory of evolution, Charles Darwin postulated that differences in cognitive function between humans and other animals were simply a matter of degree or quantity, rather than human cognitive function being of a qualitatively different "higher" type. However, the anthropocentric view of humans as unique among all other creatures or as beings created in the image of God and therefore above and separate from nature still dominates. This is found in the use of the term *animal,* even in scientific journals and books, as excluding humans, even though we are an animal species. Under the anthropocentric view, other animals and nature exist not in their own right but as resources for humans. Anthropocentrism can hinder us from critically thinking about our relationship with the rest of nature and can thereby threaten not only the survival of other species and the environment, as is happening with global warming, but our own survival as well.

> **Connections**
>
> How does the government exert influence on what gets reported in the media?
> *See Chapter 11, p. 343.*
> What is our responsibility as citizens living in a democracy?
> *See Chapter 13, p. 401 and p. 406.*

HIGHLIGHTS

TYPES OF RESISTANCE AND NARROW-MINDEDNESS

Resistance: The habitual use of immature defense mechanisms when our worldviews are challenged.

Avoidance	Denial	Struggle
Anger	Ignorance	Rationalization
Clichés	Conformity	Distractions

Narrow-mindedness: Rigid beliefs that interfere with critical analysis of our worldviews.

Absolutism	Egocentrism
Anthropocentrism	Fear of challenge
Ethnocentrism	

➤ *APPLICATION: Identify an example in the text of each of the types of resistance and narrow-mindedness.*

Sunando Sen, of Queens, New York, was pushed to his death in front of a train in December 2012 by a woman who told police she had pushed him off the subway platform because she has hated Muslims ever since September 11th. Sen was from India.

The belief that artificial intelligence, in which a computer, robot, or other device is programmed to learn and make decisions, will never match human intelligence is also a product of anthropocentrism. We'll be looking at artificial intelligence and reason in Chapter 2.

Rationalization and Doublethink

While sometimes the best alternative is clear, it's often the case that competing claims require our analysis before we can come to a decision. When presented with conflicting alternatives, some people make a decision quickly because of their bias in favor of one of the alternatives. In doing so, they justify or rationalize their choice on the basis of personal preferences or opinion, rather than on a critical analysis of the competing claims. In an experiment on making choices, psychologist A. H. Martin found that with rationalization the decision is often accompanied by a "rush" of satisfaction, thus convincing the person that his or her preference was correct.[54]

We may also use rationalization in an attempt to justify past actions that are inconsistent with our image of ourselves as a decent, rational person. Child molesters may see themselves as affectionate and loving people whom children enjoy being with. A person may cheat on a sweetheart and then, when confronted, lie about the affair, justifying the lie on the grounds that he or she is a caring person who is looking out for the best interests of the sweetheart by not saying something that will hurt his or her feelings.

Because rationalization involves ignoring competing claims, people who engage in it often get caught up in doublethink. **Doublethink** involves holding two contradictory views, or "double standards," at the same time and believing both to be true. This is particularly prevalent in response to highly charged issues. Rather than analyze the arguments surrounding these issues, people may unwittingly engage in doublethink.

For example, when asked, most college students state that they believe in equality of men and women. However, when it comes to lifestyle and career, the same students who claim to believe in equality and freedom of choice also say that women should be the primary caretakers of children. Most teachers, even the most ardent feminists, treat their female students differently from their male students, calling on boys and praising their accomplishments more often, and having more tolerance of boys' disruptive behavior.[55] When shown videotapes of their classes, many of these teachers are horrified at the extent to which they ignore the girls and downplay their contributions and achievements.

Similarly, the majority of white Americans champion equality as a principle when it comes to race but may harbor unconscious prejudice. Unexamined prejudices can distort our perception of the world. In a study, people were asked to match negative and positive words with names associated with Americans of both European and African descent. The more implicitly prejudiced the subjects were, the more likely they were to match the negative words with African Americans and the positive words with European Americans.[56]

Doublethink can have an impact on our real-life decisions. According to the U.S. Bureau of Labor Statistics, women, including those who work full time outside the home, still perform the great majority of housework and child care.[57] At work, women and minorities suffer from job discrimination and earn significantly less than white men earn. The wage disparity between men and women increases with age. Yet, in spite of the evidence to the contrary, many college students, when asked, maintain that sex-based and race-based discrimination in the work-place are things of the past.

doublethink Holding two contradictory views at the same time and believing both to be true.

cognitive dissonance A sense of disorientation that occurs in situations where new ideas directly conflict with a person's worldview.

social dissonance A sense of disorientation that occurs when the social behavior and norms of others conflict with a person's worldview.

Connections

To what extent is anthropocentrism implicit in the scientific worldview? *See Chapter 12, p. 366.* How does the news media influence and reinforce narrow-minded worldviews? *See Chapter 11, p. 336.*

Cognitive and Social Dissonance

We are most likely to critically analyze or modify our views when we encounter **cognitive dissonance** and **social dissonance**, situations where new ideas or social behavior directly

U.S. Median Income by Race, Ethnicity, and Gender, 2011

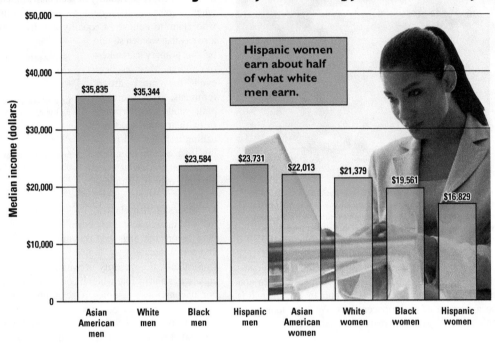

Hispanic women earn about half of what white men earn.

$35,835	$35,344	$23,584	$23,731	$22,013	$21,379	$19,561	$16,829
Asian American men	White men	Black men	Hispanic men	Asian American women	White women	Black women	Hispanic women

The average income, except for Hispanic females, who made a slight gain, is lower than it was in 2008 for all groups. The most significant drop in income was among white males, whose average income dropped by $2,065 over the three-year period.

Source: U.S. Census Bureau, 2011.

conflict with our worldviews. People who are forced to live or work in an integrated community, be it a dorm, college classroom, or a public housing project, often encounter occasions and behavior that conflict with their ethnocentric attitudes. Evidence indicates that once a person's behavior is changed—that is, after they share a meal or discuss issues in class with people of other races or ethnicities—a change in belief is likely to follow.[58] Exposing yourself to role models who are skilled in critical thinking can also strengthen your motivation to think clearly rather than engage in resistance.

Stress as a Barrier

While some stress can be good in motivating us, when we experience excessive stress our brain—and our ability to think critically—slows down. Researchers have found that when people get caught up in disasters, such as an airplane crash, hurricane, flood, or fire, the vast majority freeze up. According to Mac McLean of the FAA and Civil Aerospace Medical Institute, instead of taking action to remove themselves from the danger, most people are "stunned and bewildered."[59] (See Thinking Outside the Box: Captain Chesley "Sully" Sullenberger.)

We can counteract the effect of stress by mentally rehearsing our responses to different stressful scenarios.[60]

People, such as Captain Sullenberger, who have mentally rehearsed the best route for evacuating their building repeatedly are far more likely than those who haven't rehearsed to take action and escape in cases of emergencies, such as a fire or a terrorist attack. More importantly, mental rehearsal can enhance our performance on familiar tasks. For example, basketball players who engaged in fifteen minutes of mental rehearsal on most days and fifteen minutes of actual practice on the other days actually performed better after twenty days than players who only engaged in physical practice each day.[61]

Did You Know

In a study, college students were shown a picture of a black man in a business suit standing on a subway next to a white man who is holding a razor. When asked later what they had seen, the majority reported seeing a black man with a razor standing next to a white man in a business suit.

THINKING

CAPTAIN CHESLEY "SULLY" SULLENBERGER, *Pilot*

On January 9, 2009, shortly after takeoff from LaGuardia Airport, US Air flight 1549 struck a large flock of geese, disabling both engines. After quickly determining that neither returning to LaGuardia nor continuing on to the next closest airport was feasible, Captain Chesley "Sully" Sullenberger made the decision to attempt to land the plane in the Hudson River. With the help of his co-pilot, he successfully landed the disabled plane in the river. While some passengers and crew sustained injuries, there was no loss of life. Sullenberger remained aboard until he was sure everyone had been safely evacuated before disembarking himself.

Three years later, in January 2012, the cruise ship *Costa Concordia* navigated too close to the coast of Italy. The ship struck a rock, tearing a huge gash in the side of the ship, causing it to capsize onto its side. Unlike Sullenberger's, Captain Francesco Schettino's reaction intensified the disaster. Schettino failed to order passengers to evacuate the ship until over an hour after the accident. He also abandoned the ship before all passengers were evacuated. Thirty-two passengers died in the accident. When later questioned about his actions, Schettino blamed his helmsman for the incident. As for his abandoning the ship, he claims he accidently fell into one of the lifeboats. Rather than accepting Schettino's excuses, the Costa cruise company places the blame squarely on Captain Schettino for taking the ship off course and for the aftermath.

Why did Captain Schettino so mishandle the *Costa Concordia* incident, whereas Captain Sullenberger remained calm and in control? Sullenberger credits his years of experience and practice as an aviation safety expert and accident investigator. In a February 8, 2009 news interview, Sullenberger told Katie Couric, "One way of looking at this might be that for 42 years, I've been making small regular deposits in this bank of experience, education, and training. And on January 15 the balance was sufficient so that I could make a very large withdrawal."

DISCUSSION QUESTIONS

1. Compare and contrast the responses of Captains Sullenberger and Schettino. Relate your answer to the types of resistance. Discuss how the development of your critical thinking skills might make you less prone to using resistance in a stressful situation.

2. What deposits are you making in your "bank of experience, education, and training" that will help you respond effectively to stressful situations or a crisis? Be specific. Discuss how these "deposits" will help you achieve this objective.

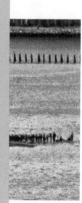

EXERCISE 1-4

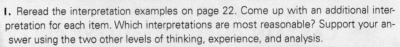

STOP AND ASSESS YOURSELF

1. Reread the interpretation examples on page 22. Come up with an additional interpretation for each item. Which interpretations are most reasonable? Support your answer using the two other levels of thinking, experience, and analysis.

2. Using the three-tiered model of thinking, discuss the experiences listed below. The interpretations that you list for each experience do not have to be ones that you personally accept. Share your interpretations with others in the class. Discuss how your past experiences have been shaped by your interpretations and how applying critical-thinking skills to analyze this issue might affect your future actions.

a. Affirmative action in college admissions discriminates against white males.

b. When I invited Chris to go to the movies with me last weekend, Chris said, "No thanks."

c. College tuition is rising faster than the cost of living in the United States.

d. According to CNN, more than half of the agricultural workers in the United States are illegal aliens.

e. Marijuana use has been decriminalized in Canada.

f. In 2012, 53 percent of college graduates under the age of 25 were unemployed or underemployed.

g. The college graduate rate for female student athletes is significantly higher than the rate for male student athletes.

h. In a recent survey, 45 percent of Americans stated that they feel that their pet listens to them better than their spouse does.

i. More and more men are going into nursing as a profession.

j. People who cohabitate before marriage are more likely to get divorced than those who do not.

3. According to the International Energy Commission, North Americans use more energy per person than any other people in the world. As a class, discuss ways in which we use rationalization or other types of resistance to justify our high energy-consumption lifestyle.

4. At the opposite end of the spectrum from egocentric people are those who sacrifice their needs and dreams for others. Harvard professor of education Carol Gilligan maintains that women in particular tend to be self-sacrificing—putting others' needs before their own. How does the tendency to be self-sacrificing interfere with effective critical thinking? Use examples from your own experience to illustrate your answer.

5. Douglas Adams (1952–2001), author of *The Hitchhiker's Guide to the Galaxy,* compared humans to a puddle of water as a way of illustrating anthropocentric thinking, or what he called "the vain conceit" of humans. He wrote:

> Imagine a puddle waking up one morning and thinking, "This is an interesting world I find myself in, an interesting hole I find myself in. It fits me rather neatly, doesn't it. In fact, it fits me staggeringly well. It must have been made to have me in it." Even as the sun comes out and the puddle gets smaller, it still frantically hangs on to the idea that everything is going to be all right; that the world was made for it since it is so well suited to it.[62]

Are humans, in fact, a lot like the puddle in Adams's analogy? Support your answer, using examples from your own experience. Discuss how this type of anthropocentric thinking shapes or distorts our interpretation of the world.

6. Working in small groups, expand on the list of barriers to critical thinking presented in the text. Come up with examples of each barrier and explain how they get in the way of critical thinking.

7. Think of a stressful situation—such as a job interview, breaking bad news, asking someone for a date, or giving a presentation in front of a class—that you will be facing in the next few weeks. Write down the task at the top of a page. Spend 15 minutes a day over the next week mentally rehearsing the task. Note the dates and times you spent mentally rehearsing the task. After you have performed the actual task, write a short essay on how well you did. Were you satisfied with the outcome? Discuss the extent to which mental rehearsal helped you perform this task, compared with similar tasks you performed in the past.

EXERCISE 1-4 CONT.

8. Write down three experiences relating to yourself and your life goals. For example, "I am good at science," "I am shy," "I haven't chosen a major yet," or "I want a job in which I can make a lot of money." Now write down at least three interpretations of each of these experiences. Analyze your interpretations. Are the interpretations reasonable? Share your interpretations with others in the class or with friends or family. Do they agree with your interpretations? If not, why not?

9. Working in small groups, discuss the types of resistance or narrow-mindedness that you are most likely to engage in when your views are challenged and steps you might take to overcome your resistance and narrow-mindedness.

10. Compare and contrast the reaction of Captain Sullenberger to a potential disastrous situation to that of Captain Schettino. Discuss how improving your critical thinking skills might improve your response to stressful situations and what deposits you are putting in your "bank of experience, education, and training," to use Sullenberger's words, to help you when you encounter situations beyond your control.

THiNK AGAIN

1. What are the characteristics of a skilled critical thinker?
   - A skilled critical thinker is well informed, open-minded, attentive, and creative, and has effective analytical, research, communication, and problem-solving skills.

2. What are the three levels of thinking?
   - The three levels are experience, which includes first-hand knowledge and information from other sources; interpretation, which involves trying to make sense out of our experiences; and analysis, which requires that we critically examine our interpretations.

3. What are some of the barriers to critical thinking?
   - Barriers include narrow-mindedness, such as absolutism, egocentrism, anthropocentrism, and ethnocentrism, as well as the habitual use of resistance, such as avoidance, anger, clichés, denial, ignorance, conformity, rationalization, and distractions.

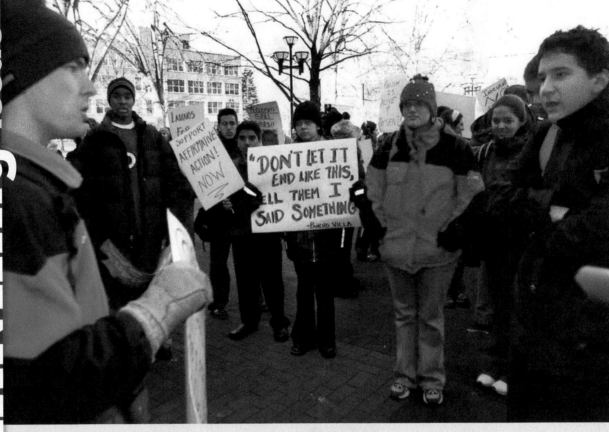

Perspectives on Affirmative Action in College Admissions

Affirmative action involves taking positive steps in job hiring and college admissions to correct certain past injustices against groups such as minorities and women. In 1954, the Supreme Court ruled in *Brown v. Board of Education* that school segregation was unconstitutional and that black children have a right to equal education opportunities. The first affirmative action legislation was proposed by Vice President Richard Nixon in 1959. Affirmative action programs and legislation were expanded during the civil rights era in the 1960s.

In 1978, Allan Bakke, a white man, sued the University of California at Davis Medical School because his application was rejected while minority students with lower test scores were admitted. The Supreme Court agreed with Bakke, ruling that reverse discrimination was unconstitutional. In 1996, with the passage of Proposition 209, California became the first state to ban affirmative action in the public sector, including admission to state colleges. Washington, Texas, and other states have also passed referenda banning affirmative action in state college admissions.

In June 2003, in *Grutter v. Bollinger,* the Supreme Court found that the admissions policy of the University of Michigan Law School, which awarded points to applicants based on race, was flawed. However, in its final ruling the court permitted race to be considered as one among many factors when considering individual applications. On June 24, 2013, the Supreme Court ruled on *Fisher v. University of Texas,* which was brought in response to *Grutter v. Bollinger* and requested overturn of the use of affirmative action in college admissions. It sent the case back to the lower court and ordered it to review the university's admission policy.

According to a 2012 Rasmussen Report, the majority of Americans aged 18 to 25 years (55 percent) oppose college affirmative action programs that give preference in admissions to blacks and other minorities, arguing that it constitutes reverse discrimination and, as such, is unjust. In contrast, in 2012 the Obama administration weighed in with briefs in support of affirmative action at the University of Texas, arguing that race should be one of many factors considered in admission. Proponents of affirmative action note that a ban on affirmative action in college admissions will cause a 2 percent drop in admissions of minorities at American colleges, including a 10 percent drop at the most elite colleges, and that this is unacceptable.[63]

Affirmative Action and Higher Education

BEFORE AND AFTER THE SUPREME COURT RULINGS

ON THE MICHIGAN CASES   NANCY CANTOR

Nancy Cantor is chancellor of Syracuse University. She was provost of the University of Michigan when the affirmative action cases were filed with the U.S. Supreme Court. In this article, published in the *Chicago Tribune* on January 28, 2003, she presents an argument for affirmative action in college admissions.

Integration takes hard work, especially when we have little other than collective fear, stereotypes and sins upon which to build. It is time America sees affirmative action on college campuses for what it is: a way to enrich the educational and intellectual lives of white students as well as students of color. We must not abandon race as a consideration in admissions.

The debate now before the U.S. Supreme Court over admissions at the University of Michigan is about the relative advantages people are getting, and it is a debate that misses the point. College admission has always been about relative advantage because a college education is a scarce resource, and the stakes are high.

In this era of emphasis on standardized tests, it may be easy to forget that colleges and universities have always taken into account many other aspects of students' experiences, including the geographic region from which they come, their families' relationship to the institution and their leadership experiences.

It is appropriate, and indeed critical, for the best institutions in the world to create the broadest possible mix of life experiences. Race is a fundamental feature of life in America, and it has an enormous impact on what a person has to contribute on campus. College admissions should be race-conscious to take the cultural and historical experiences of all students—Native American, African-American, Hispanic, Asian-American and white—and build on these in an educational setting. President Bush was wrong when he labeled the affirmative-action programs at the University of Michigan "quota systems.". . .

. . . There are no quotas at Michigan. All students compete for all seats. Race is used as a plus factor, along with other life experiences and talents, just as the president has suggested should happen. The percentages of students of color at Michigan vary annually.

Bush says he believes college admissions should be "race neutral," and he says he supports the principles of

Regents of the University of California vs. Bakke. He cannot have it both ways. Race is not neutral in the Bakke decision; it is front and center, just as it was nearly 50 years ago in *Brown vs. Board of Education*. In both cases, the Supreme Court urged our nation to boldly and straightforwardly take on the issue of race. . . .

The decision by Justice Lewis F. Powell in *Bakke* brought more than students of color to the table. It brought race in America to the table, urging educators to join hands in creating a truly integrated society of learners.

How are we to fulfill the dream of Brown and Bakke, to build a positive story of race in America, if we are told to ignore race—to concoct systems constructed around proxies for race such as class rank in racially segregated public school districts or euphemisms such as "cultural traditions" that both avoid our past and fail to value the possibility that race can play a constructive role in our nation's future?

. . . We want to include, not exclude. We want to use race as a positive category, as one of many aspects of a life we consider when we sit down to decide which students to invite to our table.

REVIEW QUESTIONS

1. According to Cantor, how does affirmative action benefit both white students and students of color?

2. What does Cantor mean which she says that "college admissions should be race-conscious"?

3. What is President Bush's stand on affirmative action, and why does Cantor disagree with him?

4. How does Cantor use the Supreme Court's rulings to bolster her argument for affirmative action in college admissions?

Achieving Diversity on Campus

U.S. SUPREME COURT JUSTICE SANDRA DAY O'CONNOR

In the following excerpt U.S. Supreme Court Justice Sandra Day O'Connor delivers the majority opinion in the landmark Supreme Court case *Grutter v. Bollinger,* in which it was argued that the use of affirmative action in college admissions is constitutional if race is treated as one factor among many and if the purpose is to achieve diversity on campus.

The University of Michigan Law School (Law School), one of the Nation's top law schools, follows an official admissions policy that seeks to achieve student body diversity through compliance with *Regents of Univ. of Cal. v. Bakke,* . . . Focusing on students' academic ability coupled with a flexible assessment of their talents, experiences, and potential, the policy requires admissions officials to evaluate each applicant based on all the information available in the file, including a personal statement, letters of recommendation, an essay describing how the applicant will contribute to Law School life and diversity, and the applicant's undergraduate grade point average (GPA) and Law School Admissions Test (LSAT) score. Additionally, officials must look beyond grades and scores to so-called "soft variables," such as recommenders' enthusiasm, the quality of the undergraduate institution and the applicant's essay, and the areas and difficulty of undergraduate course selection. The policy does not define diversity solely in terms of racial and ethnic status and does not restrict the types of diversity contributions eligible for "substantial weight," but it does reaffirm the Law School's commitment to diversity with special reference to the inclusion of African-American, Hispanic, and Native-American students, who otherwise might not be represented in the student body in meaningful numbers. By enrolling a "critical mass" of underrepresented minority students, the policy seeks to ensure their ability to contribute to the Law School's character and to the legal profession.

When the Law School denied admission to petitioner Grutter, a white Michigan resident with a 3.8 GPA and 161 LSAT score, she filed this suit, alleging that respondents had discriminated against her on the basis of race in violation of the Fourteenth Amendment, Title VI of the Civil Rights Act of 1964, and 42 U.S.C. § 1981; that she was rejected because the Law School uses race as a "predominant" factor, giving applicants belonging to certain minority groups a significantly greater chance of admission than students with similar credentials from disfavored racial groups; and that respondents had no compelling interest to justify that use of race. The District Court found the Law School's use of race as an admissions factor unlawful. The Sixth Circuit reversed, holding that Justice Powell's opinion in *Bakke* was binding precedent establishing diversity as a compelling state interest, and that the Law School's use of race was narrowly tailored because race was merely a "potential 'plus' factor" and because the Law School's program was virtually identical to the Harvard admissions program described approvingly by Justice Powell and appended to his *Bakke* opinion.

Held: The Law School's narrowly tailored use of race in admissions decisions to further a compelling interest in obtaining the educational benefits that flow from a diverse student body is not prohibited by the Equal Protection Clause, Title VI, or §1981.

In the landmark *Bakke* case, this Court reviewed a medical school's racial set-aside program that reserved 16 out of 100 seats for members of certain minority groups. . . . expressed his view that attaining a diverse student body was the only interest asserted by the university that survived scrutiny. . . . Grounding his analysis in the academic freedom that "long has been viewed as a special concern of the First Amendment," . . . Justice Powell emphasized that the "'nation's future depends upon leaders trained through wide exposure' to the ideas and mores of students as diverse as this Nation.". . . However, he also emphasized that "[i]t is not an interest in simple ethnic diversity, in which a specified percentage of the student body is in effect guaranteed to be members of selected ethnic groups," that can justify using race. . . . Rather, "[t]he diversity that furthers a compelling state interest encompasses a far broader array of qualifications and characteristics of which racial or ethnic origin is but a single though important element." Since *Bakke,* Justice Powell's opinion has been the touchstone for constitutional analysis of race-conscious admissions policies. Public and private universities across the Nation have modeled their own admissions programs on Justice Powell's views. . .

The Court endorses Justice Powell's view that student body diversity is a compelling state interest that can justify using race in university admissions. The Court defers to the Law School's educational judgment that diversity is essential to its educational mission. . . . Attaining a diverse student body is at the heart of the Law School's proper institutional mission, and its "good faith" is "presumed" absent "a showing to the contrary.". . . Enrolling a "critical mass" of minority students simply to assure some specified percentage of a particular group merely because of its race or ethnic origin would be patently unconstitutional. . . . But the Law School defines its critical mass concept by reference to the substantial, important, and laudable educational benefits that diversity is designed to produce, including cross-racial understanding and the breaking down of racial stereotypes. The Law School's claim is further bolstered by numerous expert studies and reports showing that such diversity promotes learning outcomes and better prepares students for an increasingly diverse workforce, for society, and for the legal profession. Major American businesses have made clear that the skills needed in today's increasingly global marketplace can only be developed through exposure to widely diverse people, cultures, ideas, and viewpoints. High-ranking retired officers and civilian military leaders assert that a highly qualified, racially diverse officer corps is essential to national security. Moreover, because universities, and in particular, law schools, represent the training ground for a large number of the Nation's leaders . . . the path to leadership must be visibly open to talented and qualified individuals of every race and ethnicity. Thus, the Law School has a compelling interest in attaining a diverse student body. . . . (d) The Law School's admissions program bears the hallmarks of a narrowly tailored plan. To be narrowly tailored, a race-conscious admissions program cannot "insulat[e] each category of applicants with certain desired qualifications from competition with all other applicants." . . . Instead, it may consider race or ethnicity only as a "'plus' in a particular applicant's file"; *i.e.,* it must be "flexible enough to consider all pertinent elements of diversity in light of the particular qualifications of each applicant, and to place them on the same footing for consideration, although not necessarily according them the same weight," . . . It follows that universities cannot establish quotas for members of certain racial or ethnic groups or put them on separate admissions tracks. . . . The Law School's admissions program, like the Harvard plan approved by Justice Powell, satisfies these requirements. Moreover, the program is flexible enough to ensure that each applicant is evaluated as an individual and not in a way that makes race or ethnicity the defining feature of the application. See *Bakke, supra,* at 317 (opinion of Powell, J.). The Law School engages in a highly individualized, holistic review of each applicant's file, giving serious consideration to all the ways an applicant might contribute to a diverse educational environment. . . . Also, the program adequately ensures that all factors that may contribute to diversity are meaningfully considered alongside race. Moreover, the Law School

frequently accepts nonminority applicants with grades and test scores lower than underrepresented minority applicants (and other nonminority applicants) who are rejected. . . . The Court is satisfied that the Law School adequately considered the available alternatives. The Court is also satisfied that, in the context of individualized consideration of the possible diversity contributions of each applicant, the Law School's race-conscious admissions program does not unduly harm nonminority applicants. . . . The Court takes the Law School at its word that it would like nothing better than to find a race-neutral admissions formula and will terminate its use of racial preferences as soon as practicable. The Court expects that 25 years from now, the use of racial preferences will no longer be necessary to further the interest approved today.

REVIEW QUESTIONS

1. Why did Grutter maintain that she had been treated unfairly by the University of Michigan Law School?
2. Why is Justice Powells's opinion in the *Bakke* case considered a landmark decision regarding college admissions?
3. On what grounds did the Supreme Court argument argue that attaining a diverse student body is part of an important part of institution's mission?
4. What conditions and limitations did the court place on using race in college admissions?

[THiNK AND DISCUSS

PERSPECTIVES ON AFFIRMATIVE ACTION

1. Agreeing on a definition is one of the first steps in debating an issue. How are the Supreme Court justices and Nancy Cantor each using the term *affirmative action*?
2. Discuss whether affirmative action has a place in a democracy that is built on equal rights for all citizens, or if it is a violation of the fundamental principle of fairness.
3. Compare and contrast the arguments used by Nancy Cantor and U.S. Supreme Court justice Sandra Day O'Connor regarding the use of affirmative action in college admissions. Which person makes the best argument? Support your answer.
4. Some people argue that instead of race, we should use an economic or class-based criterion for affirmative action. How would you support that premise?
5. Research the policy at your college regarding affirmative action in admission. To what extent has this policy had an impact on diversity in the student body and the quality of your education? Support your answer using specific examples.
6. What criteria (for example, experiences, talents, alumni status of parents) do you think should be used in college admissions? Working in small groups, develop a list of relevant criteria and assign each criterion a point value (for example, 10 or 20) out of a total of 100 points based on how important each criterion is to the admissions decision.

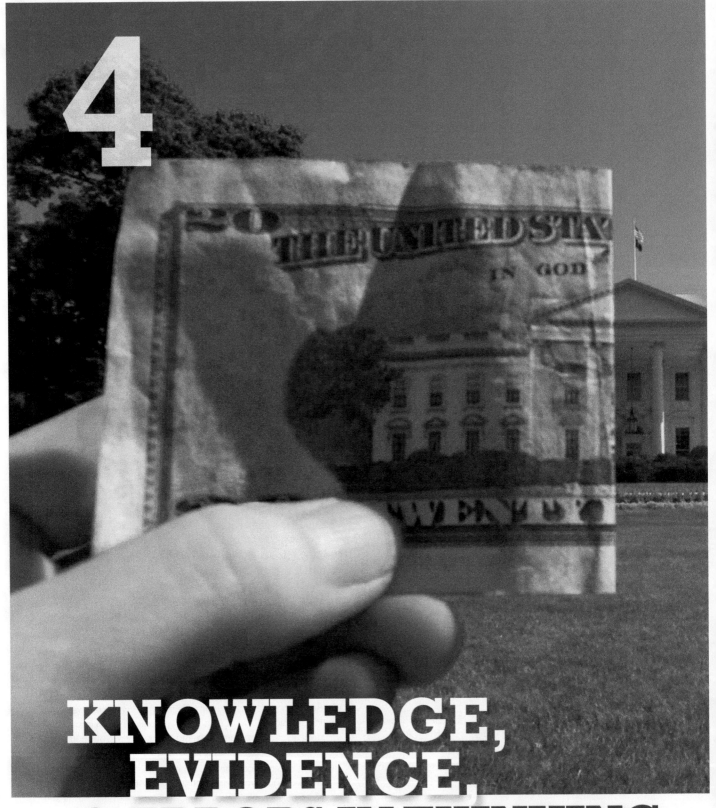

4

KNOWLEDGE, EVIDENCE, & ERRORS IN THINKING

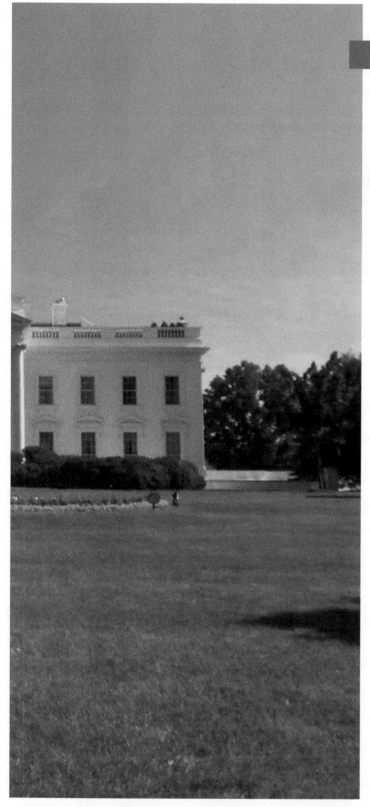

Our eyes want to join the picture of the White House on this $20 bill with the actual building, but our minds tell us that the continuation is an illusion.

In what became one of the most publicized cases of medical error, in 1995 a surgeon at University Community Hospital in Tampa, Florida, mistakenly amputated the wrong leg of 52-year-old Willie King. More recently, a surgeon at Milford Regional Medical Center in Massachusetts removed a woman's right kidney instead of her gallbladder as planned. In a high-profile case, actor Dennis Quaid's newborn twins nearly died from a dose of the blood-thinner heparin that was 1,000 times the prescribed dose. Each of these unfortunate incidents was the culmination of a chain of errors, many of them avoidable. Indeed, Healthgrades, an independent health care rating company, estimates that almost 3 percent of hospital patients in the United States are victims of potentially preventable medical errors.[1]

How can this happen? Cognitive errors, such as those we will be studying in this chapter, are the leading contributing

THiNK FIRST

- What are some of the sources of knowledge?
- In what ways might experience be misleading?
- What are some of the types of cognitive and social errors in our thinking?

>> factor in medical mistakes, many of which result in death and long-term disability.[2] It is estimated that diagnostic errors alone result in 40,000 to 80,000 hospital deaths per year in the United States.[3]

Following the 1995 incident with Willie King, hospitals have started taking extra precautions, including double back-up identification systems, computerized error-tracking systems, and the use of patient safety officers to monitor and educate medical professionals. Many medical schools are also teaching their students about cognitive biases and training them to think about how they are thinking (meta-analysis) as well as how to better communicate with and get feedback from other staff.

The prevalence of medical mistakes illustrates how cognitive errors can lead otherwise highly trained professionals to make erroneous decisions.

Good critical-thinking skills require that we evaluate evidence thoroughly and be aware of social and cognitive errors in our thinking to effectively evaluate any given situation and avoid jumping to a conclusion or acting hastily based on preconceived ideas. In Chapter 4 we will:

- Learn about the nature and limitations of human knowledge
- Distinguish between rationalism and empiricism
- Learn about different types of evidence
- Set guidelines for evaluating evidence
- Look at sources for researching claims and evidence
- Study different types of cognitive/perceptual errors, including self-serving biases
- Learn how social expectations and group pressure can lead to erroneous thinking

Finally, we will examine the evidence and arguments regarding unidentified flying objects (UFOs) and what type of proof would be necessary to establish their existence.

Actor Dennis Quaid's newborn twins were given a dose of blood thinner that was ten times that prescribed.

HUMAN KNOWLEDGE AND ITS LIMITATIONS

Knowledge is information or experience that we believe to be true and for which we have justification or evidence. Understanding how we acquire knowledge as well as having an awareness of the limitations of human understanding are essential in logical reasoning.

Rationalism and Empiricism

Our views of ourselves and the world around us are shaped by our understanding of the nature of truth and the ultimate sources of knowledge. **Rationalists** claim that most human knowledge comes through reason. Greek philosopher Plato (427–347 BCE) believed that there is an unchanging truth we can know through reason and that most of us confuse truth with worldly appearance.

The empiricists reject the rationalists' claim that it is through reason that we discern truth. **Empiricists** instead claim that we discover truth primarily through our physical senses. Science is based primarily on empiricism. The scientific method involves making direct observations of the world, and then coming up with a hypothesis to explain these observations.

Structure of the Mind

German philosopher Immanuel Kant (1724–1804) argued that how we experience reality is not simply a matter of pure reason (rationalism) or of using physical senses (empiricism) but depends on the structure of our minds. Like computers—which are designed to accept and process particular kinds of inputs from the outside world—our brains must have the correct "hardware" to accept and make sense of incoming data.

Most neurologists believe, as did Kant, that we do not see "reality" directly as it is but that instead our mind or brain provides structure and rules for processing incoming information. In other words, as we noted in Chapter 1, we *interpret* our experiences rather than directly perceiving the world "out there."

> **knowledge** Information which we believe to be true and for which we have justification or evidence.
>
> **rationalist** One who claims that most human knowledge comes through reason.
>
> **empiricist** One who believes that we discover truth primarily through our physical senses.

> **Connections**
>
> **How is the assumption of empiricism reflected in the scientific method?**
> *See Chapter 12, p. 363.*

SELF-EVALUATION QUESTIONNAIRE*

Rate yourself on the following scale from 1 (strongly disagree) to 5 (strongly agree)

1 2 3 4 5   Knowledge comes primarily through reason rather than the senses.

1 2 3 4 5   I have a tendency to look only for evidence that confirms my assumptions or cherished worldviews.

1 2 3 4 5   The most credible evidence is that based on direct experience, such as eyewitness reports.

1 2 3 4 5   When I look at a random shape such as a cloud or craters on the moon, I tend to see meaning or an image in it.

1 2 3 4 5   The probability that there are two students in a class of twenty-four who have a birthday on the same day and month is about 50 percent.

1 2 3 4 5   When I buy a lottery ticket, I use my lucky number.

1 2 3 4 5   I can truly enjoy life only if I have perfect control over it.

1 2 3 4 5   I am better than most at getting along with other people.

1 2 3 4 5   Americans are more trustworthy than other people, especially people from non-Western cultures.

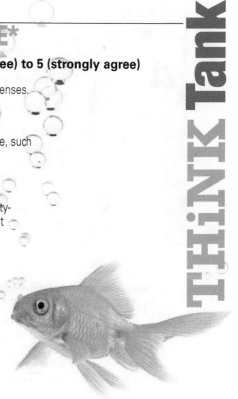

THiNK Tank

* Keep track of your results. As you read this book and gain a better understanding of critical thinking, you'll find out what your responses to each of these statements mean. A brief summary of the meaning of each rating can also be found at the back of the book.

While our brain helps us make sense of the world, it also limits us. For example, according to the new string theory in physics, there are at least nine spatial dimensions.[4] However, our brains are structured to perceive a three-dimensional world. Consequently, it is difficult, if not impossible, for us to imagine a nine-dimensional world. Because of the structure of our brains, we are also prone to certain perceptual and cognitive errors. We'll be studying some of these errors later in this chapter.

Effective critical thinking requires that we be aware of our strengths and limitations and that we strive to improve our style of inquiry and our understanding of the world. Because complete certainty is almost always an impossible goal, we need to learn how to assess evidence and to remain open to multiple perspectives.

evidence Reasons for believing that a statement or claim is true or probably true.

Connections

How can you tell if a news story is credible? *See Chapter 11, p. 337.* How do scientists go about collecting evidence? *See Chapter 12, pp. 368–369.*

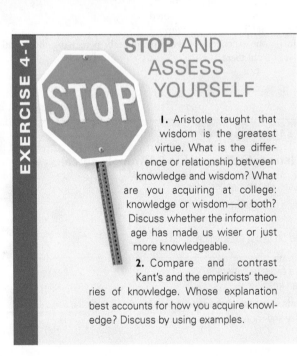

EXERCISE 4-1

STOP AND ASSESS YOURSELF

1. Aristotle taught that wisdom is the greatest virtue. What is the difference or relationship between knowledge and wisdom? What are you acquiring at college: knowledge or wisdom—or both? Discuss whether the information age has made us wiser or just more knowledgeable.

2. Compare and contrast Kant's and the empiricists' theories of knowledge. Whose explanation best accounts for how you acquire knowledge? Discuss by using examples.

EVALUATING EVIDENCE

Evidence is something that tends to prove or disprove a particular view. In arguments, evidence is used as the grounds or premises for our belief in a particular conclusion. While analytical skills are essential in evaluating an argument and

are addressed in greater detail in subsequent chapters, we first need to make sure the evidence on which we base our analysis is accurate and complete. Evidence can come from many different sources, some more reliable than others.

Evidence can be based on information from other sources or on firsthand experience. It is reasonable to use our experience as credible evidence for a claim, *if* it is not contradicted by other evidence. Likewise, if a claim conflicts with our experience, then we have good reason to be suspicious of that claim. Learning how to evaluate the credibility and accuracy of evidence is a key skill in critical thinking and logic.

Direct Experience and False Memories

Effective critical thinking requires that we be willing to check the accuracy of our experience. As we noted earlier, our brains interpret rather than directly record sensory experience. Consequently, direct sensory experience is not infallible. Even though we may remember major events "as

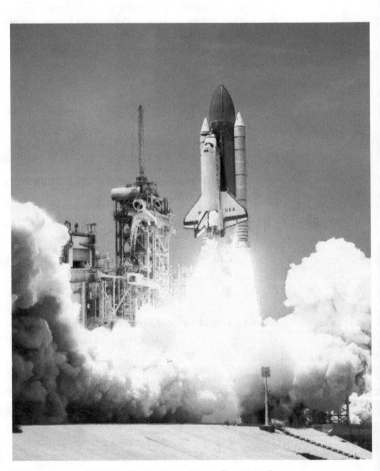

False memories can significantly alter how witnesses "remember" an event, as happened in the case of the Challenger explosion.

though they were yesterday," these memories are not as stable as scientists once thought. A study done four years after the 1986 *Challenger* explosion found that many of the witnesses had dramatically altered their memories of the shuttle disaster, even to the point of "seeing" things that had never happened.[5]

Language can also alter memories. This is particularly problematic when police inadvertently use leading questions that can bias a person's testimony or even alter the person's memories of an incident.

The power of words to shape our reality is poignantly illustrated by how leading questions can alter eyewitnesses' perception of a particular event. In a study, participants were shown a film of a car accident.[6] They were then asked one of the following questions about the speed of the cars. Their averaged responses are given in parentheses after each question:

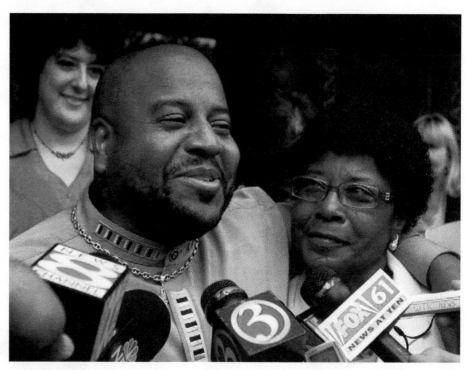

James Calvin Tillman was released from prison in July 2006, with the help of the Innocence Project, after serving 16 years for a rape he did not commit. His conviction was based on a false eyewitness report.

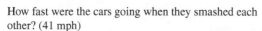

How fast were the cars going when they smashed each other? (41 mph)

How fast were the cars going when they collided? (40 mph)

How fast were the cars going when they bumped each other? (38 mph)

How fast were the cars going when they hit each other? (35 mph)

How fast were the cars going when they contacted each other? (32 mph)

Despite the fact that they had all seen the same film, participants responded with higher speeds based on the intensity of the verb. Those who were told the cars smashed or collided reported significantly higher speed estimates than those who were told that the cars merely contacted each other.

Inaccurate or false memories can be as compelling and believable as real memories. In police work, eyewitness identifications are incorrect up to 50 percent of the time. Mistaken eyewitness identifications of a suspect are the greatest single cause of wrongful convictions. Although jurors regard eyewitness identification as trustworthy, scientists have found that eyewitness reports are notoriously unreliable. According to The Innocence Project, an organization dedicated to exonerating wrongfully convicted individuals through DNA testing, misidentification by eyewitnesses is the most common cause of wrongful convictions in the U.S. It is estimated that even under the best conditions, eyewitness are incorrect about half the time.[7]

Indeed, we are so suggestible that we may go beyond inadvertently altering memories to vividly recalling events that never happened, a phenomenon known as **false memory syndrome**. Psychologists have found that after only three sessions in which there are repeated suggestions about a nonexistent childhood event, such as being lost in a mall at age 5 or spilling grape juice on a guest at a wedding, about 25 percent of the subjects will "recall" the event, and many will provide details. What's more, there is little connection between their confidence in their memory and the truth of their memory.[8]

Why are some people more prone than others to memory distortions? Elizabeth Loftus, one of the foremost researchers in the field, suggests that false memory is most likely to occur in people who don't engage in critical thinking about their memories but just accept them as reported.[9] The use of memorization strategies, such as those discussed in "Critical Thinking in Action: Memorization Strategies," can help us in accurately remembering new information. By being more attentive and analyzing events as they happen and by being alert to inconsistencies in our "memories," we are less likely to be taken in by false or distorted memories.

> **false memory syndrome** The recalling of events that never happened.

Critical THiNKing in Action

Memorization Strategies

In a study of why some people are better at accurately memorizing new information, magnetic resonance brain imaging was used to determine which brain regions are correlated with specific memorization strategies.* Researchers found that most people use one or a combination of the following four strategies for remembering the picture to the right.

1. **Visualization inspection.** Participants carefully study the visual appearance of an object. Some people are much better at this strategy and are able to commit pictures as well as pages of books to visual memory.

2. **Verbal elaboration.** Individuals construct sentences about the objects or material they are trying to memorize. For example, they may say to themselves, "The pig is key to this image."

3. **Mental imagery.** Individuals form interactive mental images, much like an animated cartoon. For example, they may imagine the pig jumping into a pool off the end of a diving board shaped like a key.

4. **Memory retrieval.** People reflect and come up with a meaning for the object or association of the object with personal memories.

Participants who use one or a combination of these different strategies performed better at learning new material than those who used these strategies only rarely or not at all. In addition, it was found that each of these strategies used different parts of the brain and that people seem to have different learning styles that work best for them.

DISCUSSION QUESTIONS

1. What strategy, if any, do you use for learning new information? For example, what strategy might you use for remembering the picture below? Evaluate the effectiveness of the strategy or strategies in helping you be a better critical thinker and in your performance in classes.

2. Think of a time when you later discovered that a memory you had was inaccurate or false. Discuss how the use of these strategies might make you less prone to memory distortions. Be specific.

The Unreliability of Hearsay and Anecdotal Evidence

We should be skeptical of what others tell us, especially if it's hearsay evidence or comments taken out of context. **Hearsay**, evidence that is heard by one person and then repeated to another person and so on until you hear it, is notoriously unreliable. As children, we've probably all played the game of "telephone," in which we whisper something to one person and she whispers the message to the next person and so on down the line until the last person says what he has heard. It is almost always different, often amusingly so, from the original message.

Anecdotal evidence, which is based on personal testimonies, is also unreliable because of the problem of inaccurate memory as well as the human tendency to exaggerate or distort what we experience to fit our expectations. For example, many people have reported seeing UFOs and, in some cases, being abducted by aliens. However, despite the apparent sincerity of their beliefs, anecdotal evidence in the absence of any physical evidence cannot be used as proof that UFOs and aliens exist. We'll be looking at

hearsay Evidence that is heard by one person and then repeated to another.

anecdotal evidence Evidence based on personal testimonies.

different perspectives on the credibility of the evidence for UFOs in the readings at the end of this chapter.

Experts and Credibility

One of the most credible sources of information is that of experts. When turning to an expert, it is important that we find someone who is knowledgeable in the particular field under question. When we use the testimony of a person who is an expert in a different field, we are committing the fallacy of *appeal to inappropriate authority.* We'll study fallacies in more depth in Chapter 5.

For example, many students believe, on the basis of the testimony of their friends, that marijuana use is harmless and that it is perfectly safe to drive after smoking a joint. In fact, research by medical experts shows that, although marijuana does not impair driving as much as alcohol, reaction time is reduced by 41 percent after smoking one joint and 63 percent after smoking two joints.[10] Despite evidence from experts, most people will still base their judgments on smoking marijuana on information from their peers until they develop stronger critical-thinking skills.

In seeking out experts, we should look at their credentials, including:

1. *Education* or training from a reputable institute

2. *Experience* in making judgments in the field

3. *Reputation* among peers as an expert in the field

4. *Accomplishments* in the field such as academic papers and awards

Unfortunately, expert testimony is not foolproof. Experts may disagree, in which case we will have to reserve judgment or look to others in the field. Furthermore, sometimes experts are biased, particularly those who are being paid by special-interest groups or corporations who stand to gain financially from supporting a particular position.

For example, it has long been assumed that milk and dairy products help maintain strong bones in adults. However, this claim has not been supported by scientific research. Instead this claim has been mainly promoted by groups that financially depend on the sale of dairy products. While the National Dairy Council extols the benefits of milk for people of all ages, many medical experts, including researchers at the Harvard School of Public Health[11] and the Physicians Committee for Responsible Medicine, argue, based on research, that milk may actually accelerate the process of bone loss in adults. In light of these findings, the Federal Trade Commission, a government agency charged with protecting consumers and eliminating unfair and deceptive marketplace practices, ordered the National Dairy Council to withdraw its ads that claimed drinking milk can prevent bone loss in adults.

Preconceived ideas can also influence how experts interpret evidence. Brandon Mayfield, an Oregon lawyer and a Muslim convert, was taken into custody in Portland, Oregon, after the March 2004 train bombing in Madrid, Spain, when what appeared to be his fingerprint mysteriously turned up on a plastic bag used by the bombers. Although Spanish law-enforcement agencies expressed doubt that the fingerprint was Mayfield's, U.S. officials insisted that it was an "absolutely incontrovertible match."[12] As it later turned out, the fingerprint belonged to an Algerian living in Spain. The U.S. officials succumbed to preconceived notions in making a false arrest of Mayfield.

The game "telephone" is an amusing example of how hearsay can result in misinterpretation.

Connections

How can you determine whether a science news story is well done and accurate? *See Chapter 11, p. 346.*

How do scientists design experiments to avoid bias? *See Chapter 12, p. 369.*

How can you recognize and avoid being taken in by misleading advertisements? *See Chapter 10, pp. 318–321.*

238

got milk?

Liquid Gold.

9 essential nutrients to
make big waves.

Inadequate research can lead to misrepresentation of a product—advertisers, for example, claimed that milk built strong bones in adults, a claim that was later proven false. The above ad also contains the fallacy of appeal to inappropriate authority, since Olympic swimmer Michael Phelps is not an expert on the health benefits of milk.

While experts are usually a good source of credible evidence, even experts can be biased and can misinterpret data, as we noted in the opening scenario on medical errors. Because of this, it is important that we be able to evaluate claims, especially those that may be slanted or that conflict with other experts' analysis.

confirmation bias The tendency to look only for evidence that supports our assumptions.

Evaluating Evidence for a Claim

Our analysis of the evidence for a claim should be accurate, unbiased, and as complete as possible. Credible

evidence is consistent with other relevant evidence. In addition, the more evidence there is to support a claim, the more reasonable it is to accept that claim. In critical thinking, there is no virtue in rigid adherence to a position that is not supported by evidence (see "Thinking Outside the Box: Rachel Carson, Biologist and Author")

Sometimes we don't have access to credible evidence. In cases like these, we should look for contradictory evidence. For example, some atheists reject the belief that there is a God because, they argue, it is contradicted by the presence of so much evil in the world. When there is evidence that contradicts a claim, we have good reason to doubt the claim. However, if there is no contradictory evidence, we should remain open to the possibility that a position may be true.

In evaluating a claim, we need to watch out for **confirmation bias**, the tendency to look only for evidence that confirms our assumptions and to resist evidence that contradicts them. This inclination is so strong that we may disregard or reinterpret evidence that runs contrary to our cherished beliefs.[13] In research about people who were opposed to and those who supported capital punishment, both sides interpreted the findings of a study on whether capital punishment deterred crime to fit their prior views. If the evidence did not fit, they focused on the flaws in the research and dismissed its validity or, in some cases, actually distorted the evidence to support their position.[14] Politicians may also cherry-pick the evidence, reading only reports and listening to evidence that supports their previous beliefs. This happened in 2002 when the Bush administration claimed there was conclusive proof that Iraq had weapons of mass destruction. Newscasters and journalists who have strong beliefs about particular issues may also engage in confirmation bias.

Sources that are usually reliable can inadvertently pass on incorrect information. A friend of mine told me that women in their 20s now earn more than men. My friend went on to tell me that he had read this in an opinion piece by a *New York Times* columnist.[15] When I checked out the information in the article, I found that, according to the National Labor Statistics, women in their 20s, despite the fact that they are better educated, earn only about 92 percent of what men earn. While my friend would normally have checked out the sources of the columnist's claims, confirmation bias kept him from doing so. He believed, prior to reading the article, that boys are getting a raw deal in school, since the majority of teachers are women, and that we are entering an age of reverse sexism. The "fact," albeit incorrect, that women in their 20s are now earning more than men are "confirmed" his views.

Confirmation bias may also take the form of more rigorously scrutinizing contrary evidence than that which supports our position. Peter Jennings, of ABC's *World News Tonight*, presented a study that "disproved" therapeutic touch, a healing method used extensively in India that involves a therapist's using the "energy" in his or her hands to help correct the "energy field" of a sick person.[16] The study, which was previously quoted in a prestigious medical journal, had been carried out by a fourth grader, Emily Rosa, as a project for her science class. On the basis of this single fourth grader's project, the editor of

RACHEL CARSON, *Biologist and Author*

After graduating with a master's degree in Zoology from Johns Hopkins University, Rachel Carson (1907–1964) was hired as a writer by the U.S. Fish and Wildlife Service. The success of her 1951 book, *The Sea Around Us*, allowed her to leave her job and concentrate on her life goal of becoming a writer.

As early as 1945 she had become concerned about the overuse of chemical pesticides, such as DDT. Although others before her had tried to warn the public about the dangers of these powerful pesticides, it was her reputation as a complete and meticulous researcher, along with her intellectual curiosity, that contributed to her success. She began by examining the existing research on the effect of pesticides. Her reputation also allowed her to enlist the expertise and support of scientists in the field.

When *Silent Spring* was published in 1962, it created an immediate uproar and backlash. A huge counterattack was launched by the big chemical companies, including Monsanto and Velsicol, which denounced her as a "hysterical woman" unqualified to write on the topic. Despite threats of lawsuits, Carson didn't back down. Because her research was informed and accurate, her opponents were unable to find holes in her argument. *Silent Spring* changed the course of American history and launched a new environmental movement.

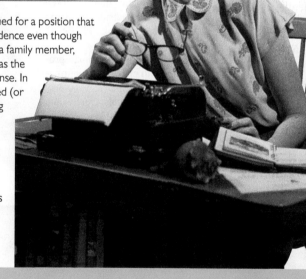

DISCUSSION QUESTIONS

1. Think of a time when you argued for a position that was supported by credible evidence even though doing so angered or alienated a family member, teacher, or employer. What was the outcome? Evaluate your response. In particular, discuss how you used (or didn't use) your critical thinking skills in responding to criticism of your position.

2. Rachel Carson is an example of how one person can make a huge difference. Looking into your future, think of ways in which you might be able to use your talents and critical-thinking skills to make the world a better place.

the journal had declared that therapeutic touch was bogus. Because the editor had a bias against nontraditional therapies, he held "studies" that suggested therapeutic touch might be ineffective to a lower standard of proof.

Even scientists sometimes look for evidence that supports their theories rather than evidence that challenges their thinking. Models used for testing hypotheses may promote confirmation bias and questionable interpretation of data. Science writer Matt Ridley, in his article "How Bias Heats up the [Global] Warming Debate," writes regarding the controversy over global warming:

> The late novelist Michael Crichton, in his prescient 2003 lecture criticizing climate research, said: "To an outsider, the most significant innovation in the global-warming controversy is the overt reliance that is being placed on models. . . . No longer are models judged by how well they reproduce data from the real world—increasingly, models provide the data. As if they were themselves a reality."
>
> It isn't just models, but the interpretation of

Connections

How do scientists use evidence to test a hypothesis? *See Chapter 12, p. 369.*

How do we as consumers reinforce confirmation bias in the news media? *See Chapter 11, p. 353.*

real data, too. The rise and fall in both temperature and carbon dioxide, evident in Antarctic ice cores, was at first thought to be evidence of carbon dioxide driving climate change. Then it emerged that the temperature had begun rising centuries earlier than carbon dioxide. Rather than abandon the theory, scientists fell back on the notion that the data jibed with the possibility that rising carbon dioxide levels were reinforcing the warming trend in what's called a positive feedback loop. Maybe—but there's still no empirical evidence that this was a significant effect compared with a continuation of whatever first caused the warming.[17]

Brain imaging studies have found that when we come to a conclusion that confirms our prior bias, the decision is associated with a pleasure response and a feeling of emotional comfort, even though our conclusion is erroneous.[18] When theories are disproved, it is generally by other scientists rather than by the scientists who proposed the theories (see "Thinking Outside the Box: Stephen Hawking, Physicist" in Chapter 1).

Because of the human propensity to engage in confirmation bias, many scholarly scientific journals require that researchers report disconfirmatory evidence as well as contradictory interpretations of their data. As critical thinkers,

we need to develop strategies that compel us to examine evidence, especially that which confirms our prior views, and to be more open-minded about evidence that contradicts our views.

In evaluating evidence, the degree of credibility required depends on the circumstances. The greater the impact our actions might have, the greater the degree of credibility and certainty we should demand. Courts of law require a high degree of credibility for evidence of guilt because of the dire consequences of declaring an innocent person guilty.

Connections

How do scientists gather evidence to test their hypotheses? *See Chapter 12, pp. 368–369.*

What are the "rules of evidence" in a court of law? *See Chapter 13, pp. 414–415.*

How reliable is the news media as a source of information? *See Chapter 11, pp. 338–341.*

Hot or Not?

Do you tend to distort evidence to fit with your beliefs?

Research Resources

We live in an age where information is proliferating at an astounding rate. We are inundated on a daily basis with information from newspapers, television, the Internet, and other media sources. When using evidence from the media—especially the mass media—we need to consider the sources and their slant, if any.

In addition, some writing, such as novels, poetry, movie scripts, and even some editorials, is not intended to be taken as factual. For example, the film *Zero Dark Thirty*, which recounted the search for and assassination of Osama bin Laden, drew considerable criticism from some people for portraying the CIA as using water boarding techniques on terrorist suspects in Guantanamo Bay. However, the movie was never intended as a documentary. Instead it was a dramatization, and as such a fusion of fact and fiction.[19]

Assessing claims, including distinguishing between fact and fiction, requires good research skills and competence in gathering, evaluating, and synthesizing supporting evidence. Like scientists, good critical thinkers spend a lot of time researching claims and collecting information before drawing a conclusion. Apply the criteria listed in the CRAAP test (which stands for currency, relevance, authority, accuracy, and purpose) to evaluate the reliability of information you find.

As you begin your research, try to set up an interview with someone who is an expert in the field under investigation, such as a faculty member or an

The film **Zero Dark Thirty**, *about the search for Osama bin Laden, was a blend of fact and fictional dramatization.*

outside expert. An expert can provide you with information as well as point you to reputable publications. When interviewing the expert, don't rely on your memory. Take accurate notes; repeat what you think you heard if you are unsure. Librarians are also a valuable source of information. In addition to their wealth of knowledge regarding resources, some college librarians have Ph.D.s in specialized fields.

Dictionaries and *encyclopedias* are another good place for you to start your research. Specialized reference books often contain extensive bibliographies of good source material. They may be accessed online or used in the reference section of your library. If you are doing time-sensitive research, make sure the reference sources are up-to-date. Make sure you use reputable encyclopedias. While sites such as Wikipedia might be a good starting point, Wikipedia entries, because they are not necessarily written by experts in their fields, cannot be used as references in research.

Library catalogues—most of which are online—are invaluable in research. Use key words to find your subject in the catalogue. In selecting resources, check the date of publication. If your library doesn't have a particular book or journal, you can usually get it through interlibrary loan.

Scholarly journals, also known as peer-reviewed journals, contain articles that have been reviewed by fellow experts in the field. Most scholarly journals are indexed on specialized databases that you can access through your library Internet home page. In some cases, the full journal articles are available on the Internet. For more general information, the Expanded Academic Index is a good place to start.

Government documents are also reputable sources of information about such things as employment statistics and demographics. You can access many of the government documents through Internet databases. Go to http://www.usa.gov/ to search for topics of interest.

Internet Web sites contain a wealth of information. Millions of new pages are added every week to the Internet. There are also specialized Web sites, such as Academic Search Complete, which are not available through search engines such as Google, Bing, and Yahoo, but that can generally be accessed through your college or university library's Web site. Many Web sites are sponsored by reputable organizations and individuals. The top-level domain at the end of a Web site's address (URL, or uniform resource locator) can help you in evaluating its reliability. All URLs for U.S. government sites end with the top-level domain *.gov*. URLs for sites ending with the top-level domain *.edu* indicate that the source of the information is a U.S. educational institution. Both of these types of sites can generally be counted on to provide reliable and accurate information. The global top-level domain *.org* indicates that the site belongs to a private or nonprofit organization such as Amnesty International or possibly a religious group. The information on these sites may or may not be reliable, depending on the reputability of the organization sponsoring

Evaluating Information – Applying the CRAAP Test
Meriam Library 📖 California State University, Chico

When you search for information, you're going to find lots of it . . . but is it good information? You will have to determine that for yourself, and the **CRAAP Test** can help. The **CRAAP Test** is a list of questions to help you evaluate the information you find. Different criteria will be more or less important depending on your situation or need.

Key: ■ indicates criteria is for Web

Evaluation Criteria

Currency: *The timeliness of the information.*
• When was the information published or posted?
• Has the information been revised or updated?
• Does your topic require current information, or will older sources work as well?
■ Are the links functional?

Relevance: *The importance of the information for your needs.*
• Does the information relate to your topic or answer your question?
• Who is the intended audience?
• Is the information at an appropriate level (i.e. not too elementary or advanced for your needs)?
• Have you looked at a variety of sources before determining this is one you will use?
• Would you be comfortable citing this source in your research paper?

Authority: *The source of the information.*
• Who is the author/publisher/source/sponsor?
• What are the author's credentials or organizational affiliations?
• Is the author qualified to write on the topic?
• Is there contact information, such as a publisher or email address?
■ Does the URL reveal anything about the author or source?
  examples: .com .edu .gov .org .net

Accuracy: *The reliability, truthfulness and correctness of the content.*
• Where does the information come from?
• Is the information supported by evidence?
• Has the information been reviewed or refereed?
• Can you verify any of the information in another source or from personal knowledge?
• Does the language or tone seem unbiased and free of emotion?
• Are there spelling, grammar or typographical errors?

Purpose: *The reason the information exists.*
• What is the purpose of the information? Is it to inform, teach, sell, entertain or persuade?
• Do the authors/sponsors make their intentions or purpose clear?
• Is the information fact, opinion or propaganda?
• Does the point of view appear objective and impartial?
• Are there political, ideological, cultural, religious, institutional or personal biases?

The CRAAP Test for Evaluating Information. 9/17/10

the Web site. The global top-level domain *.com* indicates that the site is sponsored by a commercial organization such as a corporation or private business, at least in the United States. In these cases you must try to determine the companies' motives in providing the information—for example, is it for advertising purposes? Generally, blogs should not be used as references. Blogs are notoriously unreliable and often based on opinion rather than facts. If you have any doubts about a site's credibility, it is best to ask a reference librarian or expert in the field about the most reliable sites to look at for information on an issue.

Connections

How do scientists go about gathering information and evidence? *See Chapter 12, pp. 368–369*
How does the Internet affect our lives? *See Chapter 11, pp. 347–348.*

While doing your research, no matter what resource you are using, take accurate notes or make copies of articles. Keep full citation information for your sources so that you can refer to them later and cite them if necessary. If, in presenting your research, you use material word for word, always put it in quotation marks and acknowledge the source. You should also cite the source of paraphrased information that is not widely known. In addition, remember to cite sources for any surveys, statistics, and graphics.

Researching a claim or issue requires that we be able to sort through and analyze the relevant data. Good research skills also help us make better decisions in our lives by providing us with the tools for evaluating different claims and available courses of action we might take.

EXERCISE 4-2

STOP AND ASSESS YOURSELF

1. What evidence might be sufficient for you to conclude that an intelligent computer or android is conscious and has free will? Would this same evidence be sufficient to prove to you that another human you met was conscious and had free will? Explain using the criteria for evaluating evidence discussed in the chapter.

2. Think of a time when you saw something and were convinced that your interpretation of the event was true, but you later came to have doubts about your interpretation. Discuss the factors that contributed to your doubts.

3. Working in small groups, evaluate the following list of claims. If there are any ambiguous terms, define them as well as possible. Next, make a list of types of evidence you would need to support or reject each claim. State how you would go about doing the research.

   a. Genetically modified food is dangerous.

   b. Men are more aggressive by nature than are women.

   c. Prayers are answered.

   d. Toast is more likely to fall butter-side down.

   e. Asian Americans are better at math than European Americans are.

   f. Living together before marriage is associated with a lower divorce rate.

   g. Human life begins at conception.

   h. A flying saucer crashed over Roswell, New Mexico, in 1947.

   i. Canadians, on average, live longer than Americans do.

   j. God exists.

   k. The sea level has risen almost a foot over the past century as a result of global warming.

   l. Yawning is contagious.

   m. Capital punishment deters crime.

   n. Debbie was born under the sign Aquarius. Therefore, she must love water.

4. Select one of the following topics and research it.

   a. The impact of global warming on your city or state

   b. The average age of marriage for men and women now and when your parents got married

   c. The number of members in the U.S. House of Representatives

   d. The percentage of American college athletes who become professional athletes

   e. The changes over the past 30 years in majors of college students

   Make a list of the resources, including experts, books, journals, search engines, databases, and Web sites you used in your research. Rate each of the sources you used in terms of which generated the most credible and unbiased evidence. Compare your results with those of others in your class. To what extent did the topic chosen determine which research resources, including the Internet, were most useful?

5. Choose one of the claims from exercise 3 or a recent news story and research the evidence. Write a short essay or present your results to the class for evaluation.

6. Imagine that you are backing out of a parking spot on campus. Your view is somewhat obscured by an SUV parked beside you. As you back out, you hit another car that was driving through the parking lot. Write a paragraph describing the event for the police report.

   Now imagine that you are the other person whose car was hit. Write a paragraph describing the event for the police report. Compare and contrast the two reports. Analyze how the words you chose in each report were selected to influence the perception of the police officer regarding what happened.

COGNITIVE AND PERCEPTUAL ERRORS IN THINKING

On the evening of October 30, 1938, a play based on H. G. Wells's novel *War of the Worlds* about a Martian invasion was broadcast to the nation on radio. Many of the people who listened to the show believed that the invasion was real. Some people even "smelled" the poisonous Martian gas and "felt" the heat rays being described on the radio. Others claimed to have seen the giant machines landing in New Jersey and the flames from the battle. One panicked person told police he had heard the president's voice on the radio ordering them to evacuate.

Our perceptions of the world around us are easily skewed by social influences. Most people underestimate the critical role that cognitive and social factors play in our perception and interpretation of sense data. Although emotion has traditionally been regarded as the culprit when reason goes astray, studies suggest that many of the errors in our thinking are neurological in nature.[20] In this section, we'll be looking at some of these cognitive and perceptual errors.

Perceptual Errors

Our minds are not like blank sheets of paper or recording devices, such as cameras or video recorders, as the empiricists claimed. Instead, our brains construct a picture of the world much as an artist does. Our brains filter our perceptions and fill in missing information based in part on our expectations, as occurred in the broadcast of *War of the Worlds*.

Some skeptics believe that UFO sightings are based on perceptual errors, including optical illusions (see "Analyzing Images: The St. Louis Arch"). In 1969, an Air National Guard pilot spotted what he thought was a squadron of UFOs within several hundred feet of his plane.

> **Connections**
>
> As a consumer, how can you avoid being taken in by cognitive and perceptual errors used by marketers? *See Chapter 10, p. 306.*

When the radio show based on the novel The War of the Worlds *was broadcast, many of the listeners believed that the invasion was real.*

ANALYZING IMAGES

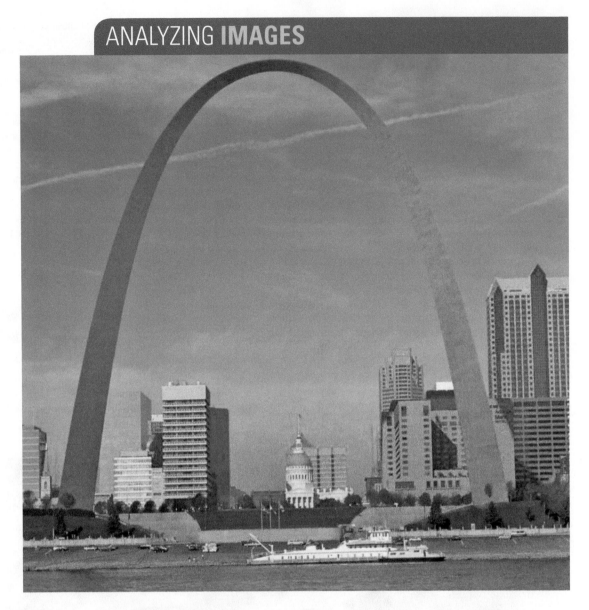

The St. Louis Arch Designed by architect Eero Saarinen, the St. Louis Arch in St. Louis, Missouri, was completed in 1965 on a site overlooking the Mississippi River. Although the height of the arch and its width at the base are both 630 feet, the graceful catenary creates the illusion that the arch is taller than it is wide. Even if we are told that its height and width are the same, we still have great difficulty making the cognitive adjustment to correct what is known as the vertical/horizontal illusion. Because of this optical illusion we also tend to overestimate the height of trees and tall buildings.

DISCUSSION QUESTIONS

1. *What was your first reaction when you were told that the height and width of the arch were the same? Did they look the same after you were told the dimensions of the arch? Share with the class other optical illusions that you have encountered in architecture or elsewhere.*

2. *Working in small groups, discuss why we might experience optical illusions such as the vertical/horizontal illusion. Discuss what resources you could use in developing your hypothesis (a hypothesis is an educated guess based on evidence and experimentation). Share your hypothesis with the class for analysis.*

ANALYZING **IMAGES**

Inkblots In an inkblot test such as in the one above, a psychologist asks a person to describe what he or she sees. The psychologist uses the descriptions to learn more about a person's motivations and unconscious drives.

DISCUSSION QUESTIONS

1. *What do you see when you look at the above inkblot? Why do you think you saw what you did?*

2. *Discuss how the inkblot test illustrates our tendency to impose order on random data. Think of a time when you fell for this error in your everyday life. Come up with two or three critical-thinking strategies you might use to make yourself less prone to being taken in by our tendency to impose meaning on random data.*

He later described the UFOs as the color of "burnished aluminum" and "shaped like a hydroplane." As it turned out, the "squadron of UFOs" was most likely a meteor fireball that had broken up in the vicinity of the plane.[21] However, while being able to provide alternative explanations for most UFO sightings makes their existence less probable, we cannot conclude with certainty that *all* sightings are a result of perceptual errors. We'll be looking at the issue of the existence of UFOs in the "Critical Thinking Issue: Perspectives on Evaluating Evidence for the Existence of Unidentified Flying Objects" section at the end of this chapter.

Our minds may also distort objects we perceive. A straight stick, when inserted in water, appears to bend. A full moon appears to be much larger when it is near the

Connections

What tools and strategies do scientists use to minimize perceptual errors? *See Chapter 12, p. 369.*

Radar photo of 2005 Hurricane Katrina that had an object that looked like a "fetus facing to the left in the womb" to some, leading some anti-abortion advocates to draw the conclusion that the hurricane was punishment for the presence of abortion clinics in the city.

horizon, a phenomenon that NASA refers to as the "moon illusion."

Misperception of Random Data

Because our brains loathe absence of meaning, we may "see" order or meaningful patterns where there are none. For example, when we look at clouds or see unexplained lights in the sky, our brains impose meaning on the random shapes we see. When we look at the moon, we see a "face," popularly known as the man in the moon. In 2004, a piece of toast with cheese, allegedly bearing the image of the Virgin Mary, sold on eBay for $28,000.

One of the most famous examples of this type of error is the "Martian Canals," first reported as channels by Italian astronomer Giovanni Schiaparelli in 1877. Many astronomers continued to believe in the existence of these canals up until 1965, when the spacecraft *Mariner 4* flew close to Mars and took photos of the planet's surface. No canals showed up in the photos. It turned out that the

"canals" were a combination of an optical illusion, the expectation that there were canals, and the brain's tendency to impose order on random data. Because of our brain's inclination to impose meaning on random data, we should maintain a stance of skepticism about what we see.

The combination of the error of misperceiving random data with confirmation bias—interpreting data in a way that confirms our cherished views—is illustrated by the next example. After the devastation of New Orleans by Hurricane Katrina in 2005, a group known as the Columbia Christians for Life announced that God's purpose in sending the hurricane was to destroy the five abortion clinics in the city. Their proof was a radar photograph taken of the hurricane in which they claimed to have seen what looked like "a fetus facing to the left (west) in the womb, in the early weeks of gestation."[22]

Stress as well as preconceptions about the world can affect our perception. How many of us, walking alone at night, have seen a person or dog standing in a shadow, only to discover it was a bush or other object?

Critical THiNKing in Action

Food for Thought: Perception and Supersized Food Portions

Obesity is becoming an epidemic in the U.S. More than one-third of Americans adults are obese—more than double the rate in 1980, according to the U.S. Centers for Disease Control and Prevention. Supersized portions of junk food, such as potato chips, hamburgers, and sodas, have been blamed, in part, for this trend.* Do supersized portions lead to supersized people, or is this just all hype so that we can place the blame for our weight problems on Lay's potato chips and McDonald's burgers? In fact, studies show that downsizing our food portions does work to keep our weight down because it takes advantage of a perceptual error. Appetite is not a matter of just the physiological state of hunger but also a matter of perception—what we see in front of us. Most of us eat more when the table or our plates are loaded with food.

Humans are not the only species who make this error. When a researcher places a pile of 100 grams of wheat in front of a hen, she will eat 50 grams and leave 50. However, if we put 200 grams of wheat in front of a hen in a similar hunger condition, she will eat far more—83 to 108 grams of wheat or, once again, about half of what is in front of her.** Furthermore, if the food is presented as whole grains of rice, rather than cracked rice, where the grains are one quarter the size of whole rice grains, the hen will eat two to three times as much as she would otherwise.

In other words, by cutting down your portion sizes and cutting your food into smaller pieces, your brain will think you're full on less food.

DISCUSSION QUESTIONS

1. Many students put on weight in their first year of college, a phenomenon known as the "freshman 15." Critically evaluate your college environment and ways in which it promotes or hinders good eating habits. Make a list of suggestions for improving the environment so students are not so vulnerable to perceptual errors and overreact as a result. Carry out one of the suggestions or pass it on to someone who is in a position to make the change.

2. Examine your own eating habits. Evaluate ways in which being more aware of your thinking process, including inbuilt perceptual errors, can help you to maintain healthier eating habits.

*Nancy Hellmich, "How to Downsize the Student Body," *USA Today,* November 15, 2004.
**George W. Hartmann, *Gestalt Psychology* (New York: Ronald Press, 1935), pp. 87–88.

Memorable-Events Error

The **memorable-events error** involves our ability to vividly remember outstanding events. Scientists have discovered channels in our brains that actually hinder most long-term memories by screening out the mundane incidents in our everyday life.[23] However, these memory-impairing channels appear to close down during outstanding events. For example, most Americans recall exactly where they were and what they were doing on the morning of September 11, 2001. However, if you ask someone what they were doing on an ordinary weekday two months ago, most

> **memorable-events error** A cognitive error that involves our ability to vividly remember outstanding events.

people would be unable to remember or would remember only if they could think of something special that happened on that day.

To use another example, airplane crashes and fatalities are reported in the national media, whereas automobile fatalities generally are not. However, per mile traveled, airplane travel is far safer. We're sixteen times more likely to be killed in an automobile accident than in an airplane accident. In fact, traffic accidents are one of the leading causes of death and disability of people between the ages of 15 and 44.[24] However, the memorable-events error exerts such control over our thinking that even after being informed of these statistics, many of us still continue to be more nervous about flying than about driving.

The memorable-events error is sometimes tied in with confirmation bias, in which we tend to remember events that confirm our beliefs and forget those that are contrary to our beliefs. A popular belief in the United States is that "death takes a holiday" and that terminally ill patients can postpone their death until after an important holiday or birthday. In fact, this belief is based purely on wishful thinking and anecdotal evidence. In an analysis of the death certificates of more than a million people who died from cancer, biostatisticians Donn Young

> **probability error** Misunderstanding the probability or chances of an event by a huge margin.
>
> **gambler's error** The belief that a previous event affects the probability in a random event.

and Erinn Hade found no evidence that there is a reduction in death rates prior to a holiday or important event.[25] Personal and social beliefs are remarkably strong even in the face of empirical evidence that logically should be devastating. When their results were published, Young and Hade received several angry e-mails criticizing them for taking away people's hope.

Probability Errors

What is the probability that two people in your class have a birthday on the same month and day? Most people guess that the probability is pretty low. In fact, in a class of 23, the probability is about 50 percent. In larger classes, the probability is even higher. When we misestimate the probably of an event by a huge margin, we are committing **probability error**.

Humans are notoriously poor at determining probability. We are inclined to believe that coincidences must have paranormal causes when actually they are consistent with

> According to the Association for Psychological Science, 1.2 percent of the adult population are pathological gamblers and at least another 2.8 percent are problem gamblers.

probability. For example, you are thinking of a friend whom you haven't seen for a year when the phone rings and it's your friend on the other line. Are you psychic? Or is it just a coincidence? You've probably thought of your friend hundreds or even thousands of times over the course of the past year without receiving any phone calls, but we tend to forget such times because nothing memorable occurred.

One of the most insidious forms of probability error is **gambler's error**—the erroneous belief that previous events affect the probability in a random event. Research suggests that gambling addiction is based on gambler's error. In a study participants were invited to think aloud while gambling. Of the verbalized perceptions, 70 percent were based on erroneous thinking such as "The machine is due; I need to continue," "Here is my lucky dealer," "Today I feel great; it is my lucky day," "It's my turn to win." These statements reveal a failure to understand the random nature of probability.

When questioned about their verbalizations, nonproblem gamblers realized that their beliefs were wrong. They were able to use accumulated evidence to critically evaluate and modify their perceptions. Problem gamblers, in contrast, processed

Statistically, there is a far greater chance per mile traveled of being killed in a car accident than in an airplane crash, yet most people have a greater fear of flying.

249

the evidence much differently. They believed what they had said and interpreted their occasional random wins as confirming their belief that the outcome of a game can be predicted and controlled. The solution? Work to improve problem gamblers' critical-thinking skills. By making gamblers aware of their erroneous perceptions and the reasons why they continue to cling to these beliefs, clinicians work to help gamblers overcome their addiction.[26]

Self-Serving Biases

There are several types of self-serving biases or errors that impede our thinking and pursuit of truth, including:

- The misperception that we are in control

- The tendency to overestimate ourselves in comparison to others

- The tendency to exaggerate our strengths and minimize our weaknesses

We are predisposed to believe that we are in control of events that are outside our control. "I knew it would rain today," you groan. "I didn't bring my umbrella." Recently, the Powerball lottery jackpot reached over $100 million. I was standing in line at a mini-mart when I overheard the following conversation between the people in front of me, who were waiting to buy lottery tickets.

> **Person 1**: "What are you going to do? Are you going to pick your own numbers or let the computer do it for you?"
> **Person 2**: "Pick my own. It gives me a better chance of winning."

People who are poor critical thinkers may fall prey to more than one error in thinking in the same situation. In this case the control error was compounded by the probability error, which we discussed earlier. Although logically we know that lottery numbers are selected randomly, many of us also believe that choosing our own numbers—especially using our "lucky" numbers—increases our chances of

Gambler's error and an addiction to gambling is based on a misunderstanding of the random nature of probability.

winning. In fact, 80 percent of winning lottery tickets have numbers randomly generated by the computer, not so-called lucky numbers picked by the winners.[27]

The misperception that we are in control of random events also plays out in superstitious behavior such as wearing our lucky shirt during a big game or bringing a

Following the disastrous April 2010 oil rig explosion in the Gulf of Mexico, British Petroleum (BP) engaged in self-serving bias by grossly underestimating the amount of crude oil that flowed from the disabled well into the Gulf. BP also overestimated its control of the situation and its ability to stop the oil flow and clean up the oil spill without outside help.

good-luck charm to an exam. Before a game, most college and professional athletes engage in ritualistic superstitious behavior such as using a particular color shoelace or tape. Some baseball players sleep with their bats to break out of a hitting slump or to keep up their batting average. To some extent, the belief that we are in control can boost our confidence in achieving our goals. In fact, ritualistic behaviors have been found to have a calming effect on athletes before a game.

However, if we carry the belief that we are in control too far, it can distort our thinking and lead to poor decisions in our lives. The self-serving bias, and misjudgment about our ability to handle a challenge, can work against our rational self-interests. For example in the case of the British Petroleum oil leak, BP lost billions of dollars as well as the public confidence because of their erroneous belief in the beginning that they were in control of the situation and didn't need outside help. Thousands of people have died in wildfires and in hurricanes, despite repeated warnings to evacuate, because they thought they were in control of the situation and could ride out the storm.

This error is also expressed in the often-heard cliché "You can do anything you want if you put your mind to it," the implication being that if only we wanted to enough, we would have perfect control. Self-help gurus have become wealthy catering to this self-serving error. In her book *The Secret* (2006), Rhonda Byrne claims to have found the secret to happiness in what she calls "the law of attraction." According to Byrne, each of us has complete control over what happens to us in our lives. If we think positive thoughts, then like a magnet, we will attract whatever we want—whether it be a parking spot, a million dollars, a sexy figure, or a cure for cancer. The downside is that if we are not successful in getting what we want, then we have only ourselves and our negative thinking to blame.

The belief that we are in control of situations where we actually have little or no control can contribute to irrational guilt or posttraumatic stress syndrome.[28] A survivor of a traumatic event may believe that he or she should have been able to predict and do something to prevent an event such as sexual abuse, domestic violence, or the death of a loved one, especially an accidental or suicidal death.

Although genetic, physical, and environmental factors play a role in the onset of depression, the belief that we should be in control of our lives can also contribute to depression (see "Critical Thinking in Action: Irrational Beliefs and Depression"). People who are depressed may cling to the irrational belief that the only alternative to not having perfect control is having no control. Because they feel they lack any control over their lives, they tend to attribute their misfortune or sadness to other people's actions. A side effect of this negative behavior is that their behavior often alienates other people, thereby confirming a second irrational belief common to depressed people that they are worthless and unlikable. Thus, their distorted expectations lead to a self-fulfilling prophecy, a cognitive error we'll be studying in the next section.

A second self-serving bias is the tendency to overestimate ourselves in comparison to others. Most people rate themselves as above average when it comes to getting along with other people. Although it obviously can't be true that the majority of people are above average—except, perhaps, in the fictional town of Lake Wobegon in Garrison Keillor's *Prairie Home Companion* on Minnesota Public Radio—this self-serving bias can bolster our self-esteem and confidence. However, if we are unaware of the bias, it can become a problem and cause us not to take responsibility for our shortcomings. A Pew Research Center survey found that while 70 percent of Americans are overweight and that nine in ten agree that most of their fellow Americans are overweight, only 39 percent of Americans consider themselves to be overweight.[29] Clearly there seems to be a disconnect between being overweight and people's estimation of their own weight.

Another example of the self-serving bias

Critical THiNKing in Action

Irrational Beliefs and Depression

Albert Ellis (b. 1913), founder of rational emotive behavioral therapy, maintains that irrational ideas are the primary source of depression, rage, feelings of inadequacy, and self-hatred. Some of these irrational beliefs are:

- "I must be outstandingly competent, or I am worthless."
- "Others must treat me considerately, or they are absolutely rotten."
- "The world should always give me happiness, or I will die."
- "I must have perfect control over things, or I won't be able to enjoy life."
- "Because something once strongly affected my life, it will indefinitely affect my life."

According to Ellis, a depressed person feels sad because he (or she) erroneously thinks he is inadequate and abandoned, even though depressed people have the capacity to perform as well as nondepressed people. The purpose of therapy is to dispute these irrational beliefs and replace them with positive rational beliefs. To achieve this, the therapist asks questions such as:

- Is there evidence for this belief?
- What is the evidence against this belief?
- What is the worst that can happen if you give up this belief?
- And what is the best that can happen?

To assist the clients in changing their irrational beliefs, the therapist also uses other techniques such as empathy training, assertiveness training, and encouraging the development of self-management strategies.

DISCUSSION QUESTIONS

1. Discuss how cognitive errors contribute to irrational beliefs. Make a list of other irrational beliefs people hold that are based on cognitive errors.

2. Do you have any irrational beliefs that interfere with your achieving your life goals? If so, what are they? Discuss how you might use your critical-thinking skills to work toward overcoming these beliefs. Be specific.

See Albert Ellis, *The Essence of Rational Emotive Behavior Therapy*. Ph.D. dissertation, revised, May 1994.

is that most people take personal credit for their successes and blame outside forces for their failures. College students often attribute their "A" grades to something about themselves—their intelligence, quick grasp of the material, or good study skills. In contrast, they usually attribute their poor grades to something outside their control such as having an unfair teacher or having a touch of the flu on the day of the exam.[30] Similarly, when it comes to being overweight, many people blame a slow metabolism as the main reason why they can't lose weight, rather than their lifestyle or factors under their control. However, when overweight people do lose weight, they rarely attribute their success to a peppy metabolism but instead credit their willpower and good choices.

This type of self-serving bias can be found in the workplace. When office employees were asked in a survey "if they ever experienced backstabbing, rudeness, or incivility in the workplace," 89 percent said "yes." However, in the same survey 99 percent said that "they were never rude or the cause of the conflict."[31] In other words, most of us are quick to complain about other's irritating behaviors but give little thought to how our behavior might be the cause of workplace conflict.

According to the Institute of Medicine of the National Academy of Sciences, medical errors are responsible for an estimated 44,000 to 98,000 deaths a year in the United States.

Connections

What is cognitive dissonance and when are people most likely to engage in it? *See Chapter 1, p 27.*

According to Carol Tavris and Elliot Aronson, social psychologists and authors of *Mistakes Were Made (But Not By Me): Why We Justify Foolish Beliefs, Bad Decisions and Hurtful Acts*, being made aware of the gap between our self-image and our actual behavior creates cognitive dissonance and discomfort. To minimize this discomfort and maintain our good opinion of ourselves, we instinctively minimize the discrepancy through denial or by blaming someone else for our shortcomings. This sort of rationalization can prevent us from realizing that we're clinging to a mistaken belief.[32] As critical thinkers, we need to deal constructively with the discomfort that comes from cognitive dissonance and to work toward overcoming our mistaken beliefs about ourselves.

A third related self-serving bias is our inclination to exaggerate or place a greater value on our strengths and underestimate or downplay our weaknesses. In a study of intellectually gifted boys who thought they hadn't done well in class, the boys downplayed the importance of academics and instead emphasized the importance of other pursuits such as sports.[33] Seeing ourselves as having those traits and abilities that are important in life increases our sense of worth and helps us to achieve our life goals. This tendency, however, can also contribute to overconfidence and failure to seek or acknowledge other people's skills.

As we noted in the introduction to this chapter, overconfidence in physicians and jumping to a conclusion has been identified as one of the key factors in diagnostic errors. Unless we are willing, as critical thinkers, to make an honest evaluation of ourselves, it is unlikely that we are going to take steps toward overcoming our shortcomings.

Self-Fulfilling Prophecy

A self-fulfilling prophecy occurs when our exaggerated or distorted expectations reinforce actions that actually bring about the expected event. Expectations can have a profound influence on our behavior. Rumors of impending bank failures during the Great Depression in the early 1930s led to mass panic in which people rushed to take their money out of banks before the banks crashed. As a result, lots of banks went bankrupt. Since banks invest some of the deposits rather than keeping all the money in the vault, the frenzy caused the collapse of the banks—the very thing the customers feared.

To use another example of a self-fulfilling prophecy, let's say a literature professor has a star football player in her class. On the basis of her (mistaken) expectations about college athletes, she assumes that he is not academically inclined but is taking the course only because it is reputed to be easy. Because of this she calls on him less and doesn't encourage him or make an effort to include him in class discussions. She justifies this behavior on her part as not wanting to embarrass him.

To preserve our expectations, we may interpret ambiguous data in ways that meet our expectations. For example, our football star may be particularly quiet and introspective during one class. The professor assumes that he is preoccupied with thinking about the upcoming game, when instead he is deep in thought about the poem that is being discussed in class. Our football player, who initially was very interested in the class and in literature and

Panicked citizens gather to withdraw their money from a federal bank during the Great Depression. This type of thinking also contributed to a plunge in the stock market in 2008, when people pulled their money from the stock market because of fears it would crash.

had even written several poems for his high school newspaper, soon begins to lose interest in the class and ends up getting only a mediocre grade. Thus, we have a self-fulfilling prophecy in which the professor's distorted expectation comes true. Clearly, preserving our expectations can come at a cost to others.

Humans are prone to several inborn cognitive and perceptual errors, including optical illusions, misperception of random data, memorable-events errors, probability errors, self-serving biases, and self-fulfilling prophecies. Because these errors are part of the way our brain interprets the world, we may fail to notice the influence they exert over our thinking. Developing our critical-thinking skills

Rumors of impending bank failures during the Great Depression in the early 1930s led to mass panic in which people rushed to take their money out of banks before the banks crashed.

can help us be more aware of these tendencies and adjust for them when appropriate.

EXERCISE 4-3

STOP AND ASSESS YOURSELF

I. Come up with an issue—such as same-sex marriage, abortion, or legalizing marijuana—that is important to you. Discuss the extent to which cognitive errors bias the way you go about collecting and interpreting evidence regarding this issue. Discuss steps you might take to compensate for this bias.

2. Think of a "lucky" charm or ritual that you use, or have used in the past, to increase your chances of doing well on something that really matters. This can include anything from wearing your "lucky shoes" during a baseball game to rubbing your mother's ring before an important exam. Given your realization that this behavior is based on a cognitive error, why might you continue to do it? Support your answer using what you know of probability error.

3. If you have ever bought a lottery ticket or know of someone who did, why did you (or the other person) buy it? When the ticket was bought, what did you, or the other person, think the probability of winning was? Discuss the extent to which this reasoning involved a probability error.

4. Given that humans are prone to cognitive errors, should we use computers rather than physicians for medical diagnoses? Support your answer.

5. Think of a time when you studied hard for a test but ended up with a low grade. To what did you attribute your poor performance? Now think of a time when you studied hard and did very well on a test. To what did you attribute your good performance? Discuss how self-serving biases may have contributed to the difference in your reaction in each of the two situations.

6. Do you tend to overestimate the amount of control you have over your life? Give specific examples. Discuss how a distorted sense of control has had an impact on your ability to achieve your life goals. Come up with at least two critical-thinking strategies you could use to correct for this cognitive error.

7. Which cognitive error are you most like to commit? Give a specific example of your using this error. If you are willing, share your strategies for overcoming these ideas with the class.

SOCIAL ERRORS AND BIASES

Humans are highly social animals. Because of this trait, social norms and cultural expectations exert a strong influence on how we perceive the world—so much so that we tend to perceive the world differently in groups from the way we do in isolation. Groups can systematically distort both the gathering and the interpretation of evidence.[34]

As we noted in Chapter 1, ethnocentrism—the unjustified belief that our group or culture is superior to that of others—can also bias our thinking and act as a barrier to critical thinking.

Victims of the bombing of a Catholic church in Nigeria by Islamic militants in 2012.

"One of Us/One of Them" Error

Our brains seem to be programmed to classify people as either "one of us" or "one of them." We tend to treat people who are similar to us with respect and those who are different from us—whether in regard to race, sex, religion, political party, age, or nationality—with suspicion or worse. Although most of us claim to believe in human equality, in our culture the use of qualifiers such as *gay judge, female doctor, Hispanic senator,* and *Down syndrome child* betray our tacit belief that any deviation from the norm needs to be specified. We rarely hear terms such as *straight judge, male doctor, European American senator,* or *able-bodied child!*

Prejudices may operate without any conscious realization on our part. In a Harvard study, subjects were asked to quickly associate positive or negative words with black or white faces. Seven out of ten white people, despite their claims that they had no racial prejudice, showed "an automatic preference for white over black."[35]

It is all too easy for people to fall into the "us versus them" mind-set, especially when they feel threatened. In 1994, the Hutu government in Rwanda stirred up Hutus' hatred and fear of the Tutsi, inciting them to carry out a brutal three-month slaughter of the Tutsi. Neighbors killed neighbors, students killed their fellow students, and doctors killed doctors. Even priests helped with the massacre of the Tutsi in their congregations, simply

255

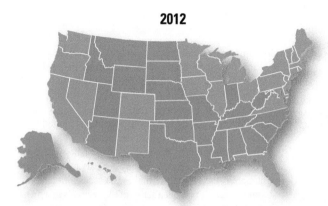

2012

Red States vs Blue States

because the Tutsi were the "other." When it was over, a million people were dead.

This error also contributes to our tendency to polarize issues into two camps. "They," whether it be "right-wing conservatives" or "far-left liberals," are irrational; there is no point in even arguing a point with them. Our group, on the other hand, holds a monopoly on Truth. There is no middle ground. During presidential elections, Americans are quick to divide up the country into two opposing camps: the red states (Republicans) and the blue states (Democrats) and to classify people in their group as "good" and "right" and those in the other group as "bad" and "mistaken."

If we are to overcome this social error we need to be aware of it in our thinking and to build in protective measures.[36] As critical thinkers, we can work toward

minimizing this error in our thinking by first critically evaluating the situation and then consciously reprogramming our brains to come up with new, more reasonable definitions of who it is that we view as "us" by seeking a more immediate and inclusive basis for a connection, such as we all attend the same college, we all are Americans, we all are human beings. We also need to make a conscious effort to be open to multiple perspectives, even those we are initially convinced must be mistaken.

Societal Expectations

The late nineteenth and early twentieth centuries were times of extraordinary technological advancement, setting in motion the expectation of ever new and revolutionary technology. On December 13, 1909, six years after the Wright brothers' epic flight, the *Boston Herald* reported the invention of an airship by a local businessman, Wallace Tillinghast.[37] Over the next several weeks, hundreds of witnesses from the New England–New York area, including police officers, judges, and businesspeople, reported sightings of the airship sailing through the skies.[38] The reported sightings led to a massive search for the airship by reporters. The search was finally called off when it was revealed that the story was a hoax perpetuated by Tillinghast.

Connections

When you serve as a juror, how can cognitive and social errors distort your analysis of the evidence? *See Chapter 13, pp. 417–418.*

Social expectations can be so powerful that they may lead to collective delusions. Sometimes these social errors may even become institutionalized.[39] Acting on social expectations without subjecting them to critical analysis can have dire consequences. The Salem witch trials in colonial Massachusetts, in which over 200 people, predominantly young women, were accused of witchcraft, were rooted in the social expectations of the seventeenth century. Those of us living in the twenty-first century may regard the witch-hunters as crazed fanatics. However, they were simply behaving in a manner that was consistent with the prevailing worldview and social expectations of their time in which certain unfortunate circumstances, such as crop failures, disease, and untimely deaths, were interpreted as being brought about by the Devil and his worldly agents—witches.

The Salem witch hunts, which took place in Massachusetts in the late 17th century, targeted those mistakenly believed to be responsible for society's ills.

The social expectations of the police who interrogated Peter Reilly, a teenager who was accused in 1973 of killing his mother, also played a role in their use of leading questions to get a "confession" out of him. Reilly's mother had been an emotionally abusive woman. In our society we expect victims of parental abuse to be violent and vengeful, even though studies suggest that it is children who witness domestic violence, rather than those who are direct victims of it, who are at highest risk, since they come to accept violence as normal.[40] In addition, it is often a family member who commits this type of violent murder. Therefore, the police jumped to the conclusion, on the basis of their expectations, that Reilly must have committed the murder.

Stereotyping is another type of social bias based on socially generated group labels. In the study mentioned in Chapter 1, page 28, in which researchers showed students a picture of a black man on a subway next to a white man who was holding an open razor, when students were later asked to recall what they had seen, half of them reported that the black man was holding the razor.

ANALYZING IMAGES

Asch Experiment

In Asch's experiment, the naive subject (left) shows puzzlement when the other subjects give what is obviously a wrong answer.

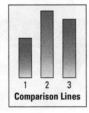

Standard Line   **Comparison Lines**

DISCUSSION QUESTIONS

1. *What do you think the naive subject in the picture above is thinking?*

2. *Think back to a time when you were in a similar situation where you thought you were correct, but everyone else with you thought something else. How did you respond to the discrepancy between your belief and theirs?*

Group Pressure and Conformity

Group pressure can influence individual members to take positions that they would never support by themselves, as happened in the Stanford prison experiment described in Chapter 1. Some religious cults exploit this tendency by separating their members from the dissenting views of family and friends. In many cults, people live together, eat together, and may even be assigned a buddy.

Group pressure is so powerful in shaping how we see the world that it can lead people to deny contrary evidence that is right before their eyes. In the 1950s, social psychologist Solomon Asch carried out a series of experiments in which he showed study subjects a screen containing a standard line on the left and three comparison lines on the right. (see "Analyzing Images: Asch Experiment"). One of the comparison lines was the same length as the standard line and the other two were of significantly different lengths.[41] In each case, an unsuspecting study subject was introduced into a group with six confederates, who had been told by the experimenter to give the wrong answer. The group was then shown the lines. The experimenter asked one of the confederates which of the three lines on the right they thought was the same length as the standard line. The confederate, without hesitation, gave a wrong answer. The next few confederates gave the same answer. By now, the naive subject was showing puzzlement and even dismay. How can six people be wrong?

After hearing six "wrong" answers, 75 percent of the naive study subjects, rather than trust the evidence of their senses, succumbed to group pressure and gave the same wrong answer. Even more surprising is the fact that when questioned afterward, some of these study subjects had actually come to believe the wrong answer was correct.

The desire for agreement is normal. However, this desire, when combined with our innate tendency to divide the world into "one of us" and "one of them," can lead to the exclusion of those who disagree with the majority, since people tend to prefer being around people who agree with them. In the corporate world, disagreement is often tacitly discouraged. "Outliers" or nonconformists who do not agree with group members may be excluded by committee chairs from further discussions or even fired.[42]

Because of our inborn tendency to conform to what others think, we cannot assume that agreement leads to truth without knowledge about the manner and conditions under which the agreement was arrived. Indeed, the current emphasis on seeking group consensus in decision making may be unreliable. In consensus seeking, the majority in a group is often able to sway the whole group to its view.

SOCIAL ERRORS AND BIASES

"One of us/one of them" errors: Our brain seems programmed to classify people as either "one of us" or "one of them." We tend to treat people who are similar to us with respect and those who are different from us with suspicion.

Social expectations: The influence of social expectations is so powerful that it can lead to collective delusions in which people attempt to fit evidence into their cultural worldview.

Group pressure and conformity: Group pressure can influence individual members to behave in ways or take positions that they would never do by themselves.

Diffusion of responsibility: A phenomenon that occurs in groups of people above a critical size where responsibility is not explicitly assigned to us so we tend to regard it as not our problem or as belonging to someone else.

➤APPLICATION: Identify an example in the text of each of the social errors and biases.

As with other errors in our thinking, we need to develop strategies to recognize and compensate for our human inclination to conform to groupthink, the tendency of members of a group to yield to the consensus of the group. When a group comes to a decision, we need to mentally step back from the group and carefully evaluate the evidence for a particular position rather than assume that the majority must be correct. In competitive ice skating and diving, because of the danger of a judge's scoring being contaminated by what other judges say, scoring is done individually, rather than as a group decision.

Diffusion of Responsibility

Diffusion of responsibility is a social phenomenon that occurs in groups of people above a critical size. If responsibility is not explicitly assigned to us, we tend to regard it as not our problem but as belonging to someone else. We are much more likely to come to someone's aid if we are alone than if we are in a crowd.

> **diffusion of responsibility** The tendency, when in a large group, to regard a problem as belonging to someone else.

This phenomenon is also known as *bystander apathy* or the *Kitty Genovese syndrome*. In 1964, 28-year-old Kitty Genovese was murdered outside her New York City apartment building. In the half hour that lapsed during the attack, none of Genovese's many neighbors,

5/30/2008 5:49:42 PM

The phenomenon of "diffusion of responsibility" was regrettably illustrated when no one came to the aid of a seriously injured man lying in a busy street in Hartford, Connecticut, after being struck by a hit-and-run driver in May 2008. The victim, Angel Torres, later died from the injuries he sustained.

who had heard her repeated cries for help, called the police. More recently, in June 2008, an elderly man was struck by a hit-and-run driver on a busy street in Hartford, Connecticut. The man lay in the street paralyzed and bleeding from his head while bystanders gawked at or

---

We are much more likely to come to someone's aid if we are alone than if we are in a crowd.

---

ignored him. Motorists drove around his body without stopping. No one offered any assistance until an ambulance finally turned up. Diffusion of responsibility can

also occur in group hazing at fraternities where no one comes to the rescue of a pledge who is clearly in distress.

As social beings, we are vulnerable to the "one of us/one of them" error, social expectations, and group conformity. When in groups, we also tend to regard something as not our problem unless responsibility is assigned to us. Although these traits may promote group cohesiveness, they can interfere with effective critical thinking. As good critical thinkers we need to be aware of these tendencies, and to cultivate the ability to think independently while still taking into consideration others' perspectives. Errors in our thinking also make us more vulnerable to falling for or using fallacies in arguments. We'll be studying some of these fallacies in the following chapter.

EXERCISE 4-4

STOP AND ASSESS YOURSELF

1. Whom do you define as "us" and whom do you put in the category of "them"? Discuss how you might go about widening the "us" category to include more people who are now in your "them" category.

2. Humans seem to have inborn biases toward particular types of people. According to a University of Florida study, when it comes to hiring, employers have a more favorable view of tall people. When it comes to earnings, every extra inch of height above the norm is worth almost $1,000 a year. In fact, nine of ten top executives are taller than the typical employee.[43] Given this cognitive error and its impact on hiring practices, discuss whether or not affirmative action policies should apply to very short people. Relate your answer to the discussion in the text of the effect of this cognitive error on our thinking.

3. Think of a time when your social expectations led you to misjudge a person or a situation. Discuss strategies for improving your critical-thinking skills so that this is less likely to happen.

4. Think of a time when the public got caught up in a "witch hunt." Identify the worldviews and social expectations that supported this "witch hunt." Which critical-thinking skills would make you less likely to go along with a "witch hunt"? Discuss what actions you could take to develop or strengthen these skills.

5. Polls before elections can influence how people vote by swaying undecided voters to vote for the candidate who is in the lead. Analyze whether election polls should be forbidden prior to the election itself.

6. The democratic process depends on social consensus. Given people's tendency to conform to social expectations and what others think, is democracy the best form of government? If so, what policies might be put in place to lessen the effect of social biases? Be specific.

7. Think of a time when you failed to speak out against an injustice or failed to come to someone's aid simply because you were in a large group and felt it wasn't your responsibility. Discuss ways in which improving your critical-thinking skills may make you less susceptible to the diffusion of social responsibility error.

8. Computers (AI) programmed with an inductive logic program can, after sufficient experience working with the ups and downs of the financial market, predict the market with greater accuracy than most experienced financial planners. Given that these computers are not as prone to cognitive errors as are humans, critically evaluate whether we should rely more on AI to make decisions about such issues as college admissions, medical diagnoses, matchmaking, and piloting an airplane.

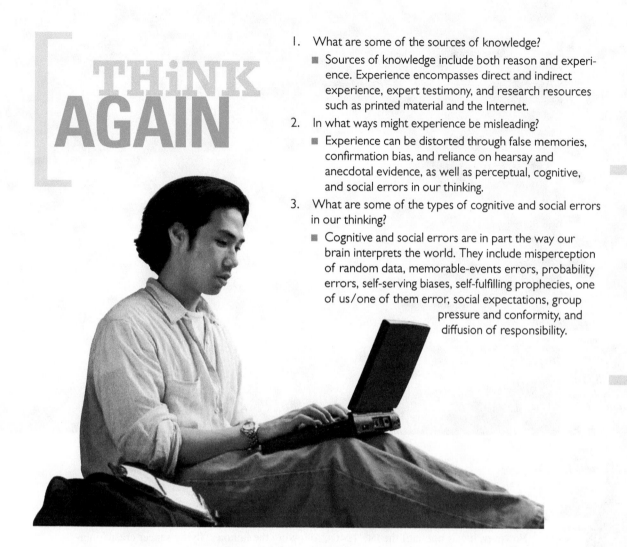

1. What are some of the sources of knowledge?
   - Sources of knowledge include both reason and experience. Experience encompasses direct and indirect experience, expert testimony, and research resources such as printed material and the Internet.

2. In what ways might experience be misleading?
   - Experience can be distorted through false memories, confirmation bias, and reliance on hearsay and anecdotal evidence, as well as perceptual, cognitive, and social errors in our thinking.

3. What are some of the types of cognitive and social errors in our thinking?
   - Cognitive and social errors are in part the way our brain interprets the world. They include misperception of random data, memorable-events errors, probability errors, self-serving biases, self-fulfilling prophecies, one of us/one of them error, social expectations, group pressure and conformity, and diffusion of responsibility.

Perspectives on Evaluating Evidence for the Existence of Unidentified Flying Objects (UFOs)

Sightings of unexplained phenomena in the sky have been reported since ancient times. However, it was not until the late 1940s, following the famous "flying saucer crash" incident in Roswell, New Mexico, that UFO reports began to proliferate. There is little doubt that sensationalist media coverage stimulated reports of more UFO sightings, just as the 1909 story in the *Boston Herald* of the invention of an airship was followed by hundreds of sightings of the bogus ship.

In 1948, the U.S. Air Force began to keep a file of UFO sightings as part of Project Blue Book. By 1969, the project had recorded 12,618 UFO sightings. Ninety percent of these UFO sightings have been identified with astronomical and weather phenomena, aircraft, balloons, searchlights, hot gases, and other natural events. Ten percent remain unexplained. In 1968, the U.S. Air Force commissioned a study under the direction of University of Colorado professor Edward Condon.[44] The study concluded that there was no evidence for UFOs and that scientific study of the phenomenon should be discontinued. As a result of the study, Project Blue Book was suspended.

Despite official consensus that UFOs do not exist, a 2012 National Geographic Society poll found that slightly more than one-third of Americans believe that UFOs exist.[45] In addition, 10 percent claim to have actually seen a UFO. The survey also found that 79 percent of Americans think that the government is hiding information from them about the existence of UFOs and alien life forms.

Following are readings from the U.S Air Force Blue Book Project and by Royston Paynter. Many if not most scientists believe that UFOs do not exist. These scientists argue that there are natural explanations for UFO phenomena, including meteorites, balloons, hallucinations, and perceptual and social error in our thinking. While Blue Book Project is more dismissive of UFOs, both readings leave open the possibility that UFOs may be real.

Project Blue Book: Analysis of Reports of Unidentified Aerial Objects

UNITED STATES AIR FORCE

Project Blue Book summarizes a series of studies of unidentified flying objects (UFOs) conducted by the U.S. Air Force beginning in 1952. The following selection is from the summary and conclusion of the report. To read the entire report, go to http://www.ufocasebook.com/pdf/specialreport14.pdf.

It is not possible to derive a verified model of a "flying saucer" from the data that have been gathered to date. This point is important enough to emphasize. Out of about 4,000 people who said they saw a "flying saucer," sufficiently detailed descriptions were given in only 12 cases. Having culled the cream of the crop, it is still impossible to develop a picture of what a "flying saucer" is. . . .

On the basis of this evidence, therefore, there is a low probability that any of the UNKNOWNS represent observations of a class of "flying saucers." It may be that some reports represent observations of not one but several classes of objects that might have been "flying saucers"; however, the lack of evidence to confirm even one class would seem to make this possibility remote. It is pointed out that some of the cases of KNOWNS, before identification, appeared fully as bizarre as any of the 12 cases of good UNKNOWNS, and, in fact, would have been placed in the class of good UNKNOWNS had it not been possible to establish their identity.

This is, of course, contrary to the bulk of the publicity that has been given to this problem. . . . It is unfortunate that practically all of the articles, books, and news stories dealing with the phenomenon of the "flying saucer" were written by men . . . had read only a few selected reports. This is accentuated by the fact that, as a rule, only the more lurid-sounding reports are cited in these publications. Were it not for this common psychological tendency to be captivated by the mysterious, it is possible that no problem of this nature would exist.

The reaction, mentioned above, that after reading a few reports, the reader is convinced that "flying saucers" are real and are some form of sinister contrivance, is very misleading. As more and more of the reports are read, the feeling that "saucers" are real fades, and is replaced by a feeling of skepticism regarding their existence. The reader eventually reaches a point of saturation, after which the reports contain no new information at all and are no longer of any interest. This feeling of surfeit was universal among the personnel who worked on

this project, and continually necessitated a conscious effort on their part to remain objective.

CONCLUSIONS

It can never be absolutely proven that "flying saucers" do not exist. This would be true if the data obtained were to include complete scientific measurements of the attributes of each sighting, as well as complete and detailed descriptions of the objects sighted. It might be possible to demonstrate the existence of "flying saucers" with data of this type, IF they were to exist.

Although the reports considered in this study usually did not contain scientific measurements of the attributes of each sighting, it was possible to establish certain valid conclusions by the application of statistical methods in the treatment of the data. Scientifically evaluated and arranged, the data as such did not show any marked patterns or trends. The inaccuracies inherent in this type of data, in addition to the incompleteness of a large proportion, of the reports, may have obscured any patterns or trends that otherwise would have been evident. This absence of indicative relationships necessitated an exhaustive study of selected facets of the data in order to draw any valid conclusions.

A critical examination of the distributions of the important characteristics of sightings, plus an intensive study of the sightings evaluated as UNKNOWN, led to the conclusion that a combination of factors, principally the reported maneuvers of the objects and the unavailability of supplemental data such as aircraft flight plans or balloon-launching records, resulted in the failure to identify as KNOWNS most of the reports of objects classified as UNKNOWNS.

An intensive study, aimed at finding a verified example of a "flying saucer" or at deriving a verified model or models of "flying saucers" (defined on Page 1 as "any aerial phenomenon or sighting that remains unexplained to the viewer"), led to the conclusion that neither goal could be attained using the present data.

It is emphasized that there was a complete lack of any valid evidence consisting of physical matter in any case of a reported unidentified aerial object. Thus, the probability that any of the UNKNOWNS considered in this study are "flying saucers" is concluded to be extremely small, since the most complete and reliable reports from the present data, when isolated and studied, conclusively failed to reveal even a rough model, and since the data as a whole failed to reveal any marked patterns or trends. Therefore, on the basis of this evaluation of the information, it is considered to be highly improbable that any of the reports of unidentified aerial objects examined in this study represent observations of technological developments outside the range of present-day scientific knowledge.

Review Questions

1. How does *Project Blue Book* distinguish between KNOWNS and UNKNOWNS in assessing reports of UFO sightings?

2. How do the authors account for the fact that so many people believe in UFOs?

3. What conclusion do the authors of *Project Blue Book* draw regarding the existence of UFOs and why?

Physical Evidence and Unidentified Flying Objects   ROYSTON PAYNTER

Royston Paynter has a Ph.D. in materials science from the University of Surrey in the United Kingdom and is currently a professor at the Institut National de la Recherche Scientifique in Quebec, Canada. In this article, Dr. Paynter writes that claims about the existence of UFOs and alien abductions should be conducted "according to the highest standards of scientific inquiry."[47] Without any physical evidence, he argues, we should remain skeptical about these claims.

Skeptics are sometimes criticized for demanding physical evidence of alien visitations. It is an unreasonable demand, believers say, because aliens are intelligent and cunning, and one cannot expect them to leave physical evidence of their presence on Earth.

Well, such an argument may make sense to somebody who is prepared to believe in alien visitations as an act of faith, in the same way that some people believe in angels. But the undeniable fact of the matter is that there is **no** probative physical evidence that compels us to conclude that aliens are visiting the Earth.

There simply is no alien space ship on display in a museum somewhere, in fact, there is no object in existence on Earth of which we can say "this must have been made by aliens." Of course it is possible to *believe* in alien visitations nonetheless, as an act of faith, but the great majority of scientists do not believe it, because it has not been proven in a rigorous scientific manner.

Those believers that reject the more extreme claims of popular UFOlogy, such as cattle mutilations, crop circles and even perhaps alien abductions, tend to fall back upon government and military reports obtained under the Freedom of Information Act. A well-known example is the US Air Force's own Project Sign "Estimate of the Situation," issued in 1948, that concluded that flying saucers were real and that they came from outer space.

To what extent is such a report authoritative? A scientifically trained individual looking at such a statement would ask "is this conclusion justified by the data presented?" That is to say, is such a conclusion forced upon us as the most economical way to explain that data, or is it the result of sloppy analysis and/or wishful thinking? In the case of the Project Sign "estimate,"

General Hoyt S. Vandenberg did not believe that the report's evidence was sufficient to support its conclusions, and he rejected it.

For those among us that are not prepared to believe in alien visitations simply as an act of faith, **physical evidence** is the key to everything. We **will** believe, if some artifact can be found on Earth that is demonstrably **alien**. Let us note here that "unidentified" and "demonstrably alien" are not synonymous. Just because a given UFO sighting cannot be explained it does not follow that it has been proved to be an alien space ship.

Short of a flying saucer landing on the White House lawn, where lie the best chances to obtain a demonstrably alien artifact? If we are to believe the stories told (or "remembered" under hypnosis) by those claiming to have been abducted by aliens, it seems that we should direct our attention first to those "alien implants" recovered from these people.

The stakes here are extremely high. If these "implants" can be shown to have been manufactured by aliens, then people really are being abducted by aliens. If, on the other hand, it cannot be shown that the "implants" are alien, then we must ask serious questions of the "researchers" who have elicited the testimony from the "abductees."

With the stakes so high, it is essential, in our opinion, that these analyses be conducted in accordance with the highest standards of scientific inquiry. Most importantly, we must demand that the UFOlogists prove *what they claim*. They are claiming that the "implants" have an alien origin. It is therefore not enough to show that they are "*100% pure*" or that they have an "unusual composition" or that they *contain chemical elements* also found in radio transmitters. They have to show that *aliens made them*.

One simple test would be enough to prove such a claim to the satisfaction of most scientists—an isotopic analysis of the material from which the implant is composed. We can reasonably expect that a device made by aliens from materials obtained in another solar system will exhibit isotope ratios different than those found on Earth. Such a test goes straight to the heart of the claim being made for the "implant" and would avoid all the obfuscation and hyperbole about "100% purity" and the like.

We urge the UFOlogical community to adopt properly scientific standards of investigation and proof in their work. They have to support their conclusions with probative evidence and rigorous reasoning and to confront the skeptics with the evidence they so dearly seek—a demonstrably alien artifact.

REVIEW QUESTIONS

1. Why do some believers maintain that the demand for physical evidence of alien visitations is unreasonable? How does Paynter respond to their objection?

2. What type of evidence does a scientist such as Paynter argue is necessary to establish the claim that UFOs exist?

3. What type of evidence does Paynter argue is necessary to prove the claim that people have been abducted by aliens?

THiNK AND DISCUSS

PERSPECTIVES ON THE EXISTENCE OF UNIDENTIFIED FLYING OBJECTS

1. What conclusion do both readings draw regarding the existence of UFOs? Compare and contrast the arguments used by the authors of Project Blue Book and by Paynter to support their conclusion(s). Evaluate the evidence each uses. Which reading presents the best argument? Explain.

2. Discuss the role of cognitive and perceptual errors, as well as social errors, in the debate over the existence of UFOs. Be specific.

3. Both the authors of Project Blue Book and Paynter concede that neither the lack of actual physical evidence of UFOs nor the ability to explain UFO "sightings" as sightings of familiar objects is not sufficient prove that UFOs do not exist (see fallacy of Appeal to Ignorance on page 148). Discuss what proof or evidence, if any, would be sufficient to convince a logical person that UFOs existed.

4. Do you believe in the existence of UFOs? Write down the evidence and premises you use to support your conclusion. Working in small groups, critically analyze each other's arguments.

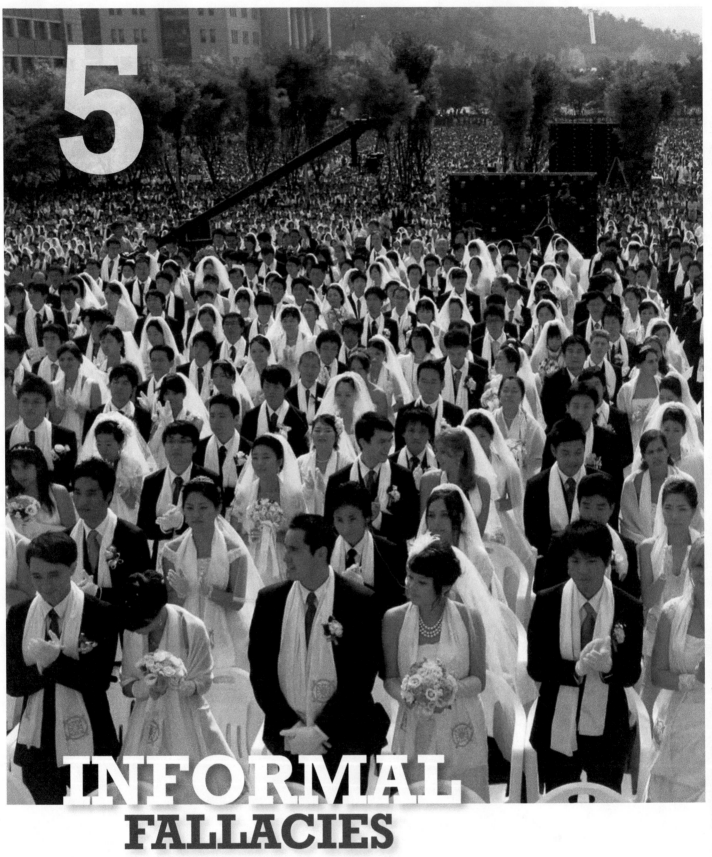

5

INFORMAL
FALLACIES

Which types of fallacies might lead someone to make a major unexpected life change such as this mass marriage conducted by the Unification Church, considered by many to be a cult?

WHAT'S TO COME

Shannon Townsend was excited about college. An honor student in high school who planned to become a physician, she finished her first semester at the University of Colorado with a 3.9 grade point average and an active social life. Then something happened to change the direction of her life. A few weeks before the end of her freshman year, she announced to her parents that she was dropping out of college to "follow Jesus." She had joined a nomadic cult known as the Jim Roberts Group, or simply the Brethren. The cult believes in disowning family and possessions, isolating themselves from society, and roaming the land (as they believe Jesus did), proselytizing and foraging for food. Over ten years have passed, and her family has not seen or heard from Shannon since she quit college to join the Brethren.[1]

Shannon's story is not that uncommon. Each year, hundreds of college students are

THiNK FIRST

- What is a fallacy, and why are we taken in by informal fallacies?
- What are three main types of informal fallacies?
- How can we avoid falling for and/or using fallacies?

 recruited into destructive cults, a particular subclass of cults, groups organized around a set of beliefs and rituals that display excessive devotion to a person or ideology, that use manipulative and deceptive recruiting techniques, and that employ fallacious reasoning—including reliance on vague language to mask their true objectives from potential members. Isolation from family and peer pressure from "new" cult friends in the form of "love bombing"—a technique by which cult members shower a recruit with unconditional love to put them into a position of making them more susceptible to accept anything the cult says—both heighten compliance and discourage critical thinking. And to retain recruits' loyalty, destructive cults also use scare tactics, emotional abuse, and guilt.

College students, especially freshmen who are having difficulty adjusting to the college environment and are experiencing separation from their families, or who are having academic or social problems, are especially vulnerable to cults. Lack of assertiveness, dependence on others, a low tolerance for ambiguity (wanting simple "right" and "wrong" answers for complex questions), and poor critical-thinking skills all make students more likely to succumb to pressure from campus recruiters for cults.[2]

The best way to avoid being targeted by a cult, according to clinical counselor and cult expert Ron Burks, is to be well informed and unafraid to ask questions. "The antidote . . . is critical thinking," he says. "Cults don't like people who are constantly thinking and asking questions."[3]

The ability to recognize fallacious arguments used by cult recruiters can go a long way toward making us less vulnerable to the lure of destructive cults and to other types of flawed arguments. In Chapter 5 we will:

- Define fallacy
- Learn how to identify fallacies of ambiguity
- Learn how to identify fallacies of relevance
- Learn how to identify fallacies with unwarranted assumptions
- Practice recognizing fallacies in everyday arguments and conversations
- Discuss strategies that can be used for avoiding fallacies

Finally, we will discuss two dramatically different proposals on how to stop gun violence and analyze these arguments for fallacies.

WHAT IS A FALLACY?

An argument is the process of supporting a claim or conclusion by providing reasons or evidence, in the form of premises, for that claim. An argument can be weak or invalid in several ways. The premises—the reasons or evidence given in support of a particular conclusion or position—may be mistaken, or the evidence may not support the conclusion. An argument contains a **fallacy** when it appears to be correct but on further examination is found to be incorrect. Fallacies may be formal or informal. In a **formal fallacy**, the form of the argument itself is invalid. For example, the following argument contains a formal fallacy: "Some high school dropouts are men. No doctors are high school dropouts. Therefore, no doctors are men." Although the premises are true, the conclusion does not follow because the form of the argument is faulty.

An **informal fallacy** is a type of mistaken reasoning that occurs when an argument is psychologically or emotionally persuasive but logically incorrect. Because fallacies can lead us to accept unsupported conclusions, being taken in by them can cause us to make poor life choices—as happened when Shannon was taken in by a destructive cult. Being able to identify informal fallacies makes it less likely that you will fall for these fallacies or use them in an argument.

In the following sections we will study three groups of informal fallacies: fallacies of ambiguity, fallacies of relevance, and fallacies with unwarranted assumptions. There are many types of fallacies in these groups. We'll be studying some of the more common ones in this chapter.

EXERCISE 5-1

STOP AND ASSESS YOURSELF

1. Think of a time when you fell for an "argument" that was emotionally persuasive but that you later realized was based on poor reasoning. Why were you initially persuaded by the argument?

2. Referring back to your example in question 1, discuss how improving your critical-thinking skills will make you less likely to fall for similar arguments that are based on fallacies and faulty reasoning.

FALLACIES OF AMBIGUITY

Arguments that have ambiguous words or phrases, sloppy grammatical structure, or confusion between two closely related concepts can lead to **fallacies of ambiguity**. People with poor language and communication skills are more likely to use or fall for these fallacies. Fallacies of ambiguity include equivocation, amphiboly, fallacies of accent, and fallacies of division.

Equivocation

Equivocation occurs when a key term in an argument is ambiguous—that is, when it has more than one meaning—and the meaning of the term changes during the course of the argument. This is most likely to happen when the meaning of the key term is not clear from the context of the argument. Verbal disputes, such as the dispute about whether a tree falling in a forest when no one is around makes a "sound," occur because of equivocation on the key term *sound*. In this case, the people who are disagreeing are each using a different definition of *sound*.

Here is another example of equivocation:

On February 23, 2010, Fox News reported that Democratic Senator Harry Reid had said that "if you're a man and out of work you may beat up your wife." From this the Fox reporters drew the conclusion that Reid thinks it is okay for men who are out of work to beat up their wives. In doing so they committed the fallacy of equivocation since the term *may* has more than one meaning. It can be used to mean "permission to" or it can be used to express "possibility." In fact, Senator Reid had actually said: "Men who are out of work tend to be abusive. Our domestic shelters are jammed." He was not giving unemployed men permission to beat their wives nor was he condoning abuse.

Here is another example of this fallacy:

Carl: Terminally ill patients have a right to decide how and when they want to die.

Juan: That's not true. There is no right to euthanasia in U.S. law.

In this argument Carl is using the term *right* as a

Hot or Not?

Is the use of fallacies a legitimate political campaign tactic?

fallacy A faulty argument that at first appears to be correct.

formal fallacy A type of mistaken reasoning in which the form of an argument itself is invalid.

informal fallacy A type of mistaken reasoning that occurs when an argument is psychologically or emotionally persuasive but logically incorrect.

fallacy of ambiguity Arguments that have ambiguous phrases or sloppy grammatical structure.

equivocation A key term in an argument changes meaning during the course of the argument.

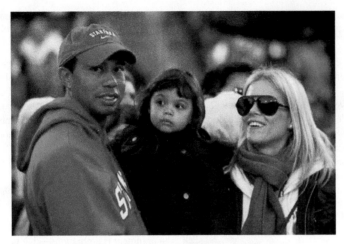

Tiger Woods is a good golfer, therefore Tiger Woods is a good husband.

moral right, whereas Juan is using a different definition of *right*—that is, as a legal right. Legal rights and moral rights are not the same. For example, we might have had a legal right to own slaves, as did southern Americans before the Civil War, but (as all Americans would today agree) not a moral right. We can also have a moral right, such as a right to faithfulness and honesty from our life partner, but not generally a legal right.

> **amphiboly** An argument contains a grammatical mistake, that allows more than one conclusion to be drawn.

The fallacy of equivocation also occurs when we misuse relative terms such as *tall*, *small*, *strong*, *big*, or *good*, as in this example:

> Two-year-old Katie is very tall. Her father, on the other hand, is not tall but about average in height. Therefore, Katie is taller than her father.
>
> Tiger Woods is a good golfer, therefore Tiger Woods is a good husband.

In these two examples, the relative terms *tall* and *good* are being used in the same argument in different contexts; it is like comparing apples and oranges. A tall toddler and a tall man are two very different things. And the fact that Tiger Woods was a good golfer does not necessarily mean that he was also a good husband. As it turned out, in 2010 it was reported that he was having an affair. He and his wife Elin Nordgren divorced shortly after.

To avoid the fallacy of equivocation, you should clearly define any ambiguous words or phrases before proceeding with the argument of discussion.

To avoid the fallacy of equivocation, you should clearly define any ambiguous words or phrases before proceeding with the argument or discussion. In addition, you need to avoid using relative terms in different contexts within the same argument.

Amphiboly

The fallacy of **amphiboly** occurs when there is a grammatical mistake in an argument, which allows more than one conclusion to be drawn. For example:

> Terri Schiavo's mother and her husband are on opposite sides of the battle over her life.[4]

In this 2005 statement regarding the issue of whether to remove the feeding tube from brain-damaged Terri Schiavo, the ambiguous wording makes it unclear which conclusion follows. Is it Terri Schiavo's husband, or her father (that is, her mother's husband), who is taking the opposite side? In this case, Terri Schiavo's husband asked to have the feeding tube removed; her mother and father, believing that Terri still had a chance of regaining consciousness, insisted that the feeding tube be kept in place.

Advertisers may use this type of fallacy, hoping you'll read more into the statement than is actually there, as in the following slogan for the Clinique fragrance Happy.

> Wear it and be happy!

The word *and* is ambiguous here. *And* can be used to mean either that they are two separate and unrelated ideas—or that a causal connection exists between two ideas: "Wear this fragrance and [if you do] you will be happy." Of course, the advertiser is hoping we'll fall for the fallacy and make the second interpretation. However, if we use the fragrance Happy and aren't any happier as a result, and so try to sue Clinique for false advertising, we can be sure that they'll say they never intended the term *and* in their ad to imply a causal connection. Instead, or so they will probably claim, they used *and* only as a conjunction between two unrelated ideas. Meanwhile, it's money out of our pockets and we're less happy than before because we've been duped by ambiguous language.

On the lighter side, humorists may use amphiboly to amuse their audiences, as in this dialogue from the 1996 movie *Spy Hard*:

> Agent: Sir, we've intercepted a very disturbing satellite transmission from our listening post on the Rock of Gibraltar.
>
> Director: What is it?
>
> Agent: It's this really big rock sticking out of the water on the south coast of Spain.

To avoid the fallacy of amphiboly, we should use language and grammar properly so the meaning of our argument is clear. When unsure of how to interpret a particular statement, we should ask the person to rephrase it more clearly.

Fallacy of Accent

The fallacy of **accent** occurs when the meaning of an argument changes according to which word or phrase in it is emphasized. For instance:

> Distraught mother: Didn't I say, "Don't play with matches"?

> Delinquent daughter: But I wasn't *playing* with the matches. I was using them to burn down Mr. Murphy's shed.

> According to our school newspaper, the administration is going to crack down on *off-campus* drinking. I'm glad to hear that they're okay with on-campus drinking.

In the first example, the delinquent daughter changes the meaning of her mother's warning by placing the accent on the word *playing*. In the second, by emphasizing the term *off-campus*, the student erroneously concludes that the college administration opposes drinking only when it's off-campus.

The fallacy of accent can also happen when we take a passage out of context, thus changing its original meaning. For instance, "proof-texting" involves taking a scriptural passage out of its original context in order to prove a particular point. Religious cults often use proof-texting to support their theological arguments. The following passage is taken from the King James Bible, which is the translation used by the Jim Roberts cult—mentioned at the beginning of this chapter—to convince recruits that they must forsake not only their worldly possessions but also their family, friends, education, and career plans.

> So likewise, whosoever of you that forsaketh not all that he hath, he cannot be my disciple. Luke 14:33

By ignoring the fact that neither Jesus nor his disciples forsook or completely disowned their family or friends, the cult leader commits the fallacy of accent.

If you are unsure about which term is being emphasized or accented in an argument, ask the person who made the argument to repeat or explain what he or she meant. If you suspect that a particular argument has been taken out of context, go back and look up the original source—in this example, the King James Version of the Bible. Arguments that take on a different meaning when read within the context of the source are fallacious.

How can you recognize the fallacy of amphiboly in advertisements? *See Chapter 10, p. 319.*

> **accent** The meaning of an argument changes depending on which word or phrase in it is emphasized.

> **fallacy of division** An erroneous inference from the characteristics of an entire set or group about a member of that group or set.

Fallacy of Division

In the **fallacy of division**, we make an erroneous inference from the characteristics of an entire set or group about a member of the group or set. In doing so we incorrectly assume that each member of a group has the characteristics of the group in general.

> Group G has characteristic C.
> X is a member of group G.
> Therefore, X has characteristic C.

For example:

> Men are taller than women.
> Danny DeVito is a man.
> Therefore, Danny DeVito is taller than the average woman.

ANALYZING IMAGES

"THANK GOODNESS! THE STUDENT LOAN COMPANY SAYS THIS IS THE LAST NOTICE I'M GOING TO GET!"

©WM. HOEST ENTERPRISES, INC. ALL RIGHTS RESERVED

Making Poor Choices

DISCUSSION QUESTIONS

1. *What fallacy is the student committing in this cartoon? Discuss how failing to recognize this fallacy might lead the student to make poor choices.*

2. *Imagine that you are the parents in the picture. Discuss what you might say to your son to call his attention to his faulty thinking.*

Obviously the concluding statement is incorrect, since the average woman—at 5 feet 4 inches tall—is 4 inches taller than Danny DeVito. Also, sometimes we may think someone or something is good (or bad) simply because of that person's or that thing's association with a particular group, as the next example illustrates:

> I hear that Canadians are really nice people. Therefore, Derek, who is from Saskatchewan, must be really nice.

Although it may be true that Canadians as a group are very nice people, we cannot infer from this that each individual Canadian, such as Derek, is really nice.

Fallacy of Composition

The **fallacy of composition** errs in the opposite direction of the fallacy of division. The fallacy of composition involves an erroneous inference from the parts to the whole by drawing a conclusion about the entire set from the characteristics of the members of that set or group, as in the following example:

> The rooms in the hotel are small. Therefore, the hotel must be small.

The fact that the rooms (parts of the hotel) are small does not mean the hotel (the whole) itself is small. In fact, rooms in some of the larger hotels in large cities like New York City tend to be smaller, albeit more elegant, than those in some

fallacy of composition An erroneous inference from the characteristics of a member of a group or set about the characteristic of the entire group or set.

small town hotels. The following is another example of this fallacy:

> Both sodium (Na) and chloride (Ca) are dangerous to humans.
>
> Therefore, table salt (NaCl), which is a combination of these two chemicals, is dangerous and should be avoided altogether.

However, the fact that sodium and chloride are dangerous on their own does not mean they are dangerous when combined. In fact, some salt in our diet is good for our health.

HIGHLIGHTS

FALLACIES OF AMBIGUITY

- *Equivocation:* An ambiguous word or phrase changes meaning during the course of the argument.

- *Amphiboly:* A grammatical error in the premises allows more than one conclusion to be drawn.

- *Fallacy of accent:* The meaning of an argument changes depending on which word or phrase is emphasized. Accent also occurs when passages are used out of context.

- *Fallacy of division:* A characteristic of an entire group is erroneously assumed to be a characteristic of each member of that group.

- *Fallacy of composition:* A characteristic of a member of a group is erroneously assumed to be characteristic of the whole group.

➤ *APPLICATION: Find an example in the text of each type of fallacy of ambiguity.*

EXERCISE 5-2

STOP AND ASSESS YOURSELF

I. Identify the fallacy of ambiguity, if any, in each of the following arguments:

*a. My parents used to get into arguments all the time, and they ended up getting divorced. Critical thinking teaches people how to make arguments. Therefore, if you want a happy marriage, don't sign up for a course in critical thinking.

b. Atoms are invisible to the naked eye. Therefore, I must be invisible since I am made up of atoms.

c. I hear that Dr. Carr is a really good teacher; therefore, it's probably a good idea for me to sign up for his course in physiology since I'm interested in the subject.

*d. Americans are among the most obese people in the world. Clyde is an American. Therefore, Clyde is one of the most obese people in the world.

e. Police officer: "Why do you rob banks?"
Willie Sutton: "[Because] that's where they keep the money."

f. The football team at State University is best in its league. Therefore, every member of the football team is one of the best football players in the league.

*g. I have no regrets for what I did. God told me to kill your children. Psalms 137 clearly says, "Happy is he who shall seize your children and dash them against the rock."

h. The sign on the deli door says "No Animals Allowed." I guess we'll have to find another place for lunch, since we're humans and humans are clearly animals.

i. You are a bad person because you are a bad student.

*j. Our town hall says it is giving out parking permits to fish at Warden's Pond. But that's ridiculous. Why would a fish need a parking permit?

k. The people of Liechtenstein have the highest personal income of any people in any nation in the world. Therefore, Liechtenstein is the richest nation in the world.

l. God created man in his own image. But you're a woman. Therefore, you aren't created in God's image.

*m Stanford is academically one of the best universities in the United States. Therefore, Claude, who is a student at Stanford, is academically one of the best students in the country.

n. "Too many doctors are getting out of business. Too many OB-GYNs aren't able to practice their love with women all across the country." George W. Bush addressing a group of people about the effects of frivolous lawsuits, September 2004.

o. The black rhino is heading toward extinction. So the black rhinos at the Cincinnati Zoo must be heading toward extinction.

*p. The Declaration of Independence states that all men are created equal. But that's certainly not the case. Studies show that people are born unequal in intelligence and athletic ability.

2. Look for examples of fallacies of ambiguity in the media, including news coverage, magazine articles, and advertisements. Identify each fallacy and discuss what purpose the writer is hoping to achieve (deliberately or unconsciously) by using this fallacy.

*Answers to selected exercises are found in the Solutions Manual at the end of the book.

FALLACIES OF RELEVANCE

In **fallacies of relevance**, one or more of the premises is logically irrelevant, or unrelated, to the conclusion. However, we may fall for these fallacies because psychologically the premises and conclusion seem to be relevant. Fallacies of relevance include personal attacks (ad hominem fallacies), appeals to force (scare tactics), appeals to pity, popular appeals, appeals to ignorance, hasty generalizations, straw man fallacies, and red herrings.

Ad Hominem (Personal Attack)

The **ad hominem fallacy** or personal attack occurs when we disagree with someone's conclusion, but instead of presenting a counterargument we attack the person who made the argument. In doing so, we try to create disapproval toward our opponent and his or her argument. This fallacy, which is sometimes referred to by the Latin phrase ad hominem, meaning "against the man," can take two forms: (1) *abusive*, when we directly attack the character of the person, or (2) *circumstantial*, when we dismiss someone's argument or accuse someone of hypocrisy because of the person's particular circumstances. People may be taken in by the fallacy because of our natural tendency to divide the world into "one of us" versus "one of them."

This fallacy often rears its ugly head in heated debates over controversial issues and in political campaigns. In the 2008 presidential campaign, the McCain campaign launched an attack ad mocking Obama as a celebrity like Britney Spears and Paris Hilton. The Democrats in turn attacked McCain as being "too old," "out of touch," and "grouchy."

People who don't conform to the accepted worldview may become the targets of personal attack, as in the following example:

> Ernst Zündel is part of the lunatic fringe. His ideas about the existence of UFOs under the South Pole are nothing short of crazy.

Instead of addressing Zündel's argument that UFOs exist under the South Pole, the person tries to discredit Zündel himself. The attempt to discredit someone's ideas by attacking his or her character and credibility is sometimes known as "poisoning the well." It is common in political campaigns.

fallacy of relevance The premise is logically irrelevant, or unrelated, to the conclusion.

ad hominem fallacy Instead of presenting a counterargument, we attack the character of the person who made the argument.

Connections

How do the "rules of evidence" protect against the use of fallacies, such as the ad hominem fallacy, in court trials?
See Chapter 13, pp. 414–415.

Critical THiNKing in Action

The Perils of Verbal Attacks in Personal Relationships

Not all uses of personal attack or the ad hominem fallacy are intentional. This fallacy may occur between people in personal relationships, because of poor communication skills.

John Gray, author of *Men Are from Mars, Women Are from Venus*, writes that we can be unwittingly abusive in personal relationships. He points out that men, rather than responding to a woman's argument, may become patronizing. Instead of addressing her concerns, the man explains why she shouldn't be upset or tells her not to worry about it. In doing so, he commits the ad hominem fallacy by dismissing her feelings. As a result, the woman becomes even more upset. He, in turn, senses her disapproval and he becomes upset as well, blaming her for upsetting him and demanding an apology before making up. She may apologize but is left wondering what happened. Or she may become even more upset at his expecting her to apologize, and before long the argument escalates into a battle, including name-calling and accusations.

In order to avoid the above scenario, Gray emphasizes the importance of good listening and communication skills in personal relationships so that we understand why the other person gets upset and can then move on from there.

1. Do you agree with Gray about men's and women's communication styles? Is this type of miscommunication also common in relationships between people of the same sex? Support your answer using specific examples.

2. Think of a time in a relationship when you said something to a person who got upset and you didn't understand why. Now think of a time when you got upset because someone casually dismissed your concerns and you were left feeling hurt. Create strategies that will make you less likely to use or fall for verbal attacks such as these and more likely to respond to them in a constructive, rational manner.

Paraphrased from John Gray, *Men Are from Mars, Women Are from Venus* (New York: HarperCollins Publishers, 1992), p. 155.

People who lack good critical-thinking skills may respond to a personal attack by returning the insult.

> Pat: I think abortion is wrong because it ends the life of a living human being.
>
> Chris: You pro-lifers are just a bunch of narrow-minded, anti-choice, religious fanatics.
>
> Pat: Oh, yeah? Well, you're an anti-life baby-killer who's no better than a Nazi.

Instead of addressing Pat's arguments against abortion, Chris turns on Pat and attacks her. Chris doesn't do much better. Instead of ignoring Chris's insult and getting the argument back on course, Pat buys into the ad hominem fallacy by returning the insult. As good critical thinkers, we must resist the temptation to respond to a personal attack by throwing abuse back at the person who attacked us.

We also commit this fallacy when we dismiss someone's argument by suggesting that their circumstances bias their thinking or when we argue that our opponent should or does accept a particular conclusion because of his or her special circumstances, such as his or her lifestyle or membership in a particular group. For example:

> Of course Raul is in favor of affirmative action in college admissions. He's Latino and will benefit from affirmative action programs.

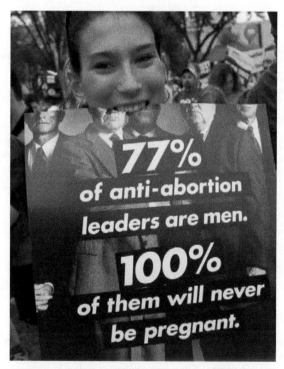

The woman carrying the placard commits the circumstantial form of the ad hominem fallacy by dismissing offhand the arguments of men. The fact that men cannot become pregnant does not mean they cannot take a position on the issue of abortion. The placard also has an ambiguous key term "leader." However, even if the term is defined, the gender of the leaders of the movement is irrelevant to the argument that abortion should be legal.

However, whether or not Raul benefits from affirmative action has no *logical* bearing on the soundness of Raul's argument in favor of affirmative action. His argument has to be evaluated independently of his circumstances.

This type of personal attack may also take the form of accusing someone of hypocrisy because of the person's circumstances.

> Father: Son, you shouldn't be smoking. It's not good for your health.
>
> Son: Look who's talking. You smoke at least a pack a day.

Here, the son dismisses his father's argument by accusing him of hypocrisy. But the fact that someone is engaging in a practice that he argues against, such as smoking, does not mean his argument is not sound. In this case, being a hypocrite or engaging in doublethink does not invalidate the father's argument that smoking is bad for the health of his son.

> **appeal to force (scare tactics)** The use or threat of force in an attempt to get another person to accept a conclusion as correct.

Not all negative statements about a person's character contain a fallacy, as in the following example.

> Jacob Robida, who allegedly attacked three men at Puzzles Lounge, a Massachusetts gay bar, and murdered two others while fleeing, was a disturbed and violent teenager who had a Nazi swastika and a coffin in his bedroom.

In this case, Robida's mental condition, his previous history of violence, and his Nazi sympathies are all relevant to the conclusion that he was probably guilty of the crime, since they help establish his motive for committing the crime.

Appeal to Force (Scare Tactics)

The fallacy of **appeal to force**, or **scare tactics**, occurs when we use or threaten to use force—whether it be physical, psychological, or legal—in an attempt to get another person to back down on a position and to accept our conclusion as correct. Like the personal attack fallacy, using an appeal to force may work in the short run. However, intimidation almost always damages trust in a relationship and is symptomatic of poor communication skills and faulty reasoning. This fallacy is illustrated by the following two examples:

Connections How do advertisers use scare tactics to get you to buy their products? *See Chapter 10, p. 318.*

> Don't disagree with me. Remember who pays your college tuition.
>
> Don't disagree with me or I'll slap your *&*% face!

ANALYZING IMAGES

THE LONDON SKETCH BOOK.

PROF. DARWIN.

This is the ape of form.
Love's Labor Lost, act 5, scene 2.

Some four or five descents since.
All's Well that Ends Well, act 3, sc. 7.

Darwin's Descent from the Apes

Fallacies can be used in nonverbal communication. After it was published in 1859, many critics of Charles Darwin's theory of evolution, rather than addressing his argument directly, responded by making personal attacks against those who supported evolution, as in this 1870 cartoon. Biologist Thomas Huxley (1825–1895), one of the most impassioned supporters of the theory of evolution, was not about to fall for this tactic. When Bishop Samuel Wilberforce allegedly asked Huxley whether "it was through his grandfather or his grandmother that he claimed descent from a monkey," Huxley used humor to deflect the attack. "If then the question is put to me," he replied, "whether I would rather have a miserable ape for a grandfather or a man highly endowed by nature and possessed of great means of influence and yet employs these faculties and that influence for the mere purpose of introducing ridicule into a grave scientific discussion, I unhesitatingly affirm my preference for the ape."

DISCUSSION QUESTIONS

1. *How successful is this cartoon in shaping your feelings or those of others about the subject of the cartoon? Did Huxley also use the ad hominem argument in his reply? Evaluate Huxley's answer. If he committed a fallacy, describe the fallacy and consider whether there was a better way of responding without resorting to fallacies or the use of rhetoric.*

2. *Given that people tend to be taken in by the ad hominem fallacy, discuss whether the media has a responsibility to refrain from publishing cartoons that attack someone's character when the real issue is the person's position on a particular issue.*

Sometimes appeals to force are more subtle than these; for example, we may threaten to withdraw affection or favors if the other person doesn't come around to our way of thinking. As we discussed at the opening of this chapter, "love bombing" by a cult—in which new recruits are showered with "unconditional" love and isolated from support systems outside the cult—leaves recruits vulnerable to this fallacy when subtle threats are later made to withdraw this love if they don't follow the cult's rules.

Appeal to force may involve scare tactics rather than overt threats. For instance, some proposed that if the U.S. Congress didn't pass a balanced budget by March 1, 2013, the country would plunge over a "fiscal cliff," resulting in massive layoffs and leaving the country vulnerable to terrorist attacks because of cuts to the military.

Filmmakers also use scare tactics to hold their audience. With advances in artificial intelligence (AI), the possibility of creating robots or androids that look or behave like

The appeal to pity on this billboard is not fallacious. Death related to smoking negatively affects victims' families as well as the person who smokes.

humans has spawned several movies, including *2001: A Space Odyssey*; *The Terminator*; *Blade Runner*; *I, Robot*; *Artificial Intelligence: AI*; the *Star Wars* and *Transformers* series; and *The Matrix* trilogy, in which machines interact intelligently with humans. Many of these movies exploit scare tactics, depicting androids and robots as evil enemies out to destroy the human race.

Not all scare tactics involve fallacies, however. For example, if you drink and drive, you might cause an automobile accident. In this case, there is a logical connection between drinking and an increased risk of an automobile accident. In addition, not all threats contain fallacies. Some threats are too blatant to be considered fallacies. For example, if someone sticks a gun in your face and says, "Hand over your wallet—or else," you generally hand over your wallet, not because the gunman has convinced you that the wallet is his but because you don't want to get shot.

People who have political, financial, or social power are more likely to use the appeal to force fallacy. Although most of us are not taken in by overt threats of force, fear is a powerful motivator and one that we are more likely to fall for than we might realize. This is particularly troublesome when those who lack power—for example, battered women or oppressed minorities—come to agree with their oppressor or blame themselves for their own oppression. Furthermore, children who witness abuse may come to believe that "might does make right" and identify with the person in power. In turn, they may use force to get their way when they are adults.

Appeal to Pity

In the fallacy of **appeal to pity**, we try to evoke a feeling of pity in the other person when pity is irrelevant to the conclusion. For example:

> Please don't give me a speeding ticket, officer. I had a really bad day: I found out that my boyfriend was cheating on me and, to top it off, I just received an eviction notice from my landlord.

However, the fact that you just found out your boyfriend was cheating on you and that you got an eviction notice from your landlord, while certainly sad, are not logically relevant to how fast you were driving. Although the officer may feel sympathy for your plight, it is not a good reason for her not to issue you a speeding ticket.

appeal to pity Pity is evoked in an argument when pity is irrelevant to the conclusion.

In previous chapters we discussed the importance in critical thinking of healthy self-esteem and assertive communication skills. People who have low self-esteem or trouble balancing their needs and those of others are particularly vulnerable to this fallacy.

> I don't have time to type up my assignment for class tomorrow morning because I promised I'd meet Justin at the movies tonight. And you know better than anyone that

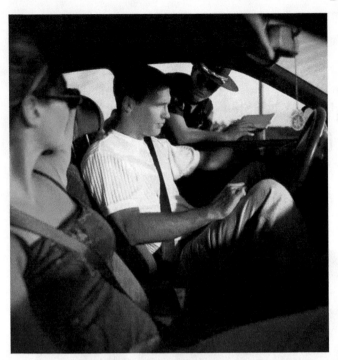

A speeding driver's pleas that "I shouldn't get a ticket because everyone speeds," or, "Please don't give me a ticket, I'm late for the party," are based on fallacious thinking and would not convince a logically thinking officer.

irresponsible behavior of someone who habitually uses this fallacy to manipulate others.

Not all appeals to pity are fallacious. There are times when a person's plight calls for a sympathetic response. For example:

> Please don't give me a speeding ticket, officer. My toddler, who is in the backseat, swallowed a nickel and is having trouble breathing. I have to get her to the hospital right away.

In this case, we would consider the officer grossly insensitive—and perhaps even criminally at fault—if she gave the parent a speeding ticket instead of escorting him and his child to the hospital as quickly as possible. Many charities also appeal to our sense of pity. Once again, there is no fallacy in cases where our pity is logically relevant to the appeal for help.

The word *critical*, as in critical thinking, is derived (as we noted at the beginning of Chapter 1) from the Greek word *kritikos*, meaning "discernment" or "the ability to judge." Being able to discern when it is appropriate for us to respond to an appeal to pity, as opposed to when we are being manipulated, involves an awareness of whether or not the reference to pity is in fact relevant.

Popular Appeal

The fallacy of **popular appeal** occurs when we appeal to popular opinion to gain support for our conclusion. The most common form is the *bandwagon approach*, in which a conclusion is assumed to be true simply because "everyone" believes it or "everyone" is doing it. Here's an example of the bandwagon form of popular appeal:

> God must exist. After all, most people believe in God.

The conclusion in this argument is based on the assumption that the majority must know what is right. However, the fact that the majority of people believe in the existence of God, or in anything else, does not mean it is true. After all, the majority of people once believed that the sun went around the earth and that slavery was natural and morally acceptable.

Popular appeal may use polls to support a conclusion, as in this example:

> Mandatory testing of students is a good measure of how academically effective a school is. A poll found that 71 percent of parents of children in grades K–12 ". . . favor mandatory testing of students in public schools each year as a way to determine how well the school is doing."[5]

The fact that most parents agree with mandatory testing is insufficient on its own to support the conclusion that it is a good measure of how well schools are doing. Instead we need a controlled

popular appeal An appeal to popular opinion to gain support for our conclusion.

Connections

How do advertisers use the fallacy of popular appeal to sell products such as "junk food" to children? *See Chapter 10, pp. 315–316.*

How can you recognize the fallacy of popular appeal in political campaigns? *See Chapter 13, p. 401.*

How can we recognize the use of snob appeal in advertisements? *See Chapter 10, p. 318.*

it's wrong to break a promise. Please type up my assignment for me. If you don't, I might fail the course. Please, please, just do this one thing for me.

People who fall for this fallacy may see themselves as caring and sensitive people who hate to say no and are always willing to go out of their way for their friends. Compassion is certainly a good trait. But there are times when, if someone makes a request like this, you need to step back and ask yourself whether pity is relevant to their argument. If not, you can still express your concern but not give into their fallacious reasoning. Falling for an appeal to pity not only hurts you but also encourages the

Hot or Not?

Does celebrity endorsement of a product make you more likely to buy that product?

ANALYZING IMAGES

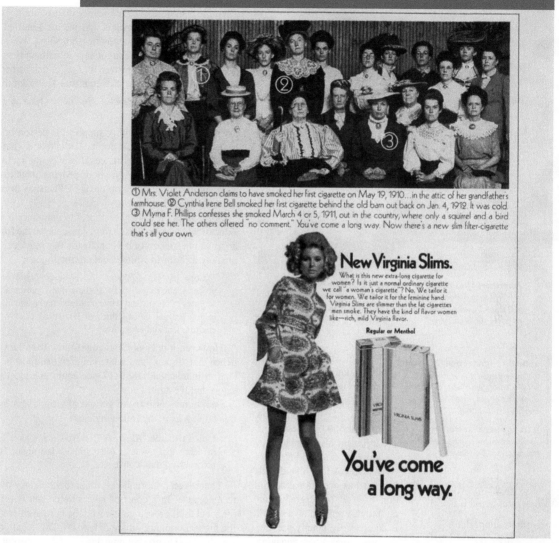

① Mrs. Violet Anderson claims to have smoked her first cigarette on May 19, 1910…in the attic of her grandfather's farmhouse. ② Cynthia Irene Bell smoked her first cigarette behind the old barn out back on Jan. 4, 1912. It was cold. ③ Myrna F. Phillips confesses she smoked March 4 or 5, 1911, out in the country, where only a squirrel and a bird could see her. The others offered "no comment." You've come a long way. Now there's a new slim filter-cigarette that's all your own.

New Virginia Slims.

What is this new extra-long cigarette for women? Is it just a normal ordinary cigarette we call "a woman's cigarette"? No. We tailor it for women. We tailor it for the feminine hand. Virginia Slims are slimmer than the fat cigarettes men smoke. They have the kind of flavor women like—rich, mild Virginia flavor.

Regular or Menthol

You've come a long way.

"You've Come A Long Way, Baby" The tobacco industry spends about $25 million a day in advertising, much of which is based on appeals to our emotions rather than to reason. In 1968, Phillip Morris introduced Virginia Slims cigarettes and the "You've come a long way, baby!" ad campaign in an attempt to expand its female market. This campaign was designed to appeal to women's growing sense of independence. It also identified smoking with being beautiful and thin. Not surprisingly, one of the main reasons women cite for smoking is weight loss.

Although the sexist overtones led to boycotts of Virginia Slims by some feminists, the ad was highly successful in getting more teenage girls to take up smoking. Virginia Slims advertising dropped the "You've come a long way, baby!" tag line during 1995–1996.

DISCUSSION QUESTIONS

1. *Discuss the use of fallacies in this ad. Make a note of your initial reaction to the above ad. To what extent did you fall prey to the fallacies in this ad and why? Analyze why this ad was successful in getting some young women to take up smoking.*

2. *If you smoke or know someone who does, what reasons do you or the other person give in support of continuing to smoke? Examine or analyze these reasons for possible fallacies.*

Advertisers often appeal to "snob appeal" in advertising, paying celebrities to endorse their products. They hope that consumers will think, "I want to be like Victoria Beckham, so I'll buy the type of purse she is carrying."

appeal to ignorance The claim that something is true simply because no one has proven it false, or that something is false simply because no one has proven it true.

hasty generalization A generalization is made from a sample that is too small or biased.

Connections

What events led U.S. courts to adopt the "innocent until proven guilty" philosophy? *See Chapter 13, p. 416.*

scientific study to determine the relationship between student test scores and how well a school is doing (see page 379 for an explanation of controlled studies). This argument also contains an ambiguous term *well*. In order to conduct a study we first need an operational definition of *well* (e.g., graduation rate) to determine how a school is doing. If we simply use student test scores we are engaging in circular reasoning, also known as the fallacy of begging the question (see page 153).

The *snob appeal* form of this fallacy involves the association of a certain idea with an elite group of people or a popular image or product. The use of supermodel Kate Upton in in the 2013 Super Bowl ads for Mercedes-Benz and of celebrities such as Mariska Hargitay of the popular television series *Law and Order: Special Victims Unit* in ads for milk are examples of snob appeal. Indeed, this fallacy is particularly prevalent in ads that attempt to create a market for products—such as fancy cars—that we wouldn't ordinarily consider purchasing.

As critical thinkers, we need to keep in mind that a particular position or conclusion is not necessarily right just because the majority or an elite group accepts it.

Appeal to Ignorance

The fallacy of **appeal to ignorance** does not imply that we are stupid. Instead, it means that we are ignorant of the means of proving or disproving something. We fall into this fallacy whenever we argue that something is true simply because no one has proven it false, or that something is false because no one has proven it true. Consider this:

> UFOs obviously don't exist. No one has been able to prove that they do.

In this example, the only support the person offers for the conclusion that UFOs don't exist is that we have been unable to prove their existence. However, the fact that we are ignorant of how to go about proving their existence does not mean that they don't exist. UFOs may or may not exist—we just don't know.

Sometimes the fallacy of appeal to ignorance is subtler. Educational psychologist Arthur Jensen used the following argument in support of his conclusion that black people are innately inferior to white people in intelligence:

> No one has yet produced any evidence based on a properly controlled study to show that representative samples of Negro and white children can be equalized in intellectual ability through statistical control of environment and education.[6]

However, it does not logically follow from *lack* of evidence that "[black] and white children can [not] be equalized in intellectual ability." Once again, the most we can say is that we don't know.

People may also try to get out of a tight spot by using this fallacy, as in the following case:

> I didn't murder Alexi, officer. You don't have any evidence that I was at Alexi's house last night. That proves that I didn't do it.

There is an important exception to the fallacy of appeal to ignorance. In a court of law, a defendant is presumed innocent until proven guilty. And the burden of proof is on the prosecution, not on the defendant. This legal principle was designed to prevent punishment of the innocent, which is considered a much greater injustice than letting a guilty person go free. In addition, because the government is much more powerful than the individual defendant, this principle helps level the playing field. It's important to note that a "not guilty" verdict is just that; it is not necessarily proof of the person's innocence.

Hasty Generalization

When used properly, generalization is a valuable tool in both the physical and social sciences. We commit the fallacy of **hasty generalization** when we generalize from a sample that is too small or biased.

Unusual cases ———————→ Odd rule about
the whole group

(premises) (conclusion)

Stereotypes are often based on this fallacy:

> My father was an abuser, and so was my ex-boyfriend John. All men are mean.

Here the speaker judges all men as "mean" on the basis of her limited experience with only two men.

As we've already seen, people tend to divide the world into "us" and "them," and rather than view people who are different from "us" as individuals, we instead label "them" on the basis of hasty generalizations. Confirmation bias, in which we seek only examples that confirm our stereotypes, reinforces this tendency.

For example, the YouTube film "Innocence of Muslims" mocked the prophet Muhammad and perpetuated the stereotype that Muslims are irrational and violent. The film, which provoked protests throughout the Muslim world, was initially and erroneously thought to be the catalyst for the attacks on the U.S. embassy in Benghazi (see page 65).

The YouTube film "Innocence of Muslims" provoked protests throughout the Muslim world by denigrating the Prophet Muhammad and showed how easily explosive material can be disseminated through the Internet.

The fallacy of hasty generalization can also interfere with cross-cultural communication and the establishment of new relationships. While on a cruise with my sister, our ship stopped at the port of Cartagena in Colombia, instead of at another Caribbean port that had originally been scheduled. When our tour director heard of the change, he quickly called our group together and warned us that we should stay on the ship while in port. If we really wanted to go ashore, he added, we should pretend to be Canadians. Colombians, he told us, hate Americans and would try to rob, assault, or arrest us on the most trivial charges, or even kill us, given the opportunity. As it turned out, Cartagena was a beautiful city, and the people we met were very friendly and helpful. Stereotypes and hasty generalizations about Colombians acted as a barrier that kept other passengers from getting to know and understand the Colombians.

Hasty generalization can also occur because we've developed stereotypes that are based on outdated information. Consider this statement:

> Most college students are liberals. I know I was, as were most of my friends, when I was in college in the mid-1970s.

Although the majority of college students identified themselves as liberal or far left politically in the 1970s, this is no longer the case. Today almost half of students—47.5 percent—are middle-of-the-road politically and another 24 percent identify themselves as conservative or far right.[7]

> Today almost half of students—47.5 percent—are middle-of-the-road politically and another 24 percent identify themselves as conservative or far right.

Before we make a generalization we should make sure that we have a sufficiently large and unbiased—as well as an up-to-date—sample. After the death of the great English poet Lord Byron in 1824, a curious physician removed his brain and weighed it. He found that Byron's brain was 25 percent larger than the average human brain. News of this discovery, which was based on only a single sample, spread throughout the scientific community, contributing to the myth that there was a connection between brain size and high intelligence.[8] We'll be studying sampling methods and the proper use of generalization in arguments in more detail in Chapter 7.

Connections

How do advertisements reinforce stereotypes? *See Chapter 10, p. 318.* What role does sampling play in scientific research and experimentation? *See Chapter 12, p. 379.*

Straw Man

The **straw man fallacy** is committed when a person distorts or misrepresents the opponent's argument, thus making it easier to knock it down or refute it. This tactic is particularly common in political rhetoric over controversial issues.

> I'm opposed to legalizing same-sex marriages. Proponents of same-sex marriage want to destroy traditional marriage and make gay marriage the norm.

This is a fallacious argument because it misrepresents the argument of those who support same-sex marriage. Supporters of same-sex marriage are not arguing that it should be an alternative to traditional marriage or that it is superior to traditional marriage. Instead, they simply want same-sex couples to have the same rights as opposite-sex couples when it comes to marriage.

Here is another example of the straw man fallacy:

> I can't believe you think genetically modified crops should be subjected to stricter regulations. If you take away farmers' ability to grow genetically modified crops, this will lead to widespread famine and starvation.

As in the previous example, this assessment of the argument in question is simplistic. It misrepresents the argument and instead sets up a straw man that is easier to knock down by arguing that without genetically modified (GM) crops, people would starve. But the opponent never argued for getting rid of GM crops, only for more regulation.

To avoid using or being taken in by this fallacy, go back and look at the argument in question as it was originally presented. Ask yourself: Has the argument been reworded or oversimplified to the point of misrepresentation? Have key parts of the original argument been omitted or key words been changed or misused?

> **straw man fallacy** An opponent's argument is distorted or misrepresented in order to make it easier to refute.

> **red herring fallacy** A response is directed toward a conclusion that is different from that proposed by the original argument.

The argument that legalizing same-sex marriage will destroy traditional marriage is based on the straw man fallacy.

Red Herring

The **red herring** fallacy is committed when a person tries to sidetrack an argument by going off on a tangent and bringing up a different issue. Thus, the argument is now directed toward a different conclusion. The red herring fallacy is named after a technique used in England to train foxhounds. A sack of red herrings is dragged across the path of the fox to distract the hounds from their prey. A well-trained hound learns not to allow distractions to divert its focus from the prey. Because the red herring issue is often presented as somewhat related to the initial one under discussion, the shift in the argument usually goes unnoticed. The original discussion may even be abandoned completely and the focus shifted to another topic without the audience realizing what is happening until it is too late.

> ### HIGHLIGHTS
> #### FALLACIES OF RELEVANCE
>
> - ***Ad hominem fallacy (personal attack):*** An attempt to refute an argument by attacking the character or circumstances of the person making the argument.
>
> - ***Appeal to force (scare tactics):*** A threat to use force—whether it be physical, psychological, or legal—in an attempt to get another person to back down on his or her position and to accept the conclusion as correct.
>
> - ***Appeal to pity:*** An attempt to gain support for a conclusion by evoking a feeling of pity, when pity is irrelevant to the conclusion.
>
> - ***Popular appeal:*** An appeal made to the opinion of the majority to gain support for the conclusion.
>
> - ***Appeal to ignorance:*** An argument that something is true simply because no one has proved it false, or that something is false simply because no one has proved it true.
>
> - ***Hasty generalization:*** A conclusion based on atypical cases.
>
> - ***Straw man:*** The distortion or misrepresentation of an opponent's argument to make it easier to knock down or refute.
>
> - ***Red herring:*** An argument directed toward a conclusion that is different from that posed by the original argument.
>
> ➤ *APPLICATION: Find an example in the text of each of the different types of fallacies of relevance.*

The use of the red herring fallacy occurs in political debates when candidates want to avoid answering a question or commenting on a controversial issue. For example, a politician who is asked about a nationalized health care plan may change the topic to the less controversial one of how important it is for all Americans to be healthy and receive good health care. In doing so, the politician avoids having to address the question of which approach to health insurance he or she supports.

Here is an example of this fallacy:

> I don't see why you get so upset about my driving after I have a few drinks. It's not such a big deal. Look at all the accidents that are caused by people talking on their cell phones while driving.

Here the person shifts the topic to accidents associated with use of cell phones, thus deflecting attention from the issue of his drinking and driving.

The red herring fallacy also occurs in discussions of ethical issues when a person changes the topic from what *should* be to what *is*. For example:

> Angelo: I don't think Mike should have lied to Rosetta about what he was doing last night. It was wrong.

> Bart: Oh, I don't know about that. If I had been in his situation, I would probably have done the same thing.

Here, Bart has changed the topic from what someone else *should* have done to what he *would* have done. In doing so, he changes the issue from a moral one to a factual one.

In the following newspaper column, the writer attempts to deflect attention away from the abuse at Abu Ghraib prison by changing the topic to the abuses under Iraqi dictator Saddam Hussein:

> The bullying and humiliation of detainees at Abu Ghraib is, as George W. Bush told Jordan's King Abdullah, "a stain on our country's honor and our country's reputation." . . . But let us also recognize what this scandal is not. There is a large difference between forcing prisoners to strip and submit to hazing at Abu Ghraib prison and the sort of things routinely done there under Saddam Hussein. This is a country where mass tortures, mass murders and mass graves were, until the arrival of the U.S. Army, a way of life.[9]

Note how the writer uses words such as *bullying*, *humiliation*, and *hazing* to downplay the torture of prisoners at Abu Ghraib, instead conjuring up an image of what happens at "harmless" college fraternity initiations. As Chris Crozier, a 21-year-old Fort Stewart mechanic stationed in Iraq, put it: "What the Iraqis may do to us is totally different. We should show them how to treat prisoners."[10] Now that's good critical thinking!

EXERCISE 5-3

STOP AND ASSESS YOURSELF

I. Identify any fallacies of relevance in the following arguments. Some of the arguments may not contain fallacies.

*a. The legal drinking age in America should be lowered to 18. After all, it's legal for you to fight and die for your country when you're 18.

b. No one has any conclusive proof that Iran has a viable nuclear weapons program. Therefore, I think we can safely assume that Iran does not have nuclear weapons.

c. Polygamy should be illegal. If polygamy is legalized in the United States, then little girls will be forced to marry older men and that is just wrong.

*d. Feminists argue for equality of men and women. That means men and women sharing the same bathrooms and locker rooms and having half of the players on professional football teams be women. But that's ridiculous. Therefore, we should reject feminism.

e. According to the news report, Jodi Arias stabbed her ex-boyfriend Travis Alexander 27 times and slit his throat while he was in the shower. Still, I don't think she shouldn't be found guilty of murder. Apparently the poor woman was a victim of domestic violence.

f. Of course Renaud is going to argue in favor of giving amnesty to illegal immigrants living in the United States. His mother came here from Haiti as an illegal immigrant twenty-five years ago.

*g. After reading the introduction to this chapter, it's obvious to me that all religious groups on campus are destructive and should be banned. After all, look what happened to Shannon.

h. I don't see why you are so concerned with global warming and switching all your light bulbs to those new energy-efficient ones. Terrorism is a much bigger threat than global warming.

i. Using animals in research isn't all that bad. Why, I just read that "if each pet cat in the United States ate only two mice, chipmunks, or baby birds each year, the number of animals slaughtered by pets would greatly exceed the number of animals used by research."[11]

*j. I think you'll agree with me that we do not want the press to find out that we're using child labor at our factory in India. You certainly wouldn't want to lose your job over this, if you get my drift.

k. Gun control is small potatoes when compared with the dangers posed by the widespread use of drones.[12]

l. You should switch from MySpace to Facebook. Facebook is the best social network because more people use it than any other social networking site.

*m. Granted, you may be a vegetarian, but you certainly can't argue against the killing of animals. After all, you do wear leather shoes and use products that were tested on lab animals.

n. I'd think twice about hiring Lucy to work the cash register in the student union cafeteria. She was fired from her last job in the bookstore for stealing, and just last week she was caught leaving the library with someone else's backpack.

o. Of course Troy voted for Obama; after all Troy is African American.

*p. You shouldn't be so concerned about street drugs. More people are killed with prescription drugs than with street drugs such as heroine and cocaine.

q. In 2010 Senator Patricia Murphy opposed the Senate health care bill on the grounds that the majority of Americans did not like the bill. Senate majority leader Harry Reid responded to her concern by arguing that she should vote for the Senate health care bill since a Kaiser Family Foundation Poll found that 57 percent of Americans "would be disappointed if Congress did not pass health care reform."

r. You wouldn't catch me visiting rural areas of British Columbia. People who live there are vicious. Why, just look at Robert Pickton, who murdered and dismembered some 27 women on his pig farm in British Columbia.

*s. Please don't count yesterday's absence against me, Professor Lee. The hot water wasn't working in our dorm and I wasn't able to take a shower.

t. "Soldiers at Fort Carson, Colorado, have been told that if they don't re-up [re-enlist] to 2007 they will be shipped out pronto for Iraq."[13]

u. I heard on the Jay Leno show that Michelle Obama buys her clothes at J. Crew. I love Michelle Obama; she's so cool. I'm going to buy my clothes at J. Crew too!

*v. Please don't count yesterday's absence against me, Professor Curto. I was struck by a car while coming home from a party and spent the day in the emergency room.

w. "[There is little] likelihood that machines, even if they reach a requisite level of complexity, will possess human attributes like consciousness and emotion. A being devoid of emotion would not feel betrayed if we kill it, nor would we regard it as a moral agent. The computer geeks in AI labs who think of themselves as nothing more than complex computer programs and want to download themselves into a computer should worry, since no one would care if they were turned off for good."[14]

x. Why are you focusing so much on Americans as the culprits in green house gas emissions. Canadians' energy use has increased by 25 percent in the past decade and they now use more energy per capita than do Americans. The Canadians also dropped their commitment to the Kyoto Protocol on reducing global warming.

*y. The Vatican, which is run by a celibate male leadership, has no moral right to take a stand on abortion.

z. "Every time you go online you're vulnerable to hackers, viruses, and cyber-thieves. Stay safe with Symantec's Norton Internet Security. It's comprehensive protection for you and your computer."

2. Discuss a time when you committed the fallacy of hasty generalization by stereotyping a particular group of people. What is the basis of this stereotype, and how is it reinforced in our language? Discuss also ways in which our language stereotypes *you*.

3. Find an editorial cartoon that contains the fallacy of personal attack. What do you think is the intent of the cartoonist? What effect does the cartoon have on your view of the subject of the cartoon? Discuss steps you might take to counter the effect of the fallacy of hasty generalization and our tendency to see the world in terms of "one of us/one of them" (see pages 148–149).

4. Which fallacy of relevance are you most likely to fall for? Give a specific example. Which fallacy of relevance are you most likely to use? Give a specific example. What steps can you take to make yourself less vulnerable to these fallacies?

*Answers to selected exercises are found in the Solutions Manual at the end of the book.

FALLACIES INVOLVING UNWARRANTED ASSUMPTIONS

A fallacy involving an **unwarranted assumption** occurs when an argument includes an assumption that is not supported by evidence. Because an unwarranted assumption is unjustified, it weakens the argument. Fallacies involving unwarranted assumptions include begging the question, inappropriate appeal to authority, loaded question, false dilemma, questionable cause, slippery slope, and the naturalistic fallacy.

Begging the Question

In **begging the question**, the conclusion is simply a re-wording of a premise. By making our conclusion the same as the premise, we are assuming that the conclusion is true rather than offering proof for it. This fallacy is also known as circular reasoning.

Premise Conclusion

Begging the question may take the form of the conclusion being a definition of the key term in the premises. In the following argument, the conclusion is simply a definition of the key term *capital punishment* rather than being an inference from the premise:

> Capital punishment is wrong because it is immoral to inflict death as a punishment for a crime.

This type of fallacy is sometimes hard to spot. At first glance, it may appear that the person has an airtight argument. On closer evaluation, however, it becomes apparent that it only *seems* this way since the conclusion and the premise(s) say essentially the same thing, as in the following argument:

> The Bible is the word of God. Therefore, God must exist because the Bible says God exists.

Here, the conclusion "God must exist" is already assumed to be true in the premise "The Bible is the word of God." To offer a rational proof of God, we cannot assume in our premise the existence of what we are trying to prove.

The begging the question fallacy can be very frustrating if we fail to recognize it, since there is no way to disprove the person's conclusion if we accept the premise. If you think an argument contains this fallacy, try reversing the conclusion and the premise(s) to see if the argument says essentially the same thing.

Inappropriate Appeal to Authority

It is generally appropriate in an argument to use the testimony of a person who is an authority or expert in the field. However, we commit the fallacy of **inappropriate appeal to authority** when we look to an authority in a field that is *not* under investigation. Young children, for example, may look to their parents as authorities even in areas where their parents have little or no expertise. Here is another example:

> My priest says that genetic engineering is not safe. Therefore, all experimentation in this field should be stopped.

Unless your priest also happens to be an expert in genetic engineering, before accepting his argument as correct you should ask him for reliable and authoritative evidence for his assertion.

We often find this fallacy in advertisements in which celebrities are used to promote products. For example, the singer Beyoncé is featured in ads promoting Pepsi, while basketball star LeBron James endorses Samsung phones; Olympic swimmer Michael Phelps appears in ads for milk (see p. 108). In none of these cases are the celebrities authorities on these products, and yet people accept their word simply because they are *experts* in unrelated fields.

Uniforms and distinguished titles such as *doctor*, *professor*, *president*, and *lieutenant* also serve to reinforce the mistaken perception that people who are experts in one field must be knowledgeable in others. This phenomenon is known as the *halo effect*. In the Milgram study explored in Chapter 1, the majority of subjects followed the orders of the experimenter primarily because he had a Ph.D. and was wearing a white lab coat, a symbol of scientific authority.

To avoid inappropriate appeals to authority, we should check out an expert's credentials in the field before using his or her testimony as authoritative.

> **unwarranted assumption** A fallacious argument that contains an assumption that is not supported by evidence.
>
> **begging the question** The conclusion of an argument is simply a rewording of a premise.
>
> **inappropriate appeal to authority** We look to an authority in a field other than that under investigation.
>
> **loaded question** A particular answer is presumed to an unasked question.

> **Connections**
>
> **How can we recognize and avoid falling for the use of inappropriate appeal to authority in advertisements?** *See Chapter 10, p. 318.*

Loaded Question

The fallacy of **loaded question** assumes a particular answer to another unasked question. This fallacy is sometimes used in a court of law when a lawyer demands a yes or no answer to a question such as

> Have you stopped beating your girlfriend?

false dilemma Responses to complex issues are reduced to an either/or choice.

However, this question makes the unwarranted assumption that you have already answered yes to a previous unasked question, "Do you beat your girlfriend?" If you don't beat your girlfriend and reply no to the question, it appears as if you are still beating her. On the other hand, if you answer yes it implies that you used to beat her.

The following example is also a loaded question:

> Do you think that the death penalty should be used only for people 18 and older?

This question is worded in a way that assumes that the people being asked approve of the death penalty when in fact they might not.

False Dilemma

The fallacy of **false dilemma** reduces responses to complex issues to an either/or choice. By doing so, this fallacy polarizes stands on issues and ignores common ground or other solutions. This slogan serves as an example:

> America—love it or leave it! If you don't like U.S. policy, then move somewhere else!

That argument makes the unwarranted assumption that the only alternative to accepting U.S. policies is to move to another country. In fact, there are many alternatives, including working to change or improve U.S. policies. In this case,

the fallacious reasoning is reinforced by the "one of us/one of them" cognitive error, in which we tend to divide the world into two opposing sides.

Poor critical-thinking skills and the tendency to see the world in black and white make it more likely that we'll fall into this fallacy. The argument that we need to raise taxes or cut medical services is based on the fallacy of false dilemma. Rather than raising taxes we can make our health care system more efficient. For example, Canada spends far less on health care per capita but has better outcomes in terms of life expectancy than the United States.

Habitual use of this fallacy restricts our ability to come up with creative solutions to problems in our personal lives as well, as the following example illustrates:

> It's Valentine's Day, and Bob didn't propose to me as I thought he would. Even worse, he said he wanted to start dating other women. I don't know what I'll do. If Bob doesn't marry me, I'll surely end up a miserable old maid.

Clearly Bob is not the only fish in the sea, although it may seem so when we are jilted by someone we care for. Overcoming personal setbacks requires that we use our critical-thinking skills to come up with a way of moving on rather than getting stuck in fallacious thinking.

We frequently find this type of fallacious thinking in all-or-nothing thinking. For example, bulimics regard eating in terms of either getting fat or bingeing and then vomiting to stay thin. They simply don't see moderation in eating as a viable alternative.

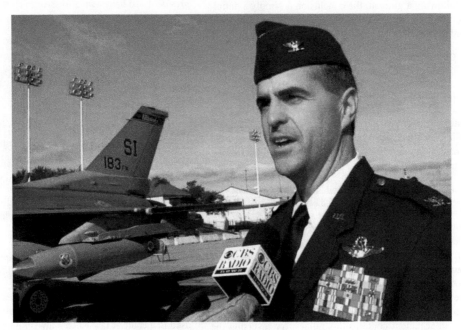

Wearing a uniform serves to reinforce the public's belief that the person is an authority in fields that may be beyond his or her actual expertise.

Some argue for wind power as the only alternative to fossil fuels. However, harnessing wind power is just one of many ways of cutting down on greenhouse emissions and reducing our dependence on foreign oil. It's not an either/or choice.

As we discussed in Chapter 4, people who suffer from depression also tend to get caught up in this type of fallacious reasoning:

"Either I'm in complete control of my life or I'm out of control."

"Either everyone likes me or everyone hates me."

Pollsters may unwittingly commit this fallacy. How options are presented in a question can influence the response. For instance, in one survey people were asked whether they felt that "the courts deal too harshly or not harshly enough with criminals." When presented with only these two alternatives, 6 percent of those surveyed responded "too harshly" and 78 percent "not harshly enough." However, when a third alternative was offered—"don't have enough information about courts to say"—29 percent chose that response and only 60 percent said "not harshly enough."[15] We'll be studying polling methods in more detail in Chapter 7.

To avoid the fallacy of the false dilemma, watch out for either/or questions that put you on the spot. If neither alternative is satisfactory, it is best to leave the response blank or check "I don't know" if that option is offered.

Questionable Cause

Because our brains tend to impose order on how we see the world, we may "see" order and causal relationships where they don't exist. When a person assumes, without sufficient evidence, that one thing is the cause of another, that person is committing the fallacy of **questionable cause**.

This can occur when we assume that because one event preceded a second event, it was the cause of the second event. This is also called the **post hoc** ("after this") fallacy.

It was divine intervention. I have a great devotion to Our Lady of Guadalupe . . . and said a little prayer to her when I hit the jackpot. Our Lady really looks out for me.[16]

—Guadalupe Lopez, mother of actress and singer Jennifer Lopez, on her $2.4 million slot-machine win at an Atlantic City casino

Superstitions are often based on this fallacy:

I wore my red sweater to the exam last week and aced it. I guess the sweater brought me good luck.

These two examples also illustrate how the self-serving bias that we are in control makes us prone to commit this fallacy.

We often see people's actions as having more causal impact on future events than they really do. For example, for more than eight decades the

How can you recognize and avoid falling for the fallacy of questionable cause in advertising? *See Chapter 10, p. 318.* **How can the scientific method be used to establish causal relationships?** *See Chapter 12, p. 367.*

questionable cause (post hoc) A person assumes, without sufficient evidence, that one thing is the cause of another.

Ryan White was a victim of questionable cause. For a time he was prohibited from attending public school because he had AIDS and people assumed that AIDS could be passed on to other students through casual contact.

THiNKing Outside the Box

JUDITH SHEINDLIN, *"Judge Judy"*

Judith Sheindlin (b. 1942), popularly known as "Judge Judy," is probably the most famous family court judge in the United States. Sheindlin attended American University and New York Law School. She graduated first in her class from law school, where she was the only woman in her class. In 1982, she was appointed a Family Court judge by then New York City Mayor Ed Koch. She quickly became renowned for her outspokenness and her quick thinking. In 1996 she was approached about presiding over cases on a television show.

The show *Judge Judy* premiered in 1996 and quickly became the number one reality court show on television. In the show, Sheindlin arbitrates small claims cases with real defendants. What fascinates many people about the show is the sheer number of illogical and fallacious arguments made by litigants. Sheindlin's responses to the use of fallacies and lame excuses by litigants has earned her a reputation as a witty but fair and logical thinker. In her book *Don't Pee on My Leg and Tell Me It's Raining: America's Toughest Family Court Judge Speaks Out,* she notes that many people fail to take responsibility for their actions, instead getting trapped in a cycle of fallacious reasoning and deteriorating and even abusive relationships. "I want people to learn to take responsibility," she says.

Judge Judy has been used in college courses for pointing out faulty logic and how to respond to it.*

1. Watch the *Judge Judy* show. List the types of fallacies made by the litigants. Note also how Judge Judy responses to the use of fallacies. Share your observations with the class.

2. Sheindlin notes that irrational and fallacious thinking can leave us trapped in abusive situations. Discuss ways in which the use of fallacious reasoning, or the inability to respond rationally to the use of fallacies by others, has left you, or someone you know, in a harmful situation, whether it be personal or at school or work.

* For example, there is a rhetoric seminar at the University of California at Berkeley entitled "Arguing with Judge Judy" that involves identifying arguments made by the litigants that are illogical or perversions of standard logic, and are used repeatedly.

Boston Red Sox lost every World Series in which they played because—so the story goes—the great baseball player Babe Ruth had jinxed the Sox when the team sold him to the Yankees in 1920.[17] When the team finally won the World Series in 2004, the victory was attributed by many fans to the "end of the curse" rather than simply to the skill and success of the team itself.

Sometimes, either because of stereotyping or ignorance, we assume two events are causally related when, in fact, they are not, as in the following example:

College students today don't participate in community service or volunteer work like we used to. That's because all they care about is getting a degree that will help them make a lot of money.

This argument commits the fallacy of questionable cause in assuming that college students, or anyone for that matter, who are concerned about making money are less likely to participate in community service as a result. While it is true that the majority of college students today are more concerned about getting a degree that will help them make money, the 2009 American freshman survey also found that a record number of incoming freshman (56.9 percent) said there was a "very good chance" they would volunteer "frequently" in college.[18]

To avoid this fallacy, we should be careful not to assume that there is a causal relationship just because two events occur near each other in time. We should also refer to well-designed studies to determine whether a causal relationship has been established between the two events. For more information on evaluating evidence, refer back to Chapter 4.

Slippery Slope

According to the **slippery-slope** fallacy, if we permit a certain action, then all actions of this type, even the most extreme ones, will soon be permissible. In other words, once we start down the slope or (to vary the metaphor) get a foot in the door, there is no holding back. We commit the slippery-slope fallacy when evidence does not support this predicted outcome, as illustrated by these two examples:

> You should never give in to your child. If you do, soon she will have you wrapped around her little finger. You need to stay in control.

> If we allow any form of human cloning, then before we know it there will be armies of clones taking over our jobs.

In the first argument, there is no credible evidence that giving in to our children's demands once in a while will lead to their dominating us.

The second argument regarding the effects of human clones is also implausible. Much of the concern about human cloning leading us down the slippery slope to armies of clones taking over the world is based on inaccurate information. In reality, it would be very risky and expensive to clone a human. Even

if we could mass-produce human clones, we would need to find women who are willing to act as surrogate gestational mothers for the cloned children. Moreover, each clone, like any child, will need a family to nurture him or her after birth.[19] This scenario is unlikely to happen on a large scale, since most parents prefer to have children who are related to them. Of course, this is not to say that there are no good arguments against human cloning, but the proverbial slippery slope is not one of them.

slippery slope The faulty assumption that if certain actions are permitted, then all actions of this type will soon be permissible.

Did You Know

One of the objections to giving women the vote was the fear that the vote would then have to be extended to all animals.

Some people oppose certain government policies on the grounds that they are "a moral hazard" that would lead us down the slippery slope to communism as in the following argument:

> Government bailouts will encourage businesses to be irresponsible and take absurd risks. If we allow them we will end up having to bailout every business in the nation until we end up under communism.

Alluding to the dreaded slippery slope when it comes to communism is a common ploy, especially among some conservatives, and involves the use of scare tactics (appeal to force) as well as the slippery slope fallacy.

Expressing a concern that something will get out of hand is not always fallacious. Sometimes the prediction that a particular action or policy will start us down a slippery slope is warranted. Consider this statement:

> The United States is running . . . a series of detention centers around the world where international legal standards are not having sway. They opened the door to a little bit of torture, and a whole lot of torture walked through.[20]

ANALYZING **IMAGES**

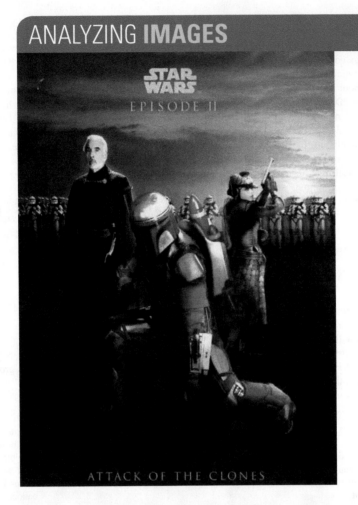

Scene From Star Wars Episode II Attack of the Clones In this sci-fi movie clones from an alien planet are portrayed as evil and a threat to the galaxy.

DISCUSSION QUESTIONS

1. *This movie is based on the assumption that mass-produced clones will be evil and destructive. What evidence, if any, is there to support this conclusion? Make a list of possible premises that people might use to support this conclusion.*

2. *Critically evaluate your argument in question 1. Identify and discuss any fallacies in this argument.*

The assumption here is that if we allow torture under these circumstances, the use of torture by the United States will become a common method of dealing with detainees.

To avoid the slippery-slope fallacy, we should carefully carry out our research and familiarize ourselves with the likely outcomes of different actions and policies. We should also watch any tendency to exaggerate forecasts of impending catastrophe.

> **naturalistic fallacy** A fallacy based on the assumption that what is natural is good.

Naturalistic Fallacy

The **naturalistic fallacy** is based on the unwarranted assumption that what is natural is good or morally acceptable and that what is unnatural is bad or morally unacceptable.* We find this fallacy in arguments that claim that no good can come from AI (artificial intelligence),

*The term naturalistic fallacy is sometimes used in a more narrow sense to convey that the concept of moral goodness cannot be reduced to descriptive or natural terms.

Same-sex parents are often discriminated against because many people only see "parents" as a mother and father. Some states still have laws prohibiting same-sex couples from adopting or taking in foster children.

simply on the grounds that AI is artificial—and hence unnatural.

Advertisers may also try to get us to conclude that their product is good or healthy simply because it is natural. An ad can claim, for example, that a tobacco product is "100 percent natural tobacco." However, it doesn't follow. *All* tobacco is natural, but that doesn't make it healthy. Arsenic, HIV, and tsunamis are also "natural," but we don't consider them to be healthy and desirable.

The naturalistic fallacy has also been used both to justify homosexuality (it occurs naturally in other animals) and to argue for its immorality, as in the following:

> Homosexual encounters do not lead to children [procreation], which is the natural end of sexual relations. Therefore, homosexuality is immoral.

In a similar manner, a person may argue that hunting is morally acceptable because other animals hunt and kill:

> I disagree that we need to protect the big cats, such as lions and tigers, from being hunted or to restrict ranchers from protecting their herds from these predators. We are only doing what the big cats do. They are predators, and so are humans.

However, the fact that other animals are predators does not justify our doing the same. Some animals also eat their young, and a few female insects even eat their male partners after mating! But these naturally occurring examples do not imply that it is morally justifiable for humans to do the same. The morality of these behaviors has to be evaluated on grounds other than that they are natural.

HIGHLIGHTS

FALLACIES INVOLVING UNWARRANTED ASSUMPTIONS

- *Begging the question:* A conclusion is simply a rewording of a premise.

- *Inappropriate appeal to authority:* An appeal based on the testimony of an authority in a field other than that under investigation.

- *Loaded question:* A question that assumes a particular answer to another unasked question.

- *False dilemma:* An argument unwarrantedly reduces the number of alternatives to two.

- *Questionable cause:* An argument that assumes without sufficient evidence that one thing is the cause of another.

- *Slippery slope:* An assumption that if some actions are permitted, all actions of that type will soon be permissible.

- *Naturalistic fallacy:* The assumption that because something is natural it is good or acceptable.

➤ *APPLICATION: Find an example in the text of each of the different types of fallacies involving unwarranted assumptions.*

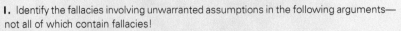

STOP AND ASSESS YOURSELF

I. Identify the fallacies involving unwarranted assumptions in the following arguments—not all of which contain fallacies!

*a. Prosecutor to defendant: Did you hide the drugs in your car?

b. Cocaine should be legalized. Cocaine, which comes from the coca plant, is all natural and therefore much safer than all these processed foods people are putting into their bodies.

c. My parents don't have a lot of money. If I don't get into Harvard with at least a partial scholarship I won't be able to go to college at all.

*d. Panhandler to person on street: "Can you spare a dime?"

e. If we allow terrorists to be tried in our civil courts instead of military tribunals, next thing you know they'll be demanding all sorts of rights given to American prisoners like free health care and a free education. If we allow this, soon terrorists from poorer countries will be flocking to our country and attacking us just so they can enjoy the higher standard of living in our prison system.

f. Clarissa has decided to drop out of college because she gained 17 pounds during her first year at college and is worried about getting diabetes. It's clear that too much education is bad for your health.

*g. My lawyer says that it looks as if I have whiplash from that automobile accident. I'm going to sue the insurance company of the person who hit my car.

h. According to the meteorologists on the Weather Channel, we might have 5 to 6 feet of flooding from heavy rain and rising river waters in the next 24 hours. I think we should pack our valuables and get out of town.

i. Do you support restricting abortion rights, thereby increasing the chances of death for thousands of women desperate enough to seek illegal abortions?

j. Splenda can't be all that bad for children. After all, it's made from all-natural sugar.

k. Conscription is wrong because people should not be compelled by the government to serve in the military.

l. Democracy is the best form of government because rule of the majority is always preferable.

*m. Boyfriend to girlfriend: So what do you want to do tonight—watch the football game on TV or grab a beer at Joe's Bar and Billiards?

n. We should not take away people's rights to own a gun. According to a 2013 Rasmussen Report, two-thirds of Americans support gun ownership as a protection against tyranny.

o. Animals can't reason, since reason is one of the things that separate humans from the beasts.

*p. Yesterday I carried an umbrella to class and it didn't rain. Today I left it home and it rained. I'd better carry my umbrella if I don't want it to rain.

q. Every time the presidential elections have been on November 6th, the Republicans have won. The elections are on November 6th this year. So a Republican will win the election.

r. New York City has proposed banning the sale of sugary drinks that are larger than 16 ounces. This would be a disaster. I mean, where's it going to stop? Next thing you know they'll be regulating everything in our life that we enjoy.

*s. Do you believe women should be drafted into the military?

t. Embryonic stem-cell research should be banned. It is a gateway to all other kinds of genetic engineering in humans and will lead to the exploitation of poor women as fetus farms.

u. If we don't cut back on energy use and our carbon emissions, global warming is going to continue getting worse and some coastal cities and towns may become uninhabitable because of the rising ocean level.

*v. My professor is leaving for a trip to Antarctica the same day that final grades are due for our class. Since this is my senior year at college, I cannot afford to get an incomplete in this class because I plan on graduating in a month. My final paper is worth 40 percent of my grade, so I can either choose to hand in the final paper before my professor leaves for Antarctica or to fail the course and therefore not graduate until next year. I don't see any other way out.

w. In Rhode Island the dropout rate at institutions of higher education is highest at the Community College of Rhode Island (CCRI). Brown University and the Rhode Island School

EXERCISE 5-4 CONT.

of Design (RISD) have the lowest dropout rates. Since CCRI has the lowest tuition and Brown and RISD have the highest tuition in the state, we should raise the tuition at CCRI if we want to lower the dropout rate there.

2. When you or your college team engages in a game or sporting event, to what extent do you attribute the win or loss to what is in actuality a questionable cause? Looking back at the cognitive errors we studied in Chapter 4, discuss which of the different kinds of errors contribute to our tendency to use or fall for this fallacy.

3. Find two advertisements containing fallacies involving two different unwarranted assumptions. Cut out or photocopy the advertisements. For each ad, write one page explaining what fallacy it contains and the target audience of the fallacious ad. Discuss how effective you think each ad is and why.

4. Which fallacy involving an unwarranted assumption are you most likely to fall for? Give a specific example. Which fallacy involving an unwarranted assumption are you most likely to use? Give a specific example. What steps can you take to make yourself less vulnerable to these fallacies?

*Answers to selected exercises are found in the Solutions Manual at the end of the book.

STRATEGIES FOR AVOIDING FALLACIES

Once you have learned how to identify informal fallacies, the next step is to develop strategies for avoiding them. Here are some strategies that can help you become a better critical thinker:

- *Know yourself.* Self-knowledge is a cardinal rule for good critical thinking. Knowing which fallacies you are most likely to fall for and which you are most likely to commit will make you less vulnerable to lapses in critical thinking.

- *Build your self-confidence and self-esteem.* Working on your self-confidence and self-esteem will make you less likely to give in to peer pressure and, in particular, to the fallacy of popular appeal. People who are self-confident are also less likely to back down when others use a fallacy on them or to become defensive and use fallacies on others.

- *Cultivate good listening skills.* Be a respectful listener of other people's views, even if you disagree with them. Do not be thinking of how you are going to respond before you have even heard the other person's argument. After the other person has presented his or her view, repeat it back to make sure you understand it correctly. Look for common ground. If you notice a fallacy in the argument, respectfully point it out. If the argument appears to be weak, ask the person for better support or evidence for his or her position rather than simply dismissing it.

- *Avoid ambiguous and vague terms and faulty grammar.* Cultivate good communication and writing skills. Clearly define your key terms in presenting an argument. And expect the same of others. Don't be afraid to ask questions. If you are unclear about the definition of a term or what someone else means, ask the person to define the term or rephrase the sentence.

- *Do not confuse the soundness of an argument with the character or circumstances of the person making the argument.* Focus on the argument that is being presented, not on the person presenting the argument. Also, resist the temptation to counterattack if another person attacks your character or threatens you because of your position on a particular issue. When two people trade insult for insult instead of focusing on the real issue, an argument may escalate out of control and both people may end up feeling frustrated and hurt. The tacit belief that if the other person is using fallacies or is being illogical then it's okay for you to do the same is a sign of immature thinking. If another person attacks your character, step back and take a deep breath before responding.

- *Know your topic.* Don't jump to a conclusion without first doing your research. Knowing your subject makes it less likely that you will commit a fallacy simply because you are unable to defend your position. This strategy involves being familiar with the relevant evidence, as well as a willingness to learn from others. In evaluating new evidence, make sure that it is based on credible sources.

- *Adopt a position of skepticism.* We should be skeptical but not close our minds to claims we disagree with, unless there is clear evidence that contradicts that claim. Don't just take people's word for it, especially if they are not authorities in the field under discussion. Also, remain skeptical about your own position and open to the possibility that you are mistaken or don't have the whole truth.

- *Watch your body language.* Fallacies need not be written or spoken. For example, the fallacies of personal attack and appeal to force can be conveyed through body language, such as rolling your eyes, glaring, looking away, and even walking away when someone is speaking.

- *Don't be set on "winning."* If your purpose is to win the argument rather than get to the truth about the issue, you're more likely to use fallacies and rhetoric when you can't rationally defend your position.

Learning how to recognize and avoid fallacies will make you less likely to fall victim to faulty arguments, whether those of cult recruiters, advertisers, politicians, authority figures, friends, or family. It is especially important to be able to identify and avoid using fallacies in your own life, thereby improving your critical-thinking skills.

The habitual use of fallacies can damage relationships and leave people feeling upset and frustrated. By avoiding fallacies, your relationships will be more satisfying and your arguments stronger and more credible. This, in turn, will make it easier for you to achieve your life goals.

EXERCISE 5-5

STOP AND ASSESS YOURSELF

1. Discuss ways in which being aware of and avoiding fallacies can improve your personal life.

2. Discuss how lack of self-knowledge and self-confidence makes you or others you know more vulnerable to fallacious reasoning. Use specific examples to illustrate your answer.

3. Working in small groups, select one or two of the following issues or one of the issues already raised in this chapter. Identify which fallacy the argument might contain. Discuss how you would go about collecting evidence to determine whether the argument is fallacious.

*a. Boys don't do as well in school as girls because almost all the teachers in elementary schools are women.

b. The beheading of infidels in Iraq, such as Western journalists, was sanctioned by Islam's holiest text, the Qur'an, which urges Muslims to resist Western occupation by stating, "Slay them . . . and drive them out of the places whence they drove you."[21]

c. "The big financiers have been the pampered pets for too long, and the mainstream figures who say 'depression . . . depression . . . depression' have been Chicken Littleing for too long; Wall Street won't change its ways without a bloodbath, and it's time they finally got one." (Argument against giving government bailouts to struggling financial institutions.)[22]

*d. "We now face a wave of education reforms based on the belief that school choice, test-driven accountability, and the resulting competition will dramatically improve student achievement. . . . [T]here is empirical evidence, and it shows clearly that choice, competition, and accountability as education reform levers are not working. But with confidence bordering on recklessness, the Obama administration is plunging ahead, pushing an aggressive program of school reform—codified in its signature Race to the Top program that relies on the power of incentives and competition. This approach may well make schools worse, not better."[23]

e. I don't think an ice cream social is appropriate for our next meeting since several of the students who will be attending are Japanese Americans, and from what I know, most of them don't eat ice cream.

f. Some people think prostitution should be legalized in the United States. However, if we legalize prostitution, sexually transmitted diseases like AIDS will run rampant and everyone will start to die out.

*g. Lawyers for the American Civil Liberties Union (ACLU) want the words *under God* removed from the Pledge of Allegiance. The Supreme Court should not support the ACLU's request. The ACLU is clearly antireligion and would like to see every trace of religion and faith in God removed from American life.

h. Support for stem-cell research by celebrities such as Michael J. Fox and Ronald Reagan Jr. has been in part responsible for the swing in public opinion in favor of the research.

i. Prayer works. Our church group prayed for Maxine after her operation, and she recovered from her surgery faster than the person in the bed beside her who had the same operation.

4. Select two of the strategies for avoiding fallacies and discuss as a class or write a short essay describing ways in which these strategies can help you become a better critical thinker. Discuss how the strategies that you plan to use to make yourself less vulnerable to using or falling for fallacies might make it easier for you to achieve your life goals.

*Answers to selected exercises are found in the Solutions Manual at the end of the book.

THiNK AGAIN

1. What is a fallacy, and why are we taken in by informal fallacies?
   - A fallacy is a type of incorrect thinking. We are taken in by informal fallacies because they are psychologically persuasive. The use of our critical-thinking skills makes us less likely to fall for fallacies.

2. What are three main types of informal fallacies?
   - One type is fallacies of ambiguity, which occur when there is ambiguous wording, sloppy grammatical structure, or confusion between two closely related concepts. In fallacies of relevance, one of the premises is logically unrelated to the conclusion. The third type is fallacies involving unwarranted assumptions in which one of the premises is not adequately supported by evidence.

3. How can we avoid falling for and/or using fallacies?
   - There are several strategies that can be used, including honing our analytical and argumentation skills, being aware of our strengths and weaknesses, building our self-confidence, cultivating good listening skills, avoiding ambiguous terms, adopting a position of skepticism, and having knowledge of the topic under discussion.

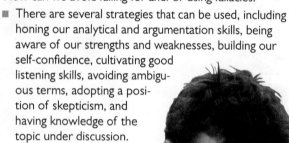

Critical THiNKing Issue

Perspectives on Gun Control

The United States has more guns per person–about one for every American–than any other country in the world, second only to Yemen. The United States also has a higher homicide rate by gun than any other developed nation. The gun homicide rate in the United States is 3.2 per 1,000 people, compared to 0.1 in Canada, 0.5 in Norway, 0.6 in Japan, and 0.7 in Great Britain. In addition, almost half of the mass shootings around the world have taken place in the United States.[24] The Centers for Disease Control (CDC) predicts that by 2015 shooting deaths in the United States will rise to 33,000, more than fatalities caused by automobiles.[25]

Following the December 2012 elementary school shooting in Newtown, Connecticut, in which 20 children and 6 adults were killed by 20-year-old Adam Lanza, there have been calls to rethink our gun laws and our interpretation of the Second Amendment of the U.S. Constitution, which states: "A well-regulated militia, being necessary to the security of a free state, the right of the people to keep and bear arms, shall not be infringed." The National Rifle Association (NRA) responded to the school shooting by calling for armed guards in schools, while others argue that more guns simply put our children at greater risk.

While most countries have responded to mass shootings by severely tightening gun control laws, most Americans do not favor an across-the-board rethinking of the Second Amendment. While about 61 percent of Americans in a 2013 poll stated that they wanted stricter laws covering the sale of firearms,[26] the country is evenly split over which is most important: protecting the right to own guns or controlling ownership of guns.[27]

In the following readings, Wayne LaPierre, executive vice president of the NRA argues in favor of laws permitting gun ownership. Mark Kelly, husband of former U.S. Representative Gabrielle Gifford, disagrees. He argues that we need stricter gun control laws.

National Rifle Association Press Release (Dec. 21, 2012)   WAYNE LAPIERRE

Wayne LaPierre is CEO and executive vice president of the National Rifle Association. In the following press release, he argues in favor of laws permitting gun ownership and for having armed guards in schools. An advocate of Second Amendment rights, LaPierre has an M.A. in government from Boston College.

The National Rifle Association's 4 million mothers, fathers, sons and daughters join the nation in horror, outrage, grief and earnest prayer for the families of Newtown, Connecticut . . . who suffered such incomprehensible loss as a result of this unspeakable crime. . . .

Now, we *must* speak . . . for the safety of our nation's children. Because for all the noise and anger directed at us over the past week, no one—nobody—has addressed the most important, pressing and immediate question we face: How do we protect our children *right now*, starting today, in a way that we know *works*?

The only way to answer that question is to face up to the *truth*. Politicians pass laws for Gun-Free School Zones. They issue press releases *bragging* about them. They post signs *advertising* them. And in so doing, they tell every insane killer in America that schools are their *safest* place to inflict maximum mayhem with minimum risk.

How have our nation's priorities gotten so far out of order? Think about it. We care about our money, so we protect our banks with armed guards. American airports, office buildings, power plants, courthouses—even sports stadiums—are all protected by armed security. We care about the President, so we protect him with armed Secret Service agents. Members of Congress work in offices surrounded by armed Capitol Police officers.

Yet when it comes to the most beloved, innocent and vulnerable members of the American family—our children—we as a society leave them *utterly defenseless*, and the monsters and predators of this world know it and exploit it. That must change now!

The truth is that our society is populated by an unknown number of genuine monsters—people so deranged, so evil, so possessed by voices and driven by demons that no sane person can possibly *ever* comprehend them. They walk among us every day. And does anybody really believe that the next Adam Lanza isn't planning his attack on a school he's already identified *at this very moment*?

How many *more* copycats are waiting in the wings for their moment of fame—from a national media machine that *rewards* them with the wall-to-wall attention and sense of identity that they crave—while provoking others to try to make *their* mark? . . .

And the fact is, that wouldn't even begin to address the much larger and more lethal *criminal* class: Killers, robbers, rapists and drug gang members who have spread like cancer in every community in this country. Meanwhile, federal gun prosecutions have decreased by 40 percent—to the lowest levels in a decade.

So now, due to a declining willingness to prosecute dangerous criminals, violent crime is *increasing* again for the first time in 19 years!

. . . And here's another dirty little truth that the media try their best to conceal: There exists in this country a callous, corrupt and *corrupting* shadow industry that sells, and sows, violence against its own people. Through vicious, violent video games with names like Bulletstorm, Grand Theft Auto, Mortal Kombat and Splatterhouse.

. . . Then there's the blood-soaked slasher films like "American Psycho" and "Natural Born Killers" that are aired like propaganda loops on "Splatterdays" and *every* day, and a thousand music videos that portray life as a joke and murder as a way of life.

. . . A child growing up in America witnesses 16,000 murders and 200,000 acts of violence by the time he or she reaches the ripe old age of 18. And throughout it all, too many in our national media . . . their corporate owners . . . and their stockholders . . . act as silent enablers, if not complicit co-conspirators. Rather than face their own moral failings, the media *demonize* lawful gun owners, *amplify* their cries for more laws and fill the national debate with misinformation and dishonest thinking that only delay meaningful action and all but guarantee that the next atrocity is only a news cycle away.

. . . As parents, we do everything we can to keep our children safe. It is now time for us to assume responsibility for their safety at school. The only way to stop a monster from killing our kids is to be personally involved and invested in a plan of absolute protection. The *only* thing that stops a *bad* guy with a gun is a *good* guy with a gun.

. . . A gun in the hands of a Secret Service agent protecting the President isn't a bad word. A gun in the hands of *a* soldier protecting the United States isn't a bad word. And when you hear the glass breaking in your living room at 3 a.m. and call 911, you won't be able to pray hard enough for a gun in the hands of a good guy to get there fast enough to protect you.

So why is the idea of a gun *good* when it's used to protect our President or our country or our police, but *bad* when it's used to protect our children in their schools?

. . . [W]hat if, when Adam Lanza started shooting his way into Sandy Hook Elementary School last Friday, he had been confronted by qualified, armed security?

Will you at least admit it's *possible* that 26 innocent lives might have been spared? Is that so abhorrent to you that you would rather continue to risk the alternative?

. . . I call on Congress today to act immediately, to appropriate whatever is necessary to put armed police officers in every school—and to do it now.

. . . Every school in America needs to immediately *identify*, *dedicate* and *deploy* the resources necessary to put these security forces in place right now. And the National Rifle Association, as America's preeminent trainer of law enforcement and security personnel for the past 50 years, is ready, willing and uniquely qualified to help.

. . . If we truly cherish our kids more than our money or our celebrities, we must give them the greatest level of protection possible and the security that is only available with a *properly trained—armed—good guy.*

REVIEW QUESTIONS

1. Why does LaPierre oppose making schools gun-free zones?
2. What is LaPierre's view regarding violence in the media and video games?
3. What does LaPierre mean when he says: "The *only* thing that stops a *bad* guy with a gun is a *good* guy with a gun"?
4. On what grounds does LaPierre argue that we should have armed guards in our schools?

Testimony by Mark Kelly, Senate Judiciary Committee Hearing on Gun Violence on Jan. 30, 2013

Mark Kelly is a retired astronaut and captain in the U.S. Navy. He is also the husband of former Arizona congresswoman Gabrielle Gifford, who was shot in the head by Jared Lee Loughner while she was speaking at an event in Tucson, Arizona, on January 8, 2011.

As you know, our family has been immeasurably affected by gun violence. Gabby's gift for speech is a distant memory. She struggles to walk and she is partially blind. And a year ago, she left a job she loves, serving the people of Arizona.

But in the past two years, we have watched Gabby's determination, spirit and intellect conquer her disabilities. We aren't here as victims. We're speaking to you today as Americans. . . .

We're both gun owners and we take that right and the responsibilities that come with it very seriously. And we watch with horror when the news breaks to yet another tragic shooting. After 20 kids and six of their teachers were gunned down in their classrooms at Sandy Hook Elementary, we said: "This time must be different; something needs to be done." We are simply two reasonable Americans who have said "enough."

On January 8th of 2011, a young man walked up to Gabby at her constituent event in Tucson, leveled his gun and shot her through the head. He then turned down the line and continued firing. In 15 seconds, he emptied his magazine. It contained 33 bullets and there were 33 wounds.

. . . The killer in the Tucson shooting suffered from severe mental illness, but even after being deemed unqualified for service in the Army and expulsion from Pima Community College, he was never reported to mental health authorities.

On November 30, 2010, he walked into a sporting goods store, passed the background check, and walked out with a semiautomatic handgun. He had never been legally adjudicated as mentally ill, and even if he had, Arizona, at the time, had over 121,000 records of disqualifying mental illness that it had not submitted into the system.

. . . Gabby is one of roughly 100,000 victims of gun violence in America each and every year. Behind every victim lays a matrix of failure and inadequacy in our families, in our communities, in our values, in our society's approach to poverty, violence, and mental illness and yes, also in our politics and in our gun laws.

One of our messages is simple, the breadth and complexity of gun violence is great, but it is not an excuse for inaction. There's another side to our story, Gabby is a gun owner and I am a gun owner. We have our firearms for the same reasons that millions of Americans just like us have guns, to defend ourselves, to defend our families, for hunting, and for target shooting.

We believe wholly and completely in the second amendment and that it confers upon all Americans the right to own a firearm for protection, collection, and recreation. We take that right very seriously and we would never, ever give it up, just like Gabby would never relinquish her gun and I would never relinquish mine. But rights demand responsibility and this right does not extend to terrorists, it does not extend to criminals, and it does not extend to the mentally ill.

When dangerous people get guns, we are all vulnerable at the movies, at church, conducting our everyday business, meeting with a government official. And time after time after time, at school, on our campuses, and in our children's classrooms. When dangerous people get dangerous guns, we are all the more vulnerable. Dangerous people with weapons specifically designed to inflict maximum lethality upon others have turned every single corner of our society into places of carnage and gross human loss. Our rights are paramount, but our responsibilities are serious. And as a nation, we've not taken responsibility for the gun rights that our founding fathers have conferred upon us.

Now we have some ideas on how we can take responsibility. First, fix our background checks. The holes in our laws make a mockery of the background check system. . . . Second, remove the limitations on collecting data and conducting scientific research on gun violence. Enact a tough federal gun trafficking statute; this is really important. And finally, let's have a careful and civil conversation about the lethality of fire arms we permit to be legally bought and sold in this country.

Gabby and I are pro-gun ownership. We are also anti-gun violence, and we believe that in this debate, Congress should look not toward special interests and ideology, which push us apart, but towards compromise which brings us together. We believe whether you call yourself pro-gun, or anti-gun violence, or both, that you can work together to pass laws that save lives.

REVIEW QUESTIONS

1. What does Kelly mean when he says that "behind every victim [of gun violence] lays a matrix of failure and inadequacy in our families, in our communities, in our values, in our society"?
2. What is Kelly's view regarding the Second Amendment?
3. Why does Kelly think background checks are important?
4. What compromise does Kelly propose we make in our gun ownership laws?

THiNK AND DISCUSS

PERSPECTIVES ON GUN CONTROL

1. Make a list of the arguments LaPierre uses in support of armed guards in schools. List the arguments Kelly uses in support of stricter gun control laws. Critically analyze both arguments for fallacies. Which person makes the most compelling argument and why?
2. Critically analyze LaPierre's argument that schools should have armed guards. In addition to looking for fallacies, check to make sure that his premises are true. This may require some independent research on your part: Are there armed guards at the Sidwell Friends School, where President Obama's daughters go to school? Are there any important premises that are missing from his argument? Discuss how Kelly would most likely respond to LaPierre's position.
3. Marko Kloos, an ex-Marine, argues in his article "Why the Gun Is Civilization" that "human beings only have two ways to deal with one another: reason and force." He proposes that in a society where not everyone is reasonable guns may be necessary as a means to protect ourselves. Do you agree? Discuss also how both LaPierre and Kelly might each response to Kloos's argument.

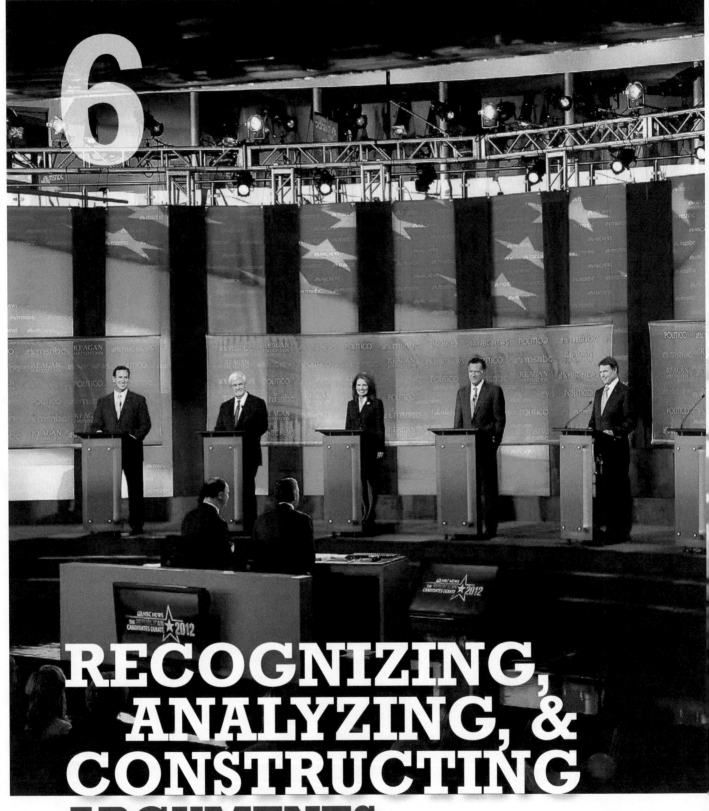

6

RECOGNIZING, ANALYZING, & CONSTRUCTING ARGUMENTS

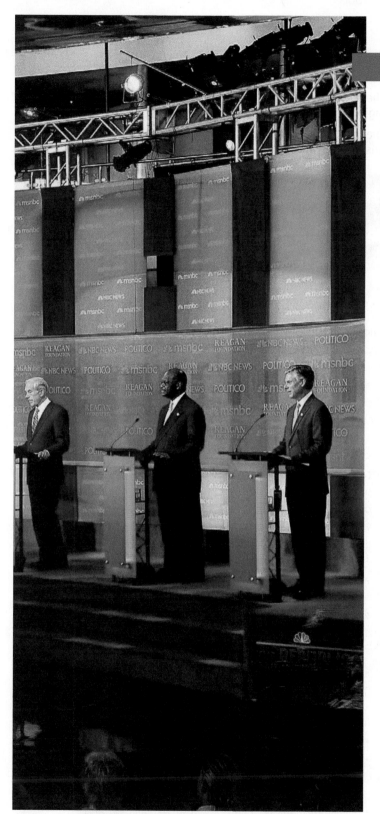

Abraham Lincoln and the incumbent Illinois senator, Stephen A. Douglas, held a series of seven political debates during the 1858 senatorial race. The debates addressed the hottest political issues of the day: whether slavery should be allowed to expand into western territories, whether states should have the authority to allow or ban slavery within their borders, and the wisdom of the U.S. Supreme Court's 1857 *Dred Scott* decision, which had ruled that a slave is "property in the strictest sense of the term" and had declared it unconstitutional for Congress to ban slavery in the western territories. Douglas argued for "popular sovereignty," claiming that the people of states and territories had the right to determine their own laws and policies on slavery. Lincoln opposed the expansion of slavery into the territories, arguing that slavery was "a moral, social and a political wrong."

How do politicians use logical arguments and rhetoric in political debates? How can developing skill in logical argumentation make us more effective in presenting and defending our positions?

THiNK FIRST

- What is an argument?
- What is the purpose of breaking down and diagramming arguments?
- What are some of the factors to take into consideration in evaluating an argument?

Although Lincoln lost the senatorial election, he emerged from the debates as a nationally renowned orator and critical thinker. Lincoln went on, as president of the United States, to issue the Emancipation Proclamation, which declared that all those enslaved in Confederate states were to be free. His skill in argumentation and debate, and his refusal to back down in the face of weak counterarguments, culminated in the passage in 1865 of the 13th Amendment, which abolished slavery in the United States.

The ability to recognize, construct, and analyze arguments is one of the most basic skills in critical thinking. To many of us, the word *argument* brings to mind images of quarreling and shouting. However, in logic and in critical thinking, argument refers to the use of reason and evidence to support a claim or conclusion. Arguments are a form of inquiry that provides us with reasons to accept or reject a particular position, so that we can make up our own minds about an issue.

In this information age we are constantly bombarded with arguments on issues from the Internet, television, newspapers, advertisers, politicians, and other sources. As citizens in a democracy, we need to develop the skills to critically analyze arguments and to make informed decisions that are based on our evaluations.

Skill in argumentation can help us make better decisions in our personal choices as well as in our public lives.

In Chapter 6 we will learn how to recognize, analyze, and construct arguments. Specifically, we will:

- Learn how to identify an issue
- Learn how to recognize the parts of an argument, including the premise, the conclusion, and premise and conclusion indicators
- Distinguish among an argument, an explanation, and a conditional statement
- Break down an argument into its premises and conclusion

- Diagram arguments
- Construct our own arguments
- Explore the basics of evaluating arguments

Finally, we will read about the issue of same-sex marriage and analyze arguments that approach that controversial question from different perspectives.

More than 50 years after the Brown v. Board of Education decision that declared segregation unconstitutional, many feel that African Americans still don't have the same opportunities for quality education as whites. This young woman is one of the "Little Rock Nine," of the first nine blacks to attend Central High in Little Rock, Arkansas, despite threats, scare tactics, and the necessary presence of the National Guard for protection.

WHAT IS AN ISSUE?

Arguments help us to analyze issues and to determine whether a particular position on an issue is reasonable. An **issue** is an ill-defined complex of problems involving a controversy or uncertainty.

One problem that many college students have in writing an essay or preparing a presentation on an issue is failing to define the issue clearly. An unfocused discussion about smoking, for example, may jump from health risks of secondhand smoking to the problem of addiction to corporate responsibility to subsidies for tobacco farmers. As a result, the discussion is shallow, and deeper insights into any one of these smoking-related issues are overlooked. Because of this, it is important that we first decide what issue we want to focus on.

Identifying an Issue

Identifying an issue requires clear thinking as well as good communication skills. We've probably all had the experience of finding ourselves arguing at cross-purposes with someone we care about. One person is upset because he or she feels the other isn't showing enough affection, while the other person perceives the issue as an attack on his or her ability as a provider. Because it is not clear what the real issue is, the argument goes nowhere and both people end up feeling frustrated and misunderstood.

Sometimes we don't have the opportunity to clarify an issue by talking to another person. This is often the case with written material, such as magazine or newspaper articles. In these cases, you may be able to determine the writer's focus by examining the title or the introductory paragraph. For example, Sohail H. Hashmi begins his article "Interpreting the Islamic Ethics of War and Peace" thus:

> Muslim writers of many intellectual persuasions have long argued that Westerners hold an inaccurate, even deliberately distorted, conception of *jihad*. In fact, however, the idea of *jihad* (and the ethics of war and peace generally) has been the subject of an intense and multifaceted debate among Muslims themselves.[1]

From this, you can presume that the issue Hashmi is addressing is something like "What is the best and most accurate interpretation of the Islamic concept of *jihad* and of war and peace in general?"

Asking the Right Questions

How we word our questions about an issue will influence how we go about seeking a resolution to it. During his debates with Senator (or, as he called him, "Judge") Douglas, Lincoln changed the national controversy about slavery by reframing

issue An ill-defined complex of problems involving a controversy or uncertainty.

the issue so that it was not simply a controversy over state sovereignty but a burning question that affected the very existence of the nation. In the final debate, Lincoln summed up the issue with these words:

> I have said and I repeat it here, that if there be a man amongst us who does not think that the institution of slavery is wrong in any one of the aspects of which I have spoken, he is misplaced and ought not to be with us. Has anything threatened the existence of the Union save and except this very institution of slavery? That is the real issue. That is the issue that will continue in this country when these poor tongues of Judge Douglas and myself shall be silent.[2]

In an article written 50 years after school segregation was declared unconstitutional by the Supreme Court in *Brown v. Board of Education* (1954), journalist Ellis Cose writes about the current lack of good schools for African American children: "When it comes to children of color, we ask the wrong question. We ask, 'Why are you such a problem?' when we should ask, 'What have we not given you that we routinely give to upper-middle-class white students?' What do they have that you don't?"[3]

To use another example, suppose you come back to your dorm room after class and find that your wallet is missing. You think that you left it on your dresser, but it isn't there. What is the issue? When asked, many students answer that that the issue is "Who stole my wallet?"[4] However, this question is a loaded question based on an as-yet-unfounded assumption—that someone stole your wallet. Maybe you misplaced your wallet or you lost it on your way to class or it got knocked behind the dresser. For now, all you know is that the wallet is missing. Therefore, rather than making assumptions you can't support, it would be better to state the issue as "What happened to my wallet?" rather than "Who stole my wallet?" Remember, one of the traits of a good critical thinker—and of great detectives—is open-mindedness.

THiNKing Outside the Box

ABRAHAM LINCOLN, *U.S. President*

Abraham Lincoln (1809–1865) was the sixteenth president of the United States. Self-educated, Lincoln had a knack for asking the right questions about important issues, such as slavery and war, and then examining all sides of the arguments before coming to a conclusion.

Lincoln's election as president in 1860 led to the secession in 1861 of southern slave-owning states (the Confederacy) and to a 4-year civil war that cost 600,000 American lives, North and South. Although Lincoln had long agreed that slavery should be permitted in states where it was already legal, in the course of the Civil War he concluded that if slavery is immoral, then it should not be legal at all in the United States. Lincoln also realized that taking a position on issues was not simply an intellectual exercise but should have real-life consequences. A man of action as well as strong principles, he issued the Emancipation Proclamation in 1863, freeing slaves in the Confederate states.

Lincoln's struggle to end slavery is depicted in the *movie Lincoln* (2012).

DISCUSSION QUESTIONS

1. Was Lincoln's decision to stand by his conclusion that slavery should be illegal a wise one, given that it escalated the hostilities in the Civil War? Are there times when it is best, from the point of view of critical thinking, to back down on an argument rather than risk conflict? Explain using specific examples.

2. Has there ever been a time when you stood your ground on an issue despite the risk of losing your friends or even a job? Discuss how your critical-thinking skills helped you to stand firm?

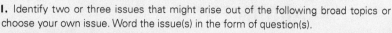

STOP AND ASSESS YOURSELF

EXERCISE 6-1

1. Identify two or three issues that might arise out of the following broad topics or choose your own issue. Word the issue(s) in the form of question(s).

*a. Freedom of speech on college campuses

b. Genetic engineering of food

c. Cohabitation among college students

*d. Downloading music from the Internet

e. Global warming

f. Decriminalizing marijuana

*g. Prayer in public schools

h. The preponderance of male science and engineering faculty at elite colleges

i. Illegal immigration

2. Identify the issues in the following passages. Word all issues in the form of short questions.

*a. "The price of college education in Minnesota is going up again this fall. The University of Minnesota and the state's two- and four-year colleges are raising tuition by double digits. . . . Higher education officials say while most students are coming up with the extra cash for college the trend toward higher tuition is not sustainable in the long run."[5]

b. There is a law pending in the Uganda legislature that would allow homosexuality to be punished with imprisonment and in certain circumstances even execution.

c. More than 700,000 Americans die each year from heart disease. Fifty percent of people given cholesterol-lowering drugs don't use them as prescribed, and the more they have to pay, the more they stop taking them. It seems obvious that probably tens of thousands of Americans are dying today because they can't afford drugs.

*d. "By next June, over a million [college students] will graduate, many lost forever to the world of inertia and learned habits. While the debate rages about how the vegetarian movement can tailor its message to reach resistant adults, open-minded college students who care about animals are being neglected at an astounding rate. Our [animal rights] movement has not yet made a massive, organized effort to reach our best audience. We could be making tremendous progress among this group of people using animal-related literature that has been shown to work."[6]

e. President Obama's educational reform agenda calls for longer school days and extending the school year in order to meet the challenges of the 21st century.

f. It is now possible to track a person's location by using their cell phone.

*g. "Tibet is backward. It's a big land, rich in natural resources, but we lack the technology or expertise [to exploit them]. So if we remain within China, we might get a greater benefit, provided it respects our culture and environment and gives us some kind of guarantee."[7]

3. Working in small groups, select one of the following issues. Take a few minutes to write down different concerns that arise from the issue. To what extent does your list reflect your preconceptions on the issue? Compare your list with those of others in your group. Discuss how collaborative sharing can give you a wider perspective on the issue.

a. Should we be eating meat?

b. Should college students who are working full time be allowed to take a full-time course load?

c. Is it a desirable goal for western nations to spread democracy throughout the world?

d. What should we be doing in our own lives about global warming?

e. What criteria should colleges use in admitting students?

f. Should the United States bring back the military draft?

4. Looking back at your list of life goals in Chapter 4, identify any issues involved in achieving your life goals.

*Answers to selected exercises are found in the Solutions Manual at the end of the book.

RECOGNIZING AN ARGUMENT

When we start with a position statement, rather than with an open-ended question that invites us to explore and analyze a particular issue, we are using rhetoric. Many people mistake rhetoric for logical arguments. Thus it is important to first understand the difference between the two.

Distinguishing Between Argumentation and Rhetoric

rhetoric The defense of a particular position usually without adequate consideration of opposing evidence in order to win people over to one's position.

argument Reasoning that is made up of two or more propositions, one of which is supported by the others.

deductive argument An argument that claims its conclusion necessarily follows from the premises.

inductive argument An argument that only claims that its conclusion probably follows from the premise.

proposition A statement that expresses a complete thought and can be either true or false.

Rhetoric, also known as *the art of persuasion*, is used to promote a particular position or worldview. In English classes, the term refers more narrowly to the art of persuasive writing or speaking. Rhetoric has its place and can help us learn more about a particular position on an issue and how to clarify that position. The art of persuasion can be useful once you have thoroughly researched all sides of an issue, have come to a reasoned conclusion, and are now trying to convince others of this conclusion, as Lincoln did in his debates with Douglas.

Rhetoric becomes a problem when it is *substituted* for unbiased research and logical argumentation. When using rhetoric this way, people present only those claims that support their own position. Because it does not require that a student first thoroughly research a topic and remain open-minded, rhetoric may deteriorate into heated and overly emotional fights in which each person resorts to resistance and fallacies rather than reason in order to "win."

Whereas the purpose of rhetoric is to *persuade* people of what you consider to be the truth, the purpose of argumentation is to *discover* the truth. The goal in rhetoric is to "win"—to convince others of the correctness of our position—rather than to analyze a position critically. The purpose of an argument, in contrast, is to present good reasons for a particular position or course of action and to offer a forum for evaluating the soundness of these reasons.

Good arguments also invite feedback and analysis of an issue in light of the feedback. You are more likely to move toward truth (if necessary, through revising your arguments and views) when all sides of an issue are presented and heard.

Types of Arguments

An **argument** is made up of two or more propositions, one of which, the conclusion, is supported by the other(s), the premise(s). In a valid **deductive argument**, such as the Wason Card Problem example in Chapter 2, the conclusion necessarily follows from the premises. In an **inductive argument**, the premises provide support but not necessarily proof for the conclusion. We'll be studying these two types of arguments in more depth in Chapters 7 and 8, respectively.

Propositions

An argument is made up of statements known as propositions. A **proposition** is a statement that expresses a complete thought. It can be either true or false. If you're not sure whether a statement is a proposition, try putting the phrase *It is true that* or *It is false that* at the beginning of the statement. The following are examples of propositions:

The earth revolves around the sun.

God exists.

Chris doesn't show me enough affection.

Cheating on exams is wrong.

Toronto is the capital of Canada.

The first of these propositions is true. Today it is generally accepted fact that the Earth revolves around the sun. The truth or falsehood of the second and third propositions is less clear. We need more information as well as clarification of the word *God* in the second proposition and clarification of the term *affection* in the third proposition. The fourth proposition is less controversial: Most people, even those who cheat on exams, agree that it is true that "cheating on exams is wrong." Finally, the last proposition is false; Toronto is *not* the capital of Canada (Ottawa is).

A sentence may contain more than one proposition, as this example illustrates:

Marcos is taking four courses this semester and working in his parents' store 20 hours a week.

This sentence contains two propositions:

1. Marcos is taking four courses this semester.

2. Marcos is working in his parents' store 20 hours a week.

Hot or Not?

Is it acceptable to use rhetoric if you're sure of your position?

ANALYZING IMAGES

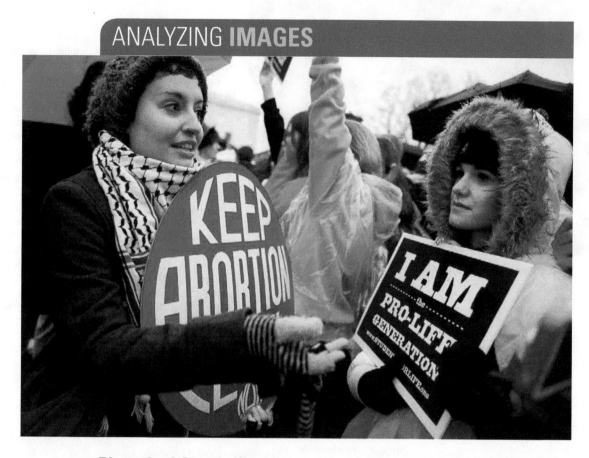

Rhetorical Standoff   Anti-abortion and pro-abortion rights demonstrators debating each other at the Supreme Court on January 23, 2012, the anniversary of the Supreme Court's *Roe v. Wade* decision, which established a women's right to an abortion.*

DISCUSSION QUESTIONS

1. *The use of rhetoric, without first researching and analyzing all perspectives on an issue, can lead to deepening polarization of an issue rather than a resolution. What do you think the two people in this photo might be saying to each other? Do you think they are engaging in rhetoric or argumentation? Working in small groups, role-play what you might say to them if you were on the scene in the capacity of resident critical thinker.*

2. *Have you ever been at a rally where people were deeply divided? If so, discuss how you responded to taunts or fallacies from those on the "other side" of the issue.*

*For more on *Roe v. Wade*, see "Critical Thinking Issues: Perspectives on Abortion" at the end of Chapter 9.

Here is another sentence with more than one proposition:

Karen is smart but not very motivated to do well in school or to try to find a job that uses her talents.

It contains three propositions:

1. Karen is smart.
2. Karen is not very motivated to do well in school.
3. Karen is not very motivated to try to find a job that uses her talents.

Not all sentences are propositions. A sentence may be directive ("Let's go out and celebrate the end of final exams"), expressive ("Wow!"), or even a request for information ("What is the capital of Canada?"). In none of these sentences is any claim being made that something is true or false. Propositions, in contrast, make claims that are either true or false. For more on the different functions of language, refer back to Chapter 3.

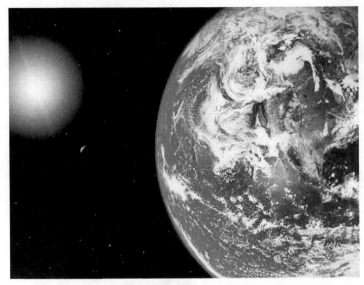

"The Earth revolves around the sun" is an example of a proposition.

Premises and Conclusions

The **conclusion** of an argument is the proposition that is supported or denied on the basis of other propositions or reasons. The conclusion is what the argument is trying to prove. Conclusions may also be called claims or positions. The conclusion can appear anywhere in an argument.

conclusion The proposition in an argument that is supported on the basis of other propositions.

premise A proposition in an argument that supports the conclusion.

descriptive premise A premise that is based on empirical facts.

A **premise** is a proposition that supports or gives reasons for accepting the conclusion. Reasoning goes from the premises to the conclusion.

Premise(s) ⎯⎯⎯⎯⎯⎯⎯→ Conclusion

Good premises are based on fact and experience, not opinion and assumptions. The more credible the premises are, the better the argument is likely to be. We considered some of the ways in which to evaluate evidence in Chapter 4. The conclusion should be supported by or follow from the premises, as in the following argument:

> *Premise*: Canada has only one capital.
> *Premise*: Ottawa is the capital of Canada.
> *Conclusion*: Therefore, Toronto is not the capital of Canada.

There are several types of premises. **Descriptive premises** are based on **empirical facts**—scientific observation and/or the evidence of our five senses. "Ottawa is the capital of Canada" and "Lisa loves Antonio" are descriptive premises.

Prescriptive premises, in contrast, contain value statements, such as "We should strive for diversity on college campuses" or "It is wrong to cheat on exams."

An **analogical premise** takes the form of an analogy in which a comparison is made between two similar events or things. In Chapter 2, we saw that the ancient Greek philosopher Plato drew an analogy between a charioteer and reason. Just as the charioteer is in charge of the horses, said Plato, so too should our reason be in charge of our emotions and passions.

Finally, a **definitional premise** contains a definition of a key term. This is particularly important when the key term is ambiguous and has different definitions, such as *right* and *diversity*, or if the key term needs a precising definition. For example, *affirmative action* is defined in a dictionary as "a policy to increase opportunities for women and minorities, [especially] in employment."[8] However, this may not be precise enough for your argument, since it is unclear about the type of policy. To clarify this, you may want to make the definition more precise in your premise. "Affirmative action is a policy of giving preference in hiring and college admissions to qualified minorities and women over a qualified white male, to increase opportunities for women and minorities."

Nonarguments: Explanations and Conditional Statements

We sometimes confuse explanations and conditional statements with arguments. An **explanation** is a statement about why or how something is the case. With an explanation, we know that something has occurred—as in the following examples:

> The cat yowled because I stepped on her tail.
> I'm upset because you promised you would meet me at the student union right after class and you never turned up.

In both examples, we are not trying to *prove* or *convince* someone through supporting evidence that the cat yowled or that we're upset; instead, we are trying to *explain* why the cat yowled and why we are upset.

We can also use explanations to describe the purpose of something, as in "iPods are useful for storing large quantities of music." In

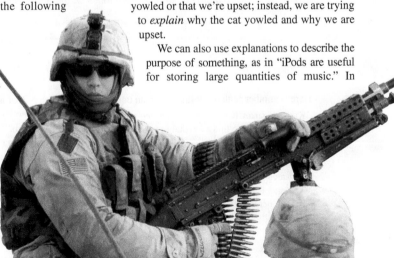

addition, we can use explanations as a means of trying to make sense of something, as in: "When Jane smiled at me, I think she was telling me that she liked me."

Good premises are based on fact and experience, not opinion and assumptions. The more credible the premises are, the better the argument is likely to be.

As with arguments, not all explanations are equally convincing. Explanations such as "I don't have my essay with me today because the dog ate it" usually raise at least a few skeptical eyebrows. Also, what might have seemed a reasonable explanation centuries or even a few decades ago may no longer be reasonable in light of new evidence. The explanation, presented to me by one of my elementary school teachers, that there have been very few famous female artists because women fulfill their creativity through having babies, is no longer considered a sound explanation.

Conditional statements may also be mistaken for arguments. A **conditional statement** is an "if . . . then . . ." statement.

> If Françoise comes from Montreal, then she understands French.

> If 18-year-olds are emotionally mature enough to go to war, then they should be allowed to drink alcohol.

A conditional statement by itself is not an argument, because no claim or conclusion follows from it. In the preceding examples, we are not drawing a conclusion that Françoise understands French or that 18-year-olds should be allowed to drink. However, conditional statements may appear as premises in an argument.

> *Premise*: If Françoise comes from Montreal, then she understands French.
>
> *Premise*: Françoise comes from Montreal.
>
> *Conclusion*: Françoise understands French.
>
> *Premise*: If 18-year-olds are emotionally mature enough to go to war, [then] they should be allowed to drink alcohol.
>
> *Premise*: Eighteen-year-olds are not emotionally mature enough to go to war.
>
> *Conclusion*: Eighteen-year-olds should not be allowed to drink alcohol.

To summarize: arguments are made up of two types of propositions—the conclusion and the premise(s). A conclusion is supported by the premise(s). The different types of premises include descriptive and prescriptive premises, analogies, and definitions. Unlike explanations and conditional statements, an argument tries to prove that something is true.

empirical fact A fact based on scientific observation and the evidence of our five senses.

prescriptive premise A premise in an argument containing a value statement.

analogical premise A premise containing an analogy or comparison between similar events or things.

definitional premise A premise containing the definition of a key term.

explanation A statement about why or how something is the case.

conditional statement An "If . . . then . . ." statement.

EXERCISE 6-2

STOP AND ASSESS YOURSELF

1. Working in small groups, select a controversial issue. After clearly defining the issue, debate it by first using rhetoric. After three minutes, stop and write a paragraph about what happened during the role-play. Now discuss the issue using argumentation instead. After three minutes, stop and write a paragraph about what happened during this role-play. Which approach worked better in terms of learning more about different perspectives on the issue? Explain.

2. It is easier to resolve a problem from a familiar context than one that is unfamiliar. Write down a problem that you encountered recently in a familiar context (for example, a social setting with friends or a class in your major). Now write down a similar problem that you encountered recently in an unfamiliar context (for example, a job interview or meeting new people). Which problem was easiest to resolve and why? How did familiarity with the context make it easier for you to resolve a problem? Write about what steps you could take to make yourself a better problem-solver and critical thinker in different contexts.

3. Which of the following statements is a proposition? Explain why or why not.

*a. Golly!

 b. I love you.

 c. The Solomon Islands were struck by an 8.0-magnitude earthquake in 2013.

*d. Most college students gain several pounds in their freshman year.

 e. Close the window.

 f. The average college student pays most of his or her own college tuition.

*g. Please keep an eye on my place while I'm away on spring break.

h. It is irresponsible to drink and drive.

i. Iran possesses nuclear weapons.

*j. Only humans are capable of language.

k. An atheist is a person who believes there is no God.

l. Excuse me.

*m. Smoking in public buildings is illegal in many states.

4. For each of the following propositions, identify which type of premise it is (descriptive, prescriptive, definitional, or analogical).

   *a. Terrorism is the unlawful use or threat of violence by individuals or groups against civilians or property to achieve an ideological or political goal through intimidating government or society.

   b. At least five of the al-Qaeda hijackers from September 11, 2001, came from Asir province in Saudi Arabia.

   c. We should constantly strive to become better critical thinkers.

   *d. The universe is like a watch created by an intelligent designer or watchmaker.

   e. The University of Toronto is the top-rated university in Canada.

   f. It's wrong to download music from the Internet without paying.

   *g. Going to Las Vegas for spring break is like going to a weeklong fraternity party.

   h. Living together before marriage for a trial period is like taking a car for a test drive.

   i. Only humans are capable of language.

   *j. Language is a type of communication that involves a set of arbitrary symbols, whether spoken, written, or nonverbal.

5. Look back at the arguments on affirmative action at the end of Chapter 1 and identify the premises and conclusion in both Nancy Cantor's and Ward Connerly's arguments.

6. Identify each of the following as an argument, an explanation, or a conditional statement.

   *a. Jasmine really likes Daniel, but because she's planning on going to Guatemala for a semester to study Spanish, she isn't interested in getting involved with him right now.

   b. The death toll in Chile following the 2010 earthquakes was not nearly as high as that in Haiti in part because the buildings in Chile were built to withstand earthquakes while those in Haiti were not.

   c. If there is a snowstorm, class will be cancelled.

   *d. If there is a snowstorm, class will be cancelled. It is snowing heavily right now, so our class will probably be cancelled.

   e. You should consider taking a trip abroad this summer while airfares are still low.

   f. In the past few decades the Catholic Church has been training more priests and bishops to perform exorcisms, in part because the pope believes that Satan is a real force in our everyday lives.

   *g. If the bay freezes over, we can go ice skating on it.

   h. It must have been colder than 28°F last week, because the ice froze in the bay last week and salt water freezes at 28°F or −2°C.

   i. Herman failed the quiz because he didn't know there was going to be one today and hadn't read the material.

   *j. If you aren't a good boy or girl, Santa won't bring you any presents this Christmas.

   k. "People react so viscerally to the decapitation executions because they identify strongly with the helpless victims, see the executioners as cruel foreigners, and are horrified by the grisly method of death."[9]

   l. Same-sex marriage should be legalized, since the U.S. Constitution guarantees citizens equal rights under the law.

   *m. If you go to the movies with me tonight, I'll help you review for your chemistry exam.

7. Write down five examples of explanations. At least one should be from your own personal experience, one from a textbook, one from a newspaper or magazine, and one from the Internet. Briefly state why each is an explanation rather than an argument.

*Answers to selected exercises are found in the Solutions Manual at the end of the book.

BREAKING DOWN AND DIAGRAMMING ARGUMENTS

Knowing how to identify the parts of and diagram an argument allows us to follow the line of thought in an argument more easily. Breaking down an argument and then using a diagram to represent the different parts of the argument lets us visualize the entire argument, its propositions, and the relationship between the premise(s) and the conclusion.

HIGHLIGHTS

HOW TO BREAK DOWN AN ARGUMENT

- **The entire argument may appear in one sentence or in several sentences.**

- **Put brackets around each proposition** in the argument.

- **Identify the conclusion.** Ask yourself: "What is this person trying to prove?" The conclusion is often, though not always, preceded by a word or phrase known as a conclusion indicator, such as

therefore	*which shows that*
thus	*for these reasons*
hence	*consequently*
so	*it follows that*

- **Identify the premises.** The premises are often, though not always, preceded by a word or phrase known as a **premise indicator**, such as

because	*may be inferred from*
since	*the reason is that*
for	*as shown by*
given that	*in view of*

- **Draw a double line under the conclusion** and a **single line under the premise(s).** Circle any conclusion or premise indicators.

▶ *APPLICATION: Identify in the text an example of (1) a conclusion indicator followed by a conclusion, and (2) a premise indicator followed by a premise.*

Breaking Down an Argument into Propositions

Before you can diagram an argument, you must first break down the argument into its propositions. Here are the steps for diagramming an argument:

1. **Bracket the Propositions.** In breaking down an argument, start by putting brackets around each proposition so that you know where each begins and ends. Remember, an entire argument can be contained in one sentence, as in the first of the following examples. Or it can contain several sentences and propositions, as in the second example.

   [I think], therefore [I am].

   [Students who sit in the front of a classroom generally earn higher grades.] Therefore [you should move up to the front of the class], since [I know you want to improve your grade point average].

2. **Identify the conclusion.** The next step is to identify which proposition is the conclusion. Some, but not all, arguments contain terms known as *conclusion indicators* that help you identify which of the propositions is a conclusion. For instance, words such as *therefore* and *thus* often serve as conclusion indicators. If there is a conclusion indicator in the argument, circle it and, if you want, put the letters *CI* above it. In the two arguments above, the word *therefore* indicates that a conclusion follows.

   When there are no conclusion indicators, ask yourself: "What is this person trying to prove or convince me of?" If you are still unsure which proposition is the conclusion, try putting *therefore* in

We can improve our arguments by testing them out on others and then modifying them in light of the feedback we receive.

front of the proposition you think may be the conclusion. If the meaning of the argument remains the same, you have located the conclusion. Once you have identified the conclusion, draw a double line under it.

CI   (Conclusion)
[I think], therefore [I am].

[Students who sit in the front of a classroom generally
                              CI   (Conclusion)
earn higher grades.] Therefore, [you should move up

to the front of the class], since [I know you want to

improve your grade point average].

3. **Identify the Premises.** The final step in breaking down an argument is to identify the premise(s). In the first argument, which is the famous cogito argument of French philosopher René Descartes (1596–1650), Descartes supports his conclusion ("I am") with the premise "I think." In other words, if he is thinking, it follows that he must exist, since someone must be doing the thinking. Draw a single line under the premise.

CI   (Conclusion)
[I think], (therefore) [I am].

Some arguments contain *premise indicators*—words or phrases that signal a premise. *Because* and *since* are common premise indicators. If there is a premise indicator, circle it and put *PI* above it. In the argument about where to sit in the classroom, the word *since* indicates that the last part of this sentence is a premise. The first sentence in the argument is also a premise because it is offering evidence to support the conclusion "you should move up to the front of the class." Draw a single line under each premise.

(Premise)
[Students who sit in the front of a classroom generally
                    CI   *(Conclusion)*
earn higher grades.] (Therefore) [you should move up to
                 PI   *(Premise)*
the front of the class], (since) [I know you want to improve

your grade point average].

Identifying the Premise(s) and Conclusion in Complex Arguments

Not all arguments are as straightforward as the ones we have looked at so far. Some passages that contain arguments also include extra material, such as background and introductory information. In the following letter to the editor, the first sentence is the conclusion of the argument. The first part of the second sentence—"Although stories of overzealous parents sometimes grab the headlines"—is not part of the actual argument; rather, it is introductory material. This introduction is followed in the same sentence by the phrase *the truth is*, which serves as a premise indicator for the first premise. The

second premise doesn't appear until the third sentence in the passage.

(Conclusion)
[Sports at the high-school level are one of the last

bastions of innocence in this century.] Although

stories of overzealous parents sometimes grab the
                              PI   *Premise*
headlines, the truth is, [most young people play for the

love of their sport and nothing more.] [Many of the
                              Premise
values that help me every day in the business world

(teamwork, unity, hard work, and tolerance) were

taught by my football and baseball coaches.][10]

Words such as *because*, *since*, *therefore*, and *so*, which sometimes serve as premise and conclusion indicators in argument, do not always play this role. *Because* and *therefore* also appear in explanations, as in this example:

Because the demographics and immigration pattern of the United States is changing, the workforce of today's college graduates will be much different from that of their parents.

In addition, the word *since* may indicate the passage of time rather than a premise.

Since the September 11, 2001, attacks on the World Trade Center and Pentagon, the nature of intercultural relationships radically changed for most Americans.

Knowing how to break down an argument into its conclusion and premise(s) makes it easier for us to analyze arguments. Although words such as *therefore* and *because* can help us in this process, it is important to remember that they do not always serve as conclusion and premise indicators.

Diagramming an Argument

Once you have mastered the basics of breaking down an argument, you are ready to diagram arguments. Sometimes arguments fail simply because the other person does not follow our line of reasoning. Diagramming an argument clarifies the relationship between the premise(s) and the conclusion, as well as the relationship between premises, so we know to present these particular premises together.

Arguments with One Premise. Begin by breaking down the argument into its propositions and drawing two lines under the conclusion and one under the premise(s). Number each proposition in the order in which it appears in the argument. Put a circle around each number.

(1) [I think], therefore (2) [I am].

ANALYZING **IMAGES**

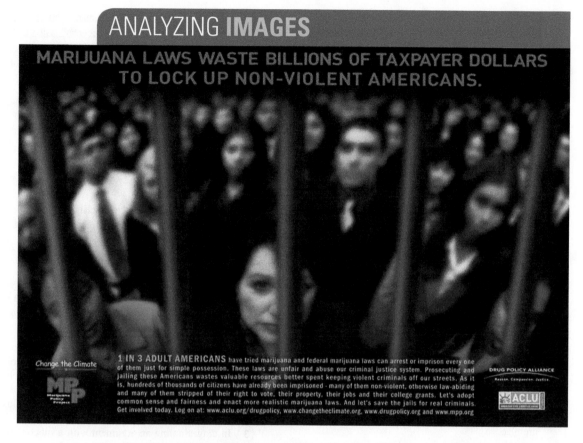

The Debate Over Marijuana

DISCUSSION QUESTIONS

1. *Identify the conclusion and premises in the argument in this advertisement. Evaluate the argument.*

2. *What is the objective of this ad? Is the ad effective in meeting its objective? Discuss the strategies, including rhetorical devices and fallacies, if any, that the creators of the ad used to try to convince the reader to accept their conclusion.*

You are now ready to diagram the argument. Begin by writing down the number of the conclusion at the bottom of a space on the page. The premise(s) go above the conclusion. When there is only one premise, place the number of the premise directly above the number of the conclusion and draw an arrow from the premise number to the conclusion number.

In this section, the parts of the diagram are identified (for example, premise, conclusion, dependent premises) purely for educational purposes. However, in the actual diagrams, only the numbers, lines, and arrows are used.

Arguments with Independent Premises. The next argument we'll be diagramming has more than one premise. Begin by breaking down the argument into its conclusion and premises, numbering each proposition in the order it appears in the argument.

(1) [Every physician should cultivate lying as a fine art]. . . . (2) [Many experiences show that patients do not want the truth about their maladies], and that (3) [it is prejudicial to their well-being to know it].[11]

In this argument, the conclusion is the first proposition—"Every physician should cultivate lying as a fine art." Write **1** at the bottom of the space below. Now examine the two premises, the second and third propositions. In this argument below, each premise supports the conclusion on its own. A premise that can support the conclusion without the other premise is known as an **independent premise**.

independent premise A premise that can support a conclusion on its own.

dependent premise A premise that supports a conclusion only when it is used together with another premise.

subconclusion A proposition that acts as a conclusion for initial premises and as a premise for the final conclusion.

You diagram an independent premise by drawing an arrow directly from each one to the conclusion.

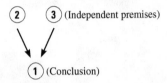

Arguments with Dependent Premises. When two or more of the premises support a conclusion only when they are used together, they are known as **dependent premises**. If you are unsure whether two premises are dependent or independent, try omitting one of them and see if the remaining premise still supports the conclusion on its own. If it does not, then it is a dependent premise.

In the argument below on Harry Potter, premises **1**, **3**, and **4** are all dependent on each other. Taken alone, they do not support the conclusion.

1 [The Bible states in Leviticus 20:26, "You should not practice augury or witchcraft."] Therefore, **2** [the Harry Potter books are not suitable reading for children.] since **3** [Harry Potter is a wizard] and **4** [wizards practice augury].

In diagramming dependent premises, you first draw a line between the premises and then draw a line from the center of this connecting line to the conclusion.

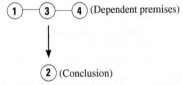

In the above argument, depending on your audience, you may not need **4**, which is a definitional premise.

Some arguments have both dependent and independent premises. Consider the following argument:

1 [Turkey should not be granted full membership in the European Union.] For one thing, **2** [the majority of the country is located in Asia, not Europe.]

3 [Turkey also has a poor human rights record.] Finally, **4** [it is a poor country with high unemployment]. **5** [Allowing it to be a full member in the European Union might spark a mass migration of people to European countries with better economies.]

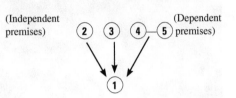

Arguments with a Subconclusion. Sometimes a premise acts as a conclusion for the final conclusion. This type of premise is known as a **subconclusion**.

1 [My granddaughter Sarah is a college freshman.]

2 [Sarah probably wouldn't be interested in hearing an AARP talk on Social Security reform.] So **3** [there's probably no point in asking her to come along with me.]

In the above argument, premise **1** offers support for proposition **2**: "My granddaughter Sarah is a college freshman. [Therefore] Sarah probably wouldn't be interested in hearing an AARP talk on Social Security." However, proposition **2**, in addition to being a conclusion for premise **1**, also serves as a premise for proposition **3**. In diagramming an argument with a subconclusion (such as proposition **2**), you put the subconclusion between the premise(s) that supports it and the final conclusion.

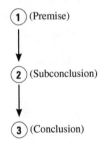

The following argument on capital punishment has a subconclusion as well as two independent premises.

1 [The death penalty does not deter criminals] because **2** [at the time the crime is done they do not expect to be arrested.] Also, since **3** [many offenders are mentally unbalanced,] **4** [they do not consider the rational consequences of their irrational actions.][12]

Here, proposition **2** is an independent premise that supports the conclusion (proposition **1**) on its own. If this were all there was to the argument, you would diagram it by placing the **2** above the **1** and drawing an arrow directly from the **2** to the conclusion.

However, the argument goes on to present additional evidence (propositions ③ and ④) for the conclusion (proposition ①) in the form of a separate supporting argument. Therefore, you'll need to adjust the diagram to allow room for this. In this case, proposition ④ is the subconclusion and proposition ③ the premise of the supporting argument. The complete argument can be diagrammed as follows:

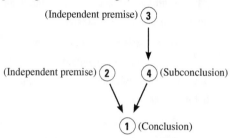

Arguments with Unstated Conclusions. In some arguments the conclusion is unstated, allowing readers to draw their own conclusions. The following argument, for example, has two premises but no conclusion:

① [Laws that permit public colleges to discriminate against applicants on the basis of race or sex are unconstitutional.] ② [The University of Michigan's affirmative action policy that awards extra points on the basis of a person's race and sex discriminates against white males.]

In determining what is the unstated conclusion, ask yourself: What is the speaker trying to prove or to convince us of? In this example, it is that the University of Michigan's affirmative action policy is unconstitutional. When a conclusion is unstated, write it in at the end of the argument and number it; in this case, since it is the third proposition, put a ③ in front of it. The broken circle indicates that the proposition is unstated. You can also add a conclusion indicator if you like.

① [Laws that permit public colleges to discriminate against applicants on the basis of race or gender are unconstitutional.] ② [The University of Michigan's affirmative action policy that awards extra points based on a person's race and sex discriminates against white males.] Therefore, ③ [the University of Michigan's affirmative action policy is unconstitutional.]

Diagramming this argument makes it apparent that neither premise can support the conclusion on its own

These people are burning Harry Potter books based on their conclusion that Harry is a wizard and witchcraft should not be practiced.

without the other premise. In other words, they are dependent premises. When diagramming an argument with an unstated conclusion, put a broken circle around the number in front of the conclusion to indicate that it was not included in the original wording of the argument. Once again, the parts of the diagram (dependent premises and unstated conclusion) are identified for clarification purposes only. They are not part of the actual diagram.

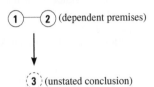

When you are arguing or discussing an issue, you usually do not have time to step back and diagram it. However, practice at breaking down and diagramming arguments will make it easier for you to recognize the conclusion and see the connections among the conclusion and premises in real-life arguments, the topic of the next section.

HIGHLIGHTS

SYMBOLS USED IN DIAGRAMMING ARGUMENTS

(1) A *circled number* is used to indicate a proposition and where it appears in the argument.

(1) A *broken circle* is used to indicate an unstated premise or conclusion.

↓ An *arrow* is used to indicate the relationship between an independent premise and the conclusion, with the conclusion appearing below the arrow.

_____ A *line* is used to connect dependent premises.

_____ A *line with an arrow* below it is used to indicate the relationship between dependent premises and the conclusion.

➤ *APPLICATION: Find an example in the text of each of these symbols being used in an argument.*

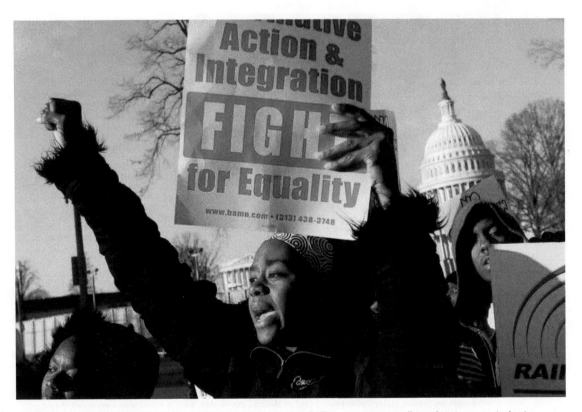

College students are divided regarding the morality and constitutionality of affirmative action in college admissions, a topic that is considered in the Critical Thinking Issue of Chapter 1.

315

STOP AND ASSESS YOURSELF

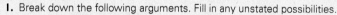

1. Break down the following arguments. Fill in any unstated possibilities.

*a. "Be an optimist. There is not much use being anything else."[13]

b. Computers may soon fade into the background, since most people prefer portable handheld devices as well as ones that turn on instantly.

c. "The right to vote is the very core of democracy. We cannot allow public apathy and political manipulation to undermine it."[14]

*d. Drinking alcohol is stupid. Alcohol has no taste at all; it's just a burning sensation. You don't drink to have a good time—you drink to forget a bad time.

e. We should not be using military drones. Drone strikes can kill innocent civilians. They are also a violation of international law.

f. Lack of experience, excessive speed, and tailgating are three of the most frequent causes of automobile accidents. For these reasons we should raise the driving age to 18, since older drivers might be more experienced and have better judgment.

*g. India should adopt a one-child policy like China. India's population has tripled in the last thirty years and it won't be long before food production will not be able to keep up with population growth.

h. All college students should routinely be tested for HIV, the virus that causes AIDS. Half of the people who carry the virus don't know that they have it. The HIV virus is transmitted primarily through sexual contact. Not only are most college students sexually active but they also have multiple partners.

i. You shouldn't date Matt. You don't want to end up with a black eye or worse.

*j. The great horned owls have just started calling to each other in the woods behind our house so it's probably the beginning of their courting season.

2. Break down and diagram the following arguments.

*a. "It is impossible to exaggerate the impact that Islam has on Saudi culture, since religion is the dominant thread that permeates every level of society."[15]

b. God does not exist. There is much evil and suffering in the world. A good and loving God would not permit so much evil.

c. I just read that Singapore is the only country in Asia where English is the first language. I know that English is also spoken throughout much of India but I guess this must mean that English is not India's first language.

*d. We should not buy a new car for Jack for his graduation. Jack is irresponsible because he doesn't care for the things he already owns. Also, we don't have enough money to buy him a new car.

e. Prostitution should be legal. Women should have the right to use their bodies as they wish. Outlawing prostitution deprives women who want to be prostitutes of their right to choose how to use their body.

f. It's unlikely that you'll find a job in manufacturing since we're in the middle of recession. You should consider going back to college to finish your degree in nursing since nursing is one of the fields where jobs are currently in demand.

*g. "An unbalanced diet can depress serotonin levels—and bingo, you're a grouch. Alcohol gives serotonin a temporary bump but then dramatically lowers it, so it pays to go easy on the sauce."[16]

h. Freedom to decide what we do in our lives, as long as we're not harming others, is a basic right in the United States. Therefore, motorcyclists should not be required by law to wear helmets, because those who don't are not harming anyone else.

i. Everything is going digital nowadays. Soon we will no longer need libraries since most journals and news sources are available online. In addition, books are being made available in electronic format.

*j. "There's a need for more part-time or job-sharing work. Most mothers of young children who choose to leave full-time careers and stay home with their children find enormous delights in being at home with their children, not to mention the enormous relief of no longer worrying about shortchanging their kids. On the other hand, women who step out of their careers can find the loss of identity even tougher than the loss of income."[17]

k. "The toughest part of buying life insurance is determining how much you need, since everyone's financial circumstances and goals are different. The best way to determine your life insurance needs is to have a State Farm Insurance professional conduct what's called a Financial Needs Analysis." (from an ad for State Farm Insurance)

l. You should learn how to speak Mandarin Chinese since you're going into international business as a career. Roughly one in five people in the world speak Mandarin. Also, learning a new language is supposed to be good for your brain.

*m. "In schools, we should give equal time with Darwinism to theories of intelligent design or creationism. Darwin's theory of evolution is a theory, not a fact. The origin of life, the diversity of species and even the structure of organs like the eye are so bewilderingly complex that they can only be the handiwork of a higher intelligence."[18]

n. The new compact fluorescent light bulbs cut down on global warming since they use 75 percent less energy than the old light bulbs. For this reason you should switch to the new bulbs. And you'll save money on your electric bill too.

o. The creation of new jobs will put the American economy back on a solid footing. Therefore, the government should launch another major stimulus program because the stimulus money will benefit the community by creating more jobs.

*p. You shouldn't bother trying out for that internship, because you won't get it. The company wants only students who are business majors. Besides, the company isn't on a bus line, and you don't own a car.

q. I saw Bob coming out of Mark's dorm room at 2 AM. Mark reported his cell phone stolen the next morning. Bob was caught stealing from a student's room once before. I think the evidence speaks for itself.

*Answers to selected exercises are found in the Solutions Manual at the end of the book.

EVALUATING ARGUMENTS

Knowing how to break down and diagram arguments makes it easier for you to evaluate them. In this section we will briefly touch on some of the main criteria for evaluating arguments: clarity, credibility, relevance, completeness, and soundness. We'll be focusing on this topic in more depth in Chapters 7 and 8.

Clarity: Is the Argument Clear and Unambiguous?

The first step in evaluating an argument is to make sure that you understand it correctly. Examine each premise and conclusion. Are they stated in terms that are clear and understandable? If any part of the argument is unclear, or if the meaning of a key term is ambiguous, ask for clarification.

For example, at a party someone told me, "Immigration is ruining this country!" When I

Hot or Not?

Does knowing how to break down and diagram arguments serve any practical purpose in your life?

asked him for clarification—"Do you mean all immigrants?" and "What do you mean by *ruin*?"—he explained that he meant that Hispanic immigrants were a financial burden on the United States.

Credibility: Are the Premises Supported by Evidence?

As we noted earlier, arguments are made up of propositions that each make a claim that can be true or false. In a good argument, the premises are credible and backed by evidence. In other words, it is reasonable for us to accept them as true. In evaluating an argument, examine each premise individually. Watch for assumptions that are being passed off as facts, especially assumptions that are widely accepted in a culture or those that are being put forth by someone who is not an authority in the field.

When my daughter was in kindergarten, the teacher asked each student what he or she wanted to be when they grew up. My daughter said that she wanted to be a doctor. The teacher shook her head and replied, "Boys become doctors; girls become nurses." Breaking down and diagramming her teacher's argument, we have

(1) [You are a girl].

(2) [Boys become doctors; girls become nurses.]

Therefore, (3) [you cannot become a doctor].

(1)———(2)

↓

(3)

A few weeks later I asked my daughter why she no longer was playing with her doctor kit. She told me what her teacher had said. Fortunately, we were able to reveal the teacher's assumption about which medical professions men and women go into and expose it as false, since today many doctors are women and many men become nurses. Because the two premises are dependent, both premises are needed to support the conclusion. And because one of the premises is false, the premises do not support the conclusion.

Often assumptions are unspoken, as in the above argument. Because of this, we tend not to be aware of them. Although some assumptions are obviously false, in most cases we may have to do some research before making a determination. Returning to the immigration example, when the speaker was asked why he felt the way he did about immigrants from Hispanic countries, he replied: "Hispanics are lazy freeloaders who burden our public welfare system, especially in states like California." Is his premise true? What were his sources of evidence? Were they credible sources?

My research turned up an academic study using statistics from the state of California. According to these statistics, Hispanic immigrants living under the poverty level are less than half as likely as American-born citizens to be collecting welfare. In addition, the study found that one of the characteristics of Hispanic immigrants was that they were generally harder working than American-born citizens and preferred to take whatever jobs were available to get by rather than collect welfare.[19] If I hadn't bothered to research his premise, which as it turns out was unfounded, I might have found myself being persuaded by his "argument" and accepting his assumption as "fact."

Relevance: Are the Premises Relevant to the Conclusion?

In addition to being true, the premises should provide relevant evidence in support of the conclusion. In other words, the premises should provide good reasons for accepting the conclusion. The statistical study cited above about Hispanic immigrants is relevant—not to the conclusion that "immigration is ruining this country" but to the opposite conclusion that "Hispanic immigrants tend to be hardworking."

A premise can be relevant without providing sufficient grounds for accepting the conclusion. The fact that when my daughter was young, most doctors were men and most nurses were women did not provide sufficient support for the teacher's conclusion that my daughter should give up her dream to become a doctor. Today, about half of all students in medical school are women.

Completeness: Are There Any Unstated Premises and Conclusions?

In evaluating an argument, ask yourself: "Are there unstated premises?" Premises may be omitted for several reasons. We may simply be unaware of a particular bit of key information related to the issue. In addition, confirmation bias may cause us to overlook important information or reject premises that do not support our worldview. In the argument about Hispanic immigrants that we've just examined, the speaker failed to include premises with actual statistics supporting his claim. In a good argument, the list of relevant premises should be complete—and backed by credible sources.

That being said, sometimes premises are obvious and don't have to be stated. Consider this argument:

> Federal funding for education should be allocated on the basis of the size of a state. Therefore, Texas should get a larger share of federal money than Rhode Island.

In this argument the unstated premise is that "Texas is larger than Rhode Island," an uncontroversial fact known by most people in the United States. However, if we were presenting the argument to someone from another country, we might want to include the premise.

Connections How can we recognize the use of faulty arguments in advertisements? *See Chapter 10, pp. 319–321.*

Leaving out a relevant premise can be problematic, especially when the premise is controversial or is based on an unfounded assumption—as in the immigration argument.

ANALYZING **IMAGES**

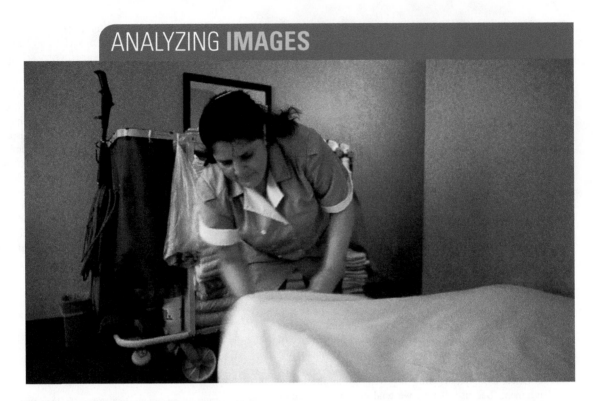

Hispanic Housekeeper   Hispanic immigrants tend to be hardworking and prefer to take low-paying jobs over collecting public assistance. In the United States they make up a significant portion of the labor force in jobs such as agricultural work, construction, and housekeeping.

DISCUSSION QUESTIONS

1. *Hispanic immigrants tend to be hardworking and prefer to take low-paying jobs, such as agricultural worker or housekeeper, rather than collect public assistance. Despite their work ethic Hispanic workers in the United States earn on the average only about two-thirds of what white workers earn. Is this fair? Create a list of premises this issue. Draw a conclusion based on your premises.*

2. *Refer to the argument you developed in the previous question and, working in small groups, evaluate your argument using the criteria listed in this section.*

Excluding relevant premises might lead us to a mistaken conclusion that is based on incomplete information.

In some cases, a premise is left out because it *is* controversial and stating it would weaken the position of the person who is making the argument. Consider:

> Abortion should remain legal. No woman should be forced to raise an unwanted child.

Breaking down and diagramming this argument, we have:

(**1**) [Abortion should remain legal.] (**2**) [No woman should be forced to raise an unwanted child.]

(2)

↓

(1)

At first glance it might look like the conclusion follows from the premise, since most people would accept this premise as reasonable. However, there is an unstated dependent premise in this argument: namely, that "a woman who gives birth to a child should also raise that child." Unlike the first premise, this one is certainly a questionable one, since adoption is an option.

Once you have identified a missing relevant premise, add it to the argument. Then go back and reevaluate the argument.

(**1**) [Abortion should remain legal.] (**2**) [No woman should be forced to raise an unwanted child.] (**3**) [A woman who gives birth to a child should also raise that child.]

In this case the unstated premise (**3**) weakens the argument, since many people do not accept it as true.

Soundness: Are the Premises True and Do They Support the Conclusion?

Finally, the reasoning process in an argument should be sound. A sound argument is one in which the premises are true and they support the conclusion. In the argument on page 187, the premise that "Hispanics are lazy freeloaders who burden our public welfare system" is false; therefore the argument is unsound. The connection between the premise(s) and conclusion should be based on reason rather than on fallacious appeals.

On the other hand, do not assume that a conclusion is false simply because it is not supported by the premises. When this happens, the most you can say is that you don't know whether the conclusion is true or false. Some issues, such as the existence of God or of consciousness in other people (or machines), probably cannot be proved or disproved through logical argumentation.

One of my most philosophically traumatic experiences as a child occurred when I was about 10 or 11 years old and realized that I could not prove the existence of anyone or anything else in the world except myself. For about a week, I wandered around in a miserable, solipsistic (the belief that I was the only being in the world) fog, estranging my concerned playmates in the process. Eventually, though, I decided that it was more practical and more conducive to my happiness just to accept on faith the existence of the world outside me. This experience also taught me that just because we can't prove something through the use of argumentation doesn't mean that it isn't true. To claim otherwise is to commit the fallacy of ignorance.

We'll be looking at additional rules for evaluating specific types of arguments in Chapters 7 and 8.

HIGHLIGHTS

GUIDELINES FOR EVALUATING AN ARGUMENT

Clarity: Is the argument clear and unambiguous?

Credibility: Are the premises supported by evidence?

Relevance: Are the premises relevant to the conclusion?

Completeness: Are there any unstated premises and conclusions?

Soundness: Are the premises true and do they support the conclusion?

➤ *APPLICATION: Find examples in the text of the application of each of these guidelines.*

EXERCISE 6-4

STOP AND ASSESS YOURSELF

I. Discuss whether the following are strong arguments. If you consider them weak, explain why.

*a. We need to protect American jobs. Therefore, we need stricter laws to keep illegal aliens from crossing the United States–Mexico border.

b. Even though the stock market crashed in 2008, stocks are still a great long-term investment. After all, the Dow Jones stock index has increased over the past 100 years.

c. People need to pass a driving test to get a license to drive a car. People should also have to take a parenting test and get a license before they can have a child. After all, parenting is a greater responsibility and requires more skill than driving.

*d. We should allow fraternities on our campus. After all, they provide volunteers to do a lot of charitable work.

e. My dog Rex growls only at people who are untrustworthy. Rex growled at Bob when he brought me home after our date. Therefore, I should not trust Bob.

f. If you're going to buy a new car, you should buy a Toyota Camry. They're one of the safest cars on the road, according to *Consumer Reports*.

*g. Abdul is a freshman at state community college. All freshmen at state community college are residents of Texas. Therefore, Abdul is a resident of Texas.

h. Marijuana use should be legal in the United States. After all, our own president, George W. Bush, as much as admitted that he had used marijuana.

i. God is all powerful. God is all good. Terrible things happen to people through no fault of their own. Therefore, God does not exist.

*j. You should stay away from Gloria because she's a troublemaker.

2. Identify the unstated premise(s) in each of the following arguments. Evaluate each of the arguments. Does leaving out the premise weaken or change the argument?

*a. Maria is a single mother. We should reject her application to the pre-med program.

b. Buck's father is a successful doctor and a graduate of State University. Buck should do well in the pre-med program.

c. If you want to save money, buy your textbooks on Amazon.com instead of the college bookstore.

*d. Cats don't bark. Therefore, Friskie doesn't bark.

e. If you're traveling in Europe you should buy a rail pass instead of renting a car.

f. I hear you'd like to do a semester in an African country. Given that the only languages you speak are Portuguese and German, you should consider doing an internship in Angola or Mozambique.

*g. I wouldn't trust Ben around children. I hear he was abused as a child.

3. Select three of the arguments from the exercises above. After identifying the missing premises, use the Internet or other resources to research the credibility of each of the missing premises. If necessary, rewrite the arguments to take into account the information you uncovered in your research.

*Answers to selected exercises are found in the Solutions Manual at the end of the book.

CONSTRUCTING AN ARGUMENT

Now that you know how to recognize, break down, and evaluate arguments, you are ready to construct your own arguments. Here is a list of steps to help you in this process:

Steps for Constructing an Argument

There are eight steps to follow when you construct an argument: (1) state the issue, (2) develop a list of premises, (3) eliminate weak or irrelevant premises, (4) establish a conclusion, (5) organize your argument, (6) try out your argument on others, (7) revise your argument, and, if appropriate, (8) put your solution or conclusion into action.

1. State the Issue. What question or issue are you going to address? Clearly identifying the issue first can help you stay on track. Word the issue in neutral terms. For example, "Should the United States have stricter gun-control laws?" and not "Should the government be doing more to keep guns out of the hands of hardened criminals?"

2. Develop a List of Premises. In coming up with possible premises, put your personal opinions aside. Avoid the trap of seeing the issue as having two sides in which rhetoric is used to settle issues, with one side winning and the other losing.

In developing a list of premises, remain objective and open-minded. Rather than select only those premises that support your particular worldview, try to explore all sides of the issue. Brainstorming with others—letting your ideas flow freely and creatively—is helpful in widening your perspective. Keep track of the premises by writing each of them down as you go along. Include references when appropriate in case you need to go back and check them.

Your premises should be relatively uncontroversial. Watch out for unsupported interpretations or assumptions. Adopt the skeptic's attitude. If you are at all unsure whether a particular premise is true, check it out. In doing your research, make sure you use only reliable sources and continue to consider all sides of the issue.

Sometimes a particular cultural world-view becomes so ingrained that we assume it is true and don't bother to question it. Dr. Joseph Collins's premise, written in 1927, that "every physician should cultivate lying as a fine art," was accepted for many years by the medical profession. The assumption that knowing the truth would harm the patient was not questioned, because it was widely accepted as true. It wasn't until 1961 that someone actually put the premise to the test and found that, in fact, the majority of cancer patients actually do better if they know the truth about their illness.[20]

Once you have established your preliminary list of premises, go back and check them. Each premise should be clearly stated, credible, and complete. Also, make sure you know the issue inside and out. You don't want to be taken by surprise by someone's question or counterargument when you present your argument. Did you leave out any important premises? For example, if your issue is whether

Before coming to a conclusion about an controversial legal issue such as allowing smoking in public places, we first need make sure our premises are based on facts.

smoking should be allowed in college dormitories, check your state's laws. Are there already laws against smoking in public buildings, and if so, is your dormitory (especially if you attend a state college) considered a public building?

If you find that your premises are heavily weighed in favor of the view you held before beginning this exercise, go back and spend more time looking at premises that support different perspectives on the issue.

3. Eliminate Weak or Irrelevant Premises.

After coming up with your list of premises, review them once again. Eliminate any premises that are weak or irrelevant to the issue. As in the proverbial chain, one weak link (premise) can destroy your whole argument. At the same time, resist the temptation to eliminate premises that don't mesh with your particular opinion regarding the issue.

Your final list of premises should be relevant to the issue. If your issue is "Should marijuana be legalized?" then you should avoid getting sidetracked by going on about how some of the legislators who oppose its legalization are hypocrites because they used marijuana when they were in college. Stick to the topic of marijuana and legalization. Also, eliminate any redundant premises—those that say essentially the same thing as another premise but in different words.

Next, form groups of closely related premises. For example, the premise "Marijuana use has been shown to decrease reaction time" should be grouped with the premise "Studies have shown that long-term use of marijuana does not have any ill effects on brain functioning"; it does not belong with the premise "The use of marijuana has been deemed immoral by the Lutheran Church." Although the first two premises take different positions on the issue, they are both similar in that they represent scientific research and not moral judgments. Ask yourself if any of the premises in your list are dependent on each other. A premise may initially appear to be weak simply because it needs to be paired with another (dependent) premise.

If your list of premises is still very long, consider your audience in deciding which premises to eliminate and which to keep. If you are doing an essay for class, the audience will be your professor. If you are doing the argument as a class presentation, the class is your audience. Your audience may also be a friend, a partner, a relative, or the readers of a newspaper or Web site.

Don't leave out a relevant premise unless it is too obvious to your audience to be stated. If in doubt, it is better to include the premise rather than assume that your audience will know about it. On the other hand, if you have only a limited amount of time to present your argument, you should include only the strongest premises. Do, however, have your other premises ready in case you are asked to expand on or clarify your argument.

Next, check the wording of your remaining premises. The wording of each premise should be clear, with no

Hot or Not?

Does the two-party system in the United States discourage the use of logical argumentation in resolving issues?

Working collaboratively with others to identify and eliminate weak or biased premises can help make your argument stronger.

Finally, your conclusion must be supported by your premises. It should not go beyond what the premises say, as in the following example:

> Most freshman on our campus own cars. The parking garage at our college does not have enough parking spots to accommodate all of their cars. Therefore, we should build another parking garage.

The conclusion that another parking garage should be built on campus does not follow from these premises. For one thing, we have no information about how many freshmen use their cars to commute to college or keep their cars on campus. And there are alternative options in dealing with a parking shortage, including mass transit, carpooling, or shuttle service from off-campus parking lots.

vague or confusing terms or emotionally loaded language. Define any ambiguous key terms in the premises and use these terms consistently throughout your argument.

4. Establish a Conclusion.
Only after you are satisfied with your list of premises should you draw a conclusion. In developing a conclusion ask yourself "What conclusion follows from these premises?" Remember to avoid looking at your issue as a contest between two sides. Look at *all* the premises in your final list and consider how the conclusion can take into account as many of the premises as possible.

For example, physician-assisted suicide is often presented as a polarized—black-and-white—issue. However, some people who are opposed to a law permitting it nevertheless think that physician-assisted suicide is justified under certain limited circumstances. Instead of splitting the issue into two sides, ask yourself how you might come up with a policy or law on the issue that takes into account the premises shared by all parties.

Be careful not to draw your conclusion too soon. This is most likely to happen if you bring a preconceived view into the argument and wear the blinders of resistance when analyzing the evidence for your conclusion. Carefully analyze your premises and make sure you've looked at all the different perspectives on the issue before drawing a conclusion. Also, make sure the connection between your conclusion and premises is reasonable, rather than based on an emotional appeal or informal fallacy.

Connections

What are the similarities between the scientific method and the use of logical argumentation in papers? *See Chapter 12, p. 383.*

5. Organize Your Argument.
There are many ways of organizing an argument. For example, you can first list or diagram your premises and conclusion, or you can present your argument in written or oral form. If you are presenting your argument in essay form, you should clearly

> Ask yourself "What conclusion follows from these premises?" Remember to avoid looking at your issue as a contest between two sides.

state the issue in the first paragraph of your essay or in your opening sentence. This will allow your audience to easily identify exactly what issue you are addressing. (See Critical Thinking in Action: Writing a Paper Based on Logical Argumentation, on page 193.).

The conclusion usually appears in the first paragraph or at the beginning of your presentation. In essays, this is sometimes called the *thesis statement*. If possible, limit your thesis statement to one sentence. Your opening paragraph can also let the reader know how you plan to defend your conclusion and organize your argument, as well as include a sentence or two to grab the reader's attention about the issue's importance.

The following excerpt from James Rachels's argument in his book *Active and Passive Euthanasia* is a good example of an opening paragraph:

> The distinction between active and passive euthanasia is thought to be crucial for medical ethics. The idea is that it is permissible, at least in some cases, to withhold treatment and allow a patient to die, but it is never permissible to take any direct action designed to kill the patient. This doctrine seems to be accepted by most

Critical THiNKing in Action

Writing a Paper Based on Logical Argumentation

Many courses require students to write an essay or thesis paper using logical argumentation. These papers are usually organized as follows:

1. **Identify the issue.** Include a brief explanation of the issue in the introductory paragraph along with definitions of key terms. The conclusion of your argument may also be stated in the first paragraph.

2. **Present premises.** This section will make up the major part of your paper. Lay out and explain the premises supporting your conclusion. Premises used should be complete, clearly stated, backed by credible evidence, fallacy-free, and logically compelling.

3. **Present and address counterarguments.** Present and respond to each of the most compelling counterarguments against your position.

4. **Conclusion and summary.** In the final paragraph, restate the issue and briefly summarize your arguments and conclusion.

5. **References.** Include a list of references for the facts and evidence used in your argument.

DISCUSSION QUESTIONS

1. Select an issue. Write a two-page draft or outline of a paper on this issue using logical argumentation. Share your draft or outline with other members of the class for feedback on how well you presented your argument. Modify your draft in light of the feedback you receive.

2. Find an article presenting an argument in a journal or newspaper. Locate in the article each of the five steps listed. Evaluate the strength of the argument. Discuss how you might improve the argument as well as its presentation.

---

doctors. . . . However, a strong case can be made against this doctrine. In what follows I will set out some of the relevant arguments, and urge doctors to reconsider their views on this matter.[21]

If you have several premises, you might want to devote a separate paragraph to each independent premise. You can discuss dependent premises in the same paragraph. In any case, let the reader know that you are introducing a new premise by using some sort of premise indicator such as *because* or *a second reason*. If appropriate, use an example to illustrate your premise. Rachels's second paragraph begins with an example of a patient who is "dying of incurable cancer of the throat [and] is in terrible pain, which can no longer be satisfactorily alleviated." He uses this example to illustrate his first premise:

> Part of my point is that the process of being "allowed to die" can be relatively slow and painful, whereas being given a lethal injection is relatively quick and painless.

Your essay or presentation should also address counterarguments. Discuss each counterargument and explain why the premises you have used are stronger. You can discuss them in the same paragraph with your supporting premises. Address the counterarguments after you present the premises that support your conclusion. For example, after presenting his premises, Rachels

summarizes his argument and then addresses the counterarguments:

> I have argued that killing is not in itself any worse than letting die; if my contention is right, it follows that active euthanasia is not any worse than passive euthanasia. What arguments can be given on the other side? The most common, I believe is the following: The important difference between active and passive euthanasia is that, in passive euthanasia the doctor does not do anything to bring about the patient death. . . . In active euthanasia, however, the doctor does something to bring about the patient's death: he kills him.

The last part of your essay may also include action that people can take to implement your conclusion or resolution to the issue. Rachels concludes his argument with this advice:

> So, whereas doctors may have to discriminate between active and passive euthanasia to satisfy the law, they should not do any more than that. In particular, they should not give the distinction any added authority and weight by writing it into official statements of medical ethics.

6. Try Out Your Argument on Others. Once you have come up with what you think is a strong argument, you are ready to try it out on someone else. In doing this, keep in mind that as critical thinkers we need to be both

Critical THiNKing in Action

The Dangers of Jumping to a Conclusion

Jumping to a conclusion too soon can have far-reaching consequences. In the middle of my freshman year in high school, my family moved to a new school district. My first assignment in the new English class was to write an epic poem in the style of the classic epic poems. Wanting to make a good first impression, and having been writing my own "books" since I was 9, I threw myself wholeheartedly into the task. When I finished, I read my poem to my mother, who had always encouraged my passion for writing.

Full of enthusiasm, I handed in my poem. The following day my teacher, a young woman fresh out of college, stood up in front of the room and read my poem. When she had finished, she glared accusingly at me and began asking in rapid succession questions about how I'd written the poem without giving me a chance to answer. She then declared that the poem was much too good for a student to have written, accused me of cheating, and ripped up my poem. She also made me sit in the back of the classroom for the rest of the year and gave me an F as a final grade. As a result, I was put in a remedial English class. It wasn't until my senior year that I was allowed to petition to be in the college-track English class. I was so traumatized by this experience that I never told my mother or anyone else what had happened. For many years after, I stopped doing any kind of creative writing and in college avoided any English or creative-writing classes.

Rather than analyzing her interpretation of my work (this was a well-written poem) and considering alternative interpretations, my teacher had jumped to the conclusion that I must have copied the epic poem from somewhere, an assumption that breached both good critical-thinking and argumentation skills.

DISCUSSION QUESTIONS

1. Imagine that you were a staff member at this school and found out from another student what had happened. Construct an argument to present to the teacher, encouraging her to reconsider her hasty generalization and come to a better-reasoned conclusion. Pair up and role play this scenario. Stop after two to three minutes and evaluate the effectiveness of your argument and your communication skills.

2. Think back on a time when a teacher or other authority figure hastily jumped to a conclusion about you or something you did. How did this event influence your life goals and decisions? Discuss ways in which your critical-thinking skills might help you to put this event in perspective.

open-minded and good listeners and not engage in resistence or resort to fallacies if others disagree with our argument. If you find that your argument is weak or that the particular conclusion you have drawn does not follow from the premises, go back and revise your argument.

7. Revise Your Argument. Revise your argument, if necessary, in light of the feedback you receive. If the other person's counterargument is more compelling, it would be irrational for you not to revise your own position in light of it. For example, a student in one of my ethics classes participated in a group presentation on capital punishment. At the end of the presentation, he was asked about his position on the issue by another student. He responded, "After doing this project I realize that capital punishment serves no purpose and that there are no good arguments for it. But," he added, "I still support capital punishment." That was poor critical thinking on his part. Stubbornly adhering to a position when there is contrary evidence is not a desirable quality.

8. Put Your Solution or Conclusion into Action.

If appropriate, put your solution or conclusion into action. Good critical thinking has a behavioral component. It involves taking critical action. For instance, if you are writing to your state senator about a need to increase community drug awareness in your hometown, you might want to suggest a realistic solution to the problem and offer to help with its implementation.

Knowing how to construct and present an argument are important skills for a critical thinker. It not only makes you more effective in presenting an argument on an issue but can also help you in resolving issues in your own life.

HIGHLIGHTS

STEPS FOR CONSTRUCTING AN ARGUMENT

1. **Clearly state the issue in the form of a question.**

2. **Develop a list of premises that address the issue.**

3. **Eliminate weak or irrelevant premises.**

4. **Establish a conclusion.**

5. **Organize your argument.**

6. **Try out your argument on others.**

7. **Revise your argument, if necessary.**

8. **If appropriate, put your solution or conclusion into action.**

➤ *APPLICATION: Identify in the text an example of each step being applied to an argument.*

Using Arguments in Making Real-Life Decisions

Arguments are useful tools for making real-life decisions, especially in situations that involve a conflict between what seem to be equally compelling alternatives. People who are poor at critical thinking not only are less likely to recognize a conflict until it gets out of control but are unable to evaluate competing alternatives to come up with an effective resolution to the problem.

Skilled critical thinkers, in contrast, are more likely to recognize a conflict. Instead of jumping to conclusions, good critical thinkers look at an issue from multiple perspectives, assigning weight when necessary to competing reasons, before reaching their final decision.

Consider this example:

> Amy was struggling with the decision of whether to go to China with her family over the summer or instead to go to summer school so that she could finish college in four years. She had been promised a job with a computer software company, following graduation in June. Unfortunately, the summer course schedule conflicted with her travel plans. What should she do?

The first thing you should do in a case like this is to come up with a list of all possible premises or reasons that are relevant to your final decision. In making her decision, Amy began by making this list:

- My grandparents, who live in China, are getting on in years, and this may be the last chance I have to see them.

- My parents are paying my fare, so the trip will not be a financial burden for me.

- I need to take a summer course to graduate next year.

- I have been promised a job with a computer software company after graduation in June.

- The summer course schedule at my college conflicts with my travel schedule.

In developing your list of premises, ask other people for ideas as well. Also, do your research and make sure that you have all the facts correct. In Amy's case, one of her friends suggested that she go to the registrar's office to see whether there was a way she could take a course that would not conflict with the trip dates. As it turned out, she could do an internship on contemporary Chinese business culture for the credits she needed to graduate. She added this option or premise to her list:

- I could do an internship for college credit while I'm in China.

After completing your list, go back and review the premises. Highlight those that are most relevant and delete those that are not. Review your final list before drawing a conclusion. Have you left anything out? Often, just by doing your research and listing various options, you may find that what first seemed to be a conflict is not a conflict at all, as happened in Amy's case.

Finally, put your decision or conclusion into action. As it turned out, Amy was able to go to China with her family *and* complete college in four years.

Arguments provide a powerful tool for analyzing issues and making decisions in our lives. As critical thinkers, we should take a stand or make an important decision only *after* we have examined the different perspectives and options. In addition, we should remain open to hearing new evidence and, in light of that evidence, to modifying our position. By trying to learn why someone holds a position different from our own, we can move closer to understanding and perhaps resolving a conflict.

EXERCISE 6-5

STOP AND ASSESS YOURSELF

1. Select an issue that is currently being discussed on your campus. After following the eight steps outlined in this chapter, write a two to three page essay or a letter to the editor of the student newspaper presenting your argument for a resolution to the issue.

2. The growing number of child pornography sites on the Internet has led to a corresponding proliferation of cyberspace sleuths—adults who pose as children and attempt to expose cyber-pedophiles. Critics of these self-appointed citizen-sleuths point out that their techniques, because they involve deception, border on entrapment. Critics also argue that it is wrong for private citizens to take the law into their own hands. Others applaud the success of these citizen-sleuths in catching sex offenders and closing down child pornography sites. Working in small groups, construct an argument on the issue of using citizen-sleuths to catch pedophiles. Share your conclusion with the rest of the class. Reevaluate your conclusion, if necessary, in light of feedback from the class.

3. Working in small groups, select a situation with which one of the students in the group is currently struggling. Using the eight-step method outlined in this chapter, generate a suggested resolution or decision.

4. Select one of the goals from your life plan that you are having difficulty achieving. Construct an argument that will enable you to achieve this goal. Put your decision or conclusion into action.

THiNK AGAIN

1. What is an argument?
   - An argument is made up of two or more propositions, including the conclusion, which is supported by the other propositions, known as premises. An argument tries to prove or convince us that the conclusion is true, whereas an explanation is a statement about why something is the case.

2. What is the purpose of breaking down and diagramming arguments?
   - Breaking down arguments helps us to recognize the different premises and the conclusion so we can identify and analyze the issue under discussion, as well as examine the premises to determine if they support the conclusion.

3. What are some of the factors to take into consideration in evaluating an argument?
   - Some of the factors in evaluating an argument are clarity, credibility, relevance, completeness, and soundness of the argument.

Perspectives on Same-Sex Marriage

The issue of legalizing same-sex marriage has divided the United States for some time. Support for same-sex marriage is increasing, with 58 percent of Americans polled in 2013 agreeing that it should be legal. Women and young people are the most likely to support same-sex marriage.[22] The change in public opinion and laws has been rapid. Indeed, until 2003, when the U.S. Supreme Court's ruling in *Lawrence v. Texas* declared antisodomy laws unconstitutional, some states had laws on the books that punished sexual intercourse between two people of the same sex with up to 25 years in prison.

Supporters of same-sex marriage argue that marriage is a basic human right that should not be denied to a person simply because of his or her sexual orientation. Same-sex marriage has been legalized in Canada, Belgium, the Netherlands, Spain, and South Africa. In addition, same-sex couples have full legal rights in many other European countries. In the United States, 13 states including California, Massachusetts, Connecticut, Iowa, Maine, Maryland, New Hampshire, New York, Washington, Minnesota, Delaware, Rhode Island, and Vermont, as well as Washington, D.C. are the only states where same-sex marriage is legal—and those marriages are not recognized by the federal government or, in most cases, by other states. However, several states, including New Jersey, Illinois, and Hawaii, have civil-union legislation for same-sex couples, and still others recognize domestic partnerships.

In 1996, during the administration of Bill Clinton, Congress passed the Defense of Marriage Act (DOMA). The act states that "the word 'marriage' means only a legal union between one man and one woman as husband and wife," thereby prohibiting the federal government from recognizing same-sex marriages. In 2004, a proposal was submitted to Congress to add a Marriage Protection Amendment to the U.S. Constitution, which would define marriage as only between a man and a woman and would also prevent state laws and courts from recognizing same-sex marriages. The amendment failed to pass. On June 26, 2013, the U.S. Supreme Court ruled that Section 3 of DOMA is unconstitutional and that same-sex married couples are entitled to federal benefits.

In the first reading Chief Justice Marshall, in *Goodridge v. Department of Public Health* (2003), argues that same-sex couples have a constitutional right to marry. In the second reading, Matthew Spalding argues that redefining marriage to a form of contract fundamentally alters the nature and purpose of marriage.

Goodridge v. Department of Public Health (2003)

CHIEF JUSTICE MARGARET H. MARSHALL, MAJORITY OPINION

Goodridge v. Department of Public Health was a landmark state appellate court case that legalized same-sex marriage in Massachusetts, the first state to do so. In the following reading former Chief Justice Margaret H. Marshall presents the majority opinion in support of the ruling.

Marriage is a vital social institution. The exclusive commitment of two individuals to each other nurtures love and mutual support; it brings stability to our society. For those who choose to marry, and for their children, marriage provides an abundance of legal, financial, and social benefits. In return it imposes weighty legal, financial, and social obligations. The question before us is whether, consistent with the Massachusetts Constitution, the Commonwealth may deny the protections, benefits, and obligations conferred by civil marriage to two individuals of the same sex who wish to marry. We conclude that it may not. The Massachusetts Constitution affirms the dignity and equality of all individuals. It forbids the creation of second class citizens. In reaching our conclusion we have given full deference to the arguments made by the Commonwealth. But it has failed to identify any constitutionally adequate reason for denying civil marriage to same-sex couples.

The Court affirmed that the core concept of common human dignity protected by the Fourteenth Amendment to the United States Constitution precludes government intrusion into the deeply personal realms of consensual adult expressions of intimacy and one's choice of an intimate partner. The Court also reaffirmed the central role that decisions whether to marry or have children bear in shaping one's identity.

Barred access to the protections, benefits, and obligations of civil marriage, a person who enters into an intimate, exclusive union with another of the same sex is arbitrarily deprived of membership in one of our community's most rewarding and cherished institutions. That exclusion is incompatible with the constitutional principles of respect for individual autonomy and equality under law.

Without question, civil marriage enhances the "welfare of the community." It is a "social institution of the highest importance." Civil marriage anchors an ordered society by encouraging stable relationships over transient ones. It is central to the way the Commonwealth identifies individuals, provides for the orderly distribution of property, ensures that children and adults are cared for and supported whenever possible from private rather than public funds, and tracks important epidemiological and demographic data.

Marriage also bestows enormous private and social advantages on those who choose to marry. Civil marriage is at once a deeply personal commitment to another human being and a highly public celebration of the ideals of mutuality, companionship, intimacy, fidelity, and family. Because it fulfils yearnings for security, safe haven, and connection that express our common humanity, civil marriage is an esteemed institution, and the decision whether and whom to marry is among life's momentous acts of self-definition.

The benefits accessible only by way of a marriage license are enormous, touching nearly every aspect of life and death. The department states that "hundreds of statutes" are related to marriage and to marital benefits. Exclusive marital benefits that are not directly tied to property rights include the presumptions of legitimacy and parentage of children born to a married couple and evidentiary rights, such as the prohibition against spouses testifying against one another about their private conversations, applicable in both civil and criminal cases Other statutory benefits of a personal nature available only to married individuals include qualification for bereavement or medical leave to care for individuals related by blood or marriage an automatic "family member" preference to make medical decisions for an incompetent or disabled spouse who does not have a contrary health care proxy, the application of predictable rules of child custody, visitation, support, and removal out-of-State when married parents divorce.

Notwithstanding the Commonwealth's strong public policy to abolish legal distinctions between marital and nonmarital children in providing for the support and care of minors, the fact remains that marital children reap a measure of family stability and economic security based on their parents' legally privileged status that is largely inaccessible, or not as readily accessible, to nonmarital children. Some of these benefits are social, such as the enhanced approval that still attends the status of being a marital child. Others are material, such as the greater ease of access to family-based State and Federal benefits that attend the presumptions of one's parentage.

It is undoubtedly for these concrete reasons, as well as for its intimately personal significance, that civil marriage has long been termed a "civil right." See, e.g., Loving v. Virginia, The United States Supreme Court has described the right to marry as "of fundamental importance for all individuals" and as "part of the fundamental 'right of privacy' implicit in the Fourteenth Amendment's Due Process Clause."

Without the right to marry—or more properly, the right to choose to marry—one is excluded from the full range of human experience and denied full protection of the laws for one's "avowed commitment to an intimate and lasting human relationship."... Because civil marriage is central to the lives of individuals and the welfare of the community, our laws assiduously protect the individual's right to marry against undue government incursion. Laws may not "interfere directly and substantially with the right to marry."...

For decades, indeed centuries, in much of this country (including Massachusetts) no lawful marriage was possible between white and black Americans. That long history availed not when the Supreme Court of California held in 1948 that a legislative prohibition against interracial marriage violated the due process and equality guarantees of the Fourteenth Amendment.

The individual liberty and equality safeguards of the Massachusetts Constitution protect both "freedom from" unwarranted government intrusion into protected spheres of life and "freedom to" partake in benefits created by the State for the common good. . . . Both freedoms are involved here. Whether and whom to marry, how to express sexual intimacy, and whether and how to establish a family—these are among the most basic of every individual's liberty and due process rights. . . . And central to personal freedom and security is the assurance that the laws will apply equally to persons in similar situations. "Absolute equality before the law is a fundamental principle of our own Constitution." . . .

REVIEW QUESTIONS

1. Why is denying same-sex couples the right to marriage incompatible with the principles of respect for autonomy and equality under the law?

2. What does Marshall mean when she says that the laws of civil marriage do not privilege procreative heterosexual intercourse between married people?

3. How is denying the right to marry between whites and blacks similar to denying the right to marry between same-sex couples?

4. How does Marshall respond to the claim that legalizing same-sex marriage will undermine the institution of marriage?

A Defining Moment for Marriage and Self-Government MATTHEW SPALDING

Matthew Spalding is vice president of American Studies and Director of the B. Kenneth Simon Center for Principles and Politics at the Heritage Foundation in Washington, D.C. In his reading, Spaulding presents arguments for why legalizing same-sex marriage will weaken traditional marriage and family.

What was once an important debate over the legal status of marriage has emerged as a critical national issue, the resolution of which will shape the future of our society and the course of constitutional government in the United States.

Family is and will always remain the building block of civil society, and marriage is at the heart of the family. Redefining marriage down to a mere form of contract fundamentally alters its nature and purpose and will usher in new threats to the liberty of individuals and organizations that uphold marriage and have moral or religious objections to its redefinition.

What Is at Stake For thousands of years, based on experience, tradition, and legal precedent, every society and every major religion have upheld marriage as the unique relationship by which a man and a woman are joined together for the primary purpose of forming and maintaining a family. This overwhelming consensus results from the fact that the union of man and woman is manifest in the most basic and evident truths of human nature. Marriage is the formal recognition of this relationship by society and its laws. While individual marriages are recognized by government, the institution of marriage pre-exists and is antecedent to the institution of government.

Society's interest in uniquely elevating the status of marriage is that marriage is the necessary foundation of the family, and thus necessary for societal existence and well-being. Family is the primary institution through which children are raised, nurtured, and educated, and developed into adults. Marriage is the cornerstone of the family: It produces children, provides them with mothers and fathers, and is the framework through which relationships among mothers, fathers, and children are established and maintained.

Moreover, because of the shared obligations and generational relationships that accrue with marriage, the institution brings significant stability, continuity, and meaning to human relationships and plays an important role in transferring basic cultural knowledge and civilization to future generations.

Redefining Marriage Redefining marriage does not simply extend benefits or rights to a larger class, but substantively changes the essence of the institution. It does not expand marriage; it alters its core meaning such that it is no longer intrinsically related to the relationship between fathers, mothers, and children. Expanding marriage supposedly to make it more inclusive, no matter what we call the new arrangement, necessarily ends marriage as we now know it by remaking the institution into something different: a mere contract between any two individuals.

Changing the definition of marriage—or even remaining neutral as to that definition—denies the very nature and purpose that gives marriage its unique and preferable status in society. If marriage becomes just one form of commitment in a spectrum of sexual relationships rather than a preferred monogamous relationship for the sake of children, the line separating sexual relations within and outside marriage becomes blurred, and so does the public policy argument against out-of-wedlock births or in favor of abstinence.

Based on current evidence and settled reasoning, it would be a terrible folly to weaken marriage either by elevating non-marital unions to the same position or by lowering the institution of marriage to the status of merely one form of household.

A Defining Moment Americans are a greatly tolerant and reasonable people. That continuing character depends on the strength of the American framework of constitutional government and the core principles of self-government—first among those the idea of religious liberty—that allow and encourage that character and our ability to govern ourselves despite our differences. Citizens and their elected representatives must be able to engage in free discussion

and deliberation on the importance of the institution of marriage for civil society and popular self-government. Activist judges must not strip them of that freedom.

We should work to rebuild and restore marriage and not allow redefinition to further weaken the institution; break its fundamental connections between husband and wife, parents and child; and thereby sever our primary link to the formation of future generations. We must act in accord with our basic principles and deepest convictions to preserve constitutional government and the foundational structure of civilization by upholding the permanent institution of marriage.

Review Questions

1. Why does Spalding regard redefining marriage to include same-sex marriage as a threat to liberty?
2. According to Spalding, what is the source of the institution of marriage?
3. Why is heterosexual marriage a necessary foundation of family?
4. According to Spalding, how would redefining marriage to include same-sex couples weaken the institution of marriage?

THiNK AND DISCUSS

PERSPECTIVES ON SAME-SEX MARRIAGE

1. Identify the key premises in *Goodridge v. Department of Public Health* (2006) and by Spalding in their arguments regarding the legalization of same-sex marriage. Identify which type of premise each is. Diagram and evaluate both of the arguments. Should the definition of marriage be limited to a man and a woman or should the definition change to take into account changing views of marriage and family? Present an argument supporting your position, referring back to the role of definitions discussed in Chapter 4 on page 124.
2. Some people oppose legalizing same-sex marriage on a federal level but support civil unions and equal rights for same-sex couples. Evaluate whether this position is consistent with a belief in equal rights and opportunities for all people, regardless of their sexual orientation. Discuss also how both Spalding and the Supreme Court in *Goodridge v. Department of Public Health* (2006) might respond to legalizing civil unions, but not marriage, for same-sex couples. Which position do you support and why?
3. Looking back at your life goals, is marriage one of your goals? If so, why? Discuss how you would respond, and why, if you were legally denied the right to marry because of your sexual orientation.
4. Cheshire Calhoun, professor of philosophy at Arizona State University, has argued that lesbians should not buy into the traditional model of marriage and family that she says is inherently oppressive to women because women take a subordinate role to men in marriage, and women are expected to do the majority of housework and childrearing, which limits their career options. Discuss her concerns. Should the institution of marriage itself be dismantled? If so, what should replace marriage as the family unit and best means for raising children? Develop arguments to support your answers.

12

SCIENCE

What do you think the scientist is thinking as she evaluates the glass flask? How can learning about scientific methodology make us better at evaluating scientific claims?

Sea levels have risen nearly 7 inches in the last hundred years because of global warming, according to the Environmental Protection Agency (EPA), and they are expected to rise another foot by 2100.[1] In the past few decades, global warming has accelerated. The hottest 9 years on record since we began recording the temperature in 1850 have occurred since 2000. Temperatures are expected to increase another 2 to 11 degrees by 2100.[2] With its widespread droughts, deadly heat waves, and massive storms, 2012 was the hottest year on record in the continental United States.

The melting of the polar ice sheets in response to the increased warming of Earth is in part responsible for rising sea levels. In 2002, a piece of the Antarctic ice shelf the size of Rhode Island broke off and fell into the ocean. If the West Antarctic ice sheet

THiNK
FIRST

- What is the scientific method?
- How does science differ from pseudoscience?
- What are some of the different types of scientific experiments and research methods?

were to completely melt—a process that has begun and is occurring at a much faster rate than previously predicted by scientists—the sea level could rise by as much as 30 inches by 2050.[3] In other words, if these trends continue, by the time today's typical college freshman retires, most of the world's coastal cities and communities will be under water.[4]

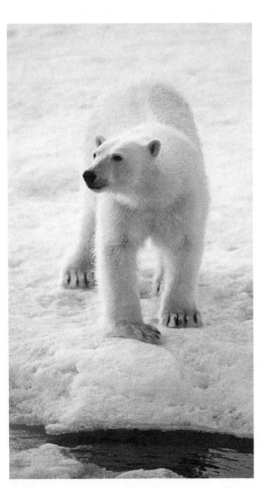

Rising sea levels will also contribute to land erosion, as well as to the salinization of freshwater and agricultural land in low-lying areas, thus disrupting our food and water supply. In addition, major storms are predicted to increase in number and intensity, while the warmer climate will ensure that infectious diseases, especially such tropical diseases as malaria, will flourish in places like the southern United States.

Some scientific research on global warming and other natural processes is more rigorous and better at explaining and predicting phenomena than other research. As critical thinkers, we need to be able to interpret and evaluate science stories in the news media, as well as research reports in scientific journals. We need to decide not only whether they are worth considering but also how scientific findings can be applied to our lives and to public policy. Even more basic to this process is the capacity to think critically about science itself as a method for discovering truth. In this chapter we'll:

- Learn about the history of science
- Identify and critically analyze the assumptions underlying science
- Study the scientific method
- Learn how to evaluate scientific explanations
- Distinguish between science and pseudoscience
- Learn about the different types of scientific experiments and how to evaluate them
- Look at ethical concerns in scientific experimentation
- Examine Thomas Kuhn's theory of normal science and paradigm shifts

WHAT IS SCIENCE?

Science rests on reasoning that moves from observable, measurable facts to testable explanations for those facts. The task of scientists is to discover, observe, and collect facts in a systematic manner and to explain relationships among them.

Modern science has a profound impact on our lives. Because it is so pervasive in our culture, we tend to assume that science is the natural method for obtaining and testing knowledge about the world. In this section, we'll examine the development of modern science, as well as some of the assumptions underlying science.

The Scientific Revolution

Prior to the seventeenth century, the teachings of Christianity, and in particular those of the Catholic Church, were regarded as the final source of truth in Western Europe. Nicolaus Copernicus (1473–1543), a Polish astronomer, launched the scientific revolution with his assertion that the sun, not the Earth, is the center of the

Copernicus launched the scientific revolution with his observation that the Earth revolves around the sun, and not vice versa.

solar system. Many historians, however, recognize English philosopher and statesman Sir Francis Bacon (1561–1626), who systematized the scientific method, as the father of modern science. In his *Novum Organum* (1620), Bacon put forth a method based on direct observation for discovering truths about the world. Bacon's scientific method, which begins with carrying out systematic observations about the world and using testing and experimentation to draw inferences that are based on these observations, has been tremendously successful in advancing our knowledge about the world and our ability to manipulate nature.

> **science** The use of reason to move from observable, measurable facts to hypotheses to testable explanations for those facts.
>
> **empiricism** The belief that our physical senses are the primary source of knowledge.
>
> **objectivity** The assumption that we can observe and study the physical world without any observer bias.

Assumptions Underlying Science

Science is the primary way in Western culture of interpreting reality. However, it is important to keep in mind that science is a system created by humans and, as such, is based on a particular worldview or set of assumptions.

Empiricism. **Empiricism**, the belief that our physical senses are the primary source of knowledge, is one of the most basic assumptions of science. Scientists consider the empirical method the only reliable method for obtaining knowledge. Consequently, the more data and observations that scientists accumulate over the generations, the greater is science's ability to correctly explain the workings of nature.

Objectivity. A related assumption underlying modern science is **objectivity**, the belief that we can observe and study the physical world "out there" as an object outside of us without bias on the part of the scientist/observer. Because the world is objective and independent of the individual observer, the presumption is that systematic observation will lead to agreement among scientists. This assumption has been called into question by quantum physics, which has found that the mere act of observing a quantum event changes it.

Connections

How can the methods of doubt and belief be used in science? *See Chapter 1, p. 10.*

What is the relationship between religious beliefs and reason? *See Chapter 2, pp. 53–54.*

What are some of the critical thinking strategies used in the reasoning process? *See Chapter 2, p. 39.*

Although early empiricists (including Bacon) thought that objectivity was achievable, most scientists now also acknowledge that past social experiences, as well as inborn cognitive and perceptual errors, can influence how even the best-trained scientists perceive the world. For example, as we noted in Chapter 4, we have a tendency to see order in random phenomena. One of the most famous examples of this type of error was the Martian canals. See Analyzing Images "The 'Canals' of Mars."

Despite the fact that complete objectivity is unattainable, scientists strive as much as possible to be aware of their biases, to be objective in their observations, and to be precise in their use of language.

Materialism. With the doctrine known as **materialism**, empiricism goes one step further. Scientific materialists argue that *everything* in the universe is physical matter. (*Materialism* in this sense has nothing to do with being obsessed with acquiring money, consumer goods, and other "material things.") According to scientific materialism, perceptions, thoughts, and emotions can all be reduced to descriptions of physical systems, such as brain waves or stimulus and response. There is no need to bring into scientific descriptions and explanations extraneous, nonmaterial concepts such as a conscious mental life. Because of its materialistic roots, science has made little, if any, progress in explaining how matter is or can become conscious.

Predictability. Scientists have traditionally assumed that the physical world is *orderly and predictable*. The universe consists of interconnected causal relationships that can be discovered through systematic observation and inductive reasoning. Quantum mechanics in particular challenges the idea of an ultimately predictable, determinist, material reality, suggesting that there are forces at play in the universe other than strictly physical causal laws. For example, the Heisenberg uncertainty principle states that it is impossible to predict both the position and momentum of a particle simultaneously, even under ideal conditions of measurement.

Unity. Associated with the belief in predictability is the assumption that there is an *underlying unity of the universe,* or a unified dynamic structure that is present in all phenomena. These unified structures can be translated into scientific laws that are universally applicable. Indeed, Albert Einstein devoted considerable effort during his lifetime in search of a grand unified theory, a search that to date has been unfruitful.

Limitations of Science

Despite its obvious strengths in enabling us to build a body of knowledge about the natural world, science has some limitations. One of these, at least from a philosophical viewpoint, is that it uses the existence of a physical world as its starting point. But as the seventeenth-century French philosopher René Descartes noted, we only have an idea in our mind of a world outside of us—not direct evidence that the world "out there" actually exists.[5] In other words, the very starting point of science—the existence of a physical world—cannot be empirically proven!

Empiricism and the use of sensory experience as the foundation of science also limits science to observable, shared phenomena. However, there are aspects of the physical world—such as dark energy and dark matter, certain electromagnetic waves, and subatomic particles—that are imperceptible to human senses and to the scientific instruments that are designed to function as extensions of our senses. In addition, according to string theorists, physicists who use mathematical reasoning, there are at least nine dimensions, not just three, that our brain is able to perceive and process.

Hot or Not?

Is science the best tool for learning about the world?

Connections

How do perception errors and personal and social bias interfer with scientific objectivity? *See Chapter 4, pp. 113–116, 126 and 130.*

materialism The belief that everything in the universe is composed of physical matter.

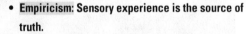

HIGHLIGHTS

ASSUMPTIONS OF SCIENCE:

- **Empiricism:** Sensory experience is the source of truth.
- **Objectivity:** We can study the physical world without bias.
- **Materialism:** Everything in the universe is made up of physical matter.
- **Predictability:** The universe is made up of interconnected causal relationships.
- **Unity:** The universe has an underlying unified dynamic structure.

➤ APPLICATION: Identify an example in the text of each of the assumptions.

ANALYZING **IMAGES**

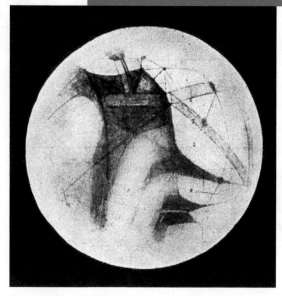

Drawing of Mars in 1895.

Photo of Mars in 2012.

The "Canals" of Mars
Many astronomers continued to believe in the Martian canals until 1965, when the space probe *Mariner 4* flew close to Mars and took photos of the planet's surface. No canals showed up in the photos. It turned out that the "canals" were a combination of an optical illusion and our brain's tendency to impose order on random data, as well as the expectation on the part of scientists that canals existed on Mars.

DISCUSSION QUESTIONS

1. *Discuss how language shapes your expectations and observations of natural phenomena, as occurred with the "canals" of Mars. Use specific examples to illustrate your answer.*

2. *Think of a time when you drew an incorrect conclusion on the basis of observation alone. How did you discover that your observation was misleading? Discuss the role scientific knowledge played in correcting your misperception?*

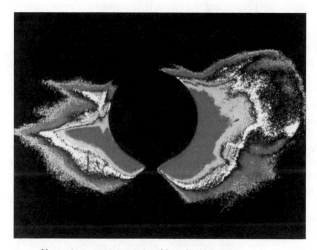

Magnetic energy is imperceptible to human senses.

Some philosophers argue that observation alone, no matter how many times we observe one event to follow another, cannot logically establish a necessary causal connectedness between the two events. Immanuel Kant in particular maintained that causality is a property of our mind, not of the outside world.* In other words, how we experience reality is dependent on the structure of our brain, which organizes and gives meaning to input from our senses.

Science and Religion

There are four basic positions regarding the relationship between science and religion: (1) science always trumps religion when there is a conflict; (2) religion always trumps

*For a review of Kant's theory of the mind and critique of empiricism, see Chapter 4, pages 103–104.

Michelangelo's rendition of the Genesis story of "The Creation of Man." The religious belief that humans are qualitatively different than other animals is one of the underlying assumptions of modern science.

science when there is a conflict; (3) science and religion operate in two separate and mutually exclusive realities; and (4) science and religion are concerned with the same reality and are compatible and complementary.

Most scientists and Western philosophers adopt the position that science always trumps religion when there is a conflict between them. This attitude has created antagonism between science and religion, especially fundamentalist religions. Many conservative Christians believe that the Bible is the literal and infallible word of God not only in the religious sphere but also in science.

People who adopt the third position, such as Judge John E. Jones (see "Critical Thinking Issue: Evolution versus Intelligent Design"), deny that there is a conflict. They argue instead that science and religion each deal with separate and mutually exclusive realms. Science deals with the objective, empirical reality; religion is concerned with values and a subjective, spiritual reality. Science asks how and what; religion asks why. Therefore, we can accept evolution without relinquishing our religious convictions regarding the special creation of human beings in the image of God. One of the problems with this approach is that in some cases science and religion make claims about the same phenomenon, whether it is the origin of human life, the effect of prayer on healing, or the occurrence of the Biblical Great Flood. When these claims are in conflict, logically they cannot both be true.

According to the fourth view, science and religion are dealing with the same reality and, as such, are compatible. This view

How does anthropocentrism act as a barrier to critical thinking? *See Chapter 1, p. 26.* **Are faith and reason compatible?** *See Chapter 2, pp. 53–55.*

Connections

> . . . how we experience reality is dependent on the structure of our brain, which organizes and gives meaning to input from our senses.

is found in Judaism, Hinduism, Islam,[6] and some mainstream Protestant denominations. If scripture conflicts with the claims of science, then scripture should be reinterpreted. For example, the creation story in Genesis should be seen as a metaphor rather than taken literally. British chemist and theologian Arthur Peacocke supports this approach. Religion and science, he argues, are both dealing with different aspects of the same reality. As such, they must always "be ultimately converging. . . . The scientific and theological enterprises [are] interacting and mutually illuminating approaches to reality."[7] With the election of Pope Francis I, who accepts the theory of evolution, the Catholic Church is expected to move closer to this view of science and religion as compatible.

Though scientists often reject religious explanations for natural phenomena, there are strands of religious belief in science. The Judeo-Christian view that God gave humans dominion over the world legitimates the use of science to control and alter nature for our benefit. In addition, *anthropocentrism*—the assumption that humans are the central reality in the universe and are qualitatively different from other animals—allows scientists to confine and use other animals in research and experiments as a means to better the lives of humans. Some scientists take anthropocentricism even further and argue that the universe exists so that conscious human life would have a place to arise—a doctrine known as the *anthropic principle.*[8]

As noted previously, science is grounded in a set of unproven assumptions. However, this does not mean that science is invalid or even that these assumptions are false. Instead, we need to keep in mind that science has limitations in addition to its strengths. As we already noted, science has been extremely successful in uncovering many of the mysteries of the universe. Science has also been responsible for producing new technology for improving our lives.

EXERCISE 12-1

STOP AND ASSESS YOURSELF

1. It has been said that science has become the religion of the twentieth and early twenty-first centuries. Critically evaluate this claim.

2. If you depended on observation with the naked eye alone, what would you most likely conclude about the relationship of the sun and the Earth? Discuss how religious assumptions influence our assumptions about the natural world.

3. Discuss whether the assumption of anthropocentrism in science is justified or if scientists should refrain from practices that exploit other animals and so-called natural resources to benefit humans.

4. Critically analyze Peacocke's claim that religion and science complement each other.

5. Inventor and computer scientist Raymond Kurzweil in his book *The Age of Spiritual Machines: When Computers Exceed Human Intelligence* rejects the assumption that only "God" or "natural forces" can create new life forms. He argues that the creation of AI by humans may be a natural step in evolution. Review his reading. Which of the assumptions of science does Kurzweil reject? Discuss whether his rejection of these assumptions is reasonable or unreasonable.

THE SCIENTIFIC METHOD

The **scientific method** involves the identification of a problem and the rigorous, systematic application of observation and experimentation in testing an explanation for the problem.

As such, it is similar to the three levels of thinking—experience, interpretation, and analysis—that we studied in Chapter 1. Alone, experience or sensory data tell us nothing. They have to be interpreted in light of existing scientific knowledge and theories. Like the three levels of thinking, the scientific method is dynamic and recursive rather than linear, with analysis returning to observation to check for consistency, and interpretation being revised in light of further analysis and observation.

Experimentation/Testing (Analysis)

⇅

Hypothesis (Interpretation)

⇅

Observation (Experience)

The scientific method includes specific steps to guide a scientist through this process of systematically analyzing his or her observations. Although there is some variation in the steps between the different scientific disciplines, the steps basically are as follows: (1) identifying the problem, (2) developing a hypothesis, (3) gathering additional information and refining the hypothesis, (4) testing the hypothesis, and (5) evaluating the results of the tests or experiments. We'll examine each of these steps in turn in this section.

Connections

How can improving our research and inquiry skills make us better scientists? *See Chapter 1, pp. 9–10.*

How does the scientific method use the three levels of thinking? *See Chapter 1, p. 21.*

What are some of the research resources scientists might use in gathering evidence? *See Chapter 4, p. 110.*

1. Identify the Problem

The scientific method begins with the identification of a problem for investigation. This requires good observation skills, an inquisitive mind, and the ability to ask the right questions. Biologist Russell Hill, in his study of athletes on British soccer teams, observed that the teams that wore red uniforms seemed to win more often. He asked the question: Might there be a causal relationship at work?[9]

scientific method A process involving the rigorous, systematic application of observation and experimentation.

A problem may also arise as the result of previous work in the field. The Human Genome Project developed out of previous genetic research, including Watson and Crick's 1953

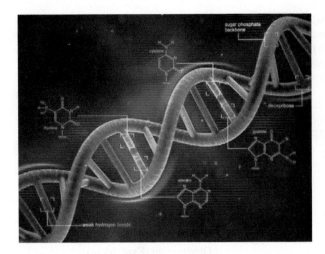

a term is generally a theoretical or operational definition. Operational definitions provide precise measures that can be used in data collection, interpretation, and testing.* For example, meteorologists studying weather and climate changes define El Niño as an oceanic condition where the temperature continues at $+0.5°C$ or higher, averaged over 3 or more consecutive months.[10] If a hypothesis introduces a new term, a stipulative definition must be provided.

A scientific hypothesis should provide a testable explanation for the problem being investigated. To facilitate this, hypotheses are often formulated as hypothetical ("If . . . then . . .") propositions. Writing Hill's soccer hypothesis as a hypothetical proposition, we have: If a team is wearing red (Antecedent), then the team is more likely to win the game than is a team wearing blue (Consequent).

> If A, then C.
> A.
> Therefore, C.

In this case we have a *modus ponens* argument.** Does the consequent or conclusion—"the team is more likely to win the game than is a team wearing blue"—regularly follow the antecedent—"a team is wearing red"? If it does follow, then the first premise (the hypothesis) is worth further testing. If it does not follow, then the first premise (the hypothesis) is false and the hypothesis should be discarded. We'll look at additional criteria for evaluating scientific explanations later in this chapter.

hypothesis A proposed explanation for a particular set of phenomena.

scientific theory An explanation for some aspect of the natural world based on well-substantiated facts, laws, inferences, and tested hypotheses.

discovery of the structure of DNA. Or a problem may be brought to the attention of a scientist by a politician, by a government agency, or by concerned citizens. For example, beginning in the fall of 2006, beekeepers in both North America and Europe began noticing that their honeybees were disappearing, with some reporting losses of as much as 90 percent of their hives.

2. Develop an Initial Hypothesis

Once a problem has been identified, the next step in the scientific method is to develop a working hypothesis. A **hypothesis** is basically an educated guess—a proposed explanation for a particular set of phenomena, which can serve as a starting point for further investigation. Several hypotheses were put forth regarding the cause of the collapse of the honeybee colonies, a phenomenon now called colony collapse disorder (CCD). Some researchers hypothesized that the use of insecticides known as neonicotinoids was responsible. Others thought a pathogen or fungus may be killing the bees. Still others suggested that radiation from cell phones may be interfering with honeybee navigation.

Hypotheses are put forth tentatively and may be changed on the basis of further observation. A scientific theory, on the other hand, is usually more complex and supported by previous work in the field. The U.S. National Academy of Sciences defines a **scientific theory** as "a well-substantiated explanation of some aspect of the natural world that can incorporate facts, laws, inferences, and tested hypotheses." Because the scientific method is inductive, scientists can never prove with absolute certainty that a theory or a hypothesis is true.

A well-formulated hypothesis uses precise language with key terms clearly defined. The scientific definition of

3. Gather Additional Information and Refine the Hypothesis

Since we cannot possibly take in all the sensory data coming at us, hypotheses are used to guide and focus the collection of additional information. Without a hypothesis to guide our observations, we don't know what is relevant and what to ignore.

*For a review of the different types of definitions, see Chapter 3, pages 74–77.

**For a review of hypothetical reasoning, see Chapter 8, pages 247–248.

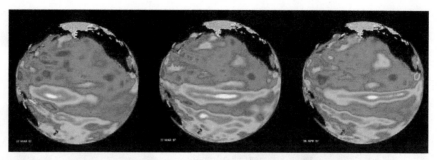

Since the 1970s, El Niño has become both more frequent and more intense. In these images, showing 3 months of sea surface temperature, the yellow and red areas indicate where waters are relatively warmer than average. El Niño contributed to massive snow blizzards in California in the winter of 2009–2010 and to the megastorms that struck the Midwest in 2012.

Scientific observation may be direct or indirect. To aid their senses and to minimize observer bias and cognitive and perceptual errors, scientists use instruments such as microscopes, telescopes, tape recorders, and stethoscopes.

The initial hypothesis may be modified on the basis of further observation. Since we can never be certain that our hypothesis is correct, collecting information is an ongoing process in science. It is vital that scientists strive to be as objective as possible and systematically record their observations without bias.

It may be only after an examination of their observations that scientists notice an unexpected pattern. When Charles Darwin as a young man of 22 traveled aboard a British naval vessel, the HMS *Beagle*, as the ship's naturalist, he collected specimens and took abundant notes on the flora and fauna of the Galapagos Islands. However, it wasn't until after he returned to England that he noticed patterns and from these, years later, developed his theory of evolution.

In collecting information, scientists avoid anecdotal and hearsay evidence. They are skeptical and do not accept at face value what people tell them, unless they have compelling firsthand evidence that what is being said is true. For example, as we learned in Chapter 7, people have a tendency to tell an interviewer what makes them look good or what they think the interviewer wants to hear.

As a graduate student in anthropology, Margaret Mead (1901–1978) was interested in finding out whether the troubles that plague adolescence in our culture are also found in so-called primitive or simpler cultures. Her hypothesis was that in these cultures, adolescence would present a different, less troubled, picture. To gather data, Mead lived with, observed, and interviewed sixty-eight young women, ages 9 to 20, in a small village in Samoa, an island in the South Pacific.

On the basis of her interviews, she concluded that Samoan girls experienced a carefree adolescence and engaged in casual sex from an early age, a finding that shocked many Westerners.[11] Many years later, the now-elderly Samoan women who had been interviewed by Mead confessed that they had lied to her, mainly as a joke. In this case, Mead's attachment to her hypothesis and her reliance on anecdotal evidence biased the way she gathered her information.

Scientists cannot rely on observations alone to determine whether a particular hypothesis is the best explanation of a phenomenon. Observations may be incomplete

Connections

What are the two types of precising definitions? *See Chapter 3, p. 75.*

What factors can bias scientists' efforts to gather evidence? *See Chapter 4, p. 116.*

How are inductive arguments using generalization used in the scientific method? *See Chapter 7, p. 206.*

Margaret Mead lived with Samoan villagers to conduct an observational study to test her hypothesis that adolescence in simpler cultures was more carefree for girls than in Western society. She is shown here, many years later, being interviewed about claims that some of the information she received was false.

ANALYZING IMAGES

1. Geospiza magnirostris.
3. Geospiza parvula.

2. Geospiza fortis.
4. Certhidea olivacea.

FINCHES FROM GALAPAGOS ARCHIPELAGO.

Darwin's Drawings of Galapagos Island Finch Beaks

DISCUSSION QUESTIONS

1. *Look at the drawings and create a list of possible explanations for the differences in the beaks of the finches.*

2. *Review the list of critical-thinking skills for reading scientific papers on page 384. Discuss the role that these skills played in Darwin's formulation of his theory of evolution.*

or biased because of poor collection methods, social expectations, or cognitive and perceptual errors. Instruments themselves may also be biased, since it is human inventors who determine what the instruments measure. For example, in the search for new life forms, both on Earth and beyond the Earth, scientists use instruments that measure the presence of DNA in soil, water, rock, and atmospheric samples. However, it is possible that non-DNA life forms exist (or once existed), such as those based on RNA.[12]

4. Test the Hypothesis

After completing the observations and data collection and refining the hypothesis, the next step in the scientific method is to test the hypothesis. Russell Hill and his fellow scientist Robert Barton tested the hypothesis about the relationship between a team's uniform color and winning by carrying out a study of team events at the 2004 Olympics.

Testing may also be done in a laboratory using a controlled experiment. To determine the effectiveness of a vaccine made from anthrax germs, Louis Pasteur designed an experiment in which he inoculated twenty-five animals with the vaccine. He also had a control group of twenty-five animals that did not receive the vaccine. Through scientific experimentation, he found that the vaccine was effective against anthrax. We'll be studying experimental design in more detail later in this chapter.

Testing a new hypothesis may take time if it depends on direct testing of empirical evidence that doesn't occur very often. For example, Einstein's theory of relativity predicted that the sun's gravitational pull would bend starlight. However, to test this prediction, scientists had to wait several years, until (in 1919) a total eclipse of the sun occurred. It may also take several years to thoroughly test a hypothesis. The Minnesota Twin Family Study is a longitudinal study begun in 1989 conducted to identify the genetic and environmental influences on psychological development. Researchers are following the development of more than 8,000 pairs of twins and their families. By carefully comparing traits in identical twins with those in fraternal twins, the researchers have been able to determine, for example, that about 40 percent of the variation in religious behavior, such as praying and attending religious services, is due to genetic rather than environmental factors.[13] The study is ongoing.

Testing and experimentation is a critical step in the scientific method, since some hypotheses that we assume to be true are, in fact, poorly supported and fall apart when tested. The more testing confirms one's hypothesis, the more confidence we can feel that the hypothesis is *probably* true. However, as we noted earlier, we will never be able to be absolutely certain that it is true.

5. Evaluate the Hypothesis on the Basis of Testing or Experimental Results

The last step in the scientific method is to evaluate the hypothesis using testing and experimentation. If the results or findings do not support the hypothesis, then scientists reject it and go back to step 2, come up with a new hypothesis, and repeat the process. We'll be learning how to interpret experimental results in the section "Evaluating an Experimental Design."

HIGHLIGHTS

THE SCIENTIFIC METHOD

1. Identify the problem

2. Develop an initial hypothesis

3. Gather additional information and refine the hypothesis

4. Test the hypothesis

5. Evaluate the hypothesis on the basis of results of testing or experimentation

➤ *APPLICATION: Identify an example in the text of each of the five steps.*

The scientific method is ongoing. Old hypotheses and theories may be revised or discarded in light of new evidence or be replaced by hypotheses with greater explanatory power. After four years of research into the cause of honeybee colony collapse, a 2010 study at Penn State College of Agriculture found unprecedented levels of a particular pesticide chemical in honeybees' pollen and hives.[14] However, this hypothesis, while one of the most promising, has yet to be substantiated. Because of uncertainty, it is important than scientists remain open-minded and do not overcommit to one hypothesis. Scientists are still exploring other explanations for CCD.[15]

Any theory, including those as well accepted as Darwin's theory of evolution or Einstein's theory of relativity, is always subject to replacement if new data contradicts it. In the next section we'll be examining some of the criteria used for evaluating scientific explanations.

STOP AND ASSESS YOURSELF

I. Working in small groups, come up with hypotheses to explain each of the following observations. Refine your hypotheses on the basis of feedback from the class.

*a. The moon looks larger when it is on the horizon than when it is high in the sky.

   b. During the past few years the number of American students attending Canadian colleges increased by 50 percent over the 2001 figure.[16]

   c. Since the 1950s, tens of thousands of people claim to have seen UFOs.

*d. Women are significantly underrepresented in senior faculty positions in science and math departments at Ivy League colleges.

   e. More than one out of eight babies in the United States is born at least 3 weeks before the due date. This represents a 36 percent increase since 1980.[17]

   f. Rates of the diagnosis of autism have risen dramatically in the past 30 years.

*g. Left-handed people die an average of 9 years earlier than the general population.[18]

   h. Eating fish regularly decreases the chance of stroke.

   i. The average person will lose five pounds a month by drinking two cups of green tea a day.

*j. Married people live about 3 years longer, on the average, than unmarried people.[19]

2. Select three of your hypotheses from the previous exercise and discuss what preliminary observations you might carry out to gather more information about them. Modify or refine your initial hypotheses on the basis of your observations and new information.

3. Select one of your hypotheses from question 2. Word the hypothesis in the form of a hypothetical argument. Discuss how you might test your hypothesis.

4. "The real purpose of [the] scientific method," writes Robert Pirsig, author of *Zen and the Art of Motorcycle Maintenance,* "is to make sure Nature hasn't misled you into thinking you know something you actually don't know." What do you think he meant by this? Relate your answer to the study of informal fallacies in Chapter 5 and the study of cognitive, perceptual, and social errors in Chapter 4.

5. Think of a problem or question in your life, such as why your car isn't getting better gas mileage, the most efficient way to study for an exam, or whether you should drink less coffee. Write an essay explaining how you would apply the scientific method to coming up with an answer to the problem.

6. Austrian zoologist Konrad Lorenz once gave the following advice: "It is a good morning exercise for a research scientist to discard a pet hypothesis every day before breakfast. It keeps him young."[†] What are some of your pet hypotheses about your life and the way the world works? Applying the characteristics of a critical thinker found in Chapter 1, decide whether you should discard some or all of these hypotheses.

*Answers to selected exercises are found in the Solutions Manual at the end of the book.
[†]Quoted in Singh Simon, "How a Big Idea Is Born," *New Scientist,* Vol. 184, Issue 2476, December 4, 2004, p. 23.

EVALUATING SCIENTIFIC HYPOTHESES

Different scientists observing the same phenomenon might come up with different hypotheses or explanations. We've already mentioned a few criteria for a good scientific hypothesis: It should be relevant to the problem under study, use precise language, and provide a testable explanation. Other criteria for evaluating a scientific explanation include consistency, simplicity, falsifiability, and predictive power.

Relevance to the Problem Under Study

First of all, a good hypothesis or explanation should be relevant to the problem under study. In other words, it should be related to the phenomenon it is intended to explain. Obviously, we cannot include all observations and facts in a hypothesis. Instead, we need to decide which are relevant to the problem under investigation. Polish chemist Marie Curie (1867–1934), for example, focused specifically on the atomic properties of radium and polonium in coming up with her initial hypothesis about the nature of radioactivity; Hill focused on the color of a sport team's uniform in his hypothesis.

Consistency with Well-Established Theories

Science is a system of logically consistent hypotheses or theories. Scientific explanations are preferred if they are consistent with well-established theories in the field—what American historian of science Thomas Kuhn refers to as "normal science." (We'll be studying Kuhn's concepts of normal science and paradigms later in this chapter.) This system forms a *paradigm*, or particular way of looking at and explaining the world. For example, the new hypothesis that "internal processes in the ocean such as the release of oceanic methane hydrate deposits that exist on the sea floor on continental margins are the primary cause of global warming" is considered a good hypothesis by environmental scientists since it is consistent with the established paradigm that global warming is the result of a combination of man-made and natural physical and chemical changes in the earth.

The intelligent design theory, on the other hand, does not meet this criterion because

it is inconsistent with the well-established theory of evolution (see "Critical Thinking Issue: Evolution versus Intelligent Design").

However, scientists do not automatically discard explanations that contradict well-established theories, especially if they meet the other criteria for a good explanation. Einstein's theory of relativity, which stated that time and space are relative, was not compatible with Newtonian physics, in which time and space are fixed and absolute. As it turned out, the theory of relativity—bizarre as it first sounded—turned out to be a better explanation of some phenomena. While Newton's theory remains a valid predictor at the level of phenomena that we can detect with our "normal" powers of observation, it fails at extreme conditions, such as those involving the speed of light (186,000 miles per second). Einstein's theory of relativity led to a radical rethinking of physics on the cosmic level.

Simplicity

If rival hypotheses or explanations both satisfy the basic criteria, scientists generally accept the one that is simpler, a logical principle known as Ockham's razor (named for the medieval philosopher William of Ockham). The great majority of scientists reject intelligent design theory because, among other reasons, the theory of evolution is simpler than that of intelligent design. The process of evolution alone, scientists argue, can explain the gradual development of complex organs such as the human eye, beginning with the light-sensitive cells that primitive organisms possess. There is no need to add the idea of an intelligent designer to the process.

Did You Know

Karl Popper believed that "Darwinism is not a testable scientific theory, but a metaphysical research program."[20]

On the other hand, there is nothing about the physical world itself that points to a preference for simplicity. Simplicity is a preference on the part of scientists. When there are competing hypotheses, the more complex hypothesis may turn out to be correct. For example, Einstein's theory of relativity failed the test of simplicity. However, it explained certain phenomena better and had more predictive power than the competing and simpler Newtonian theory of absolute space and time.

Thinking Outside the Box

ALBERT EINSTEIN, *Inventor*

One of Albert Einstein's high school teachers told his father: "It doesn't matter what he does—he will never amount to anything." However, young Einstein (1879–1955) was not one to let others' opinions determine the course of his life. A mediocre student in school, he preferred learning on his own and taught himself mathematics and science. Having a curious, creative, and analytical mind, he soon realized the inadequacies of Newtonian physics and by the age of sixteen had already developed the basics of his theory of relativity.

Einstein graduated from the Swiss Federal Polytechnic School at Zurich in 1900 with a degree in physics. Unable to find a teaching position, he accepted a job in the Swiss patent office. In his spare time he continued to work on physics and completed a doctorate in physics in 1905. In the same year he published the papers that introduced his theory of relativity and would later revolutionize physics. His papers were initially met with skepticism and ridicule. However, his theory eventually won support and in 1914 he was offered a professorship at the University of Berlin. In 1921 he won the Nobel Prize for physics.

By the 1930s Einstein, who was a Jew, was high on Hitler's enemy list. He moved to the United States in 1933 and accepted a position at the Institute for Advanced Research at Princeton, New Jersey. Einstein was a humanist and pacifist who saw science in its wider social context. Fearful that Germany was building an atomic bomb, he wrote a letter to President Franklin D. Roosevelt in 1939, urging him to develop the bomb first. He also stressed in his letters to the president that the bomb should never be used on people. He was appalled when the U.S. dropped the atomic bombs on Hiroshima, Japan.

After Hiroshima, Einstein became an anti-nuclear and anti-war activist, and a leading figure in the World Government Movement. He was invited to become president of Israel, an offer he declined. During his later years Einstein worked on the construction of a unified field theory in physics, which would reconcile his theory of relativity with the quantum theory, but never succeeded. He died in his sleep in 1955.

1. Referring to the moral principles and concerns discussed in Chapter 9, construct an argument about whether or not scientists have a moral obligation to refuse to engage in research that might be used to produce destructive technology.

2. In what ways might young Einstein's rebelliousness against authority have aided him in remaining open-minded and questioning established scientific paradigms? Relate your answer to your own attitudes toward accepted science.

Testability and Falsifiability

A hypothesis or explanation should be presented in a form that is testable and can be replicated by other scientists. In addition to being testable, an explanation must be able to be falsified.[21] Philosopher Karl Popper (1902–1994) pointed out that logically no number of positive experimental outcomes or observations can confirm a scientific theory; however, a single counter example is logically decisive since it proves that the theory is false. Therefore, one of the main tasks of a scientist in testing a hypothesis is the search for the negative, falsifying instances. For example, the hypothesis that "all swans are white" was based on observations of hundreds of thousands of swans, every one of which was white. However, the hypothesis was falsifiable, since it would take only one non-white swan to prove it false, which happened when black swans were discovered in Australia. Resistance to falsification is a constant struggle in science because of confirmation bias. A good scientist seeks evidence and carries out experiments that might falsify his or her theory.

On the other hand, theories that are able to accommodate all challenges have a critical weakness, because they cannot be tested for falsity. For example, Sigmund Freud's theories about the Oedipus complex fail the falsifiability criterion since, if a man claims that he does not have this complex, Freudians argue that he has repressed it into his unconscious.* However, unconscious thoughts, by their very nature, are untestable. Therefore, there is no way of falsifying Freud's theory.

Predictive Power

Finally, a good hypothesis or explanation has predictive power and can be used to accurately predict and explain the occurrence of similar events. The greater the predictive power, the more fruitful the hypothesis is. A hypothesis is fruitful if it suggests new ideas for future research.

The big bang theory, for example, was able to predict not only that the universe was expanding but also the amount of helium in the universe and the distribution of the galaxies. It alone was also able to explain the existence of microwave background radiation throughout the universe, which was first detected in 1965. Likewise, one of the reasons Einstein's theory of general relativity became so widely accepted was because of its predictive power. His theory of relativity predicted with greater accuracy certain eclipses than did Newton's theory.

pseudoscience A body of explanations or hypotheses that masquerades as science.

Good scientific explanations meet all or most of the criteria that we have described so far. In the subsection that follows, we'll be looking at the differences between scientific explanations or hypotheses and those of pseudoscience.

Distinguishing between Scientific and Pseudoscientific Hypotheses

Pseudoscience is a body of explanations or hypotheses that, in an attempt to gain legitimacy, masquerades as science. However, unlike science in which explanations are grounded in the scientific method, including systematic observation, reason, and testing, pseudoscience is based on emotional appeals, superstition, and rhetoric. Astrology, psychic healing, numerology (the study of numbers, such as one's date of birth or 9/11/2001, to determine their supernatural meaning), tarot card readings, and mind reading are all examples of pseudoscience.

While scientific explanations and hypotheses use precise wording, those of pseudoscience are usually framed in such ambiguous language that it is impossible to determine what would count as verification of the hypothesis. Astrological descriptions, for example, are usually so vague that they apply to anyone. Because of this, pseudoscientific claims are unfalsifiable.

Did You Know

Twenty-six percent of Americans believe in the accuracy of astrology.[22]

For the most part, no tests or experiments are carried out to check out the validity of pseudoscientific explanations. The few studies that are carried out, such as those on extrasensory perception or ghosts, are generally poorly designed and rarely replicable. Pseudoscience may also explain the failure of its explanations to stand up

*The Oedipus complex is the theory that young boys have sexual feelings toward their mothers that often involve rivalry with the father for the mother's affection. Freud considered this part of normal development.

ANALYZING **IMAGES**

Science Versus Pseudoscience

DISCUSSION QUESTIONS

1. *According to Gall polls, about ¼ of Americans believe in astrology. Referring back to Chapter 5 on informal fallacies, critically examine the claims that are used to support this conclusion.*

2. *Using the criteria discussed in this section, evaluate the hypothesis that astrology is a good scientific hypothesis.*

---

to scientific scrutiny by blaming the subject. For example, it might be said that a person was not healed by a faith healer because he or she did not have enough faith.

Pseudoscientific explanations also fail to meet the criteria of predictability. Most are so broadly worded that just about anything would bear out their predictions. Not surprisingly, most pseudoscientific predictions are done after the fact. Nostradamus, a sixteenth-century writer of prophecies, is today credited with foreseeing events such as the French Revolution, the rise of Nazism in Germany, and the September 11, 2001, attacks on the World Trade Center. Like the first two prophecies, the one that "predicted" 9/11 was brought to people's attention only *after* the attacks had already occurred.[23] Because the language used in prophecies tends to be so vague and

Nostradamus's prophecies tended to be so vague that they could only be "proven" after they had happened.

obscure, it can be manipulated to fit many similar events, as in the following example from Nostradamus that "predicted" 9/11.

> Ennosigee, fire of the center of the earth,
> Shall make an earthquake of the New City,
> Two great rocks shall long time war against each other,
> After that, Arethusa shall color red the fresh water.[24]

Despite its lack of scientific legitimacy, belief in pseudoscience is widespread.

Pseudoscience literally means "fake science." To avoid falling for the empty promises of pseudoscience, we need to know how to critically evaluate the claims of pseudoscience, using the criteria listed on page 384. We should also be aware of how cognitive and social errors can distort our thinking and make us vulnerable to the lure of pseudoscience.

HIGHLIGHTS

**CRITERIA FOR EVALUATING
A SCIENTIFIC HYPOTHESIS**

- Is it relevant to the problem under investigation?
- Is it consistent with well-established theories?
- Is it the simplest explanation for the problem?
- Does it provide a testable and falsifiable explanation of the problem?
- Can it be used to predict the outcome of similar events?

➤ *APPLICATION: Find an example in the text of an answer to each of the above questions.*

EXERCISE 12-3

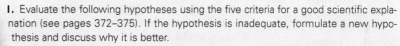

STOP AND ASSESS YOURSELF

1. Evaluate the following hypotheses using the five criteria for a good scientific explanation (see pages 372–375). If the hypothesis is inadequate, formulate a new hypothesis and discuss why it is better.

  *a. People who consume diet soda are more likely to gain weight than those who do not.

  b. Kwanda was having trouble with her computer. It would often freeze up when she was using her word processing program. She concluded that the problem must be a computer glitch.

  c. Pastor Luke Robinson believes that God inflicted his wrath on New York City in the form of Superstorm Sandy in response to Mayor Bloomberg's support of same-sex marriage.

  *d. Marijuana use leads to heroin addiction.

  e. Regular use of Facebook harms academic performance.

  f. Humans and dolphins are the only animals that engage in sex for fun.

  *g. Everything we do and everything that happens is determined by the original state of the universe.

  h. Having a pet cat or a dog increases a person's life expectancy.

  i. The avian flu is transmitted to humans through eating the flesh of an affected bird.

  *j. Whatever happens, happens for the best.

  k. The increase in carbon dioxide in the atmosphere is contributing to an increase in pollen-related allergies in people.

  l. In the new century a fire will erupt into the sky, bringing destruction on the land.

2. Polls find that young adults are more likely than older adults to believe in astrology. Why do you think this is the case? Relate your answer to the development of critical-thinking skills and the stages of cognitive development in Chapter 1.

3. Working in small groups, design and carry out an experiment to test for the existence of telepathy. Evaluate your findings.

4. Read your horoscope for the day in the newspaper or on the Internet. How accurate, in your opinion, is the prediction? Is the prediction falsifiable? Write down events that would definitively falsify the horoscope.

*Answers to selected exercises are found in the Solutions Manual at the end of the book.

RESEARCH METHODOLOGY AND SCIENTIFIC EXPERIMENTS

Scientists use research and experimentation to test their hypotheses. In this section, we'll look at the basics of research methodology and will examine three research methods that use experimentation: field experiments, controlled experiments, and single-group (pretest–posttest) experiments.

Research Methodology and Design

Research methodology is a systematic approach to gathering and analyzing information based on established scientific procedures and techniques. Experimentation is only one type of research method. **Scientific experiments** are carried out under controlled or semicontrolled conditions and involve systematic measurement and statistical analysis of data. Other research methods include observation, surveys, and interviews (see Chapter 7). For example, rather than carrying out an experiment in a laboratory under simulated sunlight or starlight, which are controlled conditions that scientists may use, ethnologist Jane Goodall used observation of chimpanzees in their natural habitat in Tanzania. Astronomer Arthur Eddington, in his research on the effect of gravity on light, used observation during a solar eclipse as a research method.

research methodology A systematic approach in science to gathering and analyzing information.

scientific experiment Research carried out under controlled or semicontrolled conditions.

independent variable The factor in a controlled experiment that is being manipulated.

dependent variable A factor in a controlled experiment that changes in response to the manipulation.

controlled experiment An experiment in which all variables are kept constant except for the independent variable(s).

In coming up with a research design, scientists need to consider which methodology is best suited to the hypothesis under investigation. For example, in astronomy and meteorology, although some experiments are carried out in laboratories using simulations, it is generally not feasible to use simulation experiments, since humans have little or no control over the variables that affect the action of celestial bodies or the weather.

In designing an experiment, scientists begin by writing up a plan in which they clearly define the purpose or objective of the experiment in terms of the hypothesis that is being tested, the variables that are going to be measured, and the type of measurement that will be used. The **independent variable** is the factor that the experimenter is manipulating, while the **dependent variable** is the one that changes in response to the manipulation. Sometimes the variables under study naturally fall into place in a relatively controlled setting without having to set up an experiment. Biologist Russell Hill, for example, was able to test his hypothesis by observing four combat events, such as boxing, at the 2004 Olympics. In these events, red and blue uniforms (the independent variable) were randomly assigned to each team. Hill found that the athletes who wore red uniforms beat the blue teams 60 percent of the time, a rate higher than probability.[25]

In a **controlled experiment**, all variables are kept constant except for the independent variable(s). Variables that are not accounted for or controlled by the experimental

Ethnologist Jane Goodall used observation as a research method to test her hypothesis that chimpanzees use tools.

design are known as **confounding variables**. This is particularly a problem in field experiments and observational research.

Experimental material is the group or class of objects or subjects that is being studied, such as pea plants, light rays, or college freshmen. If a sample is going to be used, it should be precisely defined in terms of how large it will be and how it will be selected.[26] It is also important that the sample be representative of the population under study.

In addition, ethical considerations may place restrictions on what type of experimental design is suitable. For example, it would be unethical to use a controlled experiment to research the effects of smoking on children by randomly assigning half the children to a group where they are made to smoke. Instead mice or other lab animals are used as subjects, a practice that raises ethical concerns with some people, such as animal rights activists, as well as those who note that experiments done on animal models cannot always be generalized to humans.

Field Experiments

In some cases, studying a phenomenon in its natural setting may be the best method of testing a hypothesis. Field experiments use contrived situations designed to appear to the study subjects as natural occurrences. Two or more similar groups of study subjects are nonrandomly assigned to different treatments or experimental interventions. The groups are then compared to determine the effect of the treatment variable.

For example, to test their hypothesis that "bystanders are more likely to aid victims of their own race than those of a different race," psychologists Daniel Wegner and William Crano used a field experiment. An experimenter would "accidentally" drop a deck of cards he or she was carrying in a campus building when he or she was one step away from a preselected study subject. The study subjects were unaware of the design of the experiment.[27]

If the study subject immediately helped the experimenter, the actions were recorded as an instance of helping. The data were then analyzed, comparing the difference in performance between groups on the basis of their race.

Hot or Not?

Are field experiments real scientific experiments?

The disadvantage of field experiments is that natural conditions cannot be controlled and manipulated as easily as conditions in a laboratory setting. For example, the study subjects in the Wegner and Crano field experiment might have been stressed because of final exams and therefore not as willing to stop and help as they might have otherwise been. Also, the assumption that the groups were similar in all respects except for race is questionable.

Controlled Experiments

Some people regard field experiments as quasi-experiments and maintain that controlled experiments are the only true type of scientific experiment. Controlled experiments are used to determine whether there is a causal relationship between the independent and dependent variable. To rule out other confounding causal variables that may be responsible for a change, in a controlled experiment there is generally only one independent variable. To ensure that both groups are virtually identical, study subjects are randomly assigned to an experimental or control group. The experimental group receives the treatment (independent variable), while the control group does not receive it. With human study subjects, participants do not know whether they are in the experimental or control group. The results obtained from each group are then compared and statistically analyzed to determine the effect of the treatment or independent variable.

Although there are several variations on the research design in a controlled experiment, the basic design is this:

Experimental Group:
Random Assignment ⟶ Treatment ⟶ Posttest
Control Group:
Random Assignment ⟶ Placebo ⟶ Posttest

confounding variable A factor that is not accounted for or controlled by the experimental design.

experimental material The group or class of objects or subjects that is being studied in an experiment.

Connections

What types of bias and errors in thinking are reduced by the use of an appropriate research design? *See Chapter 4, p. 108.*

What types of sampling errors might occur in scientific research? *See Chapter 5, p. 148, and Chapter 7, pp. 207–208.*

PLATE IV.—MENDELIAN INHERITANCE OF THE COLOUR OF THE FLOWER IN THE CULINARY PEA

Two flowers of a plant of a pink-flowered race.   Two flowers of a plant produced by crossing the pink with the white.   Two flowers of a plant of a white-flowered race.

How do controlled experiments involve the use of inductive causal arguments? *See Chapter 7, p. 225.*

Connections

placebo A substance used in experiments that has no therapeutic effect.

In Augustinian monk Gregor Mendel's (1822–1884) famous experiments on heredity in successive generations of pea plant hybrids, he controlled for the influence of environment on traits by carrying out his experiments in a laboratory setting where variables such as light, heat, and water were kept constant, leaving only genes as the independent variable. His methodology, which established the foundations of the modern science of genetics, was radical at the time and provided a model for future research in science.

The advantage of doing a controlled experiment is that scientists have more control over the different variables that might affect the outcome of the study. One of the potential disadvantages is that human study subjects know they are part of an experiment and adjust their expectations accordingly. This is particularly problematic in medical and psychology research.

To ensure that receiving the treatment does not confound the outcome, the control group may be given a placebo. A **placebo** is a substance, such as a sugar pill or a bogus treatment, which has no therapeutic effect.

Placebos are used because the influence of expectation and self-fulfilling prophecies is so powerful that if study subjects believe that they may be receiving a particular beneficial treatment, their condition often actually improves even though they are getting only a placebo.

Single-Group (Pretest–Posttest) Experiments

Instead of using a control group and an experimental group, a *single-group experiment* uses only one group of study subjects. The variable under investigation is measured by a pretest before the intervention and again with a posttest after the intervention. Generally the same test is used in both the pre- and posttest.

Single Group:
Pretest ⟶ Treatment ⟶ Posttest

For example, in studying the effect of community service on moral reasoning, the Defining Issues Test (DIT)—a test of moral reasoning—is administered to a group of college students before their community service and then again at the end of the semester after they complete the service. It was found that the students score significantly higher on the DIT at the end of the semester.[28] Can we conclude from this that community service (the independent variable) was responsible for the improvement in the scores (the dependent variable)? No, we can't, not with the same degree of certainty that we could if there was a control group.

One of the weaknesses of the single-group study is that without a control group, it doesn't control for other

Critical THiNKing in Action

Science and Prayer

A controlled experiment conducted by Harvard scientists found that therapeutic inter-cessory prayer provided no health benefits to patients recovering from cardiac bypass surgery.* Eighteen hundred patients were randomly assigned to experimental and control groups. The experimental group was divided into those who knew they were being prayed for and those who did not know but in fact were being prayed for. The control group did not know whether they were being prayed for and, as the control, were not being prayed for. The first names of those in the two groups receiving prayers were given to members of two Catholic monasteries and one Protestant group. They each offered up the same prayer for 30 days for the names on their lists asking for "a successful surgery and a quick, healthy recovery and no complications." There was no statistical difference in the recovery of the three groups.

Does this study prove that prayer does not work? "I am always a little leery about intercessory prayer," says Rev. Dean Marek. "What we have in mind for someone else may not be what they have in mind for themselves. . . . It is clearly manipulative of divine action and personal choice." Another critic of the study states that "science is powerful and wonderful in determining the orbit of the Earth, . . . the power of a new drug. But now we've asked science to study something that occurs outside of space and time. This shows you shouldn't try to prove the power of the supernatural."**

DISCUSSION QUESTIONS

1. Evaluate the experimental design in this study. Does this study prove that prayer does not work? Are the criticisms of the study valid? If so, explain how you might go about improving the design of the study.

2. Do you personally believe that prayer works? In answering this, provide an operational definition of *prayer*. In other words, what do you mean in terms of observable, measurable effects when you say that prayer does or does not work? Discuss what evidence supports your belief regarding the effectiveness of prayer.

*H. Benson et al., "Study of the Therapeutic Effects of Intercessory Prayer (STEP) in Cardiac Bypass Patients: A Multicenter Randomized Trial of Uncertainty and Certainty of Receiving Intercessory Prayer," *American Heart Journal*, Vol. 151, Issue 4, April 15, 2006, pp. 762–764.

**Quotes from Denise Gellene and Thomas H. Maugh II, "Largest Study of Prayer to Date Finds It Has No Power to Heal," *Los Angeles Times*, March 31, 2006, p. A-8.

variables that might be affecting the outcome, such as maturation and familiarity with the test from the pretest. For this reason, single-group studies, because they are easier to set up and administer than studies with control groups, are often used as exploratory experiments, which, if the results are promising, are followed up with a controlled experiment.

In some research, however, single-group experiments may be preferable to controlled experiments, especially when it is clear that the variable under study is having a significant positive effect on the experimental group. For example, a new cancer drug is being tested on children with leukemia using a controlled experiment. After 3 months it is found that the children taking the new drug are doing significantly better than those taking the placebo. At this point the experimenters have an ethical obligation to stop the controlled experiment and switch to a single-group experimental design in which all the children are receiving the drug.

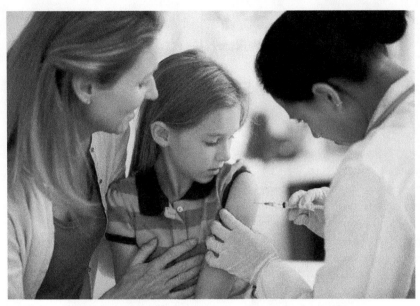

Sometimes single-group experiments are necessary, such as when a drug is found right away to be very effective.

Evaluating an Experimental Design

As we noted, there are several types of experimental design. However, good designs all have certain characteristics in common. One of the foremost is being able to *discriminate between different hypotheses*. If the same experimental results can be used to support two competing hypotheses, then the experiment was poorly designed. For example, you decide to conduct an experiment to test your hypothesis that hanging garlic on your front door will keep vampires away. You hang up the garlic and use a hidden camera to record the number of vampire visits during the next month. No vampires come to your house during the month. Does this prove your hypothesis that garlic keeps vampires away? Not necessarily, because the results of your experiment also support the competing hypothesis that vampires don't exist.

A well-designed experiment is *unbiased*. It uses checks and controls to minimize experimental error, which can result from small sample size, an unrepresentative sample, or subject or experimenter bias. A 1998 study published in the *Lancet*, a British medical journal, suggesting a link between autism and childhood vaccinations was based on testing of only twelve children with autism; there was no control group for comparison. Unfortunately, the media publicized these findings and many parents took them seriously, despite scientists' criticisms of

Why is being aware of confirmation bias and the fallacy of questionable cause important in evaluating scientific evidence?
See Chapter 1, p. 8 and Chapter 5, p. 155.

Connections

Hot or Not?
Should pregnant women, or women who might become pregnant, be allowed to participate in drug tests?

the experimental design and the lack of corroborating evidence.

This explanation of autism has since been called into question. Scientists in Denmark have carried out a 20-year unbiased study of nearly 700,000 births and have discovered that certain factors in the pregnant mother, such as rheumatoid arthritis, celiac disease, and other autoimmune disorders, significantly elevate their child's probability of having autism. These scientists have also found that women living in areas where they are exposed to parasites and microbes have stronger immune systems and are less likely to have autoimmune disorders and children with autism. While they acknowledge that what they have are correlations, scientists plan to carry out further studies to look for causal connections.[29]

A third criterion of a good design is that the *measurements of the outcome of the variable under investigation are reliable as well as accurate and precise*. Measurement tools are reliable if they provide consistency of results over time and when used by different people. An IQ test is reliable if it gives the same results when used by two different experimenters on study subjects and if the results remain consistent when the test is used on the same study subject over a period of time.

An accurate measurement is one that is consistent with other standards used for measuring a phenomenon. Measurement should also be precise. Precision depends on the problem under investigation. Days or even years may be a precise enough measurement of time in a study of the effect of global warming on the retreat of glaciers in Alaska. However, we need a more precise definition of time for calculating the timing of chain reactions in nuclear fission, which are measured in milliseconds.

Accurate and precise measurements allow the experiment to be *replicated or reproduced* by other scientists. One of the purposes of writing up experiments in a scientific journal is to provide enough details on the experimental design so that other scientists can replicate it—that is, run the same experiment and obtain the same results. Replicability is necessary because the results of one study might have occurred by chance, might have used a faulty sample, or might even have been fabricated (see pages 384–385).

The final criterion is *generalizability*. A well-designed experiment produces results that can be generalized from the sample used in the experiment. A problem with generalizability occurs when the sample in a study is not representative of the overall population that it is supposed to represent. Prior to the 1980s, most medical and psychological studies used only white males as study subjects. However, when scientists generalized the results to all people, they sometimes ran into problems. For example, we have since learned that women wake up earlier from anesthesia than do men—a fact that could have easily led to horrific surgical experiences for female patients. In 1985, the U.S. Food and Drug Administration began requiring clinical trials sponsored by drug manufacturers to include data about sex as well as age and race.

Interpreting Experimental Results

Once an experiment is complete and the data have been analyzed, the results are usually published in a scientific journal. Most scientific journals, though not all, require that articles published in them follow the organization outlined in "Critical Thinking in Action: How to Read a Scientific Paper." Some prestigious scientific journals, such as *Science* and *Nature*, which appeal to a wider audience, have space limitations, and thus some sections in articles may be condensed or combined.

The results section in a scientific paper provides information on how the data were analyzed and which findings were statistically significant. Experimental results are generally expressed in terms of averages or correlations between variables. Experimental results that falsify (that is, disprove) a hypothesis are just as important to scientific knowledge as those that support a hypothesis.

Each time an experiment is replicated with a new sample and significant results are obtained, the confidence level becomes higher, since the total sample size tested becomes larger. If the results are not replicated in subsequent experiments, the hypothesis should be reexamined.

Hot or Not?

Is it desirable, or even possible, for science to be value-neutral?

Ethical Concerns in Scientific Experimentation

A scientific experiment may be well designed and produce significant results but still be inappropriate because it violates moral principles and guidelines. Ethical considerations of informed consent, rights, and nonmaleficence (no harm) are particularly important when working with human study subjects.

Some of the most unethical scientific experiments were those performed on Jews, prisoners of war, and other captives in Nazi concentration camps. Members of marginalized groups have also been used, without their consent, in scientific experiments in other countries. Between 1930 and 1953 the U.S. Department of Health Services conducted a study of the effects of syphilis, known as the Tuskegee study, using poor black men living in Macon County, Alabama. None of the men were told that they had syphilis, and no attempt was made to treat them. The study continued even after penicillin was discovered as a cure, resulting in the death of many of the men purely for the sake of advancing scientific knowledge.

Since the 1970s there has been growing concern for the rights of human subjects in scientific experiments. Studies like the 1963 Milgram experiment and the 1971 Stanford Prison experiment (both discussed in Chapter 1), which put people at risk for psychological or physical harm, are today considered unethical.

The concept of the neutrality of science and ethical concerns over the use of scientific results for unethical purposes was poignantly raised by the creation of the atomic bomb. Albert Einstein, who was involved in launching the American effort to build a nuclear weapon during World War II, came to regret his

---

HIGHLIGHTS

CRITERIA FOR A WELL-DESIGNED EXPERIMENT

- **Unbiased:** The experiment has checks or uses controls to eliminate the possibility of subject and experimenter bias

- **Measurement:** The measurements used are appropriate and reliable as well as accurate and precise

- **Replicable:** The experiment can be reproduced by other scientists

- **Generality:** The experimental results can be generalized to the population under study

▶ *APPLICATION: Find an example in the text of the application of each of these criteria.*

Connections

How can an understanding of moral reasoning and moral principles help us recognize and avoid ethical problems in scientific experiments?
See Chapter 9, p. 274.

Critical THiNKing in Action

How to Read a Scientific Paper

A paper in a scientific journal is usually organized as follows:

- **Abstract:** A brief summary of the major findings of the study
- **Introduction:** The hypothesis under investigation and background information on similar studies
- **Methods:** Detailed description of the experimental design, including the specific procedures and methods used, and the experimental material used, such as the sample, and how it was selected
- **Results:** Review of the rationale for the experiment and an explanation of how the data were analyzed and summary of which findings were statistically significant; may include graphs and tables summarizing results
- **Discussion:** An analysis and interpretation of the data, an explanation of how the findings logically follow from the data, and a discussion of the significance of the findings and how they contribute to the field as well as the limitations of the study and suggestions for future research
- **References:** List of articles, books, and other works cited from which information was drawn

1. Select an article from a scientific journal that interests you. After reading its abstract and introduction, read the methods sections and evaluate the experimental design in terms of whether it meets the criteria of a well-designed experiment. Describe any limitations in the design and ways in which it might be improved.

2. Read the results and discussion section of the paper. Discuss whether the conclusions of the paper are supported by the experimental findings. Discuss some of the implications of this study for future research.

> It is up to the community of scientists to employ their critical-thinking skills to analyze the work of other scientists in their field and to expose frauds.

role in its creation, calling his part in it the "one great mistake" in his life. More recently, ethical concerns are being raised about genetic engineering research and the possibility of human cloning.

Ethical considerations in scientific experimentation and reporting of research findings also include integrity and honesty on the part of scientists. In cases in which research is government-funded, pressure may be brought to bear on scientists to report findings to the public in a way that is consistent with the current political agenda. For example, officials in the Bush administration had intervened to weaken and even delete sections in reports by Environmental Protection Agency scientists regarding the extent of

Scientists' role in the creation of the atomic bomb raised ethical concerns among some scientists.

global warming and the role of industry in global warming. In addition, because the promotion process is often dependent on publications—the enormous pressure to "publish or perish"—scientists may exaggerate results or be selective in what they choose to report.[30]

Research carried out on behalf of pharmaceutical companies may be unreliable because of pressure to get findings published and to get a new drug on the market. New drugs may be compared against inferior, ineffective drugs that are already on the market. In addition, observations are often carried out on a small number of cases without proper controls, and data for outcomes may be based on biased reports or self-reported symptoms ("my chest felt better") rather than survival rates. Indeed, one study estimated that "as much as 90 percent of published medical information" that doctors rely on is based on flawed research.[31]

It is up to the community of scientists to employ their critical-thinking skills to analyze the work of other scientists in their field and to expose frauds. Although peer review is an effective process for safeguarding against ethical wrongdoing, procedural errors, and fraud, reviewers tend to reject for publication scientific hypotheses and studies that fall outside the established norms in science. In the next section, we'll be looking at paradigms in normal science.

EXERCISE 12-4

STOP AND ASSESS YOURSELF

1. Discuss which type of experimental design would be best for testing each of the following hypotheses and why:

*a. Fred noticed that his hens as well as those on the neighboring farm laid more eggs when the children were away at summer camp in June and July. He hypothesized that the children's absence caused the hens to lay more eggs.

b. Students who drink a cup of coffee before a test perform better than those who do not.

c. Men are more likely to look at women who have blond hair than women who have brown or black hair.

*d. Taking antibiotics doubles a woman's risk of getting breast cancer.

e. Nonhuman mammals are able to anticipate an earthquake or tsunami hours before it strikes.

f. Good-looking couples are more likely to have daughters.

*g. Computers are conscious.

2. Read the article by Russell Hill and Robert Barton in the May 19, 2005, issue of *Nature*.[32] Evaluate the experimental design used by Hill and Barton in their study of the effect of the color red on winning, as well as the significance of their results. Working in small groups, design an experiment to test their experimental results regarding the relationship between color of team uniform and winning.

3. Millions of men take drugs such as Viagra for erectile dysfunction, but are these drugs safe? According to a 2005 report, forty-three men who had taken Viagra had developed a form of blindness. The question now facing researchers is: "Was Viagra a causal factor?" The Food and Drug Administration has hired you to come up with a controlled experiment to test this question. Working in small groups, develop an experimental design to test the hypothesis.

4. Discuss the use of placebos in controlled experiments. Is their use immoral because it involves deception? Present a logical argument to support your conclusion.

5. Psychology professors sometimes use their students as subjects in experiments or studies and may even require that students participate as part of their grade in the course. Discuss the ethical issues involved in this practice.

6. Nazi experiments on hypothermia involved submerging prisoners for long periods of time in icy water. Although the experiments resulted in the death of many of the study subjects, they were well-designed experiments that yielded valuable results, which could save the lives of people who have hypothermia. Analyze whether it is morally acceptable to use the data from these and other Nazi death camp experiments to save the lives of people.

7. Bring in an example of a graph or table from a science journal, textbook, or a Web site. Discuss how the use of visuals makes it easier to understand the significance of the results.

8. Look for an article in the mass media, or a news clip, that reports the results of a scientific study. Find a copy of the original scientific article written by the scientists who did the study. How accurately did the mass media report the study? Looking back at the discussion of mass media in Chapter 11, discuss why the media sometimes distort, either intentionally or unintentionally, scientific findings.

*Answers to selected exercises are found in the Solutions Manual at the end of the book.

THOMAS KUHN AND SCIENTIFIC PARADIGMS

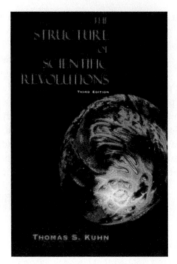

In his landmark book, *The Structure of Scientific Revolutions* (1962), American physicist and historian of science Thomas Kuhn (1922–1996) challenged the idea that the scientific method is objective and that science is progressive. He argued that science, like other human enterprises, is a social construct—a product of its society. As such, it is biased by social expectations and professional norms that determine what is an acceptable hypothesis.

Normal Science and Paradigms

Kuhn put forward three key concepts: normal science, paradigms, and scientific revolutions. **Normal science** refers to "research firmly based upon one or more past scientific achievements, achievements that some particular scientific community acknowledges for a time as supplying the foundation of its further practice."[33] Normal science is conveyed in science journals and textbooks.

> **normal science** Scientific research that is based on past achievements and is recognized by most scientists.
>
> **paradigm** The accepted view of what the world is like and how we should go about studying it.
>
> **scientific revolution** A paradigm shift in which a new scientific theory replaces a problematic paradigm.

The achievements of normal science provide paradigms or models for research in the field. A **paradigm** is the accepted view of what the world is like and how we should go about studying it. A paradigm becomes part of normal science if it is both successful in solving problems that scientists are working on and also able to attract a large group of adherents.

Paradigms, according to Kuhn, can influence not only what is considered to be a problem worth studying but also our actual perceptions of a phenomenon. For example, it is a current paradigm in science that consciousness is organically based and therefore will never be emulated by computers or artificial intelligence (AI). Consequently, the majority of scientists perceive the actions or operations of computers, even intelligent ones, in purely mechanical terms.

Although normal science is tremendously successful in generating results and new technology, Kuhn argued that it does not seek novelty. This in turn contributes to confirmation bias. When an anomaly is found, it is often dismissed out of hand, or scientists may try to reconcile it to the existing paradigm. For example, the orbit of Mars was an anomaly that could not be explained by the old geocentric (Earth-centered) paradigm of the universe and hence was ignored for many years by Western scholars until Copernicus.

Scientific Revolutions and Paradigm Shifts

Scientific progress, according to Kuhn, is not strictly linear—that is, it does not proceed in a straight line. A crisis, Kuhn argues, is necessary for the emergence of a new paradigm. If anomalies persist or cannot be explained by the current paradigm, a "crisis" may occur that leads to a rejection of the old paradigm.

A **scientific revolution**, or paradigm shift, occurs when a new scientific theory is made available to replace a problematic paradigm. Copernicus's theory that the Earth goes around the sun, Einstein's theory of relativity, German earth scientist Alfred Wegener's tectonic-plate or continental-drift theory, and Darwin's theory of human evolution all represented paradigm shifts in their respective fields.

A paradigm shift requires a new way of looking at the world and may take several decades to complete. It is

When the author was in elementary school, one of her classmates pointed to the world map on the wall and excitedly pointed out that Africa and Europe fit into North and South America like a puzzle, asking if they used to be part of one great continent. She thought that the student made a great point and was quite excited by her "discovery." However, the idea was ridiculed at length by the teacher as preposterous and unscientific (pseudoscience). It wasn't until years later that continental-drift theory, which had been proposed as early as 1912 by Alfred Wegener, became accepted by the scientific community. This experience, and the importance of keeping an open mind, has always stuck with her.

especially difficult for scientists who have been brought up and worked under the old paradigm to make the shift. Since they have invested years of their lives as well as their professional reputations in proving a particular theory, most will defend it vigorously when challenged, even in the face of contradictory evidence.

Those who fail to conform to the standards of normal science are often ridiculed as frauds, and their research findings get rejected by mainstream scientific journals. When Wegener first proposed the theory of continental drift in 1912, he too was attacked by his fellow scientists. The idea that something as large as a continent could move was considered ludicrous. However, by the early 1960s the evidence for the tectonic-plate and continental-drift theory eventually became so overwhelming that it could no longer be ignored.

New paradigms generally win adherents from young scientists and people who are new to or outside of the field and are not heavily invested in the old paradigm. For example, Einstein was only 26 when in 1905 he first published his hypothesis regarding relativity.

Kuhn's critique of normal science has been tremendously valuable in making scientists and others more aware of the role that social expectations and confirmation bias play in science. As critical thinkers, we need to be aware of the assumptions and paradigms of normal science and to remain open-minded to hypotheses that might not conform to these norms. In evaluating a new hypothesis, we should apply the criteria discussed in this chapter rather than dismissing the hypothesis because it does not conform to the paradigms of normal science.

EXERCISE 12-5

STOP AND ASSESS YOURSELF

1. Looking back at the list of assumptions at the beginning of this chapter on pages 363–364, discuss how they have shaped the current paradigms in science. Use specific examples.

2. In Chapter 2 we studied artificial intelligence (AI). Identify at least one hypothesis in this relatively new field that challenges some of the accepted paradigms of normal science. Discuss what scientific findings regarding AI would be most likely to precipitate a scientific revolution and why.

3. Discuss, hypothetically, what evidence in the field of human evolution would result in a paradigm shift and giving up the savannah theory (that humans originated on the grassy plains of Africa) for a new paradigm.

THiNK AGAIN

1. What is the scientific method?
   - The scientific method, which was first systematized by Francis Bacon, involves the identification of a problem and the rigorous, systematic application of observation and experimentation in testing an explanation for the problem.

2. How does science differ from pseudoscience?
   - Pseudoscience is a body of explanations or hypotheses that are based on emotional appeals, superstition, and rhetoric rather than scientific observation, reasoning, and testing. Furthermore, unlike scientific hypotheses, those of pseudoscience are often worded so vaguely as to be untestable.

3. What are some of the different types of scientific experiments and research methods?
   - Scientific experiments are carried out under controlled or semicontrolled conditions and involve systematic measurement and statistical analysis of data. Other research methods include observation, surveys, and interviews.

Evolution versus Intelligent Design

The legal conflict between religion and science in the classrooms dates back to 1925 when the judge in the Scopes Monkey Trial ruled that it was illegal for public schools to teach anything that contradicted the Biblical story of creation. In 1987, this ruling was reversed in *Edwards v. Aguillard* when the U.S. Supreme Court ruled that creationism was a religious theory and that teaching it in schools violated the Constitutional separation of church and state.

The conflict has recently resurfaced under the banner of intelligent design (ID) versus evolution. The theory of ID was developed in the 1980s by a group of scientists who argued that some biological structures are so complex that they can't be the result of natural selection but can be explained only by the existence of an intelligent designer.

ID is presented by its proponents as an evidence-based scientific theory. Evolutionists argue that ID is not a scientific theory at all but a religious viewpoint, since it requires a supernatural explanation of the beginning of life. In addition, evolution by natural selection does a better job of explaining the available fossil and DNA evidence and is supported by 150 years of research.

The majority of scientists (87 percent) believe that living things have evolved due to natural processes, a belief that is shared by only about one-third (32 percent) of the public.* A 2012 poll showed that 46 percent believe the ID view that God created humans in their present form within the last 10,000 years.**

*Pew Research Center for People & the Press, "Public Praises Science; Scientists Fault Public, Media," July 9, 2009. http://www.people-press.org/2009/07/09/public-praises-science-scientists-fault-public-media.
**Gallup Poll, Evolution, Creationism, Intelligent Design. http://www.gallup.com/poll/21814/evolution-creationism-intelligent-design.aspx.

In a highly publicized trial, the American Civil Liberties Union brought suit against the School Board of Dover, Pennsylvania, for requiring high school biology teachers to teach ID theory alongside the theory of evolution. In 2005, Judge John E. Jones ruled against the school board, stating that there was "overwhelming evidence" that intelligence design was not a scientific theory and that "ID cannot uncouple itself from its creationist, and thus religious antecedents."[†] As such, it violates the First Amendment clause regarding separation of church and state.

Both Michael Behe and Kenneth Miller, whose views are included here, participated as expert witnesses in the Dover School Board trial. In the first reading, Michael Behe argues that ID theory and the concept of irreducible complexity is the best scientific explanation for life. Kenneth Miller's article offers a response to Behe's argument. In it, Miller contends that scientific evidence does not support ID theory but rather is consistent with the theory of evolution.

[†]Kitzmiller v. Dover Area School District, United States District Court for the Middle District of Pennsylvania, December 20, 2005, Case No. 04cv2688. http:www.pamd.uscourts.gov/kitzmiller/kitzmiller_342.pdf.

Irreducible Complexity: Obstacle to Darwinian Evolution*

MICHAEL BEHE

Biochemist Michael Behe is a professor of biological sciences at Lehigh University. He maintains that Darwin's theory of evolution is unable to explain the origin of life and that only an intelligent designer could have created the irreducible complexities of cellular organisms.

In his seminal work *On the Origin of Species*, Darwin hoped to explain what no one had been able to explain before—how the variety and complexity of the living world might have been produced by simple natural laws. His idea for doing so was, of course, the theory of evolution by natural selection. . . .

It was an elegant idea, and many scientists of the time quickly saw that it could explain many things about biology. However, there remained an important reason for reserving judgment about whether it could actually account for all of biology: the basis of life was as yet unknown. . . .

In light of the enormous progress made by science since Darwin first proposed his theory, it is reasonable to ask if the theory still seems to be a good explanation for life. In *Darwin's Black Box: The Biochemical Challenge to Evolution* (Behe 1996), I argued that it is not. The main difficulty for Darwinian mechanisms is that many systems in the cell are what I termed "irreducibly complex." I defined an irreducibly complex system as: a single system that is necessarily composed of several well-matched, interacting parts that contribute to the basic function, and where the removal of any one of the parts causes the system to effectively cease functioning (Behe 2001). As an example from everyday life of an irreducibly complex system, I pointed to a mechanical mousetrap such as one finds in a hardware store. Typically, such traps have a

number of parts: a spring, a wooden platform, a hammer, and other pieces. If one removes a piece from the trap, it can't catch mice. . . .

Irreducibly complex systems seem very difficult to fit into a Darwinian framework, for a reason insisted upon by Darwin himself. In the *Origin*, Darwin wrote that "[i]f it could be demonstrated that any complex organ existed which could not possibly have been formed by numerous, successive, slight modifications, my theory would absolutely break down. But I can find out no such case" (Darwin 1859, 158). Here Darwin was emphasizing that his was a gradual theory. Natural selection had to improve systems by tiny steps, over a long period of time. . . . However, it is hard to see how something like a mousetrap could arise gradually by something akin to a Darwinian process. For example, a spring by itself, or a platform by itself, would not catch mice, and adding a piece to the first nonfunctioning piece wouldn't make a trap either. So it appears that irreducibly complex biological systems would present a considerable obstacle to Darwinian evolution.

The question then becomes, are there any irreducibly complex systems in the cell? Are there any irreducibly complex molecular machines? Yes, there are many. In *Darwin's Black Box*, I discussed several biochemical systems as examples of irreducible complexity: the eukaryotic cilium, the intracellular transport system, and more. Here I will just briefly describe the bacterial flagellum. . . . The flagellum can be thought of as an outboard motor that bacteria use to swim. It was the first truly rotary structure discovered in nature. It consists of a long filamentous tail that acts as a propeller; when it is spun, it

*Michael Behe, "Irreducible Complexity: Obstacle to Darwinian Evolution." In W. A. Dembski and M. Ruse, *From Darwin to DNA* (Cambridge, MA: Cambridge University Press, 2004), pp. 352–370.

pushes against the liquid medium and can propel the bacterium forward. The propeller is attached to the drive shaft indirectly through something called the hook region, which acts as a universal joint. The drive shaft is attached to the motor, which uses a flow of acid or sodium ions from the outside to the inside of the cell to power rotation. Just as an outboard motor has to be kept stationary on a motorboat while the propeller turns, there are proteins that act as a stator structure to keep the flagellum in place. . . .

As with the mousetrap, it is quite difficult to see how Darwin's gradualistic process of natural selection sifting random mutations could produce the bacterial flagellum, since many pieces are required before its function appears. . . .

Second, a more subtle problem is how the parts assemble themselves into a whole. The analogy to an outboard motor fails in one respect: an outboard motor is generally assembled under the direction of a human—an intelligent agent who can specify which parts are attached to which other parts. The information for assembling a bacterial flagellum, however (or, indeed, for assembling any biomolecular machine), resides in the component proteins of the structure itself. . . . Thus, even if we had a hypothetical cell in which proteins homologous to all of the parts of the flagellum were present (perhaps performing jobs other than propulsion) but were missing the information on how to assemble themselves into a flagellum, we would still not get the structure. The problem of irreducibility would remain.

Because of such considerations, I have concluded that Darwinian processes are not promising explanations for many biochemical systems in the cell. Instead, I have noted that, if one looks at the interactions of the components of the flagellum, or cilium, or other irreducibly complex cellular system, they look like they were designed—purposely designed by an intelligent agent. . . .

Rather than showing how their theory could handle the obstacle, some Darwinists are hoping to get around irreducible complexity by verbal tap dancing. . . . Kenneth Miller actually claimed . . . that a mousetrap isn't irreducibly complex because subsets of a mousetrap, and even each individual part, could still "function" on their own. The holding bar of a mousetrap, Miller observed, could be used as *a toothpick*, so it still has a "function" outside the mousetrap. Any of the parts of the trap could be used as a paperweight, he continued, so they all have "functions." And since any object that has mass can be a paperweight, then any part of anything has a function of its own. *Presto*, there is no such thing as irreducible complexity!

. . . Of course, the facile explanation rests on a transparent fallacy, a brazen equivocation. Miller uses the word "function" in two different senses. Recall that the definition of irreducible complexity notes that removal of a part "causes the *system* to effectively cease functioning." Without saying so, in his exposition Miller shifts the focus from the separate function of the intact *system* itself to the question of whether we can find a different use (or "function") for some of the *parts*. However, if one removes a part from the mousetrap I have pictured, it can no longer catch mice. The *system* has indeed effectively ceased functioning, so the *system* is irreducibly complex. . . .

With the problem of the mousetrap behind him, Miller then moved on to the bacterial flagellum—and again resorted to the same fallacy. . . . Without blinking, Miller asserted that the flagellum is not irreducibly complex because some proteins of the flagellum could be missing and the remainder could still transport proteins, perhaps independently. . . . Again, he was equivocating, switching the focus from the function of the system, acting as a rotary propulsion machine, to the ability of a subset of the system to transport proteins across a membrane. . . .

Future Prospects of the Intelligent Design Hypothesis

The misconceived arguments by Darwinists that I have recounted here offer strong encouragement to me that the hypothesis of Intelligent Design is on the right track. . . .

The important point here for a theory of Intelligent Design is that molecular machines are not confined to the few examples that I discussed in *Darwin's Black Box*. Rather, most proteins are found as components of complicated molecular machines. Thus design might extend to a large fraction of the features of the cell, and perhaps beyond that into higher levels of biology.

Progress in twentieth-century science has led us to the design hypothesis. I expect progress in the twenty-first century to confirm and extend it.

References

Behe, M. J. 1996. *Darwin's Black Box: The Biochemical Challenge to Evolution.* New York: The Free Press.

———. 2001. Reply to my critics: A response to reviews of *Darwin's Black Box: The Biochemical Challenge to Evolution. Biology and Philosophy* 16: 685–709.

Darwin, C. 1859. *The Origin of Species.* New York: Bantam Books.

REVIEW QUESTIONS

1. What does Behe mean by an "irreducibly complex system"?
2. According to Behe, why is it difficult to fit this concept into a Darwinian framework of evolution through natural selection?
3. According to Behe, how do both the mousetrap and the bacterial flagellum illustrate the concept of irreducibly complex systems?
4. Why does Behe believe there must be an intelligent designer of life?
5. How does Behe respond to Kenneth Miller's criticism of ID theory?

Answering the Biochemical Argument from Design*

KENNETH R. MILLER

Kenneth Miller is a professor of biology at Brown University. Miller critically examines Behe's concept of irreducible complexity in biological structures, concluding that such complexity is not irreducible and can be explained through the evolutionary mechanism of natural selection. Therefore, there is no need to evoke the existence of an intelligent designer.

One of the things that makes science such an exhilarating activity is its revolutionary character. As science advances, there is always the possibility that some investigator, working in the field or at a laboratory bench, will produce a discovery or experimental result that will completely transform our understanding of nature. . . .

In 1996, Michael Behe took a bold step in this scientific tradition by challenging one of the most useful, productive, and fundamental concepts in all of biology—Charles Darwin's theory of evolution. Behe's provocative claim, carefully laid out in his book, *Darwin's Black Box*, was that whatever else Darwinian evolution can explain successfully, it cannot account for the biochemical complexity of the living cell. . . .

Behe's argument is crafted around the existence of complex molecular machines found in all living cells. Such machines, he argues, could not have been produced by evolution, and therefore must be the products of intelligent design. . . . What I propose to do in this brief review is to put this line of reasoning to the test. I will . . . pose the most fundamental question one can ask of any scientific hypothesis—does it fit the facts?

An Exceptional Claim

For nearly more than a century and a half, one of the classic ways to argue against evolution has been to point to an exceptionally complex and intricate structure and then to challenge an evolutionist to "evolve this!" Examples of such challenges have included everything from the optical marvels of the human eye to the chemical defenses of the bombardier beetle. At first glance, Behe's examples seem to fit this tradition. . . .

Given that the business of science is to provide and test explanations, the fact that there are a few things that have, as yet, no published evolutionary explanations is not much of an argument against Darwin. Rather, it means that the field is still active, vital, and filled with scientific challenges. Behe realizes this, and therefore his principal claim for design is quite different. He observes, quite correctly, that science has not explained the evolution of the bacterial flagellum, but then he goes one step further. No such explanation is even *possible*, according to Behe. Why? Because the flagellum has a characteristic that Behe calls "irreducible complexity."

. . . To make his point perfectly clear, Behe uses a common mechanical device, the mousetrap, as an example of irreducible complexity. . . .

Since every part of the mousetrap must be in place before it is functional, this means that partial mousetraps,

ones that are missing one or two parts, are useless—you cannot catch mice with them. Extending the analogy to irreducibly complex biochemical machines, they also are without function until all of their parts are assembled. What this means, of course, is that natural selection could not produce such machines gradually, one part at a time. They would be non-functional until all of their parts were assembled, and natural selection, which can only select functioning systems, would have nothing to work with. . . .

In Behe's view, this observation, in and of itself makes the case for design. If the biochemical machinery of the cell cannot be produced by natural selection, then there is only one reasonable alternative—design by an intelligent agent. . . .

If Behe's arguments have a familiar ring to them, they should. They mirror the classic "Argument from Design," articulated so well by William Paley nearly 200 years ago in his book *Natural Theology*. Darwin was well aware of the argument . . ., Darwin's answer, in essence, was that evolution produces complex organs in a series of fully functional intermediate stages. If each of the intermediate stages can be favored by natural selection, then so can the whole pathway. . . .

Getting to the Heart of the Matter

To fully explore the scientific basis of the biochemical argument from design, we should investigate the details of some of the very structures used in Behe's book as examples of irreducibly complex systems. One of these is the eukaryotic cilium, an intricate whip-like structure that produces movement in cells as diverse as green algae and human sperm. . . .

Remember Behe's statement that the removal of any one of the parts of an irreducibly complex system effectively causes the system to stop working? The cilium provides us with a perfect opportunity to test that assertion. If it is correct, then we should be unable to find examples of functional cilia anywhere in nature that lack the cilium's basic parts. Unfortunately for the argument, that is not the case. Nature presents many examples of fully functional cilia that are missing key parts. One of the most compelling is the eel sperm flagellum, which lacks at least three important parts normally found in the cilium. . . .

The key element of Behe's claim was that "any precursor to an irreducibly complex system that is missing a part is by definition nonfunctional." But the individual parts of the cilium, including tubulin, the motor protein dynein, and the contractile protein actin, are fully functional elsewhere in the cell. What this means, of course, is that a selectable function exists for each of the major parts of the cilium, and therefore that the argument is wrong. . . .

*Kenneth R. Miller, "Answering the Biochemical Argument from Design," in Neil Manson, ed., *God and Design* (New York: Routledge Press, 2003) pp. 291–306.

Disproving Design

. . .

As we have seen, these facts demonstrate that the one system most widely cited as the premier example of irreducible complexity contains individual parts that have selectable functions. What this means, in scientific terms, is that the hypothesis of irreducible complexity is falsified. . . .

Caught in the Mousetrap

Why does the biochemical argument from design collapse so quickly upon close inspection? I would suggest that this is because the logic of the argument itself is flawed. Consider, for example, the mechanical mousetrap as an analogy of irreducibly complex systems. Behe has written that a mousetrap does not work if even one of its five parts is removed. However, with a little ingenuity, it turns out to be remarkably easy to construct a working mousetrap *after* removing one of its parts, leaving just four. . . .

. . . It is possible, in fact, to imagine a host of uses for parts of the "irreducibly complex" mousetrap.

The meaning of this should be clear. If portions of a supposedly irreducibly complex mechanical structure are fully functional in different contexts, then the central claim built upon this concept is incorrect. . . . Natural selection could indeed produce elements of a biochemical machine for different purposes. The mousetrap example provides, unintentionally, a perfect analogy for the way in which natural selection builds complex structures. . . .

What Is the "Evidence" for Design?

What follows is the logical chain of reasoning leading from the observation of biochemical complexity to the conclusion of intelligent design.

1. *Observation:* the cell contains biochemical machines in which the loss of a single component may abolish function. *Definition:* such machines are therefore said to be "irreducibly complex."

2. *Assertion:* any irreducibly complex structure that is missing a part is by definition non-functional, leaving natural selection with nothing to select for.

3. *Conclusion:* therefore, irreducibly complex structures could not have been produced by natural selection.

4. *Secondary conclusion:* therefore, such structures must have been produced by another mechanism. Since the only credible alternate mechanism is intelligent design, the very existence of such structures must be evidence of intelligent design.

When the reasoning behind the biochemical argument from design is laid out in this way, it becomes easy to spot the logical flaw in the argument. The first statement is true—the cell does indeed contain any number of complex molecular machines in which the loss of a single part may affect function. However, the second statement, the assertion of non-functionality, is demonstrably false. As we have seen, the individual parts of many such machines do indeed have well-defined functions within the cell. Once this is realized, the logic of the argument collapses. If the assertion in the second statement is shown to be false, the chain of reasoning is broken and both conclusions are falsified.

The cell does not contain biochemical evidence of design.

References

Behe, M. (1996a) *Darwin's Black Box*, New York: The Free Press.

REVIEW QUESTIONS

1. How is the "revolutionary character" of science relevant to Behe's challenge of Darwin?

2. What does Miller mean when he says that Behe's argument mirrors the classic "Argument from Design"?

3. According to Miller, what are the two principle claims of ID?

4. According to Miller, what evidence disproves the argument of irreducible complexity?

5. How does Miller summarize the chain of reasoning from the observation of biochemical complexities to the conclusion that they are evidence of an intelligent designer, and what is his analysis of the reasoning?

THiNK AND DISCUSS

PERSPECTIVES ON EVOLUTION VERSUS INTELLIGENT DESIGN

1. Using the criteria for evaluating an analogy in an inductive argument listed in Chapter 7, pages 217–218, evaluate the mousetrap analogy used by Behe. Discuss whether the analogy supports his conclusion regarding irreducible complexity in biology and the existence of an intelligent designer.

2. Was Miller successful in disproving ID and irreducible complexity? Evaluate his argument. Discuss how effective Behe's counterarguments were in responding to Miller's criticisms.

3. Evaluate both the theory of evolution and the theory of intelligent design using the criteria for evaluating a hypothesis listed on page 377. Discuss what evidence or experimental findings might falsify the ID theory/hypothesis. Discuss what evidence or experimental findings might falsify the theory of evolution by natural selection.

4. Former President George W. Bush endorsed the teaching of ID alongside evolution, stating, "Both sides ought to be properly taught so people can understand what the debate is all about." Author and physicist Robert Ehrlich disagrees. He writes that "to require intelligent design to be taught alongside evolution makes as little sense as requiring flat-Earth theory to be taught in science courses, so that students 'can make up their own minds' whether the Earth is round or flat." Discuss whether access to all sides of an argument, even ones that may be mistaken, is important in developing students' critical-thinking skills in science.

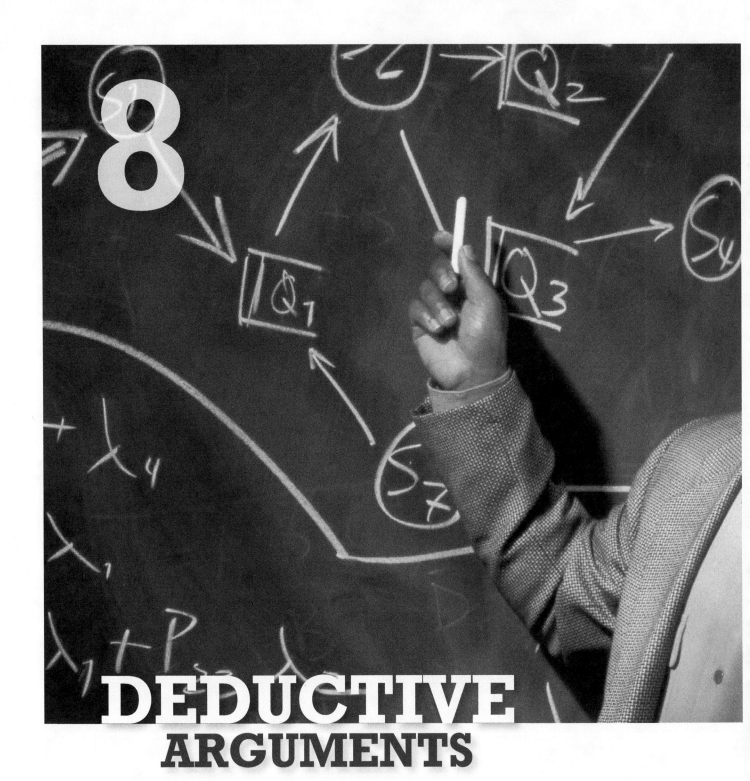

8

DEDUCTIVE
ARGUMENTS

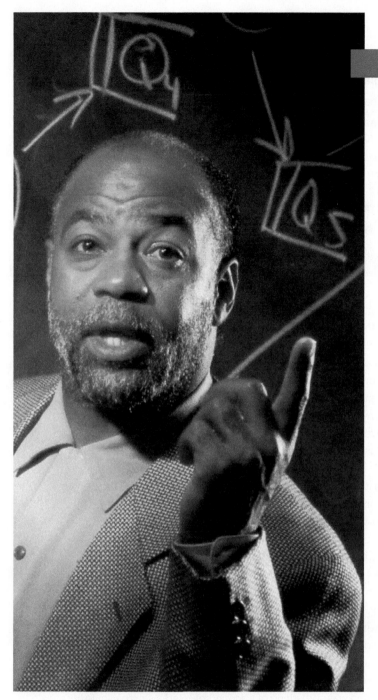

How is the professor using logical argumentation in coming up with mathematical proofs?
How can learning about deductive logic, such as arguments based on mathematics, help us make better-informed decisions?

In Sir Arthur Conan Doyle's mystery story "Silver Blaze," detective Sherlock Holmes uses his extraordinary powers of deductive logic to solve the mystery of the disappearance of racehorse Silver Blaze and the murder of the horse's trainer, John Straker. His head shattered by a savage blow, Straker's body was found a quarter mile from the King's Pyland stables where Silver Blaze was kept. A search is carried out of the surrounding moors and of the neighboring Mapleton stables for the horse.

After interviewing everyone who might have been involved and collecting all the facts, Holmes concludes that Silver Blaze is still alive and hidden in the Mapleton stables, even though the earlier search of the stables had failed to turn up the missing horse.

THiNK FIRST

- What is a deductive argument?
- What are some of the types of deductive arguments?
- What is a syllogism, and how do we know if it is valid?

>>

"It's this way, Watson," [says Holmes]. "Now, supposing that [Silver Blaze] broke away during or after the tragedy, where could he have gone to? The horse is a very gregarious creature. If left to himself his instincts would have been either to return to King's Pyland or go over to Mapleton. Why would he run wild upon the moor? He surely should have been seen by now . . . He must have gone to King's Pyland or to Mapleton. He is not at King's Pyland. Therefore, he is at Mapleton."[1]

As it turns out, Holmes's deduction is right. The missing racehorse is at Mapleton, the silver blaze on its nose covered over to disguise its appearance.

Sherlock Holmes also solves the "murder" of the horse's trainer through deductive logic. He learns from the stable hand that the guard dog did not bark when Silver Blaze was "stolen" from the stables. Therefore, Holmes concludes, the person who took Silver Blaze must have been familiar to the dog. This eliminated suspects who were strangers. Holmes then eliminates, one by one, the other suspects, leaving only the horse. As Holmes stated in another story: "When you have eliminated the impossible, whatever remains, however improbable, must be the truth."[2] He concludes that the horse must have accidentally killed its trainer when Straker, who was something of a scoundrel, used a surgical knife found in his possession to nick the tendons of Silver Blaze's ham so the horse would develop a slight limp and lose the upcoming race. Holmes explains, "Once in the hollow, [Straker] had got behind the horse and had struck a light; but the creature, frightened at the sudden glare, and with the strange instinct of animals feeling that some mischief was intended, had lashed out, and the steel shoe had struck Straker full on the forehead."[3]

To generations of mystery readers, Sherlock Holmes has epitomized the skilled reasoner. In this chapter we'll learn how to evaluate deductive arguments and practice some of the strategies used by Holmes and others who are skilled in deductive argumentation. In Chapter 8 we will:

- Identify the essential attributes of a deductive argument
- Distinguish between validity, invalidity, and soundness in a deductive argument
- Learn how to recognize and evaluate arguments by elimination, mathematical arguments, and argument from definition
- Study the different types of hypothetical syllogisms, including *modus ponens, modus tollens,* and chain arguments
- Learn how to recognize standard-form categorical syllogisms
- Reevaluate categorical syllogisms using Venn diagrams
- Practice putting arguments that are in ordinary language into standard form

Finally, we will analyze different arguments regarding the justification of the death penalty (capital punishment).

WHAT IS A DEDUCTIVE ARGUMENT?

Unlike inductive arguments, in which the premises offer only support rather than proof for the conclusion, in a valid deductive argument the conclusion necessarily follows from the premises. Deductive arguments sometimes contain words or phrases such as *certainly, definitely, absolutely, conclusively, must be,* and *it necessarily follows that.* For example:

> Marilyn is definitely not a member of the swim team, since no freshmen are members of the swim team and Marilyn is a freshman.

Deductive Reasoning and Syllogisms

Deductive arguments are sometimes presented in the form of **syllogisms,** with two supporting premises and a conclusion. For the purpose of analysis, in this chapter the premises and conclusion of a syllogism will usually be presented on separate lines, with the conclusion last.

1. *Premise: All men are mortal.*
2. *Premise: All fathers are men.*
3. *Conclusion: Therefore, all fathers are mortal.*

Deductive arguments may also be diagrammed using the guidelines we learned on pages 181–184. In the case of a syllogism, the two premises are always dependent:

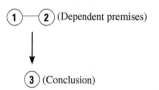

Some deductive arguments are more involved and may have several dependent premises and subconclusions.

Valid and Invalid Arguments

A deductive argument is **valid** if the form of the argument is such that the conclusion *must* be true *if* the premises are true. The **form** of an argument is determined by its layout or pattern of reasoning. In the above case, the form is:

> **syllogism** A deductive argument presented in the form of two supporting premises and a conclusion.
>
> **valid** A deductive argument where the form is such that the conclusion must be true if the premises are assumed to be true.
>
> **form** The pattern of reasoning in a deductive argument.

All X (men) are Y (mortal).
All Z (fathers) are X (men).
Therefore, all Z (fathers) are Y (mortal).

This argument is a valid form no matter what terms we use for X, Y, and Z. Because the form is valid, if we substitute different terms for *men, mortal,* and *fathers, and* the premises are still true, then the conclusion *must* be true, as in the following example.

All cats (X) are mammals (Y).
All tigers (Z) are cats (X).
Therefore, all tigers (Z) are mammals (Y).

A false conclusion does not necessarily mean that a deductive argument is invalid. In the two arguments we've examined so far, the conclusions were both true because the premises were true *and* the form was valid. The conclusion of a valid argument

Hot or Not?

Are deductive arguments better than inductive arguments?

can be false only if one of the premises is false. In the following example, which uses the same form as our initial argument, we end up with a false conclusion:

> All men are tall people.
>
> Tom Cruise is a man.
>
> Therefore, Tom Cruise is a tall person.

The conclusion in the above argument is false *only* because there is a false premise, not because the form of the argument is invalid. The first premise, "All men are tall people," is false.

If both premises are true and the conclusion is false, then the argument, by definition, is invalid. For example:

> All dogs are mammals.
>
> Some mammals are not poodles.
>
> Therefore, some poodles are not dogs.

It is also possible to have an invalid argument in which the premises are true and the conclusion just happens to be true. Consider this:

> No seniors are freshmen.
>
> All freshmen are college students.
>
> Therefore, some college students are seniors.

In this argument, the premises and conclusion are true. However, the premises do not logically support the conclusion. The invalidity of a form can be demonstrated by substituting different terms for *senior*, *freshman*, and *college students*, and then seeing whether we can come up with an argument using this form in which the premises are true but the conclusion false, as in the following substitutions:

> No fish are dogs.
>
> All dogs are mammals.
>
> Therefore, some mammals are fish.

Sound and Unsound Arguments

An argument is **sound** if (1) it is valid *and* (2) the premises are true. The argument on page 239 about fathers being mortal is a sound argument because it is valid and the premises are true. On the other hand, although the argument about Tom Cruise uses a valid form, it is not a sound argument because the first premise is false. Invalid arguments, because they do not meet the first criterion, are always unsound.

sound A deductive argument that is valid and that has true premises.

Logic is primarily concerned with the validity of arguments. As critical thinkers, we are also interested in the soundness of our arguments and in having our premises supported by credible evidence and good reasoning. We have already discussed in previous chapters guidelines for ensuring that our premises are accurate and credible. In this chapter we'll learn how to

identify the different types of deductive arguments and how to use Venn diagrams to evaluate these arguments for validity.

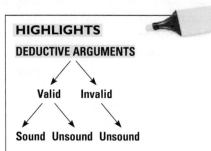

HIGHLIGHTS

DEDUCTIVE ARGUMENTS

Valid   Invalid

Sound   Unsound   Unsound

Valid argument: The form or layout of the argument is such that if the premises are true, then the conclusion must necessarily be true.

Sound argument: The form of the argument is valid and the premises are true.

➤ *APPLICATION: Identify in the text an example of an argument that is (a) valid and sound, (b) valid and unsound, and (c) invalid.*

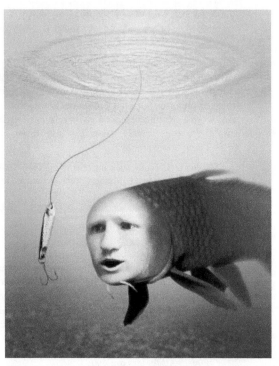

"Some mammals are fish" is an example of a false conclusion.

EXERCISE 8-1

STOP AND ASSESS YOURSELF

1. What do you mean when you say that you can prove something with certainty? Give a specific example of a proof from your everyday experience (keep it as brief as possible). What type of logic does the proof use—inductive or deductive?

2. In the story "Silver Blaze," Sherlock Holmes tells Watson that when it comes to the art of reasoning, many people rely on opinion and unsupported assumptions. The difficulty, he maintains, is to detach the framework of undeniable fact from the embellishments of hearsay and reporters. What do you think he meant by this? Explain using examples from your personal experience.

3. Using substitution, show that the form of each of the following deductive arguments is invalid. Remember: To establish invalidity, your premises must be true when you are substituting new terms for the ones in the original argument.

*a. All fraternity members are men.
   No women are fraternity members.
   Therefore, no women are men.

b. If it is raining, then it is cloudy.
   It is cloudy.
   Therefore, it is raining.

c. No mice are humans.
   Some mice are rodents.
   Therefore, no humans are rodents.

*d. Some married people are college students.
   All wives are married people.
   Therefore, some wives are college students.

e. All flowers are plants.
   All orchids are plants.
   Therefore, all orchids are flowers.

f. If my baby sister is a college student, then she is a high school graduate.
   My baby sister is not a college student.
   Therefore, my baby sister is not a high school graduate.

4. The following arguments are all valid arguments. Determine whether each argument is sound or unsound.

*a. No mammals are birds. Some penguins are mammals. Therefore, some penguins are not birds.

b. Some twins are sisters. All twins are siblings. Therefore, some siblings are sisters.

c. All students are dormitory residents. No dormitory residents are birds. Therefore, no birds are students.

*d. If Mexico is in South America, then Mexico is not a country bordering the United States. Mexico is in South America. Therefore, Mexico is a not country bordering the United States.

e. All people living in England are citizens of the European Union.
   All members of the British royal family are people living in England.
   Therefore, all members of the British royal family are citizens of the European Union.

f. All millionaires are rich people. Some Americans are not rich people. Therefore, some Americans are not millionaires.

*Answers to selected exercises are found in the Solutions Manual at the end of the book.

TYPES OF DEDUCTIVE ARGUMENTS

There are several types of deductive arguments. In this section, we'll be looking at three types of deductive arguments used in everyday reasoning:

- Arguments by elimination
- Arguments based on mathematics
- Arguments from definition

Arguments by Elimination

An **argument by elimination** rules out different possibilities until only one possibility remains. In the

> **argument by elimination** A deductive argument that rules out different possibilities until only one remains.

introduction to this chapter, we saw Sherlock Holmes using an argument by elimination. He reasoned that Silver Blaze had to be at one of the two stables. Since it wasn't at King's Pyland, it must be at Mapleton. In "Thinking Outside the Box: Bo Dietl" we profile a New York City detective who is skilled in this type of deductive reasoning.

Like detectives, physicians are trained in this type of deductive logic. In diagnosing an illness, a physician starts by doing a physical examination and, often, by ordering tests. If the examination and test results eliminate the most common explanations of the symptoms, then the physician moves on to check out less obvious possibilities until the mystery is solved. Indeed, Dr. Joseph Bell, one of Sir Arthur Conan Doyle's professors at the University of Edinburgh Medical School, was the inspiration for the character Sherlock Holmes.

Arguments by elimination are frequently used in everyday life. For instance, suppose it is the first day of the semester and you arrive on campus with 10 minutes to spare.

THiNKing Outside the Box

BO DIETL, *Top Cop*

Bo Dietl is a modern Sherlock Holmes. Born in Queens, New York, in 1950, Dietl wanted a job where he could make a real difference in people's lives. When he learned about the test to get into the police academy, he decided to give it a try and became a police officer.

One of the most highly decorated detectives in the history of the New York Police Department, Dietl investigated numerous high-profile murders and other felonies, obtaining evidence through research, interviews, and other investigative techniques. He attributes much of his success in solving more than 1,500 felonies to what he calls his "sixth sense—a nontangible feeling good detectives use in solving cases."*

One of the most famous crimes he solved was the 1981 rape and torture of a Catholic nun in an East Harlem convent. Dietl concluded from the evidence that the crime was a burglary gone wrong, rather than a sex crime, thus narrowing his search to people with burglary records. He also knew, from interviewing witnesses, that one of the men was probably tall and that the other had a limp. Days later he received a tip that the two men who committed the crime lived somewhere on 125th Street in Harlem. However, there were hundreds of buildings and thousands of people living on this street. He began the process of elimination by going to the local hangouts and tenements, knocking on doors, giving a brief description of the suspects, and asking questions. He also passed out hundreds of business cards. His efforts paid off, and the two suspects were apprehended and arrested. The 1998 movie *One Tough Cop* is based on Dietl's autobiography of the same name.

DISCUSSION QUESTIONS

1. Discuss how Dietl's method of solving the murder of the nun in the East Harlem convent demonstrates deductive reasoning using an argument by elimination.

2. In Chapter 2 we learned that much of reasoning is unconscious and automatic and that scientists and mathematicians, as well as great detectives, often resolve complex problems without any conscious deliberation. However, to develop this ability, they have spent years consciously resolving problems and mentally rehearsing solutions. Think of a type of problem in your life that you find easy to resolve with little or no conscious deliberation. Discuss what factors, such as your familiarity and experience with the problem, contributed to your ease of resolution.

*Conversation with Bo Dietl on August 8, 2005.

You check your schedule and see that your first class, Introduction to Psychology, is in Winthrop Hall. However, on your schedule the room number is smudged and you can't read it. What do you do? It would take too long to get a new schedule. Instead, you head over to Winthrop Hall and check out the building directory. It lists twelve room numbers. Nine of them are faculty offices, so you eliminate those nine. The remaining three are classrooms A, B, and C. You go into classroom A and ask some students what class it is. They tell you that it's English Literature. You proceed to classroom B and repeat the process; it turns out to be a course in Business Statistics. When you get to classroom C, you just go inside and take a seat. How do you know this is the correct classroom? Through the use of an argument by elimination. Assuming that your premises are true (that your psychology course is being taught somewhere in Winthrop Hall), the third classroom *by necessity* must be your classroom.

> My class is either in room A, B, or C.
>
> My class is not in room A.
>
> My class is not in room B.
>
> Therefore, my class must be in room C.

In the previous example, there were three alternatives. If there are only two alternatives, the argument is referred to as a **disjunctive syllogism**. A disjunctive syllogism takes one of two forms:

> Either A or B. Either A or B.
>
> Not A. Not B.
>
> Therefore, B. Therefore, A.

In determining the whereabouts of Silver Blaze, Sherlock Holmes used a disjunctive syllogism:

> Either Silver Blaze is at King's Pyland or Silver Blaze is at Mapleton.
>
> Silver Blaze is not at King's Pyland.
>
> Therefore, Silver Blaze is at Mapleton.

Here is another example of a disjunctive syllogism:

> Either you finished cleaning your room or you're staying in tonight.
>
> You are not staying in tonight.
>
> Therefore, you finished cleaning your room.

In a disjunctive syllogism, the two alternatives presented in the first premise—clean your room or stay in tonight—must be the only two possibilities. If there are other possible alternatives that have not been stated, then the argument commits the *fallacy of false dilemma*. For example:

> Either we keep Obamacare or we balance the budget.
>
> We are keeping Obamacare.
>
> Therefore, we will not have a balanced budget.

A mouse locates the prize at the end of the maze through the deductive process of elimination.

In this argument, the two alternatives in the first premise do not exhaust all possible alternatives. There are many areas of the federal budget we could cut other than healthcare spending. Because the argument commits the fallacy of false dilemma, it is not a sound argument.

Arguments Based on Mathematics

In an **argument based on mathematics**, the conclusion depends on a mathematical or geometrical calculation. For example:

> My dormitory room is rectangular in shape.
>
> One side measures 11 feet and the side adjacent to it measures 14 feet in length.
>
> Therefore, my room is 154 square feet.

You can also draw conclusions about your new roommate, Chris, even before you meet, using this type of deductive reasoning. You know from e-mail correspondence that Chris plans on trying out for the basketball team and is 6′ 2″ tall. Since you are 5′ 6″ tall, you can conclude (assuming that Chris's information is correct) that Chris is 8 inches taller than you.

These are relatively simple examples. Arguments based on mathematics may be quite complex and require

disjunctive syllogism A type of deductive argument by elimination in which the premises present only two alternatives.

argument based on mathematics A deductive argument in which the conclusion depends on a mathematical calculation.

mathematical expertise. For example, scientists at NASA needed to calculate the best time to launch the two *Mars Explorer Rovers*—robotic geologists—so that they would arrive at the Red Planet when Mars would be closest to Earth. Mars takes 687 days to complete a revolution of the Sun, compared to 365 days for Earth. Also, because their orbits differ and because Mars has a slightly eccentric orbit, the distance between Mars and Earth varies widely, ranging from about 401 million miles to less than 55 million miles.[4] The two rovers, *Spirit* and *Opportunity,* were launched from Cape Canaveral, Florida, in the summer of 2003 and landed on Mars in January 2004. The landing was remarkably smooth, thanks to the deductive reasoning skills of the NASA scientists. As of 2013 NASA has lost contact with the rover *Spirit*, which has become stuck in a sand trap. *Opportunity* is still transmitting scientific data back to Earth.

Knowing how to make arguments based on mathematics can help you make better-informed decisions, such as calculating the cost of a vacation to Cancun or determining what type of payment method for your educational expenses is most cost-effective. For example, by taking out a student loan instead of using a credit card to pay for your college expenses, you can save thousands of dollars (see "Critical Thinking in Action: Put It on My Tab: Paying College Tuition by Credit Card—a Wise Move?").

Not all arguments using mathematics are deductive. As we learned in Chapter 7, statistical arguments that depend on probability, such as generalizations, are inductive because we can conclude from these only that something is *likely*—not certain—to be true (see pages 207–209).

How can an understanding of arguments based on mathematics help you evaluate science news? *See Chapter 11, pp. 345–346.*

Connections

argument from definition A deductive argument in which the conclusion is true because it is based on the definition of a key term.

Arguments from Definition

In an **argument from definition**, the conclusion is true because it is based on a key term or essential attribute in a definition. For example:

> Paulo is a father.
> All fathers are men.
> Therefore, Paulo is a man.

This conclusion is necessarily true because a father is, by definition, "a male parent." Being male is an essential attribute of the definition of *father*.

As we discussed in Chapter 3, language is dynamic and definitions may change over time. Consider this example:

> Marilyn and Jessica cannot be married, since a marriage is a union between a man and a woman.

This conclusion of this argument was necessarily true at one time, before some states legalized same-sex marriage. Today, because the legal definition of marriage is undergoing change, this argument may no longer be sound.

Arguments by elimination, arguments based on mathematics, and arguments from definition are only three types of deductive arguments. In logic, deductive arguments are often written in syllogistic form, such as the disjunctive syllogism. In the following sections, we'll learn about two other types of syllogisms—hypothetical and categorical—and how to evaluate arguments using these forms.

Critical THiNKing in Action

Put It on My Tab: Paying College Tuition by Credit Card—A Wise Move?

Have you ever wondered why credit-card companies are so keen on signing up college students? According to CreditKarma.com, an online credit tracking site, people between the ages of 18 and 29 have the poorest credit ratings of all age groups. In fact, credit-card companies make most of their money from people who don't pay off their balance each month, which is the case with 80 percent of college students. Many parents and students regard credit cards as a convenient way to pay for tuition. However, if you think carrying a balance on a credit card or charging college expenses such as tuition to a credit card is a smart move, consider the following argument, based on mathematics:

> Your credit card bill is $1,900. This includes $1,350 for tuition and fees at your community college and $550 for books for two semesters. Being frugal, you decide not to use your credit card again, since you don't want to get too far into debt. The minimum monthly payment due on your balance is 4 percent, which comes to $75 the first month. You pay the minimum due faithfully each month.
>
> At this rate, how long will it take you to pay off your first-year college expenses? If the annual percentage rate on your card is 17.999 percent, it will take you 7 years to pay off that balance on your credit card!* In addition to the principal (the amount you charged to the card), you'll have paid a total of $924.29 in interest. This means that the amount of money you actually paid for your first year of college expenses was $2,824!**

What if you had taken out a student loan instead? The annual interest rate on a federal student loan is about 8 percent. If you put $75 a month toward paying off your student loan, it would take you 2 years and 4 months to pay off the loan. Furthermore, you don't have to start paying off your student loan until you graduate. By taking out a student loan to cover your college expenses instead of charging them to a credit card, you wouldn't have to pay anything for the 2 years while you are in college. Even then you would pay off the loan almost 3 years before you would pay off your credit card—and the total interest would come to only $188. In other words, you paid $736 for the "convenience" of charging your tuition, fees, and books for your first year at community college. Multiply this times 2 or even 4 years, and you could be paying out several thousand dollars just in interest simply because you didn't apply your logic and your critical-thinking skills when deciding how to pay for your college expenses.

DISCUSSION QUESTIONS

1. Several colleges, including Tufts University, Boston College, Sarah Lawrence College, and Arizona State University, have discontinued credit-card payments for tuition. In part this is because the credit-card companies charge the college a 1 percent to 2 percent fee on each charge, which ultimately gets added on to the cost of tuition. What is the policy at your college or university? Do you agree with the policy? Construct an argument supporting your answer.

2. Examine your own credit-card use. Discuss ways in which you can use deductive logic to be more economical in your spending habits.

*To calculate what you'll pay on a credit-card balance, go to http://cgi.money.cnn.com/tools/debtplanner/debtplanner.jsp; for what you'll pay on a student loan, go to http://cgi.money.cnn.com/tools/studentloan/studentloan.html.

**For information on applying for federal and private college loans, see http://www.collegeboard.com/student/pay/loan-center/414.html.

STOP AND ASSESS YOURSELF

I. Identify what type of argument each of the following is. If it is a deductive argument, state which type of deductive argument. If the argument is not a deductive argument, explain why. (See Chapter 7 if you need to review inductive arguments.)

*a. Clem either walked to the bookstore or took the shuttle bus. He couldn't have taken the shuttle bus, since it is out of service today. Therefore, he walked to the bookstore.

b. Hisoka is a psychiatrist. Therefore, Hisoka is a physician.

c. A 64-ounce carton of mint chocolate chip ice cream costs $5.99. A 16-ounce carton costs $1.49. Therefore, I'll actually save money by buying four 16-ounce cartons instead of one 64-ounce carton.

*d. Let's see; it's the triplets' third birthday. We have six presents for Matthew, five for Andrew, and one for Derek. If we want to be fair and give each of the triplets the same number of presents, we'll have to take two of the presents we now have set aside for Matthew and one of the presents we have set aside for Andrew and give them to Derek instead.

e. Tokyo, New York City, and Mexico City have the highest populations of any cities in the world. Tokyo has a higher population than New York City. Mexico City has a lower population than New York City. Therefore, Tokyo has the highest population of any city in the world.

f. I was told that Mary is probably in class right now and that if she were not there, to check the library where she spends most of her afternoons. However, Mary isn't in class. So she is most likely at the library.

*g. Jessica is the daughter of Joshua's uncle. Therefore, Jessica and Joshua are cousins.

h. Either Roy Jones Jr. or John Ruiz won the 2003 world heavyweight championship boxing match in Las Vegas. John Ruiz did not win the fight. Therefore, Roy Jones Jr. was the 2003 world heavyweight champion.

i. A = 5. B = 8. C = −11. Therefore, A + B + C = 2.

*j. Forrest Gump said that his mother always told him that "life was like a box of chocolates. You never know what you're gonna get." Therefore, there's no point in trying to plan for the future, since you can never know what it holds for you.

k. I know that Singapore uses either the dollar or the British pound as their currency. I checked out the countries that use the British pound and Singapore was not listed. Therefore, Singapore uses the dollar as its currency.

l. Professor Cervera told us that he was born in one of the four largest cities in Cuba, but I can't remember which one. I remember him mentioning that it was in the southeastern part of Cuba and that he could see the ocean from his bedroom window. I checked my almanac, and the four largest cities in Cuba are Havana, Santiago de Cuba, Camagüey, and Holguin. He couldn't have been born in Havana, since it is on the northwestern coast of Cuba. Camagüey and Holguin are both located inland. So Professor Cervera must have been born in Santiago de Cuba.

*m. We should ask Latitia if she is interested in working part time in our marketing department. I read that about 80 percent of freshmen said there was at least some chance they'd have to get a job to pay for college expenses. In addition, women are far more likely to have to seek employment during college than are men. Therefore, Latitia will probably be looking for a part-time job to help with her college expenses.

n. I agree that the storm we had last week was pretty bad, but it was not a hurricane since the winds never got above 70 miles per hour.

o. Either the tide is coming in or the tide is going out. The tide is not coming in. Therefore, the tide is going out.

*p. A Harvard University survey of more than 10,000 teenagers found that 8 percent of girls and 12 percent of boys have used dietary supplements, growth hormones, or anabolic steroids. Therefore, teenage boys are 50 percent more likely than are teenage girls to use products such as steroids to build muscle mass.

2. Select three of the arguments from exercise 1 and diagram them (see Chapter 6).

EXERCISE 8-2 CONT.

3. You're having lunch with some friends and mention that you're studying deductive logic. One of your friends rolls his eyes and says, "You can prove anything you want to with logic. Why, you can even prove that cats have thirteen tails. Here's how it works: One cat has one more tail than no cat. And no cat has twelve tails. Therefore, one cat has thirteen tails." Evaluate your friend's argument.

4. At a picnic, Mike went for soft drinks for Amy, Brian, Lisa, and Bill, as well as for himself. He brought back iced tea, grape juice, Diet Coke, Pepsi, and 7-Up. Using the following information (premises), determine which drink Mike brought for each person:

> Mike doesn't like carbonated drinks.
>
> Amy would drink either 7-Up or Pepsi.
>
> Brian likes only sodas.
>
> Lisa prefers the drink she could put lemon and sugar into.
>
> Bill likes only clear drinks.[5]

5. How do you pay for your tuition and other college expenses? Go to http://www.money.cnn.com/tools and calculate how much it will cost you to pay off your entire debt on the basis of the average you pay each month, or estimate what you will pay monthly after graduation. Given your financial situation, decide what would be the most economical way for you to pay for your college and personal expenses.

*Answers to selected exercises are found in the Solutions Manual at the end of the book.

HYPOTHETICAL SYLLOGISMS

Hypothetical thinking involves "If . . . then . . ." reasoning. According to some psychologists, the mental model for hypothetical thinking is built into our brain and enables us to understand rules and predict the consequences of our actions.[6] We'll be looking at the use of hypothetical reasoning in ethics in greater depth in Chapter 9. Hypothetical arguments are also a basic building block of computer programs.

According to some psychologists, the mental model for hypothetical thinking is built into our brain and enables us to understand rules and predict the consequences of our actions.

A **hypothetical syllogism** is a form of deductive argument that contains two premises, at least one of which is a hypothetical or conditional "if . . . then" statement.

Hypothetical syllogisms fall into three basic patterns: *modus ponens* (affirming the antecedent), *modus tollens* (denying the consequent), and chain arguments.

Modus Ponens

In a *modus ponens* argument, there is one conditional premise, a second premise that states that the antecedent, or *if* part, of the first premise is true, and a conclusion that asserts the truth of the consequent, or the *then* part, of the first premise. For example:

> *Premise 1*: *If* I get this raise at work, *then* I can pay off my credit-card bill.
>
> *Premise 2*: I got the raise at work.
>
> *Conclusion*: Therefore, I can pay off my credit-card bill.

A valid *modus ponens* argument, like the one above, takes the following form:

> If A (antecedent), then B (consequent).
>
> A.
>
> Therefore, B.

Sometimes the term *then* is omitted from the consequent, or second, part of the conditional premise:

> If the hurricane hits the Florida Keys, we should evacuate.
>
> The hurricane is hitting the Florida Keys.
>
> Therefore, we should evacuate.

Modus ponens is a valid form of deductive reasoning no matter what terms we substitute for A and B. In other words, if the premises are true, then the conclusion must be true. Thus:

> If Barack Obama is president, then he was born in the United States.
>
> Barack Obama is president.
>
> Therefore, he was born in the United States.

In this case, the first premise is true because the U.S. Constitution requires that the president be "a natural born citizen." Therefore, the argument is a sound argument.

> **hypothetical syllogism** A deductive argument that contains two premises, at least one of which is a conditional statement.
>
> **modus ponens** A hypothetical syllogism in which the antecedent premise is affirmed by the consequent premise.

Deductive Reasoning and Computer Programming

In computer programming, special computer languages are used to create strings of code which are comprised almost entirely of deductive logic. Some popular computer languages include C++, Java, JavaScript, Visual Basic, and HTML. Many others exist that specialize in specific tasks. In the following program using C++, a game has been created using hypothetical statements:

```
int main()
{int number = 5}
        int guess;
        cout << "I am thinking of a number between 1 and 10" << endl;
        cout << "Enter your guess, please";
        cin >> guess;
        if (guess == number)
                        {cout << "Incredible, you are correct" << endl;}
                else if (guess < number)
                        {cout << "Higher, try again" << endl;}
                else // guess must be too high
                        {cout << "Lower, try again" <<endl;}
        return 0:}
```

In the game, the computer asks the user to guess a number between 1 and 10. If the user guesses a 5 (the correct answer), the computer will congratulate the user with the message, "Incredible, you are correct." Otherwise, the computer tells the user whether his/her answer was too high or too low.

---

modus tollens A hypothetical syllogism in which the antecedent premise is denied by the consequent premise.

chain arguments A type of imperfect hypothetical argument with three or more conditional propositions linked together.

It is important not to deviate from this form in a *modus ponens* argument. If the second premise affirms the consequent (B) rather than the antecedent (A), the argument is invalid and the conclusion may be false, even though the premises are true.

If Oprah Winfrey is president, then she was born in the United States.

Oprah Winfrey was born in the United States.

Therefore, Oprah Winfrey is president.

But of course, as we all know, Oprah Winfrey is not president of the United States. This deviation from the correct form of *modus ponens* is known as the *fallacy of affirming the consequent.*

Modus Tollens

In a *modus tollens* argument, the second premise denies the consequent, and the conclusion denies the truth of the antecedent:

If A (antecedent), then B (consequent).

Not B.

Therefore, not A.

Here is an example of a *modus tollens* argument:

If Morgan is a physician, then she has graduated from college.

Morgan did not graduate from college.

Therefore, Morgan is not a physician.

Like *modus ponens*, *modus tollens* is a valid form of deductive reasoning. No matter what terms we substitute for the antecedent (A) and consequent (B), if the premises are true, then the conclusion must be true. If we change the form by changing the first premise to read "If not A, then B," we commit the *fallacy of denying the antecedent.*

Chain Arguments

Chain arguments are made up of three conditional propositions—two premises and one conclusion—linked together. A chain argument is a type of imperfect hypothetical syllogism since it may contain more than three propositions.

If A, then B.

If B, then C.

Therefore, if A, then C.

Critical THiNKing in Action

Empty Promises: If This, Then That—Making Promises and Threats

Promises are often framed as hypothetical statements: "If you do . . . , then I'll . . ." Because hypothetical syllogisms are deductive arguments, the conclusion necessarily follows from the premises. Therefore, we should think twice about the consequences (conclusion) of having to keep such a promise. For example, President Obama vowed before at an international meeting in Prague in 2009 to punish Iran for pursuing a nuclear weapons program, stating that "Rules must be binding. Violations must be punished . . . The world must stand together to prevent the spread of these weapons." When it came to light that Iran may already have a nuclear weapons program, Obama reiterated his position in his May 2009 State of the Union address: "As Iran's leaders continue to ignore their obligations, there should be no doubt: They, too, will face growing consequences. That is a promise." Four years later, despite tighter sanctions against Iran and Obama's continued assurance that he is determined to prevent Iran from getting a nuclear weapon, Iran remains undeterred in its nuclear program and may be only months away from having a nuclear weapon. In failing to follow through effectively on his promise, Obama has damaged his credibility regarding this issue.

People may also use hypothetical statements as threats to try to get their children to behave or to get their boyfriend, girlfriend, partner, or spouse to change their ways. For instance, an exasperated parent may say to a boisterous child: "If you keep misbehaving and making so much noise, Mommy is never going to get better." The child, being a typical child, misbehaves again. A few weeks later, the mother dies of cancer. In such a case, the child will likely draw the logical conclusion that she is to blame for her mother's death (never getting better).

DISCUSSION QUESTIONS

1. Imagine you had been in Obama's position. Using a hypothetical syllogism, discuss how you might word your response to Iran's nuclear program so it does not become an empty promise but one that can be acted on in a responsible manner.

2. Think of a time when you were given an ultimatum in the form of a hypothetical statement in a relationship. What conclusion logically followed from the ultimatum? Did the ultimatum hurt or enhance your relationship? Explain why or why not.

The following is an example of a chain argument:

If it rains tomorrow, then the beach party is canceled.

If the beach party is canceled, we're having a party at Rachel's house.

Therefore, if it rains tomorrow, we're having a party at Rachel's house.

Just as some arguments by elimination are syllogisms and others are not, we can have a longer chain argument that is still a deductive argument but not a syllogism because it has more than two premises. For example:

If A, then B.

If B, then C.

If C, then D.

Therefore, if A, then D.

Here is an example of a chain argument with three premises:

If you don't go to class, you won't pass the final exam.

If you don't pass the final exam, then you won't pass the course.

If you don't pass the course, then you won't graduate this year.

Therefore, if you don't go to class, you won't graduate this year.

A chain argument is valid if it follows the form of using the consequent of the previous premise as the antecedent in the next premise, and so on, with the conclusion using the antecedent from the first premise (A) and the consequent in the last premise (D).

Evaluating Hypothetical Syllogisms for Validity

Not all hypothetical syllogisms are laid out in standard syllogistic form. If an argument isn't already in standard form, put it in standard form with the conditional premise first and the conclusion last. In the case of a chain argument, begin by listing the premise containing the antecedent from the conclusion. In 1758, Ben Franklin included a version of this proverb in his famous *Poor Richard's Almanac*:

For the want of a nail, the shoe was lost;

For the want of the shoe, the horse was lost;

For the want of the horse, the rider was lost.

Let's test the validity of Franklin's argument by writing it out as a hypothetical syllogism, in this case a chain argument:

If a nail is missing (A), then the horseshoe will be lost (B).

If the horseshoe is lost (B), then the rider is lost (C).

If the nail is missing (A), then the rider is lost (C).

By rewriting this as a hypothetical syllogism, we can see that it is a valid argument. In some cases, it may be too awkward to restate each use of the antecedents and consequents using the exact same language as in the proverb. In these

cases, it is acceptable to use everyday language as long as the meaning remains the same each time it is used. Otherwise, the argument commits the fallacy of equivocation.

A hypothetical syllogism is valid if it follows one of the forms discussed in this chapter—*modus ponens*, *modus tollens*, or chain argument. If you are uncertain whether a hypothetical syllogism is valid, you can also try substituting different terms for those used in the argument under evaluation.

Not all valid arguments are sound. As we noted earlier, a deductive argument can be valid by virtue of its form but still be unsound because one of the premises is false. Rewording arguments in ordinary language in the form of a hypothetical syllogism can help you expose the faulty

---

Rewording arguments in ordinary language in the form of a hypothetical syllogism can help you expose the faulty premises.

---

premises. Suppose you are looking for a new cell phone and find two models that seem to suit your needs—a Samsung and a Motorola. Both have similar features, but the Samsung costs more than the Motorola. So you think: *The Samsung cell phone costs more, so it should be the better phone. I think I'll buy the Samsung.* Putting your argument in the form of a hypothetical syllogism, we have this:

If a product is expensive, then it must be good.

This brand of cell phone is expensive.

Therefore, it must be good.

However, the first premise is false. Not all expensive products are good, nor are all inexpensive products of poor quality. Therefore, this is an unsound argument. Unfortunately, many people fall for this line of reasoning. Indeed, some clever marketers have found that when they increase the price of certain items, such as jewelry or clothing, it actually sells better!

Putting an argument in the form of a hypothetical syllogism can be helpful in clarifying what's at stake. Consider this argument from the abortion debate:

If a being is a person (A), then it is morally wrong to kill that being except in self-defense (B).

The fetus is a person (A).

Therefore, it is morally wrong to kill the fetus except in self-defense (B).

Judith Jarvis Thomson, in her essay "A Defense of Abortion" recognizes the strength of this type of deductive reasoning and acknowledges that she must accept the conclusion if she accepts the premises as true. She also realizes that the only way to reject this argument—since it is a valid argument—is to show that one of the premises is false and therefore the argument is unsound. Otherwise, she *must* accept the conclusion. Since she can't prove that the fetus is not a person, she tentatively accepts the second premise as true. Instead, she questions the first premise, arguing that there may be circumstances when we can kill another person for reasons other than self-defense.

Hypothetical arguments are common in everyday reasoning. In addition to being used in promises and ultimatums (see "Critical Thinking in Action: Empty Promises: If This, Then That—Making Promises and Threats" on page 249), they can be used to spell out the outcomes of certain choices you make in your life: for example, the necessary antecedents you'll need to graduate from college or go on graduate school.

HIGHLIGHTS

VALID FORMS OF HYPOTHETICAL SYLLOGISMS

Modus Ponens	*Modus Tollens*	*Chain Argument*
If A, then B.	If A, then B.	If A, then B.
A.	Not B.	If B, then C.
Therefore, B.	Therefore, not A.	Therefore, if A, then C.

➤ *APPLICATION: Find an example in the text of each of the three types of hypothetical syllogisms.*

EXERCISE 8-3

STOP AND ASSESS YOURSELF

1. Sometimes the conclusion and/or one of the premises is unstated in a deductive argument, leaving you to complete the argument. Complete the following arguments, using valid forms of hypothetical syllogisms and stating which form you are using:

*a. If Sam enlists in the army, then he'll have to go to boot camp.
But Sam does not have to go to boot camp.

b. "If you look at another woman one more time, I'm going to leave you." Mike looks at another woman.

c. If it didn't rain today, I'd have to water the garden. I won't have to water the garden.

*d. If I call Lisa, then she'll know I'm interested in her.
If she knows I'm interested in her, then she might notice me more around campus.

e. If we as a nation don't do something about our unprecedented deficit problem, then we will not be able to pay off our national debt for decades. If we are not able to pay it off, then our children are going to be burdened with an intolerable debt. If our children are burdened with an intolerable debt, then they will have a lower standard of living than that enjoyed by their parents.

f. If the exchange rate is good I'm traveling to Italy and Greece over winter break. The exchange rate is favorable.

*g. If I buy a new car, then I'll have to get a job. I bought a new car.

h. If I take statistics this semester, I'll have enough credits to complete a major in accounting. Then I'll be able to apply to do an MBA in accounting.

i. If you don't stop harassing me I'm going to call the police. I'm calling the police right now.

*j. If Seattle replaced its conventional buses with hybrid-powered buses, they would save several thousands of gallons of fuel annually. In Seattle, the local transit authority has begun taking delivery of 235 hybrid-powered buses.[7]

2. Identify and evaluate each of the following hypothetical syllogisms for validity and soundness.

*a. Zachary did not get the promotion. If Zachary had gotten the promotion, he would be earning an extra $200 a month. But he is not earning an extra $200 a month.

b. If the temperature of freshwater at sea level is below 32° Fahrenheit, then it is frozen. The water in our neighbor's freshwater pond is below 32° Fahrenheit. Therefore, the water in the pond must be frozen.

c. If a newborn baby is diagnosed with AIDS, then he or she will die during the first year of life. Baby Meg was diagnosed with AIDS when she was born. Therefore, she has less than a year to live.

EXERCISE 8-3 CONT.

*d. If you love John, you'll listen to what he says. If you listen to what he says, you'll know that John is trying to lose weight. If you know he is trying to lose weight, you'll avoid offering him sweets. If you love John, you'll avoid offering him sweets.

 e. If Jamiel is a freshman at State College, then he is a student.
    However, Jamiel is not a freshman at State College. Therefore, Jamiel is not a student.

 f. If my short story gets accepted by my college literary journal, I'm going to celebrate by going to Seven Moons Restaurant. I just found out that it didn't get accepted. I guess I'm not going to be celebrating at Seven Moons Restaurant.

*g. You told me that if I helped you pay off this month's rent so you didn't get evicted, then you'd do anything for me that I wanted. Well, I paid your rent. So here's what I want you to do for me: I know you work part time in the registrar's office. So I want you to break into the registrar's office computer system and change my grades to all A's.

 h. If you smoke marijuana, then you're breaking the law. You're not smoking marijuana; therefore, you're not breaking the law.

 i. If a person is a politician, then he always lies. Joe is a politician. Therefore, Joe denies being a politician.

 j. If a person commits a murder in Rhode Island, he or she cannot be given the death penalty. Craig Price murdered three women in Rhode Island. Craig Price cannot be given the death penalty.

 k. If Chad has a fever, then Chad will stay home today. Chad doesn't have a fever. Therefore, Chad will not stay home today.

*l. If John is a Leo, then John is brave. John is a Leo. Therefore, John is brave.

*m. If I become a member of the band Alien Autopsy, then I'll probably have an opportunity to play my steel drums in front of a live audience. If I have an opportunity to play my steel drums in front of a live audience, then I'm more likely to be noticed by a talent scout. Therefore, if I become a member of the band Alien Autopsy, I'm more likely to be noticed by a talent scout.

3. Think of an issue or goal that is important in your life. Write a hypothetical syllogism related to the issue or goal. Evaluate the syllogism for validity and soundness.

*Answers to selected exercises are found in the Solutions Manual at the end of the book.

CATEGORICAL SYLLOGISMS

categorical syllogism A deductive argument with two premises and three terms, each of which occurs exactly twice in two of the three propositions.

subject (S) term In a categorical syllogism, the term that appears first in the conclusion.

predicate (P) term In a categorical syllogism, the term that appears second in the conclusion.

Categorical syllogisms are a type of deductive argument that categorizes or sorts things into specific classes, such as mammals, students, or countries. A categorical syllogism is composed of a conclusion, two premises, and three terms, each of which occurs exactly twice in two of the three propositions. In the following categorical syllogism, each of the three classes or terms—in this case "mammals," "cats," and "tigers"—appears in two propositions.

> All tigers are cats.
> Some mammals are not cats.
> Therefore, some mammals are not tigers.

Did You Know

Categorical syllogisms can be written in any of 256 standard forms or combinations. Although 256 may seem to be an unwieldy number, putting syllogisms in standard form greatly simplifies the process of evaluations.

Standard-Form Categorical Syllogisms

When a categorical syllogism is put into standard form, the terms in the conclusion are given the label *S* for the **subject** of the conclusion and *P* for the **predicate** of the conclusion. The term that occurs only in the two premises is labeled *M*, for **middle term**. The premise containing the *P* term from the conclusion is listed first, and the premise with the *S* term is listed second. Because it is found in the first premise, the *P* term is referred to as the **major term**, and the premise in which it appears is the **major premise**. The *S* term is also known as the **minor term**, and the premise in which it appears is called the **minor premise**. In addition, the verb in a standard-form categorical syllogism is always a form of the verb *to be*, such as *is* or *are*. Using these guidelines, the above argument written in standard form would look like this:

> All tigers (*P*) are cats (*M*).
>
> Some mammals (*S*) are not cats (*M*).
>
> Therefore, some mammals (*S*) are not tigers (*P*).

In other words:

> All *P* are *M*.
>
> Some *S* are not *M*.
>
> Some *S* are not *P*.

As with hypothetical syllogisms, if the form of a categorical syllogism is valid, as it is in this case, the argument will be valid no matter what terms we substitute for *S*, *P*, and *M*. If the form is valid and the premises are true, the conclusion is necessarily true.

Quantity and Quality

Each proposition in a standard-form categorical syllogism is written in one of four forms, determined on the basis of its **quantity** (universal or particular) and **qualifier** (affirmative or negative). If a proposition refers to *every* member of a class, then the quantity is universal. "All *S* are *P*" and "No *S* are *P*" are universal propositions. If a proposition refers only to *some* members of the class, then it is particular. "Some *S* are *P*" and "Some *S* are not *P*" are particular propositions. The **quality** of a proposition is either affirmative or negative. "No *S* are *P*" and "Some *S* are not *P*" are negative propositions.

The quantity and quality of the proposition is determined by its form, not by which terms (*S*, *P*, and *M*) appear as subject and predicate. For example, "All *P* are *M*" and "No *M* are *S*" are both universal propositions.

Quality and Quantity of Standard-Form Propositions

Universal affirmative:	All *S* are *P* (e.g., All oak trees are plants).
Universal negative:	No *S* are *P* (e.g., No squirrels are fish).
Particular affirmative:	Some *S* are *P* (e.g., Some Americans are Muslim).
Particular negative:	Some *S* are not *P* (e.g., Some nurses are not women).

Diagramming Propositions with Venn Diagrams

Each of the four types of propositions can be represented using a **Venn diagram**, in which each term appears as a circle. The class of *S*, for example, can be represented as follows:

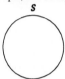

If there are no members of the class *S* (*S* = 0), the circle is shaded in. The following diagram states that there are no members of the class "unicorns," which is represented here by the term *S*.

If there is at least one member of the class (*S* = 0), you put an *X* in the circle. For example, to diagram the class "dogs," we would use an *X*, since there exists at least one dog in the world.

You can follow the same procedure for diagramming any other class represented in a syllogism. Using this method, you can represent each of the four types of propositions in a categorical syllogism using two overlapping circles, since each proposition has two terms. The intersection of the two classes *S* and *P* is the class *SP*, which contains all things that are members of both classes *S* and *P*.

The universal propositions are represented using shading. For example, "All *S* are *P*" says essentially the same thing as "There is no such thing as an *S* that is not a *P*." To represent this, you shade

middle (M) term In a categorical syllogism, the term that appears once in each of the premises.

major term The predicate (P) term in a categorical syllogism.

major premise The premise in a categorical syllogism that contains the predicate term.

minor term The subject (S) term in categorical syllogism.

minor premise The premise in a categorical syllogism that contains the subject term.

quantity Whether a categorical proposition is universal or particular.

qualifier A term such as *all, no,* or *not,* which indicates whether a proposition is affirmative or negative.

quality Whether a categorical proposition is positive or negative.

Venn diagram A visual representation of a categorical syllogism used to determine the validity of the syllogism.

in the part of the *S* circle that does not overlap with the *P* circle.

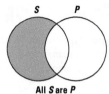

All *S* are *P*

The proposition "No *S* are *P*" states that the class *SP* is empty, or *SP* = 0. To represent this proposition, you shade in the area where the two circles overlap.

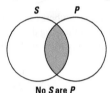

No *S* are *P*

The particular propositions are represented by using an *X*. The proposition "Some *S* are *P*" states that there is at least one member of the class *S* that is also a member of the class *P*. To diagram this, you put an *X* in the area where the two circles overlap.

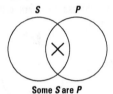

Some *S* are *P*

The proposition "Some *S* are not *P*" tells us that there is at least one *S* that is not a member of the class *P*. To diagram this proposition, you put an *X* in the *S* circle where it does not overlap the *P* circle.

If the proposition stated "Some *P* are not *S*," you would instead put the *X* in the *P* circle where it does not overlap the *S* circle.

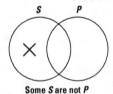

Some *S* are not *P*

Only the Venn diagrams for particular propositions state that there exist members in a class. Venn diagrams for universal propositions, in contrast, only show what doesn't exist. For instance, when we say something like "All tyrannosauruses are dinosaurs," we're not implying that tyrannosauruses actually still exist, just that there is (and was) no such thing as a tyrannosaurus that is *not* a dinosaur.

Venn diagrams engage our spatial reasoning and help us to visualize relationships between classes of things.

Using Venn Diagrams to Evaluate Categorical Syllogisms

Venn diagrams can be used for evaluating the validity of a categorical syllogism. As we noted earlier, Venn diagrams use overlapping circles to represent the terms in a proposition. Since there are three terms (*S*, *P*, and *M*) in a syllogism, you'll need to use three overlapping circles, one for each term. To do this, first draw the two intersecting circles representing the *S* and *P* terms. Then draw the circle representing the *M* term below so that it intersects both the *S* and *P* circles. The area where the *S* and *P* circles overlap makes up the class *SP*, the area where the *S* and *M* circles overlap makes up the class *SM*, and the area where the *P* and *M* circles overlap makes up the class *PM*. The area where all three circles overlap is the class *SPM*.

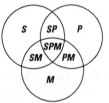

Before diagramming a syllogism, you will need to identify the terms in each proposition. Remember, always start with the conclusion. The first term in the conclusion is *S* and the second term is *P*.

     P   *M*
No (dogs) are (cats).
         S   *M*
Some (mammals) are (cats).
              S   *P*
Therefore, some (mammals) are not (dogs).

The next step is to diagram the two premises. If one of the premises is a universal proposition, start by diagramming that premise. In this case, the first premise, "No *P* are *M*," is a universal proposition. To diagram it, you are going to use only the *P* and *M* circles in the Venn diagram. The proposition "No *P* are *M*" tells you that the class *PM*—the area where the *P* (dogs) and the *M* (cats) circles intersect— is empty. In other words, there are no members of the class *PM* or, in this case, there is no such being as a dog that is a cat. To diagram this, shade in the area where the *P* and *M* circles intersect.

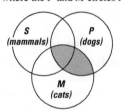

Now diagram the remaining premise "Some *S* are *M*." This proposition tells you that there exists at least one member of the class *S*. In other words, there exists at least one *S* (mammal)

that is also an *M* (cat). To diagram this premise, you put an *X* in the area *SM* where the *S* and *M* circles intersect. Ignore the shaded area where *SM* overlaps *P*, since we know from the first premise that there are no members in *SPM*.

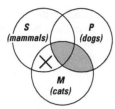

The final step is to determine if the circles contain the diagram for the conclusion, which, in this case, is "Some *S* are not *P*." The conclusion states that there is at least one *S* (mammal) that is not a member of the class *P* (dogs). Diagrammed, this means that there is an *X* in the *S* circle where it does not intersect *P*. Checking this against the diagram of the premises above, we find that there is in fact an *X* in this area. Therefore, this and all other syllogisms of this form are valid.

The following syllogism has already been broken down into its three terms for you:

M   *P*

Some (college students) are (smokers of marijuana).

S   *M*

All (freshmen) are (college students).

S   *P*

Therefore, some (freshmen) are (smokers of marijuana).

In this syllogism the first premise is a particular proposition and the second premise a universal proposition. Therefore, you start by diagramming the second premise. The premise "All *S* are *M*" states that there is no *S* that is not a member of the class *M*. Using only the *S* and *M* circles, shade in the area where the *S* circle does not intersect the *M* circle to show that there are no freshmen who are not also college students.

Next, working only with the *M* and *P* circles, diagram the other premise, "Some *M* are *P*." Place an *X* in the area *MP* where the *M* and *P* circles intersect. Since the *S* circle makes a line through the intersection, draw the *X* on the line to indicate that an *M* (college student) who is a member of the class *P* (smoker of marijuana) may be on either side of this line.

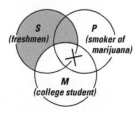

The conclusion states that "some freshmen are smokers of marijuana." In other words, there is an *X* in the class *SP* where the *S* circle and the *P* circle overlap. Looking at the

diagram of the premises, you can see that the conclusion is not contained in the premises, since all that the premises tell us is that there is a member of the class *MP* who may or may not also be a member of the class *SP*. Because the *X* in the premises falls on the line, it is possible that there is a freshman who smokes marijuana, but we can't be sure, since the *X* in the premises may be either in the *SP* circle or only in the *P* circle. Therefore, this argument and all syllogisms that follow this form are invalid.

In using Venn diagrams to determine the validity of a syllogism with two universal or two particular premises, you can start by diagramming either premise. The following is an argument with two universal premises. Begin by labeling the terms in the argument:

P   *M*

All (Americans) are (humans).

S   *M*

No (space aliens) are (humans).

S   *P*

Therefore, no (space aliens) are (Americans).

The first premise states that there are no members of the class *P* (Americans) that are not members of the class *M* (humans). To diagram this, you shade in the area of *P* that does not overlap the *M* circle. The second premise states that there are no *S* (space aliens) that are *M* (humans). Therefore, the area *SM* (human space aliens) is an empty class. To diagram this, you shade in the space where the *S* and the *M* circles overlap, like this:

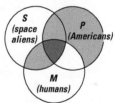

The conclusion states that there are no members of the class *SP* (American space aliens). For this syllogism to be valid, the diagram of the premises must show that *SP* is an empty class. In fact, the area *SP* is shaded in. Therefore, this argument and all syllogisms that follow this form are valid.

Let's look at one last syllogism with two particular premises.

M   *P*

Some (ranchers) are not (horse lovers).

S   *M*

Some (Texans) are (ranchers).

S   *P*

Therefore, some (Texans) are not (horse lovers).

The first premise states that there is at least one rancher who is not a horse lover. To diagram this, place an *X* in the *M* circle where it does not intersect the *P* circle. Remember to put the *X* on that part of the *S* circle where it intersects the *M* circle, since you can't tell from this premise whether this rancher is a Texan. The second premise states that there is at least one Texan (*S*) who is a rancher (*M*). But since this premise does not tell you whether this Texan is a horse lover, put the X on the line in the S circle where the P circle intersects the M circle, since we're not sure which side of the line the Texan belongs on.

Do the premises support the conclusion? To diagram the conclusion, put an X on the line where S intersects M but not P. The conclusion is invalid because the X's from the two premises may be only in the P and M circles. Therefore, this argument is invalid—as are all arguments of this form.

Putting an argument in the form of a categorical syllogism makes it easier to evaluate its validity, either by checking it for formal fallacies or by drawing Venn diagrams. Many everyday arguments can be put into standard-form categorical syllogisms, as discussed in the next section.

EXERCISE 8-4

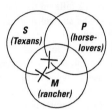

STOP AND ASSESS YOURSELF

1. For each of the following propositions, indicate the form of the proposition (universal affirmative, universal negative, particular affirmative, or particular negative), and then draw a Venn diagram for each proposition.

*a. All beagles are dogs.

b. Some Democrats are socialists.

c. Some members of the Tea Party movement are not Republicans.

*d. No android is a natural object.

e. Some college students are retired people.

f. Some scientists are not atheists.

*g. No atheist is a person who believes in God.

h. All suns are stars.

i. Some people who smoke cigarettes are people who get lung cancer.

*j. Some drugs are not illegal substances.

k. All professional basketball players are people who are more than 5 feet tall.

l. No city or town in Australia is a city or town in the Northern Hemisphere.

2. Using Venn diagrams, determine which of the following syllogisms are valid and which are invalid.

*a. All published authors are writers.
Some writers are professors.
Therefore, some professors are published authors.

b. Some scholars are not geniuses.
Some scholars are football players.
Therefore, some football players are not geniuses.

c. Some Latinos are Republicans.
All Republicans are American citizens.
Therefore, some American citizens are not Latinos.

*d. All members of fraternities are male.
Some college students are not male.
Therefore, some college students are not members of fraternities.

e. Some terrorists are citizens.
No cats are citizens.
Therefore, no cats are terrorists.

f. All members of Congress who voted for the health-care bill are Democrats.
No members of Congress who voted for the health-care bill are Republicans.
Therefore, no Republicans are Democrats.

*g. Some UFO sightings are hallucinations.
Some UFO sightings are sightings of airplanes.
Therefore, some sightings of airplanes are hallucinations.

EXERCISE 8-4 CONT.

h. No nations that allow capital punishment are members of the European Union.
   No European nations are nations that allow capital punishment.
   Therefore, all European nations are members of the European Union.

i. All people living in the Netherlands are people living in the European Union.
   All people living in Amsterdam are people living in the Netherlands.
   Therefore, all people living in Amsterdam are people living in the European Union.

*j. Some Olympic athletes are professional athletes.
   No high school cheerleaders are professional athletes.
   Therefore, no high school cheerleaders are Olympic athletes.

k. Some actors are comedians.
   All comedians are funny people.
   Therefore, some funny people are actors.

l. Some scientists are believers in UFOs.
   No irrational people are scientists.
   Therefore, some irrational people are not believers in UFOs.

*m. Some women are mothers.
   No women are men.
   Therefore, no men are mothers.

n. All pacifists are opponents of capital punishment.
   All pacifists are opponents of war.
   Therefore, all opponents of war are opponents of capital punishment.

*Answers to selected exercises are found in the Solutions Manual at the end of the book.

TRANSLATING ORDINARY ARGUMENTS INTO STANDARD FORM

Most of the deductive arguments that we hear or read in our everyday lives are not expressed as standard-form syllogisms. For example, you and your roommate are discussing whether to buy hamburgers or veggie burgers for a picnic you're throwing. She wants to buy veggie burgers, arguing that "it's wrong to eat meat from animals that are capable of reason, such as cows." Is this a valid argument? To answer this question, you first need to rewrite her argument as a standard-form categorical syllogism with three propositions.

Rewriting Everyday Propositions in Standard Form

Start by identifying the conclusion and rewriting it in standard form. Your roommate is trying to prove that it's wrong to eat meat from animals that are capable of reason. To translate this into a standard-form proposition, ask yourself: "What is the quantity (universal or particular) and the quality (positive or negative) of this statement?" Since her conclusion is referring to only some instances of meat eating, the quantity is particular. The quality of her conclusion is positive—she is saying that it *is* wrong to eat meat, as opposed to *is not*. Her conclusion, therefore, is something like this: "Some meat-eating is wrong."

However, this proposition still isn't in standard form. Standard-form propositions have a subject term and a predicate term that are both either nouns or noun clauses and that are connected by a form of the verb *to be*. In this case, the predicate term *wrong* is an adjective. You can rewrite the adjective as a noun phrase by rewording it as *a wrongful act*. The conclusion is now written as a standard-form proposition:

$$S \qquad\qquad P$$

Some (meat-eating) is (a wrongful act).

Determining the quality and quantity of a proposition is not always as straightforward as in the above example. In some instances, you will need to examine the context of the proposition to determine the quality. Consider the following two statements:

Teenagers have more automobile crashes.

Kangaroos are marsupials.

In the first example, does the speaker mean *all* teenagers or only *some* teenagers? In all likelihood, the speaker is referring to only some teenagers. Translating the statement into a standard-form proposition, you have this:

Some (teenagers) are (people who have more automobile crashes than the average driver).

When people intend or interpret statements such as this to be universal, or about *all* young people, they commit the *fallacy of hasty generalization*. We cannot go from a statement about the reckless driving habits of some to a generalization about all teenagers, since many teenagers are safe drivers and some older drivers are a danger on the road.

In the second example, the speaker is making a statement about all kangaroos, since, by definition, a kangaroo is a marsupial. Consequently, this proposition can be translated as a universal positive (*A*) proposition:

All kangaroos are marsupials.

Phrases in ordinary language that indicate that a proposition is universal include the following:

Every *S* is a *P*.   Each *S* is a *P*.

Only *P* are *S*.   *S* are all *P*.

No *P* are *S*.   Whatever is an *S* is a *P*.

Any *S* is a *P*.   If anything is an *S*, then it is a *P*.

Phrases that indicate that a proposition is particular include these:

Some *S* are *P*.   A few *S* are *P*.

Many *S* are *P*.   Most *S* are not *P*.

Not all *S* are *P*.   With few exceptions, *S* are *P*.

Quantity (positive or negative) is usually easier to determine than quality. When the quantity of a proposition is negative, one of the following terms almost always appears somewhere in the original proposition: *no, nothing, not, none.* However, this isn't a hard-and-fast rule. The term *no* may also appear in a universal positive statement, as in this example:

No valid syllogisms are syllogisms with two negative premises.

Translated into standard form, this statement becomes a universal positive proposition:

All syllogisms with two negative premises are invalid syllogisms.

Therefore it is important, when translating a statement into a standard-form proposition, to go back and check to make sure it says the same thing as the original statement.

Identifying the Three Terms in the Argument

The next step is to identify the three terms. If you have already translated the conclusion into a standard-form proposition, you have identified two of the terms.

In the opening argument about whether to buy veggie burgers or hamburgers, we recast the conclusion as a standard-form proposition: "Some (meat-eating) is (a wrongful act)." You will notice that there is a term from the original argument that does not appear in the conclusion: "Animals that are capable of reason, such as cows." This term is the middle term (*M*) in the argument. In some ordinary arguments, not all the propositions are explicitly stated. In this case, there is a missing premise that might be worded something like this: "It is wrong to eat animals that are capable of reason." That proposition

HIGHLIGHTS

GUIDELINES FOR TRANSLATING ARGUMENTS INTO STANDARD CATEGORICAL FORM

- **Rewrite each proposition in standard form, starting with the conclusion.**
- **Use the context and grammar of the original argument to decide which quantifier *(all, some,* or *no)* to use.**
- **Identify the three terms in the argument.**
- **Where necessary, rewrite each term as a noun or noun phrase.**
- **Each proposition should use a form of the verb *to be (is, are).***
- **Put the syllogism in standard form with the major premise (P) first, followed by the minor premise (S), and then the conclusion.**

➤ *APPLICATION: Identify an example in the text of the application of each guideline.*

is universal and affirmative. Putting it in standard form, you have:

All (killing of animals that are capable of reason, such as cows,) is (a wrongful act).

The second premise can be written as a particular affirmative proposition, since your roommate is saying that only particular types of meat-eating, rather than all meat-eating, are wrong.

Some (meat-eating) is (killing of animals that are capable of reason, such as cows).

Although the verb *involves* would be better English usage here, remember that the verb in a syllogism must be a form of the verb *to be.* Although the wording of this premise is a little awkward, it will do for the purpose of evaluation.

Sometimes there are more than three terms in an ordinary argument. In these cases you will need to reduce the terms to three. If there are two terms that are synonyms, use the same term for both. If there are two terms that are antonyms, or mean the opposite of each other, reduce them to one term by using *not* in front of the antonym. When there are terms that are not essential to the argument, you can simply eliminate them. Consider the following argument:

Not all birds migrate. The spot-breasted oriole, for example, lives on the east coast of Florida year-round.

There are four terms in this argument: *birds, beings that migrate, spot-breasted oriole,* and *beings that live on the east coast of Florida year-round.* In this argument you can combine the second and fourth terms into one by rewriting *beings that live on the east coast of Florida year-round* as *not beings that migrate*. The fact that they live in Florida is not essential to the argument and can be eliminated. The argument now has three terms:

> No (spot-breasted orioles) are (beings that migrate).
>
> All (spot-breasted orioles) are (birds).
>
> Therefore, some (birds) are not (beings that migrate).

Putting the Argument into Standard Form

After you have identified the three terms and translated all of the propositions into standard form, you can rewrite the argument as a standard-form categorical syllogism. Going back to our original argument, we have:

> All (killing of animals that are capable of reason, such as cows,) is a (wrongful act).
>
> Some (meat eating) is (killing of animals that are capable of reason, such as cows).
>
> Therefore, some (meat-eating) is a (wrongful act).

Once you've set up the argument as a standard-form syllogism, you can easily determine whether it is valid. In this case, it is a valid syllogistic form. In other words, if you agree with the premises, you *must* accept the conclusion. However, you may disagree with the conclusion, even though the argument is valid—but only if you believe that one of the premises is false and the argument therefore unsound. For example, you may argue that the second premise is untrue because only humans are capable of reason and therefore no animals we eat for meat are beings capable of reason. But you'll need evidence to support your position.

Recognizing and evaluating deductive arguments are important skills for everyday decision-making. Using mathematical arguments, arguments by elimination, arguments based on definition, hypothetical syllogisms, and chain arguments, you can use *known* information to discover—with absolute certainty—*unknown* information. Additionally, ordinary arguments used by other people can be translated into standard form to be analyzed for soundness and validity. In Chapter 9, we will discuss the use of critical thinking in moral decision making and in the discussion of ethical issues.

STOP AND ASSESS YOURSELF

EXERCISE 8-5

1. Translate the following arguments into standard-form categorical syllogisms. Identify the form of each syllogism. Determine the validity of each syllogism using Venn diagrams.

*a. "Since man is made in the image of God, then the taking of a man's life is the destruction of the most precious and the most holy thing in the world."[8]

b. If something is a bird then it has feathers. That means my hat must be a bird because it has feathers!

c. The majority of college students are civic-minded, since most college students do some sort of volunteer work and since people who volunteer tend to be civic-minded.

*d. Not everyone who smokes marijuana goes on to use hard drugs. All of my college roommates smoked marijuana, and none of them went on to use hard drugs.

e. Although it's true that most Hispanics are Democrats, this isn't always the case. Cubans, for example, are more likely to vote Republican.

f. Not all parents are heterosexual. I know at least half a dozen gay and lesbian parents.

*g. Teams that wear red uniforms are more likely to win than those who don't. Our team, the Blue Jays, is certain to lose the tournament tonight because we wear blue uniforms, while the opposing team, the Cardinals, will be wearing red uniforms.

h. Not all people who take more than five years to complete a degree are lazy. Some college students take more than five years to complete their degree and no college students are lazy.

i. Many of the abnormal weather patterns we've been experiencing in the past decade are a result of global warming. We've experienced an unprecedented number of droughts and heat spells during the past decade. Many of them are no doubt due to global warming.

*j. Despite what you may have heard, not all college professors are liberals. Some of the professors I know actually voted in favor of free-speech zones on campus, which is something no liberals would do.

2. Find an argument on the Internet or in a newspaper, magazine, or book. Translate the argument into a standard-form categorical syllogism.

*Answers to selected exercises are found in the Solutions Manual at the end of the book.

THiNK AGAIN

1. What is a deductive argument?
   - A deductive argument is one in which its conclusion necessarily follows from the premises if the argument is sound. A sound argument is one in which the premises are true and the form of the argument is valid.

2. What are some of the types of deductive arguments?
   - There are many types of deductive arguments, including arguments by elimination, mathematical arguments, arguments from definition, hypothetical syllogisms, and categorical syllogisms.

3. What is a syllogism, and how do we know if it is valid?
   - A syllogism is a deductive argument with exactly two premises and one conclusion. To be valid, the different types of syllogisms have to conform to particular forms. Venn diagrams can be used to determine if the form of a categorical syllogism is valid.

Perspectives on the Death Penalty

In 2011, 93 percent of all known executions worldwide took place in five countries: China, Iran, Iraq, Saudi Arabia, and the United States.[9] The United States is the only Western democracy that still uses the death penalty. More than two-thirds of countries have abolished the death penalty in law or practice, including[10] most Latin American and African countries. Both the European Union and the United Nations support worldwide abolition of the death penalty.

The death penalty was abolished in the United States in 1972 by the U.S. Supreme Court, which ruled that, given the arbitrary and often racially biased patterns in which it was applied, it was "cruel and unusual" punishment.[11] However, the death penalty was reinstated by the U.S. Supreme Court in *Gregg v. Georgia* (1976), which ruled that the death penalty does not violate the U.S. Constitution and for certain extreme crimes is the "only adequate response." Since that time, more than a thousand convicts have been executed. Although as of 2013 capital punishment is legal in thirty-two states, only eleven states and the federal government actually carry out capital punishment, with Texas leading in the number of executions. As of October 2012, there were 3,146 prisoners on death row in the United States.

Even though opposition to the death penalty remains strong among other Western nations, currently the death penalty has widespread support among Americans. A 2013 Gallup Poll found that 63 percent of Americans support the death penalty, up from 47 percent in 1965. Opposition to the death penalty is highest among women and minorities.

In the United States, most executions today are carried out through lethal injection. Because of the lengthy appeal process and the time prisoners spend on death row, the average cost associated with a death penalty case can amount to several million dollars. According to the ACLU, it can cost as much as three times more to keep a prisoner on death row before execution than to maintain a prisoner with a life sentence.

In the following readings, Ernest van den Haag presents arguments for the death penalty, while the American Civil Liberties Union (ACLU) argues against its use.

The Ultimate Punishment: A Defense of Capital Punishment

ERNEST VAN DEN HAAG

Ernest van den Haag is a retired professor of jurisprudence and public policy at Fordham University. An advocate of the death penalty, van den Haag argues that the primary purpose of the death penalty is to satisfy the demands of retributive justice. In his article, he also responds to abolitionists' arguments that capital punishment discriminates against minorities.[12]

The death penalty is our harshest punishment. It is irrevocable: it ends the existence of those punished, instead of temporarily imprisoning them. Further, although not intended to cause physical pain, execution is the only corporal punishment still applied to adults. These singular characteristics contribute to the perennial, impassioned controversy about capital punishment.

I. Distribution Consideration of the justice, morality, or usefulness of capital punishment is often conflated with objections to its alleged discriminatory or capricious distribution among the guilty. Wrongly so. If capital punishment is immoral *in se*, no distribution among the guilty could make it moral. If capital punishment is moral, no distribution would make it immoral. Improper distribution cannot affect the quality of what is distributed, be it punishments or rewards. Discriminatory or capricious distribution thus could not justify abolition of the death penalty. Further, maldistribution inheres no more in capital punishment than in any other punishment.

. . .

Maldistribution of any punishment among those who deserve it is irrelevant to its justice or morality. Even if poor or black convicts guilty of capital offenses suffer capital punishment, and other convicts equally guilty of the same crimes do not, a more equal distribution, however desirable, would merely be more equal. It would not be more just to the convicts under sentence of death.

Punishments are imposed on persons, not on racial or economic groups. Guilt is personal. The only relevant question is: does the person to be executed deserve the punishment? Whether or not others who deserve the same punishment, whatever their economic or racial group, have avoided execution is irrelevant. . . .

Equality, in short, seems morally less important than justice. And justice is independent of distributional inequalities. The ideal of equal justice demands that justice be equally distributed, not that it be replaced by equality. Justice requires that as many of the guilty as possible be punished, regardless of whether others have avoided punishment. . . .

II. Miscarriages of Justice In a recent survey Professors Hugo Adam Bedau and Michael Radelet found that 1,000 persons were executed in the United States between 1900 and 1985 and that 25 were innocent of capital crimes.

. . . Despite precautions, nearly all human activities, such as trucking, lighting, or construction, cost the lives of some innocent bystanders. We do not give up these activities, because the advantages, moral or material, outweigh the unintended losses. Analogously, for those who think the death penalty just, miscarriages of justice are offset by the moral benefits and the usefulness of doing justice. For those who think the death penalty unjust even when it does not miscarry, miscarriages can hardly be decisive.

III. Deterrence Despite much recent work, there has been no conclusive statistical demonstration that the death penalty is a better deterrent than are alternative punishments. However, deterrence is less than decisive for either side. Most abolitionists acknowledge that they would continue to favor abolition even if the death penalty were shown to deter more murders than alternatives could deter.

. . . Deterrence is not altogether decisive for me either. I would favor retention of the death penalty as retribution even if it were shown that the threat of execution could not deter prospective murderers not already deterred by the threat of imprisonment. Still, I believe the death penalty, because of its finality, is more feared than imprisonment, and deters some prospective murderers not deterred by the threat of imprisonment. Sparing the lives of even a few prospective victims by deterring their murderers is more important than preserving the lives of convicted murderers because of the possibility, or even the probability, that executing them would not deter others.

IV. Incidental Issues: Cost, Relative Suffering, Brutalization . . . Some believe that the monetary cost of appealing a capital sentence is excessive. Yet most comparisons of the cost of life imprisonment with the cost of execution, apart from their dubious relevance, are flawed at least by the implied assumption that life prisoners will generate no judicial costs during their imprisonment. At any rate, the actual monetary costs are trumped by the importance of doing justice.

Others insist that a person sentenced to death suffers more than his victim suffered, and that this (excess) suffering is undue according to the *lex talionis* (rule of retaliation). We cannot know whether the murderer on death row suffers more than his victim suffered; however, unlike the murderer, the victim deserved none of the suffering inflicted. Further, the limitations of the *lex talionis* were meant to restrain private vengeance, not the social retribution that has taken its place. Punishment—regardless of the motivation—is not intended to revenge, offset, or compensate for the victim's suffering, or to be measured by it. Punishment is to vindicate the law and the social order undermined by the crime. . . .

Another argument heard . . . is that by killing a murderer, we encourage, endorse, or legitimize unlawful killing. Yet, although all punishments are meant to be unpleasant, it is seldom argued that they legitimize the unlawful imposition of identical unpleasantness. Imprisonment is not thought to legitimize kidnapping; neither are fines thought to legitimize robbery. . . .

V. Justice, Excess, Degradation We threaten punishments in order to deter crime. We impose them not only to make the threats credible but also as retribution (justice) for the crimes that were not deterred. . . . By committing the crime, the criminal volunteered to assume the risk of receiving a legal punishment that he could have avoided by not committing the crime. The punishment he suffers is the punishment he voluntarily risked suffering and, therefore, it is no more unjust to him than any other event for which one knowingly volunteers to assume the risk. Thus, the death penalty cannot be unjust to the guilty criminal.

There remain, however, two moral objections. The penalty may be regarded as always excessive as retribution and always morally degrading.

. . .

Justice Brennan has insisted that the death penalty is "uncivilized," "inhuman," inconsistent with "human dignity" and with "the sanctity of life," that it "treats members of the human race as non-humans, as objects to be toyed with and discarded," that it is "uniquely degrading to human dignity" and "by its very nature, [involves] a denial of the executed person's humanity."

. . . Yet philosophers, such as Immanuel Kant and G. F. W. Hegel, have insisted that, when deserved, execution, far from degrading the executed convict, affirms his humanity by affirming his rationality and his responsibility for his actions. They thought that execution, when deserved, is required for the sake of the convict's dignity. (Does not life imprisonment violate human dignity more than execution, by keeping alive a prisoner deprived of all autonomy?)

. . . This degradation is self-inflicted. By murdering, the murderer has so dehumanized himself that he cannot remain among the living. The social recognition of his self-degradation is the punitive essence of execution. To believe, as Justice Brennan appears to, that the degradation is inflicted by the execution reverses the direction of causality.

Execution of those who have committed heinous murders may deter only one murder per year. If it does, it seems quite warranted. It is also the only fitting retribution for murder I can think of.

REVIEW QUESTIONS

1. How does van den Haag respond to the argument that capital punishment is wrong because it is applied in a discriminatory manner?

2. How does van den Haag respond to the argument that capital punishment is wrong because an innocent person may be executed?

3. How does van den Haag respond to the argument that capital punishment may not be an effective deterrent to crime?

4. According to van den Haag, why do justice and the principle of retribution require capital punishment for some crimes?

The Case Against the Death Penalty

AMERICAN CIVIL LIBERTIES UNION (ACLU)

The American Civil Liberties Union believes the death penalty inherently violates the constitutional ban against cruel and unusual punishment and the guarantees of due process of law and of equal protection under the law. In the following statement, issued on December 11, 2012, the ACLU presents six arguments against the death penalty.

Capital punishment is an intolerable denial of civil liberties and is inconsistent with the fundamental values of our democratic system. The death penalty is uncivilized in theory and unfair and inequitable in practice. Through litigation, legislation, and advocacy against this barbaric and brutal institution, we strive to prevent executions and seek the abolition of capital punishment.

The ACLU's opposition to capital punishment incorporates the following fundamental concerns:

. . .

Capital punishment is cruel and unusual. It is cruel because it is a relic of the earliest days of penology, when slavery, branding, and other corporal punishments were commonplace. Like those barbaric practices, executions have no place in a civilized society. It is unusual because only the United States of all the western industrialized nations engages in this punishment. It is also unusual because only a random sampling of convicted murderers in the United States receive a sentence of death.

Capital punishment denies due process of law. Its imposition is often arbitrary, and always irrevocable—forever depriving an individual of the opportunity to benefit from new evidence or new laws that might warrant the reversal of a conviction, or the setting aside of a death sentence.

The death penalty violates the constitutional guarantee of equal protection. It is applied randomly—and discriminatorily. It is imposed disproportionately upon those whose victims are white, offenders who are people of color, and on those who are poor and uneducated and concentrated in certain geographic regions of the country.

The death penalty is not a viable form of crime control. When police chiefs were asked to rank the factors that, in their judgment, reduce the rate of violent crime, they mentioned curbing drug use and putting more officers on the street, longer sentences and gun control. They ranked the death penalty as least effective. Politicians who preach the desirability of executions as a method of crime control deceive the public and mask their own failure to identify and confront the true causes of crime.

Capital punishment wastes limited resources. It squanders the time and energy of courts, prosecuting attorneys, defense counsel, juries, and courtroom and law enforcement personnel. It unduly burdens the criminal justice system, and it is thus counterproductive as an instrument for society's control of violent crime. Limited funds that could be used to prevent and solve crime (and provide education and jobs) are spent on capital punishment.

Opposing the death penalty does not indicate a lack of sympathy for murder victims. On the contrary, murder demonstrates a lack of respect for human life. Because life is precious and death irrevocable, murder is abhorrent, and a policy of state-authorized killings is immoral. It epitomizes the tragic inefficacy and brutality of violence, rather than reason, as the solution to difficult social problems. Many murder victims do not support state-sponsored violence to avenge the death of their loved one. Sadly, these victims have often been marginalized by politicians and prosecutors, who would rather publicize the opinions of pro-death penalty family members.

. . .

A society that respects life does not deliberately kill human beings. An execution is a violent public spectacle of official homicide, and one that endorses killing to solve social problems—the worst possible example to set for the citizenry, and especially children. Governments worldwide have often attempted to justify their lethal fury by extolling the purported benefits that such killing would bring to the rest of society. The benefits of capital punishment are illusory, but the bloodshed and the resulting destruction of community decency are real.

© ACLU, 125 Broad Street, 18th Floor, New York NY 10004
This is the website of the American Civil Liberties Union and the ACLU Foundation.

REVIEW QUESTIONS

1. According to the ACLU, how does capital punishment deny due process of law and violate the Constitution?

2. What does the ACLU mean when it claims that capital punishment is ineffective in controlling crime?

3. How does capital punishment waste limited resources?

4. In what ways does the death penalty violate respect for human life?

THiNK AND DISCUSS

PERSPECTIVES ON THE DEATH PENALTY

1. Working in small groups, summarize the arguments from the readings. Which side presents the strongest argument? Evaluate the arguments.

2. Find a hypothetical argument and a categorical syllogism in one of the readings. Rewrite the argument as a standard-form deductive argument. Evaluate the argument for both validity and soundness.

3. Van den Haag maintains that justice in the form of retribution demands capital punishment for murderers. Do you agree? Discuss how van den Haag would most likely respond to the call from the ACLU to abolish capital punishment.

4. One of the criticisms of the death penalty in the United States is that it is racist. Is this a strong enough concern for abolishing the death penalty? Critically evaluate van den Haag's counter-argument to this concern.

5. Clarence Darrow, a famous American criminal defense attorney (1857–1938), believed that human behavior is determined by circumstances out of our control. In his "Address to the Prisoners in the Cook County (Chicago) Jail," Darrow told the inmates:

   > In one sense, everybody is equally good and equally bad. . . .
   > There were circumstances that drove you to do exactly the thing which you did. You could not help it any more than we outside can help taking the position we take. . . .
   >   I will guarantee to take from this jail, or any jail in the world, five hundred men who have been the worst criminals and law-breakers who ever got into jail. And I will go down to our lowest streets and take five hundred of the most abandoned prostitutes, and go out somewhere where there is plenty of good land, and will give them a chance to make a living, and they will be as good people as the average in the community.

   Identify the premises and conclusion in Darrow's argument. Evaluate the soundness of his argument. Discuss how van den Haag might respond to Darrow's claim that criminals are simply products of their environments and do not deserve to be punished.

6. Should a criminal's level of cognitive development be considered in sentencing? Discuss whether murderers who lack effective critical-thinking skills or who are cognitively immature should receive the death penalty.

9

ETHICS & MORAL
DECISION MAKING

The use of performance-enhancing drugs, substances that are taken to perform better athletically, is prevalent among professional and Olympic athletes. In recent years there also has been a trend toward their use among college athletes, and a study claims that around 5 percent of middle and high school students have used a type of drug called anabolic steroids to bulk up muscle.[1, 2]

Anabolic steroids are synthetic versions of the hormone testosterone and are used to stimulate muscle growth and increase strength, and help athletes recover between workouts or races. However, use of these steroids also increases the risk of heart attacks and strokes and may contribute to the development of liver disease.[3] In addition, some scientists believe that steroid use may contribute to depression, paranoia, and aggressive behavior. In 2007, professional wrestler Chris Benoit strangled his wife and suffocated his 7-year-old son before hanging

What do you think motivated Sean "Diddy" Combs to volunteer his time helping others? How can improving our moral reasoning skills help us to make effective moral decisions that motivate us to take action to improve our lives and those of others?

THiNK
FIRST

- How does conscience help us to make moral decisions?
- What is the stage theory regarding the development of moral reasoning?
- In what ways can the different moral theories help us in formulating moral arguments?

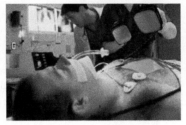

>> himself from a pulley in his basement weight room. His autopsy revealed a high concentration of steroids in his body.[4]

The possession or sale of anabolic steroids without a valid prescription is illegal, and their use is banned by most professional sports leagues as well as the International Olympic Committee (IOC) and National Collegiate Athletic Association (NCAA).

Suppose you are the captain and star player on your college basketball team, and you've made it into the finals. A wealthy entrepreneur, who is an avid basketball fan and alumnus of your college, has promised to make a $60 million donation to your school *if* your team wins the finals. Your college desperately needs the money. It is currently in serious financial trouble and has been forced to cut back on academic programs.

A few weeks before the game, the same entrepreneur offers you a banned performance-enhancing substance known as tetrahydro-gestrinone, or THG, one of the new "designer" steroids. When you express concern about getting caught, he assures you that you won't get caught, since THG has been cloaked to avoid detection by drug tests. He also tells you that he will make a $6 million donation, one-tenth of the original amount, even if your team loses, but only on the condition that you take the drug for the next 2 weeks and give the game your best effort. The team you are playing has won the finals the past 3 years in a row.

What should you do? Your school desperately needs the money, and you could do a lot of good for your school by taking the drug. On the other hand, what about possible physical harms of the steroids to yourself? Also, would it be fair to the other team or to sports fans if you had an advantage because of taking this banned drug?

This situation is an example of a moral conflict that requires you to engage in moral reasoning. We are confronted with moral decisions every day of our lives. Fortunately, most of these decisions are fairly straightforward. For the most part we keep promises, don't steal someone else's laptop when their backs are turned, wait our turn in line, and offer a helping hand to those in need. Although we may be unaware of having consciously made these decisions, we have nonetheless engaged in moral reasoning.

Perhaps in no other area are people so prone to engage in rhetoric and resistance as in debates over controversial moral issues such as capital punishment or abortion. Skill in critical thinking can help us to evaluate moral issues from multiple perspectives as well as break through patterns of resistance. In this chapter, we'll be learning how to make moral decisions in our everyday lives as well as how to think about and discuss controversial moral issues. In Chapter 9 we will:

- Examine the relationship between morality and happiness
- Distinguish between moral values and non-moral values
- Learn about the role of conscience and moral sentiments in moral decision making
- Study the stages in the development of moral reasoning
- Examine moral reasoning in college students
- Evaluate the different moral theories
- Learn how to recognize and construct moral arguments
- Apply strategies for resolving moral dilemmas

Finally, we will read and evaluate arguments regarding the morality of abortion and work toward seeking possible resolutions of the issue.

WHAT IS MORAL REASONING?

We engage in **moral reasoning** when we make a decision about what we ought or ought not to do, or about what is the most reasonable or just position or policy regarding a particular issue. Effective moral decision making depends on good critical-thinking skills, familiarity with basic moral values, and the motivating force of moral sentiments.

Aristotle, shown on left, taught that morality is the most fundamental expression of our rational nature and that we are happiest when we put moral values above nonmoral values.

Moral Values and Happiness

Aristotle believed that morality is the most fundamental expression of our rational human nature. It is through being moral, he argued, that we are happiest. The association of morality with happiness and a sense of well-being is found in moral philosophies throughout the world.

Studies support the claim that people who put moral values above nonmoral concerns are happier and more self-fulfilled.[5] **Moral values** are those that benefit yourself and others and are worthwhile for their own sake. They include altruism, compassion, tolerance, forgiveness, and justice. **Nonmoral (instrumental) values** are goal-oriented. They are a means (an instrument) to an end we wish to achieve. Nonmoral values include independence, prestige, fame, popularity, and wealth, which we desire for the most part because we believe they will bring us greater happiness.

> **moral reasoning** Used when a decision is made about what we ought or ought not to do.
>
> **moral values** Values that benefit oneself and others and are worthwhile for their own sake.
>
> **nonmoral (instrumental) values** Values that are goal oriented—a means to an end to be achieved.

ANALYZING **IMAGES**

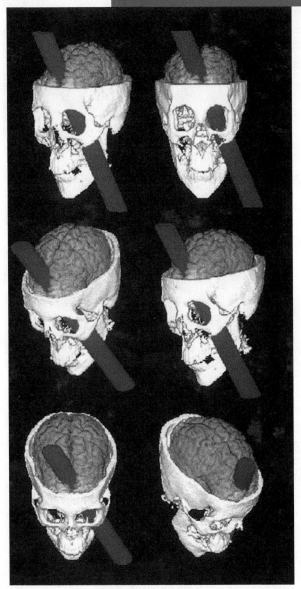

The Brain and Moral Reasoning: The Case of Phineas P. Gage
The frontal lobe cortex in the brain plays a key role in moral decision making. One of the most fascinating studies on the relation between the brain and morality was carried out by a team of scientists on the skull of a nineteenth-century railroad worker, Phineas P. Gage. In 1848, Gage was working on a railway track in Vermont when one of the explosives accidentally went off. The impact sent a long metal rod through his skull just behind his left eye. The rod passed through the frontal lobes of his brain and landed several yards away. This photo shows computer-generated images of the most likely path the rod took as it passed through Gage's skull.

After Gage recovered from the accident, his intellectual and motor skills were found to be unaffected. However, he was no longer able to engage in moral reasoning. Before the accident Gage had been well liked, responsible, and a good worker, whereas afterward he was untrustworthy and obscene and seemed incapable of making even the simplest moral decisions.

DISCUSSION QUESTIONS

1. *Neurologist Jonathan Pincus conducted a study of 14 death row inmates who committed their first murder before the age of 18, and 119 teenagers living in a reform school for delinquents. He found that violent crime is strongly correlated with neurological abnormalities in the brain. If our ability to engage in moral reasoning is dependent on our brain structure, should people such as Gage and criminals whose frontal lobes are abnormal be held morally responsible or punished for their harmful actions? Discuss how we should respond to people who seem to lack a moral sense and hurt others without compunction.*

2. *We expect people to behave morally. When they don't, we're generally taken aback. Think of a situation where you've been surprised because someone seemed to lack a sense of morality. What was your reaction to this person? Discuss why you reacted as you did.*

---

moral tragedy This occurs when we make a moral decision that is later regretted.

conscience A source of knowledge that provides us with knowledge about what is right and wrong.

affective The emotional aspect of conscience that motivates us to act.

moral sentiments Emotions that alert us to moral situations and motivate us to do what is right.

helper's high The feeling that occurs when we help other people.

When buying a car, a person who places nonmoral values above moral values might base his or her decision on stylishness, cost, and a desire to impress other people. A person who places moral values above nonmoral values, in contrast, might place more emphasis on fuel efficiency and environmental friendliness. Although many Americans regard nonmoral values such as career success, financial prosperity, and flashy materialism as the means to happiness, there is in fact little correlation between prosperity or level of income and happiness, except at the lowest levels of income.

On the other hand, there is a positive correlation between level of moral reasoning and critical-thinking ability.[6] This is not surprising, given that critical thinking requires not only that we be aware of our own values but also that we be open-minded and willing to respect the concerns of others.

When we fail to take appropriate moral action or make a moral decision that we later regret, we commit what is called a **moral tragedy**. In the Milgram study on obedience

The Montgomery Bus Boycott began as a protest against the unjust segregation on buses and ended with the U.S. Supreme Court outlawing segregation on buses.

and shaped by our family, religion, and culture.

Conscience has an **affective** (emotional) element that motivates us to act on this knowledge of right and wrong. In Chapter 2, we learned that healthy emotional development can predispose us to make better decisions. Effective moral reasoning involves listening to the affective side of our conscience as well as to the cognitive or reasoning side. Indeed, research shows that psychopaths intellectually recognize right from wrong when presented with a moral dilemma. However, they act violently anyway because they lack the emotional components of sympathy and guilt.[7]

Moral sentiments are emotions that alert us to moral situations and motivate us to do what is right. They include, among others, "helper's high," empathy and sympathy, compassion, moral outrage, resentment, and guilt.

When you help other people, you feel happy and good about yourself. This is known as **helper's high**. The feeling of helper's high is accompanied by the release of or increase in endorphins—morphinelike chemicals that occur naturally in your body. This is followed by a period of increased relaxation and improved self-esteem, which, as we learned in Chapter 1, enhances critical thinking.[8]

Empathy, or *sympathy*, is the capacity for imagining and the inclination to imagine the feelings of others. This moral sentiment expresses itself as joy at another's happiness and sadness at their despair. **Compassion** is sympathy in action and involves taking steps to relieve others' unhappiness. Although most of us are able to feel empathy or sympathy for those who are similar to us, we have a tendency (as we learned in Chapter 4) to divide the world into "us" and "them."

Not all moral sentiments are warm and fuzzy. **Moral outrage**, also known as moral indignation, occurs when we witness an injustice or violation of moral decency. Moral outrage motivates us to correct an unjust situation by demanding that *justice* be done. **Resentment** is a type of moral outrage that occurs when we ourselves are treated unjustly. For example, Rosa Parks's resentment, as well as her courage, motivated her to refuse to give up her seat on the bus to a white man. Her actions sparked the 1955–1956 bus boycott

(see Chapter 1), most of the study subjects who continued to deliver "shocks" to the "learner" knew that what they were doing was morally wrong. However, they lacked the necessary critical-thinking skills to come up with counterarguments to the researcher's argument that "the experiment requires that you must continue."

compassion Sympathy in action.

moral outrage Indignation in the presence of an injustice or violation of moral decency.

resentment A type of moral outrage that occurs when we ourselves are treated unjustly.

Conscience and Moral Sentiments

For most people, a well-developed conscience is the essence of the moral life. The word *conscience* comes from the Latin words *com* ("with") and *scire* ("to know"). A well-developed **conscience** provides us with knowledge about what is right and wrong. Like language, whose basic structure is innate, conscience is nurtured (or neglected)

Connections

What are some of the moral issues involved in a decision to engage in civil disobedience? *See Chapter 13, pp. 410–413.*

SELF-EVALUATION QUESTIONNAIRE: MORAL REASONING*

Case I: Man with an Assault Rifle

Carlos is walking to class one afternoon when he notices a man heading toward a large lecture hall brandishing an assault rifle and swearing under his breath. Carlos, who is interested in pursuing a career in law enforcement, has just come from the shooting range where he enjoys target practice. However, he still has his bag containing his handgun with him, despite the fact that no firearms of any kind are allowed on his campus. No one else has noticed the man with the rifle. If the man starts shooting, should Carlos use his gun on the assailant?

Looking at the following list, determine which considerations are most important to you in deciding what to do. Also determine whether each (1) appeals to personal interests, (2) maintains norms, or (3) appeals to moral ideals or principles. Finally, discuss what other considerations and arguments are important to you in making your decision.

  a. Whether stopping the potential assailant or observing the campus's gun code would be better for Carlos's future career in law enforcement

  b. Whether the campus's gun code is unjust and getting in the way of protecting unsuspecting students' right to life

  c. Whether Carlos's using his gun will anger the public and give his college a bad name

  d. Whether Carlos is more responsible to those who created the university's gun code or instead to the students whose lives are in danger

  e. Whether Carlos is willing to risk being expelled or going to jail

  f. What the basic values are that dictate how people treat one another

  g. Whether the man brandishing the rifle deserves to be shot for posing a threat to students

Case II: Buying an Essay from the Internet

Jennifer, a college junior, is taking five courses and doing an internship while trying to maintain her 4.0 grade-point average so that she can get into a good law school and become a civil-rights lawyer. After staying up all night to complete a fifteen-page term paper, Jennifer realizes that she forgot to write a four-page response paper due for an English literature class she's taking. Strapped for time and not wanting to damage her grade in the course, she remembers another student in her class telling her about a Web site that sells essays. She goes to the Web site and finds an essay that fits the assignment. Should Jennifer buy the paper and turn it in as her own?

Looking at the following list, determine which considerations are most important to you in deciding what to do. Also determine whether each (1) appeals to personal interests, (2) maintains norms, or (3) appeals to moral ideals or principles. Finally, discuss what other considerations and arguments are important to you in making your decision.

  a. Whether the campus rules against plagiarism should be respected

  b. How big the risk is that Jennifer will get caught

  c. Whether it is fair to the other students applying to law school if Jennifer isn't caught and gets accepted instead of them because she turned in a plagiarized essay

  d. Other students in the class are plagiarizing

  e. Whether turning in the paper from the Internet will be best for her future career

  f. Whether she is violating the rights of the professor and other students in the class by turning in the essay

  g. Whether the professor brought this on himself by placing too many demands on his students

* See page 432 to learn which stage of moral reasoning each answer represents.

in Montgomery, Alabama—one of the turning points in the modern American struggle for civil rights.

While moral outrage calls our attention to an injustice, without effective moral reasoning and critical-thinking skills we may fail to act or may respond ineffectively. Moral outrage or resentment that is not guided by reason may degenerate into feelings of bitterness, blame, or helplessness.

Guilt both alerts us to and motivates us to correct a wrong we have committed. Guilt is a lot like pain. When you cut yourself, you feel pain at the site where the injury occurred. The pain motivates you to repair the injury before it becomes infected and festers. Guilt also motivates us to avoid harming ourselves and others. We refrain from cheating on an exam or from stealing someone's laptop—even when no one is around to see us take it—because the very thought of doing so makes us feel guilty.

Guilt is frequently regarded as a barrier to personal freedom and happiness. Some of us respond to guilt with resistance, either trying to ignore it entirely or getting angry at the person who "made" us feel guilty. But at the same time, we generally regard a person who feels no guilt—such as a

sociopath—as inhuman and a monster. This uncertainty about the nature of guilt stems in part from a confusion of guilt with shame.

Guilt is often broadly defined to include shame. However, the two are different. **Guilt** results when we commit a moral wrong or violate a moral principle. **Shame**, on the other hand, occurs as a result of the violation of a social norm, or not living up to someone else's expectations for us. Teenagers who are lesbian, gay, or bisexual may feel shame for not living up to the expectations of their family, church, or society—but they generally do not feel moral guilt. Rather than motivating us to do better, shame leaves us feeling inadequate, embarrassed, and humiliated. As good critical thinkers, it is important that we distinguish between guilt and shame.

Conscience, which has both a cognitive and an affective aspect, can aid in moral decision making. The affective side of conscience includes moral sentiments that motivate us to take action. In the next section, we'll be studying the cognitive or reasoning side of our conscience.

> **guilt** A moral sentiment that alerts us to and motivates us to correct a wrong.
>
> **shame** A feeling resulting from the violation of a social norm.

Hot or Not?
Is guilt good or is it a barrier to our happiness?

Connections
How do marketers manipulate our sense of guilt to get us to buy products we might not otherwise purchase? *See Chapter 10, p. 313.*

EXERCISE 9-1

STOP AND ASSESS YOURSELF

1. Working in small groups, come up with a list of moral values and a list of nonmoral values. Discuss which values are most important to you and why. Discuss also how these values influence your life plan and everyday decisions.

2. Discuss this quotation from Irish poet W. B. Yeats: "Hate is a kind of 'passive suffering,' but indignation is a kind of joy."

3. People who are depressed can become self-preoccupied to the point of becoming indifferent to the consequences of their actions for themselves and others. According to psychiatrist Peter Kramer, author of *Listening to Prozac*, treatment with an antidepressant drug such as Prozac can in some cases "turn a morally unattractive person into an admirable one."[9] In cases where people are depressed to the point of making poor moral decisions, discuss whether it is morally acceptable, or even obligatory, for them to use Prozac or similar drugs to improve their reasoning capacity.

4. Reformers such as Mahatma Gandhi and Martin Luther King, Jr., argued that violence can never be justified by moral outrage. Instead, they insisted, we need to use our moral reasoning to develop nonviolent strategies for responding to violence. Do you agree? Come up with an argument (inductive or deductive) supporting your position.

5. Think of a specific time when you felt guilty and a time when you felt shame. How did you respond in each case? Was your response appropriate, from the point of view of effective critical thinking? If not, discuss how you might develop more appropriate responses to these feelings as well as learn how to better differentiate between them.

6. Looking back at the list of values from your life plan, identify which of these values are moral values and which are nonmoral values. If appropriate, reevaluate and reorganize your values and goals.

THE DEVELOPMENT OF MORAL REASONING

Many psychologists believe that we progress through different stages of moral development during our lives. In this section we'll be looking at theories on moral development and research on moral development in college students.

Lawrence Kohlberg's Stage Theory of Moral Development

According to Harvard psychologist Lawrence Kohlberg (1927–1987), people advance though distinct stages in the development of their moral reasoning capabilities. These stages are transcultural—that is, they are found in every culture of the world.[10] Each new stage represents increased proficiency in critical-thinking skills and greater satisfaction with one's moral decisions.

Kohlberg identified three levels of moral development, each with two distinct stages (see Highlights on page 275). In the first two stages, what Kohlberg called the **preconventional stages**, morality is defined egotistically in terms of oneself. People at this level expect others to treat them morally but generally do not treat other people with moral respect unless doing so benefits them. Most people outgrow the preconventional stages by high school.

People at the **conventional stages** look to others for moral guidance. Earning the approval of others and conforming to peer-group norms are especially important to people at stage 3, the first stage of conventional reasoning. For example, Lynndie England, one of the American guards in the Abu Ghraib prison scandal in Iraq, at her court-martial stated in her defense that she "chose to do what my friends wanted me to."[11] The judge rejected that plea. England completed her three-year prison sentence. She continues to blame the media and others for the scandal.

Most high school seniors and college freshmen are at stage 3 (good boy/nice girl) in their moral development. This stage is associated with the first stage of cognitive development in which students believe that there are right and wrong answers and that those in authority know the right answers.

The next stage of conventional moral reasoning involves substituting the norms and laws of the wider culture for peer-group norms. This type of moral reasoning is also known as *cultural relativism*. The majority of American adults are at this stage. Rather than thinking through decisions about moral issues, they adopt the prevailing view. The mere fact that "everyone" agrees with them confirms, for them, that they must be right.

At the **postconventional stages** of moral reasoning, people recognize that social conventions need to be justified. The fact that something is the law does not make it moral or just. Instead, moral decisions should be based on universal moral principles and on concerns such as justice, compassion, and mutual respect.

A person's stage of moral development is correlated with his or her behavior. Researchers found that only 9 percent of people at stage 2 (egoist) and 38 percent of people at stage 4 (society-maintaining) would offer help to someone who appeared to be suffering from drug side effects; yet all the subjects at stage 6 offered their assistance.[12] Less than 10 percent of American adults ever reach the postconventional level of moral reasoning.[13]

How does democracy contribute to "tyranny of the majority" and the belief that the majority must know what is right? *See Chapter 13, p. 400.*

Connections

preconventional stages Stage of moral development in which morality is defined egotistically.

conventional stages Stage of moral development in which people look to others for moral guidelines.

postconventional stages Stage in which people make moral decisions on the basis of universal moral principals.

HIGHLIGHTS

STAGES IN THE DEVELOPMENT OF MORAL REASONING

Level—Kohlberg's Description*: Gilligan's Description**

Preconventional

Stage 1—Avoid punishment*: Fear of punishment**
   Self-centered *: View your own needs as all that matters**

Stage 2—Egoist *: Put self first; satisfy your own needs; consider needs of others only if it benefits you: "You scratch my back, I'll scratch yours."**

Me   Others

Conventional

Stage 3—Good boy/nice girl *: Put others first; please and help others; maintain good relationships and earn others' approval; conform to peer norms**
   Self-sacrificing *: View others' needs as more important than your own**

Stage 4—Society maintaining*: Respect authority and society rules; maintain the existing social order**

Me   Others

Postconventional

Stage 5—Social contract or legalistic*: Obey useful, albeit arbitrary, social rules; appeal to social consensus and majority rule as long as minimal basic rights are safeguarded** Mature care ethics*: able to balance your own needs and the needs of others**

Stage 6—Conscience and universal moral principles*: Autonomously recognize universal rules, such as justice and equality, that are rational and logically consistent and reflect a respect for equal human rights and the dignity of each individual**

Me   Others

➤**APPLICATION:** *Identify in the text examples of reasoning at the preconventional, conventional, and postconventional stages.*

*Description of Kohlberg's stages adapted from Barbara Panzl and Timothy McMahon, "Ethical Decision-Making Developmental Theory and Practice," speech delivered at a meeting of the National Association of Student Personnel Administrators, Denver, March 1989.

**Description of Gilligan's stages adapted from Carol Gilligan's *In a Different Voice: Psychological Theory and Women's Development* (Cambridge, MA: Harvard University Press, 1982).

People at the lower levels of moral reasoning tend to come up with simplistic solutions. When these solutions don't work or backfire, they become baffled.

People outgrow their old way of thinking when it becomes inadequate for resolving the more complex problems and issues that they encounter in life. Movement to a higher stage is usually triggered by new ideas or experiences that conflict with their worldview.

Carol Gilligan on Moral Reasoning in Women

Kohlberg carried out his research only on men. Psychologist Carol Gilligan argued that women's moral development tends to follow a different path. Men, she said, tend to be duty- and principle-oriented, an approach

she called the **justice perspective**. Women, in contrast, view the world in terms of relationships and caring. She called this the **care perspective**.

Gilligan outlined three stages or levels in the development of moral reasoning in women. Like boys, girls at the preconventional stage are self-centered, putting their own needs first. Women at the conventional stage of moral reasoning, in contrast, tend to be self-sacrificing, putting the needs and welfare of others before their own. The desire to please others can backfire as we saw in the case of Lynndie England (see page 274). Finally, women at the postconventional stage are able to balance their needs and those of others—what Gilligan calls **mature care ethics**.

Although some studies support Gilligan, others have found sex differences to be insignificant.[14] Some women have a strong justice perspective, while some men prefer the care perspective. In addition, most people make use of *both* perspectives in their moral reasoning. Just as the cognitive and the affective sides of our conscience work together, the two types of moral reasoning work and complement each other, helping us to make better decisions.

> **justice perspective** The emphasis on duty and principles in moral reasoning.
>
> **care perspective** The emphasis in moral development and reasoning on context and relationships.
>
> **mature care ethics** The stage of moral development in which people are able to balance their needs and those of others.

THiNKing Outside the Box

GLORIA STEINEM, *Feminist and Writer*

Feminist and writer Gloria Steinem (b. 1934) is a good example of a creative problem solver who was willing to step up to a challenge. Steinem, who was 29 at the time and a struggling journalist, wanted to find a way to make the public aware of how Playboy Clubs exploited women. However, instead of just writing another article, she agreed to participate in a creative solution by going undercover as a Playboy Bunny. Steinem's persistence and willingness to take a risk led to an exposé of the poor working conditions at the Playboy Clubs.

Now in her late 70s, Steinem continues to work for social justice. She also writes and lectures about the importance of strong self-esteem in women's personal development.

DISCUSSION QUESTIONS

1. Discuss how Steinem's actions in going undercover as a Playboy Bunny relate to the post-conventional stage of moral development as explicated by both Kohlberg and Gilligan.

2. Think of an injustice on your campus or in the world that is of concern to you. Come up with a creative action you might take to make others more aware of this injustice or to change public policy. Share and evaluate your plan of action with others in the class. Discuss how, if at all, working with others helped you come up with a better plan. If appropriate, modify your plan in light of the feedback you receive.

THINKING Outside the Box

MOHANDAS GANDHI, *Nonviolent Activist*

Mohandas Gandhi (1869–1948), popularly known as Mahatma, or "Great Soul," was born in India, which at the time was ruled by England. As a young lawyer, Gandhi was prohibited by British segregationist practices from sitting where he wanted to on the train and from walking beside his "noncolored" friends. Even worse, he saw people of lower classes or castes being treated with utter contempt by both the Europeans and higher-caste Indians. But rather than acquiesce to cultural norms or internalize his resentment, he responded with moral outrage guided by reason.

His response sparked one of the most effective nonviolent moral reform movements in the history of the world. Following the Massacre at Amritsar in 1919, in which hundreds of unarmed Indian civilians were gunned down by soldiers in the British army, Gandhi launched a policy of nonviolent noncooperation against the British who were occupying India. As a result of his efforts, India gained its independence in 1947.

Gandhi also strove to get rid of the oppressive caste system in India. His respect for the equal dignity of all people and his use of nonviolent resistance as a strategy for political and social reform has had a lasting influence on later civil rights movements, including the 1960s civil rights movement in the United States.

DISCUSSION QUESTIONS

1. Discuss how Gandhi's resolutions to moral issues he confronted in his life reflect thinking at both Kohlberg's and Gilligan's postconventional stages.

2. Think back on a time when you were tempted to respond or responded to violence (verbal or physical) against you with violence. Discuss how a person at the postconventional stage of moral reasoning would most likely have responded and how their reasoning uses the critical thinking skills.

The Development of Moral Reasoning in College Students

A college education is positively correlated with moral development. Many young people in college go through a time of crisis—sometimes called "cognitive disequilibrium"—when they leave home and enter college. They may initially respond to the disruption of their world-views by conforming to their peer culture. The propensity of some freshmen, at the urging of their peers, to engage in self-destructive behavior—smoking, binge-drinking, reckless driving—reflects this conformity.

As we've already seen, freshmen tend to be more black-and-white in their thinking. In a study of moral reasoning in college students, students were presented with the fictional case of "Joe."[15] One day a neighbor discovers that Joe, who has been living the life of a model citizen for several years, is actually an escaped prisoner. Students were then asked, "Should the neighbor turn him in to the authorities?" Freshmen were more likely to say yes because it's what the law dictates. By the time college students reach their senior year, they are still concerned about what the law states; however, they also question whether it would be *fair* for the law to be applied in this case. Those who had reached the postconventional level wanted to know more about Joe and if he had been truly rehabilitated. They also asked which action—reporting or not reporting Joe to the authorities—would most benefit society.

Connections

Why is moral reasoning important for college students in deciding how to use social networking on the Internet? *See Chapter 11, p. 348.*

Hot or Not?

Does our current education system inhibit moral development?

Peer relations at college are important in the development of moral reasoning. Students who have diverse friendships with people different from themselves tend to make greater gains.[16] Discussions of moral issues in classrooms, in which students' ideas are challenged and they are required to support their conclusions, also have the potential to enhance moral reasoning.[17]

Despite these positive influences, most college students do not make the transition to postconventional moral reasoning. Instead, college tends to push students up into a higher stage of conventional reasoning, where they shift to conforming to wider societal norms rather than to those of their peer culture.

Moral reasoning plays an important role in our everyday decisions. Level of moral reasoning is positively correlated with self-esteem, mental health, satisfaction with career goals, honesty, and altruistic behavior.[18] In the next section we will study moral theories that guide our thinking.

EXERCISE 9-2

STOP AND ASSESS YOURSELF

1. Which scheme of moral development—Gilligan's or Kohlberg's—best describes your style and stage of moral reasoning? Discuss situations you've encountered where this stage was adequate for resolving a particular problem or conflict, as well as some situations in which it was inadequate.

2. College tends to move students up to a higher stage of conventional moral reasoning. Working in small groups, discuss why you think this is the case. Make a list of specific suggestions for changes in the curriculum and campus life in general that might promote postconventional moral reasoning.

3. How did you respond to the question on this page about whether you should report "Joe," the escaped prisoner, to the authorities? Are you satisfied with your answer? Explain, referring to the different stages of moral development.

4. Are you less susceptible to peer pressure in making moral decisions than you were in high school or when you first started college? Discuss what factors might have contributed to your ability to think more independently in making moral decisions during your transition from high school to college.

5. Since entering college, have you encountered a situation or problem in which your style of moral reasoning was inadequate? How did you respond? Would you respond differently now? Relate your answers to the stages of moral reasoning.

MORAL THEORIES: MORALITY IS RELATIVE

Moral theories provide frameworks for understanding and explaining what makes a certain action right or wrong. They also help us clarify, critically analyze, and rank the moral concerns raised by moral issues in our lives. There are two basic types of moral theories: (1) those that claim that morality is relative and (2) those that claim that morality is universal. Moral relativists claim that people *create* morality and that there are no universal or shared moral principles. Universalists, in contrast, maintain that there are universal moral principles that hold for all people.

> There are two basic types of moral theories: (1) those that claim that morality is relative and (2) those that claim that morality is universal.

The inability of many people to make universal moral judgments on issues such as abortion and capital punishment contributes to the widespread feeling that our positions on moral issues are simply matters of personal opinion and that there is little room for discussion when differences of opinion exist. Critical evaluation of the different theories, however, soon makes it clear that some moral theories are better than others for explaining morality and providing solutions to moral problems.

Ethical Subjectivism

According to **ethical subjectivists**, morality is nothing more than personal opinion or feelings. What *feels* right for you *is* right for you at any particular moment. Consider J. L. Hunter ("Red") Roundtree, who died in 2004 in a Missouri prison at the age of 92. A retired business tycoon, Roundtree pulled his first bank robbery at age 86. "Holdups," he said, "made me feel good, awful good."[19] Did the fact that robbing banks made Roundtree "feel good" morally justify what he did? The ethical subjectivist would have to say yes. If Roundtree felt "awful good" about robbing banks, then his actions were morally correct, just as are the actions of a serial killer who feels good about torturing and killing his victims.

Do not confuse ethical subjectivism with the observation that people *believe* in different moral values. Ethical subjectivism goes beyond this by claiming that sincerely believing or feeling something is right *makes* it right for that person. While robbing banks or torturing and killing

people may not be right for you, these actions—according to ethical subjectivism—*are* morally right for Roundtree and serial killers. Since personal feelings are the only standard for what is right or wrong for each individual, a person can never be wrong.

Also, do not confuse ethical subjectivism with tolerance. Ethical subjectivism, rather than encouraging tolerance, allows a person to exploit and terrorize the weak and vulnerable, as long as the perpetrator believes that doing so is right.

Ethical subjectivism is one of the weakest moral theories. Having a right to our own opinion is not the same as saying that all opinions are equally reasonable. Indeed, most people who support ethical subjectivism usually feel quite differently when they are unfavorably affected by someone else's harmful actions.

> **ethical subjectivist** One who believes that morality is nothing more than personal opinion or feelings.
>
> **cultural relativism** People look to societal norms for what is morally right and wrong.

In the previous chapter on deductive reasoning, we learned that hypothetical reasoning can be used to analyze a moral theory by providing us with a means of examining its implications. Consider the following argument:

Premise 1: *If* ethical subjectivism is true, *then* I am always behaving morally when I act on my personal feelings and opinions, including torturing and raping young children.

Premise 2: Ethical subjectivism is true.

Conclusion: Therefore, I am always behaving morally when I act on my personal feelings and opinions, including torturing and raping young children.

In the above valid hypothetical syllogism, if we are not willing to accept the conclusion as true, then we *must* reject as false the premise: "Ethical subjectivism is true." Ethical subjectivism, if taken seriously, is a dangerous theory. It not only isolates the individual but permits people to exploit and hurt others without ever having to justify their actions or stand in judgment.

Connections

Do we as a society have a moral obligation to restrict certain types of advertising and television shows that may exploit young children? *See Chapter 10, pp. 315–316.*

Cultural Relativism

Cultural relativism, the second form of moral relativism, looks to public opinion and customs rather than to private opinion for moral standards. According to cultural relativists, there are no universal moral principles. Instead, morality is nothing more than socially approved customs. Something that is regarded as morally wrong in one culture—such as polygamy, slavery, spousal abuse, or homosexuality—may be morally neutral or even praiseworthy in another culture.

Is the "social contract" the source of morality in a culture? *See Chapter 13, p. 397.* How should we respond when there is a conflict between moral principles and the laws of our society? *See Chapter 13, p. 410.*

If you are a cultural relativist, you need only ask what the customs and laws of your culture or society are at this point in time to know what is right and wrong. One hundred and fifty years ago, slavery was considered morally acceptable in the southern part of the United States; today, Americans everywhere condemn slavery as highly immoral. Cultural relativists are not just saying that Americans once *believed* that slavery was morally acceptable. They are claiming that slavery actually *was* moral prior to 1863 when it was outlawed by the Emancipation Proclamation. Indeed—according to the cultural relativists—it was not the slave owners who were immoral but the abolitionists, who opposed the cultural standards of their time.

Cultural relativism can be used to legitimate the oppression of certain groups, as well as perpetuate ethnocentrism (see "Analyzing Images: A Ku Klux Klan Lynching, Indiana, 1930"). The belief that people from other cultures do not have the same basic moral standards that we have can lead to distrust. If two cultures disagree about what is morally right, there are no rational grounds for discussion, since there are no shared universal moral values. If a culture feels offended or threatened by another, the only solutions are isolationism or war.

Cultural relativism corresponds to the conventional stages of moral reasoning. Like ethical subjectivism, cultural relativism is not a correct description of how we make moral judgments. We often pass judgment on our own culture, whether it be about a particular war, abortion, same-sex marriage, or capital punishment.

Slaves being auctioned. Slavery was once justified as moral by cultural relativists, despite its glaring violation of human rights.

ANALYZING IMAGES

A Ku Klux Klan Lynching, Indiana, 1930
Members of the Ku Klux Klan (KKK) identify morality with the white-supremacist values of their subculture. These values are expressed in hate crimes against African Americans, Hispanic immigrants, Jews, Muslims, illegal aliens, and homosexuals, all of whom the KKK sees as a threat to the American way of life.

The Ku Klux Klan was founded in the South in 1866 and officially disbanded in 1869. It was reorganized in 1915. By the mid-1920s the KKK had 5 million members and had expanded its reign of terror to the northern states as well. In the 1920s, many prominent politicians, including governors, senators, and congressmen, were members of the KKK. It experienced another surge of popularity in the 1950s and the 1960s in opposition to the civil-rights movement. It declined again in the 1980s, only to experience a resurgence following the election of President Obama.

DISCUSSION QUESTIONS

1. *Cultural relativists equate morality with the values of their culture or subculture. However, what happens when the values of one's culture and one's subculture come into conflict with each other? Is the fact that the white-supremacist values of the KKK are currently considered immoral by the government and the majority of American people morally relevant? Would the Klan's values and activities be morally admirable if the majority of Americans believed in them? Support your answers.*

2. *You probably experienced a strong emotional reaction when you first saw this image. What moral sentiments did you experience? Discuss to what extent your response was shaped by cultural values and to what extent it was informed by values that are not culture-bound. Relate your answer to the theory of cultural relativism.*

STOP AND ASSESS YOURSELF

1. Philosophy professor Stephen Satris claims that "student relativism" is one of the most pervasive and frustrating problems in teaching philosophy.[20] Student relativism is manifest in such statements as "What is true for one person might not be true for others. After all, who's to say what is moral? It's all relative." Satris believes that student relativism is not a genuine moral position but a type of mental laziness or resistance that protects students from having to critically analyze or pass judgment on their own or others' views and values. Do you agree? Relate your answer to the concept of resistance studied in Chapter 1.

2. What is the source of your moral values? Do you identify with the values of a particular group, such as your peers or religious organization? Are you satisfied with these values when it comes to making moral decisions in your life? Explain using specific examples.

3. Think of a time when you took a moral stand that conflicted with the norms of your peer group. Discuss how you justified your position. Discuss how your peers responded to you. How did you address their concerns?

4. Think of a moral decision you made this past week. Write a short essay discussing which of the values involved in making the decision were moral values and which were non-moral values. Describe also which moral sentiments played a role in motivating you to carry out this decision. Were you satisfied with your decision? Explain why or why not. If not, how might you use your critical thinking skills to come to a better decision.

*5. In August 1995, 33-year-old Deletha Word jumped to her death from the Belle Isle bridge in Detroit to escape a 19-year-old man who savagely beat her after a fender bender. Dozens of spectators stood by, some even cheering on the attacker. Discuss how an ethical subjectivist would most likely respond to this event.

6. Looking back at the steroids-in-sports question with which we began this chapter, discuss how both an ethical subjectivist and a cultural relativist would have each most likely responded to the hypothetical entrepreneur's proposal.

7. Amina Lawal, age 30, became pregnant after having an affair with her neighbor, who had agreed to marry her. However, he went back on his promise to marry her. Eight days after Lawal gave birth, the police arrested her for adultery, a capital crime in her home state of Katsina in northern Nigeria. She was tried and sentenced to be buried in the ground up to her chest and stoned to death. In her culture, in cases of adultery, typically it is only the woman who is sentenced to death by stoning. There was an outcry in some parts of the world against this practice, and the sentence, at least in Lawal's case, was dropped because of outside pressure. However, on what grounds can we, as Americans, claim that the practice is immoral? Discuss whether our claims that such practices are immoral can be reconciled with cultural relativism.

*8. Working in small groups, write a hypothetical syllogism regarding the implications of cultural relativism (*If* cultural relativism is true, *then* . . .). Share your syllogism with the class for evluation.

9. The U.S. military is grappling with the problem of post-combat guilt among soldiers in Iraq and Afghanistan who have killed in combat. These soldiers believe that the war is right and just. One officer dealing with guilt says, "I know what I did was right. But I'll never lose the sound of that grief-stricken family."[21] Discuss how both an ethical subjectivist and a cultural relativist might explain the phenomenon of guilt in these cases.

*Answers to selected exercises are found in the Solutions Manual at the end of the book.

MORAL THEORIES: MORALITY IS UNIVERSAL

Most moral philosophers believe that morality is universal—that moral principles are binding on all people regardless of their personal desires, culture, or religion. In this section, we'll look at four types of universal moral theories: utilitarianism (consequence-based ethics), deontology (duty-based ethics), natural-rights ethics (rights-based ethics), and virtue ethics (character-based ethics). Rather than being mutually exclusive, as the relativist theories are, these theories enrich and complement each other.

Utilitarianism (Consequence-Based Ethics)

In **utilitarianism**, actions are evaluated on the basis of their consequences. According to utilitarians, the desire for happiness is universal. The most moral action is that which brings about the greatest happiness or pleasure and the least amount of pain for the greatest number. This is known as the **principle of utility**, or the **greatest happiness principle**:

> Actions are right in proportion as they tend to promote happiness, wrong as they tend to produce the reverse of happiness.[22]

In making a moral decision, we need to weigh the benefits and harms (costs) to those affected by an action. English philosopher and social reformer Jeremy Bentham (1748–1832) developed the utilitarian calculus as a means of determining which action or policy is morally preferable. Using **utilitarian calculus**, each potential action is assigned a numerical value—for instance, from 1 to 10, or whatever scale you choose to use—on the basis of the intensity, duration, certainty, propinquity, fecundity, purity, and extent of the pleasure or pain. (Each of these categories is defined in "Highlights: Utilitarian Calculus: Seven Factors to Take into Consideration in Determining the Most Moral Action or Decision," on page 284). The greater the pleasure, the higher the positive numerical value it is assigned; the greater the pain, the lower the value.

Using utilitarian calculus, if a proposed policy or action has a higher total positive value than its alternatives, then it is the better policy. For example, in the case at the beginning of this chapter on using steroids, while the purity of the pleasure may be diluted by any pain to the other team if it loses the game or to you from any short-term physical effects of the drugs, this pain is outweighed by the intensity, duration, and extent of the pleasure or happiness it will bring to your college.

Utilitarian cost–benefit analysis is especially useful in developing policies for the allocation of limited resources. In 1962, there were not enough kidney dialysis machines for everyone who needed them. The Seattle Artificial Kidney Center (now known as the Northwest Kidney Centers) appointed a committee of seven—the so-called God Committee—which decided who should get kidney dialysis on the basis of each patient's capacity to benefit the community. The selection process included criteria such as age, employment history, education level, history of achievements, number of dependents, and involvement in the community. This case points out one of the weaknesses of the utilitarian calculus. While one person may regard the contributions of a poet or artist as having great value to society, another may judge a person's value solely in terms of how much money or material goods they generate.

Utilitarian Jeremy Bentham donated his estate to University College London on the condition that his preserved body (shown with a wax head in the glass cabinet) be presented at board meetings.

In deciding on the best policy, a utilitarian doesn't simply go along with what the majority wants, since people are not always well informed. Nor is happiness the same as going along with personal preferences or feelings. For example, although spending an evening partying may bring you and your friends short-term happiness, your

utilitarianism A moral philosophy in which actions are evaluated based on their consequences.

principle of utility (greatest happiness principle) The most moral action is that which brings about the greatest happiness or pleasure and the least amount of pain for the greatest number.

utilitarian calculus Used to determine the best course of action or policy by calculating the total amount of pleasure and pain caused by that action.

What are some of the utilitarian arguments for restricting—or not restricting—advertising? **See Chapter 10, p. 309.**

Connections

long-term happiness may be better served by studying for an exam you have the next day, so that you can do well in college, graduate, and get a good, well-paying job.

One of the strengths of utilitarian theory is that it requires us to be well informed about the possible consequences of our actions (or inactions) before we make moral decisions. The excuses "I didn't intend any harm" and "Don't blame me—I was just a bystander" don't pass muster with a utilitarian.

deontology The ethics of duty.

categorical imperative Kant's fundamental moral principle that helps to determine what our duty is.

On the other hand, utilitarianism fails to give sufficient attention to individual integrity and personal rights. Restoring peace by arresting and executing an innocent person may bring about the greatest happiness to the greatest number. However, this solution is wrong despite its overall benefit to society because it is wrong to use a person as a means only.

Utilitarian theory is not so much wrong as incomplete. Its primary weakness is not its claim that consequences are important but instead the claim that *only* consequences matter in making moral decisions.

Immanuel Kant is regarded as one of the greatest moral philosophers.

HIGHLIGHTS

UTILITARIAN CALCULUS: SEVEN FACTORS TO TAKE INTO CONSIDERATION IN DETERMINING THE MOST MORAL ACTION OR DECISION

1. *Intensity:* Strength of the pleasure and pain. The greater the pleasure, the higher the positive value; the greater the pain, the more negative the value.

2. *Duration:* Length of time the pain and pleasure will last.

3. *Certainty:* Level of probability that the pleasure or pain will occur.

4. *Propinquity:* How soon in time the pleasure or pain will occur.

5. *Fecundity:* Extent to which the pleasure will produce more pleasure.

6. *Purity:* The pleasure does not cause pain at the same time.

7. *Extent:* The number of sentient beings affected by the action.

➤*APPLICATION: Give an example of each of the seven factors.*

Deontology (Duty-Based Ethics)

Deontology claims that duty is the foundation of morality. Some acts are morally obligatory regardless of their consequences. We should do our duty purely out of a sense of goodwill, not because of reward or punishment or any other consequences.

According to German philosopher Immanuel Kant (1724–1804), the most fundamental moral principle is the **categorical imperative**, which (in Kant's famous words) states:

> Act only on that maxim by which you can at the same time will that it should become a universal law.[23]

The categorical imperative, said Kant, must guide our moral decision making. It is inconsistent, for example, to argue that it is wrong for others to lie but that it is okay for us. For example, it was wrong of the journalists to lie to the nurse about their relationship to Kate Middleton, Duchess of Cambridge, who had been hospitalized for morning sickness, even though the journalists may have intended it as a joke and did not expect any harm to come of their "prank" (see page 82). If it is wrong to lie, it is wrong for *everyone* to lie. Moral principles or duties apply to everyone regardless of a person's feelings or culture.

Kant believed that all rational beings will recognize the categorical imperative as universally binding. It is our ability to reason that gives us moral worth. Since humans and other rational beings have intrinsic moral worth or dignity, they should never be treated as expendable, in the way that they can be under utilitarian theory. Because each of us has intrinsic moral worth, according to Kant, our foremost duty is self-respect or proper self-esteem: If we don't respect and treat ourselves well, we're not going to treat others well. This ideal is summed up in Kant's second formulation of the categorical imperative:

> So act as to treat humanity, whether in thine own person or in that of any other, in every case as an end in itself, never as a means only.[24]

This moral obligation is found in moral philosophies and religious ethics throughout the world (see "Critical Thinking in Action: The Golden Rule—Reciprocity as the Basis of Morality in World Religions"). While religious ethics is sometimes considered different from philosophical ethics, the general moral principles recognized by the two are the same.

Kant believed that universalizing moral duties, such as a duty not to lie, requires that these duties be absolutely binding in all circumstances. Most deontologists, while agreeing that moral duties are universal, disagree with Kant, noting that there are situations where moral duties may come into conflict.

Scottish philosopher W. D. Ross (1877–1971) came up with a list of seven duties derived from the categorical imperative (see "Highlights: Seven Prima Facie Duties"). These duties include the future-looking (consequential) duties of the utilitarians, as well as duties based on past obligations and ongoing duties. Ross argued that these duties are **prima facie** (translated "at first view")—that is, they are morally binding unless overridden by a more compelling moral duty.

Let's look at an example. You have promised to pay back, by a certain date, money that you borrowed from a friend. Under ordinary circumstances, you would have a duty of fidelity to pay back the money. Your friend arrives at your door on the due date and is furious because his chemistry professor gave him a failing grade. He is carrying parts for a bomb and demands the money so he can buy the rest of the explosives he needs to blow up the science building. Should you give him the money? In situations such as these, you need to determine which moral duties are the most compelling. In this case, the duty of nonmaleficence— preventing serious harms to other people—overrides your duty to pay back the money.

> **prima facie duty** Moral duty that is binding unless overridden by a more compelling moral duty.

Deontology is a powerful moral theory, especially when it incorporates the insights of the utilitarians. While deontology is strong on moral principle and duty, one of its limitations is the failure to adequately take into account the role of sentiment and care ethics in moral decision making. On the other hand, deontology provides a solid foundation and justification for rights-based ethics— to which we now turn.

HIGHLIGHTS

SEVEN PRIMA FACIE DUTIES

FUTURE-LOOKING DUTIES

- *Beneficence:* The duty to do good acts and to promote happiness.

- *Nonmaleficence:* The duty to do no harm and to prevent harm.

DUTIES BASED ON PAST OBLIGATIONS

- *Fidelity/loyalty:* Duties arising from past commitments and promises.

- *Reparation:* Duties that stem from past harms to others.

- *Gratitude:* Duties based on past favors and unearned services.

ONGOING DUTIES

- *Self-improvement:* The duty to improve our knowledge (wisdom) and virtue.

- *Justice:* The duty to treat all people with dignity and to give each person equal consideration.

➤ *APPLICATION: Provide an example of each of the seven prima facie duties.*

Connections

What steps does our judicial process take to ensure that everyone is treated fairly? *See Chapter 13, pp. 414–415.* Do we as citizens have a moral obligation to vote? *See Chapter 13, pp. 401–402.*

Rights-Based Ethics

In rights-based ethics, moral rights are *not* identical to legal rights, as they are in cultural relativism. Because we have moral rights, others have a duty to honor these rights.

Critical THiNKing in Action

The Golden Rule—Reciprocity as the Basis of Morality in World Religions

Buddhism: "Hurt not others in ways that you yourself would find hurtful." *Udana Varga 5:18*

Christianity: "Always treat others as you would like them to treat you." *Matthew 7:12*

Confucianism: "Do not do to others what you do not want them to do to you." *Analects 15:23*

Hinduism: "This is the sum of the Dharma [duty]: do naught unto others which would cause pain if done to you." *Mahabharata 5:1517*

Islam: "None of you [truly] believes until he wishes for his brother what he wishes for himself." *Number 13 of Iman "Al-Nawawi's Forty Hadiths"*

Judaism: ". . . thou shall love thy neighbor as thyself." *Leviticus 19:18*

Native American spirituality: "Respect for all life is the foundation." *The Great Law of Peace*

DISCUSSION QUESTIONS

1. Discuss the deontologist's claim that the categorical imperative (law of reciprocity) is a universal and fundamental principle of ethics. If you are a member of a religion, discuss ways in which this fundamental principle of ethics is (or is not) expressed in your religion.

2. Most of us have been taught some form of the duty of reciprocity as young children. Using a specific example, discuss the extent to which this duty influences your everyday moral reasoning and behavior.

Welfare rights include the right to emergency medical care, regardless of ability to pay.

Connections

To what extent should media speech be protected by freedom of speech? *See Chapter 11, p. 336.* What are some of the moral conflicts raised by potential misuses of the Internet? *See Chapter 11, pp. 350–351.* Does the USA Patriot Act violate people's liberty rights, or does the government's duty to protect citizens override these rights? *See Chapter 13.*

The right to pursue our interests is limited to our **legitimate interests**—that is, those interests that do not harm other people by violating their similar and equal interests.

Moral rights are generally divided into welfare and liberty rights. **Welfare rights** entail rights to receive certain social goods, such as education, and police and fire protection, which are essential for our welfare, or well-being. At the heart of the Affordable Care Act, commonly called Obamacare, is a belief that health care is a welfare right. Welfare rights are important because without them, we cannot effectively pursue our legitimate interests.

Liberty rights entail the right to be left alone to pursue our legitimate interests. A misogynist (a man who hates women) may have an *interest* in keeping women out of the workplace, but this does not give him the *right* to do so, since it violates women's right to equal opportunity—a liberty right—and therefore his is not a *legitimate interest*. Freedom of speech, freedom of religion, freedom to choose our major and career path, the right to privacy, and the right to own property are all examples of liberty rights.

Rights ethics is an important component of a comprehensive moral theory because rights protect our equality and dignity as persons. Like duties, rights may come into conflict with each other or with other duties. When this happens, we need to use our critical-thinking skills to decide which are the more compelling moral rights and/ or duties.

HIGHLIGHTS

UNIVERSAL MORAL THEORIES

- *Utilitarianism:* Morality is based on consequences.

- *Deontology:* Duty is the foundation of morality. We have a duty to act only on principles that we would want to be universal laws.

- *Rights-based ethics:* Rights are the primary moral concern.

- *Virtue ethics:* Character is more important than right actions.

➤ *APPLICATION: Find in the text an example of the application of each theory.*

---

legitimate interests Interests that do not violate others' similar and equal interests.

welfare rights The right to receive certain social goods that are essential to our well-being.

liberty rights The right to be left alone to pursue our legitimate interests.

Virtue Ethics

Virtue ethics emphasize character over right actions. The sort of person we are constitutes the heart of our moral life. Virtue ethics are not an alternative to moral theories that stress right conduct, such as utilitarian and deontological theories. Rather, virtue ethics and theories of right action complement each other.

A *virtue* is an admirable character trait or disposition to habitually act in a manner that benefits ourselves and others. The actions of virtuous people stem from a respect and concern for the well-being of themselves and others. Compassion, courage, generosity, loyalty, and honesty are all examples of virtues. Because virtuous people are more likely to act morally, virtue ethics goes hand in hand with the other universal moral theories.

Being a virtuous person entails cultivating moral sensitivity. **Moral sensitivity** is the awareness of how our actions affect others. Morally sensitive people are more in tune with their conscience and more likely to feel guilty when they harm another person or to feel moral indignation when they witness an injustice.

Moral theories do not exist in abstraction. They inform and motivate our real-life decisions and actions. By using the universal theories together and drawing from the strengths of each, we can become more proficient at analyzing and constructing moral arguments as well as resolving moral conflicts.

> **virtue ethics** Moral theories that emphasize character over right actions.
>
> **moral sensitivity** The awareness of how our actions affect others.

ANALYZING **IMAGES**

DISCUSSION QUESTIONS

1. *According to American social theorist James Q. Wilson, the author of* The Moral Sense *(1993), some people from birth seem to have a great capacity for empathy and justice—what Aristotle called "natural virtue." People at the higher levels of moral development, like the people in the above photo, are more likely to rescue others in distress, even at a risk to their own lives. Does the duty of beneficence require that we help others in distress and, if so, what are the limits, if any, on this duty? Support your answer.*

2. *Discuss ways in which our education system might enhance our moral sensitivity as well as our capacity to help others in need.*

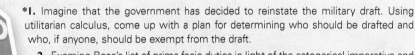

STOP AND ASSESS YOURSELF

*1. Imagine that the government has decided to reinstate the military draft. Using utilitarian calculus, come up with a plan for determining who should be drafted and who, if anyone, should be exempt from the draft.

2. Examine Ross's list of prima facie duties in light of the categorical imperative and ethics of reciprocity. Are the duties consistent with this fundamental moral principle? Working in small groups, come up with examples of each of the above moral duties in your personal lives.

3. Referring back to the case at the beginning of this chapter, use Kant's categorical imperative and Ross's prima facie duties to decide whether you ought to take the steroids.

4. What is your greatest virtue? Discuss how this virtue contributes to your ability to be a better critical thinker.

5. The majority of parents in the United States believe that it is morally acceptable, even praiseworthy, to tell their young children that Santa Claus is a real, physical person. Is it morally right to tell children this, even though it is a lie? Support your answer using the categorical imperative and duty of reciprocity.

6. After the September 11, 2001, terrorist attacks, hundreds of Arab American men were detained for questioning as a means of combating terrorism. Many were arrested and imprisoned, without being told why they were being detained. Discuss whether restricting the rights of certain groups in times of crisis is morally justified and, if so, on what grounds.

7. Utilitarian theory is often used to formulate social policies around issues such as HIV testing, free-speech zones, and the distribution of social goods such as scholarships and medical benefits. Find some examples of utilitarian reasoning in our current government policies or policies at your college. Write a short essay explaining why these policies illustrate utilitarian reasoning. Critically evaluate each policy.

*Answers to selected exercises are found in the Solutions Manual at the end of the book.

MORAL ARGUMENTS

Moral theories provide the foundation for moral arguments and their application to real-life situations.

Recognizing Moral Arguments

A moral argument, like any argument, has premises and a conclusion. However, unlike nonmoral arguments, at least one of the premises is a *prescriptive premise*—that is, it makes a statement regarding what is morally right and wrong or what *ought* to be the case. Moral arguments also contain *descriptive premises* about the world and human nature. In the following argument, the first premise is a prescriptive premise and the second premise is a descriptive (factual) premise.

> *Prescriptive premise*: It is wrong to inflict unnecessary suffering on people.
>
> *Descriptive premise*: Imprisonment causes unnecessary suffering by restricting inmates' freedom of movement.
>
> *Conclusion*: Therefore, it is wrong to imprison people.

Moral arguments may also contain premises that define key or ambiguous terms. In the above example, the argument would be stronger if it provided a definition of the ambiguous term *unnecessary suffering*. *Unnecessary suffering* may be defined as "suffering that is not essential for achieving a particular desired goal." In this case, if our goal is to prevent further harm to the community, is prison the only means of keeping this person from further harming the community, or does imprisonment constitute "unnecessary suffering"?

In making a moral argument, we should first get our facts straight. Incorrect facts or assumptions can lead to a faulty conclusion. Until recently most physicians lied to patients who were dying because they believed that telling patients the truth would upset them and hasten their deaths. It wasn't until the 1960s that a study on the effects of truth-telling showed that people with terminal cancer actually did better and lived longer if they knew the truth about their condition.[25] Good intentions, in other words, are not enough in making moral decisions. If we make unfounded assumptions without first checking our facts, we may end up actually doing more harm than good.

Constructing Moral Arguments

Constructing a moral argument is like constructing any argument, except at least one of the premises must be prescriptive. As with other arguments, begin by clearly identifying the issue. Let's use a simple example. You ride to class with one of your friends. While pulling her car into a parking spot, your friend scrapes the fender of another car. Suppose she starts to pull out and leave the scene of the accident? What should you do? You could say nothing, but by doing so you become complicit in your friend's decision to avoid taking responsibility for the accident.

After deciding that you should say something, your next step is to make a list of descriptive and prescriptive premises. In this case one of the descriptive premises could simply be a factual statement of what happened: Your friend damaged the fender of the car next to her when she pulled her car into the parking spot. In some cases the facts may be more complex and you'll need more premises, but in this case let's assume that the next car was legally parked and not moving, and no one was around to witness the accident except you and your friend.

To come up with prescriptive premises, ask yourself, "What are the moral duties, rights, and values that are relevant to this case?" The principle of reparation is relevant; if we cause harm, whether intentionally or unintentionally through carelessness, we have a moral duty to make up for that harm. The corresponding right in this case is the right of the other person to be compensated for that harm. In fact, one of the reasons we are required to carry automobile insurance is so we can honor the rights of others if we have an accident for which we are responsible.

If you are talking to someone at the postconventional level of moral reasoning, these premises may be sufficient for your friend to come to the conclusion that she ought to take steps to pay for the damage to the other car. However, what if she says, "I don't care" or "If I do, my parents will find out what happened and get angry with me"? If this happens, you need to persist in making your moral argument in a way that is respectful of your friend. You have both a duty of beneficence to be caring as well as a duty of fidelity (loyalty) to your friend. This may require gathering more information. For example, why is she worried about her parents' reaction?

You might also want to add a prescriptive premise containing an application of the principle of reciprocity by asking her, "How would you feel if someone hit your parked car and just drove off? I bet you'd be pretty upset, and rightly so." Remember not to use an accusatory tone in stating your premises—that would mean committing the abusive or ad hominem fallacy. Resorting to this fallacy tends to alienate others and moves you further from a satisfactory moral conclusion or resolution.

The issue and premises can be summarized as follows:

Issue: Your friend scraped the fender of a car in the parking lot. What should she do, and what should you do?

Descriptive premises:

- Your friend damaged the fender of the car next to her when she pulled her car into the parking spot.
- Your friend was driving her parents' car.
- Your friend is concerned that her parents will get angry when they learn about the accident.

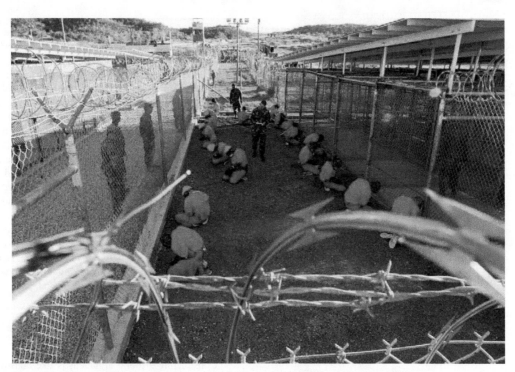

Many of the prisoners at Guantanamo Bay were denied access to legal counsel and other protections as required by the United Nations' Geneva Conventions.

Prescriptive premises:

- We have a moral duty to make up for past harms we cause others (duty of reparation).
- The person whose car your friend struck has a right to be compensated for the damage (welfare right).
- I have a duty to be kind and caring to my friend (duty of beneficence).
- I have a duty of loyalty to my friend (duty of fidelity).
- We should treat others as we would want to be treated (law of reciprocity).

In making a moral argument, the point is not to prove that you are morally superior to others but to come to a conclusion that leads to an action or a policy that is reasonable and most consistent with moral values. Do not come to a conclusion until you've developed a list of relevant premises that you can both agree on. Remain open-minded and flexible. Help your friend seek strategies that encourage her to do the right thing while minimizing possible harm to her from angry parents. Taking the premises into consideration, you may come to the following solution or conclusion:

> *Conclusion*: Your friend should leave a note on the other car with her name and phone number explaining what happened, and you should go with your friend when she tells her parents about the accident.

This is a relatively straightforward moral argument that leads to a solution, taking into account all the relevant moral principles. In a later section, we'll be studying strategies for resolving moral dilemmas, cases in which there is a conflict between moral principles and concerns.

Evaluating Moral Arguments

In evaluating moral arguments, the first step is to make sure that the argument is complete and that no important premises are omitted. In some moral arguments, the prescriptive premise(s) is unstated. A prescriptive premise may be left out because it is obvious or uncontroversial. Take this example:

> I'm so angry! I have a good grade point average but was refused a college scholarship solely on the grounds that I was a mother of a young child—and, as they said, my place is in the home. That's just not right![26]

The unstated premise in this argument involves the *duty of justice*: The college has a duty to give each student equal consideration. In this case, the only relevant criteria for consideration should have been based on grade point average, not the parental status of the student.

In some moral arguments, a prescriptive premise may be left out because it is controversial or questionable. Consider this argument:

> *Descriptive premise*: The Second Amendment to the United States Constitution protects people's right "to keep and bear arms."
>
> *Conclusion*: I have a moral right to own a handgun.

The unstated prescriptive premise in this argument is that "an action or policy is morally right if it is constitutional." In other words, this argument assumes cultural relativism is true. However, this is a questionable premise. Owning slaves was a *legal* right, at least prior to the 1865 ratification of the Thirteenth Amendment, which outlawed slavery. But most of us do not consider it to be a *moral* right—either now or before 1865. Similarly, in the argument about handguns, although you may agree with the conclusion, the premises do not support it.

The premises should also be true. If just one premise is false, the argument is unsound. For example, some people support the practice of cohabitation (living together) on the grounds that people who live together before marriage have a better chance of a successful marriage. However, research does not support this claim: The divorce rate is in fact significantly higher among married couples who lived together before their marriage or engagement.[27]

Moral arguments should also be free of informal fallacies. Consider:

> Cloning humans is wrong because it is unnatural. Therefore, human cloning ought to be illegal.

In this argument, the person is making the assumption that if something is unnatural, then it is morally wrong, thereby committing the *naturalistic fallacy*. If immorality were synonymous with what is unnatural, then the use of antibiotics, eyeglasses, or even clothing (at least in warm climates!) would be immoral.

Another fallacy that often appears in moral arguments is the *fallacy of popular appeal*. This fallacy is most likely to be used by a cultural relativist or by a person at the conventional stages of moral reasoning. The *fallacy of hasty*

Connections

What are some of the ethical concerns in designing scientific experiments? *See Chapter 12, pp. 383–384.*

moral dilemma A situation in which there is a conflict between moral values.

generalization may also be used by a cultural relativist to justify cultural stereotypes and the denial of equal treatment to certain groups of people.

Finally, the *slippery-slope fallacy* is committed in a moral argument when we argue, without sufficient evidence, against a practice on the grounds that if we allow it, then we'll have to permit other similar actions. This fallacy is most common in arguments about new technologies or practices—such as genetic engineering, same-sex marriage, and physician-assisted suicide—where we're not sure of the future consequences on society.

These are only a few of the fallacies that may appear in moral arguments. For a more in-depth review of the different informal fallacies, see Chapter 5.

Resolving Moral Dilemmas

A situation in which we have a conflict between moral values is known as a **moral dilemma**. No matter what solution you choose, it will involve doing something wrong in order to do what is right. We do *not* have a moral dilemma when the conflict is between moral values and nonmoral values, such as popularity or economic success. Solutions to moral dilemmas are not right or wrong, only better or worse.

In resolving a moral dilemma, resist the temptation to start with a "solution" and then rationalize it by selecting only the facts and principles that support it. Instead, a moral dilemma should be resolved in a systematic manner (see "Highlights: Steps for Resolving a Moral Dilemma").

Consider this classic example of a moral dilemma:

On May 19, 1894, the yacht *Mignonette* sailed from England for Sydney, Australia, where it was to be delivered to its new owner. There were four people aboard: Dudley, the captain; Stephens, the mate; Brooks, a seaman; and Parker, a 17-year-old cabin boy and apprentice seaman. The yacht capsized in the South Atlantic during a storm, but the crew managed to put out in a 13-foot lifeboat. They drifted for 20 days in the open boat. During this time, they had no fresh water except rainwater and, for the last 12 days, no food. They were weak and facing starvation. The captain called them together to make a decision about their fate. What should they do?

The first step in resolving a moral dilemma is to *clearly describe the facts*, including finding answers to any missing information. In the case of the *Mignonette* crew, you may want to know whether it was possible to catch fish (the answer is no); how much longer the crew might live (one was already dying), or whether they were near a shipping lane (no). You may also have questions about the status of the different men: Do they have families back home, how old are they, and so forth.

Next, *list the relevant moral principles and concerns*. We have a *duty to respect life*, as well as a *duty of nonmaleficence*—not to cause harm or to minimize harm. The *duty of justice* and equal treatment of all of the crew members is also relevant in this case. It's not fair to single out one crew member to kill and eat. The

Sailing before the wind: How the dinghy was managed during the last nine days.

crew members also have a *liberty right* to be left alone and not be killed unless they are interfering with someone's equal right to life. On the other hand, the captain has a *duty of fidelity* to his crew, which might put the onus on him to sacrifice his life to save his crew.

Once you have collected all your facts and made a list of the relevant moral principles, *list the possible courses of action*. Now is the time to brainstorm and get feedback from other people. List any possible actions that come to mind. In this dilemma, possible courses of action might include the following:

- The crew can wait and hope for a rescue.
- Everyone can starve to death together.
- Everyone can commit suicide together.
- The crew can eat the first person who dies.
- The crew can kill and eat the weakest person.
- The crew can kill and eat the person with the least social utility.
- Someone can volunteer to be killed and eaten.
- The crew can draw lots to see who gets eaten.

> Ideally, the best resolution to a moral dilemma is the one that honors as many moral values as possible.

HIGHLIGHTS

STEPS FOR RESOLVING A MORAL DILEMMA

1. **Describe the facts.**

2. **List the relevant moral principles and concerns.**

3. **List and evaluate possible courses of action.**

4. **Devise a plan of action.**

5. **Carry out the plan of action.**

➤ *APPLICATION: Identify an example of each of the steps in the text.*

The next step is to *devise a plan of action*. The crew has already tried the first course of action, but there seems to be no hope of rescue, and they are near death. They now face choosing from the remaining courses of action. To evaluate these, examine each in light of your list of moral principles. Ideally, the best resolution to a moral dilemma is the one that honors as many moral values as possible.

The principle of nonmaleficence requires that you try to minimize harm—in this case, the death of the crew members. Because the second and third courses of action involve the death of everyone, they're not good choices. On the other hand, killing someone without that person's permission is a violation of the person's liberty right and is unjust because it discriminates against the person. Eating the person who dies first, although gross, is not immoral—except to cultural relativists, since cannibalism is taboo in our society. Under the circumstances, it may be the best solution, since it honors the most moral principles. However, what if no one has died yet, and instead everyone is on the verge of starvation? The last two solutions both avoid the problem of injustice and may have to be the last resort.

The final step is to *carry out the plan of action*. It's also a good idea to have a backup plan in case the first plan of action doesn't work. In some moral dilemmas, people may agree on the premises but still come to different conclusions because they prioritize the relevant moral duties and concerns differently. For example, the captain may favor utilitarian theory and value the strongest members of his crew, reasoning that keeping them alive and killing the weakest member may increase the chances of at least *one* person surviving. However, the cabin boy, who lacks experience and has become extremely seasick, may value the fidelity of the captain and believe that it is the captain's tacit duty to sacrifice himself for his crew, since he was the one who was responsible for getting them into this precarious position in the first place. On the other hand, a person at the postconventional stages of moral reasoning who favors the justice perspective would probably prefer the last course of action—draw lots to see who gets eaten—since it is the most fair and just solution.

In fact, what happened is that the captain and two crew members killed Parker, the cabin boy, and ate him. The three remaining survivors were eventually rescued by a Swedish ship and returned to England, where they were tried for murder. The court ruled that the killing of Parker was not justified, since it was not in self-defense, and the men were found guilty of murder. This ruling continues to serve as a legal precedent in maritime law.

In this section, we have seen that a moral argument is much like other arguments, except that it must include at least one prescriptive premise. When trying to decide what is the best moral position or course of action, you should begin by listing the premises. Just as you would for other arguments, you must check the descriptive premises for their accuracy. If used correctly, moral reasoning can be a powerful tool for clarifying and resolving issues and dilemmas in your everyday life.

Connections

What is legal precedence, and what type of inductive reasoning is it based on? *See Chapter 13, p. 415.*

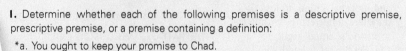

EXERCISE 9-5

STOP AND ASSESS YOURSELF

I. Determine whether each of the following premises is a descriptive premise, prescriptive premise, or a premise containing a definition:

*a. You ought to keep your promise to Chad.

b. Mary is opposed to capital punishment.

c. Torturing prisoners of war is a violation of the Geneva convention.

*d. Steroids are a type of performance-enhancing drug.

e. We are all entitled to freedom of speech.

f. School bullying is a violation of the categorical imperative and the principle of reciprocity.

*g. Doing community service work makes me feel good about myself.

h. Binge drinking is harmful because it can cause acute intoxication and even death.

i. Passive euthanasia is the withholding or withdrawing of medical treatment, resulting in a patient's death.

*j. Americans should give more money to poorer nations.

2. Discuss possible courses of action (conclusions) that your friend who scraped the fender of the car in the parking lot might take in the scenario described on page 290. Support your answer by taking into account the relevant moral duties and rights.

3. Evaluate each of the following moral arguments. If an argument is missing one or more premises, indicate what they are.

*a. You should not drink alcohol in your dorm room. After all, it's against the rules, since we're a dry campus. Also, it's against the law for anyone younger than 21 to drink alcohol, and you're only 18.

b. Euthanasia is wrong because it interferes with the natural dying process. We should wait until it is our time to die.

c. You should think of doing the optional community-service learning project for class. Studies show that doing a community-service project can actually enhance a student's level of moral development.

*d. Professor Dugan is Chris's teacher. Therefore, it would be wrong for Professor Dugan to try to initiate an intimate relationship with Chris.

e. The Affordable Care Act is a step in the right direction, but it doesn't go far enough. We ought to extend Medicare to all American citizens. That way everyone will be assured of the same basic medical coverage.

f. You're only 28. You should wait until you're in your thirties to get married. The duty of fidelity requires that we should do our best to honor our marriage vow "until death do us part," and the older you are when you get married, the less likely you are to divorce.

*g. Animals can feel pain. It is wrong to cause sentient beings pain when it can be avoided. Therefore, it is wrong to eat meat.

h. Cyberbullying is getting out of hand. Social network sites, such as Facebook, should be closely monitored and anyone caught posting intimidating remarks should lose their right to use the site and be reported to the police.

i. Those teenagers who vandalized the Van Zandt property should at least have to repay the owners for the damage and maybe even serve some time in a juvenile detention facility. It's not fair these rich students get off with just a slap on the hand while others, especially black teenagers, are sent to jail for doing the same thing.

*j. Medical research using human embryonic stem cells is morally acceptable. Recent polls show that the majority of Americans think that stem-cell research should be legal.

k. The dining hall should provide kosher meals. Several of the students in our dormitory are Orthodox Jews.

4. Working in small groups and using the five-step method discussed on page 293, resolve the following moral dilemmas:

a. Imagine that your class is on a yacht (you have a very rich professor) 3 miles offshore for an end-of-semester celebration. A storm strikes. There are only enough lifeboats to save half the people on the yacht. What should you do?

b. You are answering a hotline for the local women's resource center as part of a community-service project for school. A college student calls and tells you she is feeling suicidal. She also tells you that she has run away, because she is afraid of her boyfriend with whom she is sharing an apartment. You recognize her from her story, although she doesn't recognize your voice. You make arrangements for her to stay at the shelter belonging to the resource center. However, a few days later, you see her on campus with her boyfriend. Her face and upper arms are bruised. What should you do?

c. You are a member of the National Guard and have been told to evacuate people from an area that is predicted to be hit by a potentially devastating hurricane. You approach a family with three young children that is living in a high-risk area. The parents refuse to evacuate, saying that they rode out the last hurricane and survived and plan to do the same this time. One of the children is frightened and wants to go with you. The parents say no—the family belongs together. What should you do?

d. You are a family physician. One of your patients, a 37-year-old married man, has just found out that he has gonorrhea. He pleads with you not to tell his wife about his condition, since he is worried that she'll leave him if she finds out that he's been unfaithful. His wife is also one of your patients and has scheduled a visit for her annual checkup. The husband asks you to tell his wife, should she ask you, that he is taking antibiotics for a urinary tract infection. What should you do?

e. Tyrone, a 19-year-old college student, lost the use of both his arms and legs after an automobile accident in which his neck was broken. He has been in the hospital for 4 months when he calls in his physician and tells the physician that he no longer wants to go on living. He asks the physician to give him a lethal injection. Assisted suicide is illegal in the state. What should the physician do?

f. Megan is a college student who has been picked up for possession of a small amount of marijuana. In return for not bringing criminal charges against her, since she has no previous record, the police ask if she'll serve as an undercover agent to catch drug dealers on her campus. Should she accept the assignment?

g. Rose and Joe have been living together in a monogamous relationship for the past 2 years—since the beginning of their sophomore year at college. They both agreed, at the time they moved in together, that either could leave the relationship at any time. However, Rose unexpectedly became pregnant. Because she is opposed to abortion, she has resigned herself to having the baby. When Rose is 6 months pregnant, Joe decides to leave. He leaves a short note saying, "It was fun while it lasted, but it's time for me to move on." What should Rose do?

5. Think of a moral conflict in your life. Using the five-step method on page 293, come up with a resolution to the conflict. If you are willing, share your proposed resolution to your conflict with the class. If appropriate, make modifications to your plan on the basis of class feedback.

*Answers to selected exercises are found in the Solutions Manual at the end of the book.

1. How does conscience help us to make moral decisions?
   - Conscience has both a cognitive and an affective (emotional) aspect. The cognitive aspect provides us with knowledge and judgment of what is right and wrong, while moral sentiments or feelings, such as empathy, moral indignation, and guilt, motivate us to take action.

2. What is the stage theory regarding the development of moral reasoning?
   - Kohlberg and Gilligan proposed three levels or stages: (1) preconventional, in which people put their needs and concerns before those of others; (2) conventional, in which people conform to peer or societal norms; and (3) postconventional, in which people are able to use universal moral principles and to balance their needs and the needs of others. Most American adults and college students are at the conventional stage of development.

3. In what ways can the different moral theories help us in formulating moral arguments?
   - Moral theories provide the foundation for moral arguments and their application to real-life situations by making us aware of the different moral principles, rights, and concerns and how to prioritize them in making effective moral decisions.

Perspectives on Abortion

Prior to the 1960s, there was little support for reform of the restrictive abortion laws that had been on the books since the turn of the 19th century. Even Margaret Sanger, the founder of Planned Parenthood, opposed abortion in all but a few circumstances as "taking the life of a baby after it begins" (1963 Planned Parenthood brochure). Instead she promoted birth control (contraception) as an alternative to abortion.

In 1962, Sherri Finkbine, the star of a popular children's show, discovered that she had taken thalidomide (a sedative) during the first month of her pregnancy. Thalidomide had just been found to cause serious defects in infants if taken during the early months of pregnancy. The Finkbines decided that the best course of action was to seek an abortion, which was then illegal. Eventually, she got an abortion in Sweden. The baby was terribly deformed. Finkbine's case galvanized the movement to reform abortion laws in the United States.

Abortion was legalized throughout the United States in January 1973 by the U.S. Supreme Court's ruling in *Roe v. Wade*. The Court ruled that the right of personal privacy in the U.S. Constitution includes the abortion decision. Therefore, abortion should remain unregulated by the state, at least in the first trimester prior to viability. Rather than settling the abortion issue once and for all, however, the court ruling continues to deeply divide Americans.

A 2013 Gallup Poll found that 24 percent of Americans thought that abortion should be legal throughout pregnancy for any reason. Fifty-seven percent thought that it should be legal only under certain circumstances, while 14 percent thought that it should always be illegal.[28] Although feminism is associated in most people's minds with the "pro-choice" position, feminists are divided on the issue.

Critical THiNKiNg Issue

Since 1973 there have been several challenges to *Roe v. Wade*. Most states have passed laws restricting abortion, including parental notification for minors, and requiring waiting periods between the first visit to an abortion clinic and the actual abortion.

In the following readings we examine the abortion issue from both the legal and moral perspectives. In the excerpt from the majority opinion in Roe v. Wade, Justice Blackman maintains that abortion should be legal based on a woman's right to privacy. Fr. Clifford Stevens disagrees. He argues that abortion is unconstitutional and a violation of the rights of the unborn.

A Defense of Abortion

ROE V. WADE (1973)

In the following readings, the U.S. Supreme court, in its landmark *Roe v. Wade* decision, extends the right to privacy to include a woman's right to have an abortion. Father Clifford Stevens disagrees. He argues for the moral and constitutional rights of the unborn.

It is . . . apparent that at common law, at the time of the adoption of our Constitution, and throughout the major portion of the nineteenth century, abortion was viewed with less disfavor than under most American statutes currently in effect. . . .

Three reasons have been advanced to explain historically the enactment of criminal abortion laws in the nineteenth century and to justify their continued existence.

[First] It has been argued occasionally that these laws were the product of a Victorian special concern to discourage illicit sexual conduct. Texas, however, does not advance this justification in the present case, and it appears that no court of commentator has taken the argument seriously. . . .

A second reason is concerned with abortion as a medical procedure. When most criminal abortion laws were first enacted, the procedure was a hazardous one for the woman. . . . Modern medical techniques have altered this situation. . . . Consequently, any interest of the state in protecting the woman from an inherently hazardous procedure, except when I would be equally dangerous for her to forego it, has largely disappeared. . . .

The third reason in the state's interest—some phrase it in the terms of duty—in protecting prenatal life . . . Only when the life of the pregnant mother herself is at stake, balanced against the life she carries within her, should the interest of the embryo or fetus not prevail . . . a legitimate state interest in this area need not stand or fall on acceptance of the belief that life begins at conception or at some other point prior to live birth. In assessing the state's interest, recognition may be given to the less rigid claim that as long as at least potential life is involved the state may assert interests beyond the protection of the pregnant woman alone.

Parties challenging state abortion laws have sharply disputed in some courts the contention a a purpose of these laws, when enacted, was to protect prenatal life. Pointing to the absence of legislative history to support the contention, they claim that most state laws were designed solely to protect the woman. . . . The few state courts called upon to interpret their laws in the late 19th and early 20th centuries did focus on the State's interest in protecting the woman's health rather than in preserving the embryo and fetus. . . .

The Constitution does not explicitly mention any right of privacy. . . . [Earlier Supreme Court] decisions make it clear that only personal rights that can be deemed "fundamental" or "implicit in the concept of ordered liberty" . . . are included in this guarantee of personal privacy. They also make it clear that the right has some extension to activities relating to marriage . . . [and] procreation. . . .

The right of privacy, whether it be founded in the Fourteenth Amendment's concept of personal liberty and restrictions upon stat action, as we feel it is, . . . is broad enough to encompass a woman's decision whether or not to terminate her pregnancy. The detriment that the state would impose upo n the pregnant woman by denying this choice altogether in apparent. . . .

We therefore conclude that the right of personal privacy includes the abortion decision, but that this right is not unqualified and must be considered against important state interests in regulation.

. . . no case could be cited that holds that a fetus is a person within the meaning of the Fourteenth Amendment . . . . All this, together with our observation, supra, that throughout the majority portion of the nineteenth century prevailing legal abortion practices were far freer than they are today, persuades us that the word "person," as uses in the Fourteenth Amendment, does not include the unborn. . . .

There has always been strong support for the view that life does not begin until live birth . . . . Physicians and their scientific colleagues have ... tended to focus either upon conception or upon live birth or upon the interim point at which the fetus becomes "viable," that is, potentially able to live outside the mother's womb, albeit with artificial aid. Viability is usually places at about seven months (28 weeks) but may occur earlier. . . .

With respect to the state's important and legitimate interest in the health of the mother, the compelling point, in the light of present medical knowledge, is at approximately the end of the first trimester. This is so because of the now established medical fact . . . that until the end of the first trimester mortality in abortion is less than mortality in normal childbirth. It follows that, from and after this point, a state may regulate the abortion procedure to the extent the regulation reasonably relates to the preservation and protection of material health. Examples . . . are requirements as to the qualifications of the person who is to perform the abortion . . . .

State regulations protective of fetal life after viability have both logical and biological justifications. If the state is interested in protecting fetal life after viability, it may go so far as to proscribe abortion during that period except when it is necessary to preserve the life of health of the mother. . . .

To summarize and conclude: . . . This holding, we feel, is consistent with the relative weights of the respective interest involved with the lessons and example of medical and legal history, with the lenity of the common law, and with the demands of the profound problems of the present

day. The decision leaves the State free to place increasing restrictions on abortion as the period of pregnancy lengthens, so long as those restrictions are tailored to the recognized state interests.

REVIEW QUESTIONS

1. What are the three reasons why criminal abortion laws were in effect through most of the 19th century?
2. On what grounds does the court conclude that most of these reasons for criminalizing abortion are no longer applicable?
3. What is the right to privacy in the U.S. Constitution and how does the court apply this right to the abortion question?
4. According to the court when does life begin and how does this affect their final ruling?

The Rights of the Unborn

FATHER CLIFFORD STEVENS

Clifford Stevens is a priest in Omaha, Nebraska and author of several books on religion, religious history, and morality. In the following reading, Stevens argues that *Roe v. Wade* is a flawed ruling that failed to take into account the basic moral and constitutional rights of the unborn.

A legal victory over abortion will not be achieved by one or two cases, but only by the persistent recourse to the courts, as abortion practices are challenged with new data which demonstrate the violation of constitutional rights. What will gradually emerge as these cases are adjudicated are the facts and the principles of a new juridic development, embryonic law.

That development was opened by the Roe v. Wade decision, as the issue of civil rights was opened by Plessy v. Ferguson, workers' rights by Lochner v. New York, and children's rights by Hammer v. Dagenhart. . . .

Any opposition to abortion in the courts and in the public arena must be a *constitutional* opposition, based on principles enshrined in the Constitution of the United States, on precedents in constitutional law and on rights which the Constitution was fashioned to secure and protect.

At this point in adjudicating the dispute, only one side of the issue has really been heard, the views of those who support abortion. The only history of the question that has been examined, or even aired, is the history of the abortion laws, with an erroneous conclusion drawn from those laws.

The constitutional issue in the abortion question, the *termination of unborn life,* was not faced by the Court, in fact, the Court refused to consider that issue, much as the *Dred*

Scott Decision refused to face the question of the manner in which Black Africans were brought to the United States or the inhuman manner of their servitude. This was because *Roe v. Wade* was presented, on the basis of the briefs, as a case of law *facilitating* a basic constitutional right, rather than *constituting* one. Those arguing the case made sure that the question of unborn life and the manner of its destruction would never be faced by the Court.

In *Roe v. Wade,* there was scarcely any appeal to precedent and the precedent chosen, *Griswold v. Connecticut,* had nothing to do with the unborn. Its only link with the abortion issue was that both cases had some relationship to sexual relations and reproductive matters. The hard work of linking the abortion question with its constitutional precedents was simply not done.

In *Roe v. Wade,* abortion was accepted as standard medical practice, just as low wages, appalling working conditions and the grinding poverty of workers were accepted as standard contractual practices in *Lochner v. New York.* In both cases, the judiciary gave those exercising power over others the legal judgment over their own acts. In the case of abortion, the judiciary refused to examine the "medical" result of the surgical operation called abortion, or the claim of medical science that the procedure was merely a medical matter. The will of the patient and the willingness of the doctor were the only factors that entered into that judgment. Just as surely as the failure to recognize that Black slavery involved the oppression, exploitation and violence done to kidnapped Africans was the root of the constitutional contradiction in *Dred Scott,* so the failure to recognize that abortion involves the violent extermination of unborn life is the root constitutional contradiction in *Roe v. Wade.*

The root procedural error in adjudicating *Roe v. Wade* was to look upon the decision as *facilitative* of a basic right, rather than *constitutive* of a right, and that was because of the dependence of the Justices on the written briefs of the NARAL, which had defended the view that abortion laws were fashioned solely to protect a woman from unsafe surgery. In consequence, the abortion issue was not seen in the progression of laws securing constitutional rights, and the issue of the unborn was considered peripheral to the case. As in the case of slavery, segregation, the exploitation of workers and child labor, the constitutional issue was given a legal cover that became the focus of the dispute and the deciding factor in the majority opinion. Only by future litigation can the real constitutional issue emerge. . . .

Just as Liberty of Contract was used as a legal cover for gross injustices to workers, hiding the violation of their constitutional rights, so the Right to Privacy is used in the abortion issue as a legal cover for the violent death of the unborn. Similarly, just as the Court finally recognized that freedom of contract is not unlimited and could be used for the exploitation of others, so the Court has to be persuaded that a right to privacy has its limitations and cannot be used a legal cover for violent actions. . . .

The link that was made in the *Roe v. Wade* decision is with *abortion laws,* the formation of those laws, the purpose of those laws, the obsolescence of those laws. And a judgment was made, based on invalid historical assumptions and erroneous medical information, that those laws were purely medical matters, due to the primitive and unsafe surgical methods of the time, and that therefore the judgment in the matter is a *medical* one, and that it is for the physician to decide whether an abortion is called for in any particular case.

[T]here are no precedents relating directly to abortion. The issue of abortion has to be shown as part of a larger canvas, just as slavery and segregation had to be shown as part of the securing of the human rights laid down in the Constitution for every class of human being. . . .

UNDOUBTEDLY, ABORTION IS THE MOST VEXING constitutional question that has been brought to the Supreme Court, but it is by no means the most difficult or the most unprecedented. Slavery was a far more explosive issue, far more entrenched in legal precedents and supported by positive laws of long standing. Segregation had been given the cover of constitutional precedent and embodied in countless Supreme Court decisions, defended by statesmen and constitutional lawyers and deeply ingrained in the habits of public and private life for vast numbers of people. Child labor was part of a widely accepted economic practice, upon which families and employers depended for their livelihood, and even attempts by the federal government to eliminate the practice were overruled by the Court. There is no long-standing precedent with regard to abortion, certainly none as long-standing as liberty of contract which held as a precedent in workers' rights for almost fifty years, or separate, but equal, which supported segregation laws for fifty-eight years.

REVIEW QUESTIONS

1. On what grounds does Stevens claim that abortion is a violation of Constitutional rights?

2. What are the legal and moral similarities, according to Stevens, between the Supreme Court rulings on slavery and on abortion?

3. Why does Stevens disagree with *Roe v. Wade's* use of the right of privacy to legalize abortion?

4. Why does Stevens maintain that the *Roe v. Wade* decision was made on "invalid historical assumptions and erroneous medical information"?

THiNK AND DISCUSS

PERSPECTIVES ON ABORTION

1. Identify the main premises in both the *Roe v. Wade* majority opinion and in the reading by Stevens. Break down and diagram both arguments. Identify the different types of arguments (inductive and deductive) in both readings. For the inductive arguments, note which are generalizations, analogies, and causal arguments.

2. Referring back to Question 1, note which premises are descriptive and which are prescriptive. Identify the moral principles and rights in the prescriptive premises. Discuss the relevance of these moral principles and rights to the issue of abortion. Were any moral concerns left out of either's argument? Explain.

3. Stevens argues that the justices in *Roe v. Wade* failed to address the moral issue of the destruction of unborn life and instead focused on the will of the patients and willingness of physicians as well as the fact that abortion was accepted as standard medical practice. Critically evaluate this criticism of *Roe v. Wade*. Discuss also how the justices in *Roe v. Wade* might respond to Stevens.

4. Critically evaluate Steven's analogy between legalized slavery and legalized abortion. Did he successfully make the case that all humans, including the unborn and slaves, ought to have legal and moral rights? Support your answer.

5. Working in small groups, and referring back to the premises you identified in question 1, make a list of the premises that you found most compelling. Using these premises, come up with a policy (conclusion) for addressing the issue of abortion. Share your conclusion with your group. Modify it, if appropriate, in light of the feedback from the group.

A

accent The meaning of an argument changes depending on which word or phrase in it is emphasized.

ad hominem fallacy Instead of presenting a counterargument, we attack the character of the person who made the argument.

affective The emotional aspect of conscience that motivates us to act.

agnostic A person who believes that the existence of God is ultimately unknowable.

amphiboly An argument that contains a grammatical mistake which allows more than one conclusion to be drawn.

analogical premise A premise containing an analogy or comparison between similar events or things.

analogy A comparison between two or more similar events or things.

anecdotal evidence Evidence based on personal testimonies.

anthropocentrism The belief that humans are the central or most significant entity of the universe.

appeal to force (scare tactics) The use or threat of force in an attempt to get another person to accept a conclusion as correct.

appeal to ignorance The claim that something is true simply because no one has proven it false, or that something is false simply because no one has proven it true.

appeal to pity Pity is evoked in an argument when pity is irrelevant to the conclusion.

argument Reasoning that is made up of two or more propositions, one of which is supported by the others.

argument based on mathematics A deductive argument in which the conclusion depends on a mathematical calculation.

argument by elimination A deductive argument that rules out different possibilities until only one remains.

argument from definition A deductive argument in which the conclusion is true because it is based on the definition of a key term.

argument from design An argument for the existence of God based on an analogy between man-made objects and natural objects.

artificial intelligence The study of the computations that make it possible for machines to perceive, reason, and act.

atheist A person who does not believe in the existence of a personal God.

B

begging the question The conclusion of an argument is simply a rewording of a premise.

business An organization that makes a profit by providing goods and services to customers.

C

care perspective The emphasis in moral development on context and relationships.

case brief Researching the case under consideration and summarizing its relevant details.

categorical imperative Kant's fundamental moral principle that helps to determine what our duty is.

categorical syllogism A deductive argument with two premises and three terms, each of which occurs exactly twice in two of the three propositions.

causal argument An argument that claims something is (or is not) the cause of something else.

cause An event that brings about a change or effect.

ceremonial language Language used in particular prescribed formal circumstances.

chain arguments A type of imperfect hypothetical argument with three or more conditional propositions linked together.

civil disobedience The active, nonviolent refusal to obey a law that is deemed unjust.

cognitive development The process by which one becomes an intelligent person.

cognitive dissonance A sense of disorientation that occurs in situations where new ideas directly conflict with a person's worldview.

common law A system of case-based law that is derived from judges' decisions over the centuries.

compassion Sympathy in action.

conclusion The proposition in an argument that is supported on the basis of other propositions.

conditional statement An "If . . . then . . ." statement.

confirmation bias The tendency to look only for evidence that supports our assumptions.

confounding variable A fact that is not accounted for or controlled by the experimental design.

connotative meaning The meaning of a word or phrase that is based on past personal experiences or associations.

conscience A source of knowledge that provides us with knowledge about what is right and wrong.

controlled experiment An experiment in which all variables are kept constant except for the independent variable(s).

conventional stage Stage of moral development in which people look to others for moral guidelines.

correlation When two events occur together regularly at rates higher than probability.

cost–benefit analysis A process where the harmful effects of an action are weighed against the benefits.

critical rationalism The belief that faith is based on direct revelation of God and that there should be no logical inconsistencies between revelation and reason.

critical thinking A collection of skills we use every day that are necessary for our full intellectual and personal development.

cultural relativism People look to societal norms for what is morally right and wrong.

cyborgs Humans who are partially computerized.

D

deductive argument An argument that claims its conclusion necessarily follows from the premises.

definitional premise A premise containing the definition of a key term.

democracy A form of government in which the highest power in the state is invested in the people and exercised directly by them or, as is generally the case in modern democracies, by their elected officials.

denotative meaning The meaning of a word or phrase that expresses the properties of the object.

deontology The ethics of duty.

dependent premise A premise that supports a conclusion only when it is used together with another premise.

dependent variable The fact in a controlled experiment that changes in response to the manipulation.

descriptive premise A premise that is based on empirical facts.

diffusion of responsibility The tendency, when in a large group, to regard a problem as belonging to someone else.

direct democracy A type of democracy in which all of the people directly make laws and govern themselves.

directive language Language used to direct or influence actions.

disjunctive syllogism A type of deductive argument by elimination in which the premises present only two alternatives.

doctrine of legal precedent The idea that legal cases should be decided in the same way as previous, similar legal cases.

doublethink Involves holding two contradictory views at the same time and believing both to be true.

dysphemism A word or phrase chosen to produce a negative effect.

E

egocentrism The belief that the self or individual is the center of all things.

elitism A belief in the rule of "the best people."

emotion A state of consciousness in which one experiences feelings such as joy, sorrow and fear.

emotional intelligence The ability to perceive accurately, appraise, and express emotion.

emotive language Language that is purposely chosen to elicit a certain emotional impact.

emotive words Words that are used to elicit certain emotions.

empathy The capacity to enter into and understand the emotions of others.

empirical fact A fact based on scientific observation and the evidence of our five senses.

empiricism The belief that our physical senses are the primary source of knowledge.

empiricist One who believes that we discover truth primarily through our physical senses.

equivocation A key term in an argument changes meaning during the course of the argument.

escalation of commitment The overcommitment of marketing to a particular answer.

ethical subjectivist One who believes that morality is nothing more than personal opinion or feelings.

ethnocentrism The belief in the inherent superiority of one's own group and culture is characterized by suspicion and a lack of understanding about other cultures.

euphemism The replacement of a term that has a negative association by a neutral or positive term.

evidence Reasons for believing that a statement or claim is true or probably true.

experimental material The group or class of objects or subjects that is being studied in an experiment.

explanation A statement about why or how something is the case.

expressive language Language that communicates feelings and attitudes.

F

faith Belief, trust, and obedience to a religious deity.

fallacy A faulty argument that at first appears to be correct.

fallacy of ambiguity Arguments that have ambiguous phrases or sloppy grammatical structure.

fallacy of composition An erroneous inference from the characteristics of a member of a group or set about the characteristics of the entire group or set.

fallacy of division An erroneous inference from the characteristics of an entire set or group about a member of that group or set.

fallacy of relevance The premise is logically irrelevant, or unrelated, to the conclusion.

false dilemma Responses to complex issues are reduced to an either/or choice.

false memory syndrome The recalling of events that never happened.

federalism A system in which power is divided between the federal and state governments.

fideism The belief that the divine is revealed through faith and does not require reason.

form The pattern of reasoning in a deductive argument.

formal fallacy A type of mistaken reasoning in which the form of an argument itself is invalid.

G

gambler's error The belief that a previous event affects the probability in a random event.

generalization Drawing a conclusion about a certain characteristic of a population based on a sample from it.

groupthink The tendency to conform to group consensus.

guilt A moral sentiment that alerts us to and motivates us to correct a wrong.

H

hasty generalization A generalization is made from a sample that is too small or biased.

hearsay Evidence that is heard by one person and then repeated to another.

helper's high The feeling that occurs when we help other people.

hyperbole A rhetorical device that uses an exaggeration.

hypothesis A proposed explanation for a particular set of phenomena.

hypothetical syllogism A deductive argument that contains two premises, at least one of which is a conditional statement.

I

impeachment The process by which Congress brings charges against and tries a high-level government official for misconduct.

inappropriate appeal to authority We look to an authority in a field other than that under investigation.

independent premise A premise that can support a conclusion of its own.

independent variable The factor in a controlled experiment that is being manipulated.

inductive argument An argument that only claims that its conclusion probably follows from the premise.

informal fallacy A type of mistaken reasoning that occurs when an argument is psychologically or emotionally persuasive but logically incorrect.

informative language Language that is either true or false.

initiatives Laws or constitutional amendments proposed by citizens.

issue An ill-defined complex of problems involving a controversy or uncertainty.

J

justice perspective The emphasis on duty and principles in moral reasoning.

K

knowledge Information which we believe to be true and for which we have justification or evidence.

L

language A system of communication that involves a set of arbitrary symbols.

legitimate authority In a democracy, the right to rule given to the government by the people.

legitimate interests Interests that do not violate others' similar and equal interests.

lexical definition The commonly used dictionary definition.

liberal democracy A form of democracy emphasizing liberty of individuals.

libertarian A person who opposes any government restraints on individual freedom.

liberty rights The right to be left alone to pursue our legitimate interests.

lie A deliberate attempt to mislead without the prior consent of the target.

loaded question A fallacy that assumes a particular answer to another unasked question.

lobbying The practice of private advocacy to influence the government.

logic The study of the methods and principles used to distinguish correct or good arguments from poor arguments.

M

major premise The premise in a categorical syllogism that contains the predicate term.

major term The predicate (P) term in a categorical syllogism.

marketing research Identifying a target market and finding out if a product or service matches customer desires.

mass media Forms of communication that are designed to reach and influence very large audiences.

materialism The belief that everything in the universe is composed of physical matter.

mature care ethics The stage of moral development in which people are able to balance their needs and those of others.

media literacy The ability to understand and critically analyze the influence of the mass media.

memorable-events error A cognitive error that involves our ability to vividly remember outstanding events.

metaphor A descriptive type of analogy, frequently found in literature.

method of belief A method of critical analysis in which we suspend our doubts and biases and remain genuinely open to what people with opposing views are saying.

method of doubt A method of critical analysis in which we put aside our preconceived ideas and beliefs and begin from a position of skepticism.

middle term In a categorical syllogism, the term that appears once in each of the premises.

minor premise The premise in a categorical syllogism that contains the subject term.

minor term The subject (S) term in a categorical syllogism.

modus ponens A hypothetical syllogism in which the antecedent premise is affirmed by the consequent premise.

modus tollens A hypothetical syllogism in which the antecedent premise is denied by the consequent premise.

moral dilemma A situation in which there is a conflict between moral values.

moral outrage Indignation in the presence of an injustice or violation of moral decency.

moral reasoning Used when a decision is made about what we ought or ought not to do.

moral sensitivity The awareness of how our actions affect others.

moral sentiments Emotions that alert us to moral situations and motivate us to do what is right.

moral tragedy This occurs when we make a moral decision that is later regretted.

moral values Values that benefit oneself and others and are worthwhile for their own sake.

N

naturalistic fallacy A fallacy based on the assumption that what is natural is good.

negative correlation When the occurrence of one event increases as the other decreases.

niche media Forms of communication geared to a narrowly defined audience.

nonmoral (instrumental) values Values that are goal oriented—a means to an end to be achieved.

normal science Scientific research that is based on past achievements and is recognized by most scientists.

O

objectivity The assumption that we can observe and study the physical world without any observer bias.

operational definition A definition with a standardized measure for use in data collection and interpretation.

opinion A belief based solely on personal feelings rather than on reason or facts.

P

paradigm The accepted view of what the world is like and how we should go about studying it.

persuasive definition A definition used as a means to influence others to accept our view.

placebo A substance used in experiments that has no therapeutic effect.

politically correct The avoidance or elimination of language and practices that might affect political sensibilities.

poll A type of survey that involves collecting information from a sample group of people.

popular appeal An appeal to popular opinion to gain support for our conclusion.

populism A belief in the wisdom of the common people and in the equality of all people.

positive correlation The incidence of one event increases when the second one increases.

postconventional stages Stage in which people make moral decisions on the basis of universal moral principals.

precising definition A definition, used to reduce vagueness, that goes beyond the ordinary lexical definition.

preconventional stages Stage of moral development in which morality is defined egotistically.

predicate term In a categorical syllogism, the term that appears second in the conclusion.

premise A proposition in an argument that supports the conclusion.

prescriptive premise A premise in an argument containing a value statement.

prima facie duty Moral duty that is binding unless overridden by a more compelling moral duty.

principle of utility (greatest happiness principle) The most moral action is that which brings about the greatest happiness or pleasure and the least amount of pain for the greatest number.

probability error Misunderstanding the probability or chances of an event by a huge margin.

profit The money left over after all expenses are paid.

proposition A statement that expresses a complete thought and can be either true or false.

pseudoscience A body of explanations or hypotheses that masquerades as science.

push poll A poll that starts by presenting the pollsters' views before asking for a response.

Q

qualifier A term such as *all*, *no*, or *not*, which indicates whether a proposition is affirmative or negative.

quality Whether a categorical proposition is positive or negative.

quantity Whether a categorical proposition is universal or particular.

questionable cause (post hoc) A person assumes, without sufficient evidence, that one thing is the cause of another.

R

random sampling Every member of the population has an equal chance of becoming part of the sample.

rationalism The belief that religion should be consistent with reason and evidence.

rationalist One who claims that most human knowledge comes through reason.

reason The process of supporting a claim or conclusion on the basis of evidence.

red herring fallacy A response is directed toward a conclusion that is different from that proposed by the original argument.

referenda Laws or constitutional amendments put on the ballot by state legislators.

representative democracy A form of democracy in which people turn over their authority to govern to their elected representatives.

representative sample A sample that is similar to the larger population from which it was drawn.

research methodology A systematic approach in science to gathering and analyzing information.

resentment A type of moral outrage that occurs when we ourselves are treated unjustly.

rhetoric The defense of a particular position usually without adequate consideration of opposing evidence in order to win people over to one's position.

rhetorical devices The use of euphemisms, dysphemisms, hyperbole, and sarcasm to manipulate and persuade.

rule of law The idea that governmental authority must be exercised in accordance with established written laws.

rule of men A system in which members of the ruling class can make arbitrary laws and rules.

rules of evidence A set of rules that ensure fairness in the administration of law.

S

sampling Selecting some members of a group and making generalizations about the whole population on the basis of their characteristics.

sarcasm The use of ridicule, insults, taunting, and/or caustic irony.

science The use of reason to move from observable, measurable facts to hypotheses to testable explanations for those facts.

scientific experiment Research carried out under controlled or semicontrolled conditions.

scientific method A process involving the rigorous, systematic application of observation and experimentation.

scientific revolution A paradigm shift in which a new scientific theory replaces a problematic paradigm.

scientific theory An explanation for some aspect of the natural world based on well-substantiated facts, laws, inferences, and tested hypotheses.

self-selected sample A sample where only the people most interested in the poll or survey participate.

separation of powers A system in which three separate branches of government act as a check on one another.

shame A feeling resulting from the violation of a social norm.

slanted question A question that is written to elicit a particular response.

slippery slope The faulty assumption that if certain actions are permitted, then all actions of this type will soon be permissible.

social contract A voluntary agreement among the people to unite as a political community.

social dissonance A sense of disorientation that occurs when the social behavior and norms of others conflict with a person's worldview.

sound A deductive argument that is valid and that has true premises.

sovereignty The exclusive right of government to exercise political power.

state of nature The condition in which people lived prior to the formation of a social contract.

stereotyping Labeling people based on their membership in a group.

stipulative definition A definition given to a new term or a new combination of old terms.

strategic plan A method by which an organization deploys its resources to realize a goal.

straw man fallacy An opponent's argument is distorted or misrepresented in order to make it easier to refute.

subconclusion A proposition that acts as a conclusion for initial premises and as a premise for the final conclusion.

subject term In a categorical syllogism, the term that appears first in the conclusion.

SWOT model Used to analyze a company's strengths, weaknesses, external opportunities, and threats.

syllogism A deductive argument presented in the form of two supporting premises and a conclusion.

T

tacit consent The implicit agreement to abide by the laws of a country by remaining there.

theoretical definition A type of precising definition explaining a term's nature.

Turing test A means of determining if artificial intelligence is conscious, self-directed intelligence.

tyranny of the majority The majority impose their policies and laws on the political minorities.

U

unwarranted assumption A fallacious argument that contains an assumption that is not supported by evidence.

utilitarian calculus Used to determine the best course of action or policy by calculating the total amount of pleasure and pain caused by that action.

utilitarianism A moral philosophy in which actions are evaluated based on their consequences.

V

valid A deductive argument where the form is such that the conclusion must be true if the premises are assumed to be true.

Venn diagram A visual representation of a categorical syllogism used to determine the validity of the syllogism.

virtue ethics Moral theories that emphasize character over right actions.

W

welfare rights The right to receive certain social goods that are essential to our well-being.